MODERN PSYCHOANALYSIS

New Directions & Perspectives

MODERN PSYCHOANALYSIS

New Directions & Perspectives

edited by **Judd Marmor**

with a new introduction by the editor

Routledge
Taylor & Francis Group
LONDON AND NEW YORK

Originally published in 1968 by Basic Books, Inc.

Published 1995 by Transaction Publishers

Published 2017 by Routledge
2 Park Square, Milton Park, Abingdon, Oxon OX14 4RN
711 Third Avenue, New York, NY 10017

First issued in hardback 2018

Routledge is an imprint of the Taylor and Francis Group, an informa business

Library of Congress Catalog Number: 95-16725

Library of Congress Cataloging-in-Publication Data

Modern psychoanalysis : new directions and perspectives / edited by Judd Marmor ; with a new introduction by the editor.
p. cm.
Originally published : New York : Basic Books, 1968.
Previous ed. cataloged under: Marmor, Judd.
Includes bibliographical references and indexes.
ISBN 1-56000-825-3 (pbk. : alk. paper)
1. Psychoanalysis. I. Marmor, Judd.
RC504.M59 1995
616.89'17—dc20 95-16725
CIP

ISBN 13: 978-1-138-52821-5 (hbk)
ISBN 13: 978-1-56000-825-5 (pbk)

Contents

IV. CULTURE AND SOCIETY

Introduction to the Transaction Edition

It is a tribute to the advanced thinking of the contributors of this volume that, despite the passage of the years, it continues to be on the cutting edge of psychoanalytic theory and practice and is still highly relevant. Its thesis—that the theoretical foundations of classical psychoanalysis, rooted in metapsychology and employing concepts of libido, psychic energy, cathexis, counter-cathexis, fused and defused instincts, and the like, would have to give way to constructs of information processing, behavioral systems, adaptation, and systems-theory—is clearly in the process of being confirmed, although it may still take another decade or two for traditional ways of thinking in psychoanalysis to give way completely to the new ones.

Since this book first appeared, the most influential new development in psychoanalytic theory has been the emergence of object-relations theory and self-psychology. The former had its origins in the writings of Melanie Klein. In contrast to the Freudian emphasis on oedipal vicissitudes as the primary source of psychopathology, object-relations theory emphasized the dominant importance of the pre-oedipal relationship of the infant to the mother. Klein's thinking, however, leaned heavily on wildly unscientific hypotheses about the infant's fantasies and its innate reactions to the maternal breast. However, other leading members of the British object-relations school, such as Ronald Fairbairn and Donald Winnicott divested themselves of most of these fanciful abstractions and emphasized the *real* relationship of the pre-oedipal child to the mother and other significant persons. The subsequent development of self-psychology by Heinz Kohut carried this trend further by stressing the basic importance for healthy self-development of reinforcement of the young child's "narcissistic" needs via "mirroring" support from its caretakers. Kohut thus clearly shifted the focus of the origins of neurotic disorders away from the area of instinctual conflicts and placed it instead on deficits in developmental inputs, and on the failure of the child to acquire healthy "self-objects," that is, introjections (which Kohut calls "transmuting internalizations") of positive experiences with good authority figures.

At the theoretical level, however, as Grünbaum (1984) and Eagle (1983) have cogently pointed out, both object-relations theory and self-psychology have failed to make a clean break with Freudian meta-psychology. The concept of "infantile narcissism" is itself a vestigial remnant of libido theory; the evolutionary development of built-in behavioral systems that promote *attachments* to parenting objects in all mammalian life is much closer to the truth (Bowlby 1969, Peterfreund 1975). We simply cannot and must not ignore the growing body of knowledge about how the central nervous system functions, and our theories need to be consistent with those findings.

Despite its *theoretical* shortcomings, however, self-psychology has wrought a positive change in the *therapeutic* approach of psychoanalysis, with a recognition of the importance of the *relationship* between the analyst and the patient in contrast to the previous focus on the *interpretations and insights* given by the analyst to the patient. Thus, a renewed interest has developed in the "transference-countertransference" aspects of the analytic process, and on "intersubjectivity" in the psychoanalytic process (Stolorow, Brandschaft, and Atwood 1987)—an approach that is clearly anticipated in this volume.

In any event, it should be emphasized that the issue is not whether the adherents of the various dominant psychoanalytic schools, Freudian, neo-Freudian, object-relations, or self-psychology, help their patients therapeutically. The fact that positive therapeutic results are achieved in many ways and via a variety of techniques does not in itself validate the theoretical assumptions of any of these approaches nor give them the status of being scientifically based. The fundamental issue is whether or not the theories are rooted in heuristic concepts that are not self-validating. I have elsewhere pointed out the limitations of the sacrosanct "royal road to the unconscious" of the free-associational technique, and the way in which the clinical setting of analytic work with its transference-counter-transference matrix, tends to bring out associations in the patients of every school of therapy that validate its particular tenets (Marmor 1970).

By now it has become amply clear that when psychoanalysis works it is not because of the lifting of repressed traumatic memories, but because of a persistent relearning and reconditioning process that takes place in the context of a meaningful patient-therapist relationship (Marmor 1994a, 1994b, Eisenstein et al. 1994). This is not to imply that insight and rational understanding play no part at all in helping to motivate patients to move along the difficult road of undoing old behavioral patterns and learning new ones. But the insight that is helpful is not due to the lifting of "repressions" but rather to fuller understanding of all the factors, biological, psychological, and sociological, that have shaped their personality development, their hopes, their fears, and their interpersonal relationships. I have referred to this approach in this volume as a systems-centered one and have dealt with it in greater detail elsewhere (Marmor 1982, 1983). What I wish to emphasize is that regardless of its potential for therapeutic effectiveness, which may or may not be a factor in any individual instance, what is important in systems-thinking is that it is epistemologically and scientifically a more accurate approach to the problems of causality in normal and abnormal personality development. Traditional psychoanalytic approaches all reflect the error of *psychological reductionism* in their tendency to explain psychopathology solely on the basis of faulty relationships between the parents and the child, and in so doing, to ignore relevant neurobiological and sociocultural factors.

One consequence of this limited focus, over the past twenty-five years, has been a sharp loss of influence of psychoanalysis as a factor in the training programs of medical schools and psychiatric residencies. Where psychoanalysts used to be in charge of most of these programs, now they have been replaced largely by psychiatrists with strong biological persuasions, with a concomitant downgrading of psychotherapy as compared to pharmacotherapy. This is an unfortunate development, although this is not to deny the importance of the extraordinary advances in neurophysiology, neurochemistry, and psychopharmacology over the past several decades. However, to minimize the importance of the subjective and interpersonal experiences of patients is to fail to understand the *total* matrix in which personality and personality disorders develop. Life experiences affect the way our patients think and feel; the way they think and feel results in complex reverberations within their neurohumeral and immunological systems; these in turn have consequences for how they think, feel, and interact with other persons and with their external life situations. (See Arnold Mandell's chapter in this volume for a fuller discussion of this issue.) Such understanding is essential not merely for psychiatric disorders. It is equally relevant to the total range of human illnesses. It is precisely its potential for understanding the multifactorial impact of multiple variables on the *subjectivity* of individuals (including the psychotherapist!) that constitutes the great strength of the psychoanalytic contribution. But in order to fulfill this promise we must be prepared to broaden our investigative parameters. We must make our techniques the servants of our psychoanalytic goals rather than deify traditional rituals such as the use of the couch, a particular frequency of visits, and a refusal to interview significant others. Although the psychoanalytic method is indeed a unique investigative tool, full understanding of all of the relevant dynamic factors influencing human behavior cannot adequately be reached by an exclusively intrapsychic approach. A full appreciation of this should make it possible for psychoanalysts, *when indicated and feasible, to prescribe medication, to interview significant others,* and *to attempt to modify environmental factors without feeling that in so doing they are necessarily sacrificing the "deeper" objectives of psychoanalytic therapy.* It is my profound hope that the reissue of this volume will bring the benefit of this broader approach to a new generation of psychoanalytically oriented psychotherapists.

JUDD MARMOR

March 1995

REFERENCES

Bowlby, J. *Attachment.* New York: Basic Books, 1969.

Eagle, M. "The Epistemological Status of Recent Developments in Psychoanalytic Theory." In R. S. Cohen and L. Landau (eds.), *Physics, Philosophy and Psychoanalysis.* Boston: Reidel, 1983. Pp. 31-35.

Eisenstein, S., N. A. Levy, and J. Marmor. *The Dyadic Transaction: An Investigation Into the Nature of the Psychotherapeutic Process.* New Brunswick, NJ: Transaction Publishers, 1994.

Grünbaum, A. *The Foundations of Psychoanalysis.* Berkeley: University of California Press, 1984.

Marmor, J. "Psychoanalysis, Psychiatry, and Systems Thinking." *Journal of the American Academy of Psychoanalysis,* 10 (1982), 337-350.

———. "Systems Thinking in Psychiatry: Some Theoretical and Clinical Implications." *American Journal of Psychiatry,* 140 (1983), 833-838.

———. "Psychoanalytic Therapy and Theories of Learning." In *Psychiatry in Transition,* 2d ed. New Brunswick, NJ: Transaction Publishers, 1994a. Pp. 210-225

———. "The Nature of the Psychotherapeutic Process." In *Psychiatry in Transition,* 1994b. Pp. 296-309.

———. "The Limitations of Free-Association." In *Psychiatry in Transition,* 1994c. Pp. 265-275.

Peterfreund, E. "The Need for a New General Theoretical Frame of Reference for Psychoanalysis." *The Psychoanalytic Quarterly,* 44 (1975), 534-549.

Stolorow, R., B. Brandschaft, and G. Atwood. *Psychoanalytic Treatment: An Intersubjective Approach.* Hillsdale, NY: Analytic Press, 1987.

Preface

This book was undertaken in 1964 at the request of the Board of Trustees of The American Academy of Psychoanalysis, and under its sponsorship. The American Academy of Psychoanalysis was founded in 1956 to promote the progressive, scientific development of psychoanalysis by furthering communication among psychoanalysts of all viewpoints and their colleagues in other disciplines in science and in the humanities for the purpose of inquiring into the phenomena of individual motivation and social behavior. Additional purposes were to encourage and support research in psychoanalysis, and to foster the acceptance and integration of psychoanalysis in universities and medical schools. Its record over the past eleven years is an eloquent tribute to the success of these aims. The published proceedings of The American Academy of Psychoanalysis Meetings which appear in the annual volumes *Science and Psychoanalysis*, edited by Jules Masserman, reflect, more than anything I can say, the vitality of the scientific spirit in psychoanalysis that The American Academy of Psychoanalysis has catalytically fostered. I am deeply grateful to my colleagues in the Academy for their encouragement and support in bringing this volume into being.

Inasmuch as the Academy is an organization which does not require or expect ideological loyalty to any particular frame of reference, it is important to note that the views expressed in this volume are those of each individual author only, and do not in any way reflect any official position of the Academy or its members.

Three Fellows of the Academy, Doctors Leonard Duhl, Maurice Green, and Edwin Weinstein, served as members of a publications committee to assist me in the planning of the volume and to act as consultants during its preparation. I wish to acknowledge their invaluable assistance, as well as that of the publisher, Arthur Rosenthal and his associates, whose patience, understanding, and wise advice were enormously helpful throughout.

Most of all I must express my profound appreciation to my secretary, Mrs. Reba Berg, without whose dedicated and creative assistance this book could not have been completed.

JUDD MARMOR

February 1968

The Authors

LOUIS BREGER, Ph.D. Staff Psychologist and Assistant Clinical Professor, Langley Porter Neuropsychiatric Institute and University of California Medical School, San Francisco.

ALBERT C. CAIN, Ph.D. Associate Professor, Departments of Psychology and Psychiatry, University of Michigan; Chief Psychologist, Children's Psychiatric Hospital, University of Michigan, Ann Arbor.

LEONARD J. DUHL, M.D. Special Assistant to the Secretary, Department of Housing and Urban Development; Assistant Professor of Psychiatry, George Washington Medical School, Washington, D.C.

LEON EDEL, D.Litt. Henry James Professor of English and American Letters, New York University, New York City.

GEORGE L. ENGEL, M.D. Professor of Psychiatry and of Medicine, University of Rochester Medical Center, Rochester.

STUART M. FINCH, M.D. Professor of Psychiatry; Chief, Children's Psychiatric Service, University of Michigan Hospital, Ann Arbor.

LAWRENCE ZELIC FREEDMAN, M.D. Foundations Fund Research Professor in Psychiatry, University of Chicago Medical School, Chicago.

WELLS GOODRICH, M.D. Professor of Psychiatry, Albert Einstein School of Medicine, Montefiore Hospital, Bronx, New York.

Maurice R. Green, M.D. Training Analyst, William Alanson White Institute; Assistant Clinical Professor of Psychiatry, New York University, New York City.

Roy R. Grinker, Sr., M.D. Director, Institute for Psychosomatic and Psychiatric Research, Michael Reese Hospital and Medical Center, Chicago.

Harold Kelman, M.D. Training Analyst and Former Dean, American Institute for Psychoanalysis; Editor, *American Journal of Psychoanalysis*, New York City.

Robert L. Leopold, M.D. Director, West Philadelphia Community Mental Health Consortium; Associate Professor of Clinical Psychiatry and Director of the Division of Community Psychiatry, University of Pennsylvania, Philadelphia.

Sol Levine, Ph.D. Professor and Director, Division of Behavioral Sciences, Johns Hopkins School of Hygiene and Public Health, Baltimore.

Arnold J. Mandell, M.D. Associate Professor, Department of Psychiatry, University of California Medical Center, Los Angeles.

Judd Marmor, M.D. Director, Divisions of Psychiatry, Cedars-Sinai Medical Center; Clinical Professor of Psychiatry, University of California, Los Angeles.

Jules H. Masserman, M.D. Professor and Co-chairman, Division of Psychiatry, Northwestern University Medical School, Chicago.

Salvador Minuchin, M.D. Director, Philadelphia Child Guidance Clinic; Professor of Clinical Child Psychiatry, University of Pennsylvania School of Medicine, Philadelphia.

Morris B. Parloff, Ph.D. Chief, Section on Personality, Laboratory of Psychology, National Institute of Mental Health, Public Health Service, Department of Health, Education and Welfare, Washington, D.C.

Arnold A. Rogow, Ph.D. Graduate Professor of Political Science, City University of New York, New York City.

Jurgen Ruesch, M.D. Professor of Psychiatry and Director of Section on Social Psychiatry, Langley Porter Neuropsychiatric Institute, San Francisco.

Leon Salzman, M.D. Professor of Clinical Psychiatry, Georgetown University Medical School; Faculty, Washington School of Psychiatry, Washington, D.C.

Norman A. Scotch, Ph.D. Associate Professor of Social Anthropology, Department of Behavioral Sciences, Johns Hopkins School of Hygiene and Public Health, Baltimore.

John R. Seeley, Ph.D. Dean and Director of Program, The Center for the Study of Democratic Institutions, Santa Barbara.

Harley C. Shands, M.D. Chairman, Department of Psychiatry, Roosevelt Hospital; Clinical Professor of Psychiatry, Columbia University, New York City.

Roger L. Shapiro, M.D. Chief, Section on Personality Development, Adult Psychiatry Branch, National Institute of Mental Health; Teaching Analyst, Washington Psychoanalytic Institute, Washington, D.C.

Raymond Sobel, M.D. Professor of Psychiatry, Director of Child Psychiatry, Dartmouth Medical School, Hanover.

Hans H. Strupp, Ph.D. Professor of Psychiatry, Vanderbilt University, Nashville.

Edward S. Tauber, M.D. Fellow, William Alanson White Institute; Adjunct Professor of Psychology, Department of Psychology, Yeshiva University, New York City.

Montague Ullman, M.D. Director, Department of Psychiatry, Maimonides Medical Center; Professor of Psychiatry, State University of New York, Downstate Medical Center, New York City.

Edwin A. Weinstein, M.D. Research Associate, Washington School of Psychiatry; Attending Neurologist, Mount Sinai Hospital, New York City.

Otto A. Will, Jr., M.D. Medical Director, Austen Riggs Center, Stockbridge, Mass.

Frank S. Williams, M.D. Senior Staff Psychiatrist, Department of Child Psychiatry, Cedars-Sinai Medical Center; Assistant Clinical Professor of Psychiatry, University of Southern California School of Medicine, Los Angeles.

Lewis Wolberg, M.D. Medical Director, Postgraduate Center for Psychotherapy; Clinical Professor of Psychiatry, New York Medical College, New York City.

Joan J. Zilbach, M.D. Coordinator of Family Therapy, Judge Baker Guidance Center; Associate in Psychiatry, Boston University School of Medicine, Boston.

INTRODUCTION

New Directions in Psychoanalytic Theory and Therapy

JUDD MARMOR

The panorama of psychiatric thought in the modern era can be divided into three successive major trends. The earliest of these encompassed the somatically centered theories of the nineteenth century, in which man was conceptualized essentially as a *biological machine.* If disturbances occurred in the behavior of this machine, they were presumed due either to faulty manufacture—a hereditary defect or constitutional weakness—or to some external noxious agent—an injury, germ, or toxin.

Although many psychologists and psychiatrists had begun to question various aspects of this formulation, the major shift away from it, and the beginning of the second trend, occurred with the emergence of Freud's theoretical system at the turn of the century. Freud, without negating the importance of the organism (indeed he placed great stress on its unfolding evolutionary patterns), was the first to lay significant emphasis on the early environmental experiences of the infant and child. His focus, however, was on the intrapsychic reverberations of these experiences and his module was the *individual as a developmental unit.*

Finally, the revolutionary change that has been taking place in psychodynamic thought in the latter half of the twentieth century has been, not the gradual evolution of the Freudian model from a libido-oriented one to an ego-oriented one—although that has been important—but rather a shift from the closed system of the individual model to an *open-system module in which the individual's functioning is always examined in the context of his group or field situation.* Thus, while Freud's conceptual framework was psychodynamic but individual-centered, the emerging newer patterns of psychiatric thinking may be described as psychodynamic but system-centered. In advanced psychoanalytic circles today the focus of psychopathology is no longer being sought—at least to the same degree as formerly—within the individual's psyche, but rather in his system of relationships, his family, his small groups, his community, his society. This does not mean, however, that the valuable understanding acquired during half a century of interest and research in the dynamics of intrapsychic functioning needs to be discarded. It is my conviction and that of most of the contributing authors to this volume that these insights continue to be relevant even as we move on to concern with various other modules of human interaction. It is the purpose of this volume to indicate how some of the progressive thinkers in psychoanalysis today are adapting these insights to the new frontiers of psychodynamic interest.

This volume, then, may be considered an interim report on the evolution of current psychoanalytic thought. It is not assumed that the trends represented here are either ultimate or definitive. There are no ultimates in science. It is the exciting challenge and eternal frustration of the scientific method that the truth it pursues is an ephemeral will-o'-the-wisp which the pursuer can only approach but never totally grasp. Indeed, even in fields such as physics or chemistry, in which the variables are infinitely more controllable than those of behavioral science can ever hope to be, scientists do not assume that they are ever dealing with ultimate truths. Science is concerned with the amassing, testing, coordinating, and systematizing of data. A scientific hypothesis is considered better or "truer" than another if it fulfills three criteria more effectively than the other. (1) Does it explain all the available data with the least degree of complexity? (Parsimony.) (2) To what extent does it lend itself to experimentation and validation? (Heuristic value.) (3) To what extent does it make it possible to predict future events? (Predictive value.)

The essays in this volume, in my judgment, present approaches to psychodynamic theory that satisfy these criteria more adequately than Freud's unwieldy classical metapsychology. Of equal importance is the fact that the constructs which they are beginning to use have dispensed, for the most part, with the highly specialized jargon of cathexes, countercathexes, fused and defused instincts, repetition compulsions, and the like, that have for so long separated psychoanalysis from the rest of the behavioral sciences. The constructs of adaptation, learning, information processing, communication, and systems theory, which modern psychoanalysts are beginning to use, are bringing psychodynamic thinking back into the mainstream of modern psychobiological thought. Some readers might well ask, "That is all very well, but is it *psychoanalysis?*" I am tempted to reply irreverently that the question is an irrelevant one since what really matters is whether or not these approaches, regardless of what names or labels are attached to them, fulfill the criteria of science more effectively than previous ones. In science nothing is sacred except the method of science, and although this method challenges our most cherished beliefs, we must be prepared to trust it. Nevertheless, my response to this emotionally laden question is that all of the contributors to this volume do accept what I believe to be the essence of Freud's great contribution—the recognition that human behavior is motivated; that the nature of this motivation is often largely concealed from awareness; that our personalities are shaped not only by our biological potentials, but also by experiential vicissitudes; that functional disturbances in human cognition, affect, and behavior are the result of contradictory and conflictual inputs or feedbacks; and that early developmental experiences are of particular significance in shaping subsequent perceptions and reactions in adolescence and adulthood. In this fundamental sense, therefore, what this book is concerned with *is* psychoanalysis. If the corollary question of whether or not we do sufficient honor to Freud in these pages were a meaningful one—and basically, as far as science is concerned, it is not—I would argue that we do him greater homage by standing on his giant shoulders and trying to extend his vision than by worshipping blindly at his feet.

Psychoanalysis traditionally has been considered to be three things: a *method* of investigation of thoughts and feelings of which the subject is unaware ("the unconscious"), a *theory* of human personality, and a *technique* of therapy. At this point in history, roughly three-quarters of a century after Freud's initial contributions, the value of his psychoanalytic *method* of investigating "unconscious" mental processes remains unquestioned. No other approach to the understanding of what goes on *at a psychological level* in the "black box" of the human information-processing apparatus has been able to equal the psychoanalytic method of open-ended verbal communication ("free association"), and painstaking exploration of dreams, fantasies, parapraxes, and the like. It is my conviction that when the final chapter of the history of psychiatry is written, the development of this methodological tool will be recognized as having been Freud's greatest contribution.

However, as many of the chapters in this volume amply demonstrate (see particularly those of Breger, Green *et al.*, Grinker, Masserman, Ruesch, Salzman, and Shands), classical psychoanalysis as a *theory* of human behavior has not equally withstood the test of time; but this statement requires qualification. I do not wish to imply that all of Freud's views have become valueless. Certain of his basic constructs, such as those of conflict, repression, transference, and the "unconscious," still constitute an extremely effective foundation for an understanding of human behavior and psychopathology *despite the fact that the data upon which they were based can be dealt with just as effectively within other frames of reference, such as those of communication theory or learning theory.* What has become obsolete has been the cumbersome metapsychological superstructure that Freud erected upon these fundamental concepts—notably his theory of instincts, of libido, of the tripartite structure of the psyche, and of psychic energy. This "mythology" of psychoanalysis, as Freud once called his theory of instincts, has been rendered untenable by newer developments and findings in the behavioral sciences.

Even more regrettable is the fact that the high promises once held forth by psychoanalysis as a *technique* of *therapy* have failed to materialize. In retrospect, and with the benefit of hindsight, we ought not be surprised at this. Freud's method arose primarily out of his efforts *to understand* the meaning and origins of his patients' disturbances. There is no good reason *a priori* why a technique of investigation necessarily should be at the same time a good method of therapy. I suspect that it was largely the historical accident that Freud was attempting to earn a living as a psychiatric practitioner that drove him to utilize his investigative tool simultaneously as a therapeutic instrument. Indeed, compared to the then existent crude techniques of direct suggestion, hypnosis, electrotherapy, and repression, Freud's method of *involving* himself with the patient and the patient's life problems did have much to offer. Moreover, the fact that he brought elements of rational understanding and organization into an area that hitherto had been full of vast confusion lent a certain persuasiveness to the nineteenth-century rationalistic expectation that if the patient could but understand what his symptoms meant and from whence they came, this in itself would be enough to cure him.

Today, we have learned the difficult lesson that rational understanding alone is not enough; that people can understand why they behave in certain ways and yet be unable to alter their unsatisfactory patterns. The problem of modifying behavior has many parameters other than that of cognitive awareness (Marmor, 1962a, 1966a).

Freud's requirement that the patient appear daily at the therapist's office and open his heart and mind to him without holding anything back inevitably results in a powerful intensification of relationship between the patient and the help-giving person. Little wonder that Freud said in later years that although his initial problem had been one of getting patients to come to him, his eventual difficulty was in getting them to leave him. Kubie (1967) has pointed out that in his experience, under current analytic practices, the vast majority of analytic patients are left with unresolved transference patterns in relation to their analysts. In an earnest effort to deal with this problem, he began casting about for devices that might facilitate the "dissolution" of the transference, and ended by suggesting that the problem might be solved by a cautious socializing with patients during the termination phase, or by the utilization of a second therapist at that time, either alone or conjointly. What Kubie refused to see, however, was the fact that the problem that he was describing was inherent in the therapeutic method employed, and *was an iatrogenic artifact.*

The patient who seeks psychiatric therapy always brings with him certain basic distortions in his perceptions and feelings. These have been shaped and "learned" in the course of his early personality development in relationship to the significant people in his life. These distortions, which are the essence of the transference phenomenon, were not invented by Freud; they exist not only in the psychoanalyst's office, but in every significant human relationship. Freud's great contribution in this area was that he not only recognized transference as a factor of paramount importance, but also identified its historical sources and discovered its value in the therapeutic transaction. One of the unique aspects of psychoanalytically oriented psychotherapies is that transference reactions are consciously and deliberately used for the purpose of confronting the patient with the unreality of his interpersonal perceptions and reactions. The ultimate goal of such interpretations and confrontations is to enable the patient to become more realistic and adaptive in his interpersonal relationships. An important consequence of this should be that the patient ultimately perceives himself as more mature and is able to interact with authority figures with self-respect and on a greater basis of equality. The dissolution of the transference, therefore, should mean that the patient terminates his analysis with more comfortable feelings *not only toward the analyst but toward all authority figures.*

As I have indicated, however, the classical psychoanalytic relationship, by its very nature, tends to foster rather than resolve this core problem. Especially when the analyst adopts the model of the "neutral mirror" and carefully protects his "analytic incognito," these regressive patterns in the patient are enormously magnified. Under such circumstances, the patient tends to "perceive" the analyst as an Olympian, omniscient, God-like person in comparison to whom the patient feels less adequate than ever (Marmor, 1953). Many classical analysts believe that this regressive reaction is a basic prerequisite for good analytic therapy, and have laid down the dictum—one that Freud himself never formulated—that no psychoanalytic procedure is adequate if it has not produced in the patient a regressive "transference neurosis," which then has to be "worked through."

There is an intriguing parallel between this transaction of classical psychoanalytic technique and that which takes place between Zen masters and their pupils. In the Zen relationship the master's impersonality, strictness, and frustrating responses ultimately provoke in his pupil a regressive state akin to depersonalization. The "ego boundaries" of the Zen pupil then seem to dissolve and he experiences a sense of "oneness with the universe" that leads him to the longed-for state of "satori" (insight). In classical psychoanalysis, the patient asks questions and also is met with silence, reaches out for a relationship and also is rebuffed. The progressive frustration and helplessness that this kind of relationship produces ultimately provokes a similar kind of regressive reaction (Marmor, 1962b).

When, over the years, progressive psychoanalysts have argued that a more human kind of transaction seemed to produce better therapeutic results, the argument of the classicists has always been that such results were imperfect as compared with the profound characterological transformation that presumably emerged from the working-through of the transference regression. I can only say, after many years of experience with both techniques, that this conviction on the part of classical psychoanalysts is more an article of faith than a matter of fact. The therapeutic results of the classical psychoanalyic method simply do not warrant this assumption.

Where, then, are the newer system-centered psychodynamic concepts leading us, therapeutically speaking? The clinical section of this volume presents some answers to this question.

At the level of individual therapy, the emphasis is changing from one in which the therapist does something to the patient by "analyzing" him, to an examination of the nature of the reciprocal interaction between therapist and patient. The nature and quality of this transactional system is now seen as the crucial factor in achieving therapeutic progress, rather than the former assumption that what was crucial was the nature of the repetitive insights that the analyst gave to the patient. As a consequence, the therapist is no longer viewed as a neutral, impersonal conveyor of interpretations, but rather as an active human participant in a verbal and nonverbal, affective as well as cognitive, reciprocal interaction in which *both* participants "change" over the course of time. In this view the personality of the therapist is seen as an important factor which needs to be evaluated and understood just as fully as that of the patient (see Strupp, Chapter 12). Moreover, in recognition of the fact that both patient and therapist, as open systems, are products of their surrounding media, an understanding of class differences, value systems, group-linked verbal and behavioral patterns, and the like becomes highly relevant and indeed essential for optimal therapeutic effectiveness (see Minuchin, Chapter 21, also Kluckhohn, 1956).

Within this context, modern psychoanalytic therapists in increasing numbers have been breaking away from blind adherence to many of the traditional technical and ritualistic demands of classical analysis. The use of the couch, for example, is recognized as a tool which may be useful and necessary under some circumstances, not under others. There has been increasing experimentation with modifying the frequency of visits, also with interruptions of therapy and irregularity of appointments to see whether the finding in learning theory experiments that intermittent reinforcements of learning are more effective than regularly scheduled ones are applicable to efforts at modification of human behavior (Marmor, 1964). The long-standing shibboleth about the necessity for the patient's making a financial "sacrifice" in order for therapy to be successful has faded away in the light of experience with low-cost psychoanalytic clinics. The application of psychodynamic insights to various other modifications of therapeutic approach such as crisis-oriented therapies and short-term therapeutic approaches has also become more widespread (see Wolberg, Chapter 13). Many of the theoretical questions involved in these changes are admirably discussed by Strupp in Chapter 12.

The system-orientation of modern psychodynamics has led also to an increasing interest in the possibility of dealing with other factors within the patient's transactional life-system. Child analysts recognized early that psychoanalysis of the individual child was often an unnecessarily long, arduous, and circuitous approach to helping the child,* and that more expeditious and effective help could be forthcoming by working with the child's parents, whose participation and influence in the child's life space, after all, were considerably greater than those of the analyst could possibly be. This led to a concern with the dynamics of the entire family system, and in recent years family therapy has become an area of interest for increasing numbers of psychoanalysts who deal with children and adolescents (see Zilbach, Chapter 14; Williams, Chapter 15, and Shapiro, Chapter 18). Similarly, conjoint therapy of marital partners in conflict has begun to be employed, in contrast to the traditional approach of separate therapists treating each partner without

* The complexities of this approach are comprehensively discussed by Finch and Cain (see Chapter 17).

communicating with each other. Although many of these changes are now taken for granted, it cannot be strongly enough emphasized how great a break this kind of approach represents from the early classical psychoanalytic techniques. The student who entered psychoanalytic training in the 1930's was strongly impressed with the dangers implicit in any contact with a family member, even over the telephone, as though somehow the purity of the analyst's relationship with his patient would thereby be contaminated. As a consequence, the valuable assistance that could have been provided by enlisting the help of cooperative relatives was foregone, as well as the ability to correct some of the distortions inevitably inherent in the patient's perceptions of his milieu. Often, too, under those circumstances, the refusal of the analyst to have anything to do with the relatives unnecessarily created in them feelings of distrust and hostility that were destructive to the patient's progress.

I must emphasize here, as have many of the contributors to this volume, that such opening up of technical procedures to include other people in the patient's life system has not meant a lessening of concern with individual intrapsychic mechanisms. On the contrary, a proper awareness of the transactional operations in the patient's life systems is extremely helpful in enabling the psychoanalytically trained psychiatrist to achieve a more sophisticated understanding of his patient's psychodynamics.

Similar considerations have played a role in the development of analytic group psychotherapy. Although family therapy was extremely useful in the problems involving children and adolescents, and in marital conflicts, it did not lend itself as well to problems of the individual adult with emotional difficulties. In the therapies of such individuals, analytic group psychotherapy offered an additional dimension which could supplement or at times replace individual therapy as might be indicated (see Perloff, Chapter 20). As a result of the transference aspects of the dyadic process, the therapist becomes directly aware of the way the patient relates to authority surrogates, but many other aspects of the patient's interpersonal life—his behavior toward colleagues, juniors, members of the same and opposite sex, and the like—are presented through the spyglass of the patient's own perceptions and are consequently subject to considerable distortion which the analyst may or may not be able correctly to evaluate. In a group situation, on the other hand, the therapist has the opportunity to perceive these other transference patterns directly, and thus to evaluate the patient's perceptions of them more objectively.

As analysts have become increasingly aware of how aspects of the external environment are dynamically interwoven into the patient's intrapsychic reactions, there has been growing concern also with understanding the cultural milieu of the patient, and the technical demands that this imposes on therapeutic method. Spiegel (1959) was one of the first to call attention to the effect of class differences on transference-countertransference problems. Hollingshead and Redlich (1958) have noted that class position plays an important role in determining even what is defined as psychiatric illness, and whether or not psychodynamic psychotherapy will be prescribed for the patient. Sobel's chapter (Chapter 19) on the problems of late adolescence and the college years and Minuchin's (Chapter 21) on psychoanalytic therapy with low socioeconomic populations are examples of the awareness of such factors among modern psychoanalysts.

The relationship of schizophrenic disturbances to cultural milieu and socioeconomic levels has been frequently noted. More relevant to our psychoanalytic interests, however, are the fascinating studies of Lidz (1963), Wynne and Singer (1963), Jackson (1957), and their various co-workers, in demonstrating the way in which communication difficulties, ambiguities, and contradictions among family members of schizophrenics contribute to the development of schizophrenic disturbances. Will's sensitive description (Chapter 22) of a modern psychoanalyst's approach to the psychotherapy of schizophrenics encompasses these newer insights.

As psychoanalysts have broadened their awareness of the relevance of the nature of the social system to individual psychopathology, their interest in the institutional structures of society has also grown. The educational system, employment opportunities, racial segregation and prejudice, housing, and the like are no longer considered matters just of sociological concern. Their effects on personality development, ego strengths, social competence, and mental health have become increasingly apparent. Some of the ways in which psychoanalytic understanding is beginning to be applied to this growing field of community psychiatry are ably documented by Duhl and Leopold (Chapter 23).

The interests of modern psychoanalysts have not been limited to psychosocial areas. In the fields of ethology (Masserman, Chapter 8), neurophysiology (Weinstein, Chapter 9), psychophysiological medicine (Engel, Chapter 10), and psychopharmacology (Mandell, Chapter 11), there are numerous evidences of new levels of both theoretical and clinical sophistication. Similar refinements are taking place in the application of psychoanalytic insights to the areas of sociology and anthropology (Scotch and Levine, Chapter 24), the creative arts (Edel, Chapter 25), law (Freedman, Chapter 26), and political science (Rogow, Chapter 27).

What does the long-range future hold for psychoanalysis and psychoanalysts? I believe it is inevitable that its traditional forms will continue to be altered in the years to come (Marmor, 1966b). Psychoanalytic theory will not only move further away from Freudian metapsychology but will gradually begin employing more and more of the common language of the other behavioral sciences: the language of adaptation, learning theory, communications, and information theory. The beginning efforts to find certain theoretical common denominators that cut across all organic systems will undoubtedly continue at an enhanced rate, and the search for uniform theories of behavior, as encompassed within general systems theory, will go on. We can also anticipate new breakthroughs in neurophysiology and neuropharmacology, the implications of which will have to be integrated with psychodynamic theory.

As mental health care becomes more available to all who need it under the rapidly burgeoning mental health center programs, our society will be forced to dispense with the wasteful and inequitable luxury of having a highly trained specialist devote most of his professional life to the treatment of a handful of middle- or upper-class people while the vast majority of those in need of psychiatric care are consigned to second-class treatment or none at all. Psychoanalytically trained psychiatrists will continue increasingly to utilize their specialized skills in the various modifications of therapy that are illustrated in this volume in order to help greater numbers of people. The distinction between psychoanalysis and psychodynamic psychotherapy will continue to fade away. Ultimately there will evolve only one psychotherapy which will rest, as Knight once predicted, "on a basic science of dynamic psychology" (Knight, 1949, p. 101). Psychoanalysis itself as a formal, technical procedure will become more and more restricted, I suspect, to its investigative and training potentials; that is to say, it will be used either for purposes of research in unique and unusual problems of psychopathology, or it will be employed on a limited scale for the purpose of training psychiatrists to use it as an investigative tool.

As psychodynamic theory and practice, with the assistance of psychoanalysts, becomes more and more integrated into psychiatric residency programs (Marmor, 1961), we may anticipate that the current trend of diminishing numbers of applicants to psychoanalytic training institutes will continue. Conceivably, in time, the independent psychoanalytic institute—which after all was a kind of anachronism forced upon psychoanalysis by the original antagonism to it in organized medical and academic circles—may disappear from the scene and its role taken over by postgraduate training in medical schools, universities, and residency training programs. Psychiatrists with special interests in intensive psychotherapy will probably continue to seek personal analyses for themselves, although in all likelihood the rather rigid requirements of the "didactic analysis" in terms of minimum hours, frequency of visits, and so forth, which characterize contemporary psychoanalytic training, will become modified in terms of techniques that are more flexibly oriented to the actual clinical needs of each individual psychiatrist-in-training. Psychotherapy with other human beings, regardless of what form it takes, is one of the most emotionally and ethically demanding functions that one human being can take on in relationship to another. Its seductive potentials as well as its stresses are far greater than those in almost any other field of therapeutic practice, and I firmly believe that personal intensive psychotherapy aimed at removing, insofar as possible, the personal weaknesses, blind spots, and emotional immaturities of the would-be psychotherapist should be an essential aspect of his training.

The problem of whether or not this kind of intensive psychotherapeutic practice should be confined only to members of the medical profession will continue to be a knotty one. My guess is that in the years to come, as lines of clinical practice become increasingly blurred, it will become a greater source of controversy rather than a lesser one. There is ample justification for those who argue that since mind and body are one, a thorough knowledge of both is essential for those who would deal with disorders of the human mind. Certainly as our knowledge of how to integrate the uses of various drugs with intensive psychotherapeutic approaches increases, the value of a medical degree in this area of functioning cannot be dispensed with. And yet, assuming that a medically trained person has ruled out any causative somatic factors, can one honestly argue that *competently trained* nonmedical psychotherapists cannot, under usual circumstances, perform a psychotherapeutic function for most people equally well? In any event, the combination of shortage of adequately trained personnel plus the enormous psychiatric needs of our complex society will put ever growing pressure on the dispensers of mental health care to widen the circle of those who provide it. Indeed many are already pointing out that even present paramedical personnel—psychologists, psychiatric social workers, psychiatric nurses, and so on—will not be enough to provide sufficient care and that some kind of training for specially qualified laity may be essential in the future. Perhaps one path out of this difficult dilemma may ultimately lie in some variation of Kubie's creative suggestion (1954) which has never been given an adequate trial: the formation of a new specialty of medical psychotherapy which will dispense with much of the prolonged medical training which psychiatrists now must undertake and enable them to focus more thoroughly on only those aspects of physiology, pharmacology, psychology, sociology, and anthropology which are relevant to their future work.

There will be those who argue that this apparently inevitable dilution of the intensive one-to-one involvement in psychotherapy will constitute a tragic loss; that the uniquely humanistic aspect of devoting one's life, regardless of cost, to the improvement of another human being ought never to be sacrificed. Seeley in his eloquent closing chapter of this volume has emphasized this special value of the psychoanalytic tradition. There is indeed an important value here which must be cherished, but may we not succeed in finding other ways of retaining it? I cannot believe that it is any less humanistic to be concerned about many individuals than about only a few. We have the opportunity in the years ahead to broaden our humanistic horizons to a scale never before possible in human history. This is a challenge worth rising to; surely our generation of psychoanalysts and those who will follow us cannot fail to meet it!

References

Hollingshead, A. B., and Redlich, F. C. *Social Class and Mental Illness.* New York: Wiley, 1958.

Jackson, D. D. "The Question of Family Homeostasis." *Psychiatric Quarterly Supplement,* 31 (1957), 79–90.

Kluckhohn, Florence. "Dominant and Variant Value Orientations." In C. Kluckhohn and H. A. Murray (eds.), *Personality in Nature, Society, and Culture.* New York: Alfred A. Knopf, 1956. Pp. 342–357.

Knight, R. P. "A Critique of the Present Status of the Psychotherapies." *Bulletin of the New York Academy of Medicine,* 25 (1949), 100–114.

Kubie, L. S. "The Pros and Cons of a New Profession: A Doctorate in Medical Psychology." *Texas Reports in Biological Medicine,* 12 (1954), 692–737.

Kubie, L. S. "Unsolved Problem Concerning the Resolution of the Transference: Who Can and Who Cannot Resolve It?" Presented at the annual meeting of the American Psychoanalytic Association, Detroit, May 1967.

Lidz, T. *The Family and Human Adaptation.* New York: International Universities Press, 1963.

Marmor, J. "The Feeling of Superiority: An Occupational Hazard in the Practice of Psychotherapy." *American Journal of Psychiatry,* 110 (1953), 370–376.

Marmor, J. "Psychoanalysis and Psychiatric Practice." In J. H. Masserman (ed.), *Current Psychiatric Therapies.* New York: Grune & Stratton, 1961. Pp. 131–138.

Marmor, J. "Psychoanalytic Therapy as an Educational Process." In J. H. Masserman (ed.), *Science and Psychoanalysis.* New York: Grune & Stratton, 1962. Vol. 7, pp. 286–299. (a)

Marmor, J. "A Reevaluation of Certain Aspects of Psychoanalytic Theory and Practice." In L. Salzman and J. H. Masserman (eds.), *Modern Concepts of Psychoanalysis.* New York: Philosophical Library, 1962. Pp. 189–205. (b)

Marmor, J. "Psychoanalytic Therapy and Theories of Learning." In J. H. Masserman (ed.), *Science and Psychoanalysis.* New York: Grune & Stratton, 1964. Vol. 7, pp. 265–279. (b)

Marmor, J. "The Nature of the Psychotherapeutic Process." In G. L. Usdin (ed.), *Psychoneurosis and Schizophrenia.* Philadelphia: Lippincott, 1966. Pp. 66–75. (a)

Marmor, J. "Psychoanalysis at the Crossroads." In J. H. Masserman (ed.), *Science and Psychoanalysis,* Volume 10. New York: Grune & Stratton, 1966. Pp. 1–9 (b)

Spiegel, J. P. "Some Cultural Aspects of Transference and Countertransference." In J. H. Masserman (ed.), *Science and Psychoanalysis*. New York: Grune & Stratton, 1959. Vol. 2, pp. 160–182.

Wynne, L. C., and Singer, M. T., "Thought Disorder and Family Relations of Schizophrenics." *American Medical Association Archives of General Psychiatry*, 9 (1963), 191–198.

I
GENERAL

1

Conceptual Progress in Psychoanalysis

ROY R. GRINKER, SR.

Introduction

It should be expected, as a prelude to defining and describing any frontier, that its main body or consolidated area be defined as a structure, and as a process in development. However, thousands of published articles and books and an extensive psychoanalytic periodical literature confuse rather than clarify the recognition of definitive trends. Sheer limitation of space alone makes the task of summarization almost impossible even without including details, many of which, however, will be found in other chapters of this book. A more important difficulty, which at the same time points up the necessity for a critical survey, is the tendency of many psychoanalysts to consider abandoned concepts as integral parts of their field instead of viewing them in historical perspective.

The outstanding evidence for this fact is the pedagogical attitude in the psychoanalytic institutes where chronological ordering of Freud's[1] writ-

[1] The index to *The Standard Edition of the Complete Psychological Works of Sigmund Freud* will guide the reader to the several writings and times a particular idea is mentioned.

ings seems more important than emphasis on shifting concepts. This is an unfortunate inheritance of the "movement" phase of psychoanalysis which, for the most part, has not yet been superseded by a science willing to admit its mistakes openly and profit by them, and proud of its capacity to change. Intended to maintain the "heroic" position of Freud and his original "cooperative face-to-face group" in which his genius flourished (Mead, 1964), instead it deifies him and denies him the human privilege of error (Grinker, 1940).

Criticisms of Freud based on his personality or on the fact that he utilized many ideas of others which he read and "forgot" have little meaning because every creative man is a product of his times and uses his own and his culture's past as a base from which to move ahead. Unfortunately, however, Freud also "forgot," or in any event failed to synthesize, his own work. There is no available "package" of psychoanalytic theory. The old and abandoned are mixed with the new, which in some places is only implied. Although many of Freud's words are firmly embedded in our language, they are used in his own various writings and those of his followers to connote dissimilar ideas. The result is persistent semantic confusion. The vast majority of psychoanalytic authors repeat quotations from Freud or restate the old while only a few (Rapaport, 1959) interpret and attempt to systematize the basic theories. Some dispute the foundations of libido theory (Kardiner, Karusch, and Ovesey, 1959), some unproductively attempt to isolate discrete hypotheses (Madison, 1961), and some emphasize the new structural theory (Gill, 1963). Many authors attribute prescience to Freud of later developments in theory (Hartmann, 1939), and some even think they know what Freud meant to say but did not.

Yet all sciences, especially in their early stages, have an irregular progress. Those investigators who present their lifelong programs of research as a series of logical steps and who do not speak of failures, abandoned methods and findings, disappointments and accidental discoveries, are only deluding themselves and others. Most progress is neither smooth nor planned, but occurs in jump-steps and is difficult to follow logically. Anticipatory ideas of others are often discarded temporarily because the mainstream of thinking was not yet prepared for them—as, for example, some of the early ideas of Adler (1924) and Jung (1933).

It seems apparent, then, that the terms "development," "change," "progress," and "frontiers" are indefinable except at a moment in time and with a personal and cultural bias which lift out of context or specific background those ideas which seem significant. It is understood, of course, that change cannot be equated with progress. Posterity makes this final decision. With these reservations, I shall attempt, nevertheless, to make some broad sweeps of interpretation of what seem to be progressive changes in psychoanalysis, within the limitations of my knowledge and the space available to me.

Change from a Closed to an Open Theoretical System (Libido Theory to Structural Theory)

During the course of his lifetime Freud made many changes in psychoanalytic theory—far more than have been made since. These changes were required because of difficulties in understanding the clinical data with which he maintained close contact, although after about 1920 he practically ceased publishing the empirical source of his revisions (Gedo, Sabshin, Sadow, and Schlessinger, 1964).

The first theory was relatively simple, for it was largely derived from his early work with Breuer on patients under hypnosis. The data indicated that patients' symptoms were connected with memories associated with unpleasant, forbidden, and repressed emotions stimulated during traumatic real-life experiences. What was dammed up and "forgotten" in the unconscious mind was what society disapproved. These feelings and repressed memories returned via symptoms as symbolic substitute expressions. Therefore, abreaction of the feeling and recovery of memory for the traumatic event became a logical therapeutic procedure.

Here we have an open system composed of psychic and environmental transactions in varying degrees of equilibrium which could be modified by trauma or reversed by remembering. When unusual or excessive conflict developed from internal or external pressures a new equilibrium was achieved by shifts in gradients of the system, entailing acting out in behavior, withdrawal, or symptom formation. In any case, defenses against direct expression of feeling were the prime sources of a change, hence the term "defense neuroses."

The next theoretical advance emphasized several concepts. One was concerned with the topography of mental contents with reference to degrees of awareness or, in other words, to their relationship with consciousness (Gill, 1963). Awareness of reality and consciousness was allocated to an ego which functioned within a "reality principle" mediating between the mental and reality. Thus the ego controlled or filtered both perception and motor activity with logic and rationality in a highly organized manner. An absence of awareness and lack of contact with reality was characterized as the area of "the unconscious." A mid-process was called preconscious because its contents could by effort and recall become conscious. Between the conscious and unconscious levels of awareness a conceptual barrier, censorship or repressing function activated repression and kept reality-forbidden feelings, thoughts, and behaviors repressed. The "unconscious," later extended in its conceptual scope and termed the "id," was supposedly a reservoir of excitement in pursuit of gratification or release of tension, operating under the "pleasure principle." It had little if any organization. Its energy arose from bodily sources in the form of instinctual representatives. This transformation concept was applied in several other contexts. Pent-up sexual pressures were presumed to be converted into anxiety. Psychic energy was derived from bodily sources related to developmental stages of sensual pleasure. These traditionally include oral, anal, and phallic phases which ultimately fused into genital sexuality. The derived appetites or energies constituted what was called "libido."

Conceptually, this was an open system. It included biological, psychological, and social components. Action could turn in several directions corresponding to the early theory of dreams which was built on the analogy of reflex activity in the central nervous system. As an integrated system composed of parts, conflicts among these led to various shifts in intensity and localization of function. There was, however, an indication of what later events proved to be a closed conceptual system. The actions of the ego in opposing, controlling, restraining, and steering the primitive instinctual drives were at first allocated to an instinct of self-preservation. Thus, drives and their repression were both instinctual and internal, making it easy later, when it seemed necessary, to omit or to minimize the soma and social reality. The struggle for expression could then be viewed as entirely internal.

A gradual transition occurred due to a number of empirical findings requiring other explanations. Among these was the recognition that patients falsified memories of early parental seduction. These were actually fantasies based on wishes. The ego seemed to be invested by libidinal drives in various degrees depending on periods of maturation and on episodes of regression from traumatic experience. This seemed to explain narcissism and its variations and to indicate that there were no specific ego instincts. Traumatic neuroses and masochism required a new theory that postulated two instincts or drives—Eros (life) and Thanatos (death)—involved in conflict, neutralization, deneutralization, etc. Since Thanatos had no somatic source or object, the biological basis of psychoanalysis was weakened.

Thus, three factors seem to be responsible for the shift of the psychoanalytic conceptual model to a closed system: (1) sexual fantasies as stimuli for conflict replaced the misinterpreted actual seduction; (2) the need to align narcissism with sexual drives investing the ego, instead of the concept of independent ego instincts; and (3) the apparent need for a death instinct opposing the erotic instincts to explain masochism and sadism.

At this point Freud practically severed psychoanalysis from its biological roots. He also modified his sociological insights, for he considered that the latency period and the superego (at one time) were phylogenetic inheritances of acquired characteristics—truly a Lamarckian concept in pure form. (Compare this with the more acceptable thesis that the influences of culture are transmitted, with modifications, from generation to generation by symbols which constitute the genes of culture.) Social and cultural determinants of personality and neuroses became minimized with the result that on balance psychoanalysis gradually became a closed system of intrapsychic forces. Correspondingly, in psychoanalytic therapy analyst and patient form a closed transference system excluding contact or information from all other human informants. As a closed system psychoanalysis ignored the other behavioral disciplines and their findings. Organized psychoanalysis has never moved far from this position, even though Freud himself subsequently did.

Another shift occurred when topological theory became inadequate since the allocated functions of ego and superego could not be attributed to specific levels of awareness, occurring as they did on both conscious and unconscious levels. The structural concept of id replaced the topography of the unconscious, and the so-called structures of ego and superego were now viewed in opposition to id drives. Anna Freud's (1936) crucial studies of defenses implicated reality as the source of many defensive operations and of contributing to self-identity and the organization of reality. More and more evidence indicated not only a constitutional origin of the strength of drives, but also that hormones and drugs influenced their quality and quantity, indicating anew the biological roots of mentation.

Hartmann (1939) put the final touch on the transition from a closed system to an open one. He theorized that the ego has an autonomous derivation and does not, as previously considered, develop from the matrix of id processes through conflict. The autonomous ego carries the potentialities of cognition, perception, speech, and memory and other secondary processes which are adaptive to reality and prepare the individual for an average expectable environment. Freedom for independent development does not avoid conflict between the id forces and the restraining ego functions. It does, however, insure adaptation that is independent of basic drives or resolution of their conflict-producing pressures. Thus again, psychoanalysis conceptually resumed the position of a biopsychosocial open system.

It was not alone the structural theory which made the turn. The concept of adaptation was even more important. When mental functions were viewed not only from topological, dynamic, and economic frames of reference (degrees of awareness, mechanisms and energy), but also from the adaptive point of view, there was made explicit a biological system in transaction with the environment.

In the meantime revolt against the dominance of instinct and drive forces in psychoanalytic theory turned many analysts to a more "social" point of view. Included among these were Sullivan (1947), Horney (1939), Fromm (1941), and Thompson (1950). Often they seemed to go to the opposite extreme by apparently neglecting or minimizing the biological. Others such as Rado (1956) developed a psychosocial theory characterized by its emphasis on adaptation. Erikson's (1950) contributions heavily support the open system concept because he utilized maturational phases of development, according to psychoanalytic theory, in correlation with critical periods and phase-specific crises varying with the personal, social, and cultural environments. Erikson's work resulted in concepts closely related to value systems and ideologies from social theory when he described the processes through which ego identity is developed, and those resulting in regressive identity diffusion.

The Concept of Psychic Energy (Economic Theory)

Although Freud first used the term libido to denote a psychic sexual appetite, when the psychoanalytic model became closed, internal pressures, forces, activities, and conflicts seemed to require an explanatory or intervening variable which had both quality and quantity. Psychic energy is the term employed as synonymous with libido, and often both are combined as the "energy of libido." Arising from specific locations or "zones" of the body, as a representative of drives, it becomes the measure of the demands of the body on the mind. Libido, in this theoretical framework, can create tension or unpleasure if not discharged. It can accumulate, flow out to objects as cathexes or changes of energy, become fixed, displaced, or regressed. None of these terms has clear meanings, but they attempt to explain the storage, transmission, and expression of "libidinal energy." When the concept of separate ego instincts was abandoned and a death instinct was suggested, libido was broadened from its purely sexual connotation to become the life instinct (Bieber, 1958).

The concept of psychic energy has become extremely important in classical psychoanalytic discourse, but its validity is open to serious question. According to Colby (1961, p. 360), "Information is not matter, it is not energy, it is just information." The series of words—instinct, drive, action, force, and energy—are misconceptions. There is no relation of "psychic energy" to any known form of energy, and it is not remotely related to the physical concept of force. Wiener (1950) also states:

> In the employment of the word energy by Freud and by certain schools of physiologists, neither justification [for the use of the term energy] is present; or at the very most, no one has proved it so. There was a plethora of materialistic biological writing at the end of the last century in which the language of physics was bandied around in a very unphysical way. The same sort of quantity was now termed an energy and now a force regardless of the fact that the laws of transformation of force are widely different from those of energy (p. 189).

Lashley and Colby (1957) stated: Where instinctive activities have been analyzed experimentally, as in our studies of hunger, mating and maternal behavior, there is nothing that suggests free or transferable energy. There are variations in thresholds of activity with consequent differences in the arousing stimuli, dominance of a reaction system with suppression of other activities, and changes in the effective stimulus and the pattern of response due to observable formation of associations. The behavior can be explained without assumption of any energy other than the interaction of specific neural elements (p. 234).

The great neurophysiologist Sherrington (1940) wrote: "The mental is not examinable as a form of energy. That in brief is the gap which parts psychiatry and physiology. No mere running around the cycle of 'forms of energy' takes us across the chasm" (p. 289).

It is not difficult to understand the need at one time for a concept of "force" with heuristic value in a new motivational approach to psychology. Unfortunately libido and energy have lent themselves too easily to reification. An essential question is why the dual system of aggressive and libidinal instincts was needed. One obvious answer is the requirement of antagonistic instincts in a system based on conflict. The other possibility is that Jung had consolidated his own advocacy of a single instinct theory earlier than Freud (Glover, 1950), and the antagonism between these two giants made agreement impossible. Although Jung also used psychic energy as an explanatory device, it seems to be more necessary in a closed system based on the principles of drives-in-conflict than in an adaptational frame of reference involving interpersonal or social conflict in behavior. It should be possible to postulate some means by which organization of a system maintains itself, grows and transacts without having recourse to a "Maxwellian demon" called libido or psychic energy.

Information Theory as Replacement for for Psychic Energy or Libido

The most recently organized science of molecular biology has developed a significant prototype for biological processes. Its fundamental principle states that the DNA molecule is the structural chemical equivalent of the hereditary gene code, RNA is the messenger which transmits information from DNA to protein molecules according to exact specifications. Expressed more succinctly, information is coded, transmitted, and encoded. But even at the molecular level there are cooperative, inhibitory, and facilitatory processes and feedback systems insuring relatively effective control and regulation of information. Yet errors, disorders, and recombinations insure mutations which are inhibited or facilitated through transactions with the environment.

Information actually involves the development of organization and thereby coincides with negative entropy. Information even in the processes of its codification and transmission utilizes a minimal amount of energy. As a matter of fact, the higher levels of organization of the central nervous system are not concerned with the continuation of action, but with the crucial function of stopping or starting it.

There has been a great reluctance on the part of many psychoanalysts to give up the words "energy" and "cathexis" because of their relationship to the original psychoanalytic theory based on the then current concepts in physics. Actually a shift in language denotes a shift in conceptual thinking, and it is most important for psychoanalysts to learn how to think in terms of information and communication, without the use of energic or topological language. The result would be a lessening of reification, a decrease in esoteric speculation, and a badly needed commonality with other sciences.

Marcus (1962, 1965) has recently shown that instinctual processes may be viewed as a communication system involved in control and self-regulation through the transmission of information. Informational processes concerned with purposeful behavior require a negative feedback which enables compensatory behavior to restore the system's output to its normal state. In all information systems control is involved. Functional analysis involves the intrinsic organization of the structure and the properties of the system. Behavioral analysis considers the output of the system and its relation to input. The function of the system itself is identified by the transactional processes proceeding across its boundaries. As we shall describe later, these basic qualities of information and control identify systems theory (structural theory, in psychoanalytic terms) and nothing significant in terms of content need be lost by substituting information for energy. Instead, a greater sharpness in definition of systems of information at various levels will probably result in specific, well-defined, and testable psychoanalytic hypotheses.

Alexander (1958) proposed that the need for instinct theory utilizing inherent life and death forces has been a useful metaphor at one time and that its heuristic value needs replacement according to modern neurophysiological knowledge (Holt, 1965). The organism functions at different levels of complexity, but no level is separable from experience and none is stable (Greenfield and Lewis, 1965) since there is a constant process of organization and reorganization. The degree of ordered arrangement or freedom indicates structure. Accordingly, the so-called id functions, which are the most primitive, that is, the least affected by experience or time, are the least structured.

Alexander also suggested that the life instincts in open-living systems should be considered as processes involved in organization which is achieved by an increase in information (negative entropy). As a result there is less "freedom of choice" because of self-regulation by feedback mechanisms and more structure. Actions not coordinated and subordinated to functions of the total organism have more freedom and spill over into eroticized or sexual behavior. Thus, Alexander postulated that sexual behavior arises "when there is an amount of excitation in excess of what is needed by the organism in its survival activities and when excitations which could not be absorbed and included in the structure of the ego, because of a neurotic interruption of normal maturation, find isolated discharge either in the form of perversions or in neurotic symptoms" (1958, p. 300).

Despite Alexander's mixture of concepts and language using information in the same hypothesis with excitation and discharge of energy, it can be noted as an example that there is a growing attempt to abandon the concepts of instinct (drive) and energy. Substituting for these are the newer biological concepts of information whose dimensions and explanatory powers are still to be defined and tested (Ruesch and Bateson, 1951; Colby, 1964; Bateson and Jackson, 1962; Jaffe, 1959). *When applied to studies of development we should search for distortions in the ways in which information is communicated to the developing child rather than for conflicts in libidinal trends to determine the end point of different healthy and pathological forms of communication.*

Maturation and Development (Psychological Genetics)

Differentiation of maturation from development is as futile as separating hereditary from environmental influences. Nevertheless, psychoanalysis as a developmental psychology (Rapaport, 1960) has concentrated on the "givens" as intrinsic maturational forces untangled from experience. The focus is on instinctual drives and drive-restraining forces unrelated to actual functioning which only later refines and increases efficiency under the guidance of function (Weiss, 1939).

After Freud's theory of trauma or seduction failed, greater focus in the closed-system era was placed on internal psychological reality beyond anamnestic experience and independent of the environment (Rapaport, 1959). Maturation, although modified by reality, was traced back to specific drive elements. External factors inhibitory to drive discharge separated ego from id, followed by a relatively independent existence of ego functions and ego-id conflict. However, the restraining forces, like the instincts, were considered to be innate (Rapaport, 1960). Their relation to learning experience has not been explained in psychoanalytic theory.

Psychoanalysis, however, as a method of investigation and treatment has utilized data derived from adults to describe and categorize phases of development. Maturation and development were considered from the frame of reference of bodily zones, each one in turn presumed to be the source of libidinal energy. Firmly embedded not only in psychoanalytic but also in general psychological literature are formulations of oral, anal, phallic, and genital stages of development sometimes including urethral, and often dividing the oral stage into sucking and biting phases and the anal into expulsive and retentive phases. These stages have been used as referents of personality and character development and as fixation points for various psychopathological entities. Eventually they became linked to behavioral characteristics in social situations and various life crises through a process of epigenesis (Erikson, 1950).

This developmental or genetic core of psychoanalytic theory has been derived from analytic reconstructions of the long-distant past—a dubious and inaccurate method. Little additional help can be obtained from parental interrogation since forgetting and inadequate self-evaluation distort information obtained from parents. The psychoanalysis of children is also a reconstructive process. Although the subject is closer in time to critical periods of development, resistances to remembering are sometimes even stronger than for adults.

Thus, the theoretical statements regarding development stem from psychoanalytic methods if not from pure speculation. Other investigators such as Gesell and Amatruda (1941) studied the unfolding of patterned behavior in infants with a "psychomorphological" approach. Piaget has been the leader of direct observations of the maturational phases of children (1951). The application of the ethological approach lately has implicated learning in the earlier period of human life by "imprinting" (Tinbergen, 1951). The psychosomatic field popular in the 1930's led to a re-emphasis on zones of development, especially because of Alexander's "vector" theory. Studies were made of culturally imposed habits of feeding and elimination (Mead, 1947) in an attempt to establish correlations with the character of nonliterate cultures.

Grinker (1953) indicated that no one method of investigation—psychoanalysis, child observation or anthropological studies—can stand alone. All are necessary and require more than speculation and a wider view than that restricted to specific zones and orifices. The maturing child has a body that consists of more than mouth, anus, and genitals, and it has a vast organization of visceral functions. The infant is born with a specific inherited (constitutional) potential within its visceral, motoric, and ego subsystems. Despite their genic derivation they require potentiation and are modified through stimuli and deprivations stemming from the social and physical environment. The neonatal organism, although already somewhat differentiated, tends to react globally in response to all forms of stress and needs, including hunger, thirst, pain, and the like. In this earliest phase learning probably occurs through the process of imprinting.

Subsequent maturation is associated with differentiation into part functions following a relatively common timetable. Correspondingly, the needs of the part functions steer the infant toward the part objects necessary for gratification. These communicate by means of signs, and major learning, therefore, seems to occur through conditioning and reinforcement.

During this period internal need tensions are not clearly distinguishable from need satisfactions or need frustrations so that the inner-outer dimensions are not clear. In a later phase the actions and subsequent reactions of the infant and mother establish a transactional feedback relationship first within a symbiotic unit, later between them as separated organisms. The mother is influenced by her own developmental personality derivatives, her ethnic tradition, and the current cultural values, and has her own problems in maintaining an integrative capacity in relation to her child. The infant's requirements in its self-action influence the mother toward the role of mothering, although it may be insufficient for the particular infant, and during the process the mother herself matures (Benedek, 1959).

As the ego functions which are concerned with cognizance and communication with environment develop, the human attributes of symbolic transformation mature. At this period greater capacity for reverberating transactions with other individuals occurs, replacing the effect of child and mother on each other in simple interactions. Then human symbolic learning increases in both quantity and refinement. The later development of the psychological system accompanying neocortical functioning, involving object relationship and the formation of word symbols, integrates as well as screens or reacts against the imprints of the earliest experiences, memory traces, and primary affects. Finally, although still not yet well understood, learning through identification becomes an important factor in adaptation (Grinker, 1957; Lichtenstein, 1961).

Although the field of "child development" has become extremely active in response to the information vacuum indicated above, progress has been made mostly in the understanding of somatic rather than psychological development. The striking exception is the work of Anna Freud and her colleagues, which extends over three decades. Her monograph (1965) summarizes this extensive research and is a beacon light for current and future progress in the study of child development in health and illness. She indicates the powerful influence of the environment on the child, in contrast to many analysts who are concerned exclusively with internal innate forces (Klein, 1950). Yet, external factors alone are not pathogenic agents. In this statement we see that the continuum-concept in etiology has finally been accepted. Experience is interpreted by the growing organism according to the phase-adequate complexes, affects, anxieties, and fantasies which are aroused by them (A. Freud, 1965). The child's position in a curve of psychological growth is a resultant from maturation, adaptation, and structuralization. The child's needs require an environment which can satisfy them. In fact the child has to teach its mother how to mother him so that he may learn to differentiate from her (Des Lauriers, 1962). Anna Freud points out the error of the concept of steadily progressive maturation and adaptation. Psychological development is associated with unequal shifts and periods of regression. "Constant forward and backward movements, progression and regression, alternate and interact with each other" (1965, p. 105). The difficulty in determining criteria of health and illness and the inadequacy of our diagnostic classifications as well as our prognostic indices are stressed by her.

It is impossible to enumerate the evidences of progress in theory and practice developed by Anna Freud's group. Briefly, it has looked clearly at the processes of psychological growth, using the observational techniques of general psychiatry, the psychoanalytic techniques of child analysis, both verbal and play, and the observational techniques of the child development field. For example: "Obviously, what determines the direction of development are not the major infantile events and constellations in themselves but a multitude of accompanying circumstances, the consequences of which are difficult to judge both retrospectively in adult analysis and prognostically in the assessment of children. They include external and internal, qualitative and quantitative factors" (A. Freud, 1965, p. 193). Based on these concepts Anna Freud and her co-workers have established a useful index derived from process studies from which great advances in our knowledge of health and illness should accrue. Even more important for the progress of psychoanalysis than the broad statements made by Anna Freud of the "openness" and multifactorial processes in growth and development, in health and illness, and in therapeutic success and failure are her sharp and clear statements. All of these are so clearly defined that they may be considered as hypotheses essential for the testing of psychoanalytic theory by a variety of methods.

Despite the current attitude of pessimism concerning the possibilities of research on "mental health" because of the entanglement with value systems, considerable knowledge may be obtained about various kinds of mental health using longitudinal-descriptive, psychodynamic, behavioral, and sociocultural approaches. The implications of this statement are that the "total field" should include: hereditary and constitutional data, an accurate description of physical and emotional experiences during maturation and development, a knowledge of resulting psychodynamics insofar as possible, a study of behavior whenever maturity is reached (when growth and progress has ceased or slowed), a study of the sociocultural matrix within which development occurred, and those matrices in which the subjects function well. Rather than considering value judgments as obstacles to research, they become attributes of the culture and suitable for scientific investigation. Such a field, large as it may be, furnishes the opportunity for the study of permutations of a large number of variables which may be combined into a lesser number of categories or systems in transaction. This should permit the crystallization of types of "mental health" amid a spectrum of psychopathology and should lead to the finding and formulation of a number of specific hypotheses (Grinker, 1963). These are considered in greater detail by Offer and Sabshin (1966).

Psychoanalysis Viewed as a System (Dynamic Theory)

Rapaport (1950, 1951, 1953) attempted to categorize psychoanalysis as a system with the following generalizations: (1) the subject matter is behavior (including latent behavior); (2) behavior is integrated and indivisible (multiple components); (3) no behavior stands in isolation; (4) all behavior is part of a genetic series and is an epigenetic product; (5) the crucial determinants of behavior are unconscious; (6) all behavior is ultimately drive determined; (7) all behavior disposes of and is regulated by psychic energy; (8) all behavior has structural determinants; (9) all behavior is determined by reality (is adaptive); and (10) all behavior is socially determined (psychosocial).

How does one reconcile these sweeping global statements and how do these opposing concepts become integrated into a whole system? It is clear from many sources that organism and environment are integrated in adaptation. Constitution, personality, social factors, and specific reality situations are inseparable—drives and reality are only artificial demarcations of internal and external aspects of life. In fact, reality testing is an *act* which determines the objective or subjective nature of perception. It is only the mode of the act and the part of object with which action occurs that differentiates stages of development.

Psychoanalysts are beginning to pay more attention to behaviors (the data from which were too often neglected) because these reveal conflicts, defenses, and assets and represent observable entities of psychic reality with empirical referents which can be made public and replicable for research. Behavior as overt mentation blends knowing, feeling, and willing, none of which can be divorced from either motivational or social origins. In embryogenesis of behavior Coghill (Herrick, 1949) pointed out that differentiation from an undifferentiated matrix resulted in integration and control by the whole system and the appearance of gradients among the parts. Yet to some degree the parts as subsystems maintain actual or latent opposition or conflict with each other. This is determined by the quality and quantity of information fed into the parts.

Most psychologists have tacitly abandoned the duality of instinct representatives or drives (Eros and Thanatos) and the concept of two different energy systems. The concept of one inherited biologically undifferentiated drive (Herold, 1941, 1942) places the emphasis on part structures in the realm of motives and modes of expression. These have a natural ontogenetic history which ultimately determines the quality of the finally integrated whole. In the Jacksonian sense evolution and ontology are associated with the development of new functions associated with more control or inhibition of part functions (Grinker, 1939). Yet nothing is lost because weakening of integrative functions is accompanied by return of inhibited part functions (sensual satisfactions, memories, behaviors).

The same principle may be applied to conceptual systems in that parts tend to break away from the whole as control or attention is weakened. Such was the case when psychoanalytic theory focused strongly on purely psychological phenomena. Thus the biological part became the independent school of Klein (1950), with emphasis on early powerful biological expression of aggression, and the social part was adopted as a whole by Horney (1939), Thompson (1950), Sullivan (1947), et al. Other parts became the basic principles of dissident or splinter groups embellished by subsequent independent developments. Thus Adler preceded Freud in considerations of aggression and ego functions. Jung broke away with a single instinct theory to which modern psychoanalysis currently is veering implicitly.

I now propose to view progress in psychoanalysis from a frame of reference which is applicable to all fields of science and all biological, psychological, and social systems. Such a view does not alter the "facts" derived from observations within each discipline, but a universal or "bridging" scientific language can minimize reification of terms. It can be an antidote against scientism and humanism as artificial polarities, and it may enable different sciences to relate to each other and eventually even may facilitate the development of a "unified theory" of human behavior. The important point is that with such a frame of reference all systems including soma, psyche, group, society, culture, etc. may be subjected to analysis by a similar set of principles without contaminating their techniques or content (Grinker, 1956).

My choice of this kind of "metapsychology" is based on the conclusion that progress in psychoanalysis has been and will continue to be made through the use of "structural" theory. Unfortunately a variety of terms such as apparatus, system, organization, etc. have been used interchangeably with "structure." I prefer the term *system* used by von Bertalanffy (1962) since it constitutes the main concept in an already existing "general systems theory" and system does not, like structure, induce the image of morphology to which the term structure is most often applied. The main reason for utilizing systems theory is that it enables us to view the progress and viscissitudes of psychoanalytic theory from its dynamic beginnings which described an open system to the topological theory as a closed system and finally to the structural theory which once again is open. For this purpose I shall use only the broadest aspects of systems theory without details.

In any field serving as a background there exist organized patterned processes which we call systems, foci, or structures. These systems may be naturally occurring, empirically observable and describable, such as the nervous system. Others may be conceptual or patterned processes functioning through time and only describable in terms of their resultant effects or behaviors, such as psychoanalysis. Tangible or intangible, such a structure has boundaries which are open, with various degrees of permeability. It has extent in space and time—past, present, and future—independent of causality. Its position in space does not denote mass but the extent of its process.

Every system is composed of parts which in relationship to one another comprise the whole not simply in summation, and each part or subsystem has its own components. In and of itself, a system is a patterned process of action which has an adaptive purpose in the living economy. Each system maintains its organization or wholeness by regulatory devices which are homeostatic or equilibratory by goal-seeking, for example, drive-reducing activity. In addition goal-changing activities such as exploratory behavior are actualizations in response to external conditions impinging on the system's potentialities and which result in novel reactions as in evolution and creativity. Every system resists distintegration by realignments of gradients, partial sacrifice of structure or function, or by hardening its boundaries to decrease permeability and openness. Finally, every system is in patterned transactional processes with all others which constitute its environment, to a degree dependent on intersystemic closeness, significance for viability and external stress.

Transaction, rather than self-action or interaction, which is the effect of one system on another, is the relationship of two or more systems within a specified environment which includes both, not as specific entities, but only as they are in relatedness with each other within a specific space-time field. It is a reciprocal and reverberating process. Using such a conceptual scheme we may view relationships of structures, functions, scientific disciplines, methodologies, etc. We may subject each system in the field to inquiry concerning a variety of processes of communication. From these processes we can extrapolate principles which are clearly present in biology, psychology, and sociology. Common to all, however, are relationships which exist independent of source of energy and transmission or power structures; all systems within themselves and among each other are involved in coding, transmitting, decoding, and rearranging information.

Modern psychoanalysis requires field theory to include the transactions among multiple functions—genic, developmental, organ activities, hormones, nervous system, mental structures, social, cultural and physical environment—and to account for degrees of health and illness. One system does not exclude the other, and one alone cannot tell the whole story. How do we view the human being as a system in transaction instead of as a fractionated structure? We can view his genic system, his hormonal system, his nervous system, or his mental systems independently by means of special techniques as systems in their own right. Our modern task is to view these systems as parts of a larger whole by systematically studying the relationships among them. We do this by correlations of changes over specified time, changes in response to strains of development or to other stresses which disturb equilibrium.

Operationally the whole human being and his many subsystems can fruitfully be viewed as a *behaving* organism utilizing thoughts, feelings, gestures, postures, and total movement in relation to a variety of others in his surrounding world. Behaviors of all kinds, not only verbal, communicate information regarding all component aspects of personality, drives, conflicts, defense, ideals, since the ego functions as the final common pathway —in and out—of personality traits and states. Behavior reveals dilemmas, liabilities, assets, and compromises of the person in action. Therein lies the field for future study, awaiting appropriate scientific methods which are unbiased with regard to any specific theory.

Psychoanalysis as Science

Science augments or transcends common sense by developing hypotheses of more or less generality from which particular consequences are induced and which can be tested by observation and/or experimentation. Lower levels of generalities can be used to induce hypotheses at higher levels so that generality increases until finally theoretical concepts cease to be direct properties of things observable. Such theoretical concepts are then connected to even higher levels of logical relationships expressed sometimes in mathematical terms. Science is an enterprise to investigate the behavior of things and events under specific controlled conditions and draws conclusions about generalized behaviors from which prediction of events not yet known may be made (Kaplan, 1964). Included in the criteria of science are methods of control, replication, reliability and validity-testing, statistical soundness, and parsimony.

Theory gets its acid test by consonance with clinical findings, not alone by its internal consistency—although even in the latter respect psychoanalytic theory has many contradictions. One cannot accept the psychoanalytic paradigm completely or be convinced that the whole theoretical organization is so cohesive that its so-called unity would be destroyed by disavowing some of its parts, as Hartmann states (1964).

Countless statements both pro and con have been made concerning psychoanalysis as a science. Hilgard (1952), for example, stated that psychoanalysis as a science is bad science; most articles written are clinical studies, not research. On the other hand Gitelson (1964) believes that psychoanalysis is *the* basic science of psychiatry and that psychiatry can only progress by the use of the psychoanalytic method. Waelder (1960) believes that psychoanalysis is often misunderstood even by insiders and that analysts are resistant to criticism attributing it to emotional bias.

One of the problems requiring clarification has been the so-called metapsychology which Freud once called a witch. Metapsychology is a philosophical speculation concerned with mind—its origin, structure, function, and relationship to physiology and pathology. It is speculation that cannot be verified by direct experience and therefore cannot be influenced by observations or so-called facts. For a young science metapsychology appeared prematurely as a theory of theories or as speculative science. It has influenced observations by tending to mold them according to the dynamic, economic, topological or structural, and adaptive theories. Thus levels of discourse have been confused, shifts from observations to metapsychology are made in one jump, and observations are filtered to fit into metapsychology.

Farrell (1961) states that psychoanalysis is not unified theory and that each of its different parts, such as the theories of instincts, development, psychic structure, economics, or defenses and symptom formation, require testing. When psychoanalytic complexity is broken into its parts, its "mythical" character vanishes and each part theory can be tested.

The unscientific global sweeps of much of psychoanalysis have been evidenced by the extent to which its concepts have been applied and by the large body of its hypotheses which are still untestable or at least not yet tested. For example, Glover (1950) states that a psychological theory is worthless unless it can give an objective account of structure, function, dynamics of mind; trace stages of mental development from infancy to senescence; and isolate the main factors giving rise to mental disorder and correlate them with mechanisms of normal mental life, both individual and social! Zilboorg (1951) expresses the same global conception when he says, "Psychoanalysis seeks to penetrate into the deeper layers of human motivation and seeks to formulate general laws which govern the unconscious and its expression in or its influence on man's manifest behavior" (p. 12). Such an approach tends to apply the concepts of psychoanalysis to the individual, the family, small groups, nations, cultures, politics, history, biography, and art. Serious errors thus have been promulgated by attempting to apply to all forms of inquiry a method developed for use in a two-person situation.

Some psychoanalysts have contended that research, hypothesis-finding, and proof in their field can be accomplished only by using the psychoanalytic method. But considering that the method of psychoanalysis is appropriate only for strongly motivated, unhappy persons, and considering also the privacy of the situation and the inevitable distortions of memory and countertransference, can research worthy of the name be carried out? Where are the raw data from which modern psychoanalysts develop their theories? There are many difficulties inherent in presenting the mass of material from the psychoanalysis of a patient, but methods could be devised so that others do not feel that the conceptual thinking of today is devoid of an empirical foundation.

There is a current trend toward making auditory and visual recordings of the psychoanalytic process, which might be very helpful provided these data were not collected, stored, and forgotten. Certainly a nonparticipant observer could help to view the psychoanalytic process objectively with little interference with the technique. Actually several attempts have been made by Shakow (1960), Colby (1960), and Alexander and his co-workers (Levy, 1961) to study psychoanalytic and psychotherapeutic operations by recording and filming the process or by observations behind a one-way screen. Haggard, Hiken, and Isaacs (1965) have dealt with the problems as an investigation. Must psychoanalytic research be done only by a therapist? Does the transference languish and can the investigator maintain a dual role? They recorded sessions to determine if free association, transference, or interpretations suffered because of the research intrusion. They found that the therapist was relatively unaffected by the third-party observers and that the process could be studied with valid objectivity.

It seems necessary to introduce such scientific methods into psychoanalytic research. But many psychoanalysts seem hostile to scientific methods, as if such methods sought to vitiate intuition (which in itself is researchable). Indeed, Glover (1950) harshly states that psychoanalysts maintain an unrestricted license to interpret which results in a degree of fabrication that vitiates their conclusions.

Coincident with the increasing trend toward greater rigor in psychoanalytic and psychiatric research, there also has been an uneasy admixture of existentialism with psychoanalysis, in esoteric and confused language. There is a growing field called ontological psychoanalysis that has little to do with psychoanalysis but involves the philosophy of "becoming." Weisman (1965), for example, states that psychoanalysis is not a science but draws on the experiences of science to clarify philosophical issues; only a sense of reality and responsibility endows man's conduct with value and validity. The vacuum which such speculations fill is the lack in psychoanalytic theory of a supra-ordinate process which functions in integrating the many identifications which constitute the ego, ego ideal, and superego and which organize behavior into available social roles. The most suitable available term is the "self," which is a synthetic compound of many identifications. Erikson (1956) uses the term self-identity which, as a gestalt composed of many identifications, is greater than its parts. It is attained when the multiple identifications have permitted satisfactory interaction with family roles and when society recognizes the subject as a person. There is then self-realization and mutual recognition between self and the others, and concepts of values, ideologies, and purposes (Grinker, 1957).

Happily, there is a growing trend by some psychoanalysts to clarify the meaning of their jargon and to deal constructively with semantic confusions. The monotonously repetitive quotations of original terms from Freud seem to have emotional value to their users in that they minimize the quoter's doubts, but they add nothing. Kaplan (1964) complains that psychoanalytic terms are not constructs nor do they refer to observables but lean heavily on theory—thus tautology ensues. Bentley's words "naming is knowing" (1954, p. 345) are not accepted in psychoanalysis. Freud's metaphors, never completely pure, were substitutes for the absence in the standard European languages of words with psychological meaning, but their heuristic value has been transcended because of their reification.

Beres (1965) has attempted to clarify psychoanalytic tautologies and hypothetical constructs. For example he differentiates process, as a mode of function, from structure, as a mode of organization. The ego as a construct has no "contents," "interior," or "border." Spatial terms should not be used for functional dynamic processes. There is no objection to the use of shorthand symbols such as id or ego; physics, embryology and other sciences also have their symbols. But they require sharp definition. Waelder (1960) has defined various levels of discourse, which unfortunately are often confused and intermixed. The first, or empirical, is rarely utilized; instead there is an immediate jump to theory. The second is the level of clinical psychoanalytic theory, the third that of general psychological theory, and finally there is the level of metapsychology, which is independent of data and consists of speculations regarding the relationship of theories of lesser abstractions.

Despite the attitude of many psychoanalysts that the analytic method is the only one for research in the field, as psychoanalysis is becoming more open as a system, greater contact and receptivity in relation to other disciplines is occurring (Frenkel-Brunswik, 1952). Kubie (1963, p. 334) states that "it may be predicted that in the long run the application of principles based on models derived from modern electronic engineering, information theory, communications engineering, mathematical machinery, digital and analogic computers and electronic devices in general, will clarify much that at present is confused in psychoanalytic theory, concepts, and terminology. Eventually, these will furnish analysis with further techniques for critical self-examination." Sanford (cf. Bellak, 1959) believes that "other methods besides the psychoanalytic one are useful for testing psychoanalytic hypotheses and that these hypotheses are no less psychoanalytic for being tested outside the consulting room" (p. 993). Stanton (cf. Bellak, 1959) advocates using methods not characteristically psychoanalytic. Pumpian-Mindlin stated (1952) that psychoanalysis as a model must become an open system otherwise certain observations are blocked. Researches on sleep and dream deprivation leading to psychotic-like states (Fisher, 1965), new results evoking memories from electrical stimulation of the human cerebral cortex, handling of infantile animals leading to alterations in subsequent learning, psychophysiological studies on the menstrual cycle, experimental neuroses, and the ego psychology of academic psychologists all are contributing to modification of psychoanalytic theory (Grinker, 1964). As Ernest Jones (1936, p. 275) said:

In the field of Theory, on the other hand (in contradistinction to technique), I am inclined to anticipate very considerable changes in the course of the next twenty years or so. The scaffolding, as he modestly called it, that Freud has erected, has stood much rough weather extraordinarily well, though he has had to repair and strengthen it from time to time. But it would be counter to all our knowledge of the history and essential nature of science to suppose that it will not be extensively modified with the passage of time. The preconceptions from the world of contemporary scientific thought . . . with which Freud approached his studies had a visible influence on his theoretical structure, and they necessarily bear the mark of a given period. We must expect that other workers, schooled by different disciplines than his, will be able to effect fresh orientations, to formulate fresh correlations. In spite of our natural piety we must brace ourselves to welcome some change, fortifying ourselves with the reflection that to face new truth and to hold truth above all other consideration had been Freud's greatest lesson to us and his most precious legacy to psychological science.

Summary

There is no question that the conceptual form and contents of psychoanalysis have been changing. It cannot be affirmed that all these changes signify progress. Whether or not the abandonment of some of the old theories and the adoption of new ones represent progress or regression only the future will decide. Many among us have been impatient and dismayed with the apparent lack of progress, the repetitive quotations from Freud's writings, the un-understandable jargon, the semantic confusions, and the violation of ordinary respect for levels of discourse and for scientific principles. Nevertheless, change in every discipline has its own autonomous pace and patience becomes a necessity if not a virtue; the recognition of the need for change is in itself a sign of progress.

A crucial indication of real progress is the indication that, as a formal system of theoretical concepts, psychoanalysis has moved from an intermediate position of closure to one of openness. The move from a topological to a structural frame of reference has made psychoanalytic systems and subsystems amenable to consideration within general systems theory, thereby bringing psychoanalysis into relationship with other disciplines. The developments of ego psychology, previously the almost exclusive subject matter of academic psychology, have decreased the implication of drives and libidinal energy as the fuel for mind. Progress from libido theory to adaptational theory has brought scientific concepts of biology and sociology back into focus. Slowly but inevitably information theory is replacing libido theory and its energic concomitants. Silently but definitely the dual drive theory, never fully accepted even by its originator Freud, is being replaced by a monolithic theory of motivation (Eros) not too different from the ancient ideas of life. Life is a process that is there and necessary. Any other consideration at this time becomes speculative science, philosophy, or religion.

Another crucial advance occurred when the resolution of the Oedipus conflict and bisexuality and their "substitutive neuroses" were dethroned as the supreme indicators of successful analysis. Perhaps changing clinical experience and insights into pregenital problems was the cause of this shift in emphasis, or perhaps contemporary patients, because of profound social and cultural alterations, are being damaged by deleterious experiences earlier in life. At any rate, the focus on earlier phases of infantile transactions has revived an intense interest in re-evaluating phases of maturation and development, phases in the learning processes and a new interest in health or normality. This could not be accomplished without the aid of other disciplines such as ethology, conditioning, child development, and the use of child observations and experimentation.

Structural theory has made it possible to conceive of the mental system in open relation with other systems, of relationships of its parts to one another and to the whole, and this has made available the concepts of coding, transmission and encoding of information, with feedback to insure effective control or regulation. Exciting possibilities are evidenced by the results of some first tentative steps in this direction.

There have been concentrated efforts to define psychoanalytic terms clearly, to clean out semantic confusions, and to specify levels of discourse. At the same time, the reliance on metapsychology as an ideology, a value system, or a philosophy has been diminishing. All this requires a form of scientific rigor applied to conceptual thinking and to methodology without fear of throwing away intuition which can be investigated by newer approaches to the use of countertransference.

Above all, psychoanalysis has ceased to fulfill the hope of being a unified theory capable of explaining everything from motivation to history, from love to global war, from stubbornness to artistry. A unified theory does not exist; when it does, psychoanalytic concepts will furnish only a part of it. However, psychoanalytic concepts, even at this stage of development, are the most fruitful ones with which to view intrapsychic processes. Psychodynamic methods constitute the best method by which to study intrapsychic events. Yet these too in time will have to be altered and improved.

The main body of psychoanalysts still form a military "square" huddled together in defense against change. Those individuals who drop out are immediately replaced. Only a small body of courageous heterodox analysts have volunteered to search out new terrain to form alliances with members of other disciplines. These small patrols are often depleted by a magnetic attraction to the organizational spirit of the main body and its emphasis on "belonging." However, the emphasis on scientific education in our schools, the newer forms of medical education, and the eclectic spirit in psychiatric training centers promise to create more investigators who can follow Kubie's clarion call for a rebellious, challenging heterodoxy (1963): "The heterodoxy which counts is the heterodoxy of the fully informed and erudite scholar who rebels against orthodoxy within himself and within his own camp" (p. 314).

References

Adler, A. *The Practice and Theory of Individual Psychology.* New York: Harcourt, Brace, 1924.

Alexander, F. "Unexplored Areas in Psychoanalytic Theory and Treatment" (1958). In *The Scope of Psychoanalysis, 1921–1961: Selected Papers of . . .* New York: Basic Books, 1961. Pp. 183–201, 319–335.

Bateson, G., and Jackson, D. D. "Some Varieties of Pathogenic Organization." *Proceedings of the Association for Research in Nervous and Mental Diseases,* 42 (1962), 270–282.

Bellak, L. (ed.). "Conceptual and Methodological Problems in Psychoanalysis." *Proceedings of the New York Academy of Medicine,* 76 (1959), 971–1134.

Benedek, Therese. "Parenthood as a Developmental Phase." *Journal of American Psychoanalytic Association,* 7 (1959), 389–417.

Bentley, A. F. *Inquiry into Inquiries.* Boston: Beacon Press, 1954.

Beres, D. "Structure and Function in Psychoanalysis." *International Journal of Psychoanalysis,* 46 (1965), 53–63.

Bertalanffy, L. von. "General Systems Theory: A Critical Review." *Yearbook of the Society for General Systems Theory,* 7 (1962), 1–21.

Bieber, I. "A Critique of the Libido Theory." *American Journal of Psychoanalysis,* 18 (1958), 52–65.

Colby, K. M. "Experiment on the Effects of an Observer's Presence on the Imago System during Psychoanalytic Free-Association." *Behavioral Science,* 5 (1960), 216–232.

Colby, K. M. "Research in Psychoanalytic Information Theory." *American Scientist,* 49 (1961), 358–369.

Colby, K. M. "Experimental Treatment of Neurotic Computer Programs." *American Medical Association Archives of General Psychiatry,* 10 (1964), 217–227.

Des Lauriers, A. *The Experience of Reality in Childhood Schizophrenia.* New York: International Universities Press, 1962.

Erikson, E. H. *Childhood and Society*. New York: Norton, 1950.
Erikson, E. H. "The Problem of Ego Identity." *Journal of American Psychoanalytic Association*, 4 (1956), 56–121.
Farrell, B. A. "Can Psychoanalysis Be Refuted?" *Inquiry*, 1 (1961), 16–36.
Fisher, C. "Psychoanalytic Implications of Recent Research on Sleep and Dreaming. I. Empirical Findings, 197–271; II. Implications for Psychoanalytic Theory." *Journal of the American Psychoanalytic Association*, 13 (1965), 197–304.
Frenkel-Brunswik, Else. "Psychoanalysis and the Unity of Science." *Proceedings of the American Academy of Arts and Sciences*, 80 (1952), 80–271.
Freud, Anna. *The Ego and the Mechanisms of Defence* (1936). New York: International Universities Press, 1946.
Freud, Anna. *Normality and Pathology in Childhood*. New York: International Universities Press, 1965.
Freud, S. *The Standard Edition of the Complete Psychological Works of. . . .* London: Hogarth Press.
Fromm, E. *Escape from Freedom*. New York: Farrar & Rinehart, 1941.
Gedo, J. E., Sabshin, M., Sadow, L., and Schlessinger, N. "Studies on Hysteria." *Journal of American Psychoanalytic Association*, 12 (1964), 734–751.
Gesell, A., and Amatruda, C. S. *Developmental Diagnosis*. New York: Hoeber, 1941.
Gill, M. "Topography and Systems in Psychoanalytic Theory." *Psychological Issues* (1963), Monograph No. 3.
Gitelson, M. "On Identity Crisis in American Psychoanalysis." *Journal of American Psychoanalytic Association*, 12 (1964), 451–476.
Glover, E. *On the Early Development of the Mind*. London: Harcourt, Brace, 1933.
Glover, E. *Freud or Jung*. New York: Norton, 1950.
Greenfield, N. S., and Lewis, W. C. (eds.). *Psychoanalysis and Current Biological Thought*. Madison: University of Wisconsin Press, 1965.
Grinker, R. R., Sr. "A Comparison of Psychological 'Regression' and Neurological 'Inhibition.'" *Journal of Nervous and Mental Diseases*, 89 (1939), 765–781.
Grinker, R. R., Sr. "Reminiscences of a Personal Contact with Freud." *American Journal of Orthopsychiatry*, 10 (1940), 850–854.
Grinker, R. R., Sr. *Psychosomatic Research*. New York: Norton, 1953.
Grinker, R. S., Sr. (ed.). *Toward a Unified Theory of Human Behavior* (1956). 2nd ed.; New York: Basic Books, 1967.
Grinker, R. R., Sr. "On Identification." *International Journal of Psycho-Analysis*, 38 (1957), 1–10.
Grinker, R. R., Sr. "A Philosophical Appraisal of Psychoanalysis." In J. H. Masserman (ed.), *Science and Psychoanalysis* (1958), Vol. 1.
Grinker, R. R., Sr. "A Dynamic Study of the 'Homoclite.'" *Science and Psychoanalysis*, 5 (1963), 115–134.
Grinker, R. R., Sr. "Psychiatry Rides Madly in All Directions." *Archives of General Psychiatry*, 10 (1964), 228–237.

Haggard, E. A., Hiken, Julia R., and Isaacs, K. S. "Some Effects of Recording and Filming on the Psychotherapeutic Process." *Psychiatry*, 28 (1965), 169–191.

Hartmann, H. *Ego Psychology and the Problem of Adaptation* (1939). New York: International University Press, 1958.

Hartmann, H. *Essays on Ego Psychology*. London: Hogarth Press, 1964.

Herold, C. M. "Critical Analysis of the Elements of Psychic Functions." *Psychoanalytic Quarterly*, 10 (1941), 513–544; 11 (1942), 59–82; 11 (1942), 187–210.

Herrick, C. J. *Gregory Eliot Coghill.* Chicago: University of Chicago Press, 1949.

Hilgard, E. R. "Experimental Approaches to Psychoanalysis." In E. Pumpian-Mindlin (ed.), *Psychoanalysis as Science*. Stanford: Stanford University Press, 1952.

Holt, R. R. "A Review of Some of Freud's Biological Assumptions and Their Influence on His Theories." In N. S. Greenfield and W. C. Lewis (eds.), *Psychoanalysis and Current Biological Thought*. Madison: University of Wisconsin Press, 1965.

Horney, Karen. *New Ways in Psychoanalysis*. New York: Norton, 1939.

Jaffe, J. "Electronic Computers in Psychoanalytic Research." *Science and Psychoanalysis*, 2 (1959), 160–172.

Jones, E. "The Future of Psychoanalysis." *International Journal of Psychoanalysis*, 17 (1936), 269–277.

Jones, E. *The Life and Work of Sigmund Freud*. 3 vols.; New York: Basic Books, 1953.

Jung, C. *Modern Man in Search of a Soul.* London: Harcourt, Brace, 1933.

Kaplan, A. *The Conduct of Inquiry*. San Francisco: Chandler, 1964.

Kardiner, A., Karush, A., and Ovesey, L. "A Methodological Study of Freudian Theory: II. The Libido Theory." *Journal of Nervous and Mental Disease*, 129 (1959), 133–143.

Klein, Melanie. *Contributions to Psychoanalysis*. London: Hogarth Press, 1950.

Kubie, L. S. "Missing and Wanted: Heterodoxy in Psychiatry and Psychoanalysis." *Journal of Nervous and Mental Diseases*, 137 (1963), 311–314.

Lashley, K. S., and Colby, K. M. "An Exchange of Views on Psychic Energy and Psychoanalysis." *Behavioral Science*, 2 (1957), 231–240.

Levy, N. A. "An Investigation into the Nature of Psychotherapeutic Process." In J. H. Masserman (ed.), *Psychoanalysis and Social Process*, New York: Grune & Stratton, 1961. Vol. 4, pp. 125–149.

Lichtenstein, H. "Identity and Sexuality." *Journal of American Psychoanalytic Association*, 9 (1961), 179–260.

Madison, P. *Freud's Concept of Repression and Defense*. Minneapolis: University of Minnesota Press, 1961.

Marcus, R. L. "The Nature of Instinct and the Physical Basis of Libido." *Yearbook of the Society for General Systems Theory*, 7 (1962), 133–157.

Marcus, R. L. "Man as a Machine." *Journal of American Psychoanalytic Association*, 13 (1965), 404–422.

Mead, Margaret. "The Concept of Culture and the Psychosomatic Approach." *Psychiatry*, 10 (1947), 57–76.

Mead, Margaret. *Continuities in Cultural Evolution.* New Haven: Yale University Press, 1964.

Offer, D., and Sabshin, M. *Normality: Theoretical and Clinical Concepts of Mental Health.* New York: Basic Books, 1966.

Piaget, J. *The Child's Conception of the World.* New York: Harcourt, Brace, 1929.

Pumpian-Mindlin, E. "The Position of Psychoanalysis in Relation to the Biological and Social Sciences." In E. Pumpian-Mindlin (ed.), *Psychoanalysis as Science.* Stanford: Stanford University Press, 1952, pp. 125–158.

Rado, S. *Psychoanalysis of Behavior.* New York: Grune & Stratton, 1956.

Rapaport, D. "On the Psychoanalytic Theory of Thinking" (1950). In M. M. Gill (ed.), *The Collected Papers of. . . .* New York: Basic Books, 1967. Pp. 313–328.

Rapaport, D. "The Autonomy of the Ego" (1951). In M. M. Gill (ed.), *The Collected Papers of. . . .* New York: Basic Books, 1967. Pp. 357–367.

Rapaport, D. "On the Psychoanalytic Theory of Affects" (1953). In M. M. Gill (ed.), *The Collected Papers of. . . .* New York: Basic Books, 1967. Pp. 476–512.

Rapaport, D. "The Structure of Psychoanalytic Theory" (1959). *Psychological Issues,* No. 2 (1960).

Rapaport, D. "Psychoanalysis as a Developmental Psychology" (1960). In M. M. Gill (ed.), *The Collected Papers of. . . .* New York: Basic Books, 1967. Pp. 820–852.

Ruesch, J., and Bateson, G. *Communication, the Social Matrix of Psychiatry.* New York: Norton, 1951.

Shakow, D. "The Recorded Psychoanalytic Interview as an Objective Approach to Research in Psychoanalysis." *Psychoanalytic Quarterly,* 29 (1960), 82–97.

Sherrington, C. *Man on His Nature.* Cambridge, Eng.: Cambridge University Press, 1940.

Stanton, A. H. "Proposition Concerning Object-Choice." In L. Bellak *et al., Conceptual and Methodological Problems in Psychoanalysis.* New York: Annals of the New York Academy of Sciences, Vol. 76, Oct. 4, 1958. Pp. 1010–1038.

Sullivan, H. S. *Conceptions of Modern Psychiatry.* Washington, D.C.: William Alanson White Foundation, 1947.

Thompson, Clara. *Psychoanalysis: Evolution and Development.* New York: Hermitage Press, 1950.

Tinbergen, N. *The Study of Instinct.* Oxford: Clarendon Press, 1951.

Waelder, R. *Basic Theories of Psychoanalysis.* New York: International Universities Press, 1960.

Weisman, A. D. *The Existential Core of Psychoanalysis: Reality Sense and Responsibility.* New York: Scribner, 1965.

Weiss, P. *Principles of Development.* New York: Henry Holt, 1939.

Wiener, N. "Some Maxims for Biologists and Psychologists." *Dialectica,* 4 (1950), 184–191.

Zilboorg, G. *Sigmund Freud: His Exploration of the Mind of Man.* New York: Scribner, 1951.

2

Motivation, Energy, and Cognitive Structure in Psychoanalytic Theory

LOUIS BREGER

Psychoanalytic theory deals with many aspects of human thought and action, but above all it is a theory of motivation. Its emphasis on the basic urges and forces that underlie human psychology—on man's unconscious impulses, on sexuality and aggression—have made it the most influential theory of human motivation. Yet the conceptual underpinning of the motivational theory—the concepts of psychic energy, of libido, of conservation or economy, of the life and death instincts—has long been its weakest aspect. In fact, the evidence from a variety of sources now makes it clear that a theory based on these concepts is no longer tenable. Those officially committed to it can only defend it by a series of rear-guard actions that seem increasingly ineffectual.

Several writers (Apfelbaum, 1965; Loevinger, 1966) have pointed out that this conceptual underpinning, frequently called Freud's "metapsychology," has long lived in isolated, separate life from the "clinical theory"—the observations and hypotheses with which the psychoanalyst is concerned in his work with patients—and should simply be abandoned as unnecessary.

I would agree that the theory of psychic energy, in its present form, must be given up.

Colby (1955) presents an excellent analysis of this problem and outlines an alternative model. More recently Klein (1967) and Loevinger (1966) have presented some exciting new ideas to deal with the problems to which metapsychological theory has been applied, ideas that may more adequately encompass the observations on which the theory is based.

As will be seen shortly, a number of the problems of the psychoanalytic theory of motivation stem from Freud's consistent attempts to give his theory a biological underpinning: from his earliest efforts to trace the somatic sources of anxiety in blocked orgasm to his later attempts to tie aggression to catabolic processes in the form of a death instinct. While some writers have suggested that this biological "reductionism" itself creates difficulties, a more careful analysis will reveal that the problems stem, not from biology per se, but from the continued reliance on a nineteenth-century neurological model that has proven to be incorrect. Once this model is abandoned, the way is opened to a motivational theory which is consistent with modern conceptions of the brain and nervous system as active information-processing systems.

An area of difficulty closely tied to the motivational theory is the inconsistent treatment of emotion and affect. Emotion and affect present special problems, for it is the affective component that gives the energy theory its personal or subjective appeal. We know what it feels like to be angry or filled with passion or intense fear, and it is easy to think of these states in terms of "force" or "energy." But Freud himself has taught us that our immediate subjective experience is not always a good guide to our state of motivation, and, in fact, the sorts of motivational explanations frequently employed in psychoanalytic theory lack this direct subjective component. For example, they may refer to unconscious factors such as a repressed Oedipus complex or an unconscious sense of guilt which are inferred from certain observations, but which may not have any direct or immediate subjective components. Although affect is presumably relegated to the secondary role of "signal," in explanations of clinical data it is quite frequently affect or emotion that is used as the central motivational concept. Thus, when one speaks of a patient's impulses driving him to do something, or of the anxiety aroused over impulses that may "break through," the referents for "impulses" are typically the affects of anger or anticipations of sexual pleasure. And these referents have no further meaning—it adds nothing to speak of the unconscious impulses that "lie behind" the affects—unless one holds to the untenable model in which *all* psychological phenomena are reduced to tension reduction via stimulus discharge. This problem will become clarified, hopefully, once we see what Freud's tension reduction model is and how it can be modified in the light of modern evidence.

Freud's Biological Assumptions

It was perhaps inevitable that a psychology growing out of nineteenth-century science should formulate its theory in terms of forces and energies. Bernfeld (1944) and Amacher (1965) demonstrate how Freud incorporated into his work the basic ideas of the physicalistic physiology that he learned from Brücke and his other early teachers at the University of Vienna. Brücke's laboratory, at the time Freud worked there, was a center of the Helmholtz school, whose goal was to create a scientific physiology in the image of the successful physical sciences. As Shakow and Rapaport (1964) point out, much of this effort centered on replacing concepts such as the "vital" or "life force" (stemming from the romantic "nature philosophy") with concepts identical with, or equal in dignity to, the concepts of the physical and chemical sciences. Scientific explanations, at this point in history, were in large part synonymous with physico-mechanical systems driven by force or energy. Thus, when Freud came to write a model of the mind ("The Project for a Scientific Psychology," written in draft form in 1895 and subsequently abandoned), it took the form of a neuropsychological model that grew directly from his neurological training.[1]

As is well known, Freud abandoned, or attempted to abandon, his efforts to formulate a neuropsychology. In his next major theoretical work, *The Interpretation of Dreams* (1900), he presented the psychological model that remained basic to psychoanalytic theory thereafter. But his previous training, and perhaps the whole *Zeitgeist* of nineteenth-century scientific thought, prevented him from giving up the hope that some day his work would have a "solid grounding" in the physiology of the nervous system. This hope is revealed in a number of ways in his later writings. For example, in the model presented in Chapter 7 of *The Interpretation of Dreams*, he continues to refer to "excitations" and "innervations," neurological terms obviously carried over from "The Project." In the *Ego and the Id* (1923), in what is clearly a psychological mode of the mind, he cannot resist the neurological aside: "We might add, perhaps, that the ego wears an auditory lobe—on one side only, as we learn from cerebral anatomy" (p. 29). These small examples reveal an important strain that runs through much of Freud's work. For, while his theoretical works from 1900 on are presumably "on psychological ground," and he nowhere returns to the sort of large-scale neuropsychology that he attempted in "The Project," the background assumptions of his theorizing remain influenced by his early neurological training.

Holt, in a series of excellent papers (1965, 1966, 1967), shows how

[1] As Pribram (1962) points out, it was a tremendously sophisticated model, much ahead of its time and, perhaps of greatest significance, a model which recognized and attempted solutions for the major problems that such a model must face.

Freud's early neurological assumptions, presumably abandoned after "The Project," persist in more or less unchanging form throughout his later work. In brief summary, the main assumptions are:

1. The constancy principle—originally formulated in "The Project" as the idea that neurons or the nervous system as a whole tends to keep itself "free from stimulus. This process of discharge is the primary function of neuronic systems" (Freud, 1954, p. 357). This idea occurs later as the "pleasure principle" and forms the basis for:

2. The passive-reflex model—that the brain and nervous system (later the mind or mental apparatus) have a natural or primary direction, that stimuli impinge on it, either from the outside world or from within the body, and that it *reacts* by attempting to "discharge" them. This is related to the conception of the external world and internal drives as potentially pain-producing stimuli against which the individual must protect himself; leading to such concepts as "stimulus barriers" and "ego defense."

3. Finally, there is the assumption that quantitative increases and decreases in stimulation are directly reflected in quantitative changes in the nervous system and that increase in stimulation is painful while "discharge" is pleasurable. It is this last assumption that gives the model its "input-output" character, later seen as libido and libido economy as well as influencing other portions of the theory such as the concept of "object relations" (that is, the idea that there is a fixed quantity of energy in a more or less closed system, so that if libido is "invested" in one object it is "unavailable" for other purposes).

Energy was first defined by Freud as the physical energy of the environment which impinges on the receptors and is directly reflected in the energy state of the nervous system. A similar status was given to internal physical states, with hunger providing the chief example. (Even at this point there are difficulties with this view, for it is not clear whether there is necessarily any "less" stimulation arising from a full stomach than an empty one, and there is certainly "more" stimulation arising from sexual gratification in orgasm than its absence.) In any case, in the early model the energy system was not "closed"—that is, the energy of the environment was thought to be conducted in and "discharged" by the nervous system. Then the shift was made to libido, a hypothetical psychic energy which seems to operate in a closed system. That is, there is only so much of it available for "psychic work" so that, for example, if most of it is used up in self-love (narcissistic libido), there isn't much left over to love others (object libido). On the other hand, libido remains connected in an inconsistent way to at least one source of physical stimulation, glandular sexual excitation, that apparently is directly convertible into psychic energy. These are the kinds of contradictions, among others, that urge the abandonment of the libido concept.

Thus, the concept of force and energy pervades the theory of motivation. Psychic determinism, one of the hallmarks of Freud's system, is typically a reduction of some phenomenon (humor, a slip of the tongue, a work of art) to the "unconscious impulses" that motivate it and these, in turn, rest on the assumptions outlined above.

As Holt points out, these assumptions exerted their influence from the background as it were. Since they were primarily implicit rather than explicit, they were not readily changed when neurophysiology finally began the rapid progress that proved them incorrect. Furthermore, much of this progress has taken place since Freud's death and political considerations within the official psychoanalytic movement have imposed additional barriers to changing these major aspects of the theory (Shakow, 1962). Nevertheless, change must occur, because it is now clear that in almost every respect these assumptions are wrong. In brief summary, we know that:

1. Far from being passively reactive, the brain and nervous system are spontaneously active. Even in "deep" sleep, cortical activity is great and is not directly dependent on stimulus input.

2. It is misleading to think of the nervous system as simply "transmitting" energy. While the firing of receptor neurons is proportionally related to stimulus intensity (Miller, Ratliff, and Hartline, 1967), this energy does not "build up" nor "press for discharge." Rather, it is integrated as information in the active fields made up of reverberating neural networks. Thus, while there is electrochemical energy involved in the transmission of nerve impulses, these impulses should be conceptualized as signals which convey information.

3. In the light of the above, energy within the nervous system is quantitatively negligible. It bears no directly proportional relationship to pleasure nor to the motivational state of the person. (If it did, a bright sunny day with a lot of noise would be more "motivating" than the contemplation of an important decision in a quiet room.)[2]

As Holt puts it (1965, p. 109):

> The electrical phenomena associated with the neuron are accessible to quantitative study today, but this work offers no basis for the economic point of view—the assumption that mental events might be meaningfully examined from the standpoint of the "volumes of excitation" involved. Rather than this kind of "power engineering," "information engineering" seems to be the relevant discipline. Brücke, Meynart and Exner (Freud's teachers) were wrong, therefore, as Fechner had been before them: The nervous system is not passive, does not take in and conduct out again the energies of the environment, and shows no

[2] Space does not permit further elaboration which would entail consideration of findings relating to habituation, activation, arousal, and the role of amplification and attenuation systems such as the reticular formation and the so-called pleasure and pain centers. The reader is referred to Tomkins (1962) for one approach to motivation which utilizes these concepts and findings.

tendency to "divest itself of" its own impulses. The principle of constancy is quite without any biological basis.

It has been argued by a number of psychoanalytic writers that considerations stemming from neurophysiology have no force, since Freud's theory may be treated as a purely psychological one for which biological facts are irrelevant. This position is untenable for two reasons. First, as Holt (1965, 1966) and Amacher (1965) go to great pains to demonstrate, the model was never pure psychology in Freud's own thinking. The early neurological assumptions persisted in the form of an implicit model that guided the chief motivational explanations of the theory. Second, the pure psychology position is unsupportable on the face of it. While no psychological theorist is obliged to engage in explicit neurologizing when formulating propositions about psychological functioning, he is obligated to keep his propositions *consistent* with what is known about the way the brain works. There is no justification for clinging to a psychological theory that conceives of mental functioning in a way that is incompatible with our knowledge of brain function as, for example, traditional S-R theory has done. Further, there is a great deal to be gained on both sides when psychological theory is formulated in a fashion consistent with what is known about neurology and when neurophysiology is consistent with what is known from psychological observation. Not the least important gain may be the formulation of new hypotheses in both disciplines.

The Problem of Motivation

Motivation is essentially the problem of defining what gives the dominant and persistent directions to thought and action. All living organisms are active; activity is one of the defining characteristics of life; hence, it adds little when motivational concepts are put forth to explain activity itself. Rather, the problem is to account for the *dominant directions* of this activity; for how it is that one thing is done rather than another, or why one train of thought preoccupies us as opposed to another. This is the sort of problem that we are trying to explain with concepts such as drive or need; that is, to explain how a person stays directed toward certain goals such as financial success or sexual conquest. Freud's characteristic answers to the question of motivation are of two sorts. One, tied more closely to clinical data, attempts to explain motivated activity in terms of its unconscious meaning. Thus, a strong drive toward success may be explained as due to the unconscious effects of the internalized standards of a demanding parent. Loevinger (1966) makes the excellent point that explanations in terms of such "meanings" are the heart of psychoanalytic motivational theory.

Freud relies on another type of explanation, however, one in which motivation is explained by relating present motivated activities to earlier forms. This kind of explanation rests directly on the untenable assumptions just discussed, for it typically takes the form of reducing an observed phenomenon to its presumed initial tendency. This tendency—tension reduction via stimulus or "impulse" discharge—is assumed to characterize infancy under the domination of the pleasure principle. Thus, by reducing a symptom or any bit of motivated behavior to this initial tendency, Freud attempts to show how it stems both from the developmental history of the individual and from what he took to be the basic biological direction of the organism. As we have shown, this latter assumption rests on very insubstantial grounds.

But the problem remains—how does one account for motivated activity? A more acceptable account can be built using two key ideas from Freud, ideas that have been typically relegated to secondary positions because of the primary emphasis on drive as stimulus or energy discharge. These are: (1) the centrality of emotion and affect to activity we think of as motivated, and (2) the idea that present motivated activity is a transformation of earlier patterns. It is possible to go through a great number of examples to which the traditional energy discharge concept is applied and to show how they may more easily be dealt with in terms of *dominant direction,* a direction that may be understood as a transformation of an earlier direction, amplified by emotional or affective feedback. Such a view, however, requires some major modifications in the underlying psychological model. In what follows, I shall present some preliminary ideas concerning such modifications.

The Concept of Structure

The preceding considerations argue strongly for the abandonment of a conception of motivation based on energy, libido, conservation, or tension-reduction. In addition to the reasons reviewed here, Colby (1955), Loevinger (1966), and White (1963) discuss a number of others. When we give up the concepts of energy or libido we are faced with the prospect of explaining the central motivational phenomena to which that energy theory was applied. As is well known, no theory is abandoned because of a critical attack on its inadequacies. This is particularly true in the case of energy theory which is so central to the whole area of motivation. Rather, we must propose a new or alternative theory that can more satisfactorily deal with the problems at hand.

We can begin by conceiving of the mind as an *active system.* The direction of an ongoing, *active system* is determined by the way it is structured; that is, the mind as an information-processing apparatus which interprets (perceives) input and guides output (behavior), functions according to the way it is organized. This organization or structure, in turn, is a result of innate factors that result from evolutionary selection, interacting with factors that result from specific experiences encountered during development.

Before presenting what is essentially a new structural model, we should look briefly at two ways in which the concept of structure is used in psychoanalytic theory. What is now most frequently referred to as the "structural theory" by psychoanalytic writers is the tripartite division of the mind into id-ego-superego. While this model provides some conception of structure, it is of a rather general sort. Furthermore, the assumption of a passive reflex apparatus and of motivation as arising outside of structure (in the form of external stimuli or internal impulses that must be warded off or dealt with in some way) create serious problems for this conception. All of the assumptions of the tension-reduction model are retained in the concept of the id as a mass of excitations "pressing for discharge." The most interesting problems, those relating to the transformations of patterns (as in the development of interpersonal relationships, or changes in the way aggression is expressed) are viewed as secondary to the flow of libido. This is really one of the central paradoxes of psychoanalytic theory. Its observations and hypotheses deal with the meanings (conscious and unconscious) and symbolic transformations that characterize personality development. Yet the heart of the developmental theory, the concept of psychosexual stages, is tied to an untenable assumption concerning progressive attempts to seek "pleasure" in certain somatic zones of the body.

As Tomkins (1962, p. 12) puts it:

> The whole dependency-communion complex was unnecessarily limited to the oral complex. As an aftermath, more literal-minded psychologists have spent thousands of hours of time (theirs and their subjects') in the investigation of the details of feeding and weaning without regard for the feelings of love and hate, of distress and shame, which are the core of the earliest relationship.
>
> The whole shame complex, which can begin when the child is messy in eating and in regurgitation, was exclusively focused mistakenly on the drive of defecation, as though the countless occasions when a mother might humiliate her child were exclusively and inherently concerns or derivative concerns about the control of defecation and urination.

I would argue that the id-ego-superego model should be completely reformulated. The concept of the id as an unstructured mass of excitations is simply unsupportable (Holt, 1967). Along with the deficiencies already noted, it overlooks the potential for specific organization that is built into the human brain as a result of evolutionary development.

The concepts of ego and superego explain too much and not enough. By placing all of personality development under these rubrics, the impression is created that much more is known about the specifics of processes such as the development of "reality testing," "delay of gratification," "conscience development," and the like, than is actually the case. A further problem with the ego-superego conceptions is that they too easily lend themselves to a kind of anthropomorphism. While we should certainly know better, it is not uncommon to hear of a patient's ego "doing" something, or of his superego "causing him" to feel guilt, as if these were entities within the personality. Obviously, they are not entities but general concepts that refer to a group of processes that have certain characteristics in common. This problem might best be solved by giving up *the* ego and *the* superego and substituting more general concepts that encompass the same observations. I shall propose the memory system as such a structural concept, but first let us consider a second way in which the idea of structure has been used in psychoanalytic theory.

Structure, Biology, and Development

Freud's early model contained a number of structural concepts similar to the idea of the memory system.[3] In fact, he uses this term in the model of the mind presented in Chapter 7 of *The Interpretation of Dreams* (1900). We see here the beginnings of a structural theory with a nonanthropomorphic concept, the memory system, as the basic unit. Development can then be conceived as the progressive modification of such structures. But our modern concepts of information processing were not available to Freud, and, as might be expected in terms of his training and the general tenor of scientific thought at the time, he gave more and more preference to motivational explanations in terms of the discharge of psychic energy in his subsequent writings.

These difficulties may be avoided in large part by assuming that what is biologically basic (in Freud's terms, "instinctual") is *the direction given to thought and action by the structure or organization of the nervous system.* The ethologists (Tinbergen, 1951; Hess, 1962; Lorenz, 1966) take such an approach when they posit structural mechanisms underlying the

[3] Freud, after all, did much of his early scientific work studying the histological structure of nerve tissue. The model he worked out in "The Project" (Freud, 1954) contained at least as many structural as energy components. Holt points out that the model contains at least five feedback loops of the sort delineated by modern information theory, and Pribram's analysis of "The Project" indicates how the model can be coordinated with modern neuropsychology. For some examples in "The Project," see the treatment of memory as changes in the structure of the "contact barriers" on pages 359–360 or the discussion of the effects of experience in determining the future course of neural activity, essentially a directional concept of motivation on page 362. Similarly, the model presented in *The Interpretation of Dreams* (1900) contains a number of structural elements as, for example, the concepts of memories laid down behind the "perceptual apparatus" (Freud refers to them as "memory systems" at one point and as "physical structures" at another).

"fixed action patterns" that comprise the "instinctual behavior" of certain birds and fish. Such structures have evolved, through the process of natural selection, because of the adaptive advantages they confer on the species possessing them. That is to say, certain biological aims must be accomplished if an individual or a species is to survive. These include nourishment, escape from harm, reproduction, and others. In any species that one chooses to examine, adequate ways of achieving these aims have evolved; those species which have not are the extinct rejects of evolution. These guiding structures are embodied in the brain and nervous system and have evolved to their present state of complexity over long periods of time, just as have the other biological systems of the body. We may study these phenomena at the level of their behavioral manifestations which, in man, includes their psychological manifestations. To do this we can conceive of the processes of *perception, internal processing* of perceived input, and *output.* The achievement of basic biological goals, even in the simpler organisms, involves perception of stimuli in the environment, internal processing of perceived input (which becomes increasingly important as we ascend the phylogenetic scale to organisms with more complex nervous systems), and output. Thus, the well-adapted bird or fish or mammal has evolved neural structures which allow it to perceive certain cues associated with natural predators. These set in motion the internal processes leading to the output of "flight." Similarly with nourishment and aggression. Animals must have evolved mechanisms which lead them to attack and eat their prey or to actively seek out those plants that sustain them. It is worth stressing that even in the case of the relatively fixed action patterns, it is goals or environmental achievements, and not the rigid sequence of motor acts, that are built in.

Conceiving of "instinctual" structures in this way permits a much more unitary and consistent view than the untenable doctrine of dual life and death instincts or the confusing variety of energy concepts. The basic mechanisms which give direction to nourishment, flight, reproduction, and aggression are *all of the same form*—they are all evolved structures which insure that the basic biological aims necessary for survival will be met.

When we examine most of these "instinctual" areas in humans, it is apparent that a great deal of development and learning intervenes between birth and the achievement of "instinctual" aims such as reproduction. The concept with which we attempt to deal with this process is motivation. We must move from instinct as "fixed action pattern" in the simpler organism, to "motive" in the complex organism. Motives, like fixed action patterns, however, are structures which give direction to behavior relevant to the major survival-oriented functions. *But, they are structures which have been shaped by the long period of development and learning that humans must undergo.*

For the most part, psychoanalytic theory, like other theories of human motivation, is concerned with those human motives that are most plastic, that involve the greatest amount of change during the course of development. This is particularly true for such plastic "interpersonal" motives as love, dependency, and aggression. The study of these motives is the study of the way the long period of development operates; of how "cognitive structures" mediate the eventual achievement of basic biological aims just as culture mediates man's relationship with his environment. Much of psychoanalysis may be seen as the study of such mediational processes (the "vicissitudes of libido," the psychosexual stages of development, the development of the ego and ego abilities which remain in the "service of the id," and others). In species, such as the human, in which there is a prolonged period of development between infancy and adulthood, memory systems mediate between an original biological tendency and its eventual expression. In this way, they are intimately tied to culture, which also serves these aims in complex, mediational ways. It is from this fact that the analogies between the function of cultural customs and those of biological functions arise. For example, when we examine the mating or fighting patterns of simpler organisms such as fish or reptiles, we see that certain responses are pre-programmed to appear, given minimal amounts of maturation and the appropriate releasing stimuli. In the human, some fourteen years or more of development must take place before successful reproduction can take place. A fixed pattern for reproduction does not exist in the more direct form found in simpler species. Rather, there is a basic direction, probably associated with the satisfaction of nourishment and dependency needs that forms the pre-program for what will later, after a number of developmental transformations, become adult love and mating. On the basis of these transformations, which themselves interact and shape interchange with environment, memory systems are built up which consist of the stored material and programs guiding its various transformations that determine the individual's orientation toward males and females. Through the childhood and adolescent years of development, further transformations occur, both as new "content" is added in the form of more memory material and as new programs are acquired, such as advances in "thinking," symbolizing, and the like. When all goes well, the child emerges from adolescence with a normal sexual or reproductive orientation, that is, the *memory systems have functioned to mediate the aim of reproduction.* What they have used in this process is largely cultural material; the language, customs, fetishes, rites, rules, nuances, and so forth of the particular culture supply the material out of which the symbolic mediation is built.

Thus, it is the developmental socialization experiences that shape the motivational structures which guide the eventual sexual activities that lead to reproduction. It is in this sense that we may think of motives as mediational structures. Survival pressures operate with respect to cultures also, so that any given culture must have evolved adequate ways of mediating the eventual achievement of the basic survival functions. I would speculate that basic motivational structures relating to love and dependency that insure the care of infants have evolved in much the same way as those guiding fear and avoidance of harm. Similarly, those structures relating to aggression, curiosity, and exploration are directly related to the unique selective advantage that humans attain by way of their intelligence. Again, this shows how a structural view is able to encompass a variety of basic biological tendencies without having to posit separate "energies" or attempting the cumbersome reduction of love, curiosity, and the like to hunger and eating.

A Structural Model of Motivation

Let us turn now to the general model implied by the foregoing discussion. The concept of the memory system refers to an organized or structured mass of stored information. The memory system seems a good general term for what Piaget (Flavell, 1963) calls "schemata," what Miller, Galanter, and Pribram (1960) call "plans," or what other cognitive theorists have called "cognitive maps," "phase sequences," and the like. It would consist of memory material defined as differentiated structure. As such, it is not separable from the perceptual apparatus, since the process of perception always involves some form of matching of sensory or internal input with existing memory. On the other hand, it may be of value to think of two separate processes: (1) *perception,* which involves the coordination of input with memory; and (2) *internal transformations,* which involve various sorts of manipulations of stored information in relative independence from input (as in thinking, planning, the flow of associations, anticipations, fantasy, dreams, and the like). In addition, it is possible to think of two aspects of the memory systems: the content or stored information and the "programs" for putting it together; analogous to vocabulary on the one hand and the rules or "grammar" governing language usage on the other. While there may be value in talking about content and programs as if they were separate, in fact they are most probably intertwined with each other. Finally, we must note that, as Lashley (1950) has so convincingly shown, memory storage does not consist of the storage of specific memories in specific areas of the brain. Rather, memory material is "coded" (in some neuro-chemical fashion). A key characteristic of this coded material is its "generalizability" or "substitutability" as demonstrated by the application of old learning in novel situations, or by transposition, equipotentiality of response, displacement, the recognition and response to new symbols, language usage, and the like. We can think, then, of content as coded information which can be *trans-*

lated by the operations of different programs. Some of these would be the programs involved in the processes of object recognition whereby a particular sensory input (such as, infant sees mother's face) is tried for fit against stored memories until a match is achieved and there results "recognition" and, perhaps, some form of output such as a smile. As the memory systems become progressively differentiated, a particular input may come to involve both more content and a greater variety of programs. Thus, for the older child the sensory input of "mother's face" leads to a relatively automatic recognition, but also to the activation of other memories within the same system, such as anticipations of being fed (particularly if this input occurs simultaneously with input from hunger pangs). A number of related anticipations and outputs associated together in the same memory system may all be brought into play, including "magical," "pre-logical" expectations and anticipations, hallucinatory wish fulfillments, and so forth.

Thus, it is necessary to think in terms of several systems or levels of memory organization. On one level, coded material may exist in a state of greater fluidity, permitting a freer associating of memory elements one with another. To put it another way, we can say that the programs guiding memory organization at this level permit the loose coupling of elements, as by association in time, physical appearance, common sound, connection with a common third element, psychological similarity, and other "rules." I would hypothesize that these programs are associated with the earliest functioning of the system. At another level, the programs guiding memory organization may be more "critical," that is, they may subject the material to a screening process which permits only certain types of organized material, such as those that are more socially acceptable, to pass on to an output system such as speech. These programs may be assumed to operate hierarchically, so that information is successively processed on its way toward output (see Colby, 1965, for an attempt at an actual computer program for such a process). These two levels bear a rough resemblance to the psychoanalytic notions of primary and secondary process. It was my intent, in fact, to conceptualize these processes in terms of the operations of different programs. This forms the core of a structural model of motivational phenomena, for it is the way the neural networks in the brain have become structured as a result of experience modifying their initial tendencies, that provide the *direction* of ongoing activities that *is* motivation.

Structure and the Dominance of Motives

A chief difficulty with a formulation in terms of programs is that it does not necessarily provide any way of assigning predominance to one structure over another. In such a "cognitive" scheme every activity seems equally possible. For each, we merely talk of a particular program being in operation. In short, the model, in this sense, seems very *unmotivational,* since we typically think of motives as dominant, as guiding the major directions of activity. As Holt points out, "Pure psychology needs motivation if it is to move beyond a narrow range of cognitive problems" (Holt, 1967, p. 20). The solution utilized by Freud was to connect "the mental" to "the body" in some way; to bring in somatic sources of motivation such as hunger, or physiological fright-and-flight reactions. This is seen most clearly in his earliest theories of anxiety, where anxiety is viewed as dammed-up sexuality in the literal sense of blocked orgasm.

The alternative solution I have been discussing views the basic biological processes as built into brain structure. But in humans, where these drives are so plastic, all that exists initially is a tendency or general direction. We can assume, however, that this initial tendency sets the pattern for what comes later, and that the initial structuring, the differentiation of relatively undifferentiated structures, or what Piaget calls the accommodation of schemata, has lasting motivational consequences. The second idea that we can draw on to make our cognitive model a motivational one is that certain structures have emotional-affective systems associated with them that feedback and amplify or potentiate the activities guided by these structures.

Let me begin with a consideration of the role of emotion and then take up the issue of the importance of primary structure. It seems necessary to assume that the system of emotional responses has become attached to those structures which guide the basic survival-oriented activities of the organism to insure that these activities will be pervasive and persistent. Thus, emotion, and its psychological counterpart, affect, acts as an internal amplification system which, through a process of feedback, insures that the survival-oriented activities will become dominant over all others.

As an example, let us consider the role of fear in flight from danger. Many species are pre-programmed, as it were, to recognize and react to certain stimuli associated with a natural enemy. This means that visual, olfactory, or other cues are perceived as dangerous and produce escape output; for example, they get the animal to start running or swimming or flying. Now we can ask, "Why doesn't the animal stop escaping as soon as he turns his head and no longer perceives the enemy?" After all, he is subject to new stimulus input as soon as he leaves the immediate stimulating situation. It is here that emotion plays its central part. The perception of danger causes the stimulation of an instinctual escape *pattern.* A part of this pattern involves output to emotional response systems, such as the activation of the sympathetic nervous system, the secretion of adrenalin with its accompanying changes, and the like. These internal changes are slower acting and perseverate longer than cortical recognition. In addition, the animal reacts to them as signs of danger so that the internal feedback they provide keeps the animal in the pattern of escape even when the predator is not in sight. This is an example of how a basic survival-oriented motive has an emotional feedback system associated with it that *potentiates* its effects. The survival value of such potentiation should be obvious—those animals possessing it have lived to reproduce another day while those without it did not. This hypothesis is consistent with the clinical observation that dominant motives are those with strong emotional components.

Let us now consider the second idea with which we can make our cognitive model a motivational one. Recall that Freud's approach to the problem was to assign a primary tendency to the mental apparatus (the pleasure principle, the tendency to divest itself of stimulation) and to explain later motivational states as *transformations* of this initial tendency. While he was wrong about the pleasure principle, the idea that *what comes early shapes what comes later* may be retained to make our structural account a motivational one and to allow it to explain the major phenomenon that the traditional energy model is applied to.

We can assume that the initial structuring of the memory systems takes place along primary process dimensions, that is, that the initial coding or representation of the environment is in terms of programs that are tied to motor acts (Piaget's "sensorimotor" intelligence). In addition to building up a sense of "self" identified with one's body, such programs might facilitate freer associations between stimuli and images. The fact that such programs become structured first would give them a more basic place as guiding structures. In other words, if mental development proceeds from undifferentiated to progressively more structured stages, it is reasonable to assume that the initial dimensions of differentiation become crucial in determining later functioning of the system. This brings us back to a consideration of development.

Initially, the mental apparatus is relatively undifferentiated, although certain reflexive structures and initial tendencies are present. Structure develops as these tendencies are modified and new ones created out of an interaction with the environment. Since this interaction is constantly a function of the existing structures, the development of new ones must be based on those that already exist. Various analogies suggest themselves for describing the way initial structure shapes subsequent organization. We might think of the way the formation of the infant's skeleton determines what the adult skeleton will be, initial directions of growth or abnormalities being reflected in its final form; or we might think of proto-programs, the initial programs that are involved in the development of later programs; or of what Harlow (1949) calls "learning sets" which, in his experiments, are strategies that are acquired on the basis of past learning which cast subsequent learning in a new dimension.[4] These analogies all convey the general

[4] Psychoanalytic theory is, of course, replete with analogies in which the experiences associated with a certain activity such as feeding or toilet training structure the memory

point that initial structuring provides a sort of blueprint or framework for what develops later.

Since this early structuring is of the same form as that which develops out of the interaction of initial tendencies with environmental experiences, it is reasonable to assume that its motivational consequences are just as basic. In other words, the form taken by these early precursors to thinking and fantasy would provide blueprints, such as a "motor" conception of the world, or an identification of "self" with "body" which is what Freud means, I think, when he states that the original "ego" is "pure body ego." These *anlagen* of mental function are revealed during states favoring regression; that is, conditions where these early established programs guide psychological activity.

I have already made brief mention of the basic structures associated with hunger, love, aggression, and flight, each of which may be thought of as frameworks which shape the direction of later structures. These structures tend to involve systems of potentiating emotional response. For example, fear-producing-input sets into operation a number of physiological processes that prepare the organism for flight and assure, via internal feedback, that this reaction will be more than momentary. The fact that the basic biological goals involve these related emotional and affective systems is of the greatest importance, for it accounts, in large part, for their dominant character and persistence into adult life, even when they have become disconnected, as it were, from their original purpose.

In addition to the initial structuring along these lines, the earliest forms of cognitive development (the sensorimotor schemata) also provide a framework for the subsequent memory systems. Moreover, these different structures are far from separate. They interact and exert various constraints on one another. Thus, when the infant is extremely hungry or frightened he is unable to engage in the sort of exploration of the environment that is necessary for the development of stable perceptual structures. On the other hand, under normal conditions of development where intense hunger or fright is minimal or brief, activities in the service of cognitive and perceptual structures may take up a great deal of time.

In sum, it is the early structuring of the mind that is crucial for the development of motivation, that is, for specifying the basic *directions* that later activity will take. This early structuring takes place along several dimensions, including those defined by the major survival-oriented functions and those defined in terms of the basic perceptual, sensorimotor, and cognitive areas. Thus, the explanation for the motivationally dominant effects of certain forms of early experience is in terms of their providing the

---

system in basic ways so that a variety of later activities such as dependency or cleanliness may be guided within the framework that is laid down initially.

framework or blueprint for later development within the memory systems. For example, the infant's earliest interactions with mother, father, and siblings lead to internalized memories and to certain primary programs guiding their organization. This initial structuring of the memory systems guides the output of interpersonal perception, emotional reactions to other people, the expectations of how others will react, actions taken on the basis of these expectations, and the like. This—rather than "vicissitudes of the libido"—is the sort of underpinning needed to explain "object relations" and the importance of early family relationships.

Let us consider an overly simple example—a young man with a neurotic fear of sexually attractive older women, based on his Oedipal experiences. Traditionally this might be explained as due to the guilt and anxiety aroused by a repressed Oedipal conflict (a truly cumbersome explanation, if you analyze it in terms of psychic energy). Now consider this example in structural terms of (1) perception, (2) internal organization and transformation of information, and (3) output. First, the older woman is perceived in a particular way which is a function of the organization and structuring of the perceptual apparatus. Perception is *organizing;* it is not the registering of stimuli on a blank screen. In this example, the process of equating the input "older woman" with "mother" already begins in the process of perception. Next, this perceived input is given further meaning in terms of the organized memory systems. In this case, part of the meaning given to the input brings into play a system having to do with "mother," "sexual attraction toward mother with accompanying emotional arousal," "fear of punishment," "the idea that the attraction is wrong," and so forth. These perceptions then lead to certain ways of dealing with the perceived input, such as defense mechanisms.

This process, whereby perceived input is given meaning in terms of memories related within certain systems, provides the possibility of a number of internal *transformations,* as by symbolism. This can then lead to certain output phenomena, such as panic, overt acts such as avoiding older women or seeking them out and establishing close but intellectual relationships, thoughts and fantasies, dreams, and so forth.

In this particular example we have assumed that anxiety plays a continuing role. It is worth stressing that while anxiety may frequently be involved in the origin of such a pattern, it may not continue to be a part of the subsequent output. The passage of time, repetition, and other factors may cause the simplification and automatization of a particular pattern such as this. When this happens we may see, in the adult, a well-established (characterological) way of dealing with women that runs relatively smoothly and shows little overt emotion or anxiety; that is, what we describe as a well-defended person. What sense, then, does the traditional explanation of defenses as means to avoid anxiety have, when there is not necessarily even any anxiety present? Again, it only makes sense if we conceptualize "anxiety" as an output phenomenon of a process that involves perception, organization, transformation, and output. Although anxiety, anger, sexual arousal, and the like *may be* involved at earlier periods in the development of a particular perceptual-memory system, it is the *structuring of the systems* that determines present output, and not the affect or anxiety.

This example implies a revision of the psychoanalytic theory of neurosis. Neurotic phenomena (such as symptoms, life styles, choice of partners, forms of sexuality and of aggression) are essentially later symbolic transformations of early acquired patterns. We assume, for example, that a strong negative affect such as anxiety or guilt gets attached to the perception and internal representation of sexuality. This becomes represented in terms of early programs whereby parts of the body may stand for their function—which is what Freud refers to as the "attachment of anxiety to the sexual organs." Thus "attachment" must be interpreted as *symbolic representation.* This representation then goes through a sequence of transformations, coming out of the development of defense mechanisms, the incorporation of cultural stereotypes and beliefs, all of which, in themselves, involve symbolic substitute processes. Then, in the adult, we may see a neurotic disgust over sex or the repetitive seeking out of partners who are rejecting, or the arousal of anxiety over some "idea" that represents the whole complicated system of memory transformations. A full accounting of an adult neurosis would entail an understanding of the series of internal transformations that the initial pattern has undergone. This is extremely difficult to carry out retrospectively, but it is what psychoanalytic case histories try to do from the relatively limited data of the patient's present memory material. The foregoing presents some preliminary suggestions for the application of a structural model to the problem of neurosis. For a similar application of these ideas to dream theory, the reader is referred to Breger (1967).

Before concluding, let me devote brief consideration to some of the processes that occur in later development. In order to more fully explicate the process whereby early structuring affects subsequent reactions, we must consider some of the transformations that can occur within the memory systems as a result of subsequent experience and particularly the acquisition of language and other *symbolic* capabilities. As has been mentioned, even the simplest forms of cognitive and perceptual development involve some form of internal representation of the environment. Human beings very rapidly move beyond such simple forms, however, and, with the development of language and other symbolic modes, there develop more far-reaching modes of internal representation; that is, modes which enable one to code stored information according to different programs. The adaptive value of such processes should be obvious. Internal representation allows the child to break free from dependence on the immediate environment, and it is just this ability that leads to all of man's higher achievements. Progressive development of such internal representations may indeed become completely free from the environment, as in abstract mathematics. But without jumping to this level, we may note the type of process that develops after the first year of life as exemplified by (but not restricted to) language development. What is involved here is the ability to perform *transformations on internally stored representations of the environment.* Such transformations would, of necessity, work with existing stored symbolic material. For example, the infant develops a stored memory of a toy (this itself takes time and begins by the development of a simple object-recognition schemata). He also develops a set of expectations having to do with mother doing things for him (feeding, making him comfortable, stimulating, playing, and the like). Then, at some point, given sufficient prior experience, he brings these two bits of stored information together to create the proto-fantasy of mother getting him the toy. This "bringing together" is a process whereby the symbols for the environment can be substituted one for the other. For example, something like "I want toy," "mother satisfies wants, as when I want food," mother satisfying one can substitute for mother satisfying another to "mother gives me toy." Such a process assumes that the infant can equate "wanting" one thing with "wanting" another, as well as equating objects with each other—something that seems very simple to us *because* it so readily is facilitated by our language, that is, the concept "want" bridges the gap and we can assign toy and food to the class "objects of desire." But for the infant, during a period before language or when only its crude beginnings are present, it is no easy task to develop such a fantasy. The symbolic tools available for such substitute activities are the earliest forms in which the environment is represented. Thus, receiving something from someone may be closely tied to the memory system dealing with feeding, while states of desire could be tied to the emotional reactions accompanying hunger. In a similar fashion, the relations between objects in the environment or between one's own actions and their effects would be symbolized in the form that characterizes Piaget's "sensorimotor" stage. All of this points to a sort of "primary process thinking" as a *necessary* early way of performing transformations on stored, symbolic representations of the environment. In other words, certain programs develop to guide fantasy, expectations, and symbolic substitutions which make use of the symbolizing capabilities of the infant. These are the initial programs for performing internal, symbolic transformations on stored representations of input (from the environment and one's own body). Because of their primacy, they set the pattern for later, more complex transformations.

The possibility that the earliest forms of psychological operation could be facilitated by a "loose" or primary-process-like combining of associated material has interesting consequences. That is, the free use of just those processes such as substitutions, displacements, and lack of distinction between the internal and external environments, that are viewed as maladaptive or even psychotic in the adult might be extremely useful in the early development of thinking, planning, and the like. It has always seemed to me that so-called reality-oriented "logical" thought is highly overrated, probably because it is more familiar to us from that aspect of conscious experience to which we attend. Attempts to program computers to think like people shed some interesting light on this, for it becomes apparent that even the biggest computer imaginable cannot do some of the simple things the brain can do if it is constrained to such reality-oriented operations. It appears that other programs are necessary, and I suggest that we look to the primary process for a model. This suggests a hierarchical ordering of programs where there is the loosest combination of associations at one level with subsequent critical processing of these creations on the way to output.

Later psychological development may be viewed as a series of stages in which these processes are progressively refined. The further development of language means the internalization of new programs for manipulating symbols. Concomitantly, there are a host of developments in "thinking," "problem solving," "fantasy," and so forth, all of which may be viewed as the development of new programs that are built on or grow out of the earlier programs. Whether the early programs continue to exist along with later structures or are absorbed as the infant's skeleton is "absorbed" during growth is not certain. In any case, it seems likely that the earliest structuring exerts an influence that is central to later motivation.

References

Amacher, M. P. "Freud's Neurological Education and Its Influence on Psychoanalytic Theory." *Psychological Issues*, 4, No. 4 (1965), Monograph No. 16.

Apfelbaum, B. "Ego Psychology, Psychic Energy, and the Hazards of Quantitative Explanation in Psycho-Analytic Theory." *International Journal of Psycho-Analysis*, 46 (1965), 168–181.

Bernfeld, S. "Freud's Earliest Theories and the School of Helmholtz." *Psychoanalytic Quarterly*, 13 (1944), 341–362.

Breger, L. "Function of Dreams." *Journal of Abnormal Psychology*, Monograph, 1967.

Colby, K. M. *Energy and Structure in Psychoanalytic Theory*. New York: Ronald Press, 1955.

Colby, K. M. "Computer Simulation of Neurotic Processes." In R. W. Stacey and B. Waxman (eds.), *Computers in Biomedical Research*. New York: Academic Press, 1965. Vol. 1, pp. 491–503.

Flavell, J. H. *The Developmental Psychology of Jean Piaget*. Princeton, N.J.: Van Nostrand, 1963.

Freud, S. "The Project for a Scientific Psychology" (1895). In Marie Bonaparte, Anna Freud, and E. Kris (eds.), *The Origins of Psychoanalysis: Letters to Wilhelm Fliess, Drafts and Notes, 1887–1902*. New York: Basic Books, 1954. Pp. 347–445.

Freud, S. "The Interpretation of Dreams" (1900). *The Standard Edition of the Complete Psychological Works of. . . .* London: Hogarth Press. Vols. 4 and 5. (Also published as *The Interpretation of Dreams*. Basic Books, 1955.)

Freud, S. "Beyond the Pleasure Principle" (1920). *The Standard Edition of the Complete Psychological Works of. . . .* London: Hogarth Press. Vol. 18, pp. 8–64.

Freud, S. *The Ego and the Id* (1923). *The Standard Edition of the Complete Psychological Works of. . . .* London: Hogarth Press. Vol. 19.

Harlow, H. F. "The Formation of Learning Sets." *Psychological Review*, 56 (1949), 51–65.

Hess, E. H. "Ethology: An Approach toward the Complete Analysis of Behavior." In R. Brown *et al.*, *New Directions in Psychology*. New York: Holt, Rinehart, & Winston, 1962. Pp. 157–266.

Holt, R. R. "A Review of Some of Freud's Biological Assumptions and Their Influence on His Theories." In N. S. Greenfield and W. C. Lewis (eds.), *Psychoanalysis and Current Biological Thought*. Madison: University of Wisconsin Press, 1965. Pp. 93–124.

Holt, R. R. "Beyond Vitalism and Mechanism. Freud's Concept of Psychic Energy." In B. B. Wolman (ed.), *Historical Roots of Contemporary Psychology*. New York: Harper & Row, 1966.

Holt, R. R. "The Development of Primary Process: A Structural View." In R. R. Holt (ed.), *Motives and Thought: Psychoanalytic Essays in Memory of David Rapaport. Psychological Issues*, 5, Nos. 2–3 (1967), Monograph Nos. 18–19, pp. 345–383.

Klein, G. S. "Peremptory Ideation: Structure and Force in Motivated Ideas." In R. R. Holt (ed.), *Motives and Thought: Psychoanalytic Essays in Memory of David Rapaport. Psychological Issues*, 5, 6, Nos. 2–3 (1967), Monograph Nos. 18–19, pp. 80–128.

Lashley, K. S. "In Search of the Engram." *Proceedings of the Society for Experimental Biology and Medicine*, 4 (1950), 454–482.

Loevinger, Jane. "Three Principles for a Psychoanalytic Psychology." *Journal of Abnormal Psychology*, 71 (1966), 432–443.

Lorenz, K. Z. *On Aggression*. New York: Harcourt, Brace, & World, 1966.

Miller, G. A., Galanter, E. H., and Pribram, K. H. *Plans and the Structure of Behavior*. New York: Henry Holt, 1960.

Miller, W. H., Ratliff, F., and Hartline, H. A. "How Cells Receive Stimuli." In J. L. McGaugh, N. W. Weinberger, and R. E. Whalen (eds.), *Psychobiology: The Biological Bases of Behavior*. San Francisco: Freeman, 1967. Pp. 201–214.

Pribram, K. H. "The Neuropsychology of Sigmund Freud." In A. J. Bachrach (ed.), *Experimental Foundations of Clinical Psychology*. New York: Basic Books, 1962. Pp. 442–468.

Shakow, D. "Psychoanalytic Education of Behavioral and Social Scientists for Research." In J. H. Masserman (ed.), *Science and Psychoanalysis*. New York: Grune & Stratton, 1962. Vol. 5, pp. 146–161.

Shakow, D., and Rapaport, D. *The Influence of Freud on American Psychology*. New York: International Universities Press, 1964.

Tinbergen, N. *The Study of Instinct*. London: Oxford University Press, 1951.

Tomkins, S. S. *Affect, Imagery, Consciousness*. New York: Springer, 1962. Vol. 1.

White, R. W. "Ego and Reality in Psychoanalytic Theory." *Psychological Issues*, 3, No. 3 (1963), Monograph No. 11.

3

Psychoanalysis between Two Cultures

JURGEN RUESCH

For nearly two thousand years Greek philosophy and psychology dominated the Western world. And although we have come a long way from Aristotle's dissertation on the soul, the most significant change occurred in this century. Freud marks the turning point in that he was the last to offer us a comprehensive model of the human soul in the philosophical, theological, and literary sense, and the first to use machine analogies to describe human behavior. These two contradictory trends run throughout his work. True to humanistic tradition, for example, he inspired his pupils to band together and to accept his teachings as some sort of gospel truth. But aware of the growing impact of science, he also introduced terms such as psychical apparatus, energy, mechanism, and resistance (Freud, 1938; Freud and Breuer, 1892, Freud, 1925). In his attempts to mechanize the soul, he negated the humanistic component of psychoanalysis, perhaps its most basic and enduring feature. As a result, human relations were analyzed in a technical way, and what passed between doctor and patient no longer existed in its own right but was viewed as a repetition of earlier experiences and was termed transference and countertransference (Freud, 1912). In the same vein, psychoanalysis was considered a method and labeled a technique (Freud, 1913–1915). After Freud's death, the individualistic goal of self-realization in education and training was sacrificed to bureaucratic and organizational requirements. For years, trainees were tied down in one locale, preventing their contact with other centers and people; they had to attend scores of evening seminars disruptive to their family life; and their personal and training analyses grew longer and longer until they became practically interminable (Lewin and Ross, 1960).

These and many more are the conflicting trends that have uprooted psychoanalysis in the last few decades. Seen from the vantage point of hindsight and history, it becomes abundantly clear that psychoanalysis was shaken by what C. P. Snow refers to as the conflict of the two cultures (Snow, 1959). Freud, the nineteenth-century man (Rieff, 1959), wanted to be a universalist, embracing the humanities as well as the physical, biological, and social sciences. Today, the twentieth-century man knows that he has to choose between one and the other. The humanists are concerned with values, human experience, and action (Knapp, 1964). They are person-oriented and deeply committed to individual development. Because of this emphasis on human diversity, agreed-on standards of proof are not feasible. The scientific culture, in contrast, is concerned with machines and organizations and therefore is system-oriented. It is primarily interested in innovation and man-made order. Scientists have a single-mindedness of method and a plurality of subject matters; they believe in the quantification of methods, standards of proof, and the establishment of facts (Bridgman, 1959). To them, the experience of the individual and the insider's views matter little as long as technological progress in the world has been achieved.

The schism between humanities and science has been accentuated further by the fact that, unlike the older generation of professionals, the younger generation no longer has been educated in the humanistic tradition. Today, then, neither analysand nor analyst is likely to be grounded in the humanities. On a contemporary scene that is somewhat unfavorable to human considerations, the frontiers of psychoanalysis appear in a new perspective. Instead of striving toward external expansion and looking for new fields of application, psychoanalysis must seek internal innovations. The theory of psychoanalysis will have to be adapted to the ongoing social changes if it is to reflect modern man, and it will have to be modernized if it is to survive in a theoretically sophisticated world.

New Directions

The outstanding technological innovations of this century have been the invention of the computer and the perfection of control devices that steer machines. While in centuries past technologists developed machines that reduced physical labor (output) and invented devices that improved man's perception (input), modern engineers have perfected decision-making machines. With this augmentation of human brain capacity in terms of information storage and retrieval, computation, and technical decision-making, with the discovery of new sources of energy, and with the development of machines that do the work of slaves, the ecology of the world has changed. More and more our natural surroundings are being made over and replaced by man-made environments. To accomplish these gigantic technological tasks, our economics has also changed. The local back yard economy has given way to global economies, necessitating complex human organizations, which, as a by-product, have introduced a fantastic increase of bureaucratic practices (Benjamin, 1965; Ellul, 1964; Kerr, Dunlop, Harbison, and Myers, 1964).

Meanwhile the human being has had to adapt to these large-scale technological changes in many different ways (Ruesch, 1966). Rugged individualism has given way to mutual interdependence; the sense of security that was based on lifelong roles, human relations, and the ownership of property has been replaced by a sense of adaptability based on temporary tenure of office in organizations, time-limited membership in families, and leasing and renting of property. From long-lasting human contacts with few people, we have moved to short contacts with many people. If the former sense of security was based on stability, the modern sense of security is based on a person's ability to change. From survival of the fittest in the fight against the environment, we have moved to survival of the most adaptive in the human organization.

In scientific and intellectual fields we also have seen radical changes. The older scientific tradition was characterized by the creation of homogeneous professional groups, each group usually directed by one leader and adhering to one school of thought. The newer scientific organizations require heterogeneous, interdisciplinary groups administered by a rotating directorship and welded together by a common task. Schools of thought have given way to task orientation; cause-and-effect thinking has been replaced by transactional approaches; and psychological concerns have been overshadowed by social considerations (Horowitz, 1961).

From a variety of surveys of the behavioral sciences (Berelson, 1963; Hoselitz, 1959), it becomes abundantly clear that psychoanalysis has been based on human fundamentals that prevailed before the technological orientation became dominant. Psychoanalysis inevitably will have to make some decisions. It will have to choose sides and will have to align itself with one of the two cultures (Kaplan, 1965; Snow, 1959). It has to decide whether it is a literary movement; a spiritual, moral, or psychological exercise to influence human experience; a healing art; or a science. Depending on which side it chooses, it has to align its theories, educational philosophies, and practical procedures accordingly (Mohr, 1960). But regardless of how this decision will come out, psychoanalysis will also have to take cognizance of the revolution taking place in personality development, human relations, and social action or else share the fate of those disciplines which, like theology, have blithely ignored the human changes brought about by the march of technology.

The choices facing psychoanalysis are understood better if theory construction in the system-oriented sciences is contrasted with the theoretical views prevailing in the older person-oriented disciplines (Mohr, 1960; Mora, 1965).

Theory Construction in the Humanities

The oldest and perhaps still the most widely used method for describing behavior is the character type, the role typology, or the situational pattern. The technique of establishing a typology consists of telescoping a variety of features that were observed in different people on different occasions and under different conditions all upon one and the same person or situation. Character types thus evolved in novels, drama, and comedy—in song, mythology, and fable. Fictitious characters such as the devil, the witch, or the angel, which once upon a time were familiar to everybody, were found in the theological literature. Literary characters such as Hamlet, Faust, or Don Quixote were frequently quoted by learned people, as were mythological and legendary figures such as Siegfried, Narcissus, and Lancelot. Following in the footsteps of the humanities, psychiatrists and psychoanalysts made ample use of typologies; Freud's anal character (Freud, 1908), Abraham's oral and genital characters (Abraham, 1924; 1925), Jung's introverted and extraverted personalities (Jung, 1946), and Kretschmer's schizothymic and cyclothymic characters (Kretschmer, 1925) may serve as examples. If character types served as models for psychopathological types, role typologies such as the Trinity and the Holy Family served as models for relationships. Social-situation typologies such as the Oedipus Rex tragedy were employed to describe internal and external conflict between human beings and stages in human development (Mullahy, 1948).

Many academic disciplines employ typologies to cope with such diversified topics as values, roles, social classes, traits, or diagnoses. The shortcomings of typologies are related to the fact that divergent observations at different places and at different times are held together by one feature common to all. As a result, this feature usually suffers an arbitrary maximization. For example, if a person is caught telling a lie, he may have lied only one minute out of 525,600 minutes a year. In collecting data on another person who also lied, the observer silently establishes a hierarchy of variables whereby he assigns in all cases the highest priority to lying, a feature which then becomes the common link between a number of otherwise unrelated people. A similar distortion occurs in situational typologies such as accidents, weddings, or funerals in which people lose their individuality and are known but by their roles—e.g., the bride or the deceased. Typologies of all kinds are possible only with serious distortions in time, place or identity.

In an attempt to bridge the humanistic-scientific cleavage, some investigators tried to use individual and situational typologies as a basis for scientific operations (Marx, 1963). The procedure was as follows: individual observations were scanned against a background of typologies. The best-fitting typology was selected in each case, and at the end frequency distributions were established, the data analyzed statistically, and probabilities established. A scientific description and treatment of the observations was thought to have occurred if patterns could be reliably rated. The shortcomings of this procedure, however, are obvious. While the humanist uses types as a linguistic device and achieves precision by carefully aligning many universal verbal symbols until a unique description is achieved, the scientist wishes to define one universal by comparison with a standard so that validity and reliability of the term can be achieved. In rating procedures, the greatest error occurs in labelling, inasmuch as few observers can agree as to which typology fits a case in question best. In most instances, agreement becomes possible only after the raters have been similarly indoctrinated. As long as the initial observations are not based on measurements but on impressionistic comparisons with standards, this method obviously leaves much to be desired. Returning now to psychoanalytic procedures, it is obvious that most observations consist of labels and ratings given to the behavior of another person by trained observers. However, the rating is undertaken by only one expert, and reliability and validity checks are missing. The psychoanalytic procedure so far remains a method characteristic of the humanities in which the theories are expressed in verbal terms, the data are phrased in verbal terms, and the participants rely upon their experiences, unchecked by external points of reference. Let me consider next the ways in which psychoanalytic theory would have to be modified to become part of a unified theory of behavior.

Theory Construction in the Behavioral Sciences

The scientific approach to human behavior is based upon the ideal of an observer who stands outside of human affairs, is distant, objective, and uninvolved. However, in the pursuit of this goal scientists have run into difficulties. Among these, the limitations of the living observer, the complexities existing in multivariate approaches, the need for some stable points of reference in the field in which human behavior takes place, and the duality between action and symbolic behavior are worthy of further consideration.

THE OBSERVER AND THE OBSERVED

The modern scientist knows that at any one moment he can assume but one position (Ruesch, 1956). Either he looks at a phenomenon from the outside, ignores the unique experiences of a given particle or person, and is objective, distant, and interested in mass effects; or he is on the inside, aware of the unique circumstances and experiences of the participants, and interested in the outcome of that particular situation of which he is a part. The relationship of the observer to the observed thus is a function of the mass, time, and space scales involved. Eddington (1927) once remarked that man is half way between the mass of the atoms and the mass of the stars. Here are a few figures to illustrate the point:

The *mass* of a proton is	1.67×10^{-27} kg.
of a mole (H)	1.008×10^{-3} kg.
of a human being	7.72×10^{1} kg.
of the earth	5.983×10^{24} kg.
of the sun	1.95×10^{30} kg.
of the universe	2.14×10^{52} kg.

If we deal with the number of particles instead of with mass, we arrive at these figures:

Avogadro's number (number of molecules in a mole):	6.0249×10^{23}
Number of molecules displaced by a human being in water (77.2 liters of H_2O):	2.58×10^{27}
Number of protons in the universe	1.29×10^{79}

The relationship is termed objective when the time, space, and mass scales of the observer and the observed differ significantly, and the difference is of the order of 10^{23}. This is the case in the physical sciences. The gas laws, for example, deal with moles (6.0249×10^{23}), and astrophysics with multiples thereof (10^{52}). If the differences are smaller, we are dealing with less reliable mass effects. This is the case in the social sciences. Economics, for example, although dealing with millions of votes or stock-market transactions (10^{6}–10^{8}), certainly does not reach the objectivity level of the physical sciences. The abstractions of clinicians usually are based on a few hundred cases (10^{2}), and the abstractions of the psychoanalyst may vary from two observations ($10^{.3}$) to about ten (10^{1}). The relationship of observer to observed that involves observations or measurements of the order of 10^8 or less must be termed subjective. This is the case in the healing arts, in psychoanalysis, in psychology, and in other face-to-face operations.

THE UNIVARIATE AND THE MULTIVARIATE APPROACHES

In order to copy the procedure of the physical sciences, behavioral scientists —and notably among them the psychologists—have attempted to dissect complex patterns into their various components. For this purpose they distinguish between variables to be measured and the parameters of the field, which must be held stable during the period of observation. This procedure was successful in experimental studies as in the measurement of sensory thresholds, where easy-to-measure variables and identifiable parameters were available. But the method failed in the area of social behavior inasmuch as human beings are complex organisms who operate in even more complex fields. Subsequently, scientists came to recognize that the univariate approach of the physical and biological sciences did not yield satisfactory results in the behavioral and social sciences. So they developed the multivariate approach (Cattell, 1966). Here, then, is the contrast:

In the univariate approach we have:	(1) variables to be measured
	(2) parameters, which are kept stable
In the multivariate approach we find:	(1) transactional patterns that can be identified
	(2) complex fields governed by consistent rules

In the multivariate approach, the measurement of single variables has given way to the identification of patterns—a method borrowed from Aristotelian thinking and the humanities. And inasmuch as the social field in which this transactional pattern takes place could not be assumed to be stable, the stability was lodged in the abstract rules that govern a situation. The scheme of things in the multivariate approach, then, is as follows: Behavioral patterns are identified and their probability of occurrence is related to the field in which they are encountered. The field and the action stand in a reciprocal relation to each other. Or, to put it in other words, one or several human beings who potentially have at their disposal a variety of individual patterns of adaptation, when confronted with an identifiable situation, tend to react in predictable ways. From character typologies we have moved to interactional patterns of persons with situations. If psychoanalysis wishes to qualify as a behavioral or social science, it would have to account for the interdependence of person and situation. In classical psychoanalytic theory, the situation is given a direct place in the fantasy and an indirect place in the superego formation of the patient. But current situations happen to exert just as powerful an influence as past situations, and psychoanalytic theory will have to provide some theoretical framework for the field in which current transactions take place.

THE VARIABLE AND THE STABLE

In the physical sciences, a parameter such as temperature can be experimentally controlled and therefore can be presumed to be stable. In the behavioral sciences, the parameters not only are not stable but, unlike temperature, humidity, or speed, usually cannot be experimentally controlled. The next best solution to this lack of control is to assume that the next larger entity in terms of mass, space, and time scales will be more stable than the smaller entity. We thus arrive at a scheme in which the next larger entity serves as parameter for the next smaller entity. The series from small to large reads as follows: Nucleus—Cell—Tissue—Organ—System—Organism—Individual—Family—Group—Organization—Community—County—State—Nation—United Nations—World—Solar System—Galaxy—Universe. For example, it is presumed that the framework of a professional organization is relatively more stable and continuous than the individual membership. A society continues to exist while individuals are continuously being replaced. The frame of reference in the socal sciences thus is based upon differences in the rate of change, whereby the larger entity is thought to change more slowly. If psychoanalysis wishes to qualify as a science, it must establish a frame of reference other than the individual psychoanalyst. First, he is a participant in the situation, and second, he possesses a rate of change that is similar to that of the patient. This difficult problem has been the main reason that has kept psychoanalysis out of the universities. One of the basic tenets of the academic community is that each subject matter must be judged by a neutral body of people (Lewin and Ross, 1960). The judgments are based either on the assessment of measurements, as in the physical and social sciences, or on the consensus of experts from a variety of fields. Psychoanalysis has only one judge, and he is an insider and biased.

ACTION AND SYMBOLIC BEHAVIOR

Another very basic difficulty of the behavioral sciences bears on the fact that we simultaneously deal with actual and symbolic events. Atoms and molecules do not emit symbolic sounds as far as we know; but they do engage in physical action. But human beings are social creatures; they act, produce a physical impact, and at the same time engage in symbolic transactions. And very often the symbolic behavior does not coincide with the action behavior. To take account of this discrepancy, Freud introduced the concept of the unconscious, which in its day was an extremely versatile notion. In modern parlance, however, it is more useful to express this relationship as follows: When an action has an impact and the participants use terms that stand in a one-to-one or concordant relationship to the ongoing action, they are said to be aware of the events. When the terms are discrepant, they either are unaware of or they deliberately falsify the ongoing action.

In modern behavioral theories it must be assumed that information steers action and that a circular relationship exists between action and information. Not only is action steered by a variety of control centers, but, through feedback, action and the effects of action change the informational state of the control centers. This reciprocal and circular relationship requires that any behavioral theory make provisions for both the symbolic representation of action (information) and the action itself (physical impact). The events in turn must be subdivided into behavior (variable) and field (stable). Any behavioral theory thus has to account for a tetragonal relationship. (See Table 1.)

Table 1.

THE ORIGINAL EVENTS
are divided into

ACTUAL EVENTS which stand for themselves	and	SYMBOLIC EVENTS which stand for other events
These are studied in two ways:		These are studied in two ways:
1) STUDY OF ACTION BEHAVIOR		1) STUDY OF SIGNALING BEHAVIOR
2) STUDY OF PHYSICAL FIELD		2) STUDY OF SOCIAL ORDER

From this combination emerge
UNIFIED THEORIES

If psychoanalysis wishes to qualify as a science, it would have to make new provisions for the duality between actual and symbolic events. Although "reality testing" is a term that refers to the patient's examination of information in action, psychoanalytic theory has no place for action. As a matter of fact, "acting out" is considered an undesirable by-product and refers to the intrusion of action behavior into signaling behavior. Up to now, therefore, psychoanalysis has concerned itself mostly with the symbolic end of transactions and has not developed ways of coping with the action part of behavior.

General System Theories

In military systems the soldier comprises but a small fraction of the enterprise. Military systems include everything, ranging from weapons development to psychological warfare, from communication to transportation, and from health services to civil administration. Even more inclusive are the systems designed to explore outer space, where all conceivable aspects of living and technology have to be considered. To cope with this organized complexity, system theories were developed whereby the term "system" was used to refer to a cluster of components or units engaged in mutual interaction. However, one of the difficulties that remained was the encoding of data. In one subsystem there were people, in another there were dollars, and in a third there were machines. While the physicist possesses satisfactory conversion laws, for example, to relate mass to energy, the behavioral sciences do not have suitable devices that would enable scientists to relate sensory data to biochemical changes in the body. Before a unification of the behavioral sciences can be accomplished, the analogies, homologies, and transactional processes characteristic of cell, organ, organism, group, and society have to be expressed in terms that are applicable to all of these entities. In the life sciences this task has become the domain of general systems theory, the principal exponents of which are Bertalanffy (1966), Miller (1965), and Rapoport (1966).

While general systems theory may specify some general features shared by various subsystems, scientists nonetheless proceed as usual with the development of specific theories bearing upon their work. But in order to fit various subsystems together, the specific theories must be expressed in certain ways. For this purpose, the procedures borrowed from electrical engineering have proven extremely useful (Ashby, 1956). The "black box" containing complex electronic devices has terminals for input and output, but the internal mechanism is not open for inspection. Thus in any system provisions can be made for the insertion of "black boxes," the details of which are not covered by the general systems theory except for specification of input and output.

Modern science thus has arrived at the following broad outline for theory construction: Each major area, such as molecular biology, behavioral science, or astrophysics, contributes a general systems theory. Each specific discipline, such as cell physiology, genetics, or experimental psychology, contributes special theories. In between stand task-oriented groups that selectively combine several special fields into a unified theory to cope with their particular problems. Examples of unified theories are found in the field of psychosomatic medicine, where behavioral and physiological data of individuals are combined.

In attempting to fit psychoanalysis into the scheme of special, unified, and general systems theories it becomes clear that psychoanalytic theory is a special theory and that its data are derived from a special situation. In the 1930's and 1940's varied attempts were made to combine psychoanalytic theory with other theories. Alexander (1950) attempted to create a unified theory of psychosomatic medicine; Parsons (1952) attempted to combine social and psychoanalytic theory. More recently, Menninger (1963) attempted to bring psychoanalytic theory more in line with biological thinking and described a progression of dyscontrols in human behavior. Unfortunately many attempts remained unsatisfactory because they were based on the establishment of analogies and interpretative explanations rather than on shared variables. Returning to the consideration of the black box theory, it becomes abundantly clear that in electrical engineering input and output are expressed in terms that are shared by all components. To make psychoanalytic data and theories suitable for connection with other behavioral data, a common variable has to be found. In the past, I have suggested that inasmuch as communication is the modality that interconnects all social processes, terms derived from the communication disciplines might help in connecting psychoanalysis with other fields (Ruesch and Bateson, 1951; Ruesch, 1961).

MODERN ENGINEERING APPROACHES

A new approach to old human problems has been introduced in management, operations research, and urban design. Modern engineers simply design a new society from scratch. In contrast to the theoreticians of the older disciplines, who derived their theories from observation of existing conditions, the engineers start with a theory and then construct a brave new world. These modern utopians are not concerned with people; instead they are concerned with systems (Boguslaw, 1965). The radical departure of the system designers from previous methods of theorizing consists in their neglect of existing conditions, historical continuity, and social tradition. The new designs are dedicated to the efficiency, reliability, and predictability of the system. In these modern computerized approaches, man is no longer kingpin of the total set; instead he has become a unit, impersonal, replaceable, and expendable. The revolutionary idea thus consists in adapting the world—and this includes the human being—to the system design. This procedure, of course, leads to perfect theories, but it remains to be seen where and when the adaptability of people will reach its limits and they will cease to fit into the systems that have been designed for them.

The system design came into being after a series of theoretical developments took place in the field of communication. In 1948 Wiener published his work on cybernetics. Based on the concept of negative feedback —a notion derived from the servomechanism theory developed in electrical engineering—this theory of control in animal and machine exerted a profound influence on biological, psychological, and social research. In 1949 C. E. Shannon published his information theory (Shannon and Weaver, 1949), which provided criteria for the evaluation of different systems of communication. Concurrently evolved the theory of smoothing, filtering, and detection of the value of signals in the presence of noise—a theory that has been mostly confined to the field of engineering (Pierce, 1961). These as well as other technical discoveries led to the development of the theory of automata and computers. The latter have not only revolutionized our lives, but they have also introduced new possibilities into science. Because a computer program is made up of a series of logical statements, the machine has become a device to check the logic of the human being, and, if a theorem cannot be written as a computer program, it is not considered a proper theorem. The uses and limitations of computers have been ably reviewed in the literature (Coulson, 1962; Greenberger, 1962; Feigenbaum and Feldman, 1963; Sherman, 1963; Kent and Taulbee, 1965; Licklider, 1965).

At the present, then, theoretical advances are intimately tied to technical procedures. Re-enactment of events or simulation of natural phenomena by an external model is the path on which advances are currently made; and the results are tested in the construction of completely new worlds. The preciseness of these approaches does not permit fuzzy concepts to obscure the picture, and unworkable hypotheses immediately become apparent. According to this view, psychoanalytic theory should be translatable into a computer program, and if this is not possible the theory should be changed until it can be done (Colby, 1964).

MINIMUM REQUIREMENTS FOR A UNIFIED THEORY OF BEHAVIOR

Such a change would mean that the characteristics of human beings, like those of other living entities such as cells, organs, organisms, or organizations, would have to be specified in terms that enable the scientist to combine various entities with one another. The first set of functions to be specified would describe the communicating entities in terms of: (1) input functions, which in human behavior are identified with perception or the cognitive processes; (2) central functions, which are concerned with scanning (recognition), data processing (thinking and association), data storage (memory), and decision-making (judgment); and (3) output functions, which in human beings are identified with physical action and symbolic expression.

The second set of functions would describe the processes connecting various entities such as cells, organs, organisms, organizations, and machines with one another. Among these connecting functions are the sequential and temporal characteristics, the languages and codes, the devices for attribution of meaning to agreed-upon symbols, and the devices for interpretation. Feedback processes would arrange for relaying effects of what went on between the entities back to the sources of information storage, therefore steering future action and symbolic behavior.

The third set of functions that have to be specified are those of the outside observer. Reports of the participant (inside observer) have to be supplemented by reports of the uninvolved (outside observer). Statements about his position have to be complemented by information about his bias, description of the models he uses, and data about other features characterizing his position (Ruesch, 1967).

Summary

In recognition of the fact that the separation of the humanities from the social and physical sciences has undesirable side effects, some professionals have begun to tear down the walls separating the various disciplines from one another. Among the new developments that attempt to bridge the gulf between person orientation and system orientation has been the organization of new interdisciplinary departments in our universities. Older divisions such as philosophy, anthropology, sociology, psychology, and English alone cannot cope with subjects such as the mass media, advertising, propaganda, interpersonal relations, industrial organization, and the like. Therefore, departments of human development, social relations, and communication have been established. The common denominator of all these enterprises is their interdisciplinary nature, which enables them to draw liberally from the social, behavioral, engineering, and mathematical disciplines. These modern centers increase the probability that unified theories might be forthcoming that can connect the individual with the smaller molecular and the larger social world.

The frontiers of psychoanalysis and psychotherapy and the future development of theories concerning the individual fall into the interdisciplinary area (Stollak, Guerney, and Rothberg, 1966; Wallerstein, 1966). The immediate task is to find ways of theoretically connecting data about an individual with data about situation and group. In order to include psychoanalytic data in the pool of behaviorial information, the following modifications of psychoanalytic theory will be necessary:

1. Introduction of fixed points of reference for the psychoanalytic observer. These may consist either of standards leading to measurements or of multiple observers whose reports would increase the validity and reliability of observations.

2. Introduction of a theoretical device that places observations into a situational or contextual configuration so that psychoanalytic observations also can be made outside the standardized and controlled psychoanalytic situation.

3. Introduction of variables to account for physical action to supplement observations of symbolic expression. Both action and expression would have to be accounted for in the theoretical scheme.

4. Introduction of a simplified device similar to the "black box" of the engineers that would enable behavioral scientists to connect one individual with others, obviating the details of the internal structure. For many purposes, description of input (perception) and output (word or action) in a given situation might suffice to link the behavior of one individual to that of others.

The association of psychoanalysis with medicine and psychiatry is a historical accident brought about by the fact that Freud was a physician and neurologist. The alliance with medicine brought affluence to psychoanalysts but poverty to theoretical development. Today medicine no longer is interested in the individual but in biological and social systems that lend themselves for primary and secondary prevention. Psychoanalysis, in contrast, is a learned discipline that deals with the individual. Its welfare and development will best be served by association with other professions drawn from the humanities and behavioral sciences that also focus on the individual. Unless the body of knowledge of psychoanalysis can be included in the cumulative body of knowledge of the behavioral disciplines, the future of psychoanalysis is in doubt.

References

Abraham, K. "The Influence of Oral Erotism on Character-Formation" (1924). In *Selected Papers of. . . .* New York: Basic Books, 1953. Vol. 1, pp. 393–406.

Abraham, K. "Character-formation on the Genital Level of the Libido" (1925). In *Selected Papers of. . . .* New York: Basic Books, 1953. Vol. 1, pp. 407–417.

Alexander, F. *Psychosomatic Medicine.* New York: Norton, 1950.

Ashby, W. R. *An Introduction to Cybernetics.* London: Chapman & Hall, 1956.

Benjamin, A. C. *Science, Technology, and Human Values.* Columbia: University of Missouri Press, 1965.

Berelson, B. (ed.). *The Behavioral Sciences Today.* New York: Basic Books, 1963.

Bertalanffy, L. von. "General System Theory and Psychiatry." In S. Arieti (ed.), *American Handbook of Psychiatry.* New York: Basic Books, 1966. Vol. 3, pp. 705–721.

Boguslaw, R. *The New Utopians.* Englewood Cliffs, N.J.: Prentice-Hall, 1965.

Bridgman, P. W. *The Way Things Are.* Cambridge: Harvard University Press, 1959.

Cattell, R. B. (ed.). *Handbook of Multivariate Experimental Psychology.* Chicago: Rand McNally, 1966.

Colby, K. M. "Experimental Treatment of Neurotic Computer Programs." *American Medical Association Archives of General Psychiatry*, 10 (1964), 220–227.

Coulson, J. E. (ed.). *Programmed Learning and Computer-Based Instruction*. New York: John Wiley, 1962.

Eddington, A. S. *Stars and Atoms*. New Haven, Conn.: Yale University Press, 1927.

Ellul, J. *The Technological Society*. New York: Knopf, 1964.

Feigenbaum, E. A., and Feldman, J. (eds.). *Computers and Thought*. New York: McGraw-Hill, 1963.

Freud, S., and Breuer, J. "On the Psychical Mechanism of Hysterical Phenomena" (1892). *The Standard Edition of the Complete Psychological Works of. . . .* London: Hogarth Press. Vol. 2, pp. 3–17. (Also in *Collected Papers of. . . .* New York: Basic Books, 1959. Vol. 1, pp. 24–41.)

Freud, S. "Character and Anal Erotism" (1908). *The Standard Edition of the Complete Psychological Works of. . . .* London: Hogarth Press, Vol. 9. (Also in *Collected Papers of. . . .* New York: Basic Books, 1959. Vol. 2, pp. 45–50.)

Freud, S. "The Dynamics of the Transference" (1912). *The Standard Edition of the Complete Psychological Works of. . . .* London: Hogarth Press. Vol. 12, pp. 97–108. (Also in *Collected Papers of. . . .* New York: Basic Books, 1959. Vol. 2, pp. 312–322.)

Freud, S. "Further Recommendations in the Technique of Psycho-Analysis" (1913–1915). *The Standard Edition of the Complete Psychological Works of. . . .* Vol. 12, pp. 145–156. (Also in *Collected Papers of. . . .* New York: Basic Books, 1959. Vol. 2, pp. 342–391.)

Freud, S. "The Resistances to Psycho-Analysis" (1925). *The Standard Edition of the Complete Psychological Works of. . . .* London: Hogarth Press. Vol. 19, pp. 163–174.

Freud, S. "An Outline of Psychoanalysis" (1938). *The Standard Edition of the Complete Psychological Works of. . . .* London: Hogarth Press. Vol. 19, pp. 163–174.

Greenberger, M. (ed.). *Computers and the World of the Future*. Cambridge, Mass.: MIT Press, 1962.

Horowitz, I. L. *Philosophy, Science and the Sociology of Knowledge*. Springfield, Ill.: Charles C Thomas, 1961.

Hoselitz, B. F. (ed.). *A Reader's Guide to the Social Sciences*. New York: The Free Press of Glencoe, 1959.

Jung, C. G. *Psychological Types*. London: Kegan Paul, Trench, Trubner, 1946.

Kaplan, N. (ed.). *Science and Society*. Chicago, Ill.: Rand McNally, 1965.

Kent, A., and Taulbee, O. E. (eds.). *Electronic Information Handling*. Washington, D.C.: Spartan Books, 1965.

Kerr, C., Dunlop, J. T., Harbison, F. H., and Myers, C. A. *Industrialism and Industrial Man*, 2nd ed., New York: Oxford University Press, 1964.

Knapp, R. H. *The Origins of American Humanistic Scholars*. Englewood Cliffs, N. J.: Prentice-Hall, 1964.

Kretschmer, E. *Physique and Character*. London: Kegan Paul, Trench, Trubner, 1925.

Lewin, B., and Ross, Helen. *Psychoanalytic Education in the United States.* New York: Norton, 1960.

Licklider, J. C. R. *Libraries of the Future.* Cambridge: MIT Press, 1965.

Marx, M. H. (ed.). *Theories in Contemporary Psychology.* New York: Macmillan, 1963.

Menninger, K. *The Vital Balance.* New York: Viking, 1963.

Miller, J. G. "Living Systems: Basic Concepts; Living Systems: Structure and Process; Living Systems: Cross-Level Hypotheses." *Behavioral Science,* 10 (1965), 193–237, 337–379, 380–411.

Mohr, G. J. "Psychoanalysis: Some Present-Day Assessments." In J. H. Masserman (ed.), *Science and Psychoanalysis.* Vol. III. *Psychoanalysis and Human Values.* New York: Grune & Stratton, 1960. Pp. 1–19.

Mora, G. "The History of Psychiatry: A Cultural and Bibliographical Survey." *Psychoanalytic Review,* 52 (1965), 298–328.

Mullahy, P. *Oedipus Myth and Complex.* New York: Hermitage, 1948.

Parsons, T. "The Superego and the Theory of Social Systems." *Psychiatry,* 15 (1952), 15–25.

Pierce, J. R. *Symbols, Signals and Noise.* New York: Harper, 1961.

Rapoport, A. "Mathematical Aspects of General Systems Analysis." In *General Systems.* Ann Arbor, Michigan: Society for General Systems Research, 1966. Vol. 11, pp. 3–11.

Rieff, P. *Freud: The Mind of the Moralist.* New York: Viking, 1959.

Ruesch, J. "The Observer and the Observed: Human Communication Theory" (1956). In R. R. Grinker, Sr. (ed.), *Toward a Unified Theory of Human Behavior.* 2nd ed.; New York: Basic Books, 1967. Pp. 36–54.

Ruesch, J. *Therapeutic Communication.* New York: Norton, 1961.

Ruesch, J. "The Future of Psychologically Oriented Psychiatry." In J. H. Masserman (ed.), *Science and Psychoanalysis.* Vol. X. *The Sexuality of Women.* New York: Grune & Stratton, 1966. Pp. 144–160.

Ruesch, J. "Epilogue to the Second Edition." In R. R. Grinker, Sr. (ed.), *Toward a Unified Theory of Human Behavior.* 2nd ed.; New York: Basic Books, 1967. Pp. 376–390.

Ruesch, J., and Bateson, G. *Communication: The Social Matrix of Psychiatry.* New York: Norton, 1951.

Shannon, C. E., and Weaver, W. *The Mathematical Theory of Communication.* Urbana, Ill.: University of Illinois Press, 1949.

Sherman, P. M. *Programming and Coding Digital Computers.* New York: John Wiley, 1963.

Snow, C. P. *The Two Cultures and the Scientific Revolution.* New York: Cambridge University Press, 1959.

Stollak, G. E., Guerney, B. G., Jr., and Rothberg, M. (eds.). *Psychotherapy Research: Selected Readings.* Chicago, Ill.: Rand McNally, 1966.

Wallerstein, R. S. "The Current State of Psychotherapy." *Journal of the American Psychoanalytic Association,* 14 (1966), 183–224.

Wiener, N. *Cybernetics, or Control and Communication in the Animal and the Machine* (1948). 2nd ed.; Cambridge, Mass.: MIT Press, 1961.

4

Psychoanalysis and the Twentieth-Century Revolution in Communication

HARLEY C. SHANDS

> *Philosophy is written in that great book which lies ever before our eyes—I mean the universe—but we cannot understand it if we do not first learn the language and grasp the symbols in which it is written.*
>
> —GALILEO

The twentieth century may well take its place in history as that century in which an understanding of communicational process began to be the central topic of intellectual interest. The unbelievable expansion of computer technology, the revolutionary approaches to teaching of mathematical techniques, the automation of information-retrieval are those matters most in focus—but less conspicuously there is the perhaps more important acceleration in understanding the "human condition" as a function of human means of communication. The pioneer researches of such men as Sapir and Cassirer have taught us that the human condition is a matter of relatedness to others on the basis of an artificial system of communication. The most radical developments in the twentieth century involve an expanded understanding of communicational processes in relation to knowing and thinking. Where traditionally in the past the ideal has been that of so correcting language and thought as to allow a clear view of an unchanging "reality," modern consensus in many fields increasingly assumes that the processes of communication are inevitably *participants* in the eventual conclusion. This central understanding means that certainty becomes illegitimate *in principle*. The mathematical background of this idea has been established by Gödel; the physical theory by Heisenberg; the philosophical statement by Peirce. Comments illuminating the whole approach are to be found in the discussions by Bentley (1950), Bohr (1950), and Conant (1952).

The background of this movement involves a greater appreciation of the processes of development. From the relatively recent theoretical beginning in the New Science of Giambattista Vico in the mid-eighteenth century (Bergin and Fisch, 1961), the significance of developmental process is reaffirmed in the biological sphere by Darwin and comes to clear exposition in an unexpected way in the title of the book by Einstein and Infeld, *The Evolution of Physics* (1938). In modern cosmologies, as well as in modern theories of knowledge, we learn that the universe, instead of being a static system, may be one capable of indefinite expansion. But in the effort to manage this idea, we have to turn from the study of a presumably "objective reality" to the study of the communicational process which inevitably both reveals to and conceals from us what we investigate. The statement can be made that we have evolved to the point at which we learn to investigate communication *as such*, with the "to what" and the "of what" understood as secondary. The new view of communication differs from any previous view in that the field has no substantive content; we are concerned only with the act of *making common* to more than one participant, as implied by the etymological derivation of the term (from *cum*, "with," and *munis*, "bound" or "under obligation"—i.e., communicants are under similar obligations).

The principal importance of the artificial system of communication is that the human being by virtue of this kind of system is made extremely dependent on learned methods of relating himself to his human relatives. Where he has a normal childhood, he arrives at maturity equipped with his language as (in Sapir's phrase) an essentially perfect instrument of communication. Where he does not learn the system in childhood, he is relatively impaired, and, unless he learns some linguistic system well, he is likely never to be able to do so in later life. The person incompletely socialized in his infancy tends never to feel the serene sense of belonging which characterizes the bulk of normal human beings.

In the very first years of the twentieth century we find two very differently oriented conceptual systems of enormous importance to those portions of the world where there have been the major developments in modern science. These two are the theoretical systems initiated by Einstein in relation to the physical universe and by Freud in relation to the universe of "mental illness." The significant similarity in the two systems is that in both there is implicit the central notion of the importance of means of communication as formative of the universe "discovered" by such means. The original publication of Freud's work on dreams occurred in the same decade as the publication of the special theory of relativity. Both contributions have had enormous impact on mankind in subsequent years. The impact of Freud's ideas has been blurred and limited by the fact that Freud used an inappropriate mechanical frame of reference in which to present these insights. The conceptual system emerging from Einstein's wider view has made Newtonian mechanics obsolete as a conceptual model, as well as other systems using Newtonian theory as a conceptual model, including not only the Freudian, but also the Marxist system.

Some Differences of Opinion

In the intellectual history of the twentieth century we find a radically new emphasis on *points of view* and *methods of communication* which increasingly has superseded the earlier supposed capacity to deal with isolated *facts*. Where in the eighteenth century Hume (1748) subordinated the study of *relations of ideas* to that of *matters of fact*, in the twentieth century we have turned the world upside down as we realize that matters of fact depend on relations of ideas. Where it is still useful in simple situations to deal with ideas of "object" or of "matter in motion" (the basic scheme used by Marxism), at the frontier of knowledge we see that the *relation* is always prior to the fact and that the postulation of an objective source for any communication is simply a rationalization based on a widespread human inability to understand symbolic process.

It is ironic that the psychoanalytic institutes, deeply immersed in the fixation processes characteristic of institutionalization, should now resist the further development of the central insights to which they owe their original existence. We find in the Freudian notion of "transference" the same insight as that contained in the so-called "Sapir-Whorf" hypothesis, namely that no statement can be understood to have value independent of the situational context of its occurrence. Any such statement has to be understood in terms of the developmental histories of the *participants* and of the *linguistic systems* as well. The idea is very close as well to that of the Gestalt psychologists who emphasize that no "figure" can be understood as independent of its "ground"—but the significance of the psychoanalytic idea is that it specifically includes the developmental-historical dimension.

In the traditional view psychoanalysis is seen as a *scientific* procedure having a place in the specifically *medical* universe as a treatment of *disease*. It is couched in a language borrowed from pre-Einsteinian physics; because of this origin, it is formulated in energy-mechanical terms which in turn assume a deterministically oriented universe. The principal novel conception of psychoanalysis is that of the "unconscious" processes which underlie overt manifestations of behavior (especially at the linguistic-symbolic level). In the intense parochialism of the discipline, this conception is very generally reified into the idea of an institution ("The Unconscious") to which *belief* is directed: the comment "You don't believe in 'The Unconscious'!" tends then to become an accusation of heresy.

The contrasting series made in the following discussion begins with the assumption that psychoanalysis is a strictly limited, narrowly defined variant in the broad field of psychotherapy and that the whole field is primarily concerned with training or educational procedures of a highly complex type.[1] The reason why psychotherapy falls legitimately into the medical universe is that it is a primarily *clinical* discipline, and the training to become a psychotherapist is predominantly a clinical training. The kind of judgment and the feeling of responsibility involved are perhaps best developed in a medical setting, although they are not directly connected with the pharmacopoeia or the regular armamentarium of the medical practitioner. Clinical judgment has always to do with a relativity of therapeutic procedure and the patient's tolerance and sensitivity. Training in a clinical tradition tends to emphasize thinking and acting in terms of relations rather than in terms of objects. In psychotherapies of all sorts, the appropriate relations are those having communicational implications, and the dynamic trend in any such context is inherently purposive and goal-directed.[2]

Finally, the importance of unconscious processes is by now no longer novel in any sense. Every modern study of organ, organism, system, or computer participates in the same notion. Freud's great contribution is not the notion of unconscious process but rather his precocious, unclearly stated, but magnificently insightful awareness that "unconscious" in the psychoanalytic sense means "not-yet-symbolizable" (cf. Freud, 1915, and further discussion below).

Although Freud's work was throughout his career in the area of communicational process, it was not until very late that he began to formulate his ideas in terms which approach modern ways of thinking. Only with the publication of *Hemmung, Symptom und Angst* (1926) does it appear that he thinks of signaling as a function of feeling; prior to that time the prevailing conception is the quasi-substantive idea of transformation of a "li-

[1] To quote Sapir (1957, p. 145), "psychiatry is moving away from its historical position of a medical discipline unable to make good, to that of a discipline which is medical only by tradition and courtesy and is compelled, with or without permission, to attack fundamental problems of psychology and sociology so far as they affect the well-being of the individual. The locus, then, of psychiatry turns out to be not the human organism at all in any fruitful sense of the word but the more intangible, and yet more intelligible, world of human relationships and ideas that such relationships bring forth."

[2] It is noteworthy that a purposive approach is specifically required by communicational process; widely different approaches, such as those of Wiener (1948), in relation to the theory of computer technology, and of Granit (1955), in relation to the physiology of the special senses, insist on this basic conceptual assumption.

bido" into a feeling of anxiety. The difficulty of shifting frames of reference is well seen in the problems of modern adults attempting to cope with the "new mathematics" their children are studying; what is clear to a bright third-grader is now often entirely obscure to his father. It is of further interest to note that some contemporary investigators concerned with clinical problems have begun to use the new mathematical techniques. Piaget (1957) used the propositional calculus in his recent work in the study of thinking, and Feinstein (1963) points out that any medical clinician uses set theory in his approach to problems of diagnosis.

When the problems of psychoanalysis are treated purely at the technical level, the operations of the classical analyst and his explanations are fully consonant with the view expressed here. Psychoanalysis operates (in purest form) as solely a technique of *verbal* communication; intervention takes place through *interpretation* alone. The effect of interpretation is an increment of learning in *insight*. The "material" of observation is the patterning of the analysand's behavior (verbal and nonverbal), and the analyst's interpretation is his evaluative description of these patterns back to the analysand. His resulting insight is an interpretation of the analyst's interpretation, in a procedure ideally always assuming the circular nature of the process and the unavoidability of both "transference" and "countertransference" distortion.

The analyst, saying with deceptive simplicity "Just say what comes to mind" is in fact imposing a severe strain on the prospective patient's capacity to "play" a particularly complex "game." When the patient demonstrates a capacity to pick up this kind of procedure, he is termed (explicitly or implicitly) *suitable*, and the procedure often becomes a mutually creative and satisfying engagement; when he is found not to be suitable, he is usually rejected out of hand. The procedure is an experiment in communication, with the patient serving as *initiator* of patterns which the analyst subsequently interprets in a manner conveying at least some novelty to the analysand. By his differential responses the analyst modifies subsequent behavior both within and outside the relationship.

This mutuality, while specifically perhaps unique, still has a "family resemblance" (Wittgenstein, 1953) to many others with which we are familiar in the twentieth century. The *selection* procedure somewhat resembles that for acceptance into institutions of higher learning. After acceptance, the activity of the analyst as it might be described by a behaviorist amounts to *positive* and *negative reinforcement*. In learning-theory language, the patient is involved in a *trial-and-error* investigation, with the judgment as to when in error supplied (positively or negatively) by the analyst. In the language of evolutionary biology, every pattern exhibited by the patient becomes a *variant* or *mutation*, to be selected or rejected for survival and elaboration.

The overwhelming probability in *statistical* terms (as noted in a discussion of research in psychoanalysis by Glover, 1952) is that the opinion of the patient will come to resemble that of the analyst in depth: agreement in fact is taken to mean truth in theory!

Tokens, Abstractions, Symbols

The capacity mysteriously emergent at the evolutionary transition between primate and human being is that of dealing with pattern apparently divorced from a context, that capacity spoken of as "abstraction." When we examine the process more closely, we find that the apparent divorce is made possible only by an immediately simultaneous remarriage: the pattern removed from its original context of origin can be managed only by an immediate joining to a symbol, a verbal or mathematical sign, or a token of some other sort. Such a joining makes the symbol meaningful and at the same time makes the pattern communicable—but only in the new context of a linguistic-symbolic system in which the symbol used has a relation to its fellows. The "object" is named and can be talked about only through the use of a word which has meaning in relation to other words—and only in the setting of a social system in which the language is an accepted medium of communication. To describe any pattern divorced from its context of origin is like talking about the male or female role in sexual intercourse—it is possible to make the reference, but impossible in practice to separate either from its reciprocal. Through the development of a new relation, the act of *naming* makes *knowing* possible at the level of conceptual thought (Dewey and Bentley, 1960).

Abstracting is therefore constructing. Instead of dealing with a pattern in its natural setting, we use patterns in a new relation, one involving the *shape* of the object or event and the *shape* of the word (or verbal or mathematical sign). Freud's insight into this fact is obscured by his inability to emancipate himself from his own linguistic context. He speaks (1915) of the process of "becoming conscious" as that of the association of the "idea of the thing" with the "idea of the word." This formula is inaccurate because the notion of an "idea" already implies a symbolic process; had he said the "shape" or "pattern" rather than the idea, his comment would be astonishingly contemporary in its implication.

Modern research in computer technology leads to the idea that the basic property of the nervous system is that of the *recognition* of *pattern* (Selfridge and Neisser, 1960). All animals recognize patterns and demonstrate intelligent behavior (Bentley, 1950). The specific human advantage is that of the use of a symbolic pattern by means of which to grasp natural pattern and refer to the latter in the absence of the original context of origin. The human symbol therefore has always to be seen as existing in two universes simultaneously—the universe of nature from which it takes its original origin, and the universe of a symbolic-linguistic system in which it has communicational potentiality. The dual nature of human symbols can be seen in most concrete form in the monetary universe—every dollar or franc or mark has a value: (1) in relation to goods and services which can be bought within the system and (2) a second relation to the international, "meta"-market in which money itself is bought and sold with constantly varying rates of exchange. Perhaps the most important implication in the nature of the communicational process is that linguistic symbols (verbal or mathematical signs) never refer to particulars, but always to universals or generalizations (Locke, 1690; Vygotsky, 1934). A name establishes a category, class, or mathematical set. Where the human being originally knows his mother as a particular collection of touchings, smellings, and tastings, he knows her in the abstract universe only as a member of a class, "mother." For particular reference in symbols, the human being has to deal with *intersections* of classes: "my mother" is the intersection of the two classes of: (1) all those things which are mine and (2) all those persons referred to as mothers. The word, dealing with a pattern abstracted from an event, has to be placed in context with other words to make a particular reference. We are all inevitably involved with at least binomial process when we use a name (John Jones; *Homo sapiens;* this lean, hungry, yellow dog). For this reason alone, it is never possible to refer to any particular object without going through the roundabout method of putting the problem in general terms, then identifying the intersection of those sets involved.

It is important to note that the basic structure of this process is one which leads to extraordinary error in one direction and to many forms of novel insight in the other. In Freud's (1915) example, he points to the similarity in shape between the squeezing of a blackhead and the ejaculation of a penis. In both there is the form of spurting (both occur in the set of "spurts"). In the example, Freud points to the psychotic confusing of the two; in later discussion of the same idea, Storch (1948) and Van Domarus (1944) make similar comments. At the other side of the scale of rationality, however, we find that the same kind of assimilation can be seen in the astonishing insight of L. Boltzman (Rothstein, 1958) that *physical information* is identical with *negative entropy*. The subsequent course of the insight is the deciding factor, since the identity of spurting blackhead and ejaculating penis is of purely local interest, while the identity of information and negentropy is the theoretical basis for modern information theory. Not only does linguistic usage require generalization and subsequent binomial identification, it always requires that the subject matter be put into sequential form. The other great capacity of the abstracting process is that of grasping as an instantaneously understood whole what originally occurs as a temporally separated sequence. Any word is *heard* as a series of phonemes, but it is *understood* as a whole; to illustrate the point, let us take the sequential parts, "to" and "get" and "her"—when we hear them as a single whole, we hear "together," a totally different meaning from the sum of the parts. When we examine the perceptual process, we find a similar capacity to integrate sensations of sight, sound, touch, smell, and others into the comprehension of an *object:* but the object is always a construct, an artificial whole, and an extrapolation from minimal cues to the supposition that this object is like others previously known.

When we start with an analytical, intellectual approach to objects, we ignore the *prehistory* in which the object is first perceptually grasped, then along with the emergence of an object-concept (Inhelder and Piaget, 1958), internalized and identified for symbolic reference. Cassirer (1946), following the lead of the philologist Usener, notes that the origin of the original conception appears to be a situation in which an intense emotional experience separates out a pattern from others. Through the development of a deeply felt emotional reaction, the pattern in question is separated from its context and made available for naming. In the beginning, new patterns tend to emerge in *mythic* form—Usener speaks of "momentary deities" which command identification and persistence. The emotional setting so established uses the physiological mechanisms with which we are familiar in the establishment of a Pavlovian "temporary connection" (Shands, 1960)—but the persistence and maintenance of the temporary connection in the human species becomes a function of *consensual ratification* (or consensual validation, Sullivan, 1953), rather than that of repetition of the unconditional stimulus. In the "second signal system" the human being looks to a preceptor or authority speaking with the weight of the group consensus to maintain the relation established in the emotion of the moment. The institution of marriage, for example, is a consensually supported group method of maintaining a relation established on the basis of the evanescent frenzy of sexual excitement.

The most important implication of this method of procedure is that through repetitive reinforcement in plastic organisms at critical periods, consensual agreement is made into "reality." The enormous force of human beings in concert comes from the commitment of all to the common goal; it is notable that in every crisis situation, the group can be found to rise to an extraordinary level of achievement because of the enforced presence of a widespread consensus as to goals and values. The fragmentation of the human group by the development of different linguistic-symbolic systems is well described in the Bible.[3]

[3] The power of consensus was well known to the writer of Genesis: "And the Lord said, Behold, the people is one, and they have all one language; and this they begin to do: and *now nothing will be restrained from them, which they have imagined to do.* Go to, let us go down, and there confound their language, that they may not understand

The importance of psychoanalytic ways of thinking is perhaps primarily in the emphasis given to the process of developing insight in rational terms through the route of *personal* myth and metaphor. In a psychoanalytic undertaking, the two participants examine a personal linguistic system in order to correlate it more accurately with the larger social context in which it occurs. The patient learns new meanings for ancient patterns, and he is encouraged to experiment with previously tabooed operations and relations. In the psychoanalytic situation there may be a continuous becoming in which all the familiar patterns of one's life are reviewed and seen from a different point of view so that experimental testing of a new sort can take place. From the microcosmic establishment of insight in the therapeutic situation, the patient is enabled to try out new patterns in the macrocosmic context of his ordinary life. The patient both "acts out" and "works through" patterns of behavior in relation to developments occurring in the psychotherapeutic relationship.

It is notable that any improvement or "cure" occurring in this process has to be validated in some consensual context—originally in consensus of patient and therapist, but eventually in consensus of patient and sexual partner, patient and employer, patient and competitor. When we understand the fundamental importance of consensus for linguistic process, we can get a clearer picture of why the beginnings of human history tend to be signaled now to us by the persistence of religious artifacts and idols. These objects of veneration are primary *objects of consensus*—the original human group appears as a group of *communicants*, sharing some rudimentary version of ritual experience.

When human beings discover the universe of symbols, they discover the human *mysteries*. In the symbolic universe there appears the possibility of apparently *instantaneous* action, and apparent *action-at-a-distance*. From the beginning of time to the beginning of the twentieth century is the period required for the genius of an Einstein finally to grasp the fact that "instantaneous" is an illegitimate conception, since any event can be related to any other event only in the finite time required for light to move from the one to the other area (Toulmin and Goodfield, 1965). But the great mysteries of religion, of magic, and of faith-healing continue to assume that events occur in no-time. In another context, the sudden shift is regularly one from a positive to a negative: the last becomes the first, black becomes white. Both these processes are well seen in the central mystery of Christian theology, the eucharist. There, in an instant, the bread and wine of the mass become the flesh and blood of the crucified Christ, in the operation called *transubstantiation*. Thus symbol becomes flesh, and the

---

one another's speech. So the Lord scattered them abroad from thence upon the face of the earth; . . . Therefore is the name of it called Babel; because the Lord did there confound the language of all the earth" (Genesis 11, 6–9).

boundary between natural world and symbolic universe is said to be obliterated. Second, in this ritual, man's most horrible sin, cannibalism, is ritually reversed into man's most sacred sacrament, in a matter emphasizing the basic ambivalence of the symbolic process.

Human Communication: Human Games

The principal differences between human and lower-animal kinds of communication have to do with distance: the human being is able to transmit certain coded patterns through great distances of space and time. The communicational potentialities of all other animals are much more limited. When we follow out the studies of anatomical and physiological possibilities in evolution, we see a progressive development of distance-reception as we move up the evolutionary scale toward man. This development involves both the peripheral receptors and the central data-processors. Primates are differentiated from other mammals by their greater visual capacity; the macrosmatic mammal uses sight principally as a method of finding something to investigate by smell. In man the process takes the further step of using visually discriminated pattern as the basis for linguistic operation.

Through naming and describing, man comes to live in a symbolic universe as well as in the natural one. When in a stable social system, there is general recognition that group activity takes precedence over individual activity, and such abstract notions as patriotism, honor, and love come to be prepotent over primary needs for survival and reproduction. Man comes to live in a group separated from all others by its ritual and symbolic practices and beliefs. Since all of these have a predominant symbolic meaning, we can say that man's chief relatives are his *co-linguists* rather than (as is generally the case in lower animals) his *con-specifics*.

In man, the problems of intragroup hostility (and to some extent those of intergroup hostility) are approached through the means of ritual competition which to some degree takes the place of crude combat. It is interesting to note how many examples of somewhat similar practices have recently been observed by ethnologists, in which competition is allowed in *formes frustes* which settle the question as to which of the competitors is the "better man" without harming the loser (except in "loss of face"). The specifically human invention is that of the *game* which serves the same function as the ritual modes of competition transmitted in the animal by hereditary means. The game shows important differences from animal play. A human game is characterized by *rules* (which may or may not be consciously apparent to the players), by the use of artificial tokens or counters, by the necessary consensus as to the values and meanings involved, and, most importantly, by a learning process[4] which can be studied in detail in

[4] When one considers the "well-adjusted" adult as a competent player in his cultural

childhood and in the various educational institutions worked out by mankind over its period of existence. With adequate consensus, the human game achieves a kind of autonomous existence—but the dependence on consensus is seen in the difficulty we have in understanding alien cultural practices (Langer, 1942).

Different Genera of Games

Within the universe of games defined as above, we find a variety of both species and genera of games. The widest differentiation which can be made is that of the goal involved. Piaget notes that the two great classes of mentational activity are separated by reference to goals: he says (1950, p. 6),

> What common sense calls "feelings" and "intelligence," regarding them as two opposed "faculties," are simply behavior relating to persons and behavior affecting ideas of things; but in each of these forms of behavior, the same affective and cognitive aspects of action emerge, aspects which are in fact always associated and in no way represent independent faculties.

The consistent effort in modern science has been to develop means of avoiding human frailty, and thus removing from observation and description the primary source of error, human feeling. The scientist is a man who distrusts the approach to knowledge through the imprecise "hunches" and "intuitions" of the ordinary human being. It is of interest to find, in a review of scientists' careers after a lapse of twenty years, that Anne Roe quotes a comment indicating that in at least one prominent scientist, the preference for the abstract depends on the fact that the feeling involved is quite different from that involving human problems. One of these men, commenting on the difference between research and administration, says, "administrative work tires you more than anything else. It's the need for making decisions involving human beings . . . I don't mind it nearly so much if people aren't involved" (Roe, 1965, p. 314). Working with the abstract avoids the feelings of fatigue (cf. Shands and Finesinger, 1952).

The justification for avoiding human problems in science has been the universally accepted assumption that behind the appearance of a universe so transient and changing in perceptual terms there is a (metaphysically) real universe which can be approached through the proper use of conceptual thought. Planck (1931) states that we have to begin with an assumption of "the existence of another world of reality behind the world of the senses; a world which has existence independent of man, and which can be perceived indirectly through the medium of the world of the senses, and

---

games, then the consideration of major importance is how well he plays, in comparison with his fellows. In this rendering, the use of the health-disease rubric in behavioral context becomes an inappropriate metaphor.

by means of certain symbols which our senses allow us to apprehend" (p. 8). He says further that "it is as though we were compelled to contemplate a certain object in which we are interested through spectacles of whose optical properties we were entirely ignorant" (p. 8). Perhaps the clearest way of describing the shifting emphasis in twentieth-century preoccupations with communication is by the use of this same metaphor: we have in this epoch learned how to study the "optical properties" of the "spectacles" constituted by perceptual and symbolic process. It is notable in Planck's use of this metaphor that he selects the specifically visual and assumes that this is the primary route to "reality."

To anticipate a discussion more fully developed below, it is perhaps important to comment here that the search for superhuman or extrahuman truth and reality is common to both science and religion. Both scientists and religious experts seek invariance, eternally reliable relations, and an abstract universe—the two are separated by method, but joined by a common goal. The modern gathering of information tends to show the two as similarly preoccupied with transcending the communicational limitations of human beings—and as similarly doomed to failure in this effort.

The phasic character of human preoccupations is well seen in the context of the practice of medicine. We are now aware of the fact that, prior to the twentieth century, the armamentarium of the physician had predominantly a placebo effect; in comparison with the active drugs and precise surgical procedures of the contemporary period, the physicians of former times were of little "real" use to the patient. But in every period that we know, in every culture, there is an important therapeutic function and functionary (Kiev, 1965). The implication is that the physician is primarily related to others as a *human* practitioner. The paradoxical fact is that as the demonstrable effectiveness of modern scientific medicine has been increasingly evident, the status of the physician has declined rather than increased.

It is hypothetically possible and appealing to suppose that the elaboration of modern technical procedures has facilitated an alienation of the physician from the patient. The resistance of other cultures to *scientific* medicine is easily documented—with the emphasis upon scientific progress in both the USSR and China, there is at the same time a clinging to traditional therapeutic procedures (acupuncture, herbal medicine, etc.). The implication is that the primary cultural function of the physician is not that of the scientific healer but that of interpreter (diagnostician, prognosticator, reader of omens). In this context, one can suppose that the psychotherapist appears in a scientific culture as a disguised occupant of this cultural role: "Man does not live by bread alone!"

Games and Players

Through abstraction, patterns of games can be transported to places widely different in space and time. The typically American game of baseball found a new home in Japan at a time when other cultural practices were immensely different in the two areas. In the contemporary period we find, in spite of great resistance, that the American methods of mass production and mass distribution are increasingly being exported: the supermarket flourishes in Europe, and the first French Levittown is being built.

The movement of patterns to new contexts is somewhat like the movement of animal species to new habitats; the new conditions tend to promote acceleration in developmental trends. But where the animal species responds by increase or decrease in numbers, the pattern is either adopted or rejected by the persons already in the social system of immigration. To make an irreverent association, the United States of twenty years ago was the scene of an explosive development of interest in psychoanalysis in the latter, and of the Japanese beetle in the former, context. In the contemporary period we see in both instances a marked change in the original acceleration, with the development of a new equilibrium.

The point to be made is in the demonstration that during the period of twenty years in which psychoanalysis reached its contemporary level of influence in the intellectual and medical community in this area of immigration, it was suffering a marked decline in its original area of appearance. In 1965 there appeared two reports in *The New York Times;* in the one, Professor Horkheimer (1965) of Frankfort is quoted as deploring the lack of interest in psychoanalysis in Germany, and in the second, Joseph Wechsberg (1965) reports from Vienna that psychoanalysis has all but disappeared there. The "metastasis" has flourished in the United States during the same period that the original growth has practically disappeared from its context of origin.

The suggestion inherent in this observation is that the United States has furnished to psychoanalysis a peculiarly favoring environment, while in other parts of the world the unfavorable environment has caused the seed to fall on stony ground. Since during this same period the United States has been the major scene of an explosive development of trends inherent in Western, as opposed to Eastern, civilization, it appears worthwhile to pursue the relation. The hypothesis which I should like to examine is that psychoanalysis emerges from a scientific culture, not (as generally supposed by its practitioners) as an example of a scientific operation, but as an antithetical movement in contrast to the former dehumanizing trend of Western science.

The psychoanalytic movement is characterized by the narrowness of its zone of influence, both throughout the world and in the context of social class. It is primarily of interest to well-educated middle-class persons in the urban-industrial areas of the Western world. Within this grouping it is particularly appealing to those traditions emphasizing: (1) individualism and democracy (as contrasted with those emphasizing collectivism and authoritarian approaches), (2) Protestant rather than Roman Catholic religious institutions, and (3) rational capitalism and the rational application of technological discoveries to industrial exploitation.

If we take the broadest possible view of these separable trends, it becomes possible to say that psychoanalysis appears to appeal to those immersed in the most Western of Western movements, since it is in all of these ways that we see a kind of exaggeration of the trends which differentiate Western institutions from those of the other parts of the world. In a particularly clear statement made by a man familiar with both Western and Eastern cultures, Pandit Nehru (1964) is quoted in a recent display reviewing his life and work, as saying, referring to the English conquest of India,

> But one great benefit the English did confer upon India . . . I am sure it was a good thing for India to come in contact with the scientific and industrial West; India lacked this and without it she was doomed to decay. . . . From this point of view the Protestant individualistic Anglo Saxon English were suitable for they were more different from us than other Westerners, and could give us greater shocks.

What Nehru emphasizes here is the fact that science is uniquely Western in its origin and development. In the United States we are prone to ignore this fact as we see on every side the operation of a scientific culture.

To trace this development, it is of interest to return to a discussion made by the pioneer sociologist Max Weber. Weber (1904) outlines the derivation of Western institutions (including capitalism and science) from origins in the Protestant reformation. He comments that throughout Western history there runs the thread of rationality; he notes that in such diverse fields as theology, architecture, finance, and philosophy the original insights are present in cultures other than the West, but only in the West do these beginnings come to be exploited in the rational forms which have obviously been so powerful in shaping the industrial and technological superiority of the Western world.

Rationality in this tradition appears repeatedly in Freud's writings as the highest goal. The apparently random, irrational technical approach through "free association" is presented as the pursuit of rationality through an apparently irrational route—but the goal is always that of enhancing the power of conscious rationality. In this goal-orientation, Freud's scientific background is highly apparent; and Freud repeatedly affirms his belief that he is making a scientific contribution.

On the other hand, however, and from the methodological point of view, psychoanalysis is the antithesis of science. Scientific method is primarily oriented toward the experimental demonstration of predictable relationships in accordance with clear, consciously stated hypotheses. The philosopher of science, according to Reichenbach (1949), is "not much interested in the thought processes which lead to scientific discovery"—instead, he is only concerned with a "logical analysis of the completed theory"; the scientist, in similar fashion, is not much interested (as a specialist) in the way hypotheses emerge, but only in the manner in which the hypothesis can be rationally tested.

The central importance of rational thinking in science is well seen in the statements of the masters from whom the modern scientific tradition takes its form. The emphasis throughout is upon measurement and the statement of relations in mathematical form. Hume (1748) comments that if any book does not deal with reasoning in terms of quantity and number, it is illusion and should be cast into the flames. Planck (1949) says that the task of physics is to measure everything measurable and to render every unmeasurable thing measurable.

In this tradition, the claim that psychoanalysis is a science appears unreasonable. It is a procedure interested primarily in thought processes rather than in logical proof; it is impossible to formulate any procedure in the psychoanalytic situation so as to devise an experiment or achieve a replicable experimental result. It is a procedure by which the analyst in "free-floating attention" seizes on patterns and "tests" them only by referring them back to their source for consensual approval. It prides itself on its delving into the unconscious and the preconscious. The mass of procedures developed through three hundred years of Western science has been devised for the specific purpose of removing the influence of bias and emotion from the "facts" of measurement, usually in instrumental form. Psychoanalysis, by contrast, is antithetically interested in the emotional and human background of the material which can be elicited.

The point can be again made in a different context by noting that where the ideal of scientific inquiry is that of the demonstration in *written* form of *invariant* relations described in *mathematical* exactitude for literate *replication* and communication, the techniques of psychoanalysis emphasize the particular relatedness of the two participants in an *intimate* relation utilizing *spoken* speech and, in the consensus of many of the older generation, one spoiled by any kind of recording or record-taking. Again the differences are not merely marked, they are diametrically antithetical.

If these relations are accurately described, how can we then understand that psychoanalysis is so firmly oriented toward its own participation in a scientific universe? The answer appears to be the same as that involved in the use of the term "science" in Christian Science, namely, that the prestige of science in the West is so powerful a factor that to declare anything unscientific is similar to declaring it unreliable. The prestige of the scientific movement is borrowed by many who wish to retain their membership in this exclusive society of scientists. But the nature of psychoanalysis (and its derivative psychotherapies) is such that this claim is inherently in error.

If psychoanalysis is science, then it is necessary to change the traditional definition of science; if it is not science, it is necessary to examine the possibility of reliability of its insights in some other context. The curious fact that appears repeatedly is that the bulk of psychoanalysts, following in the footsteps of the master, make the claim and ignore the evidence. The resolution of the problem which I suggest here is that we understand science itself as a game,[5] one played primarily in the West. The emergence of psychoanalysis can then be seen as a part of a movement which in many ways runs directly counter to the traditional versions of science; these differing approaches pose an antithesis to the thesis posed by science. The understanding of this process allows us to see more directly into the interesting fact that psychoanalysis, here seen as most unscientific in its very nature, still must be understood as appearing in the context of Western science, and within that context, it has obviously achieved its greatest growth in that area in which the technical and industrial application of scientific method has been most obvious, that is, in the United States.

Science and Communication

Scientific method is essentially a restricted method of communication, using a clearly describable linear, conscious, rational approach emphasizing quantitation. In a description of the process called the technique of "strong inference," for example, Platt (1964) describes a method of serial dichotomizing in a "logical tree" at which each step is tested for accuracy, with the resulting discarding of one of the two possible alternatives. As he properly notes, this method of thinking is the "old-fashioned method of inductive inference that goes back to Francis Bacon." The result of this method of attack is to outline a series of propositions each of which is tested serially for its truth-value; the test yields a "yes" or "no" answer, and the result is that the next step can be decided on the basis of the just-previous "yes" answer.

The process thus described centers around the nature of *proof*. In prescientific methods of operation, the lack of both metallic and theoretical

[5] To the point in this connection is the comment of the Nobel prize-winner Wigner (1964) that the success of science is mainly to be traced to its practice of limiting its objectives. The scientist chooses out of all possible procedures those which test a particular limited hypothesis in a locally manageable context.

instruments made it very difficult to arrive at a decision as to truth on any basis other than that of consensus. By inserting between the sensory evidence and the final conclusion the instrumental processes of replicable measurement and strict logical control, the availability of proof was immensely enhanced. With an experimental method, proof *in limited areas* becomes easily demonstrable in reassuring fashion. With successive developments, instrumentation becomes more refined and techniques more precise —to a point at which in a total reversal of the ancient faith-oriented attitude there is now a widespread consensus that the *only* method of approaching problems is the scientific method.

It is of particular interest to note in this connection that pursuing the processes of rational inquiry in the tradition mentioned has indicated the limitations of that very method. The logical outcome of a dedication to strict logical data-processing is the development of machines which process information logically—in the modern emergence of the computer as the significant movement of this time. But the unexpected outcome of improvements in technical approaches has been the demonstration of limitations—by the masters of that method.

As emphasized by Einstein and Infeld (1938), the twentieth century is the epoch in which thinking in physical terms utilizes the notion of a field, a general matrix out of which there are differentiated the various kinds of matter and the objects into which matter is formed. The comment is made there that matter is a particularly concentrated area of the field and that it is only by a process of arbitrary definition that the dichotomy of field and matter can be made. The kind of thinking which eventuates in the notion of a field in physics is that which leads to the postulation of a system in a physiological context. Where the linearity of narrowly defined scientific method lends itself to long-range prediction, the implication of the relational situation in both the field and the system is that it is impossible to predict very far. The kinds of problems suited to the two systems can be seen to be those of astronomy in the first and of biological evolution in the latter instance. When we deal with systems, we find that any system is defined as a limited area of a larger system but in turn the larger system is defined by the possibilities of communication which reveal it to the smaller system. In thinking about systems, we find that any "cause" produces an "effect" which then becomes a "cause" in relation to its own cause—the circularity of feedback process makes linear, cause-and-effect thinking obsolete.

In Freud's own personal development we can find a movement from the linear to the circular kind of thinking, against his own obvious resistance. From an earlier stage in which he regarded "transference" manifestations as simply a contaminant and an interference, he slowly moved to a point at which the analysis of the transference-countertransference system is seen as the appropriate preoccupation of the psychoanalyst. The circularity of the process is well seen in that nothing said by either participant can be understood except in terms of previous and subsequent comments by the other. Every "fact" found is modified by considerations of emphasis, feeling, and purpose.

When the patient begins to associate, the psychoanalyst listens until the communicational flow reaches a point where, on the basis of a feeling on the part of the analyst, he interrupts to make a communication in the form of an interpretation. Such an intervention effectively removes forever any possibility of an experimental replication. The interpretation organizes material from the stream of association in a manner usually novel to the patient; it selects and rejects on a basis different from that used by the patient. It is a feedback statement having a curiously bitemporal function, since it affects both past and future. It affects the past by offering alternative meaning and thus changing the *significance* of the data.

We tend to think of the past as fixed and unchanging, but this is an idea based on the assumption of the accuracy and completeness of records. The past which is actually relevant at any point is that mass of memories, habits, attitudes, and the like which persist into the present from the presumed past. A new view of this material tends to reorganize the human being as a whole, just as the theory of evolution reorganized all of man's previously cherished ideas about his own origins. When any human being undergoes a religious conversion or a massive illumination of any sort, he is subjected to a widespread revision of his past as well as of his probable future.

It is notable that past and future are always mingled in any verbal communication, since any word, statement, or other collection of phonemes becomes meaningful only on retrospective interpretation. The English-speaking student of German is familiar with the "suspended" feeling he is likely to get in reading a long German sentence in which the verb is at the very end placed. Any kind of abstract intellectual operation depends upon the discrimination of a pattern which follows, while it seems to precede, the sequence in which it is presented. We can cite the two words "psychotherapist" and "psychotic" to indicate that the third and successive syllables often are crucially important in determining meaning, and if we split "therapist" we find "the" and "rapist." The faculty of abstraction involves (1) a prediction and anticipation on the basis of the form of the initial members of a sequence, plus (2) a retrospective interpretation after the sequence is finished. A joke instantaneously reverses a preliminary anticipation by denying it and replacing it with a totally different one, with an effect commensurate with the amount of surprise involved.

The structure of psychotherapy is one which utilizes these characteristics. It is unavoidably and inexorably a circular process which represents the transactionally intricate result of both anticipation and retrospection. The end of the procedure is stated by Hanns Sachs as that point at which the patient has internalized the process to the degree where he becomes his own analyst. The various paradoxes with which we are familiar in this area are only paradoxes as long as the attempt is made to construe circular process in linear fashion (which comes first, the chicken or the egg?).

The contemporary nature of psychotherapy is well seen in the number of relatives it has in the modern world. It is like action-painting in that it exploits the apparently random; it is like nonobjective art in that it is not supposed to represent or be anything, but rather to function as a self-expressive operation. Like these artistic movements of the twentieth century, psychotherapy puts a heavy onus on the listener-critic, involving him much more than have traditional art forms as a participant-observer. The modern artist is as wary of an observer who asks "What is it a picture *of?*" as is the psychoanalyst whose patient asks, "What comes into my mind *about what?*"

The remarkable fact which can repeatedly be found is that out of all these apparently irrational processes there does emerge to the informed and sensitive observer a series of meaningful patterns evoking a significant emotional reaction. To the patterns found in a painting by a Pollock or a Kline the appropriate response may be that of purchasing an artifact, while to the patterns found in free associational material the response may be that of formulating an interpretation. Both alike depend on a novel understanding of the communicational relationship from person to person instead of from object to person.

Religion, Science, and Psychoanalysis

There is a common assumption that science is antireligious; one of the most polemical of statements "debunking" religion is to be found in Freud's *Future of an Illusion* (1927). Here, on the other hand, I want to suggest that the movement from religion to science is a developmental movement in which what appears to be a difference is in fact only a metamorphosis of components clearly to be found in the formerly dominant field. Similarly, the twentieth-century movement from narrowly conceived descriptions of physical science to contemporary concerns with communication can be seen as a development of trends inherent in the former conception.

The preoccupation with the nature of religion on the part of the founders of modern science, Descartes, Newton, Kepler, and others, is well documented by Koestler (1959). In modern affirmation, Polanyi notes that the basis of science, as well as that of religion, is faith shared by a group of similarly prepared communicants. We tend to believe that scientific discoveries are always welcomed by scientists, but the evidence indicates that a new idea may be unwelcome even to its own discoverer. The resistance of scientists to scientific discovery has been the occasion for recent learned papers (Barber, 1961); the experiment of Michelson and Morley now often cited as the principal support of the relativity theory was regarded by them as a failure, not to be mentioned (Grünbaum, 1964).

What relates science and religion is a common pursuit of truth; what separates them is the reliance on the appropriate method. In the contemporary scene, if we take as the appropriate test of truth the test of consensus (as we do in fact even in the matter of approaching divine revelation through an ecumenical convention which votes on opinions), we find that there are many competing approaches to truth. Not only is there a major consensus as to the truth of scientific methodology; we find less widespread but similarly intensely held consensual views relating to such diverse fields as existentialism and Abstract Expressionism, phenomenology and Zen Buddhism. In each such group, the central "cement" holding the group together is the commonly shared conviction as to the validity of its own means of approach.

In order to choose between these various competing ideologies, it is generally the most useful method to approach them developmentally, seeing each as an emergence from a previous state of a system in which a predecessor ideology was cherished. It is instructive in this way to look at the origins of the Christian Church from its predecessor "parents," then to look at the Protestant reformation, the rise of rational science, and the appearance of psychoanalysis as they appear to demonstrate metamorphosis of certain patterns reappearing the same and yet different in each successive stage.

The origins of all these movements repeatedly appear in a passionate dedication which allows the founders to persist in the face of intense opposition. Throughout there is repeated the strain of opposition of the mystical to the logical, with now the one and now the other in a dominant position. The curious consequence of a more comprehensive understanding of communicational process is that we begin to see that the mystical and the logical are both consequences of the symbolic process. The magical beliefs of translation from the one to the other state of being and the sober scientific notion that a mathematical statement is eternal and universally applicable to some phenomena in nature are equally dependent on the implications of the descriptive universe in which these matters are placed by verbal and mathematical formalisms.

The Christian church is the child of Hebrew and Greek parents. The Jewish origin of the principal founders of Christianity was continuously modified by the influence of the Greek civilization in which the principal development of the early Christian church took place. Early Christian theologians sought their inspiration in the works of Plato and Aristotle, and the codification and crystallization of theology derives as much from the pagan as from the Jewish heritage. We can differentiate the strains, however. From the Jewish "parent" there appears the central notion of monotheism, with the deity as the apotheosis of the symbol ("The Great I Am"). The process, begun in Moses' selection of the tables of the law as principal object of veneration (rather than the Golden Calf tolerated by Aaron, or the idols concretely used by other religious groups), was completed in the very Greek testament of John, in which the Christ is seen as primarily a symbol, "the Word become flesh." From the Greek side there emerges the apparatus of rational discourse and the logical thinking which after a long period of development appears as the background of mathematical rigor in the physical sciences.

In the earliest days of the Christian church we find the statement of the dilemma with which we still are in major involvement. What is preferable, *faith* or *works?* Is it more important to have a passionate commitment, or a rational method of inquiry? The implication which we can find repeatedly is that the difference is important in (1) establishing an institution and (2) solving a problem. The preference of Saint Paul for faith is clearly stated in many places. His manifest success as the administrative founder of a millennially durable institution gives us reason to respect his opinion. On the other hand, faith is obviously inadequate when it is desired to attain reliable information, and the pervasive doubting and demands for proof are the basis of scientific research. But, it is the faith in this method of doubting which binds together the scientific community.

In the Catholic Church of the Middle Ages, we find more and more a resurgence of *polytheism* (in the form of the Trinity, the increasing importance of the Virgin Mary, and the host of demigods appearing in the catalogue of saints to whom prayers are directed) and the performance of *works* (as in penance, the buying of indulgences, and the like). To this trend, the ascetic doctrines of Calvin appear as a return to the strictness and the harshness of the Old Testament. As Weber notes, the Puritans, because of their preference for Old Testament doctrine, were said to practice "English Hebraism." Out of this period of reaffirmation of the importance of a direct and personal relation to the deity, and out of the implications of the bitter doctrine of predestination, there emerged the paradoxical belief in the importance of *justification* which we find reflected so precisely in Reichenbach's comment that the philosopher of science is exclusively interested in the context of justification. The passionate Puritan stands in the ambivalent stance of deep faith and anguished query, "How am I justified?" The removal of the institutional trappings of the Catholic Church leaves the Protestant much more dependent on his own resources and therefore seems to orient him to the apparatus of logical proof and experimental demonstration.

The period in which psychoanalysis appears is again a period of great turmoil in the intellectual world. Freud's psychoanalytic writings began appearing with the beginning of the twentieth century; his preoccupation was with interpretation. Within a decade, the original statement of relativity theory appeared, in the same Germanic area. The massive contribution of Einstein is similarly a contribution in the interpretative area; Einstein, as Wertheimer emphasizes, arrived at his conclusions through a process of introspective rumination.[6] He left the problems of proof to others while restricting his own activity to internal data-processing.

The point of greatest interest therefore is to be seen in the fact that psychoanalysis participates in the same process through which a grasp of relativity theory appeared, namely, through the route of wonder and questioning. Psychoanalytic technique specifically abandons the tradition of directed logical inquiry which is the hallmark of experimental science. The technique requires an original commitment purely on the basis of faith, with subsequent rationalization of the faith as significant results appear. We understand that not only do the parts of this process appear in apparently random fashion on the surface, but also that any such partial appearance is the end result of even more deeply unconscious processes. The technical process of developing and refining hypotheses and interpretations has to be substantially complete before these insights can be accurately tested in the real world—but like Einstein, the psychoanalyst leaves the testing to others. The comparison is not meant to indicate a parity of intellectual accomplishment, but simply a parallelism of method—and in both instances the method is *pre-scientific*. In a similar sense, as Simpson (1963) emphasizes, we find another of the great formative ideas of the modern world in the doctrine of evolution—but Darwin's method was never an experimental one. It depended instead on the collection of observational data with a long period of "mulling," ruminating, or "stewing," out of which the generative hypothesis emerges for subsequent testing in the specifically scientific tradition.

[6] It is notable that both Freud and Einstein were Jews with a similar history of emancipation from the specifically religious belief of the larger group, but with (especially in the case of Freud, as demonstrated in the preface he wrote to the Hebrew edition of *Moses and Monotheism*) the maintenance of a strong sense of belonging to the group. In his "autobiographical notes," which are entirely concerned with his intellectual development, Einstein notes that the preoccupation with relativity began in his adolescence, following a period of intense religiosity which ended at the age of twelve when he was convinced that the "stories in the Bible could not be true." (Schilpp, 1949.) Wertheimer (1945) quotes Einstein as saying of the derivation of the ideas of relativity, "These thoughts did not come in any verbal formulation. *I very rarely think in words at all.* A thought comes, and I *may try to express it in words afterward*" (p. 228). He notes further, "During all those years there was a *feeling* of direction, of going straight toward something concrete" (p. 228). These excerpts refer to a process which we tend to call "making the unconscious conscious" and "working through" to insight.

Western Dialectics and the Body-Mind Problem

Unless we develop an interest in our cultural background, we are prone to get the idea that the current problems with which we are concerned are novel in our own times. When we look back into history, however, we find with the Preacher that there is nothing new under the sun. Of particular interest in this matter is the "psychosomatic" problem which we may regard as recently invented. The roots to the problem are to be found in the distinction between the "concrete" and the "abstract" in thinking, and in the ways in which this problem manifests itself with reference to the early movements in Christianity.

When "psychic" is taken to mean *spiritual*, and "somatic" to mean *fleshly*, then we find in the gospel according to John the remarkable statement of a translation: "The Word was made flesh, and dwelt among us" (John 1, 14). In this statement, the crucial mystery of the Christian church, and through it the central problem of the Western world, is made clear. In the doctrine of the Eucharist, the Catholic church officially declares that the symbolic bread and wine of the mass is actually transmuted (transubstantiated) into the flesh and blood of the crucified Christ. When we mull over the implications of this statement, we find the concretistic renderings of the idea of incorporation in psychoanalytic theory to be in the same tradition.

The idea of faith-healing depends on this basic premise, namely, that there can be an instantaneous movement from one to another state of being. The ultimate of disease is death, and Saint Paul promises the faithful, in the same tradition, "Behold, I show you a mystery; we shall not all sleep [i.e., die], but we shall all be changed. In a moment, in the twinkling of an eye, at the last trump; for the trumpet shall sound, and the dead shall be raised incorruptible, and we shall be changed" (I Corinthians 15, 51–52). This promise is that the flesh shall be made spirit, the concrete shall be translated into the abstract, into an enduring pattern freed of the human limitations of decay and dissolution—precisely the same goal as that included in the scientific goal of *invariance.*

It is noteworthy here that the sacred and the profane participate equally in the symbolic process. The punch-line of a joke is often the statement of a reversal, a "switch"—as for instance in the most banal of jokes, "That was no lady, that was my wife." In the sacred setting, Paul makes precisely the same internal contradiction in saying, "For this corruptible must put on incorruption, and this mortal must put on immortality" (I Corinthians 15, 53).

When we look at these mystical statements not from the point of view of proof, but from the point of view of communicational process, we find that these mysteries are not in fact very mysterious; they depend entirely upon the nature of the symbol. A symbol defines a category, not an object—"man" or "business" or "ocean" or any other noun refers to a group, a set. It is the nature of the category that it should have dimensional limits of positive and negative extent: man is limited by the notion of "subhuman" and "suprahuman," and within the universe of man there are evaluative limits of good-bad, black-white, fat-thin. The meaning of the symbol can be *instantaneously* reversed by adding a − or a + sign or by using terms such as "hypo-" or "hyper-." The mysteries of Christian theology are mostly then explained by the confusion between the empirical and the abstract; the value of the belief in Christ is that immediate translatability is promised as a consequence of belief. To a considerable extent, this basic faith underlies all manifestations of the promise of an instantaneous change from disease to health (or from perdition to salvation) in any form of faith-healing or conversion.

The degree to which this confusion penetrates every part of the Western world at least is demonstrated in the two alternative, contradictory definitions of the term "real" to be found in the dictionary (Oxford, 1933). The two are (1) that which has an "absolute and necessary, in contrast to a merely contingent, existence" and (2) that which can be "vividly brought before the mind"—the two definitions describe as real the contradictory meanings of that which is (1) solid and concrete and (2) that which is vividly perceived. In the second definition, we have to agree that the hallucination is "real."

Progression in History

A major problem in discussing any progression in historical sequence is that the statement of developmental occurrence is often taken as meaning, as in the term "immature," something of a depreciating sort. If we say that the insight of any great leader or thinker is partial, it is not a statement of comparative or competitive implication. It is rather to be expected that any statement made by any person at any time will have to be revised, supplanted, changed to fit new conceptions, new facts, new schemata. The most important of civilizations in the ancient world, that of the Greeks, has been characterized by Piaget as at the stage of conceptualization now exemplified by the ten-year-old child; calculus, the great invention of Newton, is currently taught to the high-school student. The fact appears to be that human knowledge proceeds by a plateaulike succession, with each new point of vantage giving an entirely different perspective on the whole. The difficulty is that as Wittgenstein (1953) notes, one tends to climb on others' conceptions until one understands them—then to "throw away the ladder" and to see the contemporary stage not as one of a series, but as the truth.

When the scientist arrives at the formulation of a powerful system in which to demonstrate truth, he tends to assume that this system has no prehistory nor any subsequent history. We find repeatedly comments that science has gone about as far as it can, and that human thinking has reached an apogee from which there are no likely forward movements. All such notions are clearly contradicted by many developments in modern methods of communication. The fact appears to be that we tend to develop as far as we can in one system of communication, and that when the limitations of any such system have been pretty well established, there tends to be a revolutionary occurrence in which another system replaces the now obsolete one. A case in point is the modern use of non-Euclidean geometry. The invention of non-Euclidean systems appears to have occurred as an intellectual game, using a set of assumptions different from those chosen by Euclid. To the general surprise of many persons, when Einstein developed the notion of relativity, it appeared that some of the non-Euclidean geometries were precisely adapted to the physical notions expressed by him. The theoretical instrument shapes a thought, and a thought shapes a new theoretical instrument.

For these reasons, it is important to see that Freud's genius established new areas for intensive investigation; but at the same time we must expect that further investigation will show that he was in some sense wrong about everything that he believed. Like Moses in the desert, the discoverer and leader often sees the Promised Land from afar, forbidden to enter—while his followers, leaving him, enter without knowing that they are in his debt. For this reason it is important both to acknowledge the significance of Freud's contributions and to demonstrate that they are repeatedly in error. Of special interest is the relation between "conscious" and "preconscious" thinking, as the idea developed by Freud can be seen altered and further illuminated by an idea of the Russian linguist, Vygotsky.

Conscious and Preconscious in Development

Freud's distinction between "conscious" and "preconscious" on a "topographical" basis is often obscure. One reason which appears helpful, at least to the author, is that the spatial metaphor is entirely inappropriate. The distinction is not between regions or zones in a topographical context, but between different levels of developmental functioning. Conscious thinking, as noted previously, is characterized by the adjectives linear, rational, measurable, discursive, logical. The use of conscious thinking is closely associated with possibilities of proof; the movement is from step to step in a consciously developed argument which has as a principal objective in the strictest sense the demonstration of an identity on both sides of an equation.

Children's thinking is of a different sort. Vygotsky uses the term "chain-complex" or "complex" to describe the manner in which the child at one stage of linguistic development may be seen to skip from one idea to another on the basis of a common element in two situations. The basis of the movement is simply that the shape of pattern occurring in the one context is that also occurring in the other. We can put this in modern language by saying that the child moves from set to set on the basis of successive intersections of the previous with the current set. A beautiful example of thinking in complexes may be found in the account of the mad tea party in *Alice in Wonderland* in which changes are rung on the different senses of the word, "well" (in the well, well in). Training in logical thinking pays intensive attention to helping the child distrust this kind of chaining and subject his thought to logical dichotomization.

Preconscious thinking, ruminating in dreaming or daydreaming, uses the complex. Metaphor is specifically a technique in which the pattern separated from its original context is placed in a set with another pattern. It is apparent that the vast majority of all such relationships occur in an irrational manner; the assumed similarity is insusceptible to proof. The other side of the picture is given by the fact that it is from this kind of free-association that the novel demonstrations of identity of pattern eventually emerge—for the subsequent scientific possibilities of verification and falsification. Vygotsky's "complex" is the origin of the creative insight of the poet, the artist, and the scientific innovator. Perhaps the most important insight of Freud in the development of the techniques of psychoanalysis is that of combining the free-association of the patient with the "freely-floating attention" of the therapist in such a way that the two creative processes mutually reinforced each other. It is, on the other hand, unfortunate that the powerful intimacy involved in this relationship tends to make the result difficult to examine logically—in the usual case, the development of an emotionally ratified consensus makes the analyst and the patient regard each other with undue enthusiasm.

To illustrate something of the technique of thinking in chain complexes and the selective reinforcement practiced by at least one psychotherapist, it may be of value to cite an actually observed sequence with a highly "suitable" patient.

A medical student in the psychotherapeutic situation began a chain of free association by noticing moving leaves on a tree visible through a window. Their movement made him think of delicate skillful actions, like those of the surgeon or pianist; he remembered admiring the activity of the professor of surgery, and he commented that he wished to become a surgeon. He then returned to the idea of the pianist, remembering that he had wanted to learn the piano but that his teacher had been unable to induce him to work hard enough at practice for him to learn. He regretted having quit. The therapist, listening to this chain of ideas, inferred that the patient was referring to the present situation and that he was in a sense warning the therapist that he might abandon psychotherapy before practicing enough to gain adequate skill. The train of association then can be seen (if the therapist is right in the interpretative metamorphosis) as a warning and as a plea—the patient hopes that the skill of the therapist is adequate to the task of keeping the patient at his own task long enough to learn. The therapist's interpretation is a function of his own prediction that this patient is among those who tend to interrupt treatment, and his interpretation is in part a technical move to prevent the interruption which the patient implicitly predicts by his reference back to the piano teacher.

As common elements in the above chain, the *delicate movements* tie together leaves, surgeon, and pianist; the notion of *skill* joins the professor of surgery and the expert pianist; the idea of *learning* relates piano teacher, surgeon, and psychoanalyst. It is obvious that this kind of stream of consciousness is entirely different from the strictly logical progression in a mathematical or scientific argument—but at the same time, it is observable that it is through this kind of processing that the expert logician *begins* to approach his precise sequential data-processing. The difference between the two methods is the crucial difference between "conscious" and "preconscious" ways of approaching a problem; free association is a method of using the associational train to derive patterns of novel significance and to operate in feedback loops to change the patient's ways of thinking by introducing these patterns into the system by interpretation.

The thinking in complexes encouraged by the psychoanalytic situation has its greatest potentiality in the enhancement of creative experimentation with the shapes of one's own experience. Its reciprocal liability, however (one also exploited by many other communicational training procedures in the modern world), is that the procedure, with its attendant feelings of anxiety and alienation, fosters the structuring of experience along the guide lines presented by the nearest dependable structure. The procedure loosens habitual techniques and the loosened potentialities tend to restabilize themselves by alignment with the power apparent in the situation. This means that the patient often becomes a therapist, whereas the trainee in "thought-control" often becomes a commissar; it also means, in a reinterpretation of "suitability," that the most welcome restructuring is that which resembles what is already present. The "ideal" patient is therefore usually a middle-class person whose orientation is similar to that of the psychoanalyst.

Psychotherapy in the Twentieth Century

The conclusion with which it becomes possible to terminate this brief discussion of some of the central concerns of our time is that psychotherapy (and its more rigidly defined parent, psychoanalysis) offers a route to the understanding of communicational process available in no other undertaking. The processes observable are specifically developmental; they are not concerned with *matters of fact*, but with *relations of ideas* (Hume, 1748). The procedure is only misleadingly mixed up with notions of therapy and cure; it is primarily and dominantly concerned with training techniques of thinking.

The central "mystery" of psychotherapy is identical with the central mystery of religion or of any other learned and incorporated world-view. This mystery is always a communicational mystery, involving the necessarily interpretative step through which the human being develops his own universe in easy or uneasy relation with those of his fellows. It can easily be seen that the definition of "real" as "that which can be vividly brought before the mind" is in fact the operational definition. When societies believe in ghosts and devils, these devils and ghosts are often "realized"; they may form the basis of judicial conviction and legal execution. If the individual, dissociated from the possibility of participating in the general consensual ratifications of his group, makes consistently an interpretation of his universe which differs from that of the consensus, we say that he is "sick" and we try to persuade or coerce him into agreement with the majority as a method of "cure." But the indications appear convincing that the situation is not one of illness, but rather one of deviance. We are appalled by an interpretation which is radically novel and we tend to assign to it a term such as "unreal," "aberrant," "bizarre," "misguided." The greatest potentiality of the psychotherapeutic approach would seem in this context to be that the therapist, taking his line of approach from developmental considerations, does not conclude that the novel interpretation is necessarily wrong. Instead, he seeks to understand it in the context of its developmental history.

In these ways we see a conception of a universe progressing in dialectical process through the posing and resolving of contradiction. The underlying structure of the process can be more easily seen when we understand that any linear statement has to be in error, but at the same time it has to be made in linear form because that is the only way in which the human methods of data-processing can break down the great universal wholes into fragments which can be grasped and assimilated.

In the cycling paradoxes of human sequence, we find that new developments tend to contradict all that we think we know, but that as the new development comes to find its place in the larger view it comes to appear not as an abrupt contradiction of former views but as a logically necessary development from those views. Wisdom (as differentiated from proof) takes a long view and sees the cyclical pattern as one which inevitably characterizes the human condition. It was known to the preacher-poet and seer that there is a time to reap and a time to sow, a time to live and a time to die, and that the human destiny is to deal with the recurring relation of the new and the old. The most immediately current preoccupations with data-processing leads to essentially the same interpretation. In modern language we can say that the new induces anxiety[7] until it is known; then the novelty is destroyed and we become again aware that there is no new thing under the sun.

When Freud, using with brilliance the insights available to him in the nineteenth-century terminology, came to the conclusion that the function of the "mental apparatus" is that of abolishing stimulation and reducing the input of "energy," he was previsioning a modern interpretation which while in one sense entirely contradictory, still in translation comes to be nearly identical to the pattern implied in his comment. The more modern rendering is that any data-processing system has the function of reducing *novelty* (or, as Kuhn puts it, making the anomalous regular). Since information is inversely proportional to probability, the reduction of novelty increases the amount of stored knowledge and reduces the amount of current input information which the human being has to deal with. The transfer of symbolic information to the inner world is a function of human modes of communication; the difficulty is that any such internalized information derived from the experience of another (i.e., a preceptor) has to be, in the new context, in error to some extent. Didactic practices therefore have the dual effect of (1) reducing informational input as the transferred knowledge is found to be correct and (2) increasing informational input as the transferred knowledge is found to be incorrect. We are left with the ancient necessity of dealing with successive approximations, each in error but perhaps each a bit more nearly accurate than its predecessors. There seems to be no reason to suspect that psychoanalytic theory is exempt from this process.

Note: This work was done with the help of a fellowship from the Commonwealth Fund. Its content and form owe much to a series of discussions held at intervals over several years with the other members of the Committee on Therapy of the Group for the Advancement of Psychiatry. Although these discussions rarely eventuated in consensus, they were of great benefit to the author in clarifying his own opinions in this complex area.

[7] Trotter comments (1941) that "the mind delights in a static environment. . . . Change from without . . . seems in its very essence to be repulsive and an object of fear . . . a little self-examination tells us pretty easily how deeply rooted in the mind is the fear of the new."

References

Barber, B. "Resistance by Scientists to Scientific Discovery." *Science,* 134 (1961), 596–602.
Bentley, A. F. "Kennetic Inquiry." *Science,* 112 (1950), 775–783.
Bergin, T. G., and Fisch, M. H. *The New Science of Giambattista Vico.* New York: Doubleday, 1961.
Bohr, N. "On the Notions of Causality and Complementarity." *Science,* 111 (1950), 51–54.
Burtt, E. A. *Metaphysical Foundations of Modern Science.* rev. ed.; New York: Doubleday, 1954.
Cassirer, E. *Language and Myth.* New York: Harper, 1946.
Conant, J. B. *Modern Science and Modern Man.* New York: Columbia University Press, 1952.
Dewey, J., and Bentley, A. F. *Knowing and the Known.* Boston: Beacon, 1960.
Einstein, A., and Infeld, L. *The Evolution of Physics.* New York: Simon & Schuster, 1938.
Feinstein, A. R. "Boolean Algebra and Clinical Taxonomy." *New England Journal of Medicine,* 269 (1963), 929–938.
Freud, S. "The Unconscious" (1915). *The Standard Edition of the Complete Psychological Works of. . . .* London: Hogarth Press. Vol. 14. (Also in *Collected Papers of. . . .* New York: Basic Books, 1959. Vol. 4, pp. 98–136.)
Freud, S. "Lines of Advance in Psychoanalytic Therapy" (1919). *The Standard Edition of the Complete Psychological Works of. . . .* London: Hogarth Press. Vol. 17, pp. 159–168. (Also in *Collected Papers of. . . .* New York: Basic Books, 1959. Vol. 2, pp. 392–402.)
Freud, S. "Inhibitions, Symptoms, and Anxiety" (1926). *The Standard Edition of the Complete Psychological Works of. . . .* London: Hogarth Press. Vol. 20.
Freud, S. "The Future of an Illusion" (1927). *The Standard Edition of the Complete Psychological Works of. . . .* London: Hogarth Press. Vol. 21.
Glover, E. "Research Methods in Psychoanalysis." *International Journal of Psycho-Analysis,* 33 (1952), 403–409.
Granit, R. *Receptors and Sensory Perception.* New Haven: Yale University Press, 1955.
Grünbaum, A. "The Bearing of Philosophy on the History of Science." *Science,* 143 (1964), 1406–1412.
Horkheimer, M. quoted in article by Philip Shabecoff, *New York Times,* February 22, 1965, Sec. 2, p. 1.
Hume, D. "Enquiry Concerning Human Understanding" (1748). In E. A. Burtt (ed.), *English Philosophy from Bacon to Mill.* New York: Modern Library, 1939.

Inhelder, Bärbel, and Piaget, J. *The Growth of Logical Thinking*. New York: Basic Books, 1958.

Kiev, A. "The Study of Folk Psychiatry." *International Journal of Psychiatry*, 1 (1965), 524–548.

Koestler, A. *The Sleepwalkers*. London: Hutchinson, 1959.

Langer, S. K. *Philosophy in a New Key*. Cambridge, Mass.: Harvard University Press, 1942.

Locke, J. "Essay Concerning Human Understanding" (1690). In E. A. Burtt (ed.), *English Philosophy from Bacon to Mill*. New York: Modern Library, 1939.

Nehru, J. Quoted in Smithsonian Institute Exhibition, Museum of History and Technology, on J. Nehru, "His Life and His India." October–December, 1964.

Oxford English Dictionary (1933). London: Oxford, 1961.

Piaget, J. *The Psychology of Intelligence*. New York: Harcourt, Brace, 1950.

Piaget, J. *Logic and Psychology*. New York: Basic Books, 1957.

Planck, M. *The Universe in the Light of Modern Physics* (1931). 2nd ed.; London: Allen & Unwin, 1937.

Planck, M. *Scientific Autobiography and Other Papers*. New York: Philosophical Library, 1949.

Platt, J. R. "Strong Inference." *Science*, 146 (1964), 347–353.

Reichenbach, H. "The Philosophical Significance of the Theory of Relativity." In P. A. Schilpp (ed.), *Albert Einstein, Philosopher-Scientist*. New York: Harper, 1949. Pp. 287–312.

Roe, Anne. "Changes in Scientific Activities with Age." *Science*, 150 (1965), 313–318.

Rothstein, J. *Communication, Organization, and Science*. Indian Hills, Colo.: Falcon's Wing Press, 1958.

Sachs, H. Personal communication.

Sapir, E. *Culture, Language and Personality: Selected Essays of. . . .* Berkeley: University of California Press, 1957.

Schilpp, P. A. (ed.). *Albert Einstein, Philosopher-Scientist*. New York: Harper, 1949.

Selfridge, O. F., and Neisser, U. "Pattern Recognition by Machine." *Scientific American*, 203 (1960), 60.

Shands, H. C. *Thinking and Psychotherapy*. Cambridge, Mass.: Harvard University Press, 1960.

Shands, H. C., and Finesinger, J. E. "A Note on the Significance of Fatigue." *Psychosomatic Medicine*, 14 (1952), 309–314.

Simpson, G. G. "Biology and the Nature of Science." *Science*, 139 (1963), 81–88.

Storch, A. *The Primitive Archaic Forms of Inner Experience and Thought in Schizophrenia*. New York: Nervous and Mental Diseases Publishing Company, (1948).

Sullivan, H. S. *The Interpersonal Theory of Psychiatry*. New York: Norton, 1953.

Toulmin, S., and Goodfield, June. *The Discovery of Time*. New York: Harper & Row, 1965.

Trotter, W. *Collected Papers.* London: Humphrey Milford, 1941.
van Domarus, E. "The Specific Laws of Logic in Schizophrenia." In J. S. Kasanin (ed.), *Language and Thought in Schizophrenia.* Berkeley: University of California Press, 1944.
Vygotsky, L. S. *Thought and Language* (1934). New York: John Wiley, 1962.
Weber, M. *The Protestant Ethic and the Spirit of Capitalism.* New York: Scribner, 1904.
Wechsberg, J. "Freudian Slip." *New York Times Magazine,* June 6, 1965.
Wertheimer, M. *Productive Thinking* (1945). New York: Harper & Row, 2nd ed., 1959.
Wiener, N. *Cybernetics.* New York: John Wiley, 1948.
Wigner, E. P. "Events, Laws of Nature, and Invariance Principles." *Science,* 145 (1964), 995–998.
Wittgenstein, L. *Philosophical Investigations.* New York: Macmillan, 1953.

5

Psychoanalysis: Some Philosophical and International Concerns

HAROLD KELMAN

Psychoanalysis is theory, therapy, technique, a method of investigation, and a body of knowledge. It is people, organizations, institutions, a movement, history. It is education, training, and a profession. It is a literature, theoretical and practical, applied to and influencing a spectrum of disciplines.

A product of the Western world, psychoanalysis appeared in the late nineteenth century, and it is approaching its centenary. How is it that psychoanalysis became manifest when and where it did? What was its relation to the evolution of and revolutions in the sciences? What does the sequence from creative reason (the Greek *logos*) through ecstatic reason (the Enlightenment) to abstract reason (in the nineteenth century), to technical reason (in the twentieth century) illuminate regarding the appearance of psychoanalysis? What effects did the change in the structure of our social world, from a *Gemeinschaft* to a *Gesellschaft*, have on these progressions in reason, science, and psychoanalysis?

The transition from *Gemeinschaft* to *Gesellschaft*, begun centuries ago, was accelerated during the Renaissance and the Industrial Revolution.

> *Gemeinschaft* is a social unit which does not primarily come into being through conscious design: one finds oneself belonging to it as one belongs to one's home. . . . The purest form of *Gemeinschaft* is within the family, particularly between mother and child where unity is the first stage in development and separateness is a later phase. . . . *Gesellschaft* is a relationship contractual in its nature, deliberately established by individuals who realize that they cannot pursue their proper interests effectively in isolation and therefore band together. . . . Individuals who enter a *Gesellschaft* do so with only a fraction of their being, that is, with that part of their existence which corresponds to the specific purpose of the organization. . . . In the *Gemeinschaft* unity prevails, in spite of occasional separation; in the *Gesellschaft* separation prevails, in spite of occasional unity (Pappenheim, 1959, pp. 66–67).

In the latter phases of this transition appeared the *Wissenschaften.* The English translation "sciences" does not convey its emotional climate of rigor, vigor, scholarship, wisdom, and respect of the student for the teacher. *Wissenschaften* include the *Naturwissenschaften* and the *Geisteswissenschaften,* inadequately translated as natural sciences, and humanities or social sciences, respectively. *Geisteswissenschaften* are concerned with the mind in the broadest sense and with the spirit of man.

Freud and the Beginning of Psychoanalysis

Freud grew up in this tradition of *Wissenschaften.* Therefore psychoanalysis bears its imprint. Freud's *Weltanschauung* was of the mid-nineteenth-century European Western world—its geocentric universe replaced by a heliocentric one, its favored position in the eyes of God usurped by Darwin's evolution, and its scientific optimism sharply waning. The Enlightenment was several centuries old, and the dignity of the individual seemingly assured. The emphasis on consciousness and reason had overvaulted itself preparing the way for a corrective, Freud's concept of "the unconscious." The rational philosophies were being questioned, Descartes's bifurcation was being undercut, phenomenology and existentialism were gathering momentum. *Gemeinschaft* was being replaced by *Gesellschaft,* and the natural sciences were becoming even more dominant.

Freud was an outsider—born in Moravia, brought up in a decadent fragmenting Austro-Hungary, in an anti-Semitic Catholic Vienna which withheld professorial status, ostracized him, and still refuses him recognition and seems bent on denying his existence (Wechsberg, 1965). A male, the first born of a closely knit Jewish family and the favorite of a dominating mother (Fromm, 1959), Freud's self-confidence stems from his family environment, which gave him the courage to pioneer in the ways that brought on his exclusion and isolation during 1894–1904. Freud's confidence in himself moved him outward to France and to the world's literature through his language facility and inward to self-analysis and his creative responses. "Psycho-analysis is my creation; I was for ten years the only person who concerned himself with it" (Freud, 1914, p. 287).

Psychoanalysis is a product of world view expressed in the languages of the "sciences." It contained many paradoxes and contradictions that became evident as schisms. Psychoanalysis as an investigative tool versus psychoanalysis as therapy points up some of these issues. Freud's interest was in knowing as investigating. He was aware that therapeutic results are a secondary consequence of selfless devotion to investigating. For him the morality was in the integrity of the investigator, in the faith of the one being investigated, and in the scientific attitude guiding both, but not in the theory of the mind. About the latter he was uncompromising: It had to be in keeping with the natural science viewpoint.

But forces pushed Freud and psychoanalysis in the direction of therapy. He had to make a living, and neurotics, who could be investigated, came to doctors for help. The prestige of medicine and its organizations became essential to the movement. Other currents contributed, among which were the successes of material medicine and the inadequacy of nosological and descriptive psychiatry. A therapy for the increasing neuroses of Western man became a necessity.

Freud's stand for lay analysis could have been more powerfully motivated by his investigative bent and his attempt to keep psychoanalysis in the broader currents of the sciences than by his lack of interest in therapy and his low opinion of doctors. "The true line of division is between *scientific* analysis and its *applications* alike in medical and in non-medical fields," not "between . . . medical and applied analysis" (Freud, 1927, p. 257).

The search for a new therapy was the predominant motivation of American doctors going to Europe for analysis in the 1920's. The conflicts in the psychoanalytic movement of the late 1930's and 1940's in the United States may have been brought on partly by the sudden expansion of psychoanalysis and the influx of many European analysts, but they were significantly contributed to by differences in tradition. It was inevitable that the strongest opposition to lay analysis would come from the United States with its emphasis on the exact, the experimental, and the technological in science, with its medical traditions, and with its antiphilosophical, anti-old world and antiauthority biases.

Freud hoped to include in the training of analysts ". . . elements from the mental sciences, from psychology, the history of civilization and sociology, as well as from anatomy, biology and the study of evolution . . . anything . . . that serves as a training for the intellect and for the powers of observation" (Freud, 1927, p. 252). The current trend to move analytic training into institutes of behavioral science and under set-ups using medical and other university departments seems to provide these elements. But today psychoanalysis, medicine, welfare, and education have different meanings. As the Western world rapidly becomes one big middle class (Kelman, 1963), psychoanalysis, formerly an upper-class interest, has become a middle-class occupation. The idioms of our time revitalize the spirit of the "sciences" as practiced in a climate of *Gemeinschaft*. But psychoanalysis, following a trend paralleled in all the dedicated professions, has become too much of an applied natural science, practiced by members of a *Gesellschaft*.

Phenomenology, Existentialism, and Psychoanalysis

The emergence of phenomenology (Husserl, 1900) and existentialism (May, Angel, and Ellenberger, 1958) were fostered by the accelerated transition from a life of *Gemeinschaft* to one of *Gesellschaft*, which increased Western man's alienation. The mounting numbers of fatherless and/or motherless children, regardless of the physical presence of the parent or parents, evidence this alienation and the anachronistic inadequacy of the superego concept in the treatment of these children.

Phenomenology asserted it could restore to "the term 'scientific' its traditional broader meaning," provide a methodological basis which would "satisfy the criteria of precision and verifiability," define the limits of the natural sciences, reinstate the scientific status of the social sciences, and offer "a new dimension of human life, *Existence*," based on a "non-physicalistic conception of the world" (Tymieniecka, 1962).

The phenomenologist's approach follows the "*fundamental rule*" (Freud, 1938). "He is to tell you not only what he can say intentionally and willingly . . . but everything else besides that his self-observation presents him with. . . . If he can succeed after this injunction in putting his self-criticism out of action, he will provide us with a mass of material" (p. 174). It is reflected in Freud's attitude toward research and therapy. "One of the claims of psycho-analysis to distinction is, no doubt, that in its execution, research and treatment coincide, but still the technique required for the one begins at a certain point to diverge from that of the other. . . . The most successful cases are those in which one proceeds as it were, aimlessly, and allows oneself to be overtaken by any surprises, always meeting them with an open mind, free from any presuppositions" (Freud, 1912, p. 114). Tiebout (1958) asserted that "at various points Freud was forced to transcend . . . the anti-existentialist, mechanistic conceptual framework . . . in the direction of a phenomenalistic approach" (p. 341) and that "Freud's analysis of anxiety, narcissism, and the pleasure principle approximates the existential analysis of a finitude, anxiety, and non-being" (p. 341).

Freud took five courses (1872–1876) with Brentano and worked for him as a translator (Barclay, 1964). He also must have heard much phenomenology and existentialism during his intimate relationship (February 1907–July 1938) with Ludwig Binswanger, about which they "made little fuss" while "being loyal to each other" (Binswanger, 1957). Freud (1924) mentioned the "large extent to which psycho-analysis coincides with the philosophy of Schopenhauer" (p. 59) and he noted the value of "Nietzsche, another philosopher whose guesses and intuitions often agree in the most astonishing way with the laborious findings of psycho-analysis" (p. 60). Freud read Schopenhauer late in life, Nietzsche he "avoided" to keep his mind "unembarrassed" and because of a "constitutional incapacity . . . for philosophy proper" (p. 59).

Although descriptive phenomenology could give detailed descriptions of patients' inner states, it was recognized that more could be done with this information. Minkowski suggested the "investigation of the *structure* of states of consciousness using the methods of 'structural analysis' and of 'categorical analysis' " (Ellenberger, 1958, p. 99). Thereby the connections and interrelations of the data obtained could be recognized. Through structural analysis Minkowski and von Gebsattel concluded that the basic symptom in melancholia is that "time is no longer experienced as a propulsive energy" (Ellenberger, 1958, p. 100). In schizophrenia Minkowski felt that the "loss of vital contact with reality" was the central problem. In compulsions, von Gebsattel and Straus saw that the "patient is fighting not so much against disgusting 'things' as against a general background of disgust" (Ellenberger, 1958, p. 100). In categorical analysis, what can be gathered from an analysis of the categories of feeling, thinking, willing, and acting as well as from the categories—in the philosophic sense of this word—of time, space, cause, and substance are also used. The manner in which these categories are experienced in a spectrum of conditions and situations is described in a valuable literature.

The existential analyst's task is to make use of this phenomenological material. To understand how he functions, existential philosophy, existential psychotherapy, and Binswanger's and Boss's existential analyses must be distinguished from each other. Existentialism's concern is with man's immediate experience, variously dealt with since time immemorial. Kierkegaard's beginnings and other contributions were evolved by Heidegger into "a phenomenology of human *Dasein*." His "philosophy is based on the contrast between existence as *Vorhandensein* (characteristic of things) and as *Dasein* (for human beings). . . . Man is not a ready-made being," but becomes what he makes himself through choosing "between an *inauthentic* and an *authentic* modality of existence" (Ellenberger, 1958, p. 118).

Existential psychotherapy is an application of existential concepts to psychotherapy. Among them are the notions of *existential neurosis*, which means to be living in an inauthentic modality; encounter (*Begegnung*), which refers to a "decisive inner experience," following from the meeting of two people and happening in one or both; and *kairos*, which refers to a critical or decisive moment when a patient could be open and available to psychotherapeutic intervention that could crucially and even dramatically turn the course of his life in a constructive direction.

Binswanger's "Existential Psychoanalysis" (1963) is his "synthesis of psychoanalysis, phenomenology and existential concepts modified by original insights" (Ellenberger, 1958, p. 120). He investigates his patients' states of consciousness as well as the entire structure of their existence, defines how "one individual may live in two or more conflicting 'worlds' " (p. 121), and strives to reconstruct their development and transformation utilizing psychoanalytic methods.

Boss (1963) more rigorously follows Heidegger. In his Daseinsanalytic re-evaluation of psychoanalytic therapy and theory, he shows their "intrinsic harmony" and "the impact of Daseinsanalysis on traditional psychoanalytic techniques" (p. 230). He concludes that Daseinsanalysis is not "a new and 'hostile' school of psychotherapy . . . but that no other psychotherapeutic procedure but . . . psychoanalytic *practice* is capable of helping man to break through to and to carry out his authentic and wholesome being-wholly-himself" (p. 284). However, for this to happen "a few—though decisive—corrections . . . in the understanding of man discovered by the analysis of Dasein" (p. 284) are essential.

Phenomenology and existentialism had been intimately studied by American philosophers and theologians since the turn of the century. In the United States, Erwin Straus's classic works on phenomenological and existential psychiatry, many now available in English (Straus, 1965), have become known only since about 1950. *Existence* (May, Angel, and Ellenberger, 1958) interested American psychiatrists in phenomenology and existentialism. There followed journals, organizations, conferences, and teaching institutes concerned with the relation of phenomenology and existentialism to psychiatry. They reflect a spectrum of viewpoints, from an insistence that there is no existential psychotherapy but psychotherapy with new dimensions, to an implication that it is unique, requiring special curricula of instruction.

Existential analysis influences the therapist's attitudes, interests, and ways of using familiar techniques. The patient's experiences and worlds are entered into with other forms of participation and objectives. New dimensions are added to the therapy, evoking feelings of genuine interest and of being understood.

There are considerable differences between existential analysis and the classical psychoanalytic model, as defined. The hallmark of investigation and experimentation is objectivity in the one and subjectivity in the other. In the classical model, each instance is to reflect or help create a generalization, in the search for essence, while in existentialism, existence precedes essence and each event is experienced as unique and original. The one seeks predictable, repeatable, controllable, and quantifiable phenomena, the other seeks what is unpredictable, uncontrollable, and that which is qualitative; in short, that which is spontaneous. The factually valued phenomena concern the one, while the other, with equal vigor, describes and utilizes all phenomena in terms of their factual, moral, aesthetic, and spiritual valuations. Public verifiability of aspects of external reality through concepts characterizes the one, validation through consensual experiential referents characterizes the other. The literature of one is written in a literal prose style; the other in a poetic one replete with the figurative and the metaphorical, including the paradoxical.

In existentialism a new concept of disease emerges "as a restricted way of life . . . a greater rigidity" in a human being's "potential designs of existence" (Riese, 1961, p. 483). Etiology (Kelman, 1966) is not an isolable cause or causes but due to bad faith, as Sartre puts it. Diagnosis holds a less significant place, although the new category of existential neurosis emerged. Prognosis depends on the patient's ontogenetic guilt, his capacity for containing suffering, his ability to assume the fullest possible responsibility for his life, to make free decisions, and to experience all these in his encounter with his physician, healer, priest, friend, or nature.

Crisis means *kairos* of which there may be many, small and large, before, during and after the therapy (Kelman, 1960). Therapy involves the patient's changed attitudes toward suffering, guilt and responsibility in encounter (*Begegnung*) with his helper. The patient remains the sole and competent witness and must give "an unprejudiced and faithful picture of his inwardness" (Riese, 1961). He must "make the greatest contributions . . . his own free decisions" (Riese, 1961).

With all these differences, when we consider the extensive revisions of both theory and technique taking place now in psychoanalysis, the diversity in practice becomes significantly less. Much of what has been described in phenomenology and existentialism has been included in other theories and techniques under different names or has been utilized in therapy without awareness (Kelman, 1962). There is much in the American tradition in spirit and in fact which is congruent with it. Nonetheless, phenomenology and existentialism can contribute much to American psychotherapy. We are being impressed with the need for re-examining our premises and undercutting our antiphilosophic bias, and being confronted with correctives to mechanization of therapy and dehumanizing attempts to deal with human problems on a mass scale.

The future of psychoanalysis will be significantly determined by what happens in the United States. We can guide it more effectively to the extent that we know its history and see it in the wider context of the sociology of our ideas, our cosmologies, and our myths. Such breadth and depth of vision may give us essential correctives and wisdom in evolving its new idioms as theory, research, technique, training, and application. It will then be expressive of and find its place in the idioms and myths of a new unitive world view.

References

Barclay, J. R. "Franz Brentano and Sigmund Freud." *Journal of Existentialism*, 5 (1964), 1–36.

Binswanger, L. *Sigmund Freud: Reminiscences of a Friendship*. New York: Grune & Stratton, 1957.

Binswanger, L. *Being-in-the-World: Selected Papers of*. . . . New York: Basic Books, 1963.

Boss, M. *Psychoanalysis and Daseinsanalysis*. New York: Basic Books, 1963.

Ellenberger, H. F. "A Clinical Introduction to Psychiatric Phenomenology and Existential Analysis." In R. May, E. Angel, and H. F. Ellenberger (eds.), *Existence*. New York: Basic Books, 1958. Pp. 92–124.

Freud, S. "Recommendations for Physicians on the Psycho-Analytic Method of Treatment" (1912). *The Standard Edition of the Complete Psychological Works of*. . . . London: Hogarth Press. Vol. 12, pp. 109–120. (Also in *Collected Papers of*. . . . New York: Basic Books, 1959. Vol. 2, pp. 323–333.

Freud, S. "The History of the Psycho-Analytic Movement" (1914). *The Standard Edition of the Complete Psychological Works of*. . . . London: Hogarth Press. Vol. 14, pp. 3–66. (Also in *Collected Papers of*. . . . New York: Basic Books, 1959. Vol. 1, pp. 287–359.)

Freud, S. "An Autobiographical Study" (1924). *The Standard Edition of the Complete Psychological Works of*. . . . London: Hogarth Press. Vol. 20, pp. 3–71.

Freud, S. "Postscript to a Discussion on Lay Analysis" (1927). *The Standard Edition of the Complete Psychological Works of*. . . . London: Hogarth Press. Vol. 20, pp. 179–251. (Also in *Collected Papers of*. . . . New York: Basic Books, 1959. Vol. 5, pp. 205–214.)

Freud, S. "An Outline of Psychoanalysis" (1938). London: Hogarth Press. Vol. 23, pp. 141–205.

Fromm, E. *Sigmund Freud's Mission*. New York: Harper, 1959.

Husserl, E. *Ideas: General Introduction to Pure Phenomenology* (1900). New York: Macmillan, 1952.

Kelman, H. " 'Kairos' and the Therapeutic Process." *Journal of Existential Psychiatry* (1960), 233–239.

Kelman, H. "Perspectives on Psychoanalysis." *Journal of Existential Psychiatry*, 3, No. 9 (1962), 1–26.

Kelman, H. "Training Analysis: Past, Present and Future." *American Journal of Psychoanalysis,* 23 (1963), 205–216.

Kelman, H. "Psychoanalysis and the Study of Etiology: A Definition of Terms." In J. H. Merin (ed.), *The Etiology of Neurosis.* Palo Alto, Calif.: Science & Behavior Books, 1966.

May, R., Angel, E., and Ellenberger, H. F. *Existence.* New York: Basic Books, 1958.

Pappenheim, F. *The Alienation of Modern Man.* New York: Monthly Review Press, 1959.

Riese, W. "Phenomenology and Existentialism in Psychiatry: An Historical Analysis." *Journal of Nervous and Mental Diseases,* 132 (1961), 469–484.

Straus, E. W. *Phenomenological Psychology: Selected Papers of. . . .* New York: Basic Books, 1966.

Tiebout, H. M., Jr. "Freud and Existentialism." *Journal of Nervous and Mental Diseases,* 126 (1958), 341–352.

Tymieniecka, A. T. *Phenomenology and Science in Contemporary European Thought.* New York: Noonday Press, 1962.

Wechsberg, J. "Freudian Slip." *The New York Times Magazine,* June 6, 1965.

6

Sexuality in Psychoanalytic Theory

LEON SALZMAN

For a long time to come, Freud and psychoanalysis will be intimately associated in the minds of most people with sex, as they have been for the past fifty years. This is to be expected, for Freud truly produced a revolution in sexual education, behavior, and mores. At the very least, his work permitted the world of science to become interested in this aspect of human behavior beyond the mere anatomy and physiology of the sexual apparatus. The role of sex in human functioning became a major and, at times, a dominating interest for the psychologist.

Albeit revolutionary for their time, Freud's views were limited, however, by the lack of knowledge concerning sexual function in his day. As such knowledge has increased through biological, physiological, anthropological, sociological, and psychoanalytic studies, it has become apparent that many of Freud's early ideas are not consistent with the data derived from these disciplines.

Historical Perspectives

Prior to the Christian ethic, which viewed the body as sinful, as opposed to the soul, which was holy, sex behavior for both sexes was largely uninhibited, lusty, and thoroughly enjoyed, even if it was not talked about (Taylor, 1954; Cole, 1953). Christian morality, symbolized by the Victorian era in the West, relegated sex to the privacy of the bedroom, unavailable to the scrutiny of the scientist or physician. As the tide of liberation for the female as well as the male progressed, the swell of progress in the medical sciences in the 1900's made it inevitable that sex and sexual practices would become the subject of scientific study. There was widespread interest in the pathology of sexual practices as described in the encyclopedic researches of Krafft-Ebing (1922) and M. Hirschfield (1944).

It was not until the work of Freud, however, that human sex behavior became a focal concern of psychologists, physicians, and scientists in related disciplines. Psychoanalytic investigations took their initial impetus from the libido theory which presumed that the sexual instinct was the major directing force in human development. These investigations, however, tended to focus on sex primarily as an instinct. Sex was studied in terms of the aim or object of the drive rather than as an activity between two people in which a multitude of reactions, responses, and interactions occur (Freud, 1932). Since sex activity in man *generally* takes place in an atmosphere of tenderness and mutual regard, it resembles animal activity only to the extent that it is an act of procreation. Therefore, its biological significance in man is only a small part of its total importance. In recent years there has been a much greater emphasis on the interpersonal aspects of sex behavior, a development which takes into account the extraordinary capacity of sex to fulfill many of man's needs aside from the biological function of procreation (Alexander, 1948; Angyal, 1965; Erikson, 1950; Hoch and Zubin, 1949; Kardiner, Karush, and Ovesey, 1959). Sexual disorders, as well as other mental disorders, are thus seen as complications of personality development as a whole rather than of sexual development in particular (Boss, 1949).

The efforts to study behavior in the framework of instinct, or learning, or the concepts of maturation, or experience have not been illuminating, since they tend to become either–or dichotomies rather than a recognition of the essential role of both elements. Research in primates in general as well as in man specifically clearly indicates that the physiological mechanisms involved in coitus are functional before the individual is capable of reproduction. In addition, social experience clearly influences the capacity to perform the sex act.

The work of Yerkes (1943), Nissen (1954), Harlow (1959), and

Young, Guy, and Phoenix (1965) clearly suggest that the patterns of sexual behavior and performance depend rather heavily on learned experience through contact with parents, siblings, and other members of society. They indicate the intricate and necessary effects of social interaction for adequate sexual patterning in rhesus monkeys, guinea pigs, rats, cats, and chimpanzees. Beach (1965, p. 549) summarizes these studies:

It thus appears that normal developments of effecting mating patterns in some primates rests upon much more than simple physiological maturation and may prove dependent upon the formation of tendencies or capacities for a general social responsiveness out of which more specific types of interindividual reaction patterns can later emerge.

The tendency to move from an instinctual framework to a more culturally oriented perspective in personality theory has been reflected in a number of alternative theories regarding infantile sexuality, homosexuality, female sexuality, and sexual deviations. These approaches take into account the scientific developments in psychology, anthropology, sociology, and ethology over the past fifty years. Instinct theory is largely outmoded as a biological model for the comprehension of personality development, and the view of sex as an instinct limits the understanding of its role in human behavior (Kardiner *et al.*, 1959; Harlow, 1958, 1959; Green, 1964, Yerkes, 1943; Bieber, 1958; Mead, 1952; Money, 1960–1961; Ovesey, 1955, 1961; Bieber *et al.*, 1962; Marmor, 1942, 1965; Young, 1961; Hampson and Hampson, 1961).

It is obvious that man's sexual activity far exceeds his procreative needs. An effort has been made to account for this surplus interest by the assumption that its performance was made enjoyable *in order* to perpetuate its usage (Alexander, 1948; Kinsey, Pomeroy, and Martin, 1948; Kinsey, Pomeroy, Martin, and Gebhard, 1953), as if, to encourage man to reproduce his species, sex *had* to be made a source of pleasure. This is a teleological notion. Adaptive behavior does not require a reward to encourage its performance, since it is beyond the choice of the animal and therefore is obligatory and compulsive. Actually, unlike man's other biological needs, sex does involve choice, and *can* be abandoned. The performance of other biological functions such as eating, breathing, and defecating can also be a source of pleasure, but man has no choice in regard to them. The impetus for sex activity under ordinary circumstances rarely arises out of species preservation needs, but comes from its enormous potentialities for satisfaction of various kinds (Salzman, 1962).

Although good personal relationships may not be necessary for sexual intercourse, the establishment of warm, collaborative, mutually satisfying relations encourages repeated and more satisfactory sexual contacts. On the other hand, sex activity may be the background for exerting power and control over others even when there may be no particular interest in sex itself. The drama of human relationships and its limitless variations can be highlighted in the forced intimacy of sexual embrace. Thus, sexual activity and the attitudes and behavior which accompany it can reveal the covert feelings, fantasies, and tensions of the partners. Its function is special because of the interpersonal context in which it is carried out.

Infantile Sexuality

Freud's exposition of sexual interest and activity in children prior to the maturation of the sexual gonads came as a shocking revelation to the scientific as well as nonscientific world. Instead of the assumed purity and innocence of childhood, Freud's theories suggested that children carried on a polymorphous, perverse sexual life with, in addition, a strong sexual interest in the parent of the opposite sex. Although these notions stimulated much unwarranted criticism of Freud's theories, some of the objections represented valid doubts about his *sexual* interpretation of the *genital* activity of the infant and child.

Freud's notions about infantile sexuality were an outgrowth of his work with adults. Since it is almost impossible to get direct data from adults regarding experiences prior to age four and similarly difficult to get statements of the meaning of the four-year-old's behavior, the information is all extrapolated from later years with data derived from free association or dream analysis (Salzman, 1966). Some of the interpretations made in child analysis of three- or four-year-old behavior are heavily influenced by the preconceptions of the observer and confirm the sexual nature of the Oedipal attachment if one believes it to be present in the first place (Klein, 1948, 1949). Evidence from direct observational studies, however, is scanty and does not always confirm Freud's views (Gesell and Ilg, 1943; Gesell, 1955; Piaget, 1932, 1954; Piaget and Inhelder, 1942; Kagan and Moss, 1962; Ilg and Ames, 1955; Bailey and Shaffer, 1963, 1964). An intensive observational approach, as well as more longitudinal studies aimed at observing and describing so-called sexual items of behavior in children, is badly needed. Caution should be observed, however, in crediting interpretations of infantile behavior derived from information based on a pre-existing theory of the ubiquity of sexual behavior in the early years. Recent research by D. E. Berlyne (1966) and others suggests that much activity of higher animals, and probably man, is concerned with obtaining stimuli with no manifest goal except to maintain levels of sensory input and that traditional explanations of such behavior in terms of biological drives such as sex and survival are probably irrelevant. Much of such "exploratory" behavior involves seeking out, novelty, change, complexity, and variety and has no specific adaptive motivation, either sexual, aggressive, or defensive. These studies have direct relevance to certain pre-verbal patterns of behavior in humans that traditionally have been interpreted as sexual in nature.

In order to appraise the significance of behavior prior to a capacity to verbalize, it is necessary to examine the behavior free from preconception. The activity of the infant who passes his hand over his entire anatomy and particularly his mouth may simply be exploratory. Similarly, the handling of the genitals along with the earlobes, blanket, and so forth *may* have no special significance aside from the infant's need to explore his environment and his own body, receiving sensory input from his skin as well as from his lips, ears, penis, or genital area. At this time, and for a long time to come, the genital area is almost exclusively identified with urination. A great deal of the child's play, whether with the same or opposite sex, often involves mutual exploration or manipulation. Some games resemble adult sexual play and are often interpreted as such by the adults. However, the participants must be aware at some level of their understanding that such play is sexual in the adult sense for the observer to assume that it is something other than the playful exploratory behavior which may involve any organ or part of the body. Because of an abundance of special nerve endings, the glans of the penis may become a favorite organ for manipulation. A focus on the penis or the female genital area by anxious, prudish, or puritanical parents can give these areas undue significance and cause associations with shame, loathing, or disgust even prior to gonadal maturation (Sullivan, 1953, 1956).

The absence of the penis in the girl is regularly noted by both sexes, but it is only through questioning that the girl comes to learn about her genitalia. Although the little girl discovers her clitoris early in life, it is extremely doubtful that vaginal sensations occur prior to puberty (Sherfey, 1966). Consequently, it is inevitable that the little girl's attitude and experience with her genitals are closely tied to the prevailing knowledge, mores, and prejudices that exist in the particular culture toward the female (Thompson, 1950; Horney, 1933; Green, 1964). This suggests a strong cultural rather than an innately biological attitude toward sexual differences (Harlow, 1958, 1959; Money, 1960; Young, 1961). It is important to note in this connection that Freud not only used the male as a prototype of his psychosexual theories but that he also developed these theories almost exclusively from the male point of view, later superimposing these views on the subject of female psychosexuality.

It is important, in the interests of clarity and scientific validity, to distinguish between *genital* and *sexual* behavior. The genital serves the function of urination as well as the delivery of sperm, and therefore genital activity cannot always be presumed to be synonymous with sexual activity, even though it may often be correlated. This is equally true in the woman. Genital behavior refers to *any* activity relating to the genital, while sexual behavior refers more specifically to that in which the genital is involved, directly or indirectly, for purposes leading toward orgasm.

Beach, in his summary of the conference on sex and behavior, held in Berkeley, California, commented on this issue with regard to animal behavior (Beach, 1965, p. 546):

Many of the elements involved in the coitus of adult mammals can occur independently long before puberty. As just noted mounting behavior is not uncommonly shown by very young males and penile erection is often possible at birth, but to identify these as "sexual responses" is most strongly inadvisable. Throughout the individual's life, these reactions may occur in several different contexts with different outcomes. To assign them arbitrarily and exclusively to a single functional pattern can lead only to confusion. Defining erection in a week-old puppy as "sexual behavior" simply because the adult male has an erection while copulating is no more logical than affirming that voiding of urine by the infant male is "territorial behavior" because the adult urinates upon rocks and trees in connection with the establishment of territorial boundaries.

He suggests that this applies equally to human sexual behavior.

It can be anticipated that as data derived from observational and developmental studies accumulate, most infantile behavior will be recognized to be related to nonlibidinal adaptational needs. In the early insecure and helpless years, the infant is involved in developing skills relating to survival and interpersonal security. Exploratory activities relating to his own body are preparatory to expanding his knowledge and skill in achieving mastery of himself and his environment. The special interest in the genitals may derive from their particular accessibility in the male, or because of their profusion of nerve endings and the self-sentient capacity of genital play. Such play, however, does not differ in any substantial way from the manipulation of other body zones except for the cultural and parental attitudes which develop in connection with it (Schachtel, 1959; Sullivan, 1953).

When is the genital viewed by the child as something more than a mere somatic appendage? Does this occur when the child recognizes a difference between the male and female genital? Or does it take on special significance when the parents interpret genital play as masturbation? Can we justifiably call genital play in the infant or child masturbation? Or is this the adult's view of genital play in view of the goal of genital play in the adult? What is the expectation of such manipulation in the early years in comparison to the goal of such play in later years?

The child who goes through mother's handbag is not called a thief or presumed to have the same motives as an adult doing the same thing. Similarly, the infant suckling at his mother's breast for nutritional purposes is hardly comparable to a man sucking at the breast of his beloved. To assume that the infant suckles out of libidinal needs in addition to hunger is no more valid than to presume that the adult sucks out of nutritional needs in additional to his libidinal desires. Such interpretations can arise only out of mistaken preconceptions of human behavior. Such reductionist tendencies which relate all behavior ultimately to libidinal interests have lessened the validity and value of psychoanalytic theories of personality development (Hook, 1959; Pumpian-Mindlin, 1956).

In essence, then, the concept of infantile sexuality is derived from a few observations and a large number of extrapolations from adult sexual behavior and interpretations of behavior in the early years which could be understood in a variety of other ways (Chodoff, 1966). The paucity of critical studies on infantile sexuality has been the consequence of research taking infantile sexuality as an acknowledged fact. The evidence from direct observation of children is unconvincing either because the observations have been distorted by such preconceptions or because they are merely descriptive and speculative. Efforts to confirm infantile sexuality from the analyses of adults are equally unconvincing since they introduce the fallacies of infantile amnesias and the retrograde reconstruction of early experiences. The future has yet to decide about the validity of this concept. The issue of infantile sexuality will be most clearly illuminated by developmental studies rather than theories which take as their starting point the a priori assumption that sexual (rather than genital) activity occurs before gonadal maturity.

The Role of Sex in Human Development

The motivating power of sex toward social behavior lies in its being a biological activity which, in its proper functioning, is regularly accompanied by pleasure (Sullivan, 1953). The pleasure principle, Freud believed, dominates man's behavior until it is subordinated to a reality principle as man is forced to acknowledge the communal and social requirements of his culture.

A *physiological* hierarchy of man's functioning would demand the primacy of the respiratory or cardiac function with the sexual function being near the bottom of the list. However, unlike sex activity, respiratory and cardiac functions are autonomic, and therefore their *psychological* significance is far behind that of the sex function, where choice and postponement are possible.

Aside from any determining influence on normal or abnormal development, the role of sex in human behavior is significant by virtue of the fact that it is the only activity in man that requires physical intimacy between the sexes for its complete biological function. Any consideration of the role of sex in human behavior must take this issue into account. The autonomic functions in man, such as cardiac control, breathing, digestion, endocrine functioning, and so forth, can proceed without conscious intervention and require no interpersonal exchanges. The sex function is the only biological function that *requires* another human being for its total fulfillment. Even masturbation or nocturnal emissions are usually accompanied by the fantasied presence of another person.

The capacity of sex to be postponed, delayed, or even permanently abandoned lends itself to fantasy elaboration or symbolic transformation. It can also, therefore, become an active agent in the manipulation of human relationships. Sex can be used as a bargaining agent in dealing with nonsexual issues. It can be the grounds on which battles for power, prestige, envy and jealousy, generosity or meanness are fought. It can be used to express resentments or grievances and can be a vehicle for vengeance. Since sexual satisfactions usually depend on the cooperation and willingness of the partner, sex can be used to withhold or deny satisfaction or to administer favor or largesse to another person (Salzman, 1954). Problems, conflicts, and interpersonal struggles in any area of human functioning are apt to express themselves in sexual behavior.

Indeed, the physical intimacy required by sex may be impossible in the face of serious and overpowering resentments. At such times sexual intercourse may be impossible, or its performance markedly altered, resulting in a variety of distortions from homosexuality to premature ejaculation. Small wonder then that the neurotic or psychotic, with his elaborate difficulties in the interpersonal sphere, would also present sexual complications (Boss, 1949). The crucial question for psychological theory is which comes first, the sexual difficulties or the neurotic problem. Freud postulated the primacy of the sexual complication but more recent psychoanalytic theorists lean toward the notion that the sexual complications are the consequences rather than the causes of disordered human relationships (Horney, 1939; Sullivan, 1953; Rado, 1956).

The tendency to regard all of man's ethical, artistic, philosophical, and aesthetic interests as sublimations of sex is also seen by more recent theorists as an attempt to force facts into pre-existing theory rather than a theory growing out of the facts. Man is motivated by many forces that go beyond his purely libidinal interests (Alexander, 1948; Masserman, 1951). These forces transcend his biological needs and are not necessarily related to sex or pleasure as such.

Sex Differences

Patriarchal societies supported by theological myths of creation have supported the notion of a primal male for centuries (Frazer, 1940). Freud assumed that this was a biological fact developed through an evolutionary process (Freud, 1905). He developed his basic theory of psychosexual development around the male, then applied it to the female with some modifications. He believed that all females resented having been denied the desirable male organ and that much of their psychological life was spent in efforts to overcome this deficiency or to come to terms with it. The hopeless striving to obtain a penis was finally abandoned in childbirth, when the woman could accept her child as a substitute for it. These views were supported and amplified by many female psychoanalysts such as Helene Deutsch (1944–1945), Melanie Klein (1948), and Therese Benedek (1952).

However, in an excellent anatomical, biochemical, and physiological review of the nature of female sexuality, Sherfey (1966) has pointed out that biologically the female sex and not the male is primal. It is inaccurate to speak of a bisexual phase of embryonic development. Genetic sex is established at fertilization, but all embryos are morphologically female until the effect of the sex genes is felt during the fifth or sixth week of foetal life. At that time, if the genetic sex is male, primordial germ cells stimulate the production of testicular inductor substance which stimulates foetal androgens which *suppress* the growth of the ovaries. In this way androgens induce the male growth pattern. If the genetic sex is female, germ cells stimulate the production of follicles and estrogen. However, if the gonads are artificially removed before the seventh week, a normal female anatomy will develop even in the absence of estrogens. Therefore, female differentiation is the result of the innate, genetically determined morphology of all mammalian embryos. After twelve weeks sex reversals are impossible, since the masculine nature of the reproductive tract is fully established.

Freud's theories concerning female psychosexuality have been shaken not only by such biological studies but by many others as well (Money, 1960; Ovesey, 1956; Young, 1961). Biologically, the female is not at all inferior to the male. Indeed, in many ways she is better equipped biologically to fulfill her role than is the male (Montagu, 1953). She has a more labile nervous system and a more responsive autonomic system, physiological findings which are undoubtedly related to the need to handle the regularly recurring crises of menstruation, childbirth, and the physiological trials of childrearing. In addition, the notion of a sex-linked character structure has been rudely shaken by recent investigations concerning the female sexual apparatus (Masters, 1959, 1960; Masters and Johnson, 1961, 1962). These studies indicate that the woman, far from being passive in the sex act, is an extremely active participant to the extent that vaginal contractions are more responsible for sperm reaching the ovum than the sperm's own motile powers. In almost every phase of Freud's views on the psychology of the female there have been objections, revisions, and clarifications (Horney, 1939; Sullivan, 1953; Fromm, 1941; Rado, 1956; Marmor, 1942, 1968; Masserman, 1951; Salzman and Masserman, 1962).

The attempt to link character with gender overlooks the multicausal basis for character and the crucial significance of temporal and cultural factors. Character structure is the result of a multiple set of interactions of which biology is only one factor, and cultural determinants of a social, political, economic, and philosophical nature are others. The post-Freudian ego psychologists and psychoanalysts see character structure as the result of the interaction of culture and the individual rather than as a result of cultural pressures on libidinal development (Kardiner *et al.*, 1959). This altered view of character development is particularly significant in elucidating the psychology of the female.

The complex problem of gender role in relationship to genital morphology in sex behavior has been illuminated by a large number of physiological, biochemical, and chromosomal studies in recent years (Hampson and Hampson, 1961). There are a large number of variables which enter into the total sexual pattern: (1) sex chromatin pattern; (2) gonadal sex as indicated by morphology; (3) hormonal sex which is correlated to secondary sex characteristics; (4) external genital morphology; (5) internal accessory reproductive structure; (6) sex assignment and rearing; and (7) psychological sex or gender role.

Psychological maleness or femaleness (gender role) is not attributable to any single one of the variables and does not appear to have an innate performed instinctive basis. On the contrary, at the Gender Identity Clinic in Baltimore it has been found that sex assignment and rearing usually plays the major factor in gender role. Thus, gender role in man appears to depend on learned experience as well as on somatic variables. Hampson and Hampson (Beach, 1965, p. 125) conclude: "psychologic sex or gender role appears to be learned, that is to say it is differentiated through learning during the course of many experiences of growing up. In place of a theory of innate constitutional psychologic bisexuality we can substitute a concept of psycho-sexual neutrality in humans at birth."

Thus, the attitudes, characterological traits, and behavioral characteristics of the female are not due exclusively to her biological sex, but also to the demands, expectations, and restraints which any particular culture places on her. Biological and physiological differences, nevertheless, are significant. The marked differences in the size and bulk of the voluntary muscles obviously produce some divergent attitudes regarding the male and female when a culture requires strength and endurance. Although this was a paramount need in primitive cultures, the advent of a technology capable of replacing muscular power in recent years has obviated this advantage. Nevertheless, the major differences which revolve about the roles of the male and female in the procreative and child-rearing processes may produce distinctive characterological elements in each sex (Green, 1964). In spite of recent changes in her cultural status, child-bearing and child-rearing functions still influence a significant portion of woman's personality structure.

As child-rearing practices change, either through the use of crèches, early boarding schools, or day-care centers, major changes in this aspect of woman's maternal role may occur (Cohen, 1965). However, since there is no likelihood in the foreseeable future that the actual child-bearing role of woman will be supplanted by artificial techniques, it is fair to assume that this will remain a significant factor in feminine psychology.

Ultimately the concept of the biologically weak, helpless, and submissive female will have to be abandoned, even though many women as well as men have come to accept this notion (Lundberg and Farnham, 1947). This fact requires a chapter in itself and is related to the defense mechanism of identification with the aggressor. It is analogous to the prisoner, slave, or member of a minority group who comes to accept the derogatory view of his own status in order to achieve maximum security and advantage. Even though his status changes, there is always a time lag after a long period of subjugation in the recognition of his own power and privilege (Friedan, 1963).

Orgasm in the Female

A further complication in the comprehension of feminine psychology has been produced by the assumption, wholly unsupported by biological or physiological data, that the female is capable of two distinct types of orgasm—clitoral and vaginal. There are, indeed, quantitative differences in the female's response to the sex act, but there is no reason to assume that this is due to a "vaginal" rather than a "clitoral" orgasm (Marmor, 1954). Recent research has definitively demonstrated that the nature of orgasm in the female is the same regardless of the stimulus that produces it and consists of rhythmic contractions of the extravaginal musculature against the greatly distended circumvaginal venous plexi and vestibular bulbs surrounding the lower third of the vagina.

The extensive researches of Masters and Johnson (1961, 1962, 1966) and the highly informative article by Sherfey (1966) have illuminated many hitherto clouded and confused areas of female sexual physiology. The investigations of Masters and Johnson clearly demonstrate that, physiologically, clitoral and vaginal orgasms are not separate entities. Stimulation of the clitoral glans initiates the orgasm, which then spreads to the outer third of the vagina. Orgasm is a total body response and with marked variations in intensity and timing. Physiologically it is a physical release from vasocongestive and myotonic increments developed in response to sexual stimuli.

Regardless of the anatomical position of the clitoris, the penis rarely comes into direct contact with the clitoral glans. However, it is continuously stimulated throughout coitus even though it retracts during the plateau stage of sexual excitement. The erection and engorgement of the clitoris causes it to retract into the swollen clitoral hood, but the active thrusting of the penis and the traction on the labia minora provide stimulation and energetic friction on the glans of the clitoris. After some time, the orgasmic contractions begin. The clitoral reaction is the same, regardless of what is used to stimulate the clitoris and whether it is direct or indirect. Thus the various positions described or advocated to increase penile contact with the clitoris are superfluous. However, a female superior or lateral coital position does allow for more direct contact. It is notable in this connection that such positioning has been discredited and avoided because of the notion that the female passive role requires the male to always "be on top."

Orgasm in the male and the female is identical biologically. In the male it consists essentially of the contractions of the responding muscles against the erectile chambers containing sperm and related products. In the female the contractions produce expulsion of blood from the erectile chambers. The lower one-third of the vagina is different morphologically from the remaining two-thirds and is capable of accommodating any size of penis. It is a fallacy to assume that the larger penis will be better able to stimulate the clitoris or to be more effective in coitus. However, since the female has a slower arousal time and requires continuous stimulation for orgasm to occur there is often the anxiety that the male orgasm will come too soon to permit orgasm in the female. This has a valid biological basis and is often the cause of premature ejaculation when the anxiety of the male produces tension, which results in too early ejaculation.

The female is capable of multiple orgasm, while the male requires a refractory period before further orgasms are possible. However, there is a need for continuous stimulation until orgasm, since the sexual tension in the female can fall instantaneously if such stimulation is discontinued. This capacity for multiple orgasm and readiness to respond to sexual stimulation requires regular and consistent sexual activity in the female for her to respond most adequately. Thus it is likely that the most common cause of frigidity and difficulty in achieving orgasm in the female is due to infrequent or inadequately employed sexual intercourse.

One of the unfortunate consequences of the clitoral-vaginal orgasm notion is that it tends to encourage discontent and feelings of inadequacy in the female who experiences orgasm due to clitoral stimulation before or during sexual intercourse. She assumes that her orgasm is inferior, even though it may have been pleasurable, and that she is sexually immature. She insists on having a "vaginal" orgasm and blames either herself or her husband for her failure to experience this. Since there appears to be no validation for this whole notion, there is no reason to assume that an orgasm which is achieved by means of clitoral stimulation is necessarily inferior or imperfect, or that it can be improved on with psychoanalytic therapy.

Sex activity is a process to be enjoyed and practiced in whatever manner is conducive to the greatest mutual enjoyment. Consequently the *manner* of stimulating the glans and clitoris, whether by means of the mouth, finger, or vaginal insertion should not necessarily be viewed in terms of either normality or maturity. Although there is a preferred posture to insure procreation and mutual orgasm, a more enlightened attitude toward sex should avoid assigning priorities to particular methods of achieving sexual satisfaction. Despite the fact that laws regarding sex behavior in many parts of the world still cling to categories of "normal" or "deviant," modern psychological theory tries to avoid labeling variations of sex behavior between male and female as deviant so long as they do not prove physiologically or psychologically injurious to either partner. This is particularly applicable to variations in terms of activity or passivity in the sex act. The assumption that the male must be the aggressive one in sexual intercourse, and the female the passive one, is simply not valid. Each partner must be passive *and* aggressive, and must participate mutually and cooperatively in the interaction. The unfortunate persistence of labels attributable to one sex as opposed to another has led to untold misery in the form of feeling guilty, inferior, inadequate, or even "homosexual" when one's inclinations are somewhat different from prevailing notions concerning the role of each sex. The female has been the major victim in this hangover from Victorian morality and scientific infantilism. Since, under this notion, the mantle of being passive and submissive falls on her, she has been required to wait on the desires and demands of the male and to be subject to his particular program for sexual activity. To encourage or direct the male's sexual activity was to step outside of the "female" role; to suggest or recommend measures that might enhance her enjoyment would be aggressive, or too "masculine." Consequently, she has been expected to be patient and long-suffering and to depend on the man's good will and competence for her enjoyment. When she has refused to function in these prescribed ways, some psychologic and psychoanalytic theorists have insisted on labeling her behavior as "penis envy," "masculine protest," "latent homosexuality," or "refusal to accept her proper biological role." Such labels are remnants of outmoded conceptions of female psychology.

Simultaneous orgasm is an ideal outcome of the sex act, but unfortunately it has been made a "requirement" by some psychoanalysts who imply that when one's libidinal development is brought to maturity by treatment, simultaneous orgasm should be a regularly expected outcome of the sex act. However, because of differing rates of activation of sex interest and response in many partners, simultaneous orgasm is relatively rare even in the best of relationships. To determine sexual adjustment on the basis of success in achieving simultaneous orgasm is therefore often unfair to one or both partners. This is particularly the case with the liberated or psychoanalyzed female who, out of misinformation or misguided expectation, does not appreciate the limitations and complications of this demand. The hope for simultaneous orgasm is neither a neurotic fantasy nor a romantic dream. The desire to realize it is reasonable enough. However, if failure consistently to achieve it results in anxiety, despair, and bitter recrimination, then it may become a neurotic demand supported by unrealistic expectations.

Our understanding of feminine psychology has only just begun. We have yet to evaluate the ultimate psychological effects of the marked technological changes which are reducing the need for the gross musculature of the male. These changes will undoubtedly alter the role and status of the female. As the demand for equality of opportunity, education, and employment is met, the role of the female may radically enhance her status and her view of herself beyond the boundaries of motherhood. Profound changes can be expected in her psychology as she moves out of the confines of a minority into equal status with the male economically as well as sociologically (Marmor, 1968).

Homosexuality

The causes of homosexuality prior to Freud were centered on hereditary or constitutional factors and were thought to be the result of degeneracy (Hirschfield, 1938; Krafft-Ebing, 1922). Some speculated on the presence of a homosexual center in the brain which predisposed one to homosexuality. Freud advanced the first theory of homosexuality based on developmental factors that could theoretically be treated, or prevented if the developmental situations could be altered. It was presumed that homosexuality was directly related to the problem of object choice and fixation at the "homosexual stage" of psychosexual development (Freud, 1911, 1932).

Once the libido theory is set aside, as many psychoanalytic theorists have done, and demands are made for more precise definitions, a new set of propositions about this disorder can be developed. Such a process is now going on. Views of homosexuality are now being refined from a more operational and phenomenological point of view. In addition to being a sexual disorder it is also visualized as a symptom of a larger personality disorder. Some theorists contend that it is always a symptom of some personality warp rather than a disease entity (Salzman, and Masserman 1962; Ovesey, 1955, 1961; Bieber *et al.*, 1962; Marmor, 1965). Its origins can be traced to a conflict of standards, values, or other strivings unrelated to one's sexual life. It can therefore be symbolic of other personality difficulties and not directly related to the sexual realm of experience. These later studies universally reveal a significant influence of the culture, both in an individual, family, and community sense in the genesis of the disorder (Marmor, 1965).

Nevertheless, all the theories have a common heritage in Freud's original formulations. Some stress oral factors (Bergler, 1956; Klein, 1949), while others (Kolb and Johnson, 1955) emphasize the impetus for homosexuality as deriving from parental suggestions. Some theorists (Horney, 1950; Thompson, 1950; Sullivan, 1953) emphasize the interpersonal elements and view the disorder as an attempt to integrate one's sexual needs on whatever basis and with whatever gender may be possible. This might be the result of fear of injury from the opposite sex or withdrawal from competition with the same sex (Rado, 1940; Kardiner *et al.*, 1959; Ovesey, 1955, 1956).

While the influence of heredity has been dismissed by most theorists, the notion of a universal latent homosexual trend in all humans still persists. The concept implies that homosexuality is a possibility in everyone due to an innate psychic bisexuality (Freud, 1932). While the potentiality for homosexual development exists if certain conditions are present during an individual's development, it is not an established fact that homosexual trends are universal. Latency as *dormancy*, which is implied in Freud's concept of latent homosexuality, must be distinguished from latency as *potentiality*, which is a developmental conception and implicit in all personality theory (Salzman, 1957, 1965; Robbins, 1955). There are still many unanswered questions regarding this problem. Definitive studies of a combined clinical and statistical nature will do a great deal toward clarifying them (Bieber *et al.*, 1962; Marmor, 1965).

However, in order to facilitate such research it is first necessary to define homosexuality so that some consensus on the subject can be established. If it is viewed as a symptom of a wider personality disorder rather than a specific syndrome, it is then possible to study it in its broader social and psychological context (Hooker, 1965). Homosexuality is a manifestation of some failure in personality development in which an individual compulsively prefers and becomes exclusively involved in sexual relations with the same sex. This does not mean that the homosexual is necessarily incapable of sexual activity with the opposite sex, but only that he prefers a partner of the same sex. The term should not refer to the experimental or exploratory sexual encounters that are a common occurrence in the experience of a great many individuals. The accidental or environmental homosexual episodes that occur in prison or under the circumstances of absence of the opposite sex (Karpman, 1948; Fishman, 1930) also must be viewed in a different perspective than true homosexuality. The tendency to assign particular behavioral and sociological characteristics to each sex and to label such manifestations as homosexual when they appear in the opposite sex has led to a dangerous abuse of the concept of homosexuality. This tendency derives from an unsubstantiated notion that there are fixed and definite behavioral characteristics of each sex and that any variation of these characteristics has sexual rather than sociological significance (Money *et al.*, 1955; Money, Hampson, and Hampson, 1957). This makes homosexuality such an inclusive concept that a serious examination of it as a sexual disorder is interfered with.

The hypothesis of a ubiquitous homosexual biological phase in human development can neither be validated in anthropological or cross-cultural studies, nor universally identified within particular cultures. The maintenance of this assumption leads to an unnecessary number of complications and convoluted secondary and tertiary assumptions that do not substantially add to knowledge of homosexuality. There are alternative hypotheses that are as fruitful and heuristic as the libido theory without its contradictory complications.

In addition to the assumption of a homosexual stage of psychosexual development, Freud's concept of homosexuality rested on an outmoded theory known as the bisexual theory of sexual development. Sandor Rado (1940), in a scholarly examination of this theory, dealt it some fatal blows. The theory implied that all humans are bisexual and therefore the psychological and biological qualities of both sexes are present in everyone. It was responsible for the concept of latent homosexuality and supplied a facile answer to the etiology of homosexuality. The theory of psychic bisexuality and the concept of latent homosexuality have not been clarifying hypotheses, but labels that have impeded research in this disorder (Salzman, 1965).

The treatment of homosexuality has been difficult not only because of the prevailing ignorance of its origins, but because of the public censure and criticism that its manifestation stirs up. While it may be a widespread disorder, it is rarely offensive to the public interest. However, considering it as a crime has produced an unfortunate set of circumstances which limit the effectiveness of psychiatric and social controls (Hooker, 1965; Home Office, 1957). The success of treatment remains uncertain, but it is now clear that it is treatable. Various studies give conflicting reports, but one (Bieber *et al.*, 1962) which is well documented claims 27 per cent total recovery. Psychotherapy remains the only rational treatment modality. Physiological therapies such as hormones, drugs, or electroshock are totally ineffective. The developmental interpersonal concept of the origin of the symptom seems to hold great promise in the ultimate clarification of the disorder. Not only are more open-ended research designs necessary to an ultimate clarification of its etiology, but greater treatment programs are necessary in order to accumulate the data needed to improve theoretical formulations.

Related to the problem of homosexuality but not identical with it is the problem of those individuals who wish to change their sexual identities because of powerful gender identifications with the opposite sex. These individuals are neither homosexuals nor transvestites. They are presently called transsexual. The Gender Identity Clinic at Johns Hopkins Hospital has devised a surgical method of treatment which changes the genital anatomy in such cases to fit the psychological gender of the transsexual. The therapeutic effect has been extremely encouraging, and these individuals make successful sexual adjustments in their new gender roles even though procreation is, of course, impossible.

Sexual Deviations

Concepts of normality and deviation would be simple if sex behavior in man were merely an instinctual performance with only a minimal of learned refinements. We could then proceed to label all sexual behavior not directly involved in the biological procreative function as abnormal, and we would be spared a multitude of disagreements and criticisms from legal, theological, sociological, and psychiatric sources. However, an overview of the advances in the understanding of sexual behavior, both normal and abnormal, bears out the severe limitations of the original psychoanalytic conceptions of sex and its role in human behavior. Its deficiencies are particularly apparent in the area of sexual behavior involving the so-called perversions, deviations, or abnormalities—or less pejoratively, the variations of sexual behavior.

What is normal and what is abnormal in sex behavior? This apparently simple yet complex question requires the combined efforts of sociologists, psychiatrists, and public administrators to clarify. Normality is not simply a psychological or physiological determination. It involves definitions which evolve from the history, religious orientation, and sophistication of a culture, both in aesthetic and scientific matters. Normality in one sense is established by the prevailing theological and scientific attitudes toward sex behavior. Legal formulations can and often do change with advances or changes in theological doctrine or scientific evidence.

The definition of normal sex behavior cannot be established in absolute terms, but only as a guidepost to the study of the abnormal. A workable formulation that can serve for many years to come asserts that normal sex behavior is largely a subjective determination and consists of sexual activity which is acceptable to both partners and which produces satisfaction and pleasure without damage, either psychologically or physiologically, to either partner or the culture in which they live. This formulation, however, requires the additional dimension that such behavior should not be contrary to public interest either because of the immaturity or incapacity of one of the partners or because public displays of such behavior tend to displease or damage others. This is analogous to concepts of normality with regard to other biological activities such as assimilation or excretion, where peculiar, idiosyncratic, or statistically unpopular practices are not considered abnormal or illegal unless they impinge on others. Social value judgments have no place in regard to variations in sex activity between adult partners and under circumstances of privacy and free choice. In view of individual preferences and prejudices among people of various cultures, such matters need only come to the attention of the psychiatrist when anxiety accompanies the activity. However, such variations are qualitatively and quantitatively different from major deviations in the sex act which constitute serious social and psychiatric problems and have been minutely catalogued and described in the classic volumes such as Krafft-Ebing's (1922) *Psychopathia Sexualis* and in more recent works on sexual disorders (London and Caprio, 1940). The tendency, however, to view such deviations as separate disease entities is neither theoretically nor therapeutically sound. Such classifications are holdovers of a nosology which predated present knowledge of sex. When sex behavior is viewed from an adaptational view, a different type of classification scheme emerges (Rado, 1956; Hoch and Zubin, 1949). In this framework deviations are viewed as compromise attempts to achieve as much satisfaction in sex activity as is consistent with the anxiety surrounding the activity. Such pattern modifications may be produced by situational factors as well as developmental ones and can account for variations of the exploratory elements in sexual behavior without having to postulate "polymorphous perverse" beginnings of sexual activity. Other modifications may represent distortions of sex behavior due to the linking up of sexual satisfactions with unrelated reactions such as pain or aggression (Rado, 1956).

An alternative view concerning sexual deviations is elaborated on in the existential approach. This approach has been useful in advancing the understanding of many behavioral disorders. It endeavors to comprehend the subjective symbolic meaning of the deviate behavior instead of exploring it from a manifest behavioral point of view. In this view, sexual incapacity often represents a failure in the individual's fulfillment of his total capacities for intimacy and love, and therefore alternative sexual substitutes are attempted in order to achieve the maximum relationship that is possible. The existential approach avoids and criticizes conceptions of sex in terms of partial elements of the sex act such as impulses, libido, love objects, and so forth and sees deviant sexual behavior in terms of incapacity for loving as represented in the sexual act (Boss, 1949; May, Angel, and Ellenberger, 1958). The deviate, whatever the category, always has difficulties in the areas of intimacy, closeness, and capacity to love, trust, and to commit himself. Thus, the symptom of disordered sexual functioning is merely a reflection of the total personality defect.

Conclusion

Psychoanalytic research derived from intensive exploration of the patient's verbalizations, symbolic processes, and unconscious motivations will continue to be a fruitful source of data for the elucidation of the covert processes involved in the development of intimacy, both sexual and nonsexual. If the collection of such data can be obtained without pre-existing bias we may be able to apply alternative points of view to the data. The richness of data produced by the intensity of the analytic relationship cannot be replaced by any other research device. An inevitable and rewarding by-product of such investigations will be the development of therapeutic skills and knowledge for the amelioration of those sexual difficulties which distress individuals and disturb societies.

References

Alexander, F. *Fundamentals of Psychoanalysis.* New York: Norton, 1948.

Angyal, A. *Neurosis and Treatment: A Holistic Theory.* New York: John Wiley, 1965.

Bailey, Nancy, and Shaffer, E. "Maternal Behavior, Child Behavior and Their Intercorrelation from Infancy to Adolescence." *Child Development*, 28, No. 87 (1963), Monograph No. 3.

Bailey, Nancy, and Shaffer, E. "Correlations of Maternal and Child Behavior with Development of Mental Ability." *Child Development*, 26, No. 97 (1964), Monograph No. 6.

Beach, F. A. (ed.). *Sex and Behavior.* New York: John Wiley, 1965.

Benedek, Therese. *Psychosexual Functions in Women.* New York: Ronald Press, 1952.

Benedict, Ruth. *Patterns of Culture.* New York: Mentor Press, 1953.

Bergler, E. *Homosexuality: Disease or Way of Life?* New York: Hill & Wang, 1956.

Berlyne, D. E. "Curiosity and Exploration." *Science*, 153, No. 3731 (1966), 25–33.

Bieber, I. "A Critique of the Libido Theory." *American Journal of Psychoanalysis*, 18 (1958), 52–68.

Bieber, I., *et al. Homosexuality.* New York: Basic Books, 1962.

Boss, M. *Meaning and Content of Sexual Perversions.* New York: Grune & Stratton, 1949.

Chodoff, P. "A Critique of Freud's Theory of Infantile Sexuality." *American Journal of Psychiatry*, 123, No. 5 (1966), 507–518.

Cohen M. "Female Sexuality." Delivered at the Frieda Fromm-Reichmann Memorial Lecture, 1965.

Cole, W. G. *Sex in Christianity and Psychoanalysis*. New York: Oxford University Press, 1953.
Deutsch, Helene. *Psychology of Women: A Psychoanalytic Interpretation*, 2 vols.; New York: Grune & Stratton, 1944–1945.
Erikson, E. H. *Childhood and Society*. New York: Norton, 1950.
Fishman, J. E. *Sex in Prison*. New York: Commonwealth Fund, 1930.
Frazer, J. G. *The Golden Bough: A Study in Magic and Religion*. New York: Macmillan, 1940.
Freud, S. "Three Essays on the Theory of Sexuality" (1905). *The Standard Edition of the Complete Psychological Works of. . . .* London: Hogarth Press. Vol. 7, pp. 123–243. (Also published as *Three Essays on the Theory of Sexuality*. New York: Basic Books, 1963.)
Freud, S. "Psychoanalytic Notes upon an Autobiographical Account of a Case of Paranoia" (1911). *The Standard Edition of the Complete Psychological Works of. . . .* London: Hogarth Press. Vol. 12. (Also published in *Collected Papers of. . . .* New York: Basic Books, 1959. Vol. 3, pp. 387–466.)
Freud, S. *New Introductory Lectures on Psycho-analysis* (1932). *The Standard Edition of the Complete Psychological Works of. . . .* London: Hogarth Press. Vol. 22.
Friedan, Betty. *The Feminine Mystique*. New York: Norton, 1963.
Fromm, E. *Escape from Freedom*. New York: Farrar & Rinehart, 1941.
Gesell, A., and Ilg, Frances L. *Infant and Child in the Culture of Today*. New York: Harper, 1943.
Gesell, A. *The First Five Years of Life*. New York: Harper, 1940.
Green, M. R. (ed.). *Interpersonal Psychoanalysis: The Selected Papers of Clara M. Thompson*. New York: Basic Books, 1964.
Hampson, J. L., and Hampson, Joan G. "The Ontogenesis of Sexual Behavior in Man." In W. C. Young (ed.), *Sex and Internal Secretions*. 3rd ed.; Baltimore: Williams & Wilkins, 1961. Vol. 2, pp. 1401–1432.
Harlow, H. F. "The Nature of Love," *American Psychologist*, 13 (1958), 673–685.
Harlow, H. F. "Love in Infant Monkeys," *Scientific American*, 200 (1959), 68.
Harlow, H. F., and Harlow, Margaret R. "The Effect of Rearing Conditions in Behavior," in J. Money (ed.), *Sex Research*. New York: Holt, Rinehart, & Winston, 1965.
Hirschfield, M. *Sexual Anomalies and Perversions*. London: Encyclopaedic Press, 1944.
Hoch, P., and Zubin, J. (eds.). *Psychosexual Development in Health and Disease*. New York: Grune & Stratton, 1949.
Home Office. *Report of the Committee on Homosexual Offenses and Prostitution* (The Wolfensen Report). London: H.M.S.O., 1957.
Hook, S. (ed.). *Psychoanalysis, Scientific Method, and Philosophy*. New York: New York University Press, 1959.
Hooker, Evelyn. "Male Homosexuals and Their 'Worlds,'" in J. Marmor (ed.), *Sexual Inversion*. New York: Basic Books, 1965. Pp. 83–107.
Horney, Karen. "The Denial of the Vagina." *International Journal of Psycho-Analysis*, 18 (1933), 57–70.

Horney, Karen. *New Ways in Psychoanalysis.* New York: Norton, 1939.

Horney, Karen. *Neurosis and Human Growth.* New York: Norton, 1950.

Ilg, Frances L., and Ames, Louise B. *Child Behavior.* New York: Harper, 1955.

Kagan, J., and Moss, H. N. *Birth to Maturity.* New York: John Wiley, 1962.

Kardiner, A., Karush, A., and Ovesey, L. "A Methodologic Study of Freudian Theory." *Journal of Nervous and Mental Diseases,* 129 (1959), 11–19, 133–143, 207–221, 341–356.

Karpman, B. "Sex Life in Prison." *Journal of Criminal Law and Criminology,* 38 (1948), 475–486.

Kinsey, A., Pomeroy, W. B., and Martin, C. E. *Sexual Behavior in the Human Male.* Philadelphia: Saunders, 1948.

Kinsey, A., Pomeroy, W. B., Martin, C. E., and Gebhard, P. H. *Sexual Behavior in the Human Female.* Philadelphia: Saunders, 1953.

Klein, Melanie. *Contributions to Psycho-analysis,* 1921–1945. London: Hogarth Press, 1948.

Klein, Melanie. *The Psycho-analysis of Children.* 3rd ed.; London: Hogarth Press, 1949.

Kolb, L. C., and Johnson, A. M. "Etiology and Therapy of Overt Homosexuality." *Psychoanalytic Quarterly,* 24 (1955), 506–515.

Krafft-Ebing, R. von. *Psychopathia Sexualis.* 12th ed.; New York: Physicians and Surgeons, 1922.

Lewis, W. C. "Coital Movements in the First Year of Life." *International Journal of Psycho-Analysis,* 46 (1965), part 3, pp. 372–374.

Lief, H. I. "Sex Education in Medical Students and Physicians." *Pacific Medicine and Surgery,* 73 (1965), 52–58.

London, L. S., and Caprio, F. S. *Sexual Deviations.* Westpoint, Conn.: Associated Booksellers, 1950.

Lundberg, F., and Farnham, Marynia. *Modern Woman: The Lost Sex.* New York: Harper, 1947.

Marmor, J. "The Role of Instinct in Human Behavior." *Psychiatry,* 5 (1942), 509–516.

Marmor, J. "Some Considerations Concerning Orgasm in the Female." *Psychosomatic Medicine,* 16 (1954), 240–245.

Marmor, J. (ed.). *Sexual Inversion: The Multiple Roots of Homosexuality.* New York: Basic Books, 1965.

Marmor, J. "Changing Patterns of Femininity: Psychoanalytic Implications." S. Rosenbaum and I. Alger (eds.), *Psychoanalysis and Marriage.* New York: Basic Books, 1968.

Masserman, J. H. "Some Current Concepts of Sexual Behavior." *Psychiatry,* 14 (1951), 61–62.

Masserman, J. H. *Practice of Dynamic Psychiatry.* Philadelphia: Saunders, 1955.

Masserman, J. H. "Sex and the Singular Psychiatrist." In J. H. Masserman (ed.), *Science and Psychoanalysis.* Vol. 9. *Adolescence, Dreams and Training.* New York: Grune & Stratton, 1966. Pp. 111–125.

Masters, W. H. "The Sexual Response Cycle of the Human Female. Part II. Vaginal Lubrication." *Annals of the New York Academy of Science,* 83 (1959), 301–317.

Masters, W. H. "The Sexual Response Cycle of the Human Female. Part I. Gross Anatomic Considerations." *Western Journal of Surgery*, 68 (1960), 52–72.

Masters, W. H., and Johnson, Virginia E. "The Physiology of Vaginal Reproductive Function." *Western Journal of Surgery*, 69 (1961), 105–120.

Masters, W. H., and Johnson, Virginia E. "The Sexual Response Cycle of the Human Female. Part III. The Clitoris: Anatomic and Clinical Considerations." *Western Journal of Surgery*, 70 (1962), 248–257.

Masters, W. H., and Johnson, Virginia A. "The Sexual Response Cycle of the Human Male. Part I. Gross Anatomic Considerations." *Western Journal of Surgery*, 71 (1963), 85–95.

Masters, W. H., and Johnson, Virginia A. *The Human Sexual Response*. Boston: Little, Brown, 1966.

May, R., Angel, E., and Ellenberger, H. F. (eds.). *Existence: A New Dimension in Psychiatry and Psychology*. New York: Basic Books, 1958.

Mead, Margaret. *Sex and Temperament*. New York: Mentor, 1952.

Mead, Margaret. "Cultural Determinants of Sexual Behavior." In W. C. Young (ed.), *Sex and Internal Secretions*. 3rd ed.; Baltimore: Williams & Wilkins, 1961. Vol. 2, pp. 1383–1400.

Money, J. "Components of Eroticism in Man: Cognitional Rehearsal." In J. Wortis (ed.), *Recent Advances in Biological Psychiatry*. 2 vols.; New York: Grune & Stratton, 1960–1961. Vol. 1.

Money, J. (ed.). *Sex Research*. New York: Holt, Rinehart, & Winston, 1965.

Money, J., Hampson, Joan G., and Hampson, J. L. "Imprinting and the Establishment of Gender Role." *American Medical Association Archives of Neurology and Psychiatry*, 77 (1957), 333–336.

Money, J., Hampson, Joan G., and Hampson, J. L. "An Examination of Some Basic Concepts: The Evidence of Human Hermaphroditism." *Bulletin of the Johns Hopkins Hospital*, 97 (1955), 284–310.

Montagu, A. *The Natural Superiority of Woman*. New York: Macmillan, 1953.

Nissen, H. W. "Development of Sex Behavior in Chimpanzees." *Amherst Symposium*, 1954.

Ovesey, L. "The Pseudohomosexual Anxiety." *Psychiatry*, 18 (1955), 17–25.

Ovesey, L. "Masculine Aspirations in Women: An Adaptational Analysis." *Psychiatry*, 19 (1956), 341–351.

Ovesey, L. "The Homosexual Conflict: An Adaptational Repair." *Archives of General Psychiatry*, 5 (1961), 55–69.

Ovesey, L., Gaylen, W., and Hendlin, H. "Psychotherapy of Male Homosexuality: Psychodynamic Formulations." *Archives of General Psychiatry*, 9 (1963), 19–31.

Piaget, J. *The Language and Thought of the Child*. New York: Harcourt, Brace, 1932.

Piaget, J. *The Construction of Reality in the Child*. New York: Basic Books, 1954.

Piaget, J., and Inhelder, Bärbel. *The Child's Concept of Space*. London: Routledge & Kegan Paul, 1942.

Pumpian-Mindlin, E. (ed.). *Psychoanalysis as Science*. 2nd ed.; New York:

Basic Books, 1956.
Rado, S. "A Critical Examination of the Concept of Bi-sexuality." *Psychosomatic Medicine*, 2 (1940), 459–467.
Rado, S. *Psychoanalysis of Behavior: Collected Papers*. New York: Grune & Stratton, 1956. Vols. 1 and 2.
Robbins, B. S. "The Myth of Latent Emotions." *Psychotherapy*, 1, No. 1 (1955), 3–30.
Robbins, B. S. "The Nature of Femininity." *Psychotherapy*, 1, No. 2 (1956), 99–108.
Rosenblatt, J. S., and Aronson, L. R. "The Influence of Experience on the Behavioral Effects of Androgen in Prepubertally Castrated Male Cats." *Animal Behavior*, 6 (1958), 171.
Salzman, L. "Premature Ejaculation." *International Journal of Sexology*, 8 (1954), 69–76.
Salzman, L. "The Concept of Latent Homosexuality." *American Journal of Psychoanalysis*, 17 (1957), 161–169.
Salzman, L. "Paranoid State, Theory and Therapy." *Archives of General Psychiatry*, 2 (1960), 679–693.
Salzman, L. *Developments in Psychoanalysis*. New York: Grune & Stratton, 1962.
Salzman, L. " 'Latent' Homosexuality." In J. Marmor (ed.), *Sexual Inversion*. New York: Basic Books, 1965. Pp. 234–247.
Salzman, L. "Memory and Psychoanalysis." *British Journal of Medical Psychology*, 39 (1966), 127.
Salzman, L., and Masserman, J. H. *Modern Concepts of Psychoanalysis*. New York: Philosophical Library, 1962.
Schachtel, E. G. *Metamorphosis*. New York: Basic Books, 1959.
Schein, M. V., and Hale, E. B. "The Effect of Early Social Experience of Male Sexual Behavior of Androgen-Injected Turkeys." *Animal Behavior*, 7 (1959), 189.
Sherfey, Mary J. "The Evolution and Nature of Female Sexuality in Relation to Psychoanalytic Theory." *Journal of the American Psychoanalytic Association*, 14, No. 1 (1966), 28–128.
Sullivan, H. S. *Interpersonal Theory of Psychiatry*. New York: Norton, 1953.
Sullivan, H. S. *Clinical Studies in Psychiatry*. New York: Norton, 1956.
Taylor, G. R. *Sex in History*. New York: Vanguard, 1954.
Thompson, Clara M. *Psychoanalysis: Evolution and Development*. New York: Hermitage House, 1950.
Yerkes, R. M. *Chimpanzees: A Laboratory Colony*. New Haven: Yale University Press, 1943.
Young, W. C. "The Hormones and Mating Behavior." In W. C. Young (ed.), *Sex and Internal Secretions*. 3rd ed.; Baltimore: Williams & Wilkins, 1961. Vol. 2, pp. 1173–1239.
Young, W. C., Goy, R. W., and Phoenix, C. H. "Hormones and Sexual Behavior." In J. Money (ed.), *Sex Research*. New York: Holt, Rinehart & Winston, 1965.

7

Dreaming and Modern Dream Theory

MAURICE R. GREEN, MONTAGUE ULLMAN,
and EDWARD S. TAUBER

Historical Introduction

Dreaming, by and large, in and out of the psychiatric and psychoanalytic literature, has been approached as a different and very special thought process. In psychoanalysis, it has been regarded as a uniquely valuable therapeutic and diagnostic instrument. Freud's earliest psychoanalytic conceptions received great impetus from his investigation of dreams, although they were based, for the most part, on a neurological model of sexual excitation and frustration (Freud, 1899; Amacher, 1965). Much of what Freud formulated is still valid; there is much, however, that no longer holds true in the light of clinical and laboratory research of the last four decades. Nevertheless, the value of the dream as an instrument for probing into the intricacy of the human personality stands unquestioned today.

Literature on the meaning of dreams dates back to 2000 B.C. in Egypt, and to 700 B.C. in Assyria (Boss, 1958). The Chaldeans and other Near Eastern people lent great weight to dreams. In Homer's work and in Biblical writings dreams were regarded very seriously as communications from the Divine. They were used medically in the temples of Aesculapius to promote the ritual healing of sickness, and by Hippocrates to help diagnose diseases. Herophilus, a third-century Greek physician, even recognized that some dreams serve the function of wish-fulfillment (Dodds, 1957). Aristotle suggested that dreams might present a useful course of action that a person had not yet considered in his waking life—an early glimpse of the problem-solving potentiality of some dreams. Dreams have always been considered to have prophetic power, and even today many people use dreams to try to prophesy the winning horse in a race, or the winning number in the numbers racket. Telepathic powers were early ascribed to dreams and recently have become the subject of scientific experiment (Ullman, 1966). Dreams were also considered, even from the days of Aristotle, sometimes to be mere reflections from the waking day, expressing the same cares, hopes, preoccupations, and feelings; and from the Chaldean days to the present some dreams were regarded as foolish, misleading, or meaningless. In the Dark Ages dreams were often regarded as messages from God or the Devil. Freud reviewed much of this history up to 1900 (Freud, 1899).

In this limited space only a few of the significant contributions will be touched on, and not always will the best representation or the original source of the notion be presented. The emphasis will be on recent material and on apparent seeds of further development in the theory of dreaming and the art of dream interpretation.

Freud's self-analysis led to his investigation of his own dreams and childhood memories. His libido theory was based on the ideas he elaborated from these investigations (Tauber and Green, 1959). Although Freud did a richly detailed study of the many varieties of dreams in relation to various contexts, in the end he focused on the infantile sexuality that he believed was concealed and disguised by the manifest dream content. According to Freud, the latent content of the dream was—like the unconscious content of symptomatic behavior, the psychopathology of everyday life, and the communication between the patient and therapist—rich with oral, anal, phallic, and other instinctual strivings. Following the original breakup of Freud's group, Jung and Adler developed approaches to dreams consistent with their theoretical deviations from Freud. Adler's focus on dreams was designed to reveal the content of his theoretical preoccupation with the social and compensatory strivings of the individual (Ullman, 1962). Jung's approach to dreams focused on his concern with the collective unconscious and archaic images (see his latest statement in *Man and His Symbols*, 1964). Other approaches to dreams reflect the various other psychoanalytic theories and preoccupations.

Heinz Hartmann (1964) and Ernst Kris (1952) emphasized the importance of Freud's late writings on the participation of the ego in dreams and other unconscious processes—particularly the ego's need for intelligibility and for synthesis. However, it was Erik H. Erikson (1954) who made the first important addition to Freud's work within the classical tradition—"The Dream Specimen of Psychoanalysis." Here he followed the early lead of Stekel, Maeder, H. Silberer, and Jung in adding to the narrow, mechanistic approach of Freudian orthodoxy a purposive perspective. He said, ". . . this dream may reveal *more* than the basic fact of a disguised wish fulfillment derived from infantile sources; that this dream may, in fact, carry the historical burden of being dreamed *in order to be* analyzed . . ." (p. 8).

Erikson pleads for more respectful attention to the manifest content of the dream and its verbal report by the patient. He emphasizes the importance of its style of representation which presents the individual's personal time-space and the frame of reference for his defenses and accomplishments. However, in spite of his attention to the verbal, sensory, spatial, temporal, somatic, interpersonal, and affective aspects of the manifest content, he never abandons the more narrow concept of latent dream material. He continues to rely on the classic links of associations and symbols to reveal the latent dream thoughts. Nevertheless, he goes beyond a concern with psychosexual issues and ego defenses to stress the importance of ego identity and a life plan, thus including much of the neo-Freudian contribution. In a more recent book, *Insight and Responsibility* (1964), Erikson adds a further dimension by assimilating the phenomenological emphasis on immediate subjective experience. He criticizes Hartmann (p. 163) for following Freud in imposing a Cartesian strait jacket on the model of man. He states, "I believe we can undo this strait jacket only by separating from our concept of reality one of its more obscure implications, namely actuality, the world verified in immediate immersion and interaction" (p. 164). He presents a searching analysis of Freud's dream of Count Thun to illustrate the participation of the actual adult ego in the dream. He states, "Dream life encases the most recent dangers to the ego's sense of mastery into the tapestry of previous and distant ones, using personal delusion and private cunning to make one meaningfully patterned past of them all and to bring this past into line with anticipated actuality" (p. 200).

The existentialist approach, best represented by Medard Boss, attempts to transcend the limitations of the various psychoanalytic theories. Boss, in *The Analysis of Dreams* (1958), addresses himself to the separate and distinct mode of existence that characterizes dreaming. He points out that the person who dreams and recalls his dream is identical to the person who continues to function throughout the waking day. Dreaming characterizes a separate and distinct form of existence for a person as the waking state or nondreaming state of sleep characterizes another distinct form of human existence for the same identity. Boss is sharply critical of both Freud and Jung for what he considers to be their implicit derogation of the manifest content. He points out how the "natural scientific" bias of both of these pioneers led them away from a concern with the dream at the phenomenological level and involved them mainly in a concern with the dream as a disguised form of symbolic expression.

William James, like Medard Boss, respected the phenomenal nature of the dream as a form of existence in itself. He wrote:

The world of dreams is our real world whilst we are sleeping, because our attention then lapses from the sensible world. Conversely when we wake, the attention usually lapses from the dream-world and that becomes unreal. But if a dream haunts us and compels our attention during the day, it is very apt to remain figuring in our consciousness as a sort of sub-universe alongside of the waking world. Most people have probably had dreams which it is hard to imagine not to have been glimpses into an actually existing region of being . . . (James, 1918, p. 294).

However, James paid very little attention to dreams and dreaming in his writings. It was not until recent years that William James's approach to dreams, similar to that of Boss, became widely shared by many analysts, clinicians, and research workers.

American psychiatrists under the leadership of Adolf Meyer and William A. White eagerly received Freud's contributions to dream theory and the clinical use of dreams in the second decade of this century. But, in spite of this early enthusiasm for Freud's work, there was also keen interest and reception for the later contributions of Adler, Stekel, Jung, and others who deviated from Freud.

Sullivan considered the experience of the dream to be of a different order of experience from that of waking life—in two ways: first, it occurs in a state of sleep and thus poses an impassable barrier to accurate recall in the waking state; and second, dreaming takes place mostly in the parataxic mode of experience, which is a very generalized, oversimplified, and concrete formulation of happenings characterized by their immediate qualities without reference, necessarily, to temporal continuities, causal sequences, or logical syntax. Although Sullivan believed any attempt to translate this into statements that could be made consensually valid by mere intellectual operations was futile and wasteful, he did not minimize the significance of the reported dream. He urged that it be given full attention and weight like any other reported experience. He said, "The psychiatrist reflects back to the person what has seemed to him to be the significant statements, and then sees if it provokes any thought in the mind of the patient" (Sullivan, 1953, p. 337).

Erich Fromm, an early associate of Sullivan in Washington and New York, differs from Sullivan in many respects, including the approach to dreams. Fromm follows H. Silberer, Maeder, Stekel, and others in his use of anagogic, analogical, and metaphorical interpretation. He, too, rejects the limitations of Freud's so-called "laws of the unconscious" as a necessary prerequisite for dream interpretation. Basically, Fromm is concerned with communicating how the imagery of the dream illuminates the patient's struggle to avoid responsibility for himself and his blind tendency to live out life in false solutions, idolatrous pursuits, and evasions while it can, at the same time, reveal his hidden potentialities.

Karen Horney, who was associated with Fromm and Sullivan for a time after breaking away from Freudian orthodoxy, repeatedly emphasized the importance of dreams for developing a patient's awareness of his *real self*. She said that ". . . in dreams we are closer to the reality of ourselves; that they represent attempts to solve our conflicts, either in a neurotic or in a healthy way; that in them constructive forces can be at work, even at a time when they are hardly visible otherwise" (Horney, 1950, p. 340).

Tauber and Green (1959) proposed a deeper reconsideration of prelogical experience, especially dreaming, in the structure of thinking. They reject the scientific convention of placing concept, ideas, and grammar as central and primary. They assert vigorously that feeling values have a much broader semantic than the content expressed in discursive grammer. They insist that dreaming is not primarily a guardian of sleep; that the doctrine of wish-fulfillment interferes with appreciation of the manifest symbolic activity; that the dream is invaluable for introducing novelty in a patient's conception of himself; and that the dream is rich with details of the analyst-patient relationship, and hence is a uniquely worthy instrument for exploring the transference-countertransference vicissitudes.

Ullman (1958, 1959, 1963) early called attention to the adaptive significance of the dream occurring in an experiential state of inner vigilance and partial arousal. He sees the cyclic variations in depth of sleep during the night as an opportunity for the individual to confront some challenge to the continuity of his habitual way of life wherein cognitive preparation for reinforcing neurotic illness patterns may occur or, on the other hand, preparation for healthy change may take place. Dreaming involves a process of self-confrontation, concerned not with intelligibility and referential meaning of a given aspect of experience, but rather with the felt reactions derivative of that experience. Given a situation involving unknown operating causes, a personal myth is created through the use of familiar and manipulatable imagery. This myth and its expression in imagery has to be understood not in terms of disguise, but rather as a statement of a problem the answer to which is not within the sleeper's awareness, and at the same time as an effort at mastery. In both the dream state and the waking state we construct myths to explain things we do not understand.

Bonime, a student of Karen Horney and Bernard Robbins, wrote a practical guide (1962) to dream interpretation expressed in an interpersonal framework concerned with values, the growth of self-awareness, and a confrontation with the patient of what he is actually about in his everyday living. Bonime, too, eschews Freudian mechanics for a view of dream symbolism as metaphoric referents. He heuristically categorizes the dream content into actions, individuals, surroundings, and feelings.

French and Fromm (1964, pp. 94–95) emphasize the problem-solving tendencies of dreams wherein "wishes and wish-fulfilling fantasies are only parts or phases of a more comprehensive problem-solving effort." They explain Freud's failure to appreciate the problem-oriented thought processes of dreaming as due to a narrow preoccupation with infantile wishes and a misguided belief in the value of tracing chains of association. They present a sequence of dreams in the course of a psychoanalysis that richly illustrates the step-by-step path in which the patient manifests in his dreams the gradual unfolding and overcoming of his problems in living. The analyst in this case relies on intuition, empathy and "sympathic resonance" to grasp the gestalten of the dream imagery. French says, "What is present in the dream work, on the other hand, is a practical, empathic understanding of interpersonal relations. This kind of understanding does not need syntactical logic" (p. 162).

Basic Research on Dream Physiology

In the past we have had to rely on the questionable validity of a report of a private experience which nonetheless had a limited usefulness. Scientific research must use data that are public and repeatable in order to establish the community of consensus to which scientific knowledge belongs. Publicly, we have had the reported dream; and now we have the observations of the physiology and behavior of the dreamer as he is dreaming, thanks to the EEG monitoring technique discovered by Aserinsky and Kleitman (1953).

EEG CORRELATES OF DREAMING

Dreaming appears preponderantly in stage one EEG when it is ascending from stage two EEG, usually after at least a short period of stage four EEG (Kleitman, 1963). Dreaming may occur with or without rapid eye movements, referred to as REMs. The presence of REMs is presumably associated with the liveliness of the dream sequence. When the sleeper was both actor *and* spectator of the dream he was witnessing, he showed more REMs, as well as more small hand movements, than did the sleeper who was *only* a passive spectator of the dream. Subjects reported dreams more often when the REMs were accompanied by a large increase in the pulse rate. Slow eye movements, referred to as SEMs, are also significantly associated with dreaming. Kamiya said, "SEMs often build up in magnitude and speed . . . into REMs. Also, SEMs do not cease on the onset of REMs.

On the contrary, the REM period is really a period of heightened SEM as well as REM" (Kleitman, 1963, pp. 98–99).

Roffwarg, Dement, Muzio, and Fisher (1962) described an interesting experiment in which a judge working with the verbal report of a subject's dream could, without knowing the EEG pattern, infer, with a high degree of accuracy, the direction of the eye movements from the movement and spatial patterning occurring in the dream.

Kleitman (1963) considers the REM-EEG cycles associated with dreaming to be only one manifestation of a basic primitive periodicity of rest and activity that occurs in animals and humans alike, even in anencephalous children and in decorticated dogs. In the newborn human this cycle, of 50 to 60-minute duration, represents a coalescence of several periodicities; this cycle increases with age to 60 to 70 minutes in children of nursery school age and 80 to 90 minutes in the adult (Roffwarg, Muzio, and Dement, 1966).

Aserinsky now questions the one-to-one correspondence between REM activity and dreams. He describes bursts of REM activity that occur during a so-called REM period sometimes *not* accompanied by dreams. A twenty-minute REM stage does not mean a twenty-minute dream.

PHYSIOLOGICAL CORRELATES

Studies comparing the waking state with the REM periods (REMPs) show much more similarity than the REMPs have with the other stages of sleep. The auditory-evoked response, AER, simulates the waking state amplitude in contrast to the increased amplitude observed in N-REM sleep (Weitzeman and Kremen, 1965). Also, neocortical cells which initiate corticospinal movements have almost the same threshold (slightly lower) during REMPs as they have during states of quiet wakefulness. In the other stages of sleep the threshold is much higher than during wakefulness. In fact, all the evidence shows that there is a heightened excitability of the sensory-motor cortex in REMPs that is probably general for the entire neocortex as well as the vestibular and bulbar reticular formation during REMPs than during other stages of sleep. Although gross body movements are inhibited during REM periods, studies show that fine body movements, measured by a strain gauge, at the throat, wrist, ankle, upper arm, shoulder, and abdomen, were markedly increased. These fine body movements continued throughout the REMP and were almost completely absent during non-REMPs (Baldridge, Whitman, and Kramer, 1965). Interspersed with these fine movements are electromyographic recordings which show a reduction, often to zero, of muscle potential. The characteristic low-voltage desynchronized EEG pattern shows, in addition, 2- to 3-second "sawtooth"-shaped waves just prior to or coincident with clusters of eye movements.

Erections occurred during 80 per cent of REM periods, more frequent in the latter part of sleep time. Erections could not be accounted for by bladder pressure, local irritation, or sexual deprivation. Most of the subjects freely expressed erotic feelings in waking life, yet rarely reported any erotic content in the dreams that occurred during the erection-REM cycle. When deprived of REM-erection time, there was a compensatory increase on subsequent nights in both REM time and erection time, but more so with erection time as there were more erections during non-REM sleep (Karacan, 1965).

There were also increases in respiratory rate, systolic pressure, electrical skin resistance, and heart rate.

It seems to many research workers that the REMPs represent a qualitatively different state and process distinct from both sleep and wakefulness rather than a lighter or deeper aspect of the single state of sleep. This view is not universally accepted within the ranks of the experimentalists themselves. The notion of a qualitatively unique state of the organism differing from both the waking and the sleeping state, once introduced by Jouvet and Courjois (1959), was further developed and elaborated by Dement (1964) and Snyder (1963). An opposing point of view, however, has been put forth by Hernández-Peón (1963, p. 80) based on direct brain stem stimulation by cholinergic substances. He argues that the so-called emergent stage one simply represents the deepest stage of sleep. Thus maintaining a unitary point of view of a sleep-waking continuum, Hernández-Peón accounts for the electrocortical manifestations of the REM state as due to the spread of inhibition from the rostro-pontine segments of the arousal or vigilance system to the thalamus. The low-voltage pattern of activity is resumed when thalamic spindle-bursts are no longer sent to the cortex. "The rapid eye movements which appear in bursts during the 'desynchronized' stage of sleep can be accounted for by intermittent releases of tonic inhibition acting upon the oculo-motorneurons in the brain stem, as well as upon the motor cortex" (1963, p. 80). This has been one of the most constructive contributions made toward an understanding of the nature of sleep. Hernández-Peón demonstrated the hypnogenic pathways by placing minute crystals of acetylcholine into the brain, thereby revealing an extensive but well-defined pathway along the neuroaxis subserving sleep. This technique induced first slow sleep (N-REM) with cortical slow waves, sharp waves in the hippocampus and entorhinal cortex, a slight elevation of the arousal threshold, and a moderate diminution of muscle tonus in the nuchal muscles. Within thirty minutes, more or less, REM sleep supervened with characteristic EEG desynchronization, significant increase in arousal threshold, high amplitude theta rhythm in the entorhinal cortex, practically isoelectric electromyogram, and bursts of rapid eye movements. Subsequent studies revealed that the hypnogenic pathway extended from the forebrain down as far as the upper levels of the spinal cord. Furthermore, he demonstrated that the sleep mechanism consists essentially of a powerful inhibition of the mesodiencephalic arousing or vigilance neurons. The sleep-wakefulness continuum is conceptualized as two reciprocally antagonistic neural systems with an intrinsic rhythmic and automatic activity. The dreaming process, conceptually more speculative, has been explained on the basis of selective disinhibition of the corticolimbic system. This formulation attempts to account for the widespread electrical activity occurring in the cortical areas.

A somewhat similar neurophysiological state to the REMP has been described by Russian writers and others. It is interesting to see that much more attention has been paid recently to what Pavlov, stimulated by Zeleny, called the "orientational reflex." Many studies, mostly from the USSR, but also from elsewhere, have defined this complex as including: overt receptor-adjusting responses; the EEG arousal pattern; increased activity of the circulatory, respiratory, electrocutaneous, and pupillary responses; physicochemical and muscular processes within sense organs that increase their sensitivity and resolving power; and increased skeletal-muscle tension. Pavlov described a preliminary "arrest reaction" associated, it is now known, with stimulation of the thalamic reticular system, and a later phase, preparing for action, "including tensing of the musculature and the GSR in the palms and soles (apparently due to perspiration, which, as Darrow pointed out, facilitates gripping) . . ." (Berlyne, 1963, p. 313). More recently, Sokolov (1963) has described the changes in the EEG in their relationship to the extinction of the orienting reaction.

> Where the orienting reaction is extinguished, all the reactions disappear gradually but the EEG background is still active. If, however, the extinction process is continued further, the EEG background tends to be changed by the development of slow waves, indicative of the development of an inhibitory state in the cortex. With the development of this inhibitory background there is a paradoxical restoration and intensification of orienting reactions as revealed by exaltation of alpha-rhythm, a cutaneogalvanic reaction, respiratory changes and vascular reactions, all of which are stably maintained in this transitional state between waking and sleep (Sokolov, 1963, p. 289).

It is also noteworthy that the hippocampal gyrus seems to be necessary for gestalt type memory, although its intactness is not required for repetitive, rote-type learning. In humans, stimulation of the hippocampal gyrus does not cause any significant emotional manifestation.

It has also been shown that during the waking state REM rate is a nonspecific concomitant of attentive activity (Amadeo and Shagass, 1963). No significant differences were found between visual and nonvisual stimuli with respect to the incidence of these eye movements (Shimazano, Ando, Sakamoto, Tanaka, Eguchi, and Nakamura, 1965).

Rechtschaffen has established that visual imagery also occurs during non-REM states in stages two, three, and four, but usually with less detail, vividness, or emotional intensity than dreams reported during REM states. He and his co-workers concluded that "subjects reported unique, discrete manifest images and themes which were repeated in the reports from *different* EEG stages of sleep. We conclude that on these nights dreams are only a part of a larger body of interrelated sleep mentation" (Rechtschaffen, Vogel, and Shaikun, 1963, p. 547).

It is interesting to note that when subjects were dreaming a dream that they were instructed to dream as a posthypnotic task, the REM time was shortened from the control range of 12.5 to 34.5 minutes to the subjects' range of 2.0 to 9.5 minutes. The REM time was shortened even more by increasing the number of elements given in the posthypnotic dream suggestion. Many subjects dreamt about the suggested topic in every REM period of the night. One explanation may possibly be that scanning of recent and remote memory occurs to a greater extent in sleep not influenced by the guiding security of the hypnotist on whom the dreamer relies for emotional orientation and rapport.

DREAM CONTENT

Dream recall is directly related to the closeness of the time of awakening to the occurrence of the REMs. If the dreamer was awakened ten or more minutes after the REMs have stopped, there was complete forgetfulness in twenty-five out of twenty-six cases (Kleitman, 1963). References from the more remote past are much more frequent in dreams that occur toward the end of a night's sleep; rectal temperature is consistently lower during this type of dreaming; recall was better for these later dreams; they were longer in duration, more vivid, more emotionally intense, and were associated with a longer period of REM (Verdone, 1965). Correspondingly, the first few minutes of REMPs early in the night show much more relatively unaltered memory fragments of the preceding day or two than do dreams of the latter part of the night (Fisher, 1965).

The elements and personnel of the experimental situation are also incorporated into dreams directly and indirectly from 68.5 per cent (Whitman, Pierce, Maas, and Baldridge, 1962) to 21.9 per cent (Dement, 1963a) of the dreams, especially in the early dreams of the first night in the sequence. Certain kinds of personalities seem to dream more frequently and overtly of the laboratory experimental situation. These have been described as the field-dependent type (Witkin and Lewis, 1964) who have less differentiated personalities, have more trouble recalling their dreams and characterologically rely on defenses of repression and denial. Of this latter group who recalled no dreams at all on half or less of REMP awakenings, there was no difference in their neurophysiological behavior, during REMPs and arousals, from the other subjects (Goodenough, Lewis, Shapiro, Jaret, and Sleser, 1965).

There is some evidence that learning and conditioning can take place during an REMP. Subjects can be trained to discriminate between dreaming-REMPs and nondreaming sleep, and signal this distinction without interrupting their sleep except for a slight arousal response during the actual signaling (Antrobus, Antrobus, and Fisher, 1964). Spoken personal names presented in random order during REMPs were consistently incorporated into the manifest content of the dreams with equal frequency for the neutral names as for the emotionally charged ones. However, they were incorporated with decreasing frequency according to their mode of representation in the following order, respectively: assonance, direct, association, and symbolic representation. This incorporation was not associated with any differences from the usual physiology of REMPs (Berger, 1963).

Memory for the external stimuli (numbers) is better during REM sleep than during non-REM sleep. However, when subjects' eyes were taped open and visual stimuli presented during REMPs, there was no obvious incorporation of this into the manifest dream.

Forgetting of dreams by recallers cannot be explained simply by repression; for if it were due to repression, the recallers could not remember their dreams so readily when awakened during or shortly after a dream. Rechtschaffen (1964) suggests that the fact that "the hippocampus is not functioning during N-REM sleep, or functioning quite differently from the way it does during wakefulness, accounts for much of what we know about the forgetting of dreams" (p. 165).

The tendency to formulate the stages of sleep exclusively along an axis of arousal is misleading since the different sleep stages seem to reflect other possible meanings. Thus, most observers agree that REM sleep reflects maximal inaccessibility of the sleeper if a meaningless stimulus such as a sound stimulus (decibel level) is the test stimulus. Contradictory findings strongly suggest that, although inhibition is maximal during REM sleep, significant stimuli need not be excessive in amplitude and may gain the attention of the sleeper more easily in this stage of sleep than in any other. Recent studies reveal the complexity of the memory patterning during different sleep stages. Evans, Gustafson, O'Connell, Orne, and Shor (1966) have demonstrated that *meaningful* input during an REM phase of sleep can be recaptured at a later date during REM sleep even though there is amnesia during the waking state for the selective stimulus input introduced during REM sleep. Pending further confirmation of this study, one is tempted to speculate about the nature of memory function along levels of consciousness. Thus one can conceive of memory plateaus consistent with the plateaus of consciousness and speculate that a successful "recall" is a function of the level of consciousness at which the memory material is aimed. Crossing the boundaries makes recall more difficult, but tapping recall from the level at which the information is introduced may facilitate recall. To extend the speculation to schizophrenic episodes which not infrequently emerge from a state of sleep, these episodes seem allied with deep N-REM sleep so that on awakening the sleeper is often confused and disoriented. Abruptness in waking is normally more easily achieved from REM sleep than N-REM sleep. Additionally, somnambulism is characteristically seen in deep N-REM sleep. This resembles the "amnesic"-like quality of individuals in fugues and similar states, where gross conduct may not be too strikingly unusual but yet suggests a memory function that is tied in with highly private and implicit or dissociated processes. These thought processes are not amenable to simple articulation since they no doubt refer back to very early experience. They hint at the possibility that deep N-REM sleep is the repository of ill-defined yet significant autistic mentation for which expectation of conversion to normal dreaming and potential recapture is most improbable. We are tentatively suggesting that there are horizontal planes of memory correlating with horizontal planes of consciousness.

Hence, stage three to four, non-REM sleep is much more significant clinically in that it seems to facilitate "acting out" of the vague implicit confusion of one's individual self—in enuresis, somnambulism, night terrors, etc. Accessibility to learning during sleep has also become an area of increasing scientific interest, but its successful demonstration or the failure thereof will require an appreciation of what constitutes significant adaptive input as against nonspecific input of greater or lesser amplitude.

The area of memory has likewise acquired renewed interest in view of recent studies of the hippocampus. We suspect that memory patterns may be viable within the framework of a particular level of consciousness, but the transmission of remembered experience from one level of consciousness to another is obviously most difficult unless the time interval in change of state is extremely short. Thus, reporting dream material after one has awakened is notoriously difficult for many people. This is not to imply the time interval is the exclusively salient feature in the capacity for recall.

The relatively greater inaccessibility of the individual in REM sleep as against N-REM sleep revealed in the study of auditory-evoked potentials is convincing since Weitzman has also made similar observations (unpublished) in the monkey. One is tempted to infer that the REM state is similar in many ways to the waking state, not in the least of which is the tendency to focal attention. The dreamer is busy dreaming and inhibition at the first synapse affords relative protection against disturbing sensory input unless it is meaningful.

"PATHOLOGICAL" BEHAVIOR DURING SLEEP

Observations of sleep talking in the laboratory have been reported by Kamiya (1961) and by Rechtschaffen, Goodenough, and Shapiro (1962). The latter authors confirmed Kamiya's finding that sleep talking occurred predominantly in non-REM periods (86 to 92 per cent). They, too, found non-REM sleep talking associated with gross muscle tensions, artifacts, changes in skin resistance, and occasional alpha-activity indicating a temporary tendency toward arousal. Sleep talking that was observed during REM sleep was found to be correlated with dreams.

Bruxism (nocturnal grinding of the teeth) was also studied with the EEG monitoring technique. It was found that contractions of the jaw muscles occurred much more frequently (20.9 per hr.) during REM sleep than in non-REM sleep (5.3 per hr.). Pilot studies of normal subjects showed that tooth-grinding occurred to a lesser extent but also with the same relationship to stage of sleep. Jouvet (1966) found a similar phenomenon in cats. Normally, this may be due to a spread of activity from the pontile reticular formation to the motor nucleus of the trigeminal nerve (Reding, Rubright, Rechtschaffen, and Daniels, 1964). Enuresis, night terrors, and sleepwalking, however, occur invariably during non-REM sleep.

TIME AND COLOR

Dement and Wolpert (1958) found no distortion of time in dreams, but that the time in which the action occurs as reported by the dreamer corresponds more or less precisely to the duration of the REM activity. There is something of a tendency to overestimate short time intervals. Experimentally, it has been shown that this tendency is increased by visual deprivation or by a state of depressed affect. Tauber and Green's inference (1962) based on clinical evidence that color was present in the great majority of dreams was supported by the subsequent EEG study by Kahn, Dement, Fisher, and Barmack (1962).

DEVELOPMENTAL CHANGES

The percentage of sleeping life that is spent in stage one REM "dreaming activity" decreases as a person grows older, starting with 80 per cent in a thirty-week-old premature infant to only 13 per cent in a hundred-year-old individual.

Rapid eye movements occur when there is no possibility of any visual imagery, such as in premature infants, the newborn, and the congenitally blind, thus indicating that the rapid eye movements are an inherent mechanism whose function is not yet proved and are associated with visual imagery only later on in life when visual experience has taken place.

REM-DREAM DEPRIVATION

Dream deprivation usually results in irritability, restlessness, and increased appetite. However, Dement (1963b) has reported instances in humans and animals where dream deprivation seems to have no effect.

FUNCTION OF REM-DREAM SLEEP

It is now well established that Freud's hypothesis that the dream is created specifically in response to external or internal stimuli in order to protect sleep was completely mistaken, Dement (1964, p. 149) reported ". . . In all the recent studies of sleep, there has been no finding which confirms the notion that sleep *must* be preserved or that there is even any desire or advantage in preserving uninterrupted sleep."

Contrary to the assumption of Freud, Sullivan, and others, the physiology of dreaming has very little, if anything, in common with psychotic states. Children and adults suffering chronic psychoses have the same EEG dreaming patterns that normals do.

The fact that dreaming occurs with such great frequency early in life and gradually diminishes as the individual gets older indicates that possibly dreaming serves a developmental function in the physiological maturation of the human organism. Roffwarg, Muzio, and Dement (1966) have developed a compelling thesis favoring an interpretation of the maturational effects of dreaming sleep.

Since we still do not understand what sleep is, whether it be dreaming sleep or non-REM sleep, and since so far we have a right to assume that all living animals have to have some kind of sleep, and since from a clinician's standpoint disturbances of sleep occupy a serious part of our inquiry into a patient's health, a valid inquiry must include a very broad global sense of the sleep mechanisms in the animal kingdom. It certainly is not self-evident that dreaming sleep could be absent from the life program of any animal alive. If we conceive of dreaming sleep as a reflection of the perceptual motor experience of the waking state, this type of sleep would restate the adaptive pattern appropriate to the particular species.

The questions raised by phylogenetic studies cannot be answered easily unless a more extensive inventory of sleep behavior is made of the whole vertebrate kingdom. There are certain consistent findings in the study of placental mammals and the opossum, a marsupial, which indicate that a generalization concerning the existence of REM sleep is applicable throughout. There are species differences in respect to the precise patterns of REM sleep and the fact that the opossum spends some 80 per cent of its time in sleep, of which 20 to 30 per cent is in REM sleep, has led some investigators (i.e., F. Snyder, 1965) to emphasize the antiquity of this neurophysiological process. But if the opossum is a living fossil among mammals (no monotremes, e.g., the spiny anteater or the duckbill platypus, have been studied), certainly the turtles, which can be traced back in time further than the extinct dinosaurs, reveal no REM sleep, according to Jouvet (1965). The pigeon and the chicken show very short bursts of REM sleep. On the other hand, preliminary studies indicate the presence of eye movements during sleep in two diurnal lizard species. The fact that the latter animals have such highly developed vision and oculomotor organization has suggested that specialized receptor equipment may play a role in the eventual neural mechanisms subserving sleep. How the presence of the neocortex, whose limited beginnings are first noted in reptiles and which reaches its highest development in mammals and particularly in man, is integrated with brain stem mechanisms is still far from clear. Recent studies on the frog (Hobson, 1967) have led some to doubt whether REM sleep occurs at that level of vertebrate phylogeny. So far no studies of sleep in fish have been made and formidable technical problems no doubt have contributed to the hesitation in the exploration of sleep in fish. Furthermore, there are few reliable behavioral studies of fish sleep even though certain tropical marine fish evince states of diminished arousal akin to mammalian sleep.

At any rate the existence of REM sleep in lower mammals, decorticate humans, and infants does not preclude the notion of dreaming sleep under normal circumstances since the dreaming process need in no way be "caused" by the neural mechanisms underlying REM sleep. It is merely that certain neurophysiological states may facilitate other higher neural processes. If one conceives of dreaming sleep as a state consistent with the adaptive challenges of the particular species under consideration, one may suspect that perceptual activity of the animal in the waking state is endogenously "reviewed" during dreaming sleep.

Unexpected findings in the lower end of the vertebrate spectrum need not cast doubt on what is solidly confirmed in other areas. The life span and internal clock mechanisms in the animal kingdom are sufficiently idiosyncratic so that patience in our search *is* more important than premature attempts to resolve "crucial" questions which are only seemingly crucial because our knowledge is still so scant.

Clinical Research

Although the physiology of dreaming is fascinating, raises many questions, and serves as an invaluable instrument for monitoring dreams under experimental conditions, the content of dreams can be approached distinctly and separately as a phenomenon in its own right. The range of this content is as enormous and varied as is the range of thought in everyday waking life, encompassing everything at one time or another—every category of mental experience from simple fragmented sensations to profound, prophetic messages.

ATTITUDINAL REPRESENTATION

Sequences of dreams of patients undergoing psychoanalysis have been reported by French, Offenkrantz, and Rechtschaffen (1963), Jones (1962), and Kramer, Whitman, Baldridge, and Lansky (1965), among others. Kramer *et al.* compared the dreams that were recalled to the experimenter and later reported to a psychiatrist with those which were also recalled to the experimenter but forgotten for the psychiatrist. These latter dreams were characterized by themes of thinly disguised homogenital relations, denial of need for treatment, fear of being injured by treatment, and compulsive handwashing. Some sequences showed progressive movement in trying out in the dream drama feared longings with anticipated rejection, punishment, and later victory. Other sequences showed different statements of the same problem restated over and over again with little or no progression.

Depressed patients, even when improved on imipramine therapy, showed predominant themes of escape associated with feelings of hopelessness or helplessness. Imipramine decreased the amount of dreaming time and was associated with an increase of hostility expressed in the manifest content.

Edith Sheppard first reported in 1956 (Saul and Sheppard, 1956) a method of studying personal attitudes and defensive postures in dreams under the rubric of ego functions measured by a rating scale applied to the manifest content of dreams. She later assumed that ". . . the manifest dream is excellent for studying the ego activities, especially its unconscious activities" (Sheppard and Saul, 1958, p. 237). Ten categories of ego functions were described: Source, Object, Completion, Participation, Expression, Resolution, Logic, Reality, Body Image, and Interrelationships.

Other studies have correlated hostility in manifest dreams with essential hypertension (Saul and Sheppard, 1956); giving and taking tendencies in manifest dreams with gastrointestinal disorders (Alexander and Wilson, 1935); and exhibitionistic and voyeuristic trends in manifest dreams with skin diseases (Miller, 1948). Gordon (1953) has correlated manifest dreams with TAT stories, and Bolgar (1954) has correlated manifest dreams with Rorschach responses. Sheppard (1963) reported a subsequent study by which manifest dreams were rated independently and blindly from the association given by patients in analysis and which were also rated independently and blindly. The independent ratings correlated highly in five major categories—three of hostility, one of genitality, and one of bodily mutilation. DeMartino's study of mental defectives found that subjects with higher IQ's tended to report more complex and mature dreams than those with lower IQ's. He also found that the dreams could well be utilized in much the same manner as standard projective data (DeMartino, 1954).

Markowitz and Seiderman (1963) reported a fascinating study wherein a professional artist made drawings of dreams reported by children. These drawings were then photostated. The parents of the children were shown the dream pictures of their own child together with those of three other children and asked to comment on all four without being told that one of them was based on their own child's dream. In this pilot study they found that parents are more responsive to their own child's dream than the dreams of other children. The manifest content of the dreams of children seem to express their social reality, e.g., a child who "sugar coats" her hostility to her mother in waking life dreams of pouring hot chocolate over her dying mother.

DEVELOPMENTAL SIGNIFICANCE

In recent years, beginning with Piaget (1951), dreaming has come to be seen as part of a general spectrum of thought processes, participating in the development of mental activities from infancy through childhood into adulthood. Just as children's drawings, play, Rorschach responses, and spontaneous stories show a developmental progress from the early years of verbal communication through childhood and adolescence, so do their reported dreams. Likewise, just as spontaneous stories, figure drawings, and Rorschach responses are useful ways of approaching the various problems, difficulties, psychodynamics, and diagnostic issues among patients of all ages, so have dreams been useful in the same way. Like other projective techniques, however, the use of dreams relies heavily on the personal resources and interpretive skill of the therapist. Dreaming, which is ordinarily private, uncommunicated, and often unnoticed by the waking person, is the purest form of projective data that we have; manifesting in the cases of the treatment and the laboratory situation the interpersonal transactions that include both therapist or experimenter and the patient or subject.

There is considerable evidence (Tart, 1965) now that the content of dreaming can be modified by hypnosis, conditioning, learning, and the influence of the therapist, or, in the experimental laboratory situation, by personnel. The fact that dreaming is an inherent, cyclical, physiological activity that functions in everyone throughout his entire lifetime does not prevent dreaming any more than other cyclical, physiological processes from being influenced by the complexity of interpersonal transactions as they occur or develop in the course of one's lifetime. Unfortunately, fruitful perspective on this process has been blurred by attempts to reconcile recent research findings with Freud's concept of instinctual energies (Fisher, 1965). As Grinker (1968) and others have pointed out, thought processes, including dream activity, involve very little energy compared with other physiological processes, and have much more to do, adaptively and functionally, with the processing of information. Piaget has been uniquely valuable in this respect for pointing up the function of dreaming and play in the growing child as intermediary developmental processes in exercising symbolic skill, and in assimilating new information (Green, 1961a).

In the light of the fact that dreaming occurs with great regularity in all human beings of all ages regardless of what ails them, one cannot ascribe either the cause or purpose of this regular, cyclic, psychophysiologic process to any varying environmental stimulation, such as current emotional conflicts, unresolved infantile wishes, frustrated instinctual drives, or anticipated environmental dangers. All these variables, as well as many other factors, undoubtedly influence the manifest content of the remembered or reported dreams. However, the psychophysiological pattern continues to occur in its cyclic rhythm regardless of the presence or absence of these variables and without being diminished or increased by them. Dreaming time *can* be interfered with by drugs, by waking, or by conditioned inhibition of dreaming time. Dream deprivation studies suggest that this cyclic, psychophysiologic process we call dreaming in some way facilitates the integrity or wholeness of the discriminating personality in both feeling secure and in alertly discriminating the various aspects of the environment with appropriate capacity for attention and concentration. However, Kleitman (1963) is averse to ascribing any purpose or adaptive function to dreaming. He likens it to any habit which, when interrupted, shows similar symptoms.

COGNITIVE POTENTIAL OF DREAMING

In lieu of more precise, rigorous knowledge at this time, we may *speculate* that our dreams, however influenced they may be by persons, sounds, stimulations from our immediate or recent environment, do manifest, in some way, idiosyncratic representations of felt importance regarding our personal orientation to our values in our daily living. The type of sleep manifested by dreaming *may* be the neurophysiologic instrument of greatest importance in the lower animals for their assimilation of orienting experiences in space and time regarding food, drink, and enemies, and in their preparation for adaptive responses. Dreaming in humans may result from the cortical participation in this primitive system and probably manifests the generalization (what Freud called "condensation") and abstraction (what Freud called "displacement") of the components of day-to-day emotional experience of feelings.

Condensation, like generalization, gives a common meaning to several different items. In reference to feelings, a variety of feelings separated from one another in time can be apprehended together in a symbol that draws on something they all have in common. Condensation, therefore, is not a "law" of the unconscious, but simply the assimilation of new feelings to old, manifesting the generalization that is characteristic of all mental processes. The affective stress must be changed or displaced in this process. Freud, of course, considered the manifest dream to be *always* a disguise. Displacement of affect as a disguise can be considered separately, for it is a common literary device used in the form of irony, pseudo-objectivity, and suggestion, in everyday life or in literature, to cloak an affectionate or hostile feeling. Ella Freeman Sharpe (1951) described other psychoanalytic concepts that have been recognized forms in diction and parody for centuries—simile, metonymy, synecdoche, onomatopoeia, parallels, antitheses, repetition, implied metaphor, and dramatization.

Feelings determine direction in human living by the way in which they indicate, when genuine, what is valuable, important, or interesting to the individual, either within or outside of his awareness. These feelings can function like the sensations of animals as indicators of withdrawal, approach, detour, or highly complex presentations of an emotional position or movement in human relationships.

Piaget, like William James, appreciated this cognitive aspect of feelings. He said, "Interests, pleasures and difficulties, joy and success and disappointment and failure . . . intervene here, as regulations of the action constructed by intelligence" (Piaget, 1951, p. 206).

Many studies have shown that dreaming is paid more attention to and is even facilitated in individuals who place more value on the spectrum of feelings, on the imaginative activity which includes introspection, daydreaming, fantasy, and aesthetic activity (Singer and Schonbar, 1961). Hence, whatever the basis of the physiological necessity of dreaming activity, it remains, besides, an additional resource for those who value the cognitive dimension of feelings for enhancing the quality and extent of their living. Added to this is the cultural facilitation of recall in preliterate societies where the social exchange of dream experiences assumes salience (Eggan, 1949).

Thus, the dream, whatever its *raison d'être*, can comprise a tremendous variety of suggestive sensations and images. It can present a confusing kaleidoscopic panorama of fragmented auditory, tactile, kinesthetic, olfactory, or visual images, each of which represents an emotional feeling of some value; or it can present a coherent, complexly elaborated product that may even take on all the qualities of a work of art. The cognitive aspect of the dream may be clear and simple or mysterious and bewildering.

FORMAL ATTRIBUTES OF THE DREAM MODE

The visual mode predominates for sighted people in dreams as in language and metaphor. Visual imagery is a form of organizing information especially suitable to spatial orientation and guidance. Visual forms are also preferred for fine discrimination, as exemplified by the deviation of a needle pointer on a scale. It is also favored for presenting complex, unfamiliar material, where we frequently use diagrams and illustrations; for material that necessitates relatively simultaneous relational comparisons, such as "before" and "after" pictures; and for material from which a person must make relatively quick selections of information from a much larger supply, as in a table or a graph. It is appropriate, then, that our dreams are predominantly visual for those of us who can see (Geldard, 1960).[1]

In the kaleidoscopic presentations of the dream drama, every person, every object, every element, every quality participates in the affective expressiveness of the totality of the particular event or sequence of dreaming. In this way, the parts of a dream are like the lines in a drawing where each line, each element in the picture, whether it is part of a person or the formation of a cloud or the image of a tree, participates in the total organization of the picture; or as in a poem where the sound, meter, rhythm, as well as the sensations evoked by the words themselves, all make up a single totality of affective experience. Susanne Langer (1953) pointed out that the work of art which corresponds most closely to the process of dreaming in its formal attributes is the cinema, where the individual, seated in a darkened room, forgets himself while participating in all the various roles portrayed on the screen, responding to them and to the scenery and background music as a totality.

> The most noteworthy formal characteristic of a dream is that the dreamer is always at the center of it. Places shift, persons act and speak, or change or fade—facts emerge, situations grow, objects come into view with strange importance, ordinary things infinitely valuable or horrible, and they may be superseded by others that are related to them essentially by feeling, not by natural proximity. But the dreamer is always "there," his relation is, so to speak, equidistant from all events. Things may occur around him or unroll before his eyes; he may act or want to act, or suffer or contemplate; but the *immediacy* of everything in a dream is the same for him.
>
> This aesthetic peculiarity, this relation to things perceived, characterizes the *dream mode:* it is this that the moving picture takes over, and whereby it creates a virtual present. In its relation to the images, actions, events that constitute the story, the camera is in the place of the dreamer (Langer, 1953, p. 413).

This pervasive immediacy and self-enveloping organization by which every element of the dream is related to every other by feeling rather than by natural, scientific, or other kinds of order characterize the dream mode of experience. This is also true to a lesser extent of powerful and original metaphor. In that case an image evoked by words or sounds can correlate

[1] The question of other determinants involved in the choice of the visual mode is further explored in the section Psychophysiological Considerations.

our knowledge and experience in a way that is different from and complementary to the logical mode of correlation. Of course, dream imagery, like metaphorical expressions, can be profoundly resonant and inexhaustible in implication or it may be shallow and trite. A metaphor such as "the bawdy-house of fame" (Preminger, 1965, p. 494) makes an immediate impact which could easily be expanded into a sermon on the vanity as well as the human cost of status-striving. There are many dream sequences that could express a similar feeling.

The dream, then, is a product of mental activity, unwitting and spontaneous. Although the content may be influenced by many factors, the dream product can be studied without reducing it to any particular single influence that participated in determining this content. As in the case of any other mental product, it is a formidable research task even to try to comprise all the determinants. The dream can be studied in terms of what it expresses and how it expresses it, and of the basic elements that make up its phenomenal world, however it is represented or determined.

Piaget (1951) has described the development of intelligence in terms of the formation, refinement, modification, and elaboration of intellectual schemas from infancy throughout childhood to adolescence. Dreaming, like all representation of affect, also shows intellectual forms. There seem to be developmental changes in the phenomenal appearance of dreams, too. A recent study of stories that children have made up spontaneously between the ages of two and five describes findings similar to dreams of the same age group (Pitcher and Prelinger, 1963). Roughly summarized, one might say that the presentation of space is gradually more developed, with greater area of space and more imaginative and abstract space being referred to with increasing age. Also, the characters or persons in the dream become more generalized and more like stereotypes with increasing age—in other words, there is a movement from literal, concrete events in a small, narrow space toward more generalized and representational events in a larger, more diversified space as the small child approaches school age.

Theoretical Problems

"DREAM WORK"—MICROGENESIS

Many workers have contributed to the now well-known fact that considerable information is taken in through man's perceptual apparatus which can be demonstrated in an experimental situation, but is ordinarily not at all available for recall under any circumstances (see the review by Tauber and Green, 1959). Many of the elements that make up spontaneous drawings or that make up the imagery or speech in a dream can be traced back to perceptions that the subjects were knowingly or unwittingly exposed to in the experience of the past few days. These visual elements, as well as verbal elements, undergo transformations and metamorphoses. These transformations and metamorphoses apparently occur outside of awareness about the same time as the actual perceptual experience itself. This is then "played back," so to speak, and further elaborated, or not, in the dreams of the night.

The study of verbal utterances or phonic-like forms in dream states shows that the characteristic experiential and presentational mode of symbol formation and organization prevails even when verbal instead of pictorial forms are used. Werner and Kaplan did a careful analysis of "dream speech" collected by Kraepelin over many years and found that ". . . connotations are still diffuse and interwoven; subjective and objective domains are not sharply distinguished; logical connections are not articulated; vehicles are immersed in affective-sensory-motor states and are typically personal, idiomatic, concrete, and relatively labile in character" (Werner and Kaplan, 1963, p. 244). There is frequently a continuous transformation and metamorphosis of one mode of expression into another—bodily states, postural attitudes, gestures, images change into verbal conceptions and concrete images and vice versa—images quickly express the same notion in verbal form, postural attitude, and bodily states in an almost kaleidoscopic manner. Sometimes it is more ordered and can even be as well organized, we all know, as a theatrical presentation. Freud himself remarked on how well the pictorial and concrete use of many words makes it easy for the dream to represent these words in images, e.g., "superfluous" appearing as an image of water overflowing; "manipulated" appearing as a handshake. The reverse kind of transformation also occurs. Werner and Kaplan (1963) describe the following examples from Kraepelin's collection: the conception "let yourself go" occurred in "dream speech" as "take off the mental shirt collar"; the conception "body and spirit meeting in man" yielded the words "the mushrooms and the angels find each other."

Similar studies, better known, have been made of visual transformations. Fisher (1960) has reviewed much of the current literature. Flavell and Draguns (1957) particularly focused on a historical perspective to *microgenesis* (the sequence of phenomena taking place between the presentation or occurrence of a stimulus and the formation of a stabilized cognitive response). A recent study of tachistoscopic responses including dreams and drawings revealed a much greater variety and individuality than previous studies. The drawings included "visual after-images; tightly drawn images; loosely organized free floating imagery; and blanks. . . . graphic products are not unlike verbal products . . ." (Corman, Escalona, and Reiser, 1964). Almost 90 per cent of the subjects presented elements of the experimental situation in their dreams. The drawings were rich with imagery suggestive of danger, physical threat, and efforts to forestall some unknown disaster. Conflict areas and adaptive coping techniques were clearly evident, apparently triggered by the situation of the experiment. Diagnostic categories of personalities seem to correlate with certain expressive tendencies here as in other projective data. Subjects of a predominantly hysterical personality showed greater variety of forms; greater freedom to use the entire space of the paper in drawing; more frequent alteration in live quality; and subliminal transformations of the perceptual elements. Obsessive-compulsive persons, in contrast, showed constriction and perseveration. They produced repetitive geometic forms which sometimes became representational, a consistent subject content, constricted use of the space available, and a greater tendency to detail. The authors suggest that the altered state of consciousness produced by the experimental situation—lying still in a darkened room exposed to brief flashes of light and instructed by the authority to "draw whatever images you see"—certainly evokes strong feelings which must play some part in the form and content of the imagery produced.

ALTERED CONSCIOUSNESS

This altered state of consciousness is characterized by an absence or marked diminution of the usual waking alertness and attention to the variable requirements of the external world. Janet, Breuer, Freud, and others considered this altered state of consciousness to be one particularly vulnerable to trauma, conflict, illness, fatigue, or other stress, following which the unity of the mind is interrupted and a part of it is dissociated. This was early referred to as the hypnoid state because of its similarity to the state of heightened suggestibility and vulnerability of the hypnotic state. This hypnoid state is normally entered into preliminary to sleep. It is also one in which daydreaming and "mind-wandering" may occur. Because of its inadequacy for critical appraisal and intentional productivity, this state of mind is most likely to experience its content in the presentational and experiential form of symbolization rather than the discursive and referential. This state of mind is deliberately striven for by the shaman who needs to produce a trance, by the priest-doctors of the temple of Aesculapius, by the artist seeking inspiration from within, and by the psychoanalyst who seeks free association from his patient lying on a couch.

The evidence that the laboratory situation enters into so many dreams of subjects, together with the evidence for subthreshold perception presented by Fisher and Paul (1959) and Klein (1959), among others, makes it overwhelmingly clear that the person of the psychoanalyst, together with the entire situation in which the patient encounters him, must at times enter into the dreams of every patient whether overtly or in disguised form. The reverse, no doubt, also holds true. Thus both patient and doctor take in much more of each other than either one is aware of, and this information may be teased out of defensive and counterdefensive operations during their mutual search for truth in the patient's world of experience.

It is apparent from the foregoing that we can no longer approach the problem of dreaming with an exclusively psychological bias or with an oversimplified biological one. The range of our interests has to be extended to include, in addition to the psychological and clinical dimensions, at least two others—the psychophysiological and the social.

Psychophysiological Considerations

Much of this ground has already been covered, and it remains to suggest an over-all hypothesis whereby dreaming becomes integrated into the general adaptive capacities of the organism. We can assume that a physiological mechanism anatomically located in the brain stem enables the organism to reflect periodically on some aspect of its existence and to do this under conditions where the brain, though active, is active in a way that differs from waking consciousness. A number of derivative postulates follow from this general statement.

1. The formal characteristics of the dream have to be understood as a consequence of the altered brain milieu occurring at the time. These formal characteristics include the use of a sensory mode of expression, the sense of immediacy, and the involuntary quality of the dreamer's participation. Under conditions in which there is a relative exclusion of afferent information, cognitive processes move in an autistic and hallucinatory direction. These hallucinatory and autistic processes, whether occurring in states of sensory deprivation or while dreaming, occur because there are, at these times, only two behavioral directions open to the organism. It can seek to overcome the deficit state by achieving a higher state of arousal—one that would establish a waking organism-environment equilibrium; or it can respond in an opposite way by attempting to minimize any arousal impact of the environment. Cognition and behavior are turned about, so to speak, in their relationship to subcortical centers governing arousal and are now in the service of altering an arousal state in one direction or another. In the ordinary course of waking events, a sufficient state of arousal is maintained by everyday sensory stimulation to serve as a necessary precondition for the thought processes guiding activity in the waking state. During sleep, the important thought processes guiding activity do not lead to the actual behavior engaged in by the subject, but become manifest in the periodic alterations in an internal state, the heightened states of arousal characteristic of ascending stage one REM dreaming sleep. Thinking, under such conditions, has the unique qualities that we associate with dreaming; it is thinking in a sensory mode.

2. The possibility of manipulating through the products of an activated cortical state the unstable equilibrium existing during the REM state (unstable in the sense that it can be terminated by strong emotions generated in the dream or by an aversive signal) suggests that the organism

learns how to use this state in the service of vigilance needs. Vigilance is here used in its symbolic reference to possible threats or interference with the value systems of the organism rather than in its reference to any physical threat to bodily integrity. Reticular activation is responsive to sensory stimulation, as the now classic studies of Magoun (1952) have shown. Dell (1958) has proposed reintroducing the term vigilance to refer to the nonspecific changes in the arousal system in response to internal and external stimulation. He uses it in the sense that Head (1926) does, with no reference whatsoever to conscious experience. The nonspecific arousal state is one of vigilance and affords a basic mechanism for the translation of a bodily need into behavior. Heightened levels of activity and specificity in the sensory and motor fields that characterize vigilance operations in the waking state are replaced by heightened cortical activation during the dreaming state.

3. In line with this hypothesis, the train of events presumably occurring at the time cortical activation occurs in the REM state would begin with an affective residue of the day's experience, translated into a visual metaphor. This would undergo further development as the vigilance needs impelled a longitudinal exploration of the significant connections of the present theme to past periods of life and a horizontal exploration to test its impact on current growth potential and defensive operations. Current feelings reappearing in the dream mode evoke orienting responses, forcing on the organism a reshuffling of value systems to assimilate the intrusive affects. A new equilibrium is arrived at reflecting either positive growth or an effort at maintaining the status quo.

Since alterations in the arousal system come about involuntarily, and since this system is responsive to stimuli along a spectrum of sensory intensity, it follows that the quality of thinking evoked under these circumstances would have certain specific characteristics:

1. It would more appropriately occur in a sensory rather than a discursive mode.

2. Its behavioral effect would be a central one (influence on arousal level) rather than an external one (motor adjustment).

3. The way in which this mode of thinking is experienced would reflect the involuntary and unconscious purposes toward which it is being deployed.

4. Although the whole range of an individual's past experience may be potentially available for use in this manner, the actual material that comes into focus tends to be limited and derivative of a recent event. Such an event may have been tangential to the waking purposes of the individual, but nevertheless touches on less understood and therefore less mastered but yet significant aspects of one's life experience.

5. The essentially involuntary quality of this sensory level of thinking

establishes it as an instrument for the conscious reflection of derivatives of past experience in their unmastered and involuntary aspects.

6. Once a life situation is grasped and portrayed in this way, the subsequent development is itself determined by the dynamic quality of the resultant images. Each image is, in a sense, an emotional vector; and the principles governing their interaction and final outcome might be referred to as the principles of dynamic visual metaphor, and probably conform to similar principles in the aesthetics of architecture, painting, and poetry.

Sociocultural Considerations

Field workers in anthropology have interested themselves in dreams from the point of view of the role dreams play in a particular culture, the light they shed on the customs and traditional beliefs, their connection with the prevailing myths, and their role in cultural continuity. Since dreams are dreamed by particular individuals in a culture, the question arises as to how and in what manner the unsolved problems of the particular individual are related to the unsolved problems that characterize the particular cultural setting. In any given culture there are problems and limitations to human development that are linked to currently inappropriate or inadequate institutions or mythic beliefs in the historical development of that culture. Individuals within the culture may be totally or partially unaware of the inappropriateness or inadequacy of these beliefs and institutions for the problems and limitations they encounter. Dreams have been useful to anthropologists and other behavioral scientists concerned with these institutions and myths.

Dreams of preliterate peoples reflect fragments of the prevailing mythology in a manner that is readily detectable to an outside observer. However they may be manipulated by the individual dreamer, the fact remains that the myth exists as an entity apart from himself, and one that is consciously or unconsciously assumed as real. These socially sanctioned foci of belief come to life in the dream as sources of support or as sources of anxiety, depending on the underlying nature of the immediate conflict. Historically, we may delineate three evolutionary stages in this approach to the study of the interrelationship of dream and myth. The first stage saw the introduction of speculative hypotheses on the connection between myth and dream by nineteenth-century philosophers such as Comte and Hartmann, by psychoanalytic writers starting with Freud (Freud and Oppenheim, 1911), and further developed by Abraham (1909) and others. The second stage witnessed the emergence of ambidextrous scholars such as Rivers (1923), earlier, and Roheim (1952), Devereux (1957), and others, more recently, who were knowledgeable in both psychoanalysis and anthropology and who sought and found confirmatory evidence in their field studies, of classical psychoanalytic tenets. Current trends, characterizing stage three, reflect a radically different approach to the problem shown by an emphasis on manifest content and by the introduction of quantitative measures in the assessment of dreams and culture. The approach has become more open and exploratory and less concerned with the validation of a priori psychoanalytic concepts (cf. S. G. Lee, 1958, on social influences in Zulu dreaming; the studies of Yir Yoront dreams by David M. Schneider and R. Lauristan Sharp; the study of the Caribbean by E. A. Weinstein, 1962; and the study of dreams from Hopi informants by Dorothy Eggan, 1949, 1952, and 1961). Eggan provides many clear examples both of the general cultural referents of the dream and the specific dynamic interaction between manifest content and the Hopi myth and folklore. On the question of the general cultural referents of the dream Eggan writes (1961, p. 552): "The answer to the question of whether dreams can be used cross-culturally lies in part in the degree to which dreams can be considered both a projection of the personality and the reflection of the culture. On these points there is much affirmative evidence, both experimental and ethnographic."

Bourguignon (1954, p. 268), in a study of Haitian dreams, comes to somewhat similar conclusions: "Dreams furthermore act as channels for the development of idiosyncratic modes of worship and lend support to whatever mythology exists, which itself is largely based on anecdotal material about the gods. This mythological material, in turn, furnishes the basis for dream interpretation and for the manner in which dreams are experienced."

When we come to explore the relationship of myth and dreaming within the framework of our own existence, there are points of similarity and difference to the situation prevailing in primitive cultures. It is the same insofar as myths exist and gain expression in the content of dreaming. It is different in that, in contrast to the relative ease with which myth can be discerned in primitive society, the discovery of myth in our own milieu involves the effort of taking a look at our own insides—a feat even more difficult for a society than for an individual. Sapir (1929), Kluckhohn and Murray (1953), Opler (1956), and others have called attention to the cultural patterning that plays so large a part in our lives. We are subjected to this cultural patterning before we are aware either that it is occurring, or aware of anything about the nature of the patterning. As humans, we find ourselves in the self-conscious and often difficult position of having to take a second look at a rather fragile and vulnerable product which is not by any means completely of our own making. The overt difficulties, the symptomatology of illness at a manifest social level, are receiving more and more attention. The covert influences remain to be uncovered and understood in their influence on the individual.

Although psychoanalytic writings shed light on the mechanism of unconscious processes—namely, how the individual copes with forces influencing his behavior and which are not understood by him—there is a great deal of confusion, disagreement, and ignorance about the source and nature of these unconscious factors. It is in relation to this problem that concern with social myth assumes importance. Here we have a reservoir for what is collectively unknown or unconscious, and one that in some manner articulates with what is personally unknown or unconscious.

With regard to the dream, our main emphasis as therapists has always been on the characterologic and personal conflictual referents of the symbols. Each dream element, however, expresses not only the personal and subjective, but also a historical and social referent which actually exists or did exist. When a woman dreams of a reference to her own sexual organs as a head of lettuce (Ullman, 1960) encased in the empty shell of a cantaloupe situated on the shelf of a supermarket, she is saying something about her own personal sexual problems and at the same time making a statement about an aspect of social life. The personal referents arouse our interest. The social referents are generally not pursued to any great degree.

The personal referents may be analyzed in relation to the following variables: involvement occurs in a situation of incipient sexual activity, apart from her own will and intent, and at the instigation of her husband; affective concomitants of irritation, compulsion, guilt, and constraint; and resolution through pseudo-acquiescence and preparatory sexual activity involving the use of a diaphragm. Here we see the disunity between behavior, affect, and symbolic expression.

The important point, however, is that, although the factors predisposing this individual to this disunified reaction are imbedded in her own genetic development, they can emerge only in the presence of existing social referents that can be used or misused for the purpose of rationalization. These social referents are:

1. We live in a society where the capacities of individuals are sometimes treated as objects divorced from the person: labor, brains, beauty, talent, sex.

2. These separated capacities are bought and sold.

3. The exchange value and laws of the marketplace tend to automatize and impersonalize the transaction.

4. There exists in the nature of the external referent a detachment or separation of the individual from the commodity he needs or uses. His real relation to the commodity is obscured and his relationship to it is determined by its manifest elements—the object exists as something apart from himself which may or may not be purchased.

These external or social referents reflect significant aspects of the social structure. They assume importance when one considers that insight is not knowledge alone, but knowledge combined with the ability to change behavior. A new equilibrium through insight cannot be achieved unless and until it can be experienced in activity.

It is, of course, a relatively easier task to expose a neurotic mechanism than to change it. The difficulty of effecting the change, the working through, the struggle against resistance, is one that involves not only the exploration of how these mechanisms articulate with other dynamic aspects of the personality, but, of equal and perhaps greater importance, how this trend "pays off"—that is, the pragmatic value created by the sociopathologic environment bathing and nurturing the trend. The individual is pulled back not only by the weight of his own past experience, but also by the external reinforcement that is ever on hand in the surrounding social milieu.

The view presented differs essentially from the classical Freudian position insofar as it considers the source of unconscious motivating influences as linked to specific experiences in a given social and cultural milieu and not as originating in the biological nature of man, or as due to man's inherent vulnerability because of his extreme dependence on symbolic processes. Furthermore, it assumes no a priori identification of unconscious processes as intrinsically or potentially troublesome. This point of view is in line with Fromm's[2] notion of a social unconscious, one that is something currently re-created for each individual as he participates in the cultural matrix long before there is any clear registration in awareness of the nature of the acculturating process. It is essentially a unitary view of man's nature and predicated on the view that where pathology exists in the psychic sphere, as well as in the physical sphere, our first task is to gain an accurate knowledge of the exact nature of the noxious agents at work. When functional alterations in consciousness occur, as in states of dreaming, the key to their understanding lies not in such dualistic concepts as the return of the repressed and the corollary concepts of wish fulfillment and disguise, but in the basic notion that an individual is struggling to express under conditions of altered brain function the totality of factors, some known, some unknown, governing his reactions to a specific life experience. While dreaming, no less than while awake, we are dealing with the same unitary structure, capable of the same logical incisiveness, but functioning under different conditions of afferent input, internal organization, and behavioral effect. We are dealing not with a fragmentation or compartmentalization of the psyche, but rather with the relative dominance of a concrete and experiential mode of expression over an abstract and referential mode.

However, there is much of Freud's contribution that still stands; for

[2] We may note an interesting point of contrast between Freud and Fromm. In the case of the former, appearance was taken for essence in his interpretation of the social scene and in his use of it in the development of a psychological system. For Fromm, the appearance provided clues to what was socially unknown but not unknowable, a point of view which ultimately led to his concept of the social unconscious.

example, day-residue dreams, especially those in the early part of the night, contain much material from the previous day or two which, at the same time, express deeper feelings of a more problematic nature that the dreamer is not aware of in his daily waking life. Unresolved feelings linked to memories of early childhood are expressed in dreams, but they occur toward the later part of sleep. Spoken words in dreams are *sometimes* repetitions of actual spoken words from waking life. Freud's insight into the defensive aspect of minimizing and forgetting dreams holds true, although most failure of dream recall can no longer be ascribed to repression. Affects in dreams are much less altered or distorted than ideational material, as Freud noted. Also, Freud emphasized the fact that throughout sleep we know we are dreaming and can exercise our preconscious wishes to observe and enjoy our dreams, or to wake up for some particular condition. However, there is no convincing evidence that dreaming protects sleep from interruption, even REM sleep. Nor is there any evidence that infantile sexual wishes are a necessary, if not sufficient, condition for dreaming to take place.

The Art of Dream Interpretation

What the therapist does with a reported dream usually reflects the style with which he treats any other reported experience that the patient brings. In the classical psychoanalytic style he would wait for the patient's free association to the elements of the dream and ask questions or direct his verbal reports to the end of having the patient "discover" his infantile sexuality and aggression, and eventually his castration anxiety, primal scene, Oedipal complex, and so on. Needless to say, the literature reveals that the Jungian analyst, the Adlerian analyst, and other disciples of various psychoanalytic theories will respond in such a way as to elicit from the patient the material that will, in the course of time, be more and more expressed in the language and terms of their theory since that is the frame of reference with which the analyst himself is ordering his own experience. However, as Clara Thompson (1950) showed, nearly all the well-known psychoanalytic theories have a valuable contribution to make and need not be mutually exclusive. In fact, there is much to be gained from appreciating the contribution that each makes to the understanding of human behavior and mental illness, and it remains for current workers to see in what context and under what circumstances each contribution has its special values and limitations.

Nonetheless, it is important to have at least a heuristic framework within which a therapist can order his responses to the patient's dreams. It seems useful within the clinical setting to order the communication of dreams and other transactions to four main categories: educational or problem-solving; emergency-coping; comfort-seeking; and simply or playfully expressive and sharing for its own sake. In regard to the last-mentioned category, it is interesting to note that the word "dream" is an Anglo-Saxon noun having a primary meaning in Old English of "melody, joy, or gladness." The Swedish form "dröm" has a direct subassumption of idleness and vacuity. In old Frisian, "drām" also means "(shout of) joy."

Most of the dreaming reported by patients and published in psychoanalytic literature before and after Freud, including contributions of the neo-Freudian, have to do primarily with the problematic aspect of human relationships. This, then, is the first task of the therapist in the beginning of his treatment of any patient: that is, to use the reported dreams, his observations of the patient, his personal response to the patient, and all the usual clinical information to try, at least, to arrive at a tentative formulation of the most significant problems that life has been proposing for this patient and the choices and attempted solutions that the patient has made in the face of these problems.

As Freud observed, and many others have confirmed, the first dream or first few dreams that the patient reports more clearly express his significant interpersonal difficulties than most dreams that are reported later in treatment. However, although the patient may communicate more to the therapist at this point, via his dreams, than in other aspects of his communication, he is frequently much less receptive at this time to interpretations of this material. Without entering into the controversial problem of the timing of interpretations, it can be simply stated that the therapist endeavors to gauge the patient's receptivity and to order his own style of presentation to what the patient can most usefully receive. As one does not speak intimately to strangers (although in some circles it now seems fashionable to describe one's sexual and analytic intimacies at cocktail parties and discotheques), so the analyst must speak within the limits of the patient-therapist relationship as it exists at that point in its development. In some cases there is an early and deep rapport; in others, the therapist must work over a long period of time to develop such a rapport. In America, particularly, this endeavor may be complicated by the widespread habit of pseudo-intimacy wherein the patient and analyst may collaborate in a type of language and gestural display that tokens intimacy without actually contributing to it.

Bonime (1962) has pointed out how the dialogue between the analyst and patient concerned with interpreting a dream can become a kind of subtle clever filibuster that goes on and on without paying attention to the task at hand. Of course, these kinds of resistance also occur in the transactions between analyst and patient that do not involve dreams, but it is still useful to look at them again, including the well-known dodge of changing the subject immediately after an interpretation is made. Cynicism, of course, is a time-worn defense against responsibility; and so is the indistinct blurring of communication so that the patient's sentence that seems to have started out being meaningful ends up in a vague, drifting note with the implicit implication that the analyst is supposed to know exactly what it means. Then, of course, there are all the devices described by Stephen Potter, in the "one-upmanship" type of evasion, in trying to score on the analyst by being "one up" in one way or another. Another type of resistance that also applies to dream analysis is the intense dedication that the patient expresses, wittingly or unwittingly, to his "sick self." And, of course, there is the frequent use of the device of overwhelming the analyst with the abundance of dreams and their minute detail, or trying to sidetrack the whole focus by inappropriate documentation. Then, there is the very common escape into a preoccupation with theoretical dynamics or, even more blatantly, the verbal jargon of psychoanalysis. The more naïve patient with a less sophisticated repertoire may simply avoid the issues by an overenthusiastic acceptance that undoes the whole communication at the same time that he appears to be cooperating so eagerly. Artificial exaggeration of feelings, helplessness, and the "flight into health" are also familiar ways of dodging.

The analyst can avoid many of these resistances by taking pains to avoid certain familiar pitfalls himself. He must avoid a mutual obsessional preoccupation with trivial and irrelevant material, thus unwittingly collaborating with the resistance of the patient. He should not practice a detached avoidance of emotional engagement with the patient. He should not neglect the patient's genuine, though futile, efforts to make sense while floundering about. The analyst must actively intervene when he sees the patient is genuinely floundering and give him some information that will help him get his bearings.

Transference, one of Freud's most important discoveries, must be considered in this context. The analyst must be careful not to *arbitrarily* assign himself to all the transference problems that the patient experiences or to the various roles that authority figures and others play in the patient's dreams. As a rule of thumb, patients from the well-to-do middle classes tend to see the analyst more often symbolized by a member of the service professions than by a frightening authority figure. For example, the figure representing the analyst that frequently occurs in dreams is the train conductor, the bus driver, the taxi driver, the barber, the doorman, the headwaiter, or the beautician. Finally, it is important to state that working with dreams can be genuinely frustrating and difficult for both patient and analyst without being a reflection on the sincerity and dedication of either partner to the therapeutic enterprise. It is a mistake to misinterpret every difficulty and frustration in the course of analytic work as a conscious or unconscious "resistance" to analysis.

Although the dream is a created product by the dreamer and reflects the dreamer's personality, culture, language, and current style as much as any other product that he might create, the dream does not especially lend itself to the purpose of creating a work of art for the community to which the patient belongs. By the very privacy of the dreaming process and its exclusion from the waking life of historical continuity and communality, the activity of dreaming is handicapped for such creative production. Poems and scientific discoveries arising in dreams (Coleridge, Kekule, Poincaré, and others) are a testimony to the enormous creative power of the dreamers rather than a manifestation of a special capacity for dreaming to do this kind of creating. There may, however, be some individuals who dare to show more of their creative capacities during their sleeping life in dreams than they can show or exhibit in their waking life. But this is merely another example that the dream reveals more of the dreamer, sometimes, than any other expressions he can make in waking life. Nevertheless, it is very unusual among artists, writers, musicians, and philosophers to produce any significant work in their dreams.

As for the clinical use of dreams in the treatment of infants, children, juveniles, and adolescents, this varies according to developmental level. With very young children from two to five, reported dreams have much more to do with the immediate problems they are coping with in everyday life. Also, in the very early years dreams are not distinguished from waking life. A three-year-old once reported an experience that happened during the night involving her parents and her five-year-old sister, and she was quite annoyed and stubbornly insisted that they had participated in this experience with her, when they said they knew nothing about it and told her that she had been dreaming. In this way she learned what the word "dreaming" meant. Children's play at this age with their dolls and other toys is much more revealing of the interpersonal transactions of the family life in which they participate than their dreams. This may be true because of the limitations of their verbal conceptualization and formulation for communication. For example, a two-and-a-half-year-old little girl reported dreams of riding in a bus, playing in a playground, and other samples of everyday waking activity that she was currently enthusiastic about. However, in her doll play, with very few words, she showed the mother doll taking the pants off the father doll and putting them on herself; and in another scene showed the mother doll trying to flush herself down the toilet. From four to five, children tend to dream more of animals in a way that represents aspects of human beings, just as the animals do in the animal stories that are read to children, and the cartoons that are shown to children, and in the children's lore over the years. There are the good animals and the bad animals, and the stingy animals and the generous animals, and the timid animals and the brave animals, and so on. From five to seven, according to the Ames study in New Haven (1964), most children experience a great increase in the frequency of nightmares with many dreams of being chased by bad animals or bad people; activity with fire, water, and earth; fighting and punishment dreams; and they are beginning to examine the differences and similarities between the dreams they have during sleep and the fantasies of their waking imagination.

Like any other transaction there are many levels to the communication and interpretation of a dream. It is difficult to make clear outside the clinical context why one interpretation is preferred to another at any particular time. This becomes more clear in the sequential dream analysis reported by authors such as French, Offenkrantz, and Rechtschaffen (1963).

Considering the complex intricacy of this experience and all of the richness inherent in it at any given moment, it is remarkable and puzzling that our imagery is actually successful in evoking similar feelings in other persons. But it is only puzzling when one is confused by the myth of the isolated, gloriously unique individual. Man is not creative out of his separation from nature and other persons; that is the path to insanity and sterility. Man is creative out of his vital participation in nature and the lives of others. "Interpersonal" refers to an existential aspect of man, not a mere social qualification. When we see people participating in the same reality, then it is not puzzling that their unique personal experience of a poem or a dream is both in agreement with and different from that of others. It is at this point that the movement of the creative process from its subliminal depths of unnoticed participation, and from the private revery of sleep, has achieved its fullness in the shared interpersonal experience" (Green, 1961a, pp. 726–740).

References

Abraham, K. *Dreams and Myths* (1909). New York: Nervous and Mental Diseases Publishing Company, 1913.

Alexander, F. *Selected Papers of . . .* Vol. I. *The Scope of Psychoanalysis, 1921–1961.* New York: Basic Books, 1962. Pp. 246–257.

Alexander, F., and Wilson, G. "Quantitative Dream Studies." *Psychoanalytic Quarterly,* 4 (1935), 371–407.

Amacher, P. "Freud's Neurological Education and Its Influence on Psychoanalytic Theory." *Psychological Issues,* 4, No. 4 (1965), 9–84.

Amadeo, M., and Shagass, C. "Eye Movements, Attention and Hypnosis." *Journal of Nervous and Mental Diseases,* 136 (1963), 139–345.

Ames, Louise B. "Sleep and Dreams in Childhood." In E. Harms (ed.), *Problems of Sleep and Dream in Children.* New York: Macmillan, 1964. Pp. 6–29.

Antrobus, Judith S., Antrobus, J., and Fisher, C. "Discriminative Responses to Dreaming and Nondreaming during Different Stages of Sleep." Symposium: Research on Dreams, Clinical and Theoretical Implications, Postgraduate Center for Mental Health, March 1964, New York.

Aserinsky, E. "Periodic Respiratory Pattern Occurring in Conjunction with Eye Movements during Sleep." *Science*, 150, No. 369 (November 1965), 763–766.

Aserinsky, E., and Kleitman, N. "Regularly Occurring Periods of Eye Motility and Concomitant Phenomena during Sleep." *Science*, 118 (1953), 273–274.

Baldridge, B. J., Whitman, R. M., and Kramer, M. "The Concurrence of Fine Muscle Activity and Rapid Eye Movement during Sleep." *Psychosomatic Medicine*, 27, No. 1 (January–February 1965), 19–26.

Berger, R. J. "Experimental Modification of Dream Content by Meaningful Verbal Stimuli." *British Journal of Psychiatry*, 109 (1963), 722–740.

Berlyne, D. E. "Motivational Problems Raised by Exploratory and Epistemic Behavior." In S. Koch (ed.), *Psychology: A Study of a Science*. New York: McGraw-Hill, 1963.

Bolgar, H. "Consistency of Affect and Symbolic Expressions: A Comparison between Dreams and Rorschach Responses." *American Journal of Orthopsychiatry*, 24 (1954), 538–545.

Bonime, W. *The Clinical Use of Dreams*. New York: Basic Books, 1962.

Boss, M. *The Analysis of Dreams*. New York: Philosophical Library, 1958.

Bourguignon, E. E. "Dreams and Dream Interpretation in Haiti." *American Anthropologist*, 56, No. 2 (1954), 262–268.

Broadbent, D. E. "Information Processing in the Nervous System." *Science*, 150, No. 3695 (October 1965), 457–462.

Corman, H., Escalona, Sibylle K., and Reiser, M. F. "Visual Imagery and Preconscious Thought Processes." *American Medical Association Archives of General Psychiatry*, 10, No. 2 (1964), 160–172.

Dell, P. C. "Some Basic Mechanisms of the Translation of Bodily Needs into Behavior." In G. E. W. Wolstenholme and C. M. O'Connor (eds.), *The Neurological Basis of Behavior*. Boston: Little, Brown, 1958.

DeMartino, M. "Some Characteristics of the Manifest Dream Content of Mental Defectives." *Journal of Clinical Psychology*, 10, No. 2 (April 1954), 175–178.

Dement, W. C. *The Studies of the Experimental Subject*. New York: Association for the Psychophysiological Study of Sleep, 1963. (a)

Dement, W. C. "Studies on the Function of Rapid Eye Movement (Paradoxical) Sleep in Human Subjects." *Colloques Internationaux du Centre National de la Recherche Scientifique*, 127 (1963), 571–608. (b)

Dement, W. C. "Experimental Dream Studies." In J. H. Masserman (ed.), *Science and Psychoanalysis*. Vol. 7. New York: Grune & Stratton, 1964. Pp. 129–161.

Dement, W. C. "Recent Studies on the Biological Role of Rapid Eye Movement Sleep." *American Journal of Psychiatry*, 122, No. 4 (October 1965), 404–408.

Dement, W. C., and Wolpert, E. A. "The Relationship of Eye Movement, Body Motility, and External Stimuli to Dream Content." *Journal of Experimental Psychology*, 55 (1958), 543–553.

Devereux, G. "Dreaming, Learning and Individual Ritual Differences in Mohave Shamanism." *American Anthropologist,* 59, No. 6 (1957), 1036–1045.

Dodds, E. R. *The Greeks and the Irrational.* Boston: Beacon Press, 1957.

Domino, E. F., and Yamamoto, K. "Nicotine: Effect on the Sleep Cycle of the Cat." *Science,* 150, No. 3696 (October 1965), 637–638.

Duane, T. D., and Behrendt, T. "Extrasensory Electroencephalographic Induction between Identical Twins." *Science,* 150, No. 3694 (October 1965), 367.

Eggan, Dorothy. "The Significance of Dreams for Anthropological Research." *American Anthropologist,* 51, No. 2 (1949), 177–198.

Eggan, Dorothy. "The Manifest Content of Dreams: A Challenge to Social Science." *American Anthropologist,* 54, No. 4 (1952), 469–485.

Eggan, Dorothy. "The Personal Use of Myth in Dreams." In T. Sebeok (ed.), *Myth: A Symposium.* Philadelphia: American Folklore Society, 1955. Pp. 67–75.

Eggan, Dorothy. "Dream Analysis." In B. Kaplan (ed.), *Studying Personality Cross-Culturally.* Evanston, Ill.: Row, Peterson, 1961. Pp. 551–577.

Erikson, E. H. "The Dream Specimen of Psychoanalysis." *Journal of the American Psychoanalytic Association,* 2, No. 1 (1954), 5–56.

Erikson, E. H. *Insight and Responsibility.* New York: Norton, 1964.

Evans, F. J., Gustafson, L. A., O'Connell, D. N., Orne, M. T., and Shor, R. E., "Response during Sleep with Intervening Waking Amnesia." *Science,* 152 (1966), 666–667.

Ferenczi, S. "On the Revision of the Interpretation of Dreams" (1931). In *Selected Papers of. . . .* Vol. III. *Final Contributions to the Problems and Methods of Psycho-analysis.* New York: Basic Books, 1955. Pp. 238–243.

Fisher, C. "Preconscious Stimulation in Dreams, Associations and Images: Introduction." *Psychological Issues,* 2 (March 7, 1960), 1–41.

Fisher, C. "Psychoanalytic Implications of Recent Research on Sleep and Dreaming." *Journal of the American Psychoanalytic Association,* 13, No. 2 (1965), 197–303.

Fisher, C., and Paul, I. H. "The Effect of Subliminal Visual Stimulation on Images and Dreams: A Validation Study." *Journal of the American Psychoanalytic Association,* 7, No. 1 (1959), 35–83.

Flavell, J. H., and Draguns, J. "Microgenetic Approach to Perception and Thought." *Psychological Bulletin,* 54 (1957), 197–217.

French, T., and Fromm, E. *Dream Interpretation.* New York: Basic Books, 1964.

French, T., Offenkrantz, W., and Rechtschaffen, A. "Clinical Studies of Sequential Dreams." *American Medical Association Archives of General Psychiatry,* 8 (1963), 497–508.

Freud, S. "The Interpretation of Dreams" (1899). *The Standard Edition of the Complete Psychological Works of. . . .* London: Hogarth Press. Vol. 4, pp. 1–621, Vol. 5, pp. 687–751. (Also published as *The Interpretation of Dreams.* New York: Basic Books, 1955.)

Freud, S. *The Origins of Psychoanalysis: Letters to Wilhelm Fliess, Drafts and Notes, 1887–1902*. New York: Basic Books, 1954.

Freud, S., and Oppenheim, D. E. "Dreams in Folklore" (1911). *The Standard Edition of the Complete Psychological Works of. . . .* London: Hogarth Press. Vol. 12, pp. 180–203.

Freud, S. "Some Additional Notes upon Dream Interpretation as a Whole" (1925). *The Standard Edition of the Complete Psychological Works of. . . .* London: Hogarth Press. Vol. 19. (Also in *Collected Papers of. . . .* New York: Basic Books, 1959. Vol. 5, pp. 150–162.)

Freud, S. "New Introductory Lectures on Psychoanalysis" (1932). *The Standard Edition of the Complete Psychological Works of. . . .* London: Hogarth Press. Vol. 22.

Fromm, E. *The Forgotten Language*. New York: Rinehart, 1951.

Gaarder, K. "A Conceptual Model of Sleep." *American Medical Association Archives of General Psychiatry*, 14, No. 3 (1966), 253–260.

Geldard, F. A. "Some Neglected Possibilities of Communication." *Science*, 131, No. 3413 (1960), 1583.

Goodenough, D. R., Lewis, Helen B., Shapiro, A., Jaret, L., and Sleser, I. "Dream Reporting Following Abrupt and Gradual Awakenings from Different Types of Sleep." *Journal of Personality and Social Psychology*, 2 (1965), 170–179.

Gordon, H. L. "A Comparative Study of Dreams and Responses to the Thematic Apperception Test." *Journal of Personality*, 22 (1953), 234–253.

Green, M. R. "Prelogical Experience and Participant Communication." *Psychiatric Quarterly*, 35 (October 1961), 726–740. (a)

Green, M. R. "Prelogical Experience in the Thinking Process." *Journal of Issues in Art Education*, 3, No. 1 (1961), 66–78. (b)

Grinker, R. R., Sr. "Conceptual Progress in Psychoanalysis." In J. Marmor (ed.), *Modern Psychoanalysis*. New York: Basic Books, 1968. Pp. 19–43.

Gross, J., Byrne, J., and Fisher, C. "Eye Movements during Emergent Stage One EEG in Subjects with Lifelong Blindness." *Journal of Nervous and Mental Diseases*, 141, No. 3 (1965), 365–370.

Hartmann, E. L. "The D-state: A Review and Discussion of Studies on the Physiologic State Concomitant with Dreaming." *International Journal of Psychiatry*, 2, No. 1 (1966), 11–49.

Hartmann, H. *Essays on Ego Psychology*. New York: International Universities Press, 1964.

Head, H. *Aphasia and Kindred Disorders of Speech*. New York: Cambridge University Press, 1926. Vol. 1.

Hernández-Peón, R. "A Cholinergic Hypnogenic Limbic Forebrain-Hindbrain Circuit." *Colloques Internationaux du Centre Nationale de la Recherche Scientifique*, 127 (1963), 63–84.

Hobson, A. J. "Some Electrographic Correlates of Behavior in the Frog with Reference to Sleep." *Electroencephalography and Clinical Neurophysiology*, 1967.

Hodes, R., and Suzuki, J. I. "Comparative Thresholds of Cortex, Vestibular System and Reticular Formation in Wakefulness, Sleep and Rapid Eye

Movement Periods." *Electroencephalography and Clinical Neurophysiology,* 18 (1965), 239–248.

Horney, Karen. *Neurosis and Human Growth.* New York: Norton, 1950.

James, W. *Principles of Psychology.* New York: Dover, 1918. Vol. 2.

Jones, R. M. *Ego Synthesis in Dreams.* Cambridge: Schenkman, 1962.

Jouvet, M. F. Michel. "Bruxism in Cats." Spoken report, Association for Psychophysiological Study of Sleep Meeting, March 1966, Gainesville, Florida.

Jouvet, M. F. Michel, and Courjois, J. "Sur un Stade d'Activité Electrique Cerebral Rapide au cours du Sommeil Physiologique." *Comptes Rendus des Séances de la Societé de Biologie et de Ses Filiales,* 153 (1959), 1024–1028.

Jung, C., von Franz, M., Henderson, J., Jacobi, J., and Jaffé, A. *Man and His Symbols.* New York: Doubleday, 1964.

Kahn, E., Dement, W., Fisher, C., and Barmack, J. "Incidence of Color in Immediately Recalled Dreams." *Science,* 137 (1962), 1054–1055.

Kamiya, J. "Behavioral, Subjective and Physiological Aspects of Sleep and Drowsiness." In D. W. Fiske and S. R. Maddi (eds.), *Functions of Varied Experience.* Homewood, Ill.: Dorsey, 1961. Pp. 145–174.

Karacan, I. "The Effect of Exciting Presleep Events on Dream Reporting and Penile Erections during Sleep." Unpublished M.S.D. dissertation, May 1965. Downstate Medical Center, State University of New York, Brooklyn.

Kawamura, H., and Sawyer, C. H. "Elevation in Brain Temperature during Paradoxical Sleep." *Science,* 150, No. 3698 (November 1965), 912.

Klein, G. S. "Consciousness in Psychoanalytic Theory." *Journal of the American Psychoanalytic Association,* 7, No. 1 (1959), 5–34.

Kleitman, N. *Sleep and Wakefulness.* Chicago: University of Chicago Press, 1963.

Kluckhohn, C., and Murray, H. A. *Personality in Nature, Society and Culture.* New York: Knopf, 1953.

Kramer, M. "Dream Collection." *Frontiers of Clinical Psychiatry* (Roche Report), 2, No. 22 (November 15, 1965), 5 ff.

Kramer, M., Whitman, R. M., Baldridge, B., and Lansky, L. "Depression: Dreams and Defenses." *American Journal of Psychiatry,* 122, No. 4 (October 1965), 411–417.

Langer, Susanne K. *Feeling and Form.* New York: Scribner's, 1953.

Lee, S. G. "Social Influences in Zulu Dreaming." *Journal of Social Psychology,* 47 (1958), 265–283.

Magoun, H. W. "An Ascending Reticular Activating System in the Brain Stem." *American Medical Association Archives of Neurology and Psychiatry,* 67 (1952), 145–154.

Mandell, A. J., and Mandell, Mary P. "Biochemical Aspects of Rapid Eye Movement Sleep." *American Journal of Psychiatry,* 122, No. 4 (October 1965), 391–401.

Markowitz, M., and Seiderman, S. "An Investigation of Parental Recognition of Children's Dreams, Preliminary Report." In J. H. Masserman (ed.), *Science and Psychoanalysis.* 9 vols.; New York: Grune & Stratton, 1963. Vol. 6.

Miller, M. "A Psychological Study of a Case of Eczema and a Case of Neurodermatitis." In F. Alexander and T. French (eds.), *Studies in Psychosomatic Medicine*. New York: Ronald Press, 1948. Pp. 401–421.

Onheiber, P., White, P. T., De Myer, M. K., and Ottinger, D. R. "Sleep and Dream Patterns of Child Schizophrenics." *American Medical Association Archives of General Psychiatry*, 12, No. 6 (1965), 568–571.

Opler, M. K. "Cultural Anthropology and Social Psychiatry." *American Journal of Psychiatry*, 113, No. 4 (1956), 302–311.

Ornitz, E. M., Ritvo, E. R., and Walter, R. D. "Dreaming Sleep in Autistic and Schizophrenic Children." *American Journal of Psychiatry*, 122, No. 4 (1965), 419–424.

Piaget, J. *Play, Dreams and Imitation in Childhood*. New York: Norton, 1951.

Pierce, C. M., Mathis, J. L., and Jabbour, J. T. "Dream Patterns in Narcoleptic and Hydraencephalic Patients." *American Journal of Psychiatry*, 122, No. 4 (October 1965), 402–404.

Pitcher, Evelyn G., and Prelinger, E. *Children Tell Stories*. New York: International Universities Press, 1963.

Preminger, A. *Encyclopedia of Poetry and Poetics*. Princeton, N.J.: Princeton University Press, 1965.

Rado, S. *Collected Papers of*. . . . New York: Grune & Stratton, 1956.

Rank, O. *Art and Artist*. New York: Knopf, 1932. Pp. 119, 120, 310.

Rechtschaffen, A. "Discussion of: W. Dement, Part III, Research Studies: Dreams and Communication." In J. H. Masserman (ed.), *Science and Psychoanalysis*. Vol. 7. New York: Grune & Stratton, 1964.

Rechtschaffen, A., Goodenough, D. R., and Shapiro, A. "Patterns of Sleep Talking." *American Medical Association Archives of General Psychiatry*, 7, No. 6 (1962), 418–426.

Rechtschaffen, A., Vogel, G., and Shaikun, G. "Interrelatedness of Mental Activity during Sleep." *American Medical Association Archives of General Psychiatry*, 9, No. 6 (December 1963), 536–547.

Reding, G., Rubright, W., Rechtschaffen, A., and Daniels, R. S. "Sleep Pattern of Tooth-grinding: Its Relationship to Dreaming." *Science*, 145, No. 3633 (August 14, 1964), 725–726.

Rivers, W. H. R. *Conflict and Dream*. London: Kegan Paul, Trench, Trubner, 1923.

Roffwarg, H. P., Dement, W. C., Muzio, J. N., and Fisher, C. "Dream Imagery: Relationship to Rapid Eye Movements of Sleep." *American Medical Association Archives of General Psychiatry*, 7 (1962), 235.

Roffwarg, H. P., Muzio, J. N., and Dement, W. C. "Ontogenetic Development of the Human Sleep-dream Cycle." *Science*, 152 (April 29, 1966), 604–619.

Roheim, G. *The Gates of the Dream*. New York: International Universities Press, 1952.

Sapir, E. "The Unconscious Patterning of Behavior in Society." In E. S. Drummer (ed.), *The Unconscious: A Symposium*. New York: Knopf, 1929.

Saul, L. J., and Sheppard, Edith. "An Attempt to Qualify Emotional Forces Using Manifest Dreams." *Journal of the American Psychoanalytical Association*, 4 (1956), 486–502.

Schneider, D. M., and Sharp, R. L. "Yir Yoront Dreams." Unpublished manuscript, 1958.

Sharpe, Ella F. *Dream Analysis*. London: Hogarth Press, 1951.

Sheppard, Edith. "Systematic Dream Studies: Clinical Judgment and Objective Measurements of Ego Strength." *Comprehensive Psychiatry*, 4 (1963), 263–270.

Sheppard, Edith, and Saul, L. J. "An Approach to a Systematic Study of Ego Function." *Psychoanalytic Quarterly*, 27 (1958), 237–245.

Shimazano, Y., Ando, K., Sakamoto, S., Tanaka, T., Eguchi, T., and Nakamura, H. "Eye Movements of Waking Subjects with Closed Eyes." *American Medical Association Archives of General Psychiatry*, 13, No. 6 (December 1965), 537–543.

Singer, J. L., and Antrobus, J. S. "Eye Movements during Fantasies." *American Medical Association Archives of General Psychiatry*, 12, No. 1 (1965), 71–76.

Singer, J. L., and Schonbar, Rosalie. "Correlates of Daydreaming: A Dimension of Self-awareness." *Journal of Consulting Psychology*, 25 (1961), 1–6.

Snyder, F. "The New Biology of Dreaming." *American Medical Association Archives of General Psychiatry*, 8 (1963), 381.

Snyder, F. "Progress in the New Biology of Dreaming." *American Journal of Psychiatry*, 122, No. 4 (October 1965), 377–391.

Sokolov, Y. N. *Perception and the Conditioned Reflex*. Long Island City, N.Y.: Pergamon Press, 1963.

Stekel, W. *The Interpretation of Dreams*. Translated by Eden and Cedar Paul. 2 vols.; New York: Liveright, 1943.

Stoyva, J. M. "Posthypnotically Suggested Dreams and the Sleep Cycle." *American Medical Association Archives of General Psychiatry*, 12, No. 3 (March 1965), 287–294.

Sullivan, H. S. *The Interpersonal Theory of Psychiatry*. New York: Norton, 1953.

Tart, C. T. "Toward the Experimental Control of Dreaming." *Psychiatric Bulletin*, 64, No. 2 (August 1965), 81–92.

Tauber, E. S., and Green, M. R. *Prelogical Experience*. New York: Basic Books, 1959.

Tauber, E. S., and Green, M. R. "Color in Dreams." *American Journal of Psychotherapy*, 26 (1962), 221–229.

Thompson, Clara. *Psychoanalysis: Its Evolution and Development*. New York: Hermitage House, 1950.

Ullman, M. "The Dream Process." *American Journal of Psychotherapy*, 12, No. 4 (1958), 671–690.

Ullman, M. "The Adaptive Significance of the Dream." *Journal of Nervous and Mental Diseases*, 129, No. 2 (1959), 144–149.

Ullman, M. "The Social Roots of the Dream." *American Journal of Psychoanalysis*, 20, No. 2 (1960), 180–196.

Ullman, M. "Dreaming, Life Style and Physiology: A Comment on Adler's View of the Dream." *Journal of Individual Psychology*, 18 (1962), 18–25.

Ullman, M. "Discussion of Kleitman's Paper." In E. T. Adelson (ed.), *Dreams in Contemporary Psychoanalysis.* New York: Society of Medical Psychoanalysis, 1963.

Ullman, M. "An Experimental Approach to Dreams and Telepathy: Methodology and Preliminary Findings." *American Medical Association Archives of General Psychiatry,* 14, No. 6 (June 1966), 605–613.

Verdone, P. "Variables Related to the Temporal Reference of Manifest Dream Content." *Perceptual Motor Skill,* 20 (1965), 1253–1268.

Vogel, G., Foulkes, D., and Trosman, H. "Ego Functions and Dreaming during Sleep Onset." *American Medical Association Archives of General Psychiatry,* 14, No. 3 (March 1966), 238–248.

Weinstein, E. A. *Cultural Aspects of Delusion.* New York: The Free Press, 1962.

Weitzman, E. D., and Kremen, H. "Auditory Responses during Different Stages of Sleep in Man." *Electroencephalography and Clinical Neurophysiology,* 18 (1965), 65–70.

Werner, H., and Kaplan, B. *Symbol Formation.* New York: Wiley, 1963.

Whitman, R. M., Pierce, C. M., Maas, J. W., and Baldridge, B. "The Dreams of the Experimental Subject." *Journal of Nervous and Mental Diseases,* 134 (1962), 431–439.

Witkin, H. A., and Lewis, Helen B. "The Relation of Experimentally Induced Pre-sleep Experience to Dreams." *Journal of the American Psychoanalytic Association,* 13 (1965), 819–849.

II
BIOLOGICAL

8

The Biodynamic Roots of Psychoanalysis

JULES H. MASSERMAN

Rationale

Toward the end of his life Freud began to return to the broad biological and evolutionary interests that had characterized his earlier and most productive years. Yet only a relatively few subsequent workers (e.g., von Bertalanffy, 1955; Levy, 1954; Rioch, 1955; Rado and Daniels, 1956; Grinker, 1959; Mirsky and Katz, 1958; Heath, 1954; Pribram, 1965; Mandell, 1963) have remained deeply interested in what psychoanalysis can contribute to, or receive from, the more basic sciences of morphology and physiology, particularly the evolving higher neural functions and their correlations with the individual and social complexities of human conduct. This chapter will be largely devoted to a survey of biologic, ethologic, and comparative experimental data relevant to various psychoanalytic theories of fundamental import. Let us begin by posing a few fundamental questions:

What relationship do the "instinctive," "innate," or "unconditioned" behavior patterns of animals have to the concepts of pre-experimental "primary" or "libidinal" drives or "motivations" in man? Can the rate and order of the appearance of such patterns in young animals be correlated in any way with the postulated stages of "psychosexual maturation" in the child and adolescent? Are these phases related to metabolic processes and to the differential phylogenetic and ontogenetic development of the nervous system?

Is there determinative or presumptive evidence for the postulate of "primal aggression" or of a "death instinct"? Or may the battles over territoriality, dominance, and sexual possession in both animals and man be as readily formulated according to Simpson's (1949), Huxley's (1898), or, more recently, Montagu's (1955) concepts of a universal seeking for individual participation in an evolving social order? If so, is the ostensibly self-punitive or self-destructive behavior occasionally observed in animals (e.g., in Norwegian lemmings) based on deviant individual experiences as well as on primal atavistic resonances? Or is the relatively rare occurrence of mass intraspecies warfare (as in some varieties of ants described by Schneirla, 1929) more in accord with Freud's gloomy concepts of man's thanatotropic fate?

What bearings do the ethologic concepts of "trigger stimuli" and "social releasers" have on the early channelizations or fixations of reaction patterns in the human infant? In view of the relative impersonality of such early automatic responses, is every subsequent relationship in the human primarily a "transference" displacement or elaboration of such previous attachments and repulsions? Relevant to this, of what epistemologic significance are animal studies of modes of communication, courting customs, sexual pattern, and group behavior? Or studies on the experimental induction of patterns of "masochism," diffuse "aggression," and "animal neuroses"? Can the phenomena of the latter be characterized by clinical terms such as phobias, inhibitions, compulsions, regressions, symptom formations, "social maladaptations," and even "hallucinations" and "delusions"?

Perhaps most germane of all to our interests as clinicians is the question: Can a study of the methods that may or may not be effective in relieving these symptoms in any way contribute to the understanding of clinical psychotherapy? Indeed, how readily, in contrast to lower animals, may humans be reorientated and redirected by analytic or other techniques so that they may attain a greater versatility and adaptability in human relations?

Those of us who follow Freud in a broad scientific tradition must wish to adduce evidence from every available source that might help answer such questions. I propose to survey such evidence (although, of course, any review of this vast field must be barely indicative) from two special sources: first, *ethologic*—i.e., "naturalistic" observations; and second, *comparative biodynamics*—i.e., animal experimental studies.

Psychoanalysis and Ethology

BASIC CONCEPTS OF ETHOLOGY

The key concepts of ethology concerned with *instinct, social releaser,* and *imprinting* are generally defined as follows:

Instinct, according to a resolution of the International Ethologic Congress, refers to any mode of behavior governed by hereditary patterns of function in the central nervous system and characterized by "spontaneity . . . with modifiability through learning."

A *social releaser* is a sensory stimulus that, however fragmentary in itself, is interpreted by the organism as a meaningful gestalt and thereby furnishes an "external" objective for "instinctive" behavior.

Imprinting is a permanent modification of behavior by a *social releaser.* Konrad Lorenz (1952) observed that if he himself squatted and quacked a few times before a brood of newly hatched ducklings, they would thenceforth follow him and ignore the mother duck whose "normal" priority was thus usurped. The importance of *imprinting at optimum early periods* was highlighted by Riesen (1947), who observed that if baby chimpanzees are blindfolded for 3 to 6 months after birth, they are apparently kept from taking advantage of that phase of cortical development best suited for the acquisition of visual perceptions; consequently, when the blindfold is removed, they can no longer "learn to see" or to recognize objects, and may even make themselves physically amaurotic by staring wide-eyed and uncomprehendingly at the sun. Hess (1958, 1959) has determined within a few hours the time when imprinting is effective.

Such ethologic observations may be highly relevant to developmental phases of "libidinal cathexes," the permanent effects of early infantile experience, or Bowlby's (1959) contention that, if a child does not experience warm maternal care in the first years of life, he can neither appreciate nor seek friendly relationship with anyone thereafter, and thereby becomes "autistic" and "schizophrenic." But since parallel lines of thinking in ethology and analytic dynamics may never meet, the following sections will attempt to build bridges between them.

Comparative Neuroanatomy and Neurophysiology

Gall believed that human traits were "governed" by distinct "organs" or "centers" in the brain—a notion pursued today with regard to instincts (Ostow, 1959), emotions (Arnold, 1945), percepts (Angyal, 1941; Higgins, Mahl, Delgado, and Hamlin, 1956), memory (Penfield and Miller, 1958, 1959), and foresight (Halstead, 1947). Despite trenchant critiques by Stanley Cobb (1955), Percival Bailey (1960, 1962), David McKenzie Rioch (1955), Ralph Gerard (1957), and others, such simple topographic concepts have not been easily relinquished.

In a resonating neurophysiologic rather than a topologic approach to affect, Papez (1937) proposed his famous "mechanism of emotion" which involved recruiting pathways through the hippocampus, fornix, mammillary bodies, bundle of Vicqd'Azyr, thalamus, cingulates, and amygdalae. This circuit has more recently been elaborated by McLean (1955), Malamud (1957), and others, to include actuating fibers from the midbrain reticular nuclei of Bechterew and Gudden, elaboration of distance receptors signaling food or danger through the longitudinal striae from the septal region, sexuality by connections with the cuneus, and pathways via the laminary nuclei to the cortex for mnemonic storage, "symbolic" attribution, and operational processing.

The functions of these neural nodes and networks, however, change continuously with current motivations and additive feedbacks. To cite but two examples, Neal Miller (1957) noted that rats will press bars to actuate electrodes inserted in the median forebrain bundle (sometimes at a tempo increasing to a quasi-orgiastic peak) and then promptly rotate a wheel to turn the stimulus off, indicating that the same nerve center seemed to mediate increasingly "pleasant" and then suddenly "unpleasant" drive potentials. In later studies (1965) Miller also observed that different chemicals will activate different neurophysiologic systems running through the same diencephalic locus and so produce almost opposite behavior effects. Again to illustrate the interplay of neurohormonal and experiential influences, D. S. Lehrman (1964) demonstrated that the endocrine cycles that regulate the sexual organs and activities of the ringdove are themselves exquisitely sensitive to the courting activities of the mate.[1] From such observations, David McK. Rioch (1955) concluded: "The feelings of 'euphoria' and 'dysphoria' are apparently related to adequacy of CNS functioning in the interaction of the organism with the environment, rather than to activity in any localized area."

Two questions, then, remain: In view of the rich templating of millions of years of organismic experience in the desoxyribonucleic helices in every gene, and the complex neural networks, environmental configurations, and sensitive cybernetic feedbacks that continuously affect all behavior, can one really postulate simple conative entities called "drives" or "instincts"? And, if motivation, adaptation, maturation, and retained learning are thus indistinguishable, what becomes of our artificial "localizations" and quasi-mythologic distinctions between "conscious" and "unconscious" or "id," "ego," and "superego"?

[1] The special neurophysiology of sex will be discussed in a later section.

The Biodynamics of Learning

THE VALUE OF MOVEMENT

Eckhard Hess (1958) has observed that at an optimum time of 13 to 16 hours after hatching, wild mallard ducklings[2] can be imprinted to follow a decoy *only if they are permitted to waddle after it.* Hess therefore concluded that "the strength of the imprinting appeared to be dependent not on the durations of the imprinting period but on the effort exerted by the duckling"; the young learn by doing.

Bela Mittelmann (1958) and René Spitz (1954) emphasized the importance in human beings of free musculoskeletal activity during early childhood, since physical restraints could have neurotigenic effects. In the education of our young we teach scientific principles most effectively through learned skills; in adult life we admonish each other that "a sound mind requires an active body" (Greek *sanitas* meant indissoluble physical and psychic health), and in geriatrics we know that desuetude accelerates senile deterioration. And yet, in some forms of psychotherapy, we sometimes disparage zestful re-explorations as abjured "acting out," pretend that complex human interrelationships can be solved by supine conversation between two people respectively immobilized by chair and couch, and hope that somehow life will be improved without necessarily concomitant revisitations, relearnings, and new achievements in, quite literally, that *act*uality of living.

MODES OF COMMUNICATION

As Seboek (1965) points out, there seems to be an unbroken line of intra- and inter-species signaling at all levels of life from the relatively simple chemical or contact transfers of infusoria, through the courtship dance of the male swordtail (which the female "understands" very well), to the complex kinesics—of which the vocal cords are only the audible part—in man.

Wynne-Edwards, in a comprehensive review (1965), concludes that animals send "expressions of threat, warning, fear, pain, hunger, and at least in the highest animals, such elemental feelings as defiance, well-being, superiority, elation, excitement, friendliness, submission, dejection, and solitude [which can] be systematically analyzed." In the human, similar non-

[2] Hess (1959) contends that "all animals showing the phenomenon of imprinting will have a critical period which ends with the onset of fear. . . . In the human being one could thus theoretically place the end of maximum imprinting at about 5½ months, since [various] observers [K. M. Bridges (1932), R. A. Spitz (1954), K. M. Wolf (1946)] have placed the onset of fear at about that time."

verbal elements of communication have been systematically explored by Peter Ostwald (1965).

AESTHETIC BEHAVIOR

The contention has often been advanced that animals differ from man in two major respects: (1) they do not project, modify, or enhance their power through cherished tools, and (2) they lack, or are not interested in, "artistic creativity." But ethologists can reply that the first of these shibboleths simply distinguishes those who refuse to believe that sand spiders use pebbles to tamp their tunnels, that Geospizas pick cactus spines with which to dig out their insect prey from the bark of trees, that chimpanzees in the wild use specially fashioned twigs for probes and shovels, leaves for dishes or napkins (Goodall, 1963, 1964), and sticks and stones for defense against leopards (Kortland, 1962). In organisms with more highly potentiated nervous systems, exploration of the physical universe, presumably with a view to its control and manipulation—i.e., a technology—may take precedence over all other motivations. Thus, Butler (1954) reviews the observations by Harlow (1959), Yerkes (1943), and others to the effect that monkeys and apes—particularly young ones—would leave food and other rewards to indulge in individual and conjoint exploration and "play activities" that consisted essentially in the development of increasing knowledge about, and control of, the physical milieu. When required to do so, monkeys thus learn to open cage locks with keys and work for differently colored "coins" with which to secure grapes from vending machines (the "value" of the token, in terms of the number of grapes it can secure, determining the effort and ingenuity the monkey will put forth to earn it), and apes can be taught to assemble complex tools and drive motorcycles. Ferster (1964) taught chimpanzees to recognize numerals, write in ordinal numbers, and otherwise demonstrate high intellectual capacities, including "abstract thought." But perhaps man is the prime example of an animal that insists not only on constructing things, but also on taking them apart to see how they work—although this is sometimes comparable to smashing a Stradivarius violin to splinters in search of the exact site of its ethereally melodious tone.

DESIGN

No human engineer confined to the raw materials available to a spider, bee, or beaver can improve the plan or construction of a spiderweb, a beehive, or a beaver dam. In the field of architecture combined with domestic decoration only one of numerous examples need be cited. The bower birds of Australia and New Guinea, as reported by A. J. Marshall (1956), build elaborate landscapes, tunnels, and maypoles out of sticks, pebbles, seashells, or other materials, paint them with berry juice or charcoal mixed with saliva, and decorate them with flowers. Others construct towers up to nine feet high with tepee-like roofs and internal chambers, and improve their environs with circular lawns that they tend carefully and embellish with golden resins, garishly colored berries, iridescent insect skeletons, and fresh flowers that are replaced as they wither. The scene is thus set, as it is in human affairs, for intricate routines of courtship and coitus as discussed in the following section (see Sibol, 1957; Gillard, 1963).

Sexuality

EVOLUTION

If the basic biologic purpose of sex—usually submerged in the incidental excitement—is the interchange of genes so that an organism of duplex heredity can be generated, then sex is basically present in submicroscopic viruses. In multicellular animals, heterosexuality becomes universal, although never an unmixed blessing to the parties concerned. To cite a familiar example in the insect world: the female praying mantis combines her nuptial maneuvers with her bridal feast, the dubiously fortunate groom being utilized for both.

In mammals, this erotic-incorporative sequence varies from species to species: among ungulates the continued presence of the protective buck is welcomed by the female, whereas among the carnivores the males are generally driven off after stud as being untrustworthy when hungry, especially with succulent and defenseless young coming due. Indeed, early cannibalistic societies fattened females for a dual purpose, and Marco Polo described how a Manchu warlord served him with a lovely young harem girl—roasted whole with a pomegranate in her mouth. According to Mead (1949), Malinowski (1927), Kardiner, Linton, Du Bois, and West (1945), similar synethesias of sex and sustenance have been preserved into the 1960's by various African and Australasian tribes, and furnished sound anthropologic roots for the opportunistic orality of the Congolese Simbas and the dramaturgic deglutitions depicted in Tennessee Williams' *Suddenly Last Summer*. Were we, indeed, just a bit more conscious of our semantics, we would abandon common endearments such as "honey," "sweetie pie," or the even more specific "you look good enough to eat."

THE PHYSIOLOGY OF SEX

If psychology can be defined as physiology in action, then sexuality is again demonstrably related to nutrition. In the lower animals the same enzymes and hormones affect both: e.g., Allee (1951) has shown that a hen low in the pecking order will begin to dominate the roost for both food and mates after a few injections of testosterone. Neurologically, the spinal portion of the central nervous system controls fairly complex activity: as Sherrington demonstrated in 1900, a spinal dog can both feed and copulate quite efficiently, and a decerebrate bitch can conceive and deliver. Best and Taylor (1959) summarize the following striking physio-anatomic correlations between olfactory-gustatory and sexual processes: (1) the mucosa covering the conchae has a cavernous structure suggestive of the erectile tissue of the penis and clitoris; (2) olfactory stimuli and psychic aspects of sex are very closely associated; (3) nasal congestion (with epistaxis) occurs in many women commonly at the time of the menses, and in both sexes at puberty; (4) changes in the nasal mucosa (swelling and reddening) are common in women during pregnancy and in monkeys during the oestrus cycles; (5) stimulation of the interior of the nose in rats changes the periodicity of the oestrus cycles; (6) excision of the conchae in young animals (rats) induces hypoplasia of the sex organs; (7) castration produces degenerative changes in the nasal mucosa, which are reversed by estrogen injections; and (8) atrophic rhinitis can be successfully treated by the nasal application of the follicular hormone.

At higher paleocerebral levels that fit function with futurity, more elaborate sexual seekings are served by the circuits of Papez, through which *Homo sapiens* retain their Mesozoic heritage from the time when their ancestors sought food and mates, and avoided enemies, by utilizing the most primitive of distance receptors: the sense of smell. At the hominid level these rhinencephalic functions become largely inhibitory; as Kluver and Bucy (1939) have shown, lesions of the temporal lobes (or, as Pechtel and I demonstrated more specifically (Masserman and Pechtel, 1956a), of the amygdalae, render most monkeys overly tame, bulimic and hypersexed. But even in man the ancient oral-erotic appetites evoked in the olfactory archipallium still engender a maze of (1) alimentary and sexual reflexes channeled through the hippocampus, thalamus, cingulum, and fornix to the hypothalamus, (2) more persistent hormonal influences mediated through the portal circulation of Houssay to the pituitary, and (3) mnemonic and symbolic resonances in thought and imagery circuited through the cuneus and frontal cortex (Paul McLean, 1962). A. E. Fisher points out (1964) that the human cerebrum is sexually equipotential: "The male and female brain are essentially identical . . . both brains contain cells that can direct female behavior and other cells that direct male behavior." But since the functions of these genetically variable structures are further modified throughout life not only by wide ranges of individual experience and rate of development but also by accidents of trauma, infection, metabolic disorders, drug effects, etc., any "metapsychologic" theory that traces all human behavior solely to the overriding vicissitudes of "primal sexuality" in predetermined "libidinal phases" may be attractive in its titillating simplicity, but at the price of physiologic and biodynamic naïveté.

SEXUAL TECHNIQUES

Despite the chemical control and maturation of sexual capacities in most individuals of higher species, actual sex practices must, at least in some part, be learned. For example, male guppies will attempt to mate indiscriminately with all likely-looking objects in their territory until they find only female guppies to be receptive (Noble and Curtis, 1935–1936); young doves (Craig, 1908, 1914) and apes must also pass "through a long series of fumbling approximations that look remarkably like trial-and-error learning" (Maslow, 1936) before they achieve smooth and effective autoerotic, cross species, homosexual, or heterosexual techniques. Submissive animals of either sex may assume "feminine" coital postures toward more dominant colony mates; however, according to Lashley (1954) and others, this signals a denial of hostility and an invitation to friendship rather than a Freudian equation of submissiveness with "feminine inferiority."

As species approach domesticated man, mating patterns become more specialized. According to Jane Goodall (1963), wild chimpanzees line up for the female and never fight for mates, let alone a harem. Yerkes (1943) described the behavior of captive chimpanzees as follows: The behavior of each mate with regard to feeding and other privileges seems to change in correlation with their sexual relationships, and the female comes to claim as if it were her right what previously she had allowed the male to take, while he as if in recognition of, or in exchange for, sexual accommodation during the mating period, defers to her and unprotestingly permits her to control the food-getting situation. Conversely, a chimpanzee separated from its mate may refuse food and pine away into desuetude (Kohler, 1929).

EVOLUTION OF PARENTAL PATTERNS

Here again endocrine, ecologic, and situational influences are inextricably interrelated in governing mating, nesting, and nursing behavior. For example, progesterin plus the availability of a secluded corner promote precoital nest building in rats (Lorenz, 1952), whereas lactating cats given a pituitary hormone that diminishes mammary congestion will abandon their litters. Interparental acceptance requires special early association: Craig (1908) observed that wild pigeons, whatever their oestral status, can be crossbred only if the future mates from different varieties are raised together. Conversely, the progeny then furnish stimuli that reciprocally influence the biochemical state of the parent: Leblond (1938) could elicit "maternal" conduct in adult mice of either sex by putting them in charge of newborn litters, whereas hormonally immature males and virgin females required close "concaveation" with baby mice for from one to four days before exhibiting responses of care and protection.

Denenberg, Ottinger, and Stephens (1962) showed that in the period between birth and weaning, the behavior of the mother toward her young modifies the offspring's later emotional behavior and body weight. Denenberg and Morton (1962) demonstrated that postweaning social interaction with other organisms of the same species also affects subsequent behavior. Multiple-mothering (mother rotated between her own litter and one foster litter every twenty-four hours) caused rat pups to be more emotional in adulthood than offspring reared by a single mother (Ottinger, Denenberg, and Stephens, 1963).

INFANT DEVELOPMENT

Species-specific ontogenetic factors are again immediately relevant; for example, in animals as highly developed as canines, no conditioning can occur until the eyes and ears open at three weeks, after which, according to J. P. Scott (1962), pups can be weaned without engendering the Levy sucking effect (*vide infra*). In human parallel, no "conditioning" of the human infant can occur until six weeks after birth—an observation contrary to Kleinian theory but well in accord with René Spitz's finding (1954) that babies do not really differentiate visual configurations such as parental faces until fully six months old.

PATTERNS OF INFANT CARE

J. A. King's account (1959) of the protected maturation of the prairie dog is applicable to many "subhuman" gregarious species:

> After leaving his birthplace the emergent pup meets his father and other members of the coterie and enters a pup paradise. He plays with his siblings and the other young. All the adults kiss and groom him as his mother does, and he responds to them as he does to her. He readily accepts foster mothers and may spend the night with their broods. He attempts to suckle adults indiscriminately—males as well as females. A female will submit quietly; the male gently thwarts him and grooms him instead, rolling him over on his back and running his teeth through the pup's belly fur. . . .
>
> During these first pleasant weeks the pup may even meander into adjacent coterie territories with impunity. But as he begins to mature he wanders farther and his invasions meet with less forbearance. . . . Soon he comes to recognize the territorial boundaries and learns that not all prairie dogs treat him alike. . . . He begins to use the identification kiss to discriminate between coterie members and strangers. If his kiss is not returned by another animal in his territory, he treats it suspiciously, barks at it, runs up to smell it, and then dashes off. As he grows older this behavior elaborates into the tail-spreading ritual.

Higher intelligence among more advanced species requires more varied schooling. As reported by Barbara Harrison (1963) and Colter Rule

(1964), orangutan and gorilla mothers teach their offspring how to feed, walk, climb, and vocalize; older peers teach them care-seeking, care-giving, sexual amenities (e.g., "presenting" the pudendum to an older or dominant animal of either sex) and other necessary social customs, such as according special priority to the mates and offspring of high-ranking members of the group.

FETISHISM

Scull (Scull, Nance, and Roll, 1958) dressed a mother ape in a blanket every time her infant was given to her for breast feeding, and could later use the blanket "as a symbol for the mother . . . in weaning the infant away from her." Curtis and Jean Pechtel (1956) in our laboratory have studied such fetishism in young rhesus in great detail and observed that permanent values (cathexes) were attached to toys and other objects associated with a secure infancy and early childhood, as evidenced by recourse to their proximity during periods of stress in adolescence or even late adulthood.

DISTURBED FAMILIAL RELATIONSHIPS

It is of particular significance that early familial or other stresses can produce serious and lasting deviations of conduct in animal as well as human progeny. For example, P. F. D. Seitz (1954) has noted that rat pups raised in large litters hoarded food more strenuously and became subject to greater handicaps in adaptation than did those from smaller and better tended litters. In a particularly striking pair of experiments, Thompson and Melzock (1956) observed that, if puppies were raised with the best of metabolic care but in almost complete isolation, they grew into adults subject to periods of glazed staring, apparently illusory startles, fears, and rages, and peculiar attacks of epileptoid whirling; in contrast (Thompson and Heron, 1954), excessively protected and petted pups grew into insecure, helpless, overdependent and jealously demanding dogs—a not uncommon development in species other than the canine. Liddell (1958) reported that kids separated from the mother ewe for only two hours the first day after birth remained alien to the herd and developed such severe neurotic and psychosomatic handicaps that they died within six months; others separated for shorter periods in infancy survived, but bore kids whom they in turn neglected, and so perpetuated a "neurotic family history." Harlow's observation of infant monkeys (1959) indicates that the "psychic traumata" involved may stem not from "oral deprivations" in the usual psychoanalytic sense (all of the young animals in these studies were well nourished), but from the removal of opportunities for physical contact and cuddling as initiated by the infant; Harlow's baby macaques clearly cherished and avidly clung even to cruelly abusive mothers, or to artificial ones made only of wire and terry cloth, and used both as an essential source of comfort and security before undertaking new explorations.

POPULATION CONTROL

In animal as in human societies, a "population explosion" may have seriously deleterious effects on individual and group behavior. Overcrowded guppies eat their young and thus restore optimal survival density (Wynne-Edwards, 1965). Calhoun (1962), by the simple device of forcing rat colonies to live in half their accustomed space, induced deviant sexuality, excessive fighting for food and harems, neglect of the young, and cannibalism until the overcrowding was relieved: Thiessen and Rodgers (1961) attributed these effects to persistent endocrine dysfunctions consequent on excessive visual, olfactory, and tactile stimuli. Corresponding patterns of infanticide with or without cannibalism in overpopulated or otherwise disturbed primitive societies have been described by Malinowski (1927) and Kardiner *et al.* (1945), whereas familial abuse, abortions, and child neglect are notoriously common among crowded, underprivileged families of our own "civilized" culture.[8]

SOCIAL COLLABORATION

But even such seemingly biopathic patterns have race survival value, else none of us would be here to record let alone deplore them. Although the Darwinian phrase "survival of the fittest" has often been misinterpreted to mean the triumph of the most strong and savage, Simpson (1949), Huxley (1898), Montagu (1955), and other paleobiologists have pointed out that survival of the individual as well as of the species has in most instances been due to the emergence of conspecific empathy and collaboration. In this sense, many of the patterns of group behavior most important to social psychiatry can be traced almost to their Cambrian roots.

Observations at higher evolutionary echelons may be summarized as follows: "Antelopes place sentinels who remain continually on watch at the periphery of the herd until relieved. Wounded elephants have often been seen supported by the surrounding herd and helped to escape to the safety of the jungle; otters, too, will rescue a wounded comrade" (Katz, p. 203). Loveridge (1938, 1939) frequently observed a male baboon in flight from a predator returning to defend a wounded fellow, or a female remaining behind to protect a dead mate's body. Schaller (1963) observed that even the awesome mountain gorilla is "amiable and decent" to the weak and suffering of its own kind. In contrast, Zuckerman (1932) noted that baboons *kept in captivity rather than in their natural habitat* may act more like men in concentration camps, attack the weak, the ill and the aged, manhandle

[8] A current witticism is that modern anthropologists have finally discovered the "missing link" between apes and civilized men—the present stage of *Homo sapiens.*

the females after sexual satiation, and otherwise behave in a manner that would appear cruel and destructive to a human observer; Zuckerman added that under these concentration-camp circumstances baboons did not seem to recognize the death of adults of their own kind.

Recent work in our own laboratory on conspecific succorance indicated that midway between the above phenomena, a monkey accustomed to captivity may starve for days if working a lever for food also administers an electric shock to a friendly cagemate (Masserman, Wechkin, and Terris, 1964); however, such simian "altruism" did not extend to, nor was it exhibited among, laboratory cats.

There is also much ethologic evidence that if the young of different species are raised together, peaceable relations will continue into adulthood, Such observations call into further question Freud's postulate of a universal "aggressive" or "death" instinct and add important evolutionary projections to constructive elements in group and social dynamics—unfortunately, as yet far from their apogee in human affairs.

SOCIAL FACILITATION

Bayer (1929) noted that an apparently satiated chicken would join a companion by eating again, and Chen (1937) reported that ants worked much harder in pairs than alone. A review of many such studies led Zajonc (1965) to conclude that, since "performance is facilitated [but] learning is impaired by the presence of spectators, a student should arrange to study alone, preferably in an isolated cubicle, and to take his examinations on stage in the presence of a large audience." Allport (1924, p. 261), on the basis of human data, had similarly theorized that success is fostered by "the sights and sounds of others doing the same thing." These observations may have an interesting bearing on the alternation of successive gains of insight and reorientation as a result of solitary reflection, periodically implemented by dyadic and social interaction during psychoanalytic therapy.

COMPARATIVE BIODYNAMICS

But two questions may still be raised: Are not these ethologic observations and inferences "really subjective" and "anthropomorphized"? Also, since man alone has been regarded as capable of "higher abstractions" and the development of "mores" and "culture," is he not the only creature subject to the individual "psychosomatic" and social aberrations that constitute "true" neuroses and "functional" psychoses?

Such questions are asked sufficiently frequently and sincerely to deserve extended consideration. First, as to the pejorative use of the terms "really subjective," and "anthropomorphized," an immediate epistemologic stand can be taken, to wit: since all data, "natural" or "experimental," are simultaneously and indistinguishably "objective" and "subjective," and since all human perceptions, memories, generalizations, abstractions, theorems, inferences, judgments, conclusions, and reactions can be molded only in accordance with human concepts, terms such as "real," "true," and "anthropomorphic" become tautologic shibboleths. An analogy more directly relevant to the study of comparative behavior may be the following:

It is obvious that a man can live long and fairly happily knowing very little about the structure and function of his central nervous system; however, should he wish to become a neurologist this technical information would become essential. In his first explorations of the field it might then appear to him that the human central nervous system is far too intricate to be profitably compared with, say, the simple neuraxis of an *Amphioxus* and that therefore he had best confine his studies to human neuroanatomy and physiology as related to "clinical" problems. And yet, as his knowledge broadened and deepened, he would begin to appreciate that an antithetical position might be nearer the "truth"; namely, that he could not really understand the fundamental structure and function of the human CNS *without* studying that of the *Amphioxus*, since only then could he comprehend the basic organization common to all vertebrates in the evolutionary scale, including that of man. So also, whereas the psychiatrist and psychoanalyst obviously cannot comprehend every aspect of human conduct merely by studying mice in mazes, cats in cages, or monkeys in pharmacologic hazes, such studies can, with proper criteria and controls, lead to the discovery of fundamental biodynamic principles underlying all behavior, and thus provide as many valuable leads for behavioral science and psychotherapy as does comparative neurophysiology for neurologic theory and practice.

BIODYNAMICS

For further elaboration and validation of these theses, the reader is referred to my more detailed writings (Masserman, 1943, 1945, 1948, 1950, 1951, 1953, 1955, 1958, 1959, 1960, 1962, 1964, 1965). Here we can do little more than state that by integrating such comparative ethologic observations with reinterpreted psychologic, social, and clinical data, a welter of often vague and sometimes paradoxical metapsychologic theorems can be reduced to the following four operationally testable biodynamic principles:

Principle I—*Motivation.* All behavior is motivated by physiologic needs in various configurations of contingency and urgency: survival, procreation, and, as indicated above, aesthetic creativity.

Principle II—*Adaptation.* Every organism reacts not to an absolute "reality," but to its own interpretations of its milieu in terms of its uniquely developed capacities and experiences.

Principle III—*Displacement.* Whenever goal-directed activities are blocked by external obstacles, the organism tries either (1) different methods to reach the same objectives, or (2) partially or wholly substitutes other goals. As a corollary, an optimal milieu is one sufficiently challenging to elicit originality and creativity, but not so frustrating as to induce grossly deviant conduct.

Principle IV—*Neurotigenesis*. However, when two or more urgent motivations are in sufficiently serious opposition so that the adaptive patterns attendant to each become mutually exclusive, the organism experiences a mounting internal tension ("anxiety"), develops increasingly intense and generalized ("symbolic") inhibitions and aversions ("phobias"), limited ritualizations of conduct ("compulsions"), various musculoskeletal and organic ("psychosomatic") dysfunctions, markedly deviated social interactions (self-isolation, "paranoid" suspiciousness, sexual aberrations, excessive aggression or submission) and other persistently ambivalent, ineffectively substitutive, and poorly adaptive ("neurotic") and/or progressively disorganized, regressive, and bizarrely symbolic ("psychotic") patterns of conduct.

To most behavioral scientists and psychiatrists these principles will appear immediately relevant to human experiences—though, perhaps, no more so than other systems of thought. Let us now review various animal experimental and other data that give them more fundamental significance.

Motivation (Principle I)

As expressed in the first Biodynamic Principle, any physiologic need can be evoked to actuate experimentally observable behavior: thirst, sexual and maternal drives, physical escape from constriction or discomfort, etc. These and other conations of greater or less complexity were all tested in our experiments; in practice, however, we generally utilized hunger because, though feeding behavior is itself a relatively complex expression of direct and indirect metabolic needs, it has the advantages of being easily induced, rapidly renewed, and fractionally analyzable. Parenthetically, and only partially in accord with "libido" theory, it could be demonstrated (*vide infra*) that nutritive needs had deep motivational interrelationship with patterns of gregariousness, dominance behavior, and sexuality.

EXPERIMENTAL DESIGN

An animal was placed in a glass-enclosed compartment for easy observation and photography and trained to develop various "normal" responses and manipulative patterns to obtain specific rewards. In parallel experiments, two or more animals were placed simultaneously in such situations to elicit their interactions of "cooperation" or "hostility." Each animal was then made to contend with various obstacles and frustrations; finally, conflicts of motivation—either between almost equally attractive rewards or among nearly equally balanced attractions and aversions—were induced in order to study their etiologic and phenomenologic relationships to maladaptive and aberrant conduct. In special series of experiments these techniques were elaborated to include the effects of various drugs and of local stimulations or lesions of the central nervous system on "normal" and "neurotic" behavior. Finally, a large variety of procedures, both theoretically and empirically selected, were tested for their influence in exacerbating or ameliorating these patterns of conduct. To promote objectivity of analysis and for permanence of record, tables of data, instrumental tracings, motion-picture films (Masserman, 1938–1965; Masserman and Pechtel, 1956; Pechtel and Pechtel, 1956), and independent reports of important behavioral observations were secured in all experiments.

"NORMAL" LEARNING

In a typical experiment a dog, a cat, or a monkey which had been deprived of food for from 12 to 24 hours was taught first to open a food box in response to a sensory signal and then to circumvent various barriers and manipulate various electrical switches or other contrivances to secure its own signals and food rewards. In such preliminary studies it was found that animals could form quite complex "symbolic" associations when appropriately motivated; for instance, cats and monkeys could be taught to count (press a series of switches in a required order a definite number of times), differentiate between "signs" (German script reading "*fressen*" or "*nicht fressen*"), or distinguish single or combined odors, tones, and rhythms; for that matter, the animals often anticipated the experimenter's intentions and prepared for what he was going to do by correctly interpreting subtle clues in his behavior, of which he himself had not been aware. If the animal's perceptive, mnemonic, integrative, and reactive ("intellectual") capacities were exceeded during this training period, it became recalcitrant and resistant to further learning; indeed, it would not infrequently resort to seemingly aimless play, sporadic attempts to escape, or episodic, diffuse destructiveness. Certain experiments indicated that these characteristics may persist in young animals subjected to an overly intensive regimen of training which thereby permanently impaired their adaptive responses—a pedagogic tragedy exemplified clinically by the stultified genius of William Sidis, still disregarded by some teachers of our young and ignored in psychoanalytic theory. Nearly all of our observations, on the other hand, conformed to Principle I in that no learning took place in the absence of relevant motivation; e.g., an animal that was not hungry would pay only passing notice to the food cup, whereas one trained to manipulate the signals, barriers, and switches would cease to be directly interested in these paraphernalia for receiving food as soon as its hunger was satiated. Conversely, if the training remained in accord with the animal's needs and well within its capacities and temperament, it readily entered into the experimental situation, learned avidly and effectively, remained cooperative with the experimenter (except, in our experience, in the case of generally unfriendly Vervet, Cynamologus, or adult Mangabey monkeys) and was, on the whole, an active, contented, relatively tractable and thereby "well-adjusted" animal.

Adaptation through Experience and Symbolization (Principle II)

DEVELOPMENTAL INFLUENCES

Our studies are in accord with the generalization that the young of all organisms, including man, develop through an orderly succession of stages during which sensory modalities are distinguished, integrated concepts of the environment are developed, manipulative skills are refined, early dependencies are relinquished in favor of exploration and mastery, and peer and sexual relationships are sought through which the animal becomes normally "socialized" in its group. In continued studies over the past seven years, the growth of individual animals of various species from infancy to adulthood under differing environmental influences has been carefully recorded and progressively photographed in motion pictures; these observations have revealed the following important effects on development, again with significant clinical counterparts:

Early deprivation. Young animals subjected to prolonged periods of solitary confinement, even though otherwise physically well cared for, do not develop normal initiative, physical stamina, or social relationships.

Formative experiences. Conversely, young animals given opportunities for continuously protective and nutritive contacts with adults or peers acquire exploratory self-confidence, motor, and interpersonal skills, and social "acculturations."

Learning. The growing infants show patterns of dependency, exploration, play, fetishism (i.e., attachment to objects representing early securities), rebelliousness, developing sexuality, and other characteristics significantly parallel to those in human children. However, the surrogate parents involved, whether or not of the animal's own species, impart their own traits to the adopted young. For example, a young rhesus raised from birth in the investigator's home learns to respond sensitively and adequately to human language and action, but may never acquire some of the patterns (e.g., a fear of snakes) "normal" to rhesus monkeys raised by their own mothers.

It will be recalled that the second biodynamic principle also states that each organism interprets and evaluates its milieu in terms of its own needs, capacities, and experiences. This was particularly well illustrated by experiments in which the animal's responses, though they seemed paradoxical to a casual observer, could nevertheless be accounted for by just such a premise. For example, monkeys who ordinarily liked bananas could be made to shun them by merely having the odor of the fruit appear during a series of frustrating situations; conversely, experiences ordinarily reacted to as unpleasant could be made paradoxically attractive by direct or indirect association with a reward. A special series of such experiments produced deviations of behavior with interesting clinical parallels as follows:

"Masochism." In these studies, cats taught to depress a switch which gave them a mild electric shock signaling the availability of food could be made so eager to administer increasingly severe but apparently "symbolically substitutive" electric shocks to themselves *even when the original reward was suspended* that their behavior would almost invariably be interpreted by observers unacquainted with their "case histories" as a "seeking for pain" or for "suffering." This, of course, again raises the question as to whether many patterns of conduct usually interpreted as "masochistic" are essentially not "self-punitive," but instead rooted in expectations of previously available rewards through temporarily strenuous or even hurtful behavior. If this inference proves reasonably tenable—as it certainly has in many clinical observations—it would constitute another nail in the coffin of Thanatos.

Adaptation to External Frustration by Substitutive Methods or Goals (Principle III)

AGGRESSION

If an animal which has become accustomed to obtaining food by manipulating electrical switches, running mazes, and responding to sensory signals was subsequently kept from securing its reward by some mechanical obstruction (an impassable barrier, a nonoperative switch, etc.), its first reactions would be to expend more effort to overcome that obstacle. For example, the animal would push against the barrier, energetically work or actually jump upon the switch, try to pry open the locked food box, or use other methods of forcing a way toward its original goal. If these methods became particularly intensive (i.e., the animal would use its teeth or claws as the only tools at its command), its efforts would seem to be "attacking" its environment, yet such behavior remained on the continuum of adaptive initiative and needed no new rubric of "aggressivity" to account for its dynamics or economics.

DISPLACEMENT

A further instance of this is the fact that, when more energetic efforts did not succeed in their turn, the animal did not proceed to annihilate the switch or food box even when it had the capacity to do so; instead, it shifted to substitutive actions or goals (Principles II and III). Cats and monkeys would press other objects in lieu of the experimental switches, or try to open containers other than the food box, whereas dogs would generally attempt by barks and gestures to appeal to the experimenter to manipulate the recalcitrant gadgets. If these alternative patterns also proved ineffective, the animals temporarily relinquished striving for the food and instead sought other satisfactions such as drinking excessive quantities of water, attempting to reach an animal friend or a sexual partner, or playing with various objects, including their own bodies. However, most of these substitutive activities, comprising various displacements into diffusely exploratory or regressive behavior, disappeared rapidly whenever the external obstacles were removed and the animal once again found that normally adaptive patterns were effective. There was, then, no actual "extinction" of learned "conditional" responses in the Pavlovian sense; instead, in greater accord with analytic theory, such responses were merely held in abeyance ("repressed") when intercurrent experience showed they were temporarily ineffective. Consistent with this, they reappeared promptly ("return of the repressed") when the rewards were once again offered.

INTERANIMAL ("SOCIAL") ADAPTATIONS

Dominance and aggression. When two animals, each of which had been trained to open a food box in response to the same signal, were placed together and the feeding signal given to both of them, competition for the single reward was necessarily engendered. In nearly all cases the rivalry resulted in one of the animals becoming "dominant" in securing the reward, whereas the other became "submissive"—i.e., it adapted to its partner as an irremovable obstacle and thereafter occupied itself in other pursuits until the "dominant" animal ceased to pre-empt the food. Such hierarchies could be set up in groups of four or more animals so that the members of such groups, after a period of exploratory jockeying, would range themselves in a set order of precedence in feeding without recourse to mutually aggressive behavior. Indeed, close observation of such interactions indicated that the submissive animals treated those above them as more or less impervious barriers and adapted accordingly. This raises the interesting question as to whether organism A ever reacts to or even recognizes organism B except as B facilitates or blocks the current or anticipated satisfaction of A. Nor need B actually be an "organism"; indeed, "animate" and "inanimate" objects are, as Piaget emphasized, distinguished only relatively late in life and even then only partially: a graceful sailboat or a lovely Cremona violin are as individualized and near-living creations to their ardent devotees as are inanimate terry-cloth "mothers" to Harlow's baby monkeys (1959). If, then, the interactions are deeply gratifying, the relationship may be termed "love" ("mutual" if both parties can share the satisfactions) and lead to various forms of symbiosis; conversely, reciprocal attitudes of aversion or conflict—subjectively sensed as hostility or hatred—are accompanied by greater or lesser degrees of defensive or eliminative hostile action.

Collaboration and parasitism. One pattern of conspecific "altruism" has already been described in the section on Psychoanalysis and Ethology, but an even more intriguing paradigm of human relationships appeared in a series of experiments specifically designed to explore such patterns more thoroughly. In these, cats were individually trained to work an electric switch that flashed a signal light and deposited a single pellet of food in the food box. Two of the animals were then placed together in the experimental apparatus with a transparent barrier between the switch and food box so arranged that the animal which tried to work the switch was itself barred from feeding, whereas the food reward became readily available to its partner. Obviously, many patterns of interaction were possible under such circumstances, but the following occurred most typically: after some initial random activity and individual adjustment, both animals would discover that "cooperation" was the only way in which either would get fed, so that for a time the two alternated in working the food switch for each other. This arrangement broke down when one of the cats began to linger near the food box in order to gulp every available pellet; under such circumstances its partner, deprived of all reward, likewise refused to work the switch. The inevitable result was that each animal, in a joint caricature of a sitdown strike, remained stubbornly inactive on its own side of the barrier while both starved. Eventually, one of the animals—usually the one that had previously shown the most initiative—would make another discovery: if it worked the switch six or eight times in rapid succession and *then* hurried to the food box, it could salvage the last two or three pellets before its partner, who had waited at the box, had eaten them all. From this a unique interaction evolved: one of the pair remained a "parasite" who lived off the "worker's" toil, whereas the worker remained seemingly content to supply food for both. Finally, an even more satisfactory solution was achieved by two of the workers in this series who, in the feline world, would rank as mechanical geniuses. In what seemed to be a flash of inspiration, they so wedged the switch into a corner of the cage that it operated the automatic feeder continuously and thus provided a plenitude of pellets for both animals without further effort from either—a "technological solution" in the modern mode of a previously disruptive socioeconomic problem.

Neurotigenesis: Effects of Adaptational Conflict (Principle IV)

Prior to our investigations, Pavlov (1928), Gantt (1942), and others had induced conflicts of adaptation by the traditional method of making the "conditioned stimuli" for positive or negative "conditioned reflexes" approach too closely to each other; i.e., a circle signaled food, but an almost circular ellipse, none; alternatively, nearly synchronous metronome beats ambiguously heralded opposite events. Under such circumstances the animal, in Pavlov's words, could no longer differentiate between "positive" and "negative" stimuli and therefore became "experimentally neurotic." It may be that here Pavlov was approaching, though in his own somewhat doctrinaire fashion, perhaps the fundamental etiologic factor in all "neurotigenesis": namely, *a degree of ambiguity and unpredictability in its milieu that seriously threatens the competence and security of the organism.* This generalization would include the devastating effects of genetic errors (Ginsberg, 1957–1958), infantile metabolic stresses (Waismann and Harlow, 1965), childhood deprivations (Harlow, 1959; Spitz, 1954; Bowlby, 1959), adult communicative isolation (Hebb, 1958), information overload (J. G. Miller, 1960), delayed feedback (K. Smith, 1938), and other disruptive threats to learned and ordinarily effective methods of information-processing and environmental control as reviewed above.

In our own studies, instead of converging Pavlovian "positive" and "negative' signals, we employed direct conflicts of motivation in accordance with Biodynamic Principle IV, and thus elicited aberrations of behavior that could justifiably be called more generally, intensely, and persistently neurotic. Significantly—and in a manner inadequately covered by classical analytic theory—*these conflicts could be set up by opposing motivations of approximately equal strength even when both were "positive,"* for example, requiring an animal to choose between equally attractive but mutually exclusive foods, or by positioning a hungry lactating (or oestral) female at a motivational point equidistant between food and an importunate litter (or male) so that one attraction neatly balanced but precluded the other (Masserman *et al.*, 1963). Parenthetically, that severe anxieties, paralyzing ambivalence, futile compulsivities, and even deep depressions can be precipitated by conflicting *positive* motivations (for example, toward mutually exclusive jobs or spouses) as well as "negative" ones (a difficult choice between equally dubious modes of escape from danger) is a clinical phenomenon of special significance, since it supports the etiologic importance of adaptational *conflict* rather than—as Wolpe (1958), Eysenck (1965) and others contend—fear alone in the genesis of neurotic behavior. In animals, however, such conflicts could be more simply induced between "goal-directed" conations such as hunger, thirst, or sex on the one hand, as opposed to "aversive" ones, e.g., inertia, or fear of falling or injury on the other. In the latter instances a typical experiment would run as follows:

TECHNIQUE OF NEUROTIGENESIS

A cat, dog, or monkey, which had been long accustomed to securing its food by, say, pressing a series of switches in a definite order and obtaining appropriate signals that food was available in the food box, would one day, when opening the box to receive the reward, be subjected to a traumatically deterrent stimulus. The latter need not be somatically damaging; it could take the form of any "unpleasant" physical sensation such as a harmless condenser shock or an equally benign but startling air blast across the food box. Even more effective in the case of monkeys was a completely "psychologic" trauma such as the sudden appearance of the head of a toy rubber snake in lieu of, or accompanying, the expected reward. This last phenomenon was of such great semeiologic interest that we made it an object of special study and found that, whereas animated toys or even live frogs and lizards would rarely produce aversive effects, any object that approached resemblance to a snake (for example, a rubber tube constricted near one end) became traumatic even to laboratory-born monkeys which could have had no contact with snakes of any kind, yet nevertheless seemed to have an innate fear of anything that resembled them. The relevance of such observations to Pavlov's "unconditioned reflexes" or Jung's concepts of atavistic "racial memories" is problematic.

DEVELOPMENT OF NEUROSES

All animals were adversely affected by the conflictful experiences described, though the nature, intensity, and duration of the induced aberrations of behavior varied with the urgency of the opposing motivations, the availability of substitutive satisfactions for, or partial solutions of, the dilemma through the use of previously learned skills and many other considerations involving the severity of the stress versus the unique vulnerability or adaptabilities of the individual animal Curtis Pechtel and I (1956b) summarized our observations in this regard as follows:

A differential analysis of observations on 142 cats and 43 monkeys during the last twelve years indicates that animals which fitted well into our general laboratory routine, which learned efficiently, and which explored various substitutive maneuvers in initial efforts to resolve conflictful situations subsequently showed longer continued resistance to severe stress and resumed effective behavior more readily under therapy [*vide infra*]. Younger animals were more susceptible to the induction of neuroses than were older ones. There were definite species differences: i.e., spider monkeys and mangabeys were more vulnerable to our conflict-engineering procedures than were vervets and rhesus. Other factors which expedited neurotigenesis included repetition of the traumatic experiences at unexpectedly long intervals, minimal opportunities to escape from traumata, aversive reinforcement (e.g., rubber snake with grille shock added), and a diminution of adaptive capacities produced by cerebral lesions.

In general, however, the following series of events was observed when an animal was subjected to a typical conflict between hunger and fear:

First, the animal, after a preliminary startle, acted as if to deny the unwonted experience; it would work the switches once more, secure the signals and again open the food box, though now with some hesitation and a subtly changed mode of manipulation. The usual procedure was then to permit the animal to feed again, but after it had consumed several pellets it was once more subjected to the "traumatic" stimulus. Following a number of such conflictful experiences (2 to 7 in cats or dogs, generally more in monkeys), the animal began to develop the following patterns of aberration, so closely akin to those seen clinically that the term "experimental neurosis" could with considerable validity be applied:

Anxiety. Pervasive anxiety was indicated by a low threshold of startle with persistent hyperirritability, muscular tension, crouched body postures, mydriasis, and other measurable physiologic indexes such as hidrosis, irregularly accelerated pulse rate, raised blood pressure, and increased coagulability and 17-ketosteroid content of the blood.

Psychosomatic symptomatology. In addition to these bodily changes many animals (though, with respect to individual "psychodynamic" as opposed to species "specificity," we could never precisely predict which and when) showed recurrent asthmatic breathing, genitourinary dysfunctions, and various gastrointestinal disturbances such as persistent anorexia, flatulence, or diarrhea of so severe a degree that food would pass almost undigested in less than an hour.

Motor defensive or mimetic reactions. These were likewise protean and took the following forms: inhibitions of feeding even outside the experimental apparatus to the point of self-starvation and serious cachexia; startle or phobic escape, first from stimuli directly associated with the traumatic experiences such as sensory signals (especially odors), switches, constricted spaces, etc., and then spreading to other situations; jerking tics of the head and body; stereotyped motor compulsions such as ritualized kneeling, sitting, or turning; epileptiform seizures and, in some cases, cataleptic rigidity with partial *flexibilitas cerea.*

Sexual deviations. Sexual deviations became evident in markedly diminished heterosexual interest, accentuated homosexual activity, and, especially in the case of monkeys, greatly increased direct and vicarious masturbation. One vervet, for several months after being made experimentally neurotic, spent most of his waking hours in auto-fellatio while completely ignoring a receptive female cagemate.

Sensorial aberrations. Disturbances of the sensorium were obviously more difficult to deduce, but some neurotic animals were exceedingly sensitive to even minor changes in their surroundings, whereas others showed recurrent episodes of disorientation and confusion. Some monkeys appeared to act out wishfully vivid imagery; though they refused food readily available in their food boxes, they could be observed to pick nonexistent pellets off various surfaces of the cage or from the air, then chew and swallow these fantasied tidbits with apparent relish.

Alterations in social conduct. These generally took the form of inertia and withdrawal from competition, with consequent loss of position in the group hierarchy. Significantly, overt hostility toward group mates appeared only in neurotic animals which had been accustomed to dominance, but had then become neurotically inhibited from achieving direct oral, erotic, or other satisfactions. Under such circumstances, and in the case of monkeys, especially when allied with other frustrated cagemates (Wechkin and Masserman, 1966), they turned on more successful rivals with displaced energy furiously wielded through tooth and claw.

Regression. Specific regressive behavior was manifested by staid, relatively independent adult dogs or cats which, after being made neurotic, resumed many of their previously recorded puppyish or kittenish characteristics. Spider monkeys also tended to become more passively dependent and receptive of the experimenter's ministrations, but other species showed no such proclivities.

Constitutional influences. Animals closest to man showed symptoms most nearly resembling those in human neuroses and psychoses, but in each case the "neurotic syndrome" induced depended less on the nature of the conflict (which could be held constant) than on the constitutional predisposition of the animal. For example, under similar stresses spider monkeys reverted to infantile dependencies or catatonic immobility, cebus developed various "psychosomatic" disturbances including functional paralyses, whereas vervets became diffusely aggressive, persisted in bizarre sexual patterns, or preferred hallucinatory satisfactions such as chewing and swallowing purely imaginary meals while avoiding real food to the point of self-starvation.

FACTORS THAT ACCENTUATED NEUROTIC SYMPTOMATOLOGY

Experimentally, these were precisely those that also exacerbated the basic conflict or prevented escape from it: i.e., increase in either hunger or fear, or forced transgression of the phobic, compulsive, or regressive patterns described above. Under such circumstances anxiety mounted to panic, inhibitions became paralyzing, and psychosomatic disturbances grew serious enough to threaten the life of the animal.

PROCEDURES THAT AMELIORATED NEUROTIC ABERRATIONS

It would be inaccurate, of course, to state that the choice of methods selected for investigation was not influenced by the experimenter's psychiatric and psychoanalytic training, since certain preferences, consciously or not, undoubtedly remained operative. Nevertheless, various techniques of "therapy" were investigated as objectively as possible, of which the following, with brief mention of their possible clinical parallels, were found most effective:

1. *Satiation of one of the conflictful needs.* If a neurotic animal with marked inhibitions of feeding and corresponding symbolic aversions was tube-fed, its neurotic symptoms were temporarily relieved, only to recur when the necessity and the fear of spontaneous feeding returned simultaneously.

To cite a single clinical comparison: sexual intercourse may relieve repressed desire temporarily but does not usually dispel symbolically elaborated sexual conflicts and may, indeed, exacerbate them. It will be recalled that such observations forced Freud to abandon his early attribution of the neuroses to quasi-physiologic "toxic accumulations" of "repressed libido."

2. *Prolonged rest away from the neurotigenic situation.* This blunted the other horn of the dilemma by removing the animal from the original environs of conflict. It is significant that this form of relief was minimal in monkeys in whom, as in the case of man, neurotic reactions quickly became generalized; moreover, animals which were returned to the laboratory even after a year of relatively peaceful sojourn elsewhere soon redeveloped their neurotic patterns, even though the original traumata were not repeated.

Clinically, "rest cures" and vacations away from disturbing situations may alleviate acute symptoms, but do not necessarily dispel the underlying and potentially disruptive tensions. Soldiers with "combat neuroses" may feel relieved when removed from immediate danger but unless, as Grinker and Spiegel observed (1945), the impasse between self-preservation versus military duty is effectively resolved, exposure to any situation reminiscent of this conflict almost inevitably spells the reappearance of neurotic reactions.

3. *Forced solution.* When hunger was maximal (from one to three days of starvation), food was made particularly attractive and openly available and no escape from the temptation was possible; some neurotic animals broke through their feeding or other inhibitions, began eating spontaneously, and showed gradual relief from the various neurotic symptoms originally engendered by the hunger-fear conflict. On the other hand, animals with lesser readaptive capacities, when placed in similar situations calculated to shatter the motivational impasse, reacted instead with an exacerbation of phobias, somatic dysfunctions, destructive aggressivity, or a retreat into a quasi-cataleptic stupor.

Thus also, actively directing patients paralyzed by indecision and anxiety into some decisive course of action is occasionally necessary and effective, but may likewise present the danger of further bewilderment, panic, or even psychotic reactions, if the readaptive capacities in space, time, and modality [T. French's (1933, 1941) "ego span," or "ego strength" in other analytic terminology] are seriously exceeded.

4. *Spontaneous re-exploration and solution.* Animals which had been

trained merely to respond to an automatic food signal and which were then subjected to a counterpoised fear of feeding remained neurotic indefinitely since, without special help, they had no way of re-exploring the traumatic situation. Markedly different, however, was the case of animals that had been taught to manipulate various devices that actuated the signals and feeder, since in this way they could exert at least partial control over their environment. This stood them in crucial stead even after they were made neurotic inasmuch as, though for a time they feared almost every aspect of the apparatus, when their hunger increased they gradually made hesitant but spontaneous attempts to re-explore the operation of the switches, signals, and food boxes, and grew bolder and more successful as food began to reappear. If the fear-engendering situations were prematurely repeated, their effects were even more traumatizing, but if each animal's efforts were again rewarded with food as in its preneurotic experiences, it eventually became, to all appearances, as confident and effective in its behavior as ever.

This, perhaps, is a paradigm of how most conflicts—and "larval neuroses"—are resolved in most instances by spontaneous re-exploration of the problem situation, leading to the immensely reassuring discovery that something temporarily feared either does not recur, or may be mastered if it does. Pertinent also is the necessity all of us feel for acquiring a large variety of techniques to control our environment, not only for normal living but also as a means of trial re-entry after retreat or flight. Explicitly, we invoke this principle in preparing our children for a wide range of contingencies; pragmatically, we employ "occupational therapy" or "job training" in our correctional institutions and hospitals to give our patients the skills, whether major or minor, which they can later utilize to meet social challenges in the world outside. Implicitly, also, a comparable process is at work in psychoanalysis as the analysand, in a protective, permissive situation, re-explores his conflictful and deeply repressed interpersonal desires and fantasies both verbally and through his transference relationship (*vide infra*), finds himself not punished or rejected as he had, consciously or not, feared he might be and thus, gaining confidence and aplomb, retransfers and "works through" his relationships with things and people in the real world about him.

5. *"Transference" therapy.* This leads to the question: but what about animals that had been trained to respond only to external signals and had not been taught manipulative or social skills; or if so taught, were later rendered too inhibited to use them? In such cases, it was found possible to alleviate the neurotic behavior through the more direct influence of the experimenter, who could assume the role of a reorientative trainer or "therapist." Dynamically, this influence itself was derived from the circumstance that the animal had been raised in a provident, kindly manner either in the

laboratory by the experimenter himself, or elsewhere by someone who also liked animals. Indeed, if the latter were not the case, when the animal came to the laboratory the first requirement was to dispel its mistrust of human beings and to cultivate its confidence; in effect, convert an initial "negative transference" into a "positive" one.[4] If, then, the animal's expectancy with regard to the experimenter, based on its experience with him *or his surrogates*, became predominantly favorable ("positive transference"), that expectancy could be utilized "therapeutically," for retraining and rehabilitation, however minimal the initial steps. For example, even the most "neurotic" animal, huddled in cataleptic rigidity in a dark corner, might be led by gentle petting and coaxing to take food from the experimenter's hand. Once this initial receptivity was established, the animal might be induced to eat from the floor of the apparatus if the experimenter remained near the cage; later, it sufficed that the "therapist" was merely in the room. At any stage of this retraining the premature repetition even of a faint feeding signal could reprecipitate the conflict and disrupt the animal's recovery, perhaps irrevocably. However, if the experimenter exercised gentleness and patience and did not at any time exceed the gradually regained tolerance and capacities of the animal, he could eventually induce it in successive stages to open the food box, to begin again to respond to signals and manipulate switches, and to reassert its former skills and patterns of self-sustenance. The retraining could then be continued to include acceptance of previously traumatic stimuli, so that eventually the animals would welcome even an airblast or electric shock (though not the toy snake) as itself a harbinger of food or other rewards. After such patterns were in their turn re-established, the therapist could complete the process by gradually withdrawing from the situation as the animal reasserted its self-sufficiency, until finally his personal ministrations or presence was no longer necessary.

To claim sweeping identities between the mechanics of these experiments and the almost incomparably more complex dynamics of clinical psychotherapy and psychoanalysis would be an obvious oversimplification; however, certain clinical parallels need not be overlooked. The psychotherapist, too, is preconceived as a parental or helpful surrogate, else his aid would not be sought at all. Wishfully endowed by the patient with anticipatory concern and competence (though often this is explicitly denied), the properly trained and experienced psychiatrist gently but effectively ap-

[4] Whenever possible, all experimenters dissociated themselves (though such disassociation was rarely complete in the case of dependent dogs or the highly perceptive monkeys) from the animal's traumatizing experience by having the latter administered either by remote control or by an automatic electrical governor on the apparatus. Significantly, some experimenters were not able to secure this favorable relationship in normal animals, and were correspondingly unsuccessful in helping neurotic ones. In my laboratory, this was particularly true of an assistant who had himself been raised in an oriental country where cats and dogs were kept as guards or as scavengers, sometimes eaten, but almost never liked, respected, and protected.

proaches the patient in his neurotic retreat, fills his needs personally in so far as practicable, permits him to re-explore, retest, and re-evaluate experiential symbols and their disruptive conflicts, first in the protected therapeutic situation, then gradually—and never more rapidly than the patient's anxiety permits—in the outside world, and finally fosters and redirects his personal relationships onto people and activities that can play a favorable and permanent role in the patient's future. This done, the therapist may relinquish his Virgilian role of guide and mentor as the patient takes his place once more in the world and no longer needs the psychiatrist personally except, perhaps, as another friend among a new-found many. Words, of course, are facile but sometimes deceptive instruments of communication, and abbreviations of statement should not contain abrogations of fact; nevertheless, perhaps it will be sen that, in a field more plagued by overobfuscation than by oversimplification, these comparisons and parallelisms are more than merely rhetorical.

6. *"Social" therapy.* In some animals, the success of a sixth method dubbed, debatably but conveniently, "social" therapy or "therapy by example" indicated that one factor in the process of so-called "transference" therapy was the relatively impersonal one of making the solution of a motivational or adaptational impasse seem easier or at least possible. In this procedure, the neurotic animal was simply placed with a well-trained normal one and permitted to watch the latter work the switches and signals and then feed unharmed. After from one to several days of such observation, about half the neurotic animals would begin to approach the food box, cower less at the signals, tentatively try the switches, and finally "emulate" the normal animal in resuming effective feeding patterns. Once the conflict was thus resolved, its other neurotic expressions were also in large part—but never completely—mitigated, and the animal, aside from minor residuals such as slight furtiveness, restlessness, or tension, appeared to be recovered.

Though the method was simple and certainly took the least effort on the part of the experimenter, it seems most difficult to formulate theoretically, especially since the convenient fiction of a postulated "interanimal relationship" or "identification" was dispelled when, in a control series of experiments, the neurotic animal could also be induced to resume feeding when an appropriately furred, scented, and activated automaton mechanically "answered" the signals, opened the food box, revealed the presence of tempting pellets, and otherwise changed the neurotic animal's external and internal milieu.

Perhaps, as implied previously, this is the solipsistic nidus of all "interpersonal relationships." But whatever the dynamics, we utilize such influences empirically in our clinical work. To cite but one instance, we place a neurotic child in a foster home or a special school in the hope that our young patient may be favorably influenced by the "example" of normal children being duly rewarded for patterns of behavior we wish our patient, too, to acquire. Unfortunately, psychoanalysis has long neglected group theory and practice, though these are fundamental to the development of social and community psychiatry.

Beyond Ethology and Experiment

All these ontogenic, physiologic, ethologic, and experimental considerations may seem irrelevant to those partisans of the "classical" (as distinguished from the Freudian) spirit in psychoanalysis who prefer to regard man as a special creation unique and apart, and whose behavior can be understood only in the terms of an almost monothetic metapsychology.[5] Even this limited position is of heuristic value, however, since it must be admitted that human behavior is vastly (though not incomparably) more versatile and elaborately transactive than that of other animals. As Susanne Langer (1942) points out, all doctrines (she includes Zen Buddhism, classical Freudian "metapsychology," *Daseinsanalyse* and other arcane assertions as to the special nature of man) differ from all sciences in that the former are designed not to expand or correlate man's consensual knowledge of reality but to provide him with supposedly impervious systems of wishfully assumed "facts" and pseudo-logical derivations dogmatically ensconced as exclusive and eternal truths. As psychiatrists, we admit the necessity of such forms of security and comfort; however, as scientists, we may also seek to clarify the intriguing issues involved.

And yet, the essence of therapy may derive from a more subtle and profound insight: that, contrary to our former presumptions of analytic omniscience, we need not aim to abolish man's ever-precious delusions. Instead—and only when necessary for his own and society's welfare—we must help him gently to find happier beliefs and more creative applications of them. In effect, as man's physicians, we must transcend the simpler concepts of biology and behavior theory outlined in the earlier sections of this chapter in order to deal adequately with that most intricately constituted, sensitively reactive, and complexly vulnerable of living creatures—man himself. The wise psychiatrist and psychoanalyst therefore soon learns—along with the devoted teacher and the good minister—that the best therapy is to help troubled men rebuild, largely on their own terms, their confidences in themselves, in their fellow men, and in their wishfully conceived "scientific," philosophic, and religious systems. Mortal therapists can do no more.

[5] Allen Wheelis, in "The Vocational Hazards of Psychoanalysis" (1956), points out that among the greatest of these is the defensive isolation of the analyst in his magical self-convictions.

References

Aarons, L., Schulman, J., Masserman, J. H., and Zimmar, C. P. "Behavioral Adaptations after Parietal Cortex Ablation in the Neonate Macaque." In J. Wortis (ed.), *Recent Advances in Biological Psychiatry*. New York: Grune & Stratton, 1962. Vol. IV. Pp. 347–353.

Allee, W. C. *Cooperation among Animals*. New York: Henry Schuman, 1951.

Allport, F. H. *Social Psychology*. Boston: Houghton Mifflin, 1924.

Angyal, A. *Foundations for a Science of Personality*. New York: Commonwealth Fund, 1941.

Arnold, M. B. "Physiologic Differentiation of Emotional States." *Psychological Review*, 52 (1945), 35–48.

Bailey, P. "Modern Attitudes toward the Relationship of the Brain to Behavior." *American Medical Association Archives of General Psychiatry*, 2 (1960), 361–366.

Bailey, P. "Cortex and Mind." In J. Scher (ed.), *Theories of Mind*. New York: The Free Press of Glencoe, 1962. Pp. 3–15.

Bayer, E. "Facilitation of Feeding." *Journal of Psychology*, 112 (1929).

Bertalanffy, L. von. "An Essay on the Relativity of Categories." *Philosophy of Science*, 22 (1955), 243–263.

Best, C. H., and Taylor, N. B. *The Physiologic Basis of Medical Practice*. 6th ed.; Baltimore: Williams & Wilkins, 1959.

Bowlby, J. "The Nature of the Child's Tie to His Mother." *International Journal of Psycho-Analysis*, 39 (1959), 350–373.

Bridges, K. M. "Human Imprinting." *Child Development*, 3 (1932), 324.

Butler, R. A. "Curiosity in Monkeys." *Scientific American*, 190 (1954).

Calhoun, J. B. "Population Density and Social Pathology." *Scientific American*, 206 (1962), 139–144.

Chen, S. C. "Interaction in Ants." *Psychological Zoology*, 10 (1937), 420–427.

Cobb, S. "Instincts." *American Journal of Psychiatry*, 112 (1955), 149–156.

Craig, W. "The Crossbreeding of Pigeons." *American Journal of Sociology*, 14 (1908).

Craig, W. "Male Doves Reared in Isolation." *Journal of Animal Behavior*, 4 (1914), 121–126.

Cross, H. A., and Harlow, H. F. "Prolonged and Progressive Effects of Partial Isolation on Macaque Monkeys." *Journal of Experimental Research in Personality*, 1 (1965), 39–49.

Denenberg, V. H., and Morton, J. R. C. "Effects of Weaning on Problem-solving Behavior." *Journal of Comparative and Physiological Psychology*, 55 (1962) 1096–1098.

Denenberg, V. H., Ottinger, D. R., and Stephens, M. W. "Maternal Factors in Growth and Behavior of the Rat." *Child Development*, 33 (1962), 65–71.

Eysenck, H. J., "The Effects of Psychotherapy." *International Journal of Psychiatry*, 1 (1965), 97–143.
Ferster, C. B. "Arithmetic Behavior in Chimpanzees." *Scientific American*, 210 (1964), 98–106.
Fisher, A. E. "Chemical Stimulation of the Brain." *Scientific American*, 210 (1964), 60.
French, T. M. "Interrelations between Psychoanalysis and the Experimental Work of Pavlov." *American Journal of Psychiatry*, 12 (1933), 1165–1203.
French, T. M. "Goal, Mechanism, and Integrative Field." *Psychosomatic Medicine*, 3 (1941), 226–252.
Freud, S. *The Origins of Psychoanalysis: Letters to Wilhelm Fleiss, 1887–1902*. New York: Basic Books, 1954.
Freud, S. "Leonardo da Vinci" (1910). *The Standard Edition of the Complete Psychological Works of. . . .* London: Hogarth Press. Vol. 11, pp. 63–137.
Freud, S. "An Autobiographical Study" (1924). *The Standard Edition of the Complete Psychological Works of. . . .* London: Hogarth Press. Vol. 20, pp. 1–70.
Freud, S. "The Question of Lay Analysis" (1926). *The Standard Edition of the Complete Psychological Works of. . . .* Vol. 20, pp. 179–250.
Freud, S. "Postscript to a Discussion on Lay Analysis" (1927). *The Standard Edition of the Complete Psychological Works of. . . .* London: Hogarth Press. Vol. 20, pp. 251–258. (Also in *Collected Papers of. . . .* New York: Basic Books, 1959. Vol. 5, pp. 205–214.)
Freud, S. "An Outline of Psychoanalysis" (1938). *The Standard Edition of the Complete Psychological Works of. . . .* London: Hogarth Press. Vol. 23.
Gantt, W. H. *The Origin and Development of Behavior Disorders in Dogs.* New York: Psychosomatic Monographs, 1942.
Gerard, R. W. "Units and Concepts of Biology." *Science*, 125 (1957), 429–433.
Gillard, E. T. "The Evolution of Bowerherds." *Scientific American*, 209 (1963), 30–39.
Ginsberg, B. E. "Genetics as a Tool in the Study of Behavior." *Perspectives in Biology and Medicine*, 1 (1957–1958), 397–424.
Goodall, Jane. "Chimpanzees." *National Geographic*, 124 (1963), 293–302.
Goodall, Jane. "Chimpanzee Tool-Users." *Science*, 146 (1964), 801–802.
Grinker, R. R., Sr. "Anxiety as a Significant Variable for a Unified Theory of Human Behavior." *American Medical Association Archives of General Psychiatry*, 1 (1959), 537–546.
Grinker, R. R., Sr., and Spiegel, J. P. *Men under Stress*. Philadelphia: Blakiston, 1945.
Halstead, W. C. *Brain and Intelligence*. Chicago: University of Chicago Press, 1947.
Harlow, H. F. "Love in Infant Monkeys." *Scientific American*, 200 (1959), 68.
Harrison, Barbara. *Orang-utan*. Garden City, N.Y.: Doubleday, 1963.
Heath, R. G. *Studies in Schizophrenia: A Multidisciplinary Approach to Mind-Brain Relationships*. Cambridge, Mass.: Harvard University Press, 1954.

Heath, R. G. "Reappraisal of Biological Aspects of Psychiatry." *Journal of Neuropsychiatry*, 2 (1961), 111.

Heath, R. G., Monroe, R. B., and Mickle, W. A. "Stimulation of the Amygdaloid Nucleus in a Schizophrenia Patient." *American Journal of Psychiatry*, 111 (1955), 862.

Hebb, D. O. A *Textbook of Psychology*. Philadelphia: Saunders, 1958.

Hess, E. " 'Imprinting' in Animals." *Scientific American*, 198 (1958), 81.

Hess, E. "Imprinting." *Science*, 130 (1959), 133.

Higgins, J. W., Mahl, G. F., Delgado, J. M. R., and Hamlin, H. "Behavior Changes during Intercerebral Electrical Stimulation." *American Medical Association Archives of Neurology and Psychiatry*, 76 (1956), 319–419.

Huxley, T. H. *Man's Place in Nature*. Charles C Thomas, 1898.

Kardiner, A., Linton, R., Du Bois, Cora, and West, J. *The Psychological Frontiers of Society*. New York: Columbia University Press, 1945.

Katz, D. *Animals and Man*. New York: Longmans, Green, 1937.

King, J. A. "Parameters Relevant to Determining the Affect of Early Experiences upon the Adult Behavior of Animals." *Psychological Bulletin*, 5 (1958), 46.

King, J. A. "The Social Behavior of Prairie Dogs." *Scientific American*, 201 (1959), 128.

Kluver, H., and Bucy, P. C. "Functions of the Temporal Lobe in Monkeys." *American Medical Association Archives of Neurology and Psychiatry*, 42 (1939), 979–1000.

Kohler, W. *The Mentality of Apes*. New York: Harcourt, Brace, 1929.

Kortland, A. "Chimpanzees in the Wild." *Scientific American*, 206 (1962), 128.

Langer, Susan. *Philosophy in a New Key*. New York: Mentor, 1942.

Lashley, K. S. "Dynamic Processes in Perception." In J. F. Delafresnaze (ed.), *Brain Mechanisms and Consciousness*. Springfield, Ill.: Charles C. Thomas, 1954.

Leblond, C. P. "Extra-hormonal Factors in Maternal Behavior." *Proceedings of the Society for Experimental Biology and Medicine*, 38 (1938), 66.

Lehrman, D. S. "The Reproductive Behavior of Ring Doves." *Scientific American*, 211 (1964), 48.

Levy, D. M. "The Relation of Animal Psychology to Psychiatry." In I. Galdston (ed.), *Medicine and Science*. New York: International Universities Press, 1954. Pp. 44–75.

Liddell, H. S. "Discussion of Konrad Lorenz." *Proceedings of the Center for Post-graduate Training*, New York, October 23, 1958.

Lorenz, K. *King Solomon's Ring*. New York: Crowell, 1952.

Loveridge, A. "Notes on East African Mammals." *Journal of the East African Natural History Society*, 16 (1938); 17 (1939).

McLean, P. D. "The Limbic System ('Visceral Brain') in Relation to Central Gray and Reticulum of the Brain Stem." *Psychosomatic Medicine*, 17 (1955), 355.

McLean, P. D. "Psychosexual Evaluation in Monkeys." *Journal of Nervous and Mental Diseases*, 135 (1962), 209.

Malamud, W. "Psychiatric Symptoms and the Limbic Lobe." *Bulletin of the Los Angeles Neurological Society*, 22 (1957), 131–139.

Malinowski, B. *Sex and Repression in Savage Society*. New York: Harcourt, 1927.

Mandell, A. J. "Some Determinants of Indole Excretion in Man." *Recent Advances in Biological Psychiatry*, 5 (1963), 237.

Marmor, J. "The Role of Instinct in Human Behavior." *Psychiatry*, 5 (1942), 509–516.

Marshall, A. J. "Bower Birds." *Scientific American*, 194 (1956), 48.

Maslow, A. H. "Role of Dominance in the Social and Sexual Behavior of Infra-human Primates." *Journal of Genetic Psychology*, 48 (1936), 261.

Masserman, J. H. "Experimental Neuroses and Psychotherapy." *American Medical Association Archives of Neurology and Psychiatry*, 49 (1943), 43.

Masserman, J. H. "Report of the Committee on Animal Experimentations, 1943–1944." *Psychosomatic Medicine*, 7 (1945), 46.

Masserman, J. H. "A Biodynamic Psychoanalytic Approach to the Problems of Feeling and Emotion." In M. L. Reymert (ed.), *Feelings and Emotions*. New York: McGraw-Hill, 1950.

Masserman, J. H. "Some Current Concepts of Sexual Behavior." *Psychiatry*, 14 (1951), 67.

Masserman, J. H. "Psychoanalysis and Biodynamics—An Integration." *International Journal of Psycho-Analysis*, 34 (1953), 34.

Masserman, J. H. *Principles of Dynamic Psychiatry*. Philadelphia: Saunders, 1955.

Masserman, J. H. "Experimental Psychopharmacology and Behavioral Relativity." In P. Hoch and J. Zubin (eds.), *Problems of Addiction and Habituation*. New York: Grune & Stratton, 1958.

Masserman, J. H. "Norms, Neurotics and Nepenthics." In J. H. Masserman (ed.), *Biological Psychiatry*. New York: Grune & Stratton, 1959. Vol. 1.

Masserman, J. H. "Ethology, Comparative Biodynamics and Psychoanalytic Research." In J. H. Masserman (ed.), *Science and Psychoanalysis*. New York: Grune & Stratton, 1960. Vol. 3, p. 20.

Masserman, J. H. "Drugs, Brain and Behavior." *Journal of Neuropsychiatry*, 3 (1962), 5104.

Masserman, J. H. *Behavior and Neurosis*. New York: Hafner, 1964.

Masserman, J. H. "Anxiety: Protean Source of Communication." In J. H. Masserman (ed.), *Science and Psychoanalysis*. Vol. VIII. *Communication and Community*. New York: Grune & Stratton, 1965. P. 1.

Masserman, J. H. "Motion Picture Films on Experimental Neuroses; Alcohol; Masochism; Morphine, and Development of Behavior." Catalogue, Psychological Cinema Register. State University, Pa., 1938–1965.

Masserman, J. H., and Pechtel, C. T. "Neuroses in Monkeys; A Preliminary Report of Experimental Observations." *Annals of the New York Academy of Sciences*, 56 (1953), 253.

Masserman, J. H., and Pechtel, C. T. "How Brain Lesions Affect Normal and Neurotic Olfactory Behavior in Monkey." *American Journal of Psychiatry*, 11 (1956), 256. (a)

Masserman, J. H., and Pechtel, C. T. "Neurophysiologic and Pharmacologic Influence on Experimental Neuroses." *American Journal of Psychiatry*, 113 (1956), 510. (b)

Masserman, J. H., and Pechtel, C. T. "An Experimental Investigation of Factors Influencing Drug Action." *Psychiatric Research Report*, 4 (1956), 126. (c)

Masserman, J. H., and Pechtel, C. T. *Penrod: The Evolution of Behavior Patterns in an Infant Macaque* (motion picture). Pennsylvania Cinema Register, State University, Pa., 1956. (d)

Masserman, J. H., Pechtel, C. T., and Schreiner, L. "The Role of Olfaction in Normal and Neurotic Behavior in Animals: A Preliminary Report." *Psychosomatic Medicine*, 15 (1953), 396.

Masserman, J. H., and Jacques, M. G. "Effects of Cerebral Electroshock on Experimental Neuroses in Cats." *American Journal of Psychiatry*, 104 (1947), 92.

Masserman, J. H., and Siever, P. W. "Dominance, Neurosis and Aggression." *Psychosomatic Medicine*, 6 (1944), 87.

Masserman, J. H. "Experimental Masochism." *American Medical Association Archives of Neurology and Psychiatry*, 60 (1948), 402–404.

Masserman, J. H., and Wechkin, S. "Social Interaction and Aggression." *American Journal of Psychology* (1966), 142–146.

Masserman, J. H., Wechkin, S., and Terris, W. "Altruistic Behavior in Rhesus Monkeys." *American Journal of Psychiatry*, 121 (1964), 584.

Mead, Margaret. *Male and Female*. New York: William Morrow, 1949.

Miller, J. G. "Information Input Overload and Psychopathology." *American Journal of Psychiatry*, 116 (1960), 695.

Miller, N. E. "Experiments in Motivation." *Science*, 126 (1957), 1276.

Miller, N. E. "Chemical Coding of Behavior in the Brain." *Science*, 148 (1965), 328.

Mirsky, A. F., and Katz, M. S. "Avoidance 'Conditioning' in Paramecia." *Science*, 127 (1958), 1498.

Mirsky, I. A., Miller, R. E., and Murphy, J. V. "The Communication of Affect in Rhesus Monkeys." *Journal of the American Psychoanalytic Association*, 6 (1958), 433.

Mittelmann, B. "Psychodynamics of Motility." *International Journal of Psycho-Analysis*, 39 (1958), 196–199.

Montagu, M. F. A. "Man—and Human Nature." *American Journal of Psychiatry*, 112 (1955), 401–410.

Noble, G. K., and Curtis, B. "Sexual Selection in Fishes." *Anatomical Records*, 64 (1935–1936), 84–85.

Ostow, M. "The Biological Basis of Human Behavior." In S. Arieti (ed.), *American Handbook of Psychiatry*. New York: Basic Books, 1959. Vol. 1, pp. 58–87.

Ostwald, P. F. "Acoustic Methods in Psychiatry." *Scientific American*, 212 (1965), 212–218.

Ottinger, R., Denenberg, V. H., and Stephens, M. W. "Maternal Emotionality, Multiple Mothering and Emotionality in Maturity." *Journal of Comprehensive Physiological Psychology*, 56 (1963), 313–317.

Papez, T. W. "A Proposed Mechanism of Emotion." *American Medical Association Archives of Neurology and Psychiatry*, 38 (1937), 725.

Pavlov, I. P. *Lectures on Conditioned Reflexes*. New York: International Publishers, 1928. P. 242.

Pechtel, C., McAvoy, T., Levitt, M., Kling, A., and Masserman, J. H. "The Cingulates and Behavior." *Journal of Nervous and Mental Diseases*, 126 (1958), 148–152.

Pechtel, C., and Pechtel, Jean. In J. H. Masserman (ed.), *Penrod: The Evolution of Behavior Patterns in an Infant Macaque* (motion picture). Pennsylvania Cinema Register, State University, Pa., 1956.

Penfield, W., and Miller, B. "Cortex and Memory." *American Medical Association Archives of Neurology and Psychiatry*, 79 (1958), 475.

Penfield, W., and Miller, B. "The Interpretive Cortex." *Science*, 159 (1959), 1722.

Piaget, J. "The Child in Modern Physics." *Scientific American*, 196 (1957), 46.

Pribram, K. "Freud's Project." In N. S. Greenfield and W. C. Lewis (eds.), *Psychoanalysis and Current Biological Thought*. Madison: University of Wisconsin Press, 1965. Pp. 81–92.

Rado, S., and Daniels, G. E. *Changing Concepts in Psychoanalytic Medicine*. New York: Grune & Stratton, 1956.

Riesen, A. H. "The Development of Visual Perception in Man and Chimpanzee." *Science*, 106 (1947), 107–108.

Rioch, D. McK. "Certain Aspects of 'Conscious' Phenomena and Their Neural Correlates." *American Journal of Psychiatry*, 111 (1955), 810–817.

Rule, C. "A Biologically-Based Theory of Human Behavior." *American Journal of Psychiatry*, 121 (1964), 344.

Schaller, G. B. *The Mountain Gorilla*. Chicago: University of Chicago Press, 1963.

Schneirla, T. C. "Learning and Orientation in Ants." *Comprehensive Psychology Monographs*, 6 (1929), 139.

Scott, J. P. *The Process of Socialization in Higher Animals*. New York: Milbank Fund Publications, 1953.

Scott, J. P. "Critical Periods in Behavior Development." *Science*, 138 (1962), 949.

Scott, W. E. "Data on Song in Birds." *Science*, 14 (1901), 522.

Scull, C., Nance, M., and Roll, G. F. "Research in the Soviet Union." *Journal of the American Medical Association*, 167 (1958), 2120.

Seboek, T. A. "Animal Communication." *Science*, 147 (1965), 1906.

Seitz, P. F. D. "The Effects of Infantile Experiences upon Adult Behavior in Animal Subjects. I. Effects of Litter Size during Infancy upon Adult Behavior in the Rat." *American Journal of Psychiatry*, 110 (1954), 916.

Sherrington, C. S. "The Spinal Cord." Quoted in J. F. Fulton, *Physiology of the Nervous System*. New York: Oxford University Press, 1938. Pp. 125, 215.

Sibol, J. "The Strangest Birds in the World." *Life*, March 25, 1957, p. 88.

Simpson, G. G. *The Meaning of Evolution*. New Haven: Yale University Press, 1949.

Smith, K. "Pattern Vision and Visual Acuity." *General Psychiatry*, 53 (1938), 251–272.

Spitz, R. A. "Infantile Depression and the General Adaptation Syndrome." In P. H. Hoch and J. Zubin, (eds.), *Depression*. New York: Grune & Stratton, 1954. Pp. 93–108.

Thiessen, D. D., and Rodgers, D. A. "Endocrine Effects of Overcrowding." *Psychological Bulletin*, 58 (1961), 449.

Thompson, W. R. "Influence of Prenatal Maternal Anxiety on Emotionality in Young Rats." *Science*, 125 (1957), 698.

Thompson, W. R., and Heron, W. "Maternal Influences." *Canadian Journal of Psychology*, 8 (1954), 17.

Thompson, W. R., and Melzock, R. " 'Whirling' Behavior in Dogs as Related to Early Experience." *Science*, 123 (1956), 939.

Tinbergen, N. *The Study of Instinct*. London: Oxford University Press, 1951.

Tolman, E. C. *Purposive Behavior in Animals and Men*. New York: Century, 1932.

Toynbee, A. J. *A Study of History*. Abridged by D. C. Somervill. New York: Oxford University Press, 1957.

Waismann, H. A., and Harlow, H. F. "Experimental Phenylketonuria in Monkeys." *Science*, 147 (1965), 605.

Watson, R. E. "Experimentally-Induced Conflict in Cats." *Psychosomatic Medicine*, 16 (1954), 341.

Wheelis, A. "The Vocational Hazards of Psychoanalysis." *International Journal of Psycho-Analysis*, 37 (1956), 171.

Wolf, K. M. "Child Imprinting." *General Psychological Monographs*, 34 (1946), 57–125.

Wolpe, J. *Psychotherapy by Reciprocal Inhibition*. Palo Alto, Calif.: Stanford University Press, 1958.

Wynne-Edwards, V. C. *Animal Dispersion in Relation to Social Behavior*. New York: Hafner, 1962. P. 16.

Wynne, Edwards, V. C. "Self-Regulating Systems in Population of Animals." *Science*, 147 (1965), 1543.

Yerkes, R. M. *Chimpanzees: A Laboratory Colony*. New Haven: Yale University Press, 1943.

Zajonc, R. B. "Social Facilitation." *Science*, 149 (1965), 269–274.

Zuckerman, S. *The Social Life of Monkeys and Apes*. London: Kegan, Paul, Trench, Trunmer, 1932.

9

Symbolic Neurology and Psychoanalysis

EDWIN A. WEINSTEIN

The area of neurology most relevant to psychoanalysis is that of symbolic behavior involving organism-environmental relationships and the representation of states and events within and without the body. The disciplines have in common the study of memory, cognition, and perception, and share a lexicon that includes such terms as consciousness, attention, symbolization, and adaptation. Each discipline erects a theoretical model through which the physical-chemical processes of the brain are translated into clinical phenomena. In both orientations one deals with abnormal behavior from which tacit or explicit assumptions of normal behavior are made. Both psychoanalysis and neurology are concerned with the effects of stress and deprivation, as in the loss of need-satisfying objects and delay of gratification, on the one hand, and modes of adaptation to, and compensation for, diminished capacity, on the other.

Freud's early scheme of psychoanalysis was a neuroanatomical and neurophysiological one in which he equated clinical and neurobiological entities. He thought of the excessively intense ideas of hysteria and obsessional neuroses as indicating heightened activity in the nervous system as contrasted, say, with anxiety and depressive states. It was hoped that repression, displacement, and condensation would find their counterparts in neural mechanisms and that primary and secondary process thinking could be differentiated in terms of neural organization. Psychoanalytic principles were applied to the interpretation of behavior in general paresis and the Korsakoff psychosis or amnestic-confabulatory state, and the appearance of aggressive and overtly sexual behavior was explained on the basis of impairment of repressing and inhibiting mechanisms and the release of hitherto controlled drives. Pribram believes that Freud's neurological model adumbrated modern concepts of neural conduction and delineated the organization of the neocortical and limbic-reticular systems. In general, however, the original tenets of psychoanalysis have not found their counterparts in neurophysiology, due in part to the enormous changes in each discipline. Even among neurophysiologists the concepts of excitation and inhibition are not clearly distinguished, and any eventual equating of behavior and brain function is likely to be expressed in a quite different vocabulary.

When one seeks to correlate neurology and psychoanalysis, a great deal depends on what psychoanalytic views and what neurological phenomena are selected. The bias of this chapter is that the two disciplines are related through ego psychology rather than through early theories of drive-determined behavior. While the study of the physiology of drives and affects is important, the relevance of behaviors of feeding, drinking, temperature control, and aggressive and sexual activity to psychoanalysis concerns the way these biological processes are integrated into socially organized patterns of behavior and serve as modes of communication. The fact that penile erection may be obtained by stimulation of a very large area of the limbic-reticular system does not in itself make the phenomenon more "basic" to human behavior than, say, pupillary dilatation which has an equally large representation. Similarly, the occurrence of penile erection in the REM stage of sleep may have no more significance than a variety of concomitant physiological events. From a strictly physiological standpoint, the piloerection of a cat is a means of trapping warm air in the interstices of its coat and thus preserving body heat. For psychoanalysis, the effect on another cat might be more important.

The plan of this chapter is to take a number of neurological syndromes, to consider the way some have been formulated in psychoanalytic terms, and to note the directions in which studies of these phenomena may modify psychoanalytic concepts. In the formulation to be followed, the location, extent, and rapidity of development of the brain injury is only one of a number of dependent and independent variables. Others are the conditions in which the brain injury was sustained, the nature of the resultant incapacities, the way the consequences of the incapacities are defined in terms of previous personal experience and social role, and the conditions under which the behavior is observed. Through this approach, the use of such hypothetical functions of the brain as "insight," "judgment," and "ethical sense" to designate complex interactions in the environment is avoided. No major effort is made to differentiate "organic" from "psychogenic" features or to demarcate strictly those aspects of behavior which are due to a defect from those which represent adaptive processes, as the form of the adaptive response is determined necessarily by the level of brain function.

The Syndromes of Denial

In this area, problems of adaptation and defense are considered. While most psychoanalytic theories of ego function are more concerned with the impact of internal drives rather than the effect of external circumstances, the consideration of adaptation in states of diminished capacity following brain injury is germane to concepts of repression, regression, displacement, reality testing, and object relationships.

In neurology, the syndromes of denial are usually described under the rubrics of anosognosia—literally, lack of knowledge of disease—and inattention. While most studies concern hemiparesis and visual deficits, the range of disabilities of which the patient may appear unaware or which he may deny includes involuntary movements, incontinence, disfigurement as after severe burns, and the fact of an operation. Explicit denial of a deficit may be amplified by confabulations and rationalizations, or there may be a partial denial in which a patient with a brain tumor may attribute his weakness to overwork. The paralyzed limb may be recognized, but the patient may claim that he has no connection with it and will attribute its ownership to someone else. Patients may deny feeling obviously painful stimuli, even though they may wince and withdraw (pain asymbolia). Some patients ignore the side of a hemiparesis and only attend to stimuli from the other half of space. Others may respond to questions about illness with quips and jokes, often of a sexual nature, while some are selectively silent or barely audible in such a situation.

Patients with enduring denial of, or inattention to, major physical deficits show changes in their relationship to other aspects of the environment and these appear in the phenomena of disorientation for place and time, misidentification of persons and nonaphasic misnaming of objects. During the period in which this behavior is present, patients maintain their false statements, despite cues and corrections. Some are bland and unworried, others are euphoric, paranoid, or withdrawn. Another interesting feature of the behavior is that a patient may deny a deficit in one context of language but not in another, as in the statements that "there is nothing wrong with me" and "the doctors say I'm paralyzed" (Weinstein and Kahn, 1955; Weinstein and Cole, 1963).

The usual explanation in neurology is that anosognosia is due to a lesion in the parietal-temporal area of the dominant hemisphere which damages the representation of the body image. Thus the patient cannot recognize his paralysis because the limbs themselves have dropped out of the body scheme. However, this theory does not account for the observations that the patient may deny numerous problems and disabilities other than those relating to a part of the body; that there are disturbances in recognizing aspects of the environment other than the somatic; that the patient's responses are highly selective; and that he does not appear to be disturbed by his incapacities even though he may admit them. Redlich and Bonvicini (1908), noting early that anosognosia was associated with other changes in behavior, considered it to be one aspect of a Korsakoff psychosis. Schilder (1951) saw the mechanism of denial as a deeply rooted unconscious wish and introduced the term "organic repression."

CONFABULATIONS AND DELUSIONS

Psychoanalysts have studied such delusions and confabulations[1] as dream symbolism. The brain damage is regarded as causing a functional state comparable to that of sleep, in which a primary process thought organization takes over. Ferenczi and Hollòs (1925) saw the delusions and confabulations of patients with general paresis as wish-fulfilling fantasies of an infantile type. They interpreted certain oral, anal, and genital manifestations as evidence of regression to early modes of gratification. The limitations of this approach will be taken up later, but the authors made two highly significant observations. The first led to the finding that the bizarre grandiosity of the paretic cannot be attributed to loss of insight in the sense that the patient is unaware of his disease and its consequences in any absolute sense. Patients claimed that they had been cured of syphilis and that others had the disease. Thus, although one physician patient denied having lues, he admitted having acquired a soft chancre and described eruptions on his body through which small bugs crept to irritate him and call forth marvelous intellectual capacities! Here, in effect, the patient is referring to his disease and incapacity in a vivid image. Ferenczi and Hollòs noted that patients gave as their current age the age that they were at the onset of their disease. This error persisted even though the patient could give his correct birth date and could do the arithmetic necessary to arrive at his age. Ferenczi and Hollòs also observed that a number representing age might be repeatedly used in other seemingly irrelevant contexts.

Paul Schilder (1951) had paretics recall stories which had been read to

[1] Confabulations are distinguished from delusions in that they refer to specific events, persons, and people, whereas delusions tend to be timeless and limitless.

them. He found that errors and substitutions followed along affective needs with elimination of painful ideas. In their accounts, patients introduced motives from their own lives which were interpreted as primitive, unfulfilled wishes. A technique similar to that of Schilder was employed by Betlheim and Hartmann (1961) with other brain-damaged subjects. They reported that the distortions in repetition of stories were manifestations of the repression of sexual ideas accomplished according to the rules of Freudian dream interpretation. Because of the influence of this paper on psychoanalytic thought, it will be reviewed in detail. Brief case histories of three patients were given, the second and third being of special interest. Case 2 was that of a forty-eight-year-old woman who two months prior to admission had collapsed on the street, after which she had a left hemiparesis. On admission to the hospital, she was restless, confabulatory, and, when she tried to walk or stand, would fall over backward. The patient was asked to repeat stories of killing and sexual attack, and the distortions and omissions were then noted. The second story was as follows:

A young girl went for a walk in the fields all alone. A young man came, attacked her and threw her to the ground. The girl struggled, but it was no use. The man pulled up her skirts and pushed his stiff organ into her sheath. After the intercourse he fled, leaving the crying girl lying on the ground.

In Case 2, the patient repeated this story as follows:

A young girl went across the field; a young man went down the stairs. He let the young girl fall down and pulled up her skirts and struck his slanted knee.[2]

On another repetition she said:

A young girl went over a road, there came a young man, the girl stumbled, he let the girl stand there crying and shouting. [Why did she cry?] I told you she fell down the stairs.

On another occasion she said:

Two young men and two young ladies ran up the stairs. When the two men ran up, they stopped and struck their slanted knees into the sheath.

Betlheim and Hartmann claim that the crudely sexual material is distorted in order to make it harmless and nonthreatening to the patient. It appears in consciousness, according to their interpretation, in typically dis-

[2] Rapaport, in his translation, states that the German "steif" (stiff) has also the connotations of crooked, unfair, crippled.

guised symbols for sexual intercourse, such as climbing a staircase. They attribute the persistence of confabulations in the Korsakoff psychoses to the continuing need for repression. However, when one considers that the patient was unable to stand or walk, the references to stumbling, falling down, running upstairs, and the crooked knee all indicate that the woman is talking about her paralysis. The use of the condensed symbol "steif" to indicate the tragedy and injustice of it all is striking.

Case 3 was that of a forty-nine-year-old alcoholic woman with a paresis of all four extremities who could neither stand nor walk. There must have been marked intellectual impairment as she could not repeat any of the stories correctly. In one repetition she used the number four in cryptic fashion, saying that a young man gave her four cigarettes. In this instance the cigarette is regarded as the symbol of the male sex organ. In a footnote by the translator, David Rapaport, it is suggested that number four may represent numbers one and two, the symbols for urination and defecation. A much more economical explanation would be that the number four refers to the paralyzed extremities. If some connection with urination and defecation existed, one must consider the likelihood of a quadriparetic person also having bladder and bowel weakness.

Confabulations and delusions in brain injured patients also have been studied from the standpoint of neurological deficits such as memory and time sense, and studied in their symbolic and motivational aspects (Weinstein and Kahn, 1954; Weinstein, Kahn, and Malitz, 1956). Some delusions and confabulations can be regarded as wish-fulfillments or manifestations of repression, but in many cases the confabulation seems not to deny but to magnify the seriousness of the condition. For example, a patient with a paretic arm may maintain that his limb is a dead body in bed with him; or a person after an automobile accident may claim falsely that a member of his family was injured.

Another question is why patients maintain a delusion despite all evidence to the contrary. Most explanations based on neurological deficit are inadequate because patients with comparable deficits are not deluded or confabulatory, and patients often indicate in other contexts of language that they have knowledge of their condition. For example, Talland (1961), in a study of alcoholic psychoses, reported that hardly any of the subjects attributed their hospitalization to drinking although they readily admitted that they drank heavily and neglected their diets. It is common for patients to remain disoriented regarding place even though the name of the hospital is in full view. Another feature is that patients with confabulations are usually without overt anxiety or concern over their condition even though the presence of incapacity is explicitly recognized.

Studies of the language, personality background, and changes of language pattern during recovery of brain function and during experimental increase in neurological deficit by barbiturates (Weinstein and Malitz, 1954) have shown that confabulations, although ostensibly statements about *past* events, in some degree refer to the current situation and its anticipated consequences. This holds whether the confabulation is a complete fabrication, whether it involves actual events shifted in place and time, or whether it is an actually well-localized event used in a selective context. An example of the last is the case of a man who had sustained a crushing head injury and had been committed to the hospital by his wife. When asked how his injury had occurred, his response invariably included the fact that on their first date he had taken his wife to see the film *Samson and Delilah.*

Confabulation, disorientation for place and time, and certain types of nonaphasic misnaming of objects are *metaphors* in which experiences of the self are represented in some aspect of the physical environment. The metaphor may be a highly condensed one as in the case just cited where *Samson and Delilah* suggests the crushed skull, the downfall of a mighty man, the betrayal by the wife, and something of the patient's fundamentalist, religious background. The choice of the metaphor in an individual case is determined by the nature of the deficit or problem and what have been the most significant channels of social relatedness or sources of identity. Thus persons who are described as having been highly work-oriented and who have derived considerable prestige and status from their occupations commonly confabulate about work. They attribute their symptoms to overwork and tell stories, fictitious and otherwise, when asked how they came to the hospital. The prevailing metaphors in other cases concern the family. For example, a patient with a right hemiparesis said that his right arm was his daughter and reported that he had found his son's right arm in his pocket. Earlier he had blamed his headaches on his daughter's misconduct. A review of his personality background, obtained in an interview with his wife, showed the importance of the parent-child relationship as the major organizing principle of his social environment. He had been raised by a great-aunt after the death of his mother and had habitually attributed the difficulties of living (in a Negro, lower-class, rural area) to the loss of his parents. He was reported as expressing his own moods, needs, fears, and ambitions through his own children, alternately spoiling and criticizing them. When such a person says his child's arm is paralyzed, he is not releasing hitherto repressed hostility toward his own child or reviving feelings toward a sibling, but is using the symbol that makes the current experience most meaningful.

In this approach, delusions do not exist primarily to distort or censor reality but to express it more vividly. The symbols that have the most meaning are those which are elements in the preferred patterns of social relatedness. They form the systems of identity or "world view" according to which the events of the environment are classified and its responses anticipated. The person does not so much repress existential reality but feels that the "social-reality" is more valid. Much of the adaptive function of the language lies in its "social" character, expressed not only in delusions but in its highly idiomatic, cliché character, which enables the speaker to avoid social isolation and anomie.

The effect of the brain pathology, which involves principally the limbic-reticular system on symbolic functions, can be briefly summarized. Unlike most aphasic patients, the subject can use metaphorical speech, but he does not recognize the language as metaphorical when it pertains to himself and his problems. He does not, or cannot, recognize the cues in the situation which indicate the context in which words and gestures are being used. He is less responsive to the existential aspects of a situation and more responsive to the way the consequences of his disability are defined in terms of preexisting systems of social organization. Symbols are more condensed and their referents less differentiated. For example, in a state of panic everything is either safe or dangerous. The subject becomes less aware of the processes of interaction in the environment on which language is based and regards the product of the interaction, the metaphor, as the essence of reality. It is evident that this formulation applies not only to certain types of brain injury, but to behavior in other situations of stress.

Amnesia

This term requires some definition. Although the dictionary definition is loss of memory, in practice it is applied only to certain types of memory loss, namely, experiences that the patient *should* remember, such as where he lives, his occupation, or whether he is married. Also, the evidence is the person's verbal statement rather than the result of a memory test. In organic brain disease, amnesia is usually seen as a consequence of an acute injury with loss of consciousness. Retrograde amnesia refers to the period prior to the accident which the patient says he does not remember, and anterograde amnesia concerns the events of the period after the injury or loss of consciousness.

A major contribution of psychoanalytic and other workers is that amnesia is not to be explained simply as the failure to register and recall stimuli. It was shown that memories thought to be lost through destruction of neural tissue could be recovered under certain circumstances, such as hypnosis. The passive state of patients with the amnestic-confabulatory state was early noted, Korsakoff calling the behavior "apathetic confusion." Bonhoffer (1901) commented that, while patients were attentive in conversation, they lacked spontaneity when left alone. In interviews most patients offer few spontaneous remarks and are likely to become animated only during the telling of a confabulation. In interpreting such behavior, Buerger-Prinz and Kaila (1951) considered that the whole structure of drives and emotionality was involved. They thought that patients seemed unable to relate an event to life experience.

The introduction of electroshock treatment has given significant data. In separate studies, Carter (1953), Janis (1950), and Korngold (1953) have shown that following the convulsion and loss of consciousness, amnesia endures in areas directly related to the patient's problems. While generalized memory loss is transient, Kral (1956) suggested that the issue was the patient's inability to integrate current perceptions into a personally meaningful experience. This view follows the formulation of Bartlett (1932), who refers to memory as an imaginative reconstruction in which the new experience does not merely set up a series of reactions in a fixed temporal sequence, but acts as a cue that enables us to select out of past responses those which are most relevant to the needs of the moment.

In brain-injured subjects (Weinstein, Marvin, and Keller, 1962), the content of the amnesia most frequently concerns the event that caused the injury, such as an automobile accident or a surgical operation. In the very great majority of cases there is a period of retrograde amnesia that extends beyond the temporal bounds of the actual physical impact ranging from minutes to years. Patients who were amnesic for car accidents could not remember starting on the trip or its destination, what they had done the previous day, how long they had worked on their job, or even what kind of work they had done. The events transcended any particular time span as patients say they do not remember the make of the car or even if they owned a car. Soldiers could not remember having been in the Army, where they had been stationed, or with what units they had served. Such observations bear out Buerger-Prinz and Kaila's view that amnesia involves a change in attitude or set. The change in attitude involves not only the past, but the present and the future. The facts that the patient is in a hospital, that he has a bandage on his head and a cast on his leg, that he is being interviewed by a doctor, and that he is surrounded by other patients do not constitute a relatedness in his environment that includes a feeling of the reality of his accident or injury.

As patients grow more related in their environment, the amnesia becomes more selective and is a way of representing specific problems. These include physical disabilities, intellectual deficits, occupational status, and marital affairs. Thus, a soldier, who originally could not remember if he had been in the Army, later recalled that he had been but could not remember the kind of work he had done or the rank achieved. Another man, described as highly dependent on his wife, at first did not recognize her nor remember if he were married. Later he recalled being married, but not the church in which the ceremony had been performed (his wife subsequently left him). It is significant that, during the stage of amnesia, the patient does not refer to such problems directly. How one structures problems is closely tied up with the significant sources of identity. For example, the soldiers who could not remember the kind of work they had done were described by relatives and associates as people for whom their jobs had been major components of self-esteem. When relationships among amnesic content, problems, and channels of social relatedness are recognized, it becomes apparent why amnesia can be so selective—why patients volunteer what they do *not* remember, and why they may pick out some apparently insignificant detail to disremember.

Retrograde amnesia has been more puzzling than anterograde amnesia. One can readily understand how, with a disturbance of consciousness following a brain injury, stimuli are not registered. Russell and Smith (1961) have shown that the length of time that has elapsed from the time of injury to the regaining of consciousness is an accurate index of the severity of the brain damage. However, a severe brain injury may yield a brief retrograde amnesia, and with less severe impairment a patient may say that he does not recall anything for months prior to the accident. In our own investigation patients were asked for the last thing that they remembered prior to the accident. If the retrograde amnesia was for more than a very brief time, the last memory usually referred to some current problem or relationship. This concerned the disability itself, returning to work, going home, financial and marital problems. This "last memory" might be an actual event; it might be a condensation of several events; it might be an incident displaced in space or time or it might be a confabulation. A particularly striking "last memory" was that of "going to sleep" occurring in survivors of accidents in which there had been fatalities. The length of the retrograde amnesia should be interpreted in terms of experiential rather than chronological time. It expresses the person's feeling of relationship to events, such as a "long day." Also, the patient goes as far back into the past as it is necessary to go to find an appropriate event to apply to the current stressful situation.

Memories do not usually return in chronological sequence, nor does the temporal span of the stated memory loss progressively shrink. Rather, the lessening of the amnesia was indicated in the way the patient referred to the accident and other events and would be reflected in the number of probes it took an interviewer to elicit the facts. Recollecting, like forgetting, was also a way of referring to a problem and affirming identity, as in the case of a strongly child-oriented patient who initially could not remember his children. While convalescing in a wheel chair, he recalled pushing his child around in a baby buggy. When memories were regained in chronological order, the succession appeared determined by the exigencies of the current situation. One patient with an aphasic defect could not remember anything since he was in the fifth grade. As his speech and reading ability improved, he advanced himself through school. One can hardly say, however, that he had "regressed" to a fifth-grade level. Another young man, at the close of an interview which he felt had given him support, recalled an incident in which his uncle had taken him fishing.

The recall of forgotten memories under the influence of barbiturates is not simply a manifestation of the release of hitherto repressed material. The recalled incident may be a confabulation or, if true, may be more meaningfully interpreted as a metaphorical representation of the current situation. Similarly, in a psychoanalytic interview when the patient brings up some forgotten childhood episode, this does not mean that it has been "repressed," any more than the boy cited above had "repressed" going fishing. The incident may not have been remembered because it wasn't important at the time, but in the interview it becomes a particularly apt idiom in which to picture a feeling of closeness.

The electrical stimulation of the temporal lobe carried out by Penfield and Rasmussen (1950), by Baldwin (1962), and by Mahl Rothenberg, Delgado, and Hamlin (1964) has brought data of interest. In Penfield and Rasmussen's studies, a relatively small number of patients (10 out of 190) reported "psychical" responses in which there was altered perception of the environment, the experience of a scene from the past or the sense of reliving a past experience. Penfield and Rasmussen attributed the experience to a reactivation of the original event, such as the playing of a wire recorder or strip of cinematographic film. What seems to have been neglected in this interpretation is the relevance of the memory to the current situation. Instead of the stimulation of cells bearing a specific memory, the effect of the electrical interference may be the establishing of an organization of function in which current problems may, as in confabulation, be represented by past events. Thus one of Penfield and Rasmussen's patients remembered people laughing. Another remembered his mother telling his brother he had his coat on backward, a possible reference to the operating room personnel. Mahl and his associates used the technique of a continuous recorded interview under conditions of stimulation and nonstimulation of the temporal area. They found that the thematic content of evoked memories and hallucinations appeared in connection with the subject about which the patient had been talking at the time of, or shortly before, the application of the stimulus. For example, their patient experienced "a man speaking in a silly fashion" at a time when she was preoccupied with her own speech and her concern that she sounded silly to the interviewer.

Studies of amnesia, confabulation, and the syndromes of denial are relevant to behavior associated with iatrogenic brain damage as occurs in prefrontal lobotomy and electroshock treatment. Alteration of brain function is the central effect of electroshock and is a necessary condition for consistent behavioral change (Roth, 1951; Weinstein, Linn, and Kahn,

1952; Aird, Strait, Pace, Hernoff, and Bowditch, 1956; Kahn, Fink, and Weinstein, 1956; Ulett, Smith, and Glesser, 1956). The evaluation of improvement depends in large part on the content of the language in which the patient represents his problems and relationships under the altered conditions of brain function. When a hitherto depressed patient, who had expressed suicidal ideas, becomes jovial, friendly, and euphoric, characterizes his thoughts as "silly," refers to his problems in clichés and rationalizations about "working too hard" and "worrying too much," he is regarded as much improved. When the induced adaptive behavior involves less socially acceptable delusions and confabulations, incontinence, and highly ludic[8] behavior or complaints of pain and loss of memory, he is rated "unimproved." It is evident that "improvement" is a derivative evaluation of the induced behavioral change, dependent on the expectations of the therapist and family and on the milieu in which the behavior is observed (Fink, Kahn, and Green, 1958).

Reduplicative Phenomena

Delusional reduplication or reduplicative paramnesia commonly occurs along with amnesia, confabulation, and disorientation. In reduplication for place, the patient states that there are two or more places of the same or similar name, usually the hospital, though only one exists in actuality. Temporal reduplication is the statement that a current experience has occurred previously and is the enduring manifestation of the *déjà vu* phenomenon. Reduplication for person is the attributing of two or more identities to a single person, while in reduplication for parts of the body the patient claims that he has more than one left arm, head, and so forth. One form of reduplication is usually accompanied by another. For example, a paraparetic patient who claimed he had four legs said he had been in the hospital for paralysis previously.

The term "reduplicative paramnesia" was used by Pick (1903) to describe a patient in his clinic who claimed that she had been to a clinic in another city which was exactly the same, even headed by a professor of the same name. In such reduplication the "other" place, although bearing the same name and having many of the identical characteristics of the "original," differs in some respect which is germane to the patient's particular problem. Thus the "other" hospital is situated in the patient's home town or does not perform serious operations. Usually, only one or two persons are misidentified, indicating that there is not a generalized disturbance in perception and that a restrictive misidentification furnished an adequate vehicle for the expression of the patient's attitudes. Also, while a patient may

[8] Ludic is the term used by Jean Piaget to describe the dramatic, imitative, and play behavior of young children.

reduplicate in an interview, he may address the other person correctly in a face-to-face encounter.

In reduplication of parts of the body, as in inattention, the member of the body that is reduplicated (or to which the patient is inattentive) is one that is defective in some fashion. A patient who has had a craniotomy says he has two or three heads, and the hemiplegic person, more than one left arm and leg. Reduplication for body parts, when it occurs in enduring fashion, is invariably accompanied by other forms of reduplication. One of our patients, a nurse who claimed that she had two left arms, also stated that the hospital (named correctly) was an annex of the hospital where she had trained and that several of the nurses had been supervisors at her old hospital. This patient would usually begin the interview by crying and complaining of pain and asking that her friend Mrs. D. take her home. When speaking of the "extra" hand, she would become gay and bantering and would try to brush it away. The selective aspects of the phenomenon are indicated by the observation that when left alone the patient never seemed to notice the "other" limb. The patient may claim that his own limb is intact; he may deny it belongs to him; or he may express recognition of the defect. One of our subjects, following a craniotomy, said he had three heads—one with him and the others upstairs in a closet. He denied that his head had been operated on, but said it was "empty." This statement was made, as is usual in such instances, in a bland, matter-of-fact fashion. When the examiner's doubts were voiced, the patient commented that he did not think it more unusual to change heads than it was to change hats.

The description of the fictional parts of the body, like the "extra" places, events, and persons, is a condensed representation of the patient's relationships in his environment. One man "grew another head for protection." A limb may be said to belong to one's child, a relative, or doctor. In the case cited above the arm was designated as strong and heavy and as belonging to the patient's friend, Mrs. D. The friend was a large, motherly, protecting type and the description of the limb seemed to characterize the relationship between the two women.

The principle of reduplication is also shown in changes in object naming. This is usually confined to objects having to do with illness and hospitalization and status or identity. Patients will misname a doctor's bag, a drinking straw, and rubber gloves, while objects unconnected with surgical or hospital procedures are designated correctly. (Aphasic subjects do slightly better on the illness-connected group.) A woman who had the reputation of being an excellent cook called a syringe "an icing device for cake." The reduplicative aspects are explicit in such statements as "you might call it a bed but I call it a studio couch."

Another view of the illusory reduplication of body parts is that of Ostow (1960), who explains the phenomenon as a rebirth tendency or instinct which comes into play when a living organism or group sustains a loss. Apart from the difficulty in using such a concept as "rebirth instinct," this formulation does not explain the observation that reduplication of body parts is accompanied by other forms of reduplication; it does not explain why the patient may reduplicate in one context and not another; and it does not consider the processes of symbolic organization and social interaction that are involved. The same criticism may be made of Schilder's (1951) explanation of reduplication as a "rhythmic function of memory" or "iteration principle" manifested also in repetition compulsions, the babbling of infants, and the perseveration of aphasics.

Autoscopic phenomena may be considered as episodic forms of reduplication. In autoscopic hallucinations a person sees "himself." These may occur with brain damage or in states of fatigue, emotional tension, depression, etc. According to a review of the literature by Lukianowicz (1958), cases with known organic etiology are usually associated with epilepsy or migraine. Of his six personally observed cases, two had seizures, one had extensive sarcoidosis and a severe depression, while the others were depressed or described as emotionally blunted or withdrawn. Usually the double appears suddenly and in some cases the apparition is preceded by a feeling of unreality. Most frequently only the head or upper part of the body is seen. As in other forms of reduplication, the other self differs from the observer in some significant respect. In one of Lukianowicz' patients the autoscopic phenomena began on the day of her husband's funeral. She felt her double as more warm and alive. In another case the subject, who had a leg amputation, saw his double walking without his (own) customary limp. For others the double appears cold, sad, and weary. One of our subjects would see herself going to work while she lay in bed in the morning feeling too fatigued to get up. Another aspect of autoscopy is that the double copies the patient's movements in mirror-image fashion. It is evident that the double is a symbolic representation of the observer's own problems and feelings.

Hallucinations and Other Episodic Disturbances

It is often difficult to separate hallucinations from imagery, illusions, confabulations, delusions, and colorful metaphors. As internal states cannot be monitored, we deal with inferences from verbal descriptions. Under this heading are included various episodic phenomena: hallucinations after gross brain injury, the manifestations of temporal lobe seizures and effects of brain stimulation, the *déjà vu* and *jamais vu* phenomena, results of sensory isolation and sleep deprivation, and the phantom limb experience.

The subject of hallucinations after brain injury is a complex one, and the clinical entity includes such phenomena as completion, adaptation, visual after-imagery and after-sensation, and perseveration of visual images (Bender, 1963). Most hallucinations occur in areas of impaired vision and often in the visual field opposite the location of the brain lesion. The more formed the false perception the more symbolic value it has, but the distinction between physiological and symbolic aspects is far from clear. Conditions such as prosopagnosia, the inability to identify the faces of other people and even one's own face in a mirror, are difficult to interpret and cannot be attributed solely to the visual field defects that usually accompany the phenomenon.

In patients with brain tumors and vascular and traumatic disease, episodic hallucinations and enduring delusions and confabulations tend to bear a reciprocal relationship. Patients with a well-developed amnestic-confabulatory state rarely report hallucinations (or dreams). Those who hallucinate are usually well oriented and nondelusional, even though they may be impressed with the validity of their sensory impressions. One important factor is the severity and rate of onset of the interference in brain function. Generally speaking, hallucinations have less extensive brain destruction and are apt to appear when the onset of impairment is rapid, as in toxic deliria, and also when the return to normal brain function is rapid, as in the instance of withdrawal of drugs from an addicted person. Whitty and Lewin (1957) described the behavior of patients who following cingulectomy go through a stage when they are fully oriented and report vivid, though nonexistent, scenes. A more slowly developing tumor destroying this area usually is associated with disorientation but not with hallucinations. In the course of clinical improvement from a brain injury after the patient achieves full orientation for place in the sense of giving the correct name, address, and distance from home of the hospital, he may describe a fictitious journey out of the hospital which is pictured in vivid detail. Hallucinations in a defective hemianopic visual field may follow a period in which the patient conceptualized one side of his body and surrounding space as nonexistent, or they may appear as an early symptom (Bender and Sobin, 1963). These may range from polyopic and palinopic distortions to full-fledged scenes meaningful in terms of the patient's feelings and problems. During a period of depression one of our hemiplegic patients saw coffins in his left visual field.

The hallucinatory experiences of temporal lobe epilepsy and the effects of stimulation of the temporal lobe are germane to concepts of organism-environment interaction and the relationships of the self and the physical world. Patients describe how things look nearer or farther away, brighter or dimmer. People may appear smaller and farther away even though the rest of the scene retains perspective. The subject himself may seem far away, or he may feel both distant and yet strangely in the immediate environment. The interaction is evident in such statements as "people look the way I feel." Affectual components enter as in feelings of strangeness, familiarity, unreality, fear, and impending danger. From the standpoint of relatedness in the environment, it is useful to think of emotion in its literal sense of moving out of one's self.

Reduplicative and autoscopic aspects are prominent. The patient may see himself in a hallucination or have the feeling of being a secondary observer of what is going on. In one of the earliest descriptions of temporal lobe seizures, Hughlings Jackson's patient, a cook, saw a little black woman actively engaged in cooking. Baldwin notes that when the patient describes himself as an image in the scene, the self-description is vague and never includes the face. Another patient had had several unsuccessful operations for relief of temporal lobe seizures. In the course of three hospitalizations he visualized almost the same scene of his home. These, however, differed in some detail which could be connected with the contemporary stressful situation. For example, while awaiting his third craniotomy he had a seizure in which he saw his garage, a two-story structure, with an additional third story.

The *jamais vu* and *déjà vu* experiences have been considered as analogs of amnesia and reduplication. As has been mentioned, amnesia is not only a loss of memory but includes a sense of unfamiliarity with, and a not belonging of, things and events. When this occurs over a long period of time, it is styled amnesia, and when it appears briefly, it is called *jamais vu*. The same relationship exists between *déjà vu* and other forms of reduplication. The phenomenon may occur in the course of recovery from brain injury, with seizures and in normal persons under conditions of emotional stress. Just as amnesia and enduring reduplication commonly occur together, so may *jamais vu* and *déjà vu* be intermingled. For example, a patient may not remember his own child, but reduplicate an "extra" child and feelings of familiarity may be described along with those of strangeness, wonder, and novelty. One of our patients had the momentary feeling of being in a strange place but of knowing everybody.

In the psychoanalytic literature, *déjà vu* is explained as a substitute for a repressed Oedipal wish (Freud, 1913) and as a defense against such wishes (Arlow, 1959). The above findings, however, suggest rather that it is an adaptation to some current threat, as are the more enduring reduplicative phenomena.

Hallucinations are reported during sensory isolation. Following the original experiment of Bexton, Heron, and Scott (1945) in which all fourteen subjects described hallucinations ranging from dots and simple geometric patterns to complex scenes, there have been numerous studies with varying results. In addition to the type of sensory input, such variables as degree of drowsiness, conditions of stress, boredom, amount of activity and instructions given have proven significant. Ziskind and Augsburg (1962) regard the hallucinations of sensory deprivation as essentially fragments of normal imagery occurring in states of reduced awareness. Mendelson, Solomon, and Lindemann (1958) noted that a number of patients with paralytic poliomyelitis developed disorientation, confusion, delusions, and hallucinations while in tank-type respirators. The hallucinations were related to the patients' attitudes and anxieties about their disease and its future implications. One of their patients reported traveling about the hospital in an automobile that had the shape of a tank respirator. Another was carried about in a highly colored helicopter which had the shape and appearance of a tank respirator. She also reported running about and dancing with tank respirators on the floor and that her husband and son were in tank respirators next to her. In these cases, etiological factors include not only the sensory isolation, but also the stress of the situation and possible brain damage associated with poliomyelitis and anoxemia.

No subsequent observations have been as spectacular or as rich in obvious symbolic content. According to Freedman, Grunebaum, Stare, and Greenblatt (1962), the imagery is generally unrelated to the subject's past experience or current situation. Occasionally there is a connection as in one case, where, after thinking about food and being hungry, the subject saw sliced turkey on a plate. The authors commented that the imagery was sometimes frightening, but usually pleasant. It should be emphasized that what is regarded as "symbolic" is to a considerable degree a function of the listener's orientation and method of study.

The hallucinations occurring in sleep deprivation are also related to sensory input appearing during lapses when perceptual performance is impaired, thresholds are raised, and EEG alpha amplitude is lowered. Perceptual anomalies follow a similar course, appearing during lapses when the subject seems drowsy. As in sensory isolation, the conditions of the study are extremely important. In the original report of Tyler (1946) there was a high incidence of grossly disturbed behavior with confusion, hallucinations, and delusions of persecution. On the other hand, Williams, Morris, and Lubin (1962) at Walter Reed Hospital found that over a corresponding period, the disturbances in behavior consisted only of disturbances of depth perception, illusions of movement, and changes in size, shape, and texture constancies. Tyler's group consisted of "volunteer" military personnel selected more or less at random, while the Walter Reed population was a highly motivated group of conscientious objectors, who were members of a religious sect and maintained a high morale throughout the procedure. When some hallucinations did appear after more than sixty hours of wakefulness, they were generally not related to any emotional difficulty and contained little or no affective content.

Phantom limb has been studied by psychoanalysts and its occurrence has been attributed to the nonacceptance or denial of the lost limb. Such a view was useful at a time when the phantom was ascribed to irritation of the stump or neuroma, but more recent and more systematic observations have indicated the inadequacy of a wish or need theory. Phantoms are nearly universal and not confined to those individuals whose narcissistic investment does not allow them to renounce the integrity of the body. In the phantom, the deformity or pain which led to the amputation is commonly reproduced and amputees rarely describe the phantom as identical with a normal limb. Upper limb phantoms are perceived more vividly than those after loss of the lower limb, and the hand, fingers, especially the thumb, and toes are most prominent. This has been attributed to the greater representation of these parts in the cerebral cortex (Henderson and Smyth, 1948).

Kolb (1954) has pointed out that patients do not deny the loss of a limb (unless there is accompanying brain damage or the patient sees himself as whole in a dream), but may deny the phantom experience. Simmel (1959) estimates that such denial has a probable incidence of less than 1 per cent and regards it as a conscious refusal lest the person be thought peculiar. She comments that such persons do not have the character traits of the anosognosic personality as described by Weinstein and Kahn.

Many of the features of the phantom are still unexplained. Phantoms do not appear when parts of a limb are lost slowly as in leprosy; but when the shrunken part is amputated, phantoms occur (Simmel, 1956). Formerly it was thought that young children did not have phantoms, but it has been shown that in children phantoms occur not only after amputation, but with congenital absence of a limb. In a study of 101 cases of congenital aphasia, S. Weinstein, Sersen, and Vetter (1964) found current evidence or a history of phantoms in 18 subjects. The authors also noted that the congenital phantoms are more frequently perceived as natural whereas the acquired ones are more likely to have paresthesias. From this work it would appear that the phantom depends on a neural substrate modified further by afferent stimuli and their conceptualization. To a considerable degree the type of sensation is a product of past experience and social relationships. This may be observed especially in painful phantom limbs. In today's modern hospitals, equipped with prosthetic and rehabilitation services, the painful phantom has become a rarity.

Sexual and Aggressive Behavior

The relationship of sexual and aggressive aspects of behavior to brain function has been of renewed interest since the demonstration of changes in animals following temporal lobe and amygdala lesions and the studies on the central representation of sexual, eating, and other important biological functions in the limbic system. Disturbances of sexual and aggressive behavior have long been known to occur after brain injury and formerly were attributed to frontal lobe damage. More recently they have been noted to appear after lesions in many parts of the brain, but the information is largely in the form of case reports with few systematic studies.

Meyer (1958) found impaired performance of the sexual act in 71 of 100 patients who had had contusing or lacerating brain injuries. The major symptoms were failure to gain and hold an erection, premature ejaculation, and prolongation of time for orgasm. Meyer observed that such disturbances rarely led to marital conflicts. Meyers (1961) noted enduring loss of libido and inability to have a penile erection following unilateral and bilateral surgical lesions in the pallidopallidofugal complex performed for relief of tremor. No associated disturbances in behavior were reported. The conclusion was that a central pathway for libido and potency had been interrupted.

Another type of case involves disturbances in socially observed behavior in which there are public manifestations. Such patients make open verbal and physical advances, talk a great deal about sex, have confabulations and delusions with a sexual theme, and interpret their environment in a sexual way. They are puerile and ludic, often highly euphoric and/or paranoid, masturbate, expose themselves, and are conspicuously incontinent of urine and even feces. Such behavior has been commonly attributed to a loss of inhibiting mechanisms in which there is a release of previously controlled impulses and a regression to infantile levels of gratification.

However, certain features are present which cast doubt on this explanation (Weinstein and Kahn, 1961). The behavior is selective in terms of its relationship to the patient's disability and the situation in which it occurred. Delusions and confabulations were frequently metaphorical representations of problems and incapacities as in the instance of a woman with a torticollis who claimed that two other women wearing cervical collars were men in disguise. Sexual jokes and off-color remarks were particularly apt to appear when the patient was examined physically or his mental capacities were being tested. In some instances periods of florid sexual behavior alternated with depression. The sexual remarks and gestures were addressed to a doctor or nurse rather than to another patient. There is a great deal of physical interaction with the staff. A patient may fill a urinal, but spill the contents before it can be removed by a nurse. He may complain of being hungry, but find fault with the food when it comes and refuse to eat. During interviews patients often imitate the examiner's actions and parrot his words. After release from the hospital the sexual behavior may continue to be shown in selective fashion to affirm a specific identity and implement a particular relationship. For example, patients who seemed to express their helplessness in puerile fashion may, after discharge, confine their sexual activity to molesting children. Jarvie (1954) reports a man who though eager for sexual intercourse with his wife, masturbating in front of her and threatening to rape her, did not approach other women. Some of the men report impotence, but others are quite potent.

Whether the brain injury released sexual energy is a question that depends on one's definition of sexual energy. However, the role of the behavior as a mode of adaptation to stress stems from the way sexual symbols are integrated in a pattern of language and from the manner in which the subject relates to specific people through gestures and physical contact. In such transactions the sexual elements are both a stimulus and a response. It should be pointed out that while the brain lesions involve the limbic system, most patients with such damage do not exhibit florid sexual manifestations. The premorbid background shows that patients had used a masculine-feminine dichotomy in the structuring of interpersonal events along with emphasis on the physical aspects of personal relationships, such as looks, size, and smells.

The idea of sexual behavior as symbolic of personal relationships is not new in psychoanalysis. Schilder (1951) pointed out the role of sexuality in communication and Kubie (1956) has aptly remarked on the range of emotions, needs, drives, and preoccupations which "wear the cloak of heterosexuality."

Sexual manifestations may occur in seizure states, particularly so-called temporal lobe epilepsy.[4] They are relatively uncommon and erotic sensations are not reported after brain stimulation. A particularly interesting case was reported by Mitchell and Hill (1954). Their patient had long enjoyed "thought satisfaction" from looking at a safety pin and had a history of voyeurism. Later this was followed by seizures, and, if he fantasied his fetish during intercourse or masturbation, he had a fit. Most frequently his seizures came soon after awakening with a full bladder when his "frigid" wife had refused him. Epstein (1960) has noted the occurrence of electrographic abnormalities in fetishists and transvestites and regards this evidence of brain damage as etiologically significant. He notes the altered interaction in the environment, with marked condensation of meaning in the fetish and overresponse to symbols in general. Epstein regards the fetish as the substitute for the mother's body and finds a history of unusual physical closeness. He theorizes that there is a state of increased organismic excitability and that the fetish acts both as an excitant and as a means of controlling and directing sexual and aggressive drives.

The recent investigations on the effects of lesions of the limbic system have also focused interest on aggression and violence as biological drives and primitive affects. While episodes of physical violence and rage are not uncommon after brain injuries, they are not to be explained on the basis of

[4] The term "so-called" is used because electrical abnormalities are commonly found in other areas of the brain as well.

increased neural excitability or the loss of inhibiting mechanisms. The majority of patients with hypothalamic lesions do not show openly aggressive behavior. In those that do, one finds that the behavior serves to represent problems and relationships and as a means of maintaining identity. A review of the social background indicates that overt violence and/or the expectation of such behavior in others were important components of interpersonal relationships (Weinstein, Kahn, and Slote, 1955).

An example of the use of symbols of violence in the perception of the environment is shown in the phenomenon of pain asymbolia. In this condition, stimuli which would ordinarily be perceived as painful or threatening are ignored or denied. Patients do not wince or otherwise respond to the vigorous thrust of a sharp instrument, or they may deny that it is painful. The attitude may be associated with the syndrome of akinetic mutism in which the patient is immobile, does not speak or does so in selectively inaudible fashion. Symbolic representations of death and violence also appear in the so-called thalamic syndrome, where there are complaints of spontaneous pain and hyperalgesia on the side of the body which has diminished sensation and power. The patient describes his pain as torture, says he is being "torn apart" and "caught in a vise," and also complains of deadness and coldness. In one sense the loss of sensation and hypersensitivity are contradictory, but for a person whose most meaningful representation of disability involves the language of death and violence, the feelings are complementary.

In the course of recovery from acute, closed head injuries, episodes of violence are frequently observed. These are characteristically brief, do not involve a lasting emotional reaction, and are apparently precipitated by trivial incidents. Most commonly the words and gestures of violence are directed toward another patient who has a disability comparable to that of the patient and they appear in the form of taunts, teasing, and threats. Usually, such patients are no longer confabulatory or delusional and the symbols of violence may be regarded as analogs of confabulation and delusion. Words and gestures of violence like those of sexual expression are not only expressive of feelings, but the emotional expression itself may serve to re-create, in transitory fashion, the milieu of brain dysfunction which had existed during the period of confabulation so that old adaptive patterns can again operate by reason of an altered mode of interaction in the environment.

Comment

Psychoanalysis has usefully emphasized motivation and meaning in behavior associated with organic brain deficits and has demonstrated relationships among memory, cognitive, conative, and perceptual phenomena.

However, in attempting to give a biological basis to the clinical observations, Freud and other psychoanalysts were unaware of their own metaphor. They were actually using the currently popular scientific idioms of science and reifying patterns of social interaction into biological forces. Even today there is no model of neurological events occurring wholly within the organism that can explain the behavior that has been described and it is necessary to invoke organism-environmental interactions. One could attempt, for example, to equate denial of illness with a drive for self-preservation. This approach, however, would not explain why denial occurs to a far greater degree in some people and not in others, why it takes so many different forms and why a person denies his illness in some forms of language and admits it in other words.

In Freud's view, symbols acquired their meaning from the physical qualities of the referent. Thus a long object stood for the penis, weeping and urination were equated, etc. The persistence of a symbol, as in a delusion, was held to derive from the energy of the underlying biological striving or the forces needed for their repression or distortion. Actually the content of the symbol itself was regarded as unimportant. What mattered was the "basic drive." The user of the symbol was thought to be unaware of these determinants and the purpose of the symbol was to conceal this knowledge from him. In this chapter, symbols are presented as units of social interaction. They are meaningful by reason of their place in a pattern of social relatedness and one's anticipation of the response of the environment. The symbol or metaphor is important in its own right, so to speak, and consciousness and unconscious processes are not sharply separated. They differ in the degree of condensation of the symbol and in one's awareness of the interaction. One is not so much unaware of a hidden, unfulfilled wish, or motive, but of the organization of the interactive processes, of the way we classify the environment, and the effect of our words and gestures on other people.

Whether psychoanalysis should have a physiological or social basis may well turn out to be an irrelevant question. The exploration of the environment and the ability to generalize from among the details of stimuli which form the basis of language are universal mammalian characteristics. What we call cognition, perception, and emotion are symbolic processes and language is as innate as the sexual drive.

Note: Preparation of this chapter was aided by a grant from the U.S. Army Medical Research and Development Command, Office of the Surgeon General.

References

Aird, R. N., Strait, L. A., Pace, J. W., Hernoff, M. K., and Bowditch, S. C. "Neurophysiologic Effects of Electrically Induced Convulsions." *American Medical Association Archives of Neurology and Psychiatry*, 75 (1956), 371–378.

Arlow, J. A. "The Structure of the Déjà Vu Experience." *Journal of the American Psychoanalytic Association*, 7 (1959), 611–631.

Baldwin, M. "Hallucinations in Neurologic Syndromes." In L. J. West (ed.), *Hallucinations*. New York: Grune & Stratton, 1962. Pp. 77–86.

Bartlett, F. C. *Remembering: A Study in Experimental and Social Psychology*. Cambridge, Eng.: Cambridge University Press, 1932.

Bender, M. B. "Disorders in Visual Perception." In L. Halpern (ed.), *Problems of Dynamic Neurology*. New York: Grune & Stratton, 1963. Pp. 319–375.

Bender, M. B., and Sobin, A. J. "Polyopia and Palinopia in Homonymous Fields of Vision." In M. D. Yahr (ed.), *Transactions of the Neurological Association*. New York: Springer, 1963. Vol. 88, pp. 56–59.

Betlheim, S., and Hartmann, H. "On Parapraxes in the Korsakoff Psychosis." In D. Rapaport (ed.), *Organization and Pathology of Thought*. New York: Columbia University Press, 1951. Pp. 288–310.

Bexton, W. H., Heron, W., and Scott, T. H. "Effects of Decreased Variation in the Sensory Environment." *Canadian Journal of Psychology*, 8 (1945), 70–76.

Bonhoffer, K. *Die akuten Geisteskrankheiten der Gewohnheitstrinker*." Jena: Fischer, 1901.

Buerger-Prinz, H., and Kaila, M. "On the Structure of the Amnesic Syndrome." In D. Rapaport (ed.), *Organization and Pathology of Thought*. New York: Columbia University Press, 1951. Pp. 650–688.

Carter, J. T. "Type of Personal Life Memories Forgotten Following Electro-Convulsion Therapy." *American Psychologist*, 8 (1953), 330.

Dewhurst, K., and Pearson, J. "Visual Hallucinations of the Self in Organic Disease." *Journal of Neurology, Neurosurgery and Psychiatry*, 18 (1955), 1853, 1853–1860.

Epstein, A. W. "Fetishism: A Study of Its Psychopathology with Particular Reference to a Proposed Disorder in Brain Mechanisms as an Etiological Factor." *The Journal of Nervous and Mental Disease*, 130, No. 2 (February 1960), 107–119.

Ferenczi, S., and Hollòs, S. *Psychoanalysis and the Psychic Disorders of General Paresis*. New York: Nervous and Mental Disease, 1925.

Fink, M., Kahn, R. L., and Green, M. A. "Experimental Studies of the Electroshock Process." *Diseases of the Nervous System*, 19, No. 3 (March 1958), 1–6.

Freedman, S. J., Grunebaum, H. U., Stare, F. A., and Greenblatt, M. "Imagery in Sensory Deprivation." In L. J. West (ed.), *Hallucinations.* New York: Grune & Stratton, 1962.

Freud, S. " 'Fausse Reconnaisance (Déjà Raconté),' in Psychoanalytic Treatment" (1913). *The Standard Edition of the Complete Psychological Works of. . . .* London: Hogarth Press. Vol. 13, pp. 201–207. (Also in *Collected Papers of. . . .* New York: Basic Books, 1959. Vol. 2, pp. 334–341.)

Henderson, W. R., and Smyth, G. E. "Phantom Limbs." *Journal of Neurology, Neurosurgery and Psychiatry,* 11 (1948), 88–112.

Janis, I. L. "Psychologic Effects of Electric Convulsive Treatments: I. Post-Treatment Amnesias." *Journal of Nervous and Mental Diseases,* 111 (1950), 359.

Jarvie, H. F. "Frontal Lobe Wounds Causing Disinhibition." *Journal of Neurology, Neurosurgery and Psychiatry,* 17 (1954), 14–32.

Kahn, R. L., Fink, M., and Weinstein, E. A. "Relation of Amobarbital Test to Clinical Improvement in Electroshock." *American Medical Association Archives of Neurology and Psychiatry,* 76 (1956), 23–29.

Kolb, L. C. *The Painful Phantom Psychology, Physiology and Treatment.* Springfield, Ill.: Charles C Thomas, 1954.

Korngold, M. "An Investigation of Some Psychological Effects of Electric Shock Treatment." *American Psychologist,* 8 (1953), 381–382.

Kral, V. A. "The Amnestic Syndrome." *Monatsschrift für Psychiatrie und Neurologie,* 132, Nos. 2–3 (1956), 65–80.

Kubie, L. S. "Influence of Symbolic Processes on the Role of Instincts in Human Behavior." *Psychosomatic Medicine,* 18, No. 3 (1956), 189–208.

Lukianowicz, N. "Autoscopic Phenomena." *American Medical Association Archives of Neurology and Psychiatry,* 80 (August 1958), 199–220.

Mahl, G. F., Rothenberg, A., Delgado, J. M. R., and Hamlin, H. "Psychological Responses in the Human to Electrical Stimulation." *Psychosomatic Medicine,* 26 (1964), 337–368.

Mendelson, J., Solomon, P., and Lindemann, E. "Hallucinations of Poliomyelitis Patients during Treatment in a Respirator." *Journal of Nervous and Mental Diseases,* 126, No. 5 (May 1958), 421–428.

Meyer, J. E. "Die Sexuellen Sötrungen der Hirnverletzten." *Archiv für Psychiatrie und Zeitschrift für die Neurologie,* 193S (1958), 449–469.

Meyers, R. "Evidence of a Locus of the Neural Mechanisms for Libido and Penile Potency in the Septo-Fornico-Hypothalamic Region of the Human Brain." In M. D. Yahr (ed.), *Transactions of the American Neurological Association.* New York: Springer, 1961. Vol. 86, pp. 81–85.

Mitchell, W. F., and Hill, D. "Epilepsy with Fetishism Relieved by Temporal Lobectomy," *Lancet,* 2 (1954), 626–630.

Ostow, M. "The Metapsychology of Autoscopic Phenomena." *International Journal of Psycho-analysis,* 41, Part 6 (1960), 619–625.

Penfield, W., and Rasmussen, T. *The Cerebral Cortex of Man.* New York: Macmillan, 1950.

Pick, A. "On Reduplication." *Brain,* 26 (1903), 260–267.

Pribram, K. "Freud's Project: An Open, Biologically Based Model for Psychoanalysis." In N. S. Greenfield and W. C. Lewis (eds.), *Psychoanalysis and Current Biological Thought*. Madison: University of Wisconsin Press, 1965.

Redlich, E., and Bonvicini, G. "Über das Fehlen der Wahrnehmung der eigenen Blindheit bei Hirkrankheiten." *Jahrbuch für Psychiatrie, Psychotherapie und Medizinische Anthropologie*, 29 (1908), 1–134.

Roth, M. "Changes in the EEG under Barbiturate Anesthesia Produced by Electro-Convulsive Treatment and Their Significance for the Theory of EST Action." *EEG Clinical Neurophysiology*, 3 (1951), 261–280.

Russell, W. R., and Smith, A. "Post Traumatic Amnesia in Closed Head Injury," *American Medical Association Archives of Neurology*, 5 (1961), 4–17.

Schilder, P. F. *The Image and Appearance of the Human Body*. New York: International Universities Press, 1950.

Schilder, P. F. "Studies Concerning the Psychology and Symptomatology of General Paresis." In D. Rapaport (ed.), *Organization and Pathology of Thought*. New York: Columbia University Press, 1951. Pp. 519–580.

Silverman, A. J., Cohen, S. I., Bressler, B., and Shmavonian, B. M. "Hallucinations in Sensory Deprivation." In L. J. West (ed.), *Hallucinations*. New York: Grune & Stratton, 1962.

Simmel, Marianne L. "Phantoms in Patients with Leprosy and in Elderly Digital Amputees." *American Journal of Psychology*, 69 (1956), 529–545.

Simmel, Marianne L. "Phantoms, Phantom Pain and 'Denial.'" *American Journal of Psychotherapy*, 13, No. 3 (July 1959), 603–613.

Talland, G. A. "Confabulation in the Wernicke-Korsakoff Syndrome." *Journal of Nervous and Mental Diseases*, 132, No. 5 (May 1961), 361–381.

Tyler, D. B. "Fatigue of Prolonged Wakefulness." *National Research Council Research Reports*, Part 2 (1946), 282.

Ulett, G. A., Smith, K., and Glesser, G. C. "Evaluation of Convulsive and Subconvulsive Shock Therapies Utilizing a Control Group." *American Journal of Psychiatry*, 112 (1956), 795–802.

Weinstein, E. A. "Symbolic Aspects of Thalamic Pain." *Yale Journal of Biological Medicine*, 28, Nos. 3–4 (1955–1956).

Weinstein, E. A. "Relationships among Seizures, Psychosis and Personality Factors." *The American Journal of Psychiatry*, 116, No. 2 (August 1959), 124–126.

Weinstein, E. A., and Cole, M. "Concepts of Anosognosia." In L. Halpern (ed.), *Problems of Dynamic Neurology*. New York: Grune & Stratton, 1963.

Weinstein, E. A., Cole, M., Mitchell, M., and Lyerly, O. "Anosognosia and Aphasia." *American Medical Association Archives of Neurology*, 10 (1964), 376–386.

Weinstein, E. A., and Kahn, R. L. *Denial of Illness: Symbolic and Physiological Aspects*. Springfield, Ill.: Charles C Thomas, 1955.

Weinstein, E. A., and Kahn, R. L. "Patterns of Sexual Behavior Following Brain Injury." *Psychiatry*, 24, No. 1 (February 1961), 69–78.

Weinstein, E. A., Kahn, R. L., and Malitz, S. "Confabulation as a Social Process." *Psychiatry*, 19, No. 4 (November 1956), 383–396.

Weinstein, E. A., Kahn, R. L., Malitz, S., and Rozanski, J. "Delusional Reduplication of Parts of the Body." *Brain*, 77 (1954), 45–60.

Weinstein, E. A., Kahn, R. L., and Slote, W. "Withdrawal, Inattention and Pain Asymbolia." *American Medical Association Archives of Neurology and Psychiatry*, 74 (September 1955), 235–248.

Weinstein, E. A., Kahn, R. L., and Sugarman, L. A. "Phenomenon of Reduplication." *American Medical Association Archives of Neurology and Psychiatry*, 67 (June 1952), 808–814.

Weinstein, E. A., Linn, L., and Kahn, R. L. "Psychosis during Electroshock Therapy: Its Relation to the Theory of Shock Therapy." *American Journal of Psychiatry*, 109 (1952), 22–26.

Weinstein, E. A., and Malitz, S. "Changes in Symbolic Expression with Amobarbital Sodium." *American Journal of Psychiatry*, 3 (1954), 198–206.

Weinstein, E. A., Marvin, S. L., and Keller, N. J. A. "Amnesia as a Language Pattern." *American Medical Association Archives of General Psychiatry*, 6 (April 1962), 259–270.

Weinstein, S., Sersen, E. A., and Vetter, R. J. "Phantoms and Somatic Sensation in Cases of Congenital Aplasia." *Cortex*, 1, No. 3 (1964), 276–290.

Whitty, C. W. M., and Lewin, W. "A Korsakoff Syndrome in the Post-Cingulectomy Confusional State." *Brain*, 83, Part 4 (1960), 648–653.

Whitty, C. W. M., and Lewin, W. "Vivid Day-Dreaming: An Unusual Form of Confusion Following Anterior Cingulectomy." *Brain*, 80, Part 1 (1957), 72–76.

Williams, H. L., Morris, G. O., and Lubin, A. "Illusions, Hallucinations and Sleep Loss." In L. J. West (ed.), *Hallucinations*. New York: Grune & Stratton, 1962.

Ziskind, E., and Augsburg, T. "Hallucinations in Sensory Deprivation—Method or Madness?" *Science*, 137, No. 3534 (1962), 992–993.

10

The Psychoanalytic Approach to Psychosomatic Medicine

GEORGE L. ENGEL

Introduction

The biologic basis of psychoanalytic theory is unmistakable. Hence it is not surprising that psychoanalysis has generated so many fruitful ideas concerning psychosomatic interrelationships, particularly in respect to somatic symptom formation. Yet the task of testing some of these ideas has at times presented almost insuperable difficulties. In large part these difficulties have been technical, for all too often it has not been possible to devise suitable methods to demonstrate the postulated relationships between psychological and somatic processes. As a result the growth and development of theory has all too often outstripped the verifiable facts in its support.

In this chapter I will first review what I consider to have been the three phases, historically, of the psychoanalytic approach to psychosomatic relationships and then shall discuss in somewhat greater detail the role of conversion and of certain specific and nonspecific psychological factors in the genesis of organic disease. The thesis, based on empirical observation, is that psychosomatic factors are involved in the genesis of a great many types of organic disease, often through a sequence of steps involving multiple determinants. This approach rejects the perspective that certain diseases, such as peptic ulcer and colitis, are "psychosomatic" while others, by implication, are not. Rather it attempts to identify what bodily systems may become activated through psychologic mechanisms and then to assay what part the consequent physical changes may play in the series of processes which may ultimately culminate in an organic disease state. A basic premise is that the degree and extent to which somatic systems are mobilized in response to psychological stress is inversely related to the success with which such stress can be dealt with by purely psychic processes (Engel, 1962b).

Psychoanalytic Approaches to Psychosomatic Medicine

Psychoanalysis *began* with the study of a psychosomatic phenomenon, namely conversion. Freud's elucidation of hysteria for the first time shed a brilliant light on the psychogenesis of certain somatic symptoms and for a time seemed to offer the promise that all psychosomatic phenomena could be understood in the framework of body language or organ symbolism (Freud, 1895, 1901, 1909, 1910). His concept of somatic compliance seemed to provide a fundamental basis for the understanding of conversion as a mechanism for the production of many kinds of organic lesions. Characteristic of this period is that such discoveries were made in the course of the analyses of patients considered to be suitable for this new form of treatment. The mechanisms underlying somatic symptom formation were not specifically selected as a subject for systematic investigation.

The second phase begins after World War I, when developing theory suggested that certain somatic conditions might be conceptualized within the psychoanalytic framework and perhaps also might be amenable to cure by this means. The names most often connected with this development are Alexander, Benedek, Daniels, Deutsch, Dunbar, French, Garma, Kubie, Schur, Sperling, and their many students. These I refer to as the second generation of analytic psychosomaticists. The theories dominating this later phase were the libido theory, adapted as the vector concept by Alexander (1950), Freud's second anxiety theory (1926), and more latterly the metapsychological formulations of Hartmann (1964) and of Rapaport (1959), particularly as expressed in the resomatization concept of Schur (1955). Certain nonanalytic theories also were drawn on, notably Cannon's emergency theory and later Selye's stress theory. During this period many analysts deliberately solicited their medical colleagues for patients with particular "psychosomatic" disorders, a step justified by the expectation that psychoanalysis would prove therapeutically useful, as indeed it did in certain instances. These were a group of diseases selected for study on the basis of an a priori assumption of consistency with psychoanalytic theory. They included peptic ulcer, colitis, dermatitis, rheumatoid arthritis, asthma, hypertension, and hyperthyroidism. Such research clearly established psychoanalytic theory as a useful frame of reference for understanding certain somatic disorders, but in time a number of factors combined to limit the usefulness of the method. Most restricting was the fact that continuation of research was dependent on the success of psychoanalysis as a therapeutic measure. Unfortunately, in spite of occasional impressive results, many analysts found the complications of analyzing somatically sick patients too burdensome, while many patients either proved not suitable for analysis or were lured away by promise of quicker relief through medical or surgical means. Further, those patients who did pursue analysis were a highly skewed sample of the disease population. In spite of these limitations, lasting insights into certain psychosomatic processes were obtained which have influenced much of psychosomatic research since then. But at the present time one finds very few reports in the literature of the analysis of such cases, and I have the impression that few analysts now have such patients in analysis.

The third period of psychoanalytic research begins in the late 1940's when analysts, frustrated by the small number and variety of somatic processes accessible for study among patients in a classical psychoanalytic framework, attempted to adapt the psychoanalytic method and apply the psychoanalytic know-how to the bedside and the laboratory. One might say that in this period patients with somatic disorders are being studied by psychoanalysts rather than by psychoanalysis.

At the outset of this period many of us had high expectations of being able to observe physiological variables during classical analysis and to establish correlations with deep unconscious elements. An apparently successful model for this approach had been accomplished in the 1930's in Benedek's study of the menstrual cycle (Benedek, 1952). But the number of reportable, much less successful, studies of this sort in the past fifteen years has been disappointingly few. They have included Margolin's female patient with a gastric fistula (1951); Mahl and Karpe's two patients whose stomachs were intubated before and after analytic hours (1953); the patients of Mirsky (Mirsky, Kaplan, and Broh-Kahn, 1950); of Fox (Fox, 1958; Fox, Murawski, Thorn, and Gray, 1959; Fox, Murawski, Bartholomay, and Gifford, 1961); and of Knapp (Knapp, 1960; Knapp and Nemetz, 1960; Knapp and Bahnson, 1963: Knapp, Carr, Mushatt, and Nemetz, 1966), who provided daily twenty-four-hour urine specimens for uropepsin or 17-OH corticosteroid determinations (Knapp's patients were asthmatics); the hypertensive patients of Moses, Daniels, and Nickerson (1956) and of Engel (1953) who had BP measurements before and after psychoanalytic sessions and those of Moses *et al.* (1956) who also had ballistocardiographic determinations during analytic sessions. In a few instances similar long-term correlative psychophysiologic studies have been carried out by analysts during psychotherapy (Karush, Hiatt, and Daniels, 1955; Stein, Kaufman, Janowitz, Levy, Hollander, and Winkelstein, 1962). From the scientific viewpoint the great difficulty with these studies has been not only the ethical and transference-countertransference problems introduced into the psychoanalytic procedure by the physiological measurements and tape recording, but even more so the difficulty of handling the vast quantity of data, physiological and psychological. Particularly elusive has been the problem of identifying which psychological attributes relate to the physiological measurement in question, and what the time span is over which the two parameters can reasonably be expected to interact.

Unable to pursue formal analysis, many analysts have attempted to develop interview approaches more appropriate to the patient material. Particularly useful has been the technique of the associative anamnesis of Deutsch (Deutsch and Murphy, 1955) and the open-ended medical interview of the Rochester group, which permit simultaneous evaluation of both somatic and psychologic elements. These approaches have made it possible to study patients with every kind of illness, acute and chronic, and in any setting. In some cases a therapeutic relationship has been established, making it possible to sustain observation for years. To be emphasized here is that the analyst, as the observing instrument, is able to garner a greater wealth of psychologic information in these briefer and less intensive contacts than is the person unfamiliar with and unskilled in the analytic approach. Little appreciated by the analyst who has not had the opportunity to interview patients seriously ill with somatic disorders is the readiness, at times even eagerness, of such patients to communicate psychological data and the extent to which the disruption of ego defenses at such times permits access to material ordinarily unconscious and relatively inaccessible. Clearly the kind of information obtained by such means is not identical with that obtained during a psychoanalysis. But on the other hand certain kinds of information become available which are not ordinarily available during analysis. For example, one may identify psychological themes across larger numbers of patients, representing a broader sample of social and cultural backgrounds. The crisis character of acute illness and the fact that the patient rarely has the defensive set typically evoked by psychiatric referral often leads to much fresher, more naïve, and less structured material than is usually obtained by an analyst on initial interview of a referred patient. And at the same time there is greater opportunity to make direct observation of behavior and interpersonal relationships as well as to secure data from other sources, especially when the patient is hospitalized.

Another approach has been to utilize analytic concepts to develop more experimental designs. Frequently this has involved the adaptation of projective techniques and collaboration with clinical psychologists. For example, Mirsky and his associates, combining interview and projective measures, were able to differentiate on the basis of psychodynamic formulations (previously developed by Alexander) subjects with high and low gastric secretory potential and to predict the development of ulcer in certain high secretors and pernicious anemia in certain low secretors (Mirsky, 1953, 1958; Weiner, Thaler, Reiser, and Mirsky, 1957). Seitz (1951, 1953) used hypnosis as a means of demonstrating that psychodynamically equivalent symptoms may replace spontaneous conversion reactions, but nonequivalent symptoms cannot be substituted in this way. Gottschalk, using clinical psychoanalytic theory, has devised a verbal behavior measure of affects based on a five-minute sample of spontaneous speech and has successfully applied this to various correlative studies (Gleser, Gottschalk, and Springer, 1961; Gottschalk and Kaplan, 1958; Gottschalk, Gleser, and Springer, 1961; Gottschalk, Gleser, D'Zmura, and Hanenson, 1964; Gottschalk, Cleghorn, Gleser, and Iacono, 1965). Knapp (1963), studying patients with asthma, attempted short-term predictions, covering the period from one psychoanalytic interview to the next, as a means of examining correlations between pulmonary symptoms and psychologic variables. Reiser, Weiner, and their associates have utilized a structured projective test situation in the laboratory as a means of investigating cardiovascular responses (Reiser, Reeves, and Armington, 1955; Weiner, Singer, and Reiser, 1962). Alexander and his colleagues used a film specifically selected to disrupt the psychodynamic balance believed to be characteristic of thyrotoxic patients as a means of differentiating physiologically and psychologically thyroid patients from controls (Alexander, Flagg, Foster, Clemens, and Blahd, 1961). Mohr focused on family dynamics as a means of studying eczema and asthma among preschool children (Mohr, Selesnick, and Augenbraun, 1963). Reichsman and Engel have used the spontaneous interactions between the experimenter and patient as a "natural" situation in which the experimenter becomes part of the experiment, as a means of correlating psychic processes and gastric secretion in fistula subjects (Engel, Reichsman, and Segal, 1956; Reichsman, Samuelson, and Engel, 1965). Kepecs was able to study exudation into the skin in relation to various emotional states by measuring fluid formation in blisters produced by cantharides cerate (Kepecs, Robin, and Brunner, 1951).

Conversion and the Involvement of Somatic Systems

Conversion continues to occupy a central position as a mechanism explaining many somatic manifestations. Although Freud originally invoked conversion to account for a wide variety of somatic processes (Freud, 1895, 1901, 1909, 1910), Alexander's differentiation of the vegetative neurotic from the conversion symptom for some time served to restrict the notion of conversion symptoms to functions mediated by the sensory and voluntary motor systems (Alexander, 1943). But since that time, many authors, including Alexander himself, have called attention to conversions involving structures not so innervated (Alexander, 1950; Alexander and Shapiro, 1952; Barchilon and Engel, 1952; Deutsch, 1959; Fenichel, 1945; Garma, 1958; Rangell, 1959; Schur, 1950, 1955; Seitz, 1951, 1953; Sperling, 1946, 1957, 1963, 1964). Further, there is now evidence as well that the conversion process may sometimes be one step or one component in the development of a localized organic lesion, which may then be considered a complication of a conversion (Engel and Schmale, 1967; Rangell, 1959; Schur, 1955). In such instances the resulting lesion itself and the symptoms arising from it neither have primary psychologic meaning as wish or fantasy nor serve a defensive function. Rather it seems that the drive and defense aspects of the conversion contribute to the timing and the choice of location of the manifestation, but are not responsible for the nature of the ultimate organic lesion itself.

What are the indispensable conditions determining which body parts may become accessible for use in conversion? This is determined by their capability of achieving mental representation. This means that any body experience which is perceived leaves behind memory traces which have the potential of becoming associated with other mental content and thereafter being used (reactivated) as body language (Deutsch, 1959; Margolin, 1953; Rangell, 1959; Sandler, 1958). The term *perceived* is a critical one, for it serves to differentiate silent physiological processes—e.g., increased gastric secretion as a response to an oral wish (Alexander, 1950)—from physiological processes which are perceived, consciously or unconsciously—e.g., nausea and vomiting as a reaction to contaminated food or even to the idea of contaminated food—and which may provide the perceptual data for subsequent conversion use. It is the use *pars pro toto* of the perception to represent a wish, a primary process operation, which constitutes the necessary first step of a conversion.

From the clinical perspective we know that the major determinants of the choice of a body part for a conversion are (1) physical processes experienced by the person himself and (2) the observation or fantasy of physical manifestations in an object, both of which have an ontogenetic background in the development of object relationships and are interchangeable and overdetermined, as is characteristic of primary process. Thus, whether the subject's experiences are projected onto the object or the object's experiences are perceived and responded to by the subject, it is the gestalt of the subject's own perceptual experience, exteroceptively and enteroceptively determined, which is crucial. To the extent that the memory traces of such perceptions become associated with a wish are they accessible for future reactivation when the pathway to thought or action is blocked. As

Freud originally proposed, the re-evoking of the memory traces of the perception becomes equivalent to re-establishing the situation of the original satisfaction and thereby the wish (Freud, 1900, pp. 565–566). The conversion process begins with these memory traces, which, as the representative of the opposed wish, in turn reactivate the original somatic processes which gave rise to the perceptions in the first place. The nature of the innervation, voluntary or involuntary, is irrelevant. Thus the compromise wish may be expressed in a motor act (e.g., paralysis) or in a sensation (e.g., pain, numbness, nausea, suffocation, coldness, heat), which may in turn evoke somatic responses (e.g., vomiting, hyperventilation, shivering, flushing). The latter commonly include physiologic processes in the service of bodily defense and adaptation not under voluntary control and as such do not have primary symbolic meaning.

From this it can be seen that the only body parts and functions which are available for the conversion process are those capable of being perceived consciously or unconsciously and thereby of giving rise to perceptual memory traces which can be used by the ego to symbolize and express hidden wishes. Silent physiological or biochemical processes and structures not accessible to either exteroceptive or enteroceptive perception cannot meet this requirement and hence cannot provide the basis for conversion even though they may be remotely involved in a chain of events initiated by a conversion (e.g., compensatory excretion of base in response to the respiratory alkalosis secondary to hyperventilation provoked by a conversion sensation of suffocation). This requirement is easily fulfilled and readily apparent in respect to the functioning of the voluntary motor system and the major sense organs, which can be utilized for complex and often idiosyncratic symbolic expressions in the form of pantomime (Freud, 1909). Perceptions of other bodily processes not under voluntary control similarly can come to represent symbolically the repressed wish, even though these processes originally constituted inborn biological systems concerned with approach, avoidance, defense, riddance, and adaptation and had no primary symbolic meaning.

Under what conditions may such systems be implicated in a conversion reaction? The first step may be only a sensation, the patient vividly re-experiencing the perceptual gestalt without any of the underlying physical changes (e.g., nausea, coldness, warmth, palpitation, dysphagia, suffocation). Here the sensation and its report carry the symbolic message and constitute the conversion reaction. Or the sensation may reactivate the corresponding somatic processes, nausea provoking vomiting; coldness, shivering; or suffocation, hyperventilation. These would be situations in which both the sensory and motor components together are utilized for the expression of the repressed wish. The motor component alone cannot be regarded as a conversion manifestation; only the complex as a whole can be so regarded. This differentiates conversion from the ubiquitous situations in which a bodily process of other etiology (e.g., the diarrhea of an enteritis or of ulcerative colitis, the respiratory obstruction of bronchitis or asthma) is utilized symbolically as the fulfillment of a wish, a process which might be referred to as secondary symbolization. It also differentiates conversion from the nonspecific concomitants of affects and tension states as well as from silent somatic processes involved in the expression of wishes and fulfillment of drives, as already noted.

As an illustration of these relationships is the case of a twenty-seven-year-old woman who, among a great variety of conversion symptoms, also experienced bouts of shaking chills, chattering of the teeth, and a subjective feeling of great coldness during which her hands and feet blanched and became icy cold. For a long time this was misinterpreted as the chill phase of some infectious disease, but no significant fever ever developed. One such episode occurred at a time when the patient was working out in psychotherapy some of her intensely ambivalent feelings toward her mother. In a sleep-talking episode she re-enacted an accident at age eleven in which she and her mother were struck by a hit-and-run driver while crossing a deserted, snowy street in the dead of winter. In sleep she recounted with terror seeing her mother's bloody face, then clutched her own face and complained bitterly of pain (face pain was another conversion symptom). A violent chill then ensued (described and reported to me by her husband). Upon awakening she recalled that in this accident her mother had been dragged several hundred feet by the car while she had been thrown into a snow pile on the side of the road, where (in the dark) she remained unnoticed for some twenty or thirty minutes. She remembers sitting alone in the snow feeling utterly deserted and shivering with the cold, and how endless it seemed before anyone came to her aid (Engel, 1959a).

In this example we would say that the conversion began with the reawakening of the memory traces of the original perceptual experience of being cold and all the implications that this held for this woman. Shivering, piloerection, and peripheral vasoconstriction constituted physiological responses to the sensation of being cold and did not in themselves have primary symbolic meaning. Rather the sense of coldness combined with the response of shivering, chattering teeth, and coldness of the extremities, and the perception of this response together constituted the total conversion reaction. The conversion process involved utilizing the memory of shivering in the cold to express symbolically the repressed wishes.

Sometimes the reactivated somatic changes bring in their wake other physical processes which have no psychological meaning and are to be considered as complications. Hyperventilation is an example, in which the common symptoms of numbness, tingling, light-headedness, or tetany are complications, not conversions (Engel, Ferris, and Logan, 1947). The conversion begins with the reactivated memory traces of some breathing experience, either underventilation or overventilation, as exhibited by oneself and/or by an object, where the percepts had become linked with a wish or fantasy which they now symbolize. Whether felt as inability to breathe (choking or suffocation) or as a need to overbreathe, the end result is hyperventilation. The conversion reaction includes both the sensation and the ventilatory response to it. But the symptoms of light-headedness, numbness, and tingling, and sometimes tetany that invariably ensue are the consequences of the respiratory alkalosis produced by the blowing off of carbon dioxide during the overbreathing and hence are complications. They have no primary symbolic meaning, though occasionally they may provide the perceptual basis for new conversion symptoms, which may later develop without hyperventilation.

These relationships are illustrated in the case of a young woman who experienced her first attack of hyperventilation on an occasion when she almost ran down an elderly woman crossing the street. She was unaware of overbreathing but was terrified by the symptoms of numbness, tingling, and light-headedness which followed rapidly upon the feeling that she could not breathe. In the course of analysis the following determinants of the respiratory conversion were elucidated. A classically hysterical neurotic with many conversion and phobic symptoms, she had succeeded in winning as her husband an older bachelor who was much attached to his widowed mother and whom he insisted come live with them. The patient was in constant conflict with her mother-in-law, toward whom her death wishes were only thinly veiled. Following a violent quarrel, the mother-in-law had a stroke from which she died. During the week's hospitalization the patient sat at the bedside literally day and night, virtually transfixed by the rhythm of the stertorous breathing of the comatose woman. As she listened with terrified fascination the last breath finally came. Subsequently she became preoccupied first with her husband's breathing, especially as he slept, and then with her own, with the accompanying fantasy that he or she would stop breathing and die. It was in this setting that the near-accident to the elderly woman occurred.

During the analysis there were uncovered as determinants of the sensation of suffocation a fantasy that she would be smothered by the mother's huge breasts; a fascination with the labored breathing of the parents whom she overheard in sexual intercourse, and to which she listened with bated breath in order better to hear, only to become terrified that she might not be able to take another breath and would die; the father's heavy breathing when he became angry at her or at the mother.

In this case the perceptions contributing to the conversion included those associated both with inhalation and with the feeling of not being able to take in a breath, of suffocating, as well as the sounds of breathing, her own and her parents', all of which became linked with sexual and sadomasochistic fantasies. Hyperventilation became the response to the reactivated memory traces of the perceptions of suffocation associated therewith, but the respiratory alkalosis and its concomitant of light-headedness, numbness, and tingling were complications and had no psychological meaning. Subsequently in the transference this woman developed new conversion symptoms of light-headedness, numbness, and tingling not preceded by overbreathing.

Even more intriguing are those instances in which a complication of the conversion ultimately results in local tissue damage. The best-known examples are those involving skin and mucous membrane (Barchilon and Engel, 1952; Engel, 1951; Robertiello, 1954; Schur, 1955; Seitz, 1951, 1953), though similar relationship may also be noted in upper and lower gastrointestinal tract, respiratory passages, joints, and even parts of the vascular system. For example, we have seen Raynaud's disease appear first in the index finger of a woman about to dial the phone and "tell off" her mother, and rheumatoid arthritis first in the ankle of a man upon the impulse to kick down the door of a rejecting girlfriend. Several writers have speculated about the role of conversion at some point in the development of the asthmatic attack (Rangell, 1959; Sperling, 1963). Dekker has shown that asthmatic wheezing can be produced by the passive compression of the membranous part of the larger air passages that occurs during the peculiar forceful expiration which is part of the characteristic breathing pattern in asthma (Dekker and Groen, 1957). Such an abnormal breathing pattern could come about through a conversion mechanism and constitute one factor responsible for narrowing the airways and producing the typical wheeze. Garma's suggestion that a primary psychological meaning of rejecting a bad introject constitutes an essential element in the pathogenesis of peptic ulcer would also fit with such a notion (Garma, 1958). The first step, according to this thesis, would be a conversion involving a perceptual experience associated with ingesting something bad. The response could be pylorospasm, which, in the presence of hypersecretion, may perhaps contribute to peptic ulcer formation (Engel, 1959b).

Recent new information on the response of skin to physical injury provides a clue as to a mechanism whereby local skin pathology might result as a complication of conversion. It is now known that the characteristic cutaneous reaction to injury, namely pain, tenderness, and inflammation, is not only a consequence of the direct effect on skin of the noxious factor, but also involves a feedback system which serves to enhance and sustain the inflammatory response beyond the period of the actual injury. This feedback is mediated by antidromic activity along the same afferent fibers which carry the nocioceptive impulses, and it results in the formation at the nerve terminals in the skin of chemical substances (neurokinin, substance P) which have the properties of facilitating the local inflammatory response, lowering the threshold for pain, and influencing clotting mechanisms (Chapman, Goodell, and Wolff, 1959). Of high importance to our thesis is that the same feedback system can also be activated by the hypnotic suggestion of injury (Chapman *et al.*, 1959), making it almost certain that the same would hold true as well for conversions that involve the fantasy of injury to the surface of the body. Such antidromic neurosecretory activity in the local area involved in reaction to fantasy could well explain the occurrence of local hyperesthesia, erythema, and swelling occasionally found at the site of conversion pain (Engel, 1951). And should there be interaction between such activity and other preexisting pathogenic mechanisms, such as those involved with immunity, allergy, or hemostasis, it might also explain certain examples of local skin lesions, including allergic, eczematoid or exudative dermatitis (Barchilon and Engel, 1952; Schur, 1950; Seitz, 1951, 1953), urticaria (Graff and Wallerstein, 1954; Moody and Lond, 1946), purpura (stigmatization) (Lifschutz, 1957), plantar warts (Yalom, 1964), the localization of which is clearly symbolically determined. The cases of Schur (1950), Seitz (1951, 1953), and Barchilon and Engel (1952) are excellent examples of symbolic determination of lesion localization on a conversion basis. Further, once a local skin area is diseased, regardless of the primary etiology, the associated perceptions readily achieve mental representation and hence may become the basis for future conversion reactions in the same location. It is well known that many such skin lesions tend to recur at the sites of origin.

As an example we cite the case of a twenty-year-old soldier with an urticarial eruption on the back of his legs, thighs, and buttocks. These lesions had a transverse linear distribution and resembled in every way what one would expect from a whipping. And indeed it developed that as a nine- or ten-year-old boy he had been whipped, while an inmate of a very strict orphanage, for the offense of peeking in the windows of the girls' dormitory. The recurrence of these lesions at age twenty took place spontaneously immediately after he had been apprehended loitering on the grounds of the nurses' dormitory on the military post. Though an enlisted man, he had wanted to date one of the nurses and was hoping to see her. He was apprehended by an officer, severely reprimanded, and ordered to return to his barracks. Within an hour the skin lesion had developed.

The patient of Barchilon and Engel is also particularly instructive (Barchilon and Engel, 1952).

This was a twenty-four-year-old, single woman with many conversion symptoms who since age ten had suffered with recurring eczematoid dermatitis usually occurring in relationship to contact with metal, to which she was alleged to be sensitive. The first lesion was around the neck and shoulders, the site of the metal chain of a crucifix presented to her by her aunt on the occasion of her confirmation. She was apprehensive about confession because she was not sure she knew whether or not she had sinned. When her aunt placed the crucifix about her neck, she felt shame, guilt, and unclean, and the eruption developed within a few hours. Subsequent skin lesions appeared in the following settings: (1) At the time of her graduation from high school her father presented her with a wrist watch and a lesion promptly developed at points of contact. (2) Two years later, while as a court stenographer recording the testimony of a case of rape, lesions appeared on both arms where they had rested on a metal plate at the judge's bench. (3) Lesions developed at the sites of venipunctures performed by physicians whom she had consulted about amenorrhea. (4) While acting as a maid of honor at a wedding, she rubbed her eyes after having held a coin in her sweaty palm. The lids promptly became the site of a new rash. To avoid contact with metal she placed a piece of cloth between her skin and such metal objects as watch, jewelry, and eyeglasses.

During psychotherapy the skin lesions not only cleared completely, but it no longer was necessary for her to use the cloth protection. But the lesions recurred dramatically under the following circumstances: A few days after having had her first sexual experience, about which she felt ashamed, she visited her mother for Christmas Eve. While helping with the dishes she was startled when her mother, having suddenly realized that her daughter was no longer wearing the cloth protection, exclaimed in an alarmed voice, "*What are you doing* not wearing the cloth under your watch?" The girl's immediate response was to the "*What are you doing* . . ." which she perceived as accusatory, referring to her recent sexual experience. Itching and burning under the watch immediately developed, followed by reappearance of lesions at all previous sites of involvement.

This case may be taken as a prototype of the situation in which a conversion becomes the trigger for a local tissue disease. Without question she had many times before had skin contact with metal; why, then, did the skin reaction occur for the first time only in relation to wearing the crucifix necklace? We know that the presentation of the crucifix evoked fantasies against which countercathexes were mobilized. We presume that the cathexes then shifted to the *perception* of the necklace on the skin around the neck, the perception then becoming a basis for a mental representation of the unconscious wish. By the same token the local skin area became the locus of projection not only of the repressed sexual wishes, but also of a second countercathexis originating from the superego, the fantasy of punishment. At this juncture the transition to an organic process became possible, if we assume that this involved a fantasy of injury to the local skin area (the punishment), with accompanying activation of the antidromic neurosecretory system of defense against local injury (Chapman, Goodell, and Wolff, 1959). This is an entirely plausible suggestion, since it has been shown that this system can be activated by the hypnotic suggestion of injury as well as by actual injury (Chapman *et al.*). In this patient we postulate in addition that some interaction with a pre-existing allergic predisposition accounted for the development of the local dermatitis. Once this had occurred, injury in response to metal became a reality, not merely a fantasy, and vividly reinforced the earlier perceptions and their association with the fantasy of injury, which could then readily be reprojected onto any skin site satisfying the symbolic requirements for a conversion. In this manner the conversion mechanism became a system whereby such loci could become the sites of dermatitis even in the absence of further contact with the allergen.

By placing at the center of the conversion process the perceptual experience of a change in one's own body or in the body of an object, it becomes possible to understand how systems with involuntary as well as voluntary innervations may become involved in conversion reactions, as either may be activated by an unconscious wish. When a voluntary system is involved, e.g., paralysis of a limb, we have no difficulty in recognizing the unconscious meaning of the paralysis. When a nonvoluntarily innervated system is involved, the meaning is to be found in the gestalt of the reaction and not in any component of the physiological processes. This is well illustrated in the case of the woman with chills, whose unconscious wish was represented in the perception of being cold and not in any of the physiological reactions of shivering, teeth chattering, piloerection, or vasoconstriction per se, which were reactions to that perception. Further, we are able to see how interactions may take place between specific physiological components and other pre-existing factors, as was discussed in relationship to the girl with dermatitis, where the location, but not the type, of the lesion is determined by unconscious fantasy. The latter must be seen as a complication of the conversion.

In this discussion I have emphasized mainly the primacy of the perceptual experience in conversion. This is not to neglect the importance of the expressive aspect of the conversion, which is intended as a communication to the object (as well as to the self). This externally directed communication may make use not only of the voluntary motor system, but also of other neural pathways active during the bodily expression of affect, thereby constituting another way in which autonomically innervated structures may become involved in conversions. Again, the perceptual experience associated with such autonomic activity itself can become a basis for new mental representations capable of reactivating the physiological processes with which they were originally associated. Thus there becomes established a vicious cycle in which the physiological concomitants of an affect (the observable manifestations of which have a communicative value to the environment) also become a vehicle for the expression of an unconscious wish.

This sequence is most apparent in skin, a prime organ of expression through blushing, blanching, sweating, etc., as well as in the gastrointestinal tract (gagging, vomiting, diarrhea) (Schur, 1955). As described above, interaction with local, predisposing factors may result in localized lesions.

The perspective presented here may be regarded as being closer to that of Rangell than to that of Deutsch and his colleagues, who apply the term *conversion* to cover all processes whereby perceptions, as symbolizations of lost external objects, are "retrojected" onto or into the body and the term, conversion symptom, to "any manifestation of this process expressed in an altered organic function" (Deutsch, 1959, p. 95; Rangell, 1959). Aside from the lack of definition of "altered organic function," which seems to refer to virtually every type of organic process known, the psychological data cited in support of this view do not distinguish a somatic change brought about by virtue of its capability to express a symbolic meaning from fantasies aroused by the experiencing of somatic changes which have no primary psychologic meaning. The latter constitutes a secondary symbolic utilization of the somatic process. Further, it implies a more exclusively psychogenic concept of the etiology of organic processes than the facts justify. On the other hand, the classical requirement of conflict and the use of a body process as a means of experiencing and expressing symbolically an unconscious fantasy (wish) yields a more discrete psychologic construct, for which criteria can be established and in relationship to which somatic processes can be studied. From the research viewpoint this has heuristic value, especially since it does not preclude overlap with other types of psychosomatic processes. Particularly does it allow for the conceptualization of more complex psychosomatic interrelationships, where the final organic process may be reached through a number of different sequences, which may or may not somewhere along the line include conversion. The postulated mechanism for certain skin reactions discussed above allows for such variability.

Specific and Nonspecific Psychosomatic Determinants of Disease Onset

The spectrum of psychosomatic mechanisms involved in somatic disease ranges from conversion to quite nonspecific situations, where we presume biochemical and physiological components of primary biologic defense systems may interact with pre-existing or coexisting pathogenic factors to eventuate in disease. Between these extremes are a group of disorders which might be designated as *somatopsychic-psychosomatic* (Engel, 1962b). These are somatic disorders in which the predisposing biological factors not only are present at birth or early in infancy, but also are directly or indirectly involved in the development of the psychic apparatus. This implies that at some point the somatic system involved comes to exert a specific influence on psychic development, sometimes in the form of derivatives of body language, sometimes through erotization processes, and sometimes through involvement in the processes of object relating or drive discharge. These in turn contribute to a characteristic constellation of preferred psychodynamic tendencies, ego defenses, drive patterns, and object-relating techniques that characterize persons with each of the disorders and confer on them a quality of psychodynamic specificity. They also insure a further measure of specificity as well in respect to the circumstances that prove psychologically stressful and the sequence of ego responses that culminates ultimately in the appearance of the specific somatic lesion (Alexander, 1950; Mirsky, 1953, 1958). Included among this group of disorders are such conditions as peptic ulcer, colitis, asthma, rheumatoid arthritis, hypertension, hyperthyroidism, and probably others as yet not delineated. These are the conditions traditionally regarded as "psychosomatic." The most telling evidence in support of such a notion has been the success of Mirsky and his colleagues in differentiating by psychological means a peptic ulcer-prone population (on the basis of high pepsinogen) from a peptic ulcer-immune group (low pepsinogen) and among the former successfully predicting for which ones the setting of induction into the army would constitute the specific psychologic stress conducive to ulcer formation (Weiner, Thaler, Reiser, and Mirsky, 1957). This study provides a model which may well be applied to other conditions where a biological indicator of disease susceptibility can be identified among persons in whom the disease has not yet developed.

Nonspecific determinants are involved in a wide variety of conditions. They include such familiar circumstances as the role of the circulatory concomitants of severe anxiety or of rage in precipitating acute pulmonary edema in the person with pre-existing marginally compensated heart disease; the facilitation of fungus infections ("athlete's foot") by virtue of the increased sweating accompanying the anxiety reaction. Or an inborn metabolic error, genically determined, involving a biologic defense system may result in disease when that system is activated in response to a nonspecific psychologic stress. An instructive example is the report of the production of a virilizing syndrome in a girl with a defect in the biogenesis of adrenal steroids, resulting in a disproportionate output of adrenogenic steroids in the course of the nonspecific pituitary-adrenal response triggered during a period of psychologic decompensation (Bush and Mahesh, 1959).

The patient's twin sister, who was found to have the same biogenetic defect, was psychologically healthy and revealed no evidence of virilization.

By far the most common setting in which illness, mental as well as physical, seems to develop is what we have designated the "giving up—given up" complex (Adamson and Schmale, 1965; Engel and Schmale,

1967; Schmale, 1958, 1965; Schmale and Iker, 1966). Saul has used the term impasse to designate what is probably a comparable state (Saul, 1966). This is an ego state during which for shorter or longer periods of time, often in a waxing and waning manner, previously effectively used defenses and adaptations are perceived as ineffectual and current sources of gratification as unavailable. In phenomenologic terms it has the following features: (1) It includes an unpleasant affective quality expressed in such terms as "it's too much," "it's no use," "I can't take it any more," "I give up," and so on. This may involve two different affective qualities, helplessness, where these feelings are ascribed more to failures on the part of the environment, and hopelessness, where they are more ascribed to failures of one-self and include the feeling of being beyond help from others (Schmale, 1958, 1965). (2) The patient perceives himself as less intact, less competent, less in control, less gratified, and less capable of functioning in a relatively autonomous fashion. (3) Relationships with objects are felt to be less secure and gratifying and the patient may feel himself given up by objects or he may give himself up. (4) The external environment may be perceived as differing significantly from expectations based on past experience, which no longer seems as useful a guide for current or future behavior. (5) There is felt to be a loss in continuity between past and future and an inability to project oneself into the future with hope or confidence. Hence, the future may be relatively bleak or unrewarding. (6) There is a tendency to revive feelings, memories, and behavior connected with occasions in the past which had a similar quality.

The "giving up—given up" complex is a transitional ego state, during which suitable defenses or coping devices are unavailable or have not yet evolved. The "giving up" phase is ushered in by a failure of the defenses and coping devices that had previously served to assure gratification and is marked by an awareness of the inability to reachieve gratification. The "given up" stage, which may or may not ensue, marks the apparent finality of the loss of gratification as a psychic reality, which for a time at least must be endured, as no other sources of supply appear to be available. The metapsychology of this complex and its relationship to issues of separation and depression are discussed more fully elsewhere (Engel and Schmale, 1967).

At the present time the bulk of the evidence linking the "giving up—given up" state to disease onset is retrospective. That is, it is reported to have occurred in the period immediately before onset of manifest disease by approximately 80 per cent of patients and their relatives (Adamson and Schmale, 1965; Schmale, 1958, 1965). In one study so far, however, it has been possible to differentiate women with cervical cancer from those without on the basis of the presence of the complex (Schmale and Iker, 1966). Additional prospective studies are needed before the true significance of this chronologic relationship can be established. At this time, therefore, the relationship between the complex and somatic illness can be considered only as presumptive, not proven. Nor can it be regarded as either necessary or sufficient for the emergence of somatic disease, but only as a contributing factor and then only when other predisposing factors are also present and operating. For example, the development of an illness such as pneumonia requires the additional chance factor that the patient be exposed to the infectious agent at the time that he is in this state. In the absence of such pre-existing or concurrent pathogenic factors either the state may resolve without the development of somatic illness or inappropriate defenses, and behavior constituting psychiatric disease may develop (Adamson and Schmale, 1965; Schmale, 1965).

At the present time nothing is known about the mechanisms whereby the "giving up—given up" complex might contribute to somatic change. We assume that biological systems concerned with defense against injury and with obtaining or conserving supplies are activited or in some way disrupted. What these systems are, whether they are unique for the "giving up—given up" complex, whether they are different for helplessness as compared for hopelessness or for the "giving up" phase as compared to the "given up" phase are issues not yet studied.

The Future Role of Psychoanalysis in Psychosomatic Research

Study by analysts of patients not suitable for classical psychoanalytic techniques and the development of methods to do so have proved amply rewarding. And much that has been learned, including some of the concepts which have evolved, now can be studied in finer detail through the microscope of psychoanalysis. The analyst is in an ideal position to note the circumstances surrounding episodes of somatic illness during the several years occupying an analysis. He has an excellent opportunity, for example, to study the so-called "giving up—given up" complex as a psychological phenomenon in its own right as well as to examine its postulated relationship to illness. Thus the analyst may observe its development in the transference, especially in relation to interruptions of the analysis, and note the occurrence of somatic illness. He is also in a position to collect examples of separations with and without the development of helplessness or hopelessness, helplessness or hopelessness with and without the development of illness, and illness with and without such antecedent psychic events. An example of such an approach is Ruddick's study of the occurrence of "colds" during analysis (1963). He reported that colds commonly were related to separations and losses, in response to which conflicts around oral and respiratory incorporation were activated. Whether transient "giving up—given up" also occurred is not reported, but it is well known that separations and losses are common settings for that reaction.

A change in the type of somatic disorder with changing psychodynamics in the course of psychoanalysis, particularly in relation to the transference, provides another means of studying the specific psychologic determinants of organic processes. Earlier investigators, for example, have reported alternations between ulcerative colitis and migraine (Engel, 1956; Sperling, 1957, 1964), and between asthma and colitis (Sperling, 1963), corresponding to different psychodynamic states. The ulcerative colitis patient characteristically bleeds in relation to loss of control and the development of the "giving up—given up" complex; he develops headache when he feels in control but is responding with guilt to overt self-assertion or aggression (Engel, 1956). Giovacchini, during the course of analysis of the transference neurosis in a thirty-seven-year-old woman, observed migraine replaced by hypertension, and then disappearance of the latter with changing relationships with the analyst (1963). Hypertension developed as she betrayed more ego disorganization, feeling isolated, desolate, lonely, and abandoned, a description suggesting the "giving up—given up" state. The blood pressure fell when she could reach out to the analyst and cling in an anaclitic fashion.

No procedure surpasses psychoanalysis as a means of elucidating intrapsychic processes over a period of time. Patients in psychoanalysis offer the best source of material for gaining insight into the unconscious determinants and the metapsychology of the critical psychic states involved in the genesis of somatic disorder. The time has again arrived for analysts to pay attention to such relationships and to report their findings. Rich lodes have been uncovered during this third period, begging for mining in depth by practicing analysts.

Note: This chapter is based in part on papers read before the American Psychoanalytic Association, December 4, 1965, and the British Psychoanalytical Society, November 16, 1966.

References

Adamson, J. D., and Schmale, A. H. "Object Loss, Giving Up, and the Onset of Psychiatric Disease." *Psychosomatic Medicine*, 27 (1965), 557.

Alexander, F. "Fundamental Concepts of Psychosomatic Research: Psychogenesis, Conversion, Specificity." *Psychosomatic Medicine*, 5 (1943), 205–210.

Alexander, F. *Psychosomatic Medicine*. New York: Norton, 1950.

Alexander, F., Flagg, G. W., Foster, S., Clemens, T., and Blahd, W. "Experimental Studies of Emotional Stress. I. Hyperthyroidism." *Psychosomatic Medicine*, 23 (1961), 104.

Alexander, F., and Shapiro, L. B. "Neuroses, Behavior Disorders and Perversions." In F. Alexander and Helen Ross, *Dynamic Psychiatry*. Chicago: University of Chicago Press, 1952. Pp. 117–139.

Barchilon, J., and Engel, G. L. "Dermatitis: An Hysterical Conversion Symptom in a Young Woman." *Psychosomatic Medicine*, 14 (1952), 295–305.

Benedek, Therese. *Psychosexual Functions in Women*. New York: Ronald Press, 1952.

Bush, I. E., and Mahesh, V. B. "Adrenocortical Hyperfunction with Sudden Onset of Hirsutism." *Journal of Endocrinology*, 18 (1959), 1.

Chapman, L. F., Goodell, Helen, and Wolff, H. G. "Augmentation of the Inflammatory Reaction by Activity of the CNS." *American Medical Association Archives of Neurology*, 1 (1959), 557.

Dekker, E., and Groen, J. J. "Asthmatic Wheezing: Compression of the Trachea and Major Bronchi as a Cause." *Lancet*, 1 (1957), 1064.

Deutsch, F. (ed.). *On the Mysterious Leap from the Mind to the Body*. New York: International Universities Press, 1959.

Deutsch, F., and Murphy, W. F. *The Clinical Interview*. Vol. II. *Therapy*. New York: International Universities Press, 1955.

Engel, G. L. "Primary Atypical Facial Neuralgia: An Hysterical Conversion Symptom." *Psychosomatic Medicine*, 13 (1951), 375.

Engel, G. L. "A Critical Definition of the Disorder Essential Hypertension." In Panel, "Problems of Hypertension." *Journal of the American Psychoanalytic Association*, 1 (1953), 562.

Engel, G. L. "Studies of Ulcerative Colitis. IV. The Significance of Headaches." *Psychosomatic Medicine*, 18 (1956), 334–346.

Engel, G. L. "Psychogenic Pain and the Pain Prone Patient." *American Journal of Medicine*, 26 (1959), 889–918. (a)

Engel, G. L. Review of A. Garma, *Peptic Ulcer and Psychoanalysis*. *American Journal of Digestive Diseases*, 4 (1959), 829. (b)

Engel, G. L. "Anxiety and Depression-Withdrawal: The Primary Affects of Unpleasure." *International Journal of Psycho-Analysis*, 43 (1962), 89. (a)

Engel, G. L. *Psychological Development in Health and Disease*. Philadelphia: Saunders, 1962. (b)

Engel, G. L., Ferris, E. G., and Logan, M. "Hyperventilation: Analysis of Clinical Symptomatology." *Annals of Internal Medicine*, 27 (1947), 683.

Engel, G. L., Reichsman, F., and Segal, Hanna. "A Study of an Infant with Gastric Fistula. I. Behavior and the Rate of Total HCl Secretion." *Psychosomatic Medicine*, 18 (1956), 374.

Engel, G. L., and Schmale, A. H. "Psychoanalytic Theory of Somatic Disorder, Conversion, Specificity, and the Disease Onset Situation." *Journal of the American Psychoanalytic Association*, 15, No. 2 (April 1967), 344–365.

Fenichel, O. *The Psychoanalytic Theory of Neurosis*. New York: Norton, 1945.

Fox, H. M. "Effects of Psychophysiological Research on the Transference." *Journal of the American Psychoanalytic Association*, 6 (1958), 413–432.

Fox, H. M., Murawski, B. J., Bartholomay, A. F., and Gifford, S. "Adrenal Steroid Excretion Patterns in 18 Healthy Subjects." *Psychosomatic Medicine*, 23 (1961), 32.

Fox, H. M., Murawski, B. J., Thorn, G. W., and Gray, S. J. "Urinary 17-OH Corticoid and Uropepsin Levels with Psychological Data." *Archives of Internal Medicine*, 101 (1959), 859.

Freud, S., and Breuer, J. "Studies on Hysteria" (1895). *The Standard Edition of the Complete Psychological Works of. . . .* London: Hogarth Press. Vol. 2, pp. 1–305. (Also published as *Studies on Hysteria*. New York: Basic Books, 1957.)

Freud, S. "The Interpretation of Dreams" (1900). *The Standard Edition of the Complete Psychological Works of. . . .* London: Hogarth Press. Vol. 9. (Also published as *The Interpretation of Dreams*. New York: Basic Books, 1955.)

Freud, S. "Fragment of Analysis of a Case of Hysteria" (1901). *The Standard Edition of the Complete Psychological Works of. . . .* London: Hogarth Press. Vol. 7, pp. 7–122. (Also in *Collected Papers of. . . .* New York: Basic Books, 1959. Vol. 3, pp. 13–146.)

Freud, S. "Some General Remarks on Hysterical Attacks" (1909). *The Standard Edition of the Complete Psychological Works of. . . .* London: Hogarth Press. Vol. 9. (Also in *Collected Papers of. . . .* New York: Basic Books, 1959. Vol. 2, pp. 100–104.)

Freud, S. "The Psychoanalytic View of Psychogenic Disturbance of Vision" (1910). *The Standard Edition of the Complete Psychological Works of. . . .* London: Hogarth Press. Vol. 11. (Also in *Collected Papers of. . . .* New York: Basic Books, 1959. Vol. 2, pp. 105–112.)

Freud, S. "Inhibition, Symptoms, and Anxiety" (1926). *The Standard Edition of the Complete Psychological Works of. . . .* London: Hogarth Press. Vol. 20.

Garma, A. *Peptic Ulcer and Psychoanalysis*. Baltimore: Williams & Wilkins, 1958.

Giovacchini, P. L. "Somatic Symptoms and the Transference Neurosis." *International Journal of Psycho-Analysis*, 44 (1963), 143.

Gleser, Goldine C., Gottschalk, L. A., and Springer, K. J. "An Anxiety Scale Applicable to Verbal Samples." *American Medical Association Archives of General Psychiatry*, 5 (1961), 593.

Gottschalk, L. A., Cleghorn, J. M., Gleser, G. C., and Iacono, J. M. "Studies of Relationships of Emotions to Plasma Lipids." *Psychosomatic Medicine*, 27 (1965), 102.

Gottschalk, L. A., Gleser, G. C., D'Zmura, T., and Hanenson, I. B. "Some Psychophysiologic Relations in Hypertensive Women." *Psychosomatic Medicine*, 26 (1964), 610.

Gottschalk, L. A., Gleser, G. C., and Springer, K. J. "Three Hostility Scales Applicable to Verbal Samples." *American Medical Association Archives of General Psychiatry*, 5 (1961), 254.

Gottschalk, L. A., and Kaplan, S. M. "A Quantitative Method of Estimating Variations in Intensity of a Psychological Conflict or State." *American Medical Association Archives of Neurology and Psychiatry*, 79 (1958), 688–696.

Graff, N. I., and Wallerstein, R. S. "Unusual Wheal Reaction in a Tattoo: Psychosomatic Aspects in One Patient." *Psychosomatic Medicine*, 16 (1954), 505–515.

Hartmann, H. *Essays on Ego Psychology*. New York: International Universities Press, 1964.

Karush, A., Hiatt, R. B., and Daniels, G. E. "Psychophysiological Correlations in Ulcerative Colitis." *Psychosomatic Medicine*, 17 (1955), 36.

Kepecs, J. G., Robin, M., and Brunner, M. J. "Relationship between Certain Emotional States and Exudation into the Skin." *Psychosomatic Medicine*, 13 (1951), 10.

Knapp, P. H. "Acute Bronchial Asthma. II. Psychoanalytic Observations on of Mood and Fantasy in Two Asthmatic Patients." *Psychosomatic Medicine*, 22 (1960), 88.

Knapp, P. H. "Short Time Psychoanalytic and Psychosomatic Predictions." *Journal of the American Psychoanalytic Association*, 11 (1963), 245.

Knapp, P. H., and Bahnson, C. B. "The Emotional Field: A Sequential Study of Mood and Fantasy in Two Asthmatic Patients." *Psychosomatic Medicine*, 25 (1963), 433.

Knapp, P. H., Carr, H. E., Mushatt, C., and Nemetz, S. J. "Steroid Excretion, Emotion and Asthmatic Crisis." *Psychosomatic Medicine*, 28 (1966), 114.

Knapp, P. H., and Nemetz, S. J. "Acute Bronchial Asthma. I. Concomitant Depression and Excitement and Varied Antecedent Patterns in 406 Attacks." *Psychosomatic Medicine*, 22 (1960), 42.

Lifschutz, J. E. "Hysterical Stigmatization." *American Journal of Psychiatry*, 114 (1957), 527–531.

Mahl, G. F., and Karpe, R. "Emotions and Hydrochloric Acid Secretion during Psychoanalytic Sessions." *Psychosomatic Medicine*, 15 (1953), 312–327.

Margolin, S. G. "The Behavior of the Stomach during Psychoanalysis." *Psychoanalytic Quarterly*, 20 (1951), 349.

Margolin, S. G. "Genetic and Dynamic Psychophysiological Determinants of Pathophysiological Processes." In F. Deutsch (ed.), *The Psychosomatic Concept in Psychoanalysis*. New York: International Universities Press, 1953. Pp. 3–36.

Mirsky, I. A. "Psychoanalysis and the Biological Sciences." In F. Alexander and H. Ross (eds.), *Twenty Years of Psychoanalysis*. New York: Norton, 1953. Pp. 155–176.

Mirsky, I. A. "Physiologic, Psychologic, and Social Determinants in the Etiology of Duodenal Ulcer." *American Journal of Digestive Diseases*, 3 (1958), 285–314.

Mirsky, I. A., Kaplan, S., and Broh-Kahn, R. H. "Pepsinogen Excretion (Uropepsin) as an Index of the Influence of Various Life Situations in Gastric Secretion." *Association for Research in Nervous and Mental Disease*, 29 (1950), 629.

Mohr, G. J., Selesnick, S., and Augenbraun, G. "Family Dynamics in Early Childhood Asthma. Some Mental Health Considerations." In H. I. Schneer (ed.), *The Asthmatic Child*. New York: Hoeber, 1963.

Moody, R. L., and Lond, M. B. "Bodily Changes during Abreaction." *Lancet*, 2 (1946), 934.

Moses, L., Daniels, G. E., and Nickerson, J. L. "Psychogenic Factors in Essential Hypertension." *Psychosomatic Medicine*, 18 (1956), 471.

Rangell, L. "The Nature of Conversion." *Journal of the American Psychoanalytic Association*, 7 (1959), 632.

Rapaport, D. "The Structure of Psychoanalytic Theory." In S. Koch (ed.), *Psychology: A Study of a Science.* New York: McGraw-Hill, 1959. Vol. 3, pp. 55–183.

Reichsman, F., Samuelson, D., and Engel, G. L. "Behavior and Gastric Secretion. II. A Study of a Four Year Old with Gastric Fistula." *Psychosomatic Medicine,* 27 (1965), 483.

Reiser, M. F., Reeves, A. B., and Armington, J. "Effects of Variations in Laboratory Procedure and Experimenter upon the BCG, BP, and Heart Rate in Healthy Young Men." *Psychosomatic Medicine,* 17 (1955), 187.

Robertiello, R. C. "Revival of Early Memories with the Appearance of Primitive Defence Reactions Including Aphthous Mouth Ulcers, Muscle Tensing and Urticaria." *Psychiatric Quarterly,* 28 (1954), 410–415.

Ruddick, B. "Colds and Respiratory Introjection." *International Journal of Psychoanalysis,* 44 (1963), 178.

Sandler, J. "Psychosomatic Pathology." *British Journal of Medical Psychology,* 31 (1958), 19–23.

Saul, L. J. "Sudden Death at Impasse." *Psychoanalytic Forum,* 1 (1966), 881.

Schmale, A. H. "Relationship of Separation and Depression to Disease." *Psychosomatic Medicine,* 20 (1958), 259.

Schmale, A. H. "Object Loss, 'Giving Up' and Disease Onset. An Overview of Research in Progress." Symposium on Medical Aspects of Stress in the Military Climate, Walter Reed Army Institute of Research. Washington, D.C. U.S. Government Printing Office, 1965, p. 433.

Schmale, A. H., and Iker, H. P. "The Affect of Hopelessness and the Development of Cancer." *Psychosomatic Medicine,* 28 (1966), p. 714.

Schur, M. "Case Analyses of Chronic, Exudative, Discoid and Lichenoid Dermatitis (Sulzberger-Garbe's Syndrome)." *International Journal of Psychoanalysis,* 31 (1950), 73–77.

Schur, M. "Comments on the Metapsychology of Somatization." *Psychoanalytic Study of the Child,* 10 (1955), 119–164.

Seitz, P. F. D. "Symbolism and Organ Choice in Conversion Reactions." *Psychosomatic Medicine,* 13 (1951), 254–259.

Seitz, P. F. D. "Experiments in the Substitution of Symptoms by Hypnosis." *Psychosomatic Medicine,* 15 (1953), 405–424.

Sperling, Melitta. "Psychoanalytic Study of Ulcerative Colitis in Children." *Psychoanalytic Quarterly,* 15 (1946), 302–329.

Sperling, Melitta. "The Psychoanalytic Treatment of Ulcerative Colitis." *International Journal of Psycho-Analysis,* 38 (1957), 341–349.

Sperling, Melitta. "A Psychoanalytic Study of Bronchial Asthma in Children." In H. I. Schneer (ed.), *The Asthmatic Child.* New York: Hoeber, 1963. P. 138.

Sperling, Melitta. "A Further Contribution to the Psychoanalytic Study of Migraine and Psychogenic Headaches." *International Journal of Psycho-Analysis,* 45 (1964), 549.

Stein, A., Kaufman, M. R., Janowitz, H. D., Levy, M. H., Hollander, F., and Winkelstein, A. "Changes in Hydrocholoric Acid Secretion in a Patient with a Gastric Fistula during Intensive Psychotherapy." *Psychosomatic Medicine,* 24 (1962), 427.

Weiner, H., Thaler, M., Reiser, M. F., and Mirsky, I. A. "Etiology of Duodenal Ulcer. "Relation of Specific Psychological Characteristics to Rate of Gastric Secretion (Serum Pepsinogen)." *Psychosomatic Medicine*, 19 (1957), 1–10.

Weiner, H., Singer, M. T., and Reiser, M. F. "Cardiovascular Responses and Their Psychological Correlates. I. A Study in Healthy Young Adults and Patients with Peptic Ulcer and Hypertension." *Psychosomatic Medicine*, 24 (1962), 477.

Yalom, I. O. "Plantar Warts: A Case Study." *Journal of Nervous and Mental Disease*, 138 (1964), 163.

11

Psychoanalysis and Psychopharmacology

ARNOLD J. MANDELL

It is significant that a chapter with the above title appears in a book under the aegis of a psychoanalytic society. The many historically based antagonisms between various workers in psychiatry that have led to "organic" versus "psychodynamic" factions and resulted in the inability of either to use the contributions of the other gradually are being resolved and being replaced by a more holistic synthesis of biological and social factors in human behavior theory as well as therapy. False dichotomies retarding the development of our science, such as the "nature-nurture" controversy, are gradually being replaced by multivariable interactional models. What is being shown is that enzyme regulation is dependent on hormones; hormone levels are a function of the complex interplay of limbic and cortical influence on the anterior pituitary; neurophysiological events in subcortical limbic structures are subject to modification by current experience in animals and man; current experience perception is a function of past experience; past experience is a function of social field forces as well as those related to the individual; and each of these representative levels is related to each other in a style consistent with a gradient interdependent modulation rather than an all-or-none trigger. Thus, in the process of teasing out or manipulating variables in a complex system of this type one can be working many places at the same time in spite of the investigator's or therapist's unimodality of orientation. It remains to be seen whether therapists or researchers in the behavioral areas will be secure enough to allow themselves at least momentary glances at a broader, multi-dimensional view while plying their profession and maintaining its assumptions in their own particular segment.

The area under present consideration is one in which an unavoidable confrontation between theoretical "sets" has taken place. Psychoanalytically based psychotherapeutic approaches to the psychoses have not been so effective as currently available psychopharmacological agents. Where now does adaptationally oriented, ego-strengthening therapy fit with a patient with a pharmacologically produced remission? What, if anything, does the effect of these drugs imply about economic and structural theories of the psychotic illness? It is becoming increasingly clear that responses to psychopharmacological agents, even the most potent ones, are a function of the personality pattern or "character" of the patient as well as the clinical syndrome involved. This is true not simply of the placebo response that the subject tends to make ("transference"), but also of the interpretation of the chemically induced alteration of his subjective state. These drug-induced subjective states often seem to have unconscious conditioned symbolic meaning to the patient, so that the superficial personality inventory approach to the prediction of therapeutic outcome to a drug has only been partially successful. The clinical pharmacologist may want to ask the psychoanalyst: What are the effects of a particular type of psychopharmacological agent on the associative trends, the fantasy life, the transference themes, and the interpersonal processes as revealed in a psychoanalytic interaction? This and many similar questions will become more prevalent and relevant in psychiatry and psychoanalysis. In the following discussion, we will attempt to deal with some of the basic issues in this confrontation between "theoretical sets" and perhaps indicate some areas of productive (as well as unproductive) interaction.

As Rapaport (1959) among others has pointed out, the connoted meaning of psychoanalysis is presently so variegated that more specific divisions must be made not only in a discussion of intrafield relationships, but even more so in one involving inter-field issues, in an attempt to insure that those involved in the communication process have a chance to be talking about the same thing. It is with this general orientation that we will divide the present topic into (1) *Institutional* issues, including historical, professional, and identity conflicts; (2) possible impact on psychoanalytic *theory* of both the data and theoretical models of psychopharmacology; (3) issues, mostly practical, involving psychoanalytic *therapy* in combination with psychopharmacological agents; (4) potential contributions of the psychoanalytic *research method* to the more sophisticated elucidation of psychopharmacological behavioral models; and (5) some rough clinical guides for typical drug usage.

Institutional Issues

Without reviewing in detail the strongly resisted emergence of psychoanalysis into psychiatry and the bitter antagonism that the psychoanalysts have felt toward the "organic" therapists, it is probably important to remind ourselves of the factionalism that still envelops various treatment modalities in psychiatry. As in many areas of medicine where ignorance of pathophysiology and effective treatment of disease exists, historical movements, dominant personalities, and various boards of control are more apt to be prime determinants of treatment modalities than objective indicators of effectiveness. In the intense atmosphere of the psychoanalytic institutes in the 1930's and 1940's in this country, a dedication to a philosophy and method of treatment (and research) emerged that tended to view the beginnings of the organic therapies as an indication of impatience, sadism, need to control, and personality limitations of their practitioners. At the same time, the group of "organic" therapists who used insulin, EST, psychosurgery, and other such procedures looked at the psychoanalytic movement as a group of nonscientific cultists. Because many of the leading proponents of both of these antagonistic groups are still living and their dedicated but often equally limited students are still prime determiners in group policy, remnants of this antagonism still appear to be present. With the increasingly good statistical reports concerning the efficacy of the major psychotropic medications in severely ill psychiatric patients, however, and the implied possibility of at least a future time when quite subtle intellectual and personality variables will be manipulable by chemical means, the analyst will have to begin to broaden his concepts of brain and personality function. At the same time, with new and elegant sociological research techniques demonstrating various categories of illness as community defined and promoted, and chronicity of mental illness as often a resultant of traditional definitions and treatment of the psychoses, the "organic" therapists must leave their over-simplified brain models and begin to consider such things as the interpersonal field and adaptation. It would seem that an area around which there is sufficient "hard" data, adequate opportunity for study with various techniques, and a good potential for verification of core constructs by converging evidence from many disciplines, would be the field of clinical psychopharmacology. As will be noted in the following pages, beginnings are being made in this direction.

Some Theoretical Issues in Dynamic Psychopharmacology

The earliest attempts to incorporate the growing body of clinical psychopharmacological data under the rubric of classical analytic theory were a series of papers and books by Ostow (Ostow and Kline, 1959; Ostow, 1960a, 1960b, 1962). The data and data collection methods he presents will be discussed in the research section. However, his attempt at theory construction and synthesis bears study in that it is an almost predictable outcome of a systematic application of the early libido model. Although Azima's work emphasizing modification of aggressive libido (Azima, Cramer-Azima, and DeVerteuil, 1956, 1959; Azima, Cramer-Azima, and Durost, 1959; Azima, 1959) and Winkleman's structure revision (1960) theory are similar, the most complete and ingenious statement is presented in Ostow's book (1962). Combining the fact of extrapyramidal actions of psychotropic drugs, the observations of change in motility and mood in drug treated patients, some neurophysiological studies in animals and man, rather insufficient objective tests (blink rate, "ego libido scale"), and a firmly entrenched commitment to topographic and energetic concepts, Ostow derives such concepts as: "depletion syndrome," "plethora psychosis," "ego libido content," edema as an attempt of the body to raise "ego libido," akithesia (the drug-induced side reaction of restlessness) as an "emergency" force of the ego, and the globus pallidus as the source of instinctual energy. These concepts, hampered by the use of nineteenth-century physical analogies, are untestable even by modern methods. In the light of modern standards of behavioral research, this kind of characterization of data, already encoded in a conceptually unoperational morass of hypothetical constructs is not helpful for scientific work. The work of Ostow, however, was useful in stimulating the intensive, objective descriptions of drug-personality interactions by many other workers. This area will be discussed in the appropriate section. Concepts of energy shifts among metapsychological structures seem neither reflective of actual physiological events nor helpful in thinking about behavior. For example, if one talks about phenothiazine restlessness as a defensive effort made by the ego in reaction to the libido-depleting actions of the drug (and if there is a motor retardant effect, then it is assumed to be the unaltered depletion phenomenon without the defense), one begins to approach the "by definition" circularity that has made psychoanalytic theory relatively untestable for the past sixty years. In attempting to construct models for use in studying complex phenomena involving variables from many bodies of thought, it behooves us to resist tying things too tightly. The exclusion by definition which one can use as a maneuver when the operations of a system are self-validating and very limited is not helpful in a field when so many observational and manipulative techniques are available for use. Perhaps different motility responses to phenothiazines (to use our previous example) could be predicted from individual differences in drug metabolism, or different perception of the subjective states felt by the individual, or a reaction to the change he feels in himself in interpersonal transactions, or differentially prone extra-pyramidal structures, or the symbolic meaning of the induced drug state, or perhaps a complex intra-system interactional resultant of all of the above and more. It would seem that the early theoretical efforts in a developing field such as clinical psychopharmacology should be pointed toward the facilitation of multiple approaches and with an open system orientation. At the same time, we must not ignore the kind of data for which the psychoanalytic method is so useful. Changes in fantasy life, defensive activity in interpersonal transactions, views of self and the world as revealed by psychoanalytic observation, and many other valuable sources of data need to be used. The fear which Ostow discusses that enlarging the scope of theory and practice may run the risk of undermining the foundation of the analytic method is another example of the rationale that has facilitated the progressive deviation of psychoanalysis from science. Since a general systems theory is not presently possible in this area, perhaps the most appropriate attempts should take the form of multiple "micro-models" relating a limited number of variables.

There are numerous examples available of more testable micro-models in dynamically oriented clinical psychopharmacology. Dimascio and Klerman (1960) have described an interesting relationship between the parameters of counterphobic "masculine" strivings and perception of the phenothiazine-induced state by normal subjects given these drugs. They have shown that for some personality types, the phenothiazine-induced "passivity" is dystonic and probably related to unconscious feminine identifications which are threatening. Sarwer-Foner (Sarwer-Foner and Ogle, 1956; Sarwer-Foner, 1957) has observed the same relationship. Klein (1964) has made some beginnings in the dissection of two groups of severe anxiety syndromes using iminodibenzyl derivatives and has found one group manifesting much more severe separation anxiety than the other. Klein suggests that this group of compounds alters the symptom by insulating the patient from the pain of object loss. He feels that the move toward assertiveness in the depressed patients treated with these drugs (1965) is facilitated by the same decrease in separation anxiety allowing more outward expression (and less internalization) of rage. Another interesting model for drug action is presented by Sarwer-Foner (1964). From clinical examples and a review of the literature, he presents a theory of drug action focusing on alterations in adaptive patterns (ego functions), such as motility, communication, interpersonal transactions, reception of communication from others, and changes in perception of the internal state.

These representative dynamic approaches are amenable to the test of converging evidence from various disciplines (from rating scales to free associative material), depend little on outmoded topographic and energetic considerations, and easily generalize to the clinical situation for test and use. Although historically significant, the classical theorizing applied to drug-induced behavioral changes in man by Ostow, Azima, Winkleman, and others is gradually being replaced by lower inferential models capable of encompassing dynamic phenomenology without limiting the scope of potential observations. A more global theoretical effort will have to await more data.

The place of psychopharmacological agents in *technique* theory is difficult to define. The general goals of the analysis of transference and resistance are unimpeded unless the drug parameter is ignored. The process of working through habitual, maladaptive interpersonal and intrapsychic defenses through the transference continues. The area which bears looking into, relative to technique theory with implications as to "structural" revision of a permanent sort, seems to center around affect-thought synthesis necessary for genuine feeling in transference expressions, insight, and process intensity. One might argue that an artificial affect state has been created by the pharmacological agent which might impede the recovery of the emotional aspect of earlier experiences and that emotional reconditioning experiences of aspects of the transference resolution will be going on against a backdrop of an artificial feeling state which will not permit generalization into the future.

One can answer some of these objections in several ways. It is important to recall that these psychopharmacological agents have been invoked in the face of either an irresolvable affect-block, or because the feeling generated has been beyond the tolerance of the patient. It therefore appears that a more optimal affective tone is needed for the analytic work. Like recommendations concerning the dosage of dystonic confrontations or interpretations, an anxiety optimum probably also exists which should not be superseded.

The drugs may help to bring an otherwise refractory patient to this state. Another interesting possibility, however, is that an entirely new affective tone is experienced in the therapeutic relationship, expanding the feeling possibilities beyond their previous limits; for example, a more comfortable relationship to an authority figure. Though partially drug induced, they are experienced within the context of a significant relationship, perhaps helping to undo previous paralyzing or disruptive feeling states associated with such relationships. Thus, combined therapy may help create an even more powerful emotional reconditioning experience than the interpersonal relationship alone. The new, more appropriate and tolerable basic affect state during combined treatment may be introjected as part of the therapeutic experience.

The use of drugs, of course, can be suppressive, suggestive, dominating, "too active," and a number of other attributes undesirable for psychoanalytic therapy. But, if used judiciously, they need not be. As in all invoked parameters (abstinence, limit setting, setting the termination date, and others), the how and why for the analyst are as important, if not more important, than the what.

SOME PRACTICAL CONSIDERATIONS IN COMBINING PSYCHOANALYTIC AND PSYCHOPHARMACOLOGICAL THERAPY

If one holds strictly to the "basic model technique" (Eissler, 1950) and carefully selects patients for psychoanalytic treatment, one could eliminate many of the difficult-to-answer questions raised by combination therapy, in that seldom would drugs be indicated by any criteria. However, holding to this strict definition for selection and treatment in analysis (following a long tradition in some psychoanalytic circles of clinical problem-solution by a "by definition" patient or concept elimination), still may present possibilities for the use of some psychotropic agents at times. An example of this kind of circumstance would be the precipitation of a psychotic decompensation during the analysis of a patient who did not reveal this potential in the initial evaluation or early analytic phases. This may take the form of a paranoid reaction with or without predominantly homosexual content, a severe depressive reaction with suicidal tendencies, hypererotic dissociative episodes, and many others. This is a situation which too often in typical analytic practice has been referred to a "psychiatrist" for hospitalization while the judgment as to whether or not the patient should be treated analytically is deferred until further evaluation has taken place. This abandonment of patient responsibility is probably multiply determined by such factors as an over-investment by the analyst in classical technique, ignorance of psychopharmacological agents and their use, perhaps a basic discomfort in dealing with psychotic patients, and a desire not to disrupt the time schedule of a busy analytic practice.

Broader definition of psychoanalytic therapy (Alexander and French, 1946) and the accompanying increase in potential patients, however, bring with them some interesting applications of psychopharmacological agents which allow for the creative use of new "parameters" as well as permitting work with otherwise inaccessible patients. The following case is illustrative.

A twenty-year-old, anergic, apathetic daughter of a very highly successful and ignoring father and a dominating and ambivalent mother was referred for therapy following a gradual weight gain, progression in lethargy, school failure, and social withdrawal spanning most of her adolescent years. The loss of the competition for attention with a more beautiful, intelligent, and energetic younger sister was only one piece of evidence that she repetitively presented to the therapist of the hopelessness of her position and of the accuracy of her description of herself as "basically fat, lazy, and stupid." She quite quickly rebuilt her genetic situation in the transference and saw the therapist as being "disgusted" with her, preferring his other patients to her, and sharing her lack of faith in her ability to be any other way. The masochistically provocative aspect of this presentation of self was only a thin adaptive attempt to use this honestly felt self-image. Repeated efforts to interpret this pattern as self-destructive, rage resulting from current and past frustrations as well as the only way to get attention, only made her more apathetic. There was too little evidence around to use as optimistic reflections of reality for contrast with her self derogatory productions. This kind of situation is reminiscent of the case material which has led many authors on technique (Glover, 1955; Wolberg, 1954) to use such chronic reality defects of body image as obesity and deformity as counterindications for psychoanalytic therapy. Another foray into a more regressive level of working which surrounded her feelings of oral deprivation was equally unsuccessful and appeared to generate the precisely wished-for syntonic interpersonal field in which an endless impasse seemed in the offing. It was at this point that the therapist suggested the possibility of using a drug that tends to bring out underlying natural potential. This was the class of drugs known as the monoamine oxodase inhibitors which, unlike the iminodibenzyl antidepressants, activate a broad range of personality types, especially those characterized by over-eating and oversleeping. The presentation of the action of the drug as helpful in bringing out underlying potential was (at least in the therapist's mind) an honest behavioral representation of the drug action, since it allowed the patient's own brain amines to act as the pharmacological agent. It was acknowledged that many dynamic factors were at work in addition to the drug action and these were to be thoroughly explored (these issues will be discussed later). The result of this maneuver, however, was a gradual increase in activity level, motivation for study, assertiveness in interpersonal interaction, and a decrease in eating and sleeping. The most important dynamic aspect was the beginning of a change in self-concept and the appearance of evidences of strength against which the therapist could begin to contrast the increasingly artificial derogatory self-characterization. "I can really study until midnight"; "imagine me playing three sets of tennis"; "It was I who organized the party this weekend." The surprise and delight with her actions were used as past evidences of ego strength might have been used with more ideal candidates; useful to the patient and therapist in promoting a more optimistic attack on the pathological characterological impediments to healthy functioning. This class of drugs can be given for several months without habituation or increasing the dosage, do not have rebound depressive effects (as do the amphetamines), and therefore were continued for a year. By this time, the patient had created a positive feedback situation in her social and scholastic life, had "taken over" the therapeutic work in an active way, and on gradual tapering of the drug, had continued to maintain her improvement. From her newly won position of strength, she was able to see her past passive-negativistic retreat, masochistic play for care, previous self-destructive, infantile, adaptive techniques. The therapeutic work will continue for considerably more time, but it is apparent that the current increment in coping strength with accompanying increase in self-esteem reduced the annihilate effects of the narcissistic injuries that come early in the process of gaining insight, allowing the therapy to move forward in a productive fashion.

Another indication for the use of a drug-treatment parameter within a psychoanalytic context would be the "borderline" patient who ordinarily might be considered a risk for uncovering work; and yet who, for reasons of sensitivity, psychological mindedness, many areas of functioning strength, and motivation for treatment may constitute in some ways an ideal candidate. In this situation, the low dosage, high potency fluorinated phenothiazines (which have adequate antipsychotic effects without decreasing functioning) can aid in at least two ways. Even without their use, the therapist can risk temporarily intense transference crises, exploration of dystonic fantasy material, and other such risky business with fragile patients with the security of the powerful antipsychotic effects of this drug family behind him. The therapist need not feel that hospitalization and the accompanying disruption of the patient's ongoing life stream are threatening. The existence of this drug family, therefore, can function as a security mechanism for the analyst even without its use; the increase in therapist comfort may be sufficient to weather the crisis. Occasionally these antipsychotic, function-maintaining drugs can be used as a stabilizing force for several months or years while the "borderline" patient works through difficult intrapsychic and transference material. The following case exemplifies this point.

The patient was referred after three previous attempts at psychoanalytic therapy during which she suffered three psychotic breaks requiring hospitalization. In each of the three previous interactions, there was a severe regression into a hypererotic, paranoid-like state involving the analyst as the object which totally occupied the patient's fantasy life. Her house and children were neglected as she constructed bizarre symbolic constructs connecting her analyst to herself. In each case, it appeared that this was partially defensive and generated from the opening up of material concerned with her passive oral wishes directed toward female figures and her rageful masculine protest. The patient presented many strengths: intelligence, psychological mindedness, a history of very adequate functioning in educational and work areas, evident warmth and capacity to make a relationship, and motivation for therapy. Her obvious competitiveness with male figures, overconcern for her sexual fantasies and obsessive-compulsive personality features seemed amenable to psychoanalytic therapy. Following her third decompensation, she was maintained on a low dosage of a fluorinated phenothiazine. Under the stabilizing influence of this medication, she was able to work through much of the material that had been so disruptive in the past. The hostile and erotic features of her transference, more tempered and under control, were evidenced in the therapeutic situation and were able to be gradually resolved without impairing her functioning.

From the standpoint of the classically oriented psychoanalyst, many objections either to the use of centrally active drugs in psychoanalysis, or perhaps more characteristically, to calling the above kind of therapeutic work psychoanalytic therapy, can be raised. One of these concerns the passive role the patient can be seen as playing in the pharmacological manipulation of his brain. This kind of theme might color the transference so that the patient may not learn that he himself is really actively bringing about what he believed he was undergoing passively (Fenichel, 1941). The hope for shift of the center of responsibility for autonomous functioning to the patient may be impaired, according to this view, by the interpretation of the drug as a depreciating symbolic gratification of his dependency wishes. Other anticipated and real problems include the possibility of increasing the resistance to direct transference work by making the drug the major focus. Side reactions may begin to take the place of verbalized negative transference; symptom rather than thought and feeling-oriented talk may begin to dominate the content; distorted overidealization may be stimulated by a "wonder cure" effect from the pharmaceutical agent; mistrust may be aroused by fear of the meaning of minor side effects. The sophisticated psychoanalytic patient is apt to be aware that this procedure is irregular; it may imply to the patient that the outlook is pessimistic. A great deal of material around medicine and doctors from childhood may be stirred up without being verbalized.

These and many other issues arising from the invocation of drug treatment parameters must be explored and their transference and historical meanings established and worked through, just as with any piece of therapist activity (a missed session, a change in schedule, or the suggestion that a phobic patient confront the feared object). The additional problem that is present in this area, however, concerns the many potential therapist feelings and the question of how free he feels in working around this particular group of variables. In the tradition-bound literature and supervision of psychoanalytic training there is little in the way of models for using drug parameters. It is interesting that in psychoanalytic case presentations in which drugs have been invoked little or nothing is discussed about them. Its status as a nonsanctioned maneuver in psychoanalysis may be partially responsible for therapists' resistances to the exploration of the area, and as such may be contributing to the whole issue "falling under the table," out of the sight of both patient and doctor by mutual, nonverbal consent. If this happens, of course, drug treatment can become a real impediment to the psychoanalytic process.

The Psychoanalytic Method as a Psychopharmacological Research Tool

The many animal behavior models for screening and research with psychotropic agents are of interest in considering potential application of the psychoanalytic method for research in this area. The effects of tranquilizers on activity level (Larsen, 1955), avoidance conditioning (Jacobsen and Sonne, 1955), instrumental conditioning (Ferster and Skinner, 1957), and taming (Henschele, 1961) may have implications for possible alterations in the ongoing associative material. More complex models have even more subtle implications. It has been shown that if a group of mice are kept in a cage for forty-eight hours they will attack a newly introduced member; this attack can be modified by some tranquilizing medication (Janssen, Jagenean, and Niemegeers, 1960). Two rats, placed together in a cage and shocked, will attack each other; this behavior can be modified by psychotropic agents. Antidepressants will increase electrical self-stimulation (Stein, 1962), augment conditioned avoidance-responses (Heise and Boft, 1960), and some conditioned approach-responses (Carlton and Didano, 1961). It is in the area of psychoanalytic observation of drug effects that Ostow, Winkleman, Azima, and others have made a most exciting beginning. If one uses the analytic material independently from his theoretical arguments, Ostow's cases are of great interest. Changes in masturbatory and heterosexual activity, alterations in the transference state, progressive and regressive fantasy and interpersonal moves, documented in some detail and related to changes in drugs and drug dosages seem indicative of a very promising frontier. In Ostow's accounts of the drug and psychoanalytic treatment of a neurotic and a paranoid patient, one is struck by shifting object-relationships manifested both in the transference and the associative material that seem to be tied to changes in kind and amount of medication. If we recognize that this is most difficult to attribute to the drug alone and that transference and reality aspects were continuously operative, his material presents a very strong case for the addition of this method to the study of drug effects on humans. In three "endogenous depression" cases I have seen in intensive, analytically oriented psychotherapy combined with psychotropic agents, the first imipramine effect observed was within the therapeutic transaction. Within a week with two of the cases and within two weeks with the other, there was a subtle shift toward an exteriorization of anger. Previous self-derogatory passive-aggressive techniques began to give way to more openly expressed doubts about my capacity, tolerance, and investment. The series of Parkinson patients I have treated with this medication (Mandell, 1962) also manifested this shift (in a more medical-style interpersonal interaction) often associated with an increase in the MMPI Pd scale (associated with more outwardly direct antagonism). This is the kind of change reported by Klein in his patients with anxiety (1965). Objective studies of drug effects on psychophysiological variables (Greiner and Burch, 1955), motility (Ulett, Hensler, and Callahan, 1961), self-rating (Tobin, 1962), personality inventories (Klerman, 1962), and minimal care ratings (Goldberg, Klerman, and Cole, 1965) can be greatly supplemented by the in-depth observations that the psychoanalytic or derived techniques can afford. The fascinating subtleties that might come to light may not only add to our knowledge of drugs but of psychopathology as well. Rubin (1965) reports a patient he followed who he felt was latently paranoid. This patient remitted quickly but on sustained management, could be "titrated" in and out of preoccupation with homosexual fantasies with changes of two milligrams of a fluorinated phenothiazine (from 4 to 6 mg. per day!). A schizophrenic patient of mine maintained in symptomatic remission with very high dosages of phenothiazines, repeatedly demonstrated a shift to a more optimistic outlook and more benign interpersonal expectation on the fluorinated versus the aliphatic phenothiazines six times over four and a half years of therapy. This kind of observation complements the behavioral observations made by others suggesting that rehabilitation requiring increased motility is facilitated by the fluorinated group.

Behavioral models for drug action would benefit a great deal from the psychoanalyst's help with the characterization of drug action. It is quite clear that a single descriptive continuum is not isomorphic with the actions of these drug families in man. The iminodibenzyl derivatives called "antidepressants" put some people to sleep, make others depressed, produce acute psychotic states in others, and produce remissions of depression in still others. If there really is an action or group of actions of the drug that could be characterized by some dynamic formulation such as "insulation from the pain of object loss" (Klein, 1965), would we not then be able to prescribe these drugs with more sophistication, making use of our psychodynamic understanding of the patient and his problem? Dimascio and Rinkel's work (1962) has suggested that patients who are the mesomorphic, hypermasculine type feel impaired by the aliphatic phenothiazines. Might this not be a contraindication in the patient whose paranoid illness comes from frightening feelings of inadequacy and fear of his passive homosexual wishes? This kind of data is not currently available except in studies which are (by psychoanalytic standards) rather superficial.

Although a number of workers have promised us systematic reports of psychoanalytic data from drug treated patients, there have been very few forthcoming. It is hoped that this additional descriptive parameter will be included in psychoanalytic case reports in the future. Research workers who are so inclined are currently in an identity bind. The rigorous psychopharmacological researcher is loath to accept psychoanalytic data as "legitimate." The classical purists that control the psychoanalytic journals are unwilling to accept such material as legitimately psychoanalytic. This leaves almost no aegis for this kind of approach. It is perhaps for their courage in beginning to break these sociological bonds that Ostow and workers like him deserve to be most admired. It is hoped that others will follow.

Some Rough Clinical Guides to Drug Choice

There are a number of approaches to drug choice with patients. For example, Cole (NIMH–PSC Collaborative Study Group, 1964) has recently shown that most phenothiazine families are equally effective (having adjusted for differing potency) in producing remissions in psychoses; here efficacy is determined by such criteria as discharge rate, psychotic symptoms, and minimal care items. However, there are differences in effects on mood, motility, initiative, and other more subtle variables in the actions of these drugs which are yet to be systematically and objectively worked out. More elegant drug choice would take these more subtle variables into consideration. The following will be a rough clinical attempt to do this.

PSYCHOPHARMACOLOGICAL TREATMENT OF DEPRESSION

The most identifiable and predictably responsive syndrome is the classical depressive syndrome. Seen under the diagnostic aegis of "involutional," "psychotic," "neurotic," "manic-depressive," and even "reactive," as a drug treatment entity, it is characterized by anorexia, weight loss, sleep loss (early morning rising), constipation, decreased salivation, motility disturbance (either agitated or retarded), and self-derogatory content (with or without "psychotic" material). This kind of patient, previously an excellent candidate for EST, now responds well to the iminodibenzyl derivatives. These include imipramine, amitriptyline, and their desmethyl derivatives. In the past, the analytic treatment of the middle-aged depressed patient (with an unrecognized early involutional depression) had occasionally to be interrupted for EST as a result of an impasse. This drug family allows the maintenance of continuity in the therapy, without the intense transference and countertransference difficulties attendant on hospitalization and EST.

The following description of another depressive syndrome is perhaps not ideal in that patients with this syndrome were candidates for conventional psychoanalytic approaches. This syndrome, responsive to drugs, is characterized by lethargy, overeating, lack of initiative, inadequate functioning, and a predominantly passive-dependent adaptation. These patients are often made more anergic by the iminodibenzyl group (as are normal subjects!), but respond with increased energy, functioning, and independence with the monoamine oxidase inhibitors. This drug family includes the aromatic hydrazines and the aromatic amines (tranylcypromine and pargyline).

A third depressive syndrome which is worthy of mention is the depressed "borderline" or schizoid patient with minimal adaptive capacities. There are often mixed manifestations of autistic withdrawal, peculiarities of thought, and flattened affectual tone. These patients may be activated into an acute, psychotic disorganization by either the iminodibenzyl or MAO inhibitor families. Though antidepressants are not definitely counterindicated in this group, their use constitutes a risk and probably should be accompanied by the least depressing of the phenothiazines.

PSYCHOPHARMACOLOGICAL TREATMENT OF SEVERE PSYCHOLOGICAL DISTURBANCE (PSYCHOSIS?)

Combining consideration of the treatment as prevention of psychosis with drug effects on adaptive function, there appear to be two kinds of phenothiazine treatment concepts that should be mentioned: (1) antipsychotic effect with control and (2) antipsychotic effects with little effect on functioning. The first instance applies to patients whose psychotic process or general impulsivity (independent from the psychotic process) makes them a risk to themselves or others. The high dosage, low potency aliphatically substituted phenothiazines (such as chlorpromazine or promazine or those with a piperidine substitution reduce motility, initiative, instinctual activity, impulsivity, and mood. The timely beginning of this drug family often heads off hospitalization for control or may allow previously quite violent patients to be handled in an open ward or general hospital.

The other phenothiazine concept concerns the use of the fluorinated group (triflupromazine, trifluoperazine, or fluphenazine) for quite effective control of a psychotic process with minimal decrease in motility, initiative, or mood. It is from this drug family that the analyst who is struggling with a decompensating patient can expect the most help. It is important to emphasize careful evaluation of the disturbance in that "transference psychoses" have been resolved with benefit without drugs for many decades. On the other hand, patients have had long lasting hospitalizations with schizophrenic reactions precipitated in analysis. With careful clinical discrimination between these two states, the risk of the overuse of these medications by anxious therapists will be minimized.

PREMATURE TERMINATION OF DRUG TREATMENT

A recent study (Forrest, Geiter, Snow, and Steinbach, 1964) has demonstrated that premature discontinuation of drug treatment is one of the commonest causes of relapse in the severe psychiatric disturbances. The psychotherapist, invested in his treatment method, may suffer a narcissistic injury in observing the efficacy of drug therapy. Anxious to stop the drug and return to the previous uncontaminated analytic field, he helps the patient decide to stop his medication. Numerous cases have been rehospitalized (2 to 3 months after stopping medication—about the time the last urinary metabolites are leaving) at our Neuropsychiatric Institute under just these circumstances. How long patients should remain on medication has not been established statistically; however, the consensus among men who have had the most experience is that phenothiazine therapy, once begun, should be continued for many months or years.

In conclusion, it is hoped that psychoanalytic researchers and therapists will develop and maintain greater interest in the new findings of psychopharmacology. The subtleties of human thinking and feeling make a most sensitive dependent variable system that analysts are best equipped to study. If this happens, it is possible that the analytic method will once more operate at a frontier of behavioral science.

References

Alexander, F., and French, T. M. *Psychoanalytic Therapy: Principles and Application*. New York: Ronald Press, 1946.

Azima, H. "Psychodynamic Alterations Concomitant with Tofranil Administration." *Journal of the Canadian Psychiatric Association*, 4 (1959), 172-176.

Azima, H., Cramer-Azima, F., and DeVerteuil, R. "A Comparative Behavioral and Psychodynamic Study of the Effect of Reserpine and Raudixin in Schizophrenia." *Monograph on Therapy* (New Brunswick, Canada), 2 (1956), 10–13.

Azima, H., Cramer-Azima, F., and DeVerteuil, R. "Effects of Rauwolfia Derivatives on Psychodynamic Structure." *Psychiatric Quarterly*, 33 (1959), 623–635.

Azima, H., Cramer-Azima, F., and Durost, H. B. "Psychoanalytic Formulations of Effects of Reserpine on Schizophrenic Organization." *American Medical Association Archives of General Psychiatry*, 1 (1959), 622–670.

Carlton, P. L., and Didano, P. "Augmentation of the Behavioral Effects of Amphetamine by Atropine." *Journal of Pharmacology and Experimental Therapy*, 132 (1961), 91–96.

Dimascio, A., and Klerman, G. "Experimental Human Psychopharmacology: The Role of Non-Drug Factors." In G. Sarwer-Foner (ed.), *The Dynamics of Psychiatric Drug Therapy*. Springfield, Ill.: Charles C Thomas, 1960. Pp. 56–90.

Dimascio, A., and Rinkel, M. "Personality and Drugs, 'Specific' or 'Nonspecific' Influence on Drug Actions." In M. Rinkel (ed.), *Specific and Non-Specific Factors in Psychopharmacology*. New York: Philosophical Library, 1962. Pp. 46–52.

Eissler, K. R. "The Chicago Institute of Psychoanalysis and the Sixth Period of the Development of Psychoanalytic Technique." *Journal of General Psychology*, 42 (1950), 103–157.

Fenichel, O. *Problems of Psychoanalytic Technique*. Albany, N.Y.: Psychoanalytic Quarterly, Inc., 1939.

Ferster, C. B., and Skinner, B. F. *Schedules of Reinforcement*. New York: Appleton-Century-Crofts, 1957.

Forrest, F. M., Geiter, C. W., Snow, H. L., and Steinbach, M. "Drug Maintenance Problems of Rehabilitated Mental Patients: The Current Drug Dosage 'Merry-Go-Round.'" *American Journal of Psychiatry*, 121 (1964), 33–40.

Glover, E. *The Technique of Psychoanalysis*. New York: International Universities Press, 1955.

Goldberg, S. C., Klerman, G. L., and Cole, J. O. "Changes in Schizophrenic Psychopathology and Ward Behavior as a Function of Phenothiazine Treatment." *British Journal of Psychiatry*, 111 (1965), 120–133.

Greiner, T. H., and Burch, N. R. "Response of the Human GSR to Drugs That Influence Reticular Formation of the Brain Stem." *Federation Proceedings*, 14 (1955), 346.

Heise, G. A., and Boft, E. "Behavioral Determination of Time and Dose Parameters of Monoamine Oxidase Inhibitors." *Journal of Pharmacology*, 129 (1960), 155–162.

Henschele, W. P. "Chlordiazepoxide for Calming Zoo Animals." *Journal of the American Veterinary Association*, 139 (1961), 996–998.

Jacobsen, E., and Sonne, E. "The Effect of Benactyzine on Stress Induced Behavior in the Rat." *Acta Pharmacologica et Toxicologica*, 11 (1955), 135–147.

Janssen, P. A. J., Jagenean, A. H., and Niemegeers, C. J. E. "Effects of Various Drugs on Isolation-Induced Fighting Behavior of Male Mice." *Journal of Pharmacology*, 129 (1960), 471–480.

Klein, D. F. "Delineation of Two Drug-Responsive Anxiety Syndromes." *Psychopharmacologia*, 5 (1964), 397–408.

Klein, D. F. Personal communication, 1965.

Klerman, G. "Rating Scales in the Measurement of Psychopathologic Pharmacologic Response." In J. Nodine and J. Moyer (eds.), *Psychosomatic Medicine*. Philadelphia: Lea & Febiger, 1962. Pp. 368–372.

Larsen, V. "The General Pharmacology of Benzilic Acid Diethyl-Aminoethylester Hydrochloride." *Acta Pharmacologica et Toxicologica*, 11 (1955), 405–420.

Mandell, A. J. "Motivation and Ability to Move." *American Journal of Psychiatry*, 119 (1962), 544–551.

NIMH–PSC Collaborative Study Group. "Phenothiazine Treatment in Acute Schizophrenia." *American Medical Association Archives of General Psychiatry*, 10 (1964), 246–261.

Ostow, M. "The Effects of the Newer Neuroleptic and Stimulating Drugs on Psychic Function." In G. Sarwer-Foner (ed.), *The Dynamics of Psychiatric Drug Therapy*, Springfield, Ill.: Charles C Thomas, 1960. Pp. 172–192. (a)

Ostow, M. "The Use of Drugs to Overcome Technical Difficulties in Psychoanalysis." In G. Sarwer-Foner (ed.), *The Dynamics of Psychiatric Drug Therapy*, Springfield, Ill.: Charles C Thomas, 1960. Pp. 443–463. (b)

Ostow, M. *Drugs in Psychoanalysis and Psychotherapy*. New York: Basic Books, 1962.

Ostow, M., and Kline, N. S. "The Psychic Action of Reserpine and Chlorpromazine." In N. S. Kline (ed.), *Psychopharmacology Frontiers*. Boston: Little, Brown, 1959. Pp. 45–58.

Rapaport, D. "The Structure of Psychoanalytic Theory" (1959). *Psychological Issues*, 2 (1960), 7–158.

Rubin, R. Personal communication, 1965.

Sarwer-Foner, G. "Psychoanalytic Theories of Activity-Passivity Conflicts and of the Continuum of Ego Defenses." *American Medical Association Archives of Neurology and Psychiatry*, 78 (1957), 413–421.

Sarwer-Foner, G. "On the Mechanisms of Action of Neuroleptic Drugs: A Theoretical Psychodynamic Explanation." In J. Wortis (ed.), *Advances in Biological Psychiatry*. Vol. 6. New York: Plenum, 1964. Pp. 217–232.

Sarwer-Foner, G., and Ogle, W. "Psychodynamic Aspects of Reserpine: Its Uses and Effects in Open Psychiatric Settings." *Canadian Psychiatric Journal*, 1 (1956), 1–8.

Stein, L. "New Methods for Evaluating Stimulants and Antidepressants." In J. Nodine and J. Moyer (eds.), *Psychosomatic Medicine*. Philadelphia: Lea & Febiger, 1962. Pp. 297–311.

Tobin, J. M. "Rating Scales in the Measurement of Behavioral Psychopharmacologic Response." In J. Nodine and J. Moyer (eds.), *Psychosomatic Medicine*. Philadelphia: Lea & Febiger, 1962. Pp. 363–367.

Ulett, G. A., Hensler, A., and Callahan, J. D. "Objective Measures in Psychopharmacology." *Journal of Neuro-Psychopharmacology*, 2 (1961), 401–408.

Winkleman, N. W., Jr. *The Use of Chlorpromazine and Prochlorperazine as Adjuncts to Psychoanalytic Psychotherapy*. Springfield, Ill.: Charles C Thomas, 1960.

Wolberg, L. *The Technique of Psychotherapy*. New York: Grune & Stratton, 1954.

III
CLINICAL

12

Psychoanalytic Therapy of the Individual

HANS H. STRUPP

The observer of the psychoanalytic[1] scene who sets himself the task of discerning new developments in technique suffers disadvantages comparable to those of the interpreter of contemporary or near-contemporary history: he is too close to the events and too much under their sway to view them in proper perspective. Personal biases and idiosyncrasies are bound to influence his evaluations and judgments, which inevitably will bear the stamp of his time. Seemingly significant advances may in the larger perspective of the history of science prove to be blind alleys; conversely, future advances may come from today's unnoticed or neglected developments. We still live under the shadow of Freud's revolutionary discoveries, in relation to which contemporary developments seem rather modest. This is not

[1] The terms *analyst* and *therapist* and their corollaries *psychoanalysis* and *psychotherapy* will be used more or less interchangeably, except where alleged differences are discussed. In general, the generic terms therapist and psychotherapy seem preferable because they are more neutral and less "loaded." Whatever the specific differences between psychoanalysis and psychotherapy may turn out to be, it seems reasonable to consider psychoanalysis a specialized form of psychotherapy.

to denigrate their actual or potential importance, but merely to accentuate the great theoretical and technical innovations which flowed from such concepts as the dynamic unconscious, transference, resistance, and narcissism. The empirical cornerstones on which the psychoanalytic edifice firmly rests have neither been shaken nor replaced since Freud's time. History may show that Freud's most basic, trenchant, and lasting contributions consist of (1) the basic conception of the neurotic conflict and symptom formation; and (2) the contrivance of the psychoanalytic situation as a laboratory for the microscopic study and therapeutic modification of interpersonal and intrapsychic processes, subsuming most prominently the discovery, understanding, and "handling" of transference phenomena. But such judgments rightfully belong to future generations.

This chapter focuses on *technical* developments in the two-person treatment relationship in psychoanalytic psychotherapy. It attempts to discern changes in technique that have occurred over the last few decades, to cite examples of relevant empirical research, and to point up significant problems for future research. Theoretical contributions will be mentioned insofar as they seem to have found their way into therapeutic practice. The events leading to World War II and its aftermath had a stifling effect on the development of psychotherapy on the European continent, and the prevailing ideology in the Iron Curtain countries since the war has perpetuated this trend. By contrast, the English-speaking countries, notably America and to a lesser extent England, have played a leading role in this field. Therefore, the American scene will occupy the foreground of this presentation, and little will be said about developments elsewhere.

Lack of Primary Data

In order to speak authoritatively of developments in the practice of psychoanalysis and psychotherapy one should be able to base his observations on *empirical* data. Furthermore, to discuss changes that have taken place over the years, it would be important to make comparisons between therapeutic techniques "then" and "now." Information permitting such comparisons unfortunately is not available. Freud's works on technique, as is well known, were not plentiful, and when he wrote on the subject he tended to speak in general terms. Besides, there is reason to believe that Freud's descriptions of technique are not an accurate guide to the manner in which psychoanalysis was practiced by him or anyone else. The descriptions tended to be "recommendations" rather than statements of what was actually done. It was assumed that any analyst, so long as he was properly trained, would follow "standard" technique in essential respects and that individual differences among therapists were negligible. In other words, therapists were regarded as interchangeable units, at least as far as their adherence to the basic tenets of psychoanalytic treatment was concerned. To be sure, Freud occasionally mentioned individual differences, but assigned them no great significance except in the context of countertransference reactions. He took it for granted that analyzed therapists were mature, reliable, and responsible individuals who in certain situations could act as mentors or serve as models to their patients (Freud, 1937). However, by and large, the personality of the therapist was seen as relatively inconsequential for the proper conduct of psychoanalytic therapy.

The view of therapists as "interchangeable units" was first challenged [2] by Glover (1940), who submitted a lengthy questionnaire to the membership of the British Psychoanalytic Association, eliciting information in their therapeutic techniques and practices. The form was sent to 29 practicing analysts, and the survey yielded responses from 24. While impressive, the results should have occasioned no surprise. Briefly, Glover found that British analysts, despite the marked homogeneity of their training, agreed on very few points, and indeed revealed marked divergence on many aspects of technique and practice. Glover had worded his questions in rather general terms and the responses reflected what the British analysts at the time *said* they did—not what they actually did. The *practical* significance of Glover's results is difficult to assess, because apparent discrepancies may have been of little practical import, but the opposite is more likely. In any event, the conclusion was justified that there are *true* differences in the techniques of therapists of comparable training and experience. There is no reason to assume that the situation is different today. The limited number of empirical studies bearing on this topic (e.g., Fey, 1958; Strupp, 1955, 1960b) suggest that inexperienced therapists as a group are more "alike" in their techniques than experienced ones following the same theoretical orientation, but that there are palpable technique differences between therapists following divergent theoretical orientations. One series of studies (Fiedler, 1950a, 1950b, 1951) is often cited in support of the view that experienced therapists, irrespective of their theoretical orientation, establish therapeutic relationships whose "atmosphere" shows greater resemblance to each other than is true of novices. However, these findings have at best limited validity. By rigorous criteria, it must be asserted that the question is as yet unanswered.

Primary data on psychotherapeutic techniques, such as transcripts or sound recordings, have been conspicuously scarce. Prior to 1940 such materials were virtually unavailable, and since that time the situation has not

[2] Anna Freud reported that "years ago, in Vienna," analysts discovered that they differed widely in their techniques. She states (1954, p. 609): "So far as I know, no one has succeeded yet in investigating and finding the causes of these particular variations. They are determined, of course, not by the material, but by the trends of interest, intentions, shades of evaluation which are peculiar to every individual analyst. I do not suggest that they should be looked for among the phenomena of countertransference."

changed substantially, some notable exceptions notwithstanding. Examples of the latter are the sound films and sound recordings of psychoanalytic treatment produced by the late Franz Alexander and his co-workers at Mt. Sinai Hospital in Los Angeles (Levy, 1961) and by the late Paul Bergman at the National Institute of Mental Health in Bethesda. Comparable records of individual hours or segments of therapy have been somewhat more plentiful, but highly experienced therapists have, for the most part, been rather reticent to submit their therapeutic operations to public scrutiny. While the privacy of psychotherapy lends justification to the desire to maintain confidentiality, the fact remains that we are largely uninformed concerning the actual practices of the "average" psychotherapist. From case reports and theoretical discussions in the literature we know to some extent what therapists *say* they do, but there is reason to believe in the existence of discrepancies between writings on technique and actual practices. For these reasons, too, it is difficult to form a clear picture of changes that may have occurred over the years. (Judd Marmor, 1967, testifies from his personal experience over a quarter of a century that many changes have indeed occurred. Most of the changes mentioned by him will be discussed in this chapter.)

The alternative is to have recourse to the writings of those individuals who seem to have exerted the greatest influence on the field. This, largely, will be the procedure followed in this chapter. However, irrespective of the impact these contributions have had, it must be kept in mind that they are the products of the most articulate spokesmen who do not necessarily reflect the thinking and the techniques of the rank and file of psychotherapists practicing today. Besides, therapists, while evolving their individual styles as their experience increases, undoubtedly are heavily influenced by their teachers, notably their training therapists, who belong to an earlier generation. For these reasons as well as the general conservatism of the field, it is probably fair to say that actual practices lag behind published writings.

Freud's Contributions to the Problems of Technique

As already noted, Freud published little on the topic of technique, and while on several occasions he toyed with the idea of writing an *Allgemeine Technik der Psychoanalyse* (a general account of psychoanalytic technique), this plan was never realized. In his introduction to Freud's works on technique, Strachey (1958) reviews Freud's contributions, noting "some feeling of reluctance on his part" to write systematically on the subject. It is of historical interest to cite Strachey's speculations concerning the basis of Freud's reluctance. Reportedly, he disliked the idea of future patients knowing "too much" about the details of his technique, suspecting that they would scan his writings for "clues." Moreover, he was highly skeptical of the value neophyte therapists would derive from an exposition of technique. He considered that the psychological factors (including the personality of the analyst) are "too complex and variable" to lend themselves to hard and fast rules. Most important, perhaps, he remained convinced that once the "mechanism" of psychoanalytic therapy was properly grasped and understood by the student, everything else would fall into place. Underlying his discussions of technique there was the firm belief that mastery of psychotherapy could only be acquired from clinical experience, and, more fundamentally, from the therapist's personal analysis. This notion was advanced tentatively at first, but gained strong affirmation as time went on. In one of his last writings Freud (1937) urged every analyst to re-enter analysis, perhaps every five years. This recommendation, it should be noted, has been honored subsequently mainly in the breach.

In the same work Freud expressed his belief that the ways in which psychoanalytic technique achieves its aims have been sufficiently elucidated and that therefore it would be more appropriate to inquire into obstacles which therapy encounters. This statement seems overoptimistic, considering the many problems that continue to engage therapists in their published articles. Both Hartmann (1951) and Rapaport (1959) observed that expositions of technique have lagged behind theoretical developments, and Rapaport noted that a comprehensive theory of psychoanalytic *technique* still remains to be written.

Freud's works specifically dealing with technique constitute a series of six brief contributions published in rather rapid succession between 1911 and 1915 (Freud, 1911, 1912a, 1912b, 1913, 1914b, 1915). While they deal with important special topics, they can hardly be regarded as a systematic exposition. In addition, relevant comments are interspersed in the case histories and Introductory Lectures.[3] Significantly, Freud gave his fullest account of technique in *Studies on Hysteria* (Breuer and Freud, 1895), but this technique (which Strachey calls the "pressure technique") was of course soon to be superseded by what has since become the prototype of "orthodox" psychoanalysis.

Psychoanalytic Therapy: Definition and Problems

One of Freud's (1914a) operational definitions of psychoanalytic therapy which is noteworthy for its simplicity and parsimony runs as follows:

> The theory of *repression* is the corner-stone on which the whole structure of psycho-analysis rests. It is the most essential part of it; and yet it is nothing but a theoretical formulation of a phenomenon which may be observed as

[3] See Appendix, pp. 172–173, *The Standard Edition of the Complete Psychological Works of Sigmund Freud*, Vol. 12, for a complete list of Freud's writings dealing mainly with technique.

often as one pleases [Note the emphasis on empirical data!] if one undertakes an analysis of a neurotic without resorting to hypnosis. In such cases one comes across a *resistance* which opposes the work of analysis and in order to frustrate it pleads a failure of memory. The use of hypnosis was bound to hide this resistance; the history of psycho-analysis proper, therefore, only begins with the new technique that dispenses with hypnosis. The theoretical consideration of the fact that this resistance coincides with an amnesia leads inevitably to the view of *unconscious mental activity* which is peculiar to psycho-analysis and which, too, distinguishes it quite clearly from philosophical speculations about the unconscious. It may thus be said that the theory of psycho-analysis [here Freud clearly speaks of the theory of psychoanalytic *therapy*] is an attempt to account for two striking and unexpected facts of observation which emerge whenever an attempt is made to trace the symptoms of a neurotic back to their sources in his past life: *the facts of transference and resistance.* Any line of investigation [that is, therapy] which recognizes these two facts and takes them as the starting-point of its work has a right to call itself psycho-analysis, even though it arrives at results other than my own. But anyone who takes up other sides of the problem while avoiding these two hypotheses will hardly escape a charge if misappropriation of property by attempted impersonation, if he persists in calling himself a psycho-analyst (p. 16; italics mine—H.H.S.).

In this definition the essential ingredients of psychoanalytic therapy are explicitly stated as (1) transference and (2) resistance, which in turn are viewed as the result of (3) repression. The theory of repression, which has remained the prototype of all defense mechanisms, is rooted in the postulate of (4) the dynamic unconscious. The only ingredient not explicitly mentioned but clearly implied is (5) the analytic situation which is prerequisite for the emergence of the foregoing phenomena.

One of the important ingredients in this definition is the absence of any attempt to differentiate "psychoanalysis" from "psychoanalytically oriented psychotherapy" (or similar terms)—distinctions which have been attempted by later writers. It seems clear that Freud espoused a broad and relatively unrestricted view of the psychoanalytic process, of which the development and resolution of the transference neurosis is *not necessarily* the touchstone. In this passage Freud undoubtedly had in mind the early dissidents whom he accused of "misappropriating" and distorting his ideas, but one cannot escape the impression that subsequent writers, in attempting to make finer distinctions, have grappled with pseudo-problems, or at least problems that were tangential to psychoanalytic therapy as Freud viewed it.

Freud's disinclination to spell out the technique of psychoanalysis was evidently based on similar considerations. In his well-known chess simile (Freud, 1913) he explicitly stated that only the opening and closing moves are susceptible to specification whereas the grand strategy of "working through" with all its intricacies must be tailored to the problems and personalities of individual patients. Yet the basic tenets guiding this strategy are contained in the above paradigm. The complexity of therapy in the individual patient does not lie in departures from the basic principles; rather, the latter run like a red thread through every utterance and intervention of the therapist. Therefore, Freud believed that the mastery of technique flows directly from, and is firmly rooted in, the therapist's understanding of the theoretical premises of psychoanalysis.

A further corollary of this position is the relative de-emphasis on individual difference among therapists. From this point of view, it is inconsequential whether a therapist advances ten interpretations that are aimed at the same transference manifestation during a single hour whereas another therapist, more sparing in his verbal interventions, attempts to achieve the same objective by making only two. Nor does the number of questions or the sheer number of words used by the therapist make a difference in and of itself so long as the immediate and long-range objectives of the therapeutic enterprise are clearly kept in mind. The immediate objective is always an answer to the question: Where is the *current resistance?* How does it manifest itself? How does it interfere with the progress of therapy? The long-range objective is to be sought in the clarification and resolution of the transference.

The foregoing are well-known restatements of psychoanalytic axioms; yet they have often been misunderstood by researchers in the area who, since approximately 1940, have focused on increasingly smaller units of the therapeutic transaction, attempting to dissect it in the belief that if an interpretation is effective, its effect must be traceable to a single interaction between patient and therapist. The same error apparently has been committed by analysts who have spent many pages discussing the proper timing and the "mutative" effect of a single interpretation. Psychoanalysis, like any form of psychotherapy, is to be viewed as a *process* extending over a prolonged period of time, and its effect—as has often been pointed out—must be sought in the prolonged working through of basic pathogenic conflicts as they make their appearance in multiform guises.

Nevertheless, the question arises: Why is this process crowned by success in some instances and doomed to failure in others? Assuredly, there are reasons attributable to the patient's personality structure, the genesis of his neurosis, his constitution, and so forth. But there are also factors in the therapist's personality, life experience, attitudes, etc., and the manner in which they meet and interact with the patient via the therapeutic technique. It appears that, apart from his emphasis on countertransference phenomena, Freud did not explicitly formulate the *interactive* aspects of the patient-therapist relationship.

The therapist must understand the patient's transference maneuvers, his resistances, and the specific structure of his neurosis. But his communications must reach and make sense to the patient on a deep emotional level. Thus, crucial errors in technique do not arise to any significant degree from premature, partially incorrect, incomplete, or even false interpretations: rather they are to be seen as a failure to reach the patient at a level where therapy becomes *an experience that makes a difference.* Perhaps such failures may be subsumed under the heading of faulty empathy or faulty technique. Yet, ultimately, it is not the technique that is at fault; rather it is the therapist's failure to communicate in terms that are to the patient *emotionally significant and meaningful.* Herein lies the skill and the art of psychotherapy. Where technique is elevated to a position of pre-eminence, the groundwork for such failures is laid. It is very likely that this is precisely what occurred around 1920, when, according to Clara Thompson (1950), psychoanalysis in its search for the "infantile amnesia" reached a low ebb. The renaissance of psychotherapy was made possible by the realization that the technical devices which Freud abstracted from his observations are only a means to an end.[4] Failure to heed this caution means courting a therapeutic impasse. Parenthetically, the latter-day popularity of existential analysis and its variants appears attributable—at least in part—to what is probably a basic misapprehension of the goals and procedures of psychoanalysis. On the other hand, it is easy to see how the reading of the typical psychoanalytic paper, with its astringent and impersonal quality, lends itself to misinterpretations of the essential goals aspired to by Freud in therapy.

A typical misapprehension concerns the nature of the transference, its technical handling, and resolution. One of the frequent criticisms of psychoanalysis by its contemporary opponents is the contention that the transference serves to resurrect problems of the past and to search for the childhood antecedents of the patient's current difficulties, usually at the expense of the therapist's interest in the patient's *current* problems in living. Evidently, this procedure was not infrequently followed by therapists a generation ago, but has been superseded by the newer emphasis on ego functions. As is well recognized, patients may dwell on the past as a resistance, just as they may become preoccupied with trivial events in their current lives. In short, resistance may take innumerable forms, and it is the therapist's task to recognize and deal with it in therapeutic ways. The latter constitutes an acid test of the therapist's skill.

An important question obviously concerns the relationship between a therapist's theoretical assumptions and his technique. To what extent does technique mirror underlying theoretical beliefs, and to what extent is it possible to make inferences about the therapist's theoretical assumptions by

[4] I am also mindful of the developments ushered in by W. Reich's (1949) emphasis on the analysis of character defenses and the resulting emphasis on the ego's defensive functions.

studying his behavior vis-à-vis a patient? Ideally, two therapists subscribing to identical theoretical tenets may be expected to employ identical therapeutic techniques, yet, as has been stated, such is not the case. Their communications will diverge on as many dimensions as one is willing to define: frequency of utterances, length, emotional quality, intonation, topics selected for comment—to name but a few. Such dimensions exemplify the kinds of variables which content analysts (see, in this connection, the reviews by Auld and Murray, 1955, and by Marsden, 1965) have attempted to define and measure over the past twenty years in an effort to compare therapeutic techniques. It may be objected that such measurable differences are not the "real" ones, since two therapists might differ in their therapeutic styles and yet practice an identical form of therapy. This position is difficult to defend because the critic may ask about the criteria by which similarities or differences are to be decided. Surely, there must be a more solid basis than someone's opinion, but even if one were to rely on expert opinion, a rater or judge will implicitly apply certain criteria, which are precisely the ones to be spelled out.

The issue is crucial because of the alleged theoretical differences between schools of psychotherapy, which their originators have done their utmost to accentuate. Typically, these systems are tied to conceptualizations about childhood development and the evolution of the adult personality. Many of these attempts, insofar as they are based on empirical clinical observations, are valuable contributions to the science of psychology, but this is not the present concern. To the extent that divergent theoretical positions include a theory of psychotherapy which gives rise to specific kinds of therapeutic interventions, the techniques must be operationally definable. Stated otherwise, the assertion that different systems lead to different therapeutic techniques is of little value unless the differences are in some way demonstrable. If a Rogerian, a Sullivanian, and a Freudian practice forms of psychotherapy which do *not* differ along the particular lines espoused by the originators of the system, then the uniqueness of the system may be a myth. To complicate matters, it may also be true that alleged differences in technique may lie along dimensions different from those postulated by the system, in which case the theoretical differences may be of negligible relevance as far as the practice of psychotherapy is concerned, and an entirely different theory of the nature of the psychotherapeutic influence may have to be written. Frank (1961) made a significant attempt to isolate common elements in diverse forms of psychological influence, including psychotherapy, religious conversion, "brainwashing," etc. Does the problem then have to be resolved by recourse to the kinds of *changes* effected by a given form of psychotherapy? Perhaps, but in that event criteria for the measurement of changes have to be evolved. The contention that orthodox analysis produces a restructuration of the psychic apparatus whereas other forms of therapy achieve modifications that are less far-reaching and profound may be plausible, but the critics have a right to be shown that this is indeed the case. Again, it is necessary to point out that at present we lack criteria by which such personality modifications can be reliably and validly judged. Thus far, available methods are inadequate for such an undertaking.

If the nature of the psychological influence exerted by different forms of psychotherapy turns out to have only a loose articulation to the system espoused by the therapist, one may wonder about the nature of the significant dimensions. One important dimension that invites attention as a strong contender is the person of the therapist, including his attitudes toward the patient (for example, interest, dedication, and investment in the patient as a person) and his ability to make therapy a significant and meaningful experience for the patient. *How* he accomplishes this feat is the crucial problem which research in this area must answer. The therapist's depth of belief in the truth and usefulness of his theoretical system and his abiding willingness and faith in his ability to help the patient, as Frank suggested, probably play an important part. It may also be surmised that, depending on the patient's personality, cultural background, values, etc., different systems of psychotherapy have different degrees of intellectual and ultimately emotional appeal—over and beyond the person of the therapist who practices them. This possibility in no way denies that some conceptions of neurosis and emotional problems in living, apart from the person of the therapist, are more fruitful, heuristic, and capable of effecting deeper personality changes than others.

The preceding discussion puts in sharper focus the question: To what extent is it necessary for a therapist to accept particular psychoanalytic tenets to practice psychoanalytic psychotherapy, including psychoanalysis? The answer, in terms of Freud's definition, is relatively simple, but troublesome questions remain.

For example, one might construct a continuum along which Freud's theoretical conceptions might be ordered on the basis of their relevance to the practice of psychotherapy. Such a dimension might coincide with the degree to which phenomena are capable of observation. At one extreme, resistance, as evidenced, say, by blocking, evasiveness, and the like, is closest to observation; at the other, a concept like the death instinct, furthest. Freud's metapsychological concepts, which he termed "our mythology," appear to be the ones least relevant to psychotherapeutic operations. For example, it is hard to see that therapeutic practice is greatly affected by the therapist's acceptance or rejection of the concept of the death instinct, or whether he subscribes to the notion of an innate conflict-free sphere. However, it is of considerable consequence whether he accepts the concept of resistance and defense. At the extremes, the question is easily resolved;

however, there is a large "gray" area where acceptance or rejection of a theoretical construct might make a practical difference. Therapy may take a different course if the therapist views the patient's "basic" problem as an "Oedipal conflict" or as a "pregenital oral conflict." Here the question may be not so much acceptance or rejection of a theoretical construct but the relative emphasis the therapist assigns to it. Or, there may be differences of opinion about the layering of defenses and the proper sequence of analyzing them. In any event, the degree of articulation between theory and therapeutic practice represents an important problem. Freud, it has been noted, left the matter in rather general terms. He did not go beyond such general statements as: defenses are to be analyzed before content; negative transference must be interpreted expeditiously; etc. While therapist-supervisors make more specific recommendations to their students, generally applicable criteria have not been set forth, nor has empirical research succeeded in illuminating the problem.

There is another important reason necessitating the isolation of dimensions for the comparative study of therapeutic techniques. I am referring to the requirement of defining the *independent variable* (see Frank, 1959). While the solution of this problem is of paramount importance for eventually comparing the effectiveness of different forms of psychotherapy, it is bound to have equally significant implications for the theory and practice of therapy. If the relative effectiveness of two medications is to be compared, it is scientifically inadequate to state that both are white, round, and weigh 2 grains. One may be a placebo and the other a potent drug, but one would not be able to tell from such a gross description. To define one form of treatment as "psychoanalysis" and another as "psychotherapy based on psychoanalytic principles" [5] is hardly more precise unless the "active ingredients" can be isolated. By this time it is apparent that the same form of therapy in the hands of two therapists, or the same form of therapy conducted by one therapist with two different patients, is *not* identical. Thus, it will be pointless to compare the relative effectiveness of different forms of psychotherapy, irrespective of real or apparent differences in outcome, as long as we cannot spell out the particular therapeutic interventions which are purported to be the operative ones.[6] The problem is of course vastly complicated by the fact that, concurrent with psychotherapy, the patient is undergoing a variety of life experiences which may have an inhibiting or facilitating effect on therapeutic progress. Among the practical consequences of isolating the nature of the psychological influences exerted by the therapist through his personality and technique, we may expect to see improved

[5] The majority of research papers in the literature still rest content with such broad designations.

[6] This is one of the major shortcomings of comparisons between behavior therapy and psychoanalytic therapy (see page 329).

selection of particular patients for particular forms of psychotherapy with particular psychotherapists. Needless to say, this would be a major achievement.

To summarize principal problem areas which during the last few decades have received the attention of clinicians and researchers, we may list the following:

1. There has been an increased emphasis on relating the childhood roots of the patient's neurosis to his contemporary functioning and adaptation, thereby rendering therapy a more vivid and potentially deeper-going process. Past events of the patient's life are of no intrinsic interest to therapy except insofar as feelings surrounding them are still alive in the present and continue to have an adverse effect upon the patient's current living. The influence of ego psychology here is particularly relevant.

2. Increasing attention is being paid to the personality of the therapist and the extent to which he succeeds in making therapy a significant experience for the patient. This interest is partly a function of a growing research interest, by sociologists and psychologists, in problems of two-person interactions in a variety of settings.

3. Intertwined with the foregoing has been the search for briefer, more economical, and more effective ways of treating patients by means of psychotherapy. Under this rubric should be mentioned attempts to regulate the length of therapy, frequency of visits, degree to which regression is fostered, and the like. More radical departures from the analytic model are exemplified by experimentation in the areas of verbal conditioning, behavior therapy, etc. (see page 329).

4. While the scope of indications for psychotherapy has undergone considerable broadening from the base of the transference neuroses, efforts have been made to arrive at better criteria for selecting patients for particular forms of therapy. This effort has as yet been neither systematic nor exhaustive.

5. The same judgment applies to the definition and measurement of outcome criteria by which the effectiveness of therapy can be assessed. The assertion that the resolution of the transference neurosis by interpretation alone leads to more pervasive and more lasting personality changes than other forms of therapy in which "suggestion" is used more freely remains a credo of "orthodox" analysts, but has been challenged by others, and as yet lacks clear-cut demonstration.

6. The philosophical assumptions and theoretical formulations underlying psychoanalytic therapy have been questioned from many quarters and for different reasons, leading to more or less radical departures from the "basic model" technique advocated by Freud. The emergence of numerous competing systems of psychotherapy (Harper, 1959, distinguished 36!) has probably contributed to the enrichment of the field as well as engendered confusion.

7. Advances of theory and research in sociology, anthropology (linguistics, kinesics), experimental psychology (learning theory, operant conditioning, etc.), information theory, communication theory, the use of psychoactive drugs in psychiatry, and in numerous other areas have been important but are hard to assess. The development of group therapy, family therapy, therapy with children, and other forms of psychotherapy, too, has had an impact on individual psychotherapy based on analytic principles. However, on the whole, these influences have led to comparatively few modifications or reformulations of basic psychoanalytic concepts and techniques.

In the following sections selected problems and trends will be elaborated in somewhat greater detail.

Influence of Ego Psychology

While the theoretical contributions of ego psychology have been made explicit in numerous publications, the technical implications are considerably less clear and more difficult to delineate. Hartmann (1951), in one of the few essays specifically devoted to this topic, notes the lag between theoretical advances and practical applications, and frankly acknowledges that trenchant technical discoveries, comparable to abreaction and analysis of resistances, are not to be found in the latest phase of analytic theory. Furthermore, he asserts that a great deal more is known on a theoretical level than can be utilized in practice.

Following Hartmann, ego psychology's major contribution to therapeutic practice has been in the area of handling resistances. The emphasis here rests on those aspects of the patient's psychic functioning that are concerned with his *adaptation to reality*. Clearly, the therapist never works with intrapsychic conflicts in isolation, but of necessity must deal with the patient's total personality in its intrapsychic as well as interpersonal struggles. To some extent this fact has always been recognized by analytic theory, but it was given increasing recognition by Freud (1926) in the *Problem of Anxiety* and by Anna Freud (1936) in *The Ego and the Mechanisms of Defence*. Both works have given direction to the theoretical developments that have since been subsumed under the heading of ego psychology.

How does the recognition that the ego serves a synthesizing and integrative function, that its structure comprises both conflicts and conflict-free components, and that stratification is one of its essential characteristics influence the therapist's technical maneuvers? These concepts, at least in rudimentary form, were spelled out in Freud's (1923) latest model of the psychic apparatus as formulated in *The Ego and the Id* and have since been elaborated rather than changed in any fundamental way. Hartmann points out that the evolution of analytic technique may be traced through gradually emerging changes in the original formula "making the unconscious conscious," already enunciated by Breuer and Freud (1895) in *Studies on Hysteria.* Subsequent developments occurred under the impact of the finding that a mere translation of the derivatives of the patient's unconscious conflict into consciousness was an inadequate therapeutic measure. Henceforth attention was directed upon the role and function of resistance, particularly of its unconscious aspects, which found its way into a broader conception of the structure and function of the ego. The practical yield lies in an improved understanding of the varieties of defense, the manner in which impulse and defense are woven into character traits, the identification and management of the manifold forms of resistance, and a clearer conception of the patient as a *total* person. Thus, in analyzing a resistance, the working formula "defense—warded-off impulsive" provides only a crude blueprint for the therapist's interventions. Therapists could not escape the recognition that they are operating within a complex psychic field and that any interpretation sets in motion reverberations of the total psychic apparatus, which have potentially far-reaching dynamic, economic, and structural implications. We have as yet only very imprecise notions about the workings of this process, particularly with respect to *structural* changes. Indeed, structural changes seem far more difficult to achieve than was formerly believed, and it is as yet an open question whether psychoanalytic therapy is better equipped than other forms of therapy in effecting such modifications.

Field theoretical concepts are of course not unique to psychoanalysis, but rather represent special instances of developments in biology and psychology, among other sciences. However, instead of simplifying the understanding of the effects of therapeutic interventions (notably interpretations of resistance), such concepts add to the complexity. Nevertheless, by giving proper emphasis to the complexity of the psychic apparatus—in its intersystemic, intrasystemic, and adaptational functioning—ego psychology has performed a valuable service, most significantly by its implicit warning against the "empty organism" approach of behaviorism, which has been pitted against the alleged cumbersomeness of psychoanalytic theory and therapy, but fails to explain many relevant phenomena pertaining to emotional disturbances and their amelioration.

Psychoanalytic theory and practice—at least within the mainstream of its development—has remained rooted in Freud's instinct theory, of which the stages of psychosexual development are an integral part. Yet, in this area, too, reformulations have occurred, which probably will have a lasting effect on psychotherapeutic practice. Here Erikson's (1959) formulations of epigenesis, stressing as they do the psychosocial and adaptational aspects of personality development, deserve emphasis. It may be said that Erikson has broadened Freud's original formulations by placing the child's instinctual development more squarely with the broader context of his normal social and interpersonal relatedness. For example, the oral period is characterized not only by passive and active incorporation (together with associated fantasies) subserving a function of the id, but coincides with a particular way of relating to the world and significant people. This "way of life" is one of close physical contact, dependency, and receptivity. One of the important implications of Erikson's thinking is the evolution of the child's sense of *identity* as he successfully completes the developmental tasks set by each stage. The growth and consolidation of the ego is a concomitant of the achievement of competence and mastery. These in turn presuppose a sense of basic trust, instilled in infancy and early childhood, which may be viewed as the matrix for personality growth in normal development as well as in psychotherapy.

While the implications of these notions for psychoanalytic therapy are not nearly so clear as one might wish, they appear to be an integral part of the renewed emphasis on the *experiential* learning aspects of psychotherapy, particularly as opposed to intellectual (cognitive) insight. To illustrate further: While it was recognized that repressions in childhood had set the stage for fixations, it was more or less taken for granted that once the repressions were removed, the patient would soon "catch up" and close the gap between a disturbed childhood and present-day reality. Insufficiently taken into account, it appears, was the fact that by having suffered severe childhood traumata (resulting in massive repressions), the patient's ego development had sustained serious—and perhaps irreversible—damage. By analogy, a child who has dropped out of school because of an illness has missed a significant portion of the curriculum. Merely to enable him to return to school after a year will not compensate deficits in learning and social maturation he has sustained. Similarly, the task of therapy in the "old" sense largely consisted of "returning" the patient to adult life. Freud initially believed that, when freed of his repressions, the patient would soon take advantage of the opportunities in social living and take his role among contemporaries. This process work smoothly where the patient's ego development is largely "intact." But, as every therapist knows, these cases are the exception rather than the rule. More typically, the patient, because of his neurosis, has been more or less seriously "retarded" in his personality growth, and ordinary life experience cannot be expected to fill the void. Psychotherapy, as part of its task, provides a new base of operations, or a new, if temporary, "home" from which the patient can venture forth, experiment in living, and return to enlist the therapist's assistance in helping him to understand errors in living he will unwittingly commit.[7]

Thus, the task of therapy is to clear away the impediments to emotional learning (repressions and other maladaptive defenses) and to create

[7] This is another problem concerning which therapists who advocate desensitization and substitution of behavioral responses have remarkably little to say.

opportunities for new and more viable experiences. The advantages over the childhood situation lie in the patient's greater introspective powers, those aspects of his ego which form the therapeutic alliance with the therapist, and the therapist's comparatively greater objectivity (as compared with a parent). The disadvantages are to be sought in the fact that the maladaptive patterns the patient has learned in childhood are deeply entrenched and extraordinarily difficult to modify (Freud's repetition compulsion).

It may be said that the ego psychologists, by stressing man's problems in growth and adaptation, have partially answered the accusation frequently leveled at Freud that he viewed *all* of man's behavior and psychological functioning as *nothing but* expressions of sexual and aggressive instinctual strivings. To be sure, one can find passages in his writings which tend to substantiate this conclusion, but the evolution of his thinking led from an emphasis on the dynamics of the unconscious to an increasing concern with the controlling functions of the ego. In keeping with this development, there has been a greater recognition that, in addition to mental functions which are embroiled in neurotic conflicts, there are parts of the personality which continue to serve important adaptive tasks, unless the person is completely incapacitated. How this shift in orientation has affected therapy practice is difficult to assess, all the more since psychoanalysis as yet lacks both an explicit learning theory and an explicit theory of psychotherapeutic change. Much remains to be learned about acquisition, maintenance, and—most important—modification of behavioral patterns (see Rapaport, 1959).

Analytic Therapy as a Learning Process

In this context it may prove helpful to compile an "operational inventory" of basic learning experiences occurring in psychoanalytic therapy.

1. The therapist *sets an example* of acceptance, respect, tolerance, nonpunitiveness, reliability, trustworthiness, punctuality, decency, nonretaliation, permissiveness, evenness of temper, predictability, truth, rationality, honesty, steady cooperation in constructive moves by the patient, nonavoidance of anxiety-provoking and "taboo" topics, reasonableness, etc. In this way he provides a certain gratification and stimulates in the patient the expression of wishes and impulses which become increasingly intense and primitive the less they are interfered with by outside pressure and the more they are guaranteed "safe" expression. The therapist says, in effect: "It is all right for wishes and impulses to be experienced in awareness, but there is no assurance that they will be gratified." In fact, the patient will reject a good many himself once he becomes conscious of them. (This paradigm of the permissiveness of the analytic situation has of course been abundantly spelled out by Freud and others.)

2. The therapist *sets limits:* He strictly limits the time he devotes to the patient; he expects payment for services rendered; he expects punctuality, respect for his property, rights, privacy, and independence. He also abstains from participating in the patient's neurotic maneuvers (e.g., sadomasochistic strivings and a wide variety of other techniques of interpersonal control).

3. Through the foregoing and other devices the therapist teaches the *delay of gratification*—perhaps the most important lesson the patient has to learn. Tolerance of delay is taught by regulated frustration, such as nongratification of dependency wishes, terminating the hour by the clock rather than in accordance with the patient's desires, etc. The principle here is to awaken in awareness strong wishes typically dating back to early childhood, and by failing to gratify them, educate the patient to tolerate the unpleasure, tension, disappointment, discomfort, and unhappiness associated with them. In speaking about this process, Menninger (1958) observed that the patient's gain in psychotherapy is the product of his frustrations.

There is little doubt that in normal childhood development, ego strength is acquired in much the same manner: The child learns to accept frustration of his wishes (for dependency, sexual gratification, etc.) because he acquiesces in the privations imposed upon him by the parents as trustworthy representatives of reality. He suffers the pain of frustration and ultimately of separation from his love objects, because his love outweighs his self-seeking, narcissistic wishes, and he adapts to reality without developing excessive defensive controls resulting in neurotic symptoms.

The emotional learning occurring in psychoanalytic psychotherapy can thus be reduced to the following basic model:

1. The therapist provides a "good" climate, which the patient can come to recognize as a safe, protective environment. Thus, the therapist fills the role of a reasonable, accepting, and caring parent.

2. The patient—at least consciously—is willing to engage with the therapist in the collaborative venture of psychotherapy.

3. To the extent that the patient can emotionally come to experience the "good" aspects of Condition 1 (although they are controlled, restrained, and dosed), he begins to experience hitherto repressed wishes, impulses, fantasies, etc., toward the therapist. Also awakened are the negativistic and obstructionistic tendencies, commonly labeled resistance, by which the patient in accordance with his early life experience tries to engage the therapist in a neurotic struggle which, if successful (from the patient's point of view), would spell the failure of therapy. This phase comprises the spectrum of transference reactions.

4. The task of the therapist is to convince the patient of the irrationality, futility, and self-defeating aspects of his defensive maneuvers, thus encouraging their abandonment. As a substitute, he implicitly offers his own ego (attitudes, beliefs, values, etc.) as a new and better model for interper-

sonal collaboration.[8] This process, to a preponderant extent, is an emotional, not a cognitive one, and as Freud repeatedly observed, the balance of forces is determined entirely by the patient's emotional relationship to the therapist. It must also be pointed out that while psychoanalytic therapy in important respects is a process of socialization, this is only a part of it. It is more correct to say that in the ordinary course of the child's socialization he comes to control (largely repress) his primitive instinctual strivings, which remain a central concern of analytic therapy. In the latter, various segments of unconscious processes are worked out in consciousness, interpreted in terms of their infantile roots, and integrated by the patient's adult, rational ego. The essence of analytic therapy is an intensive form of emotional learning in human collaboration and relatedness, carried on within an atmosphere of understanding and respect. The emotional relationship is mediated largely by the use of *language* and linguistic symbols, which raises the experiential aspects of the relationship to a more differentiated cognitive level.[9]

Psychotherapy (including psychoanalysis) appears to emerge more clearly as a learning process (Marmor, 1962, 1964), which is by no means restricted to the task of uncovering the patient's unformulated unconscious fantasies as they permeate his relationships to other people, life goals, and other facets of life. The making conscious of these derivatives (e.g., sado-masochistic, "homosexual," narcissistic trends) of course remains an undertaking central to analytically oriented therapy. It may be noted here, parenthetically, that the psychoanalytic emphasis on primitive, primordial fantasies, wishes, and fears separates this form of psychotherapy from the Neo-Freudian dissidents, who by and large view the patient's problem to a much greater extent as a function of destructive interpersonal and cultural influences. However, the "analyzing" of unconscious impulses proceeds concurrently with, or in the context of, a "good" human relationship, in which the patient has the unique opportunity to work, learn, and identify with a substitute parent-authority figure, whose function as a *model* has increasingly come to the fore. Thus, the therapist serves not only as a screen for the patient's transference projections, but in various ways (many of which have only been inadequately conceptualized so far) sets an example of strength, tolerance, patience, reliability—perhaps even wisdom!—which often pro-

[8] Clarification of *how* identification occurs appears to be another fruitful area for future research.

[9] Stone (1961) characterizes the psychoanalytic situation as a state of "deprivation-in-intimacy," adding: "In my view, it represents to the unconscious, in its primary and most far-reaching impact, the superimposed series of basic separation experiences in the child's relation to his mother" (p. 105). "Underlying the entire dynamics and structure of the psychoanalytic situation, perhaps one of the inspirations of its genesis, is the driving force of the primordial transference, in its varying phase and conflict emphases, a phenomenon which is in itself derived from the successive states of separation from the mother" (p. 106).

vides a sharp contrast to the patient's early childhood experiences with significant adults. This all-important function Freud more or less took for granted—he saw it as *selbstverständlich*—yet it is anything but self-evident. Any form of psychotherapy mediates *a new experience in living*, and it is the extent to which the patient can derive *meaning* from this relationship that psychotherapy—at least in part—achieves its beneficial results.

The manner in which the therapeutic relationship becomes a meaningful experience for the patient remains essentially an unsolved problem. To be sure, the therapist, through self-knowledge, clinical experience, and formal training can do a great deal to prevent the therapeutic encounter from entering blind alleys or ending in an impasse. In addition, on the basis of his knowledge of the patient's life experience, presenting symptoms, and character structure, he can identify basic problems which in multifarious, idiosyncratic ways create the difficulties in living from which the patient is suffering. But he cannot *ensure* the emotional significance of the patient's experience in psychotherapy. At this point, technique ends and the imponderables of the human encounter assume the ascendancy. This also appears to be the juncture at which theoretical differences reveal the greatest divergence. More concretely, the two problems concern (1) the patient's suitability for psychotherapy, or, more precisely, the compatibility between a given patient and a given therapist; and (2) the essential nature of the therapeutic influence, which, after all, represents the personal view put forth by the therapist-proponent of a given theoretical system.

Compatibility between Patient and Therapist

There has been an increasing recognition that the chances for success in psychotherapy are markedly enhanced provided the prospective patient meets certain criteria, a number of which were already recognized by Freud, and others which have been isolated by systematic research undertaken during the last decades. Therapists, it is well known, have fairly specific—and presumably valid—notions about the kind of attributes a promising patient should possess, as well as those attributes which make a patient unsuitable for the more usual forms of analytic psychotherapy (cf. Goldstein, 1962, who critically discusses empirical research on the problems of therapist-patient expectancies). As a composite, patients considered good prognostic risks tend to be young, intelligent, physically attractive, well educated members of the upper middle class; to possess a high degree of ego strength, at least some anxiety which impels them to seek help; to have no seriously disabling neurotic symptoms, to have a relative absence of deep characterological distortions or strong secondary gains, to have a willingness to talk about their difficulties, an ability to communicate well, some achievements in the social-vocational area, a value system relatively congruent with that of the therapist, and a certain psychological-mindedness which makes them of course linked to a number of the foregoing variables) plays an important work of Hollingshead and Redlich (1958) has shown, social class (which is of course linked to a number of the foregoing variables) plays an important role in the process of selecting patients for therapy. Understandably, therapists tend to select patients who, in the therapist's judgment, are likely to benefit from the kind of therapy he has to offer. As clinical accounts by Fromm-Reichmann, Searles, Will, and others demonstrate, these are not necessarily the "easy" patients.

Furthermore, a cautionary note is essential to avoid the misinterpretation that promising candidates for psychotherapy are not really "sick." This inference would be quite unwarranted, and is in part a reflection upon the primitive status of currently available assessment techniques. By superficial standards a person may be described as "mentally healthy" if he meets gross behavioral criteria of performance, such as functioning in a particular social role, earning a living, absence of gross disturbances in interpersonal relations, or gross overt psychopathology. Yet, such conformity or seeming adaptation to the culture may be achieved at tremendous psychic cost, since the person may feel intensely unhappy, conflicted, inhibited, and ill at ease. There can be no doubt that psychoanalytic psychotherapy pays the closest attention to, and evinces the greatest respect for, the individual's intrapsychic organization and its function in the person's *fine* adjustment to himself and others. The latter is completely lost sight of in ordinary statistical tabulations of "improvement," as used in governmental statistics, outpatient clinic reports, and studies involving psychopharmacological agents.

Unfortunately, there are no adequate measures of self-respect, a sense of worthwhileness as a person, emotional well-being arising from an ability to be at peace with oneself and others, a sense of relatedness, identity, and true productivity—values which appear to become increasingly evanescent in the nuclear age. While existential analysts and therapists subscribing to related views have correctly called attention to the importance of these values, the impression has been conveyed that they are inconsistent with the goals of psychoanalytic psychotherapy. I do not think that this is so. As a corollary, symptom relief, while certainly important, should not be regarded as the ultimate goal of psychotherapy, no matter how often it may have to be compromised and modified for practical reasons. Rather, the integration and full unfolding of the human personality is worth striving for via psychotherapy, even though in the vast majority of cases, it may have to remain an unrealizable ideal. In this sense, Freud's conception of the psychoanalytic situation may be one of the few remaining bulwarks of the humanistic spirit in the twentieth century, for in no other human relationship is as much purposeful and dispassionate effort devoted to the "education" of a single human being.

The Therapist-Patient Relationship and the Therapist's Personality: Changing Concepts

The dynamics of the therapist-patient relationship are the sine qua non of psychoanalytic psychotherapy, and all major contributions have taken as their point of departure Freud's conceptions of transference and countertransference. (See Orr, 1954; Thompson, 1950; Wolstein, 1954, 1959, for critical reviews.) It is clear that under the impact of operationalism in science certain modifications have occurred since the time of Freud. In general, there is an increasing tendency to deal with the dynamics of the therapeutic situation in process terms, to think of transference and countertransference as phenomena along continua instead of regarding them as either "positive" or "negative." Furthermore, greater emphasis is being placed on the here-and-now experience in the therapeutic relationship. Janet MacK. Rioch's (1943) formulation may serve as an example of this trend:

> The therapeutic aim in this process is not to uncover childhood memories which will then lend themselves to analytic interpretation. . . . Psychoanalytic cure is not the amassing of data, either from childhood, or from the study of the present situation. Nor does cure result from a repetition of the original injurious experience in the analytic relationship. What is curative in the process is that in tending to reconstruct with the analyst that atmosphere which obtained in childhood, the patient actually achieves something new. He discovers that part of himself which had to be repressed at the time of the original experience. He can only do this in an interpersonal relationship with the analyst, which is suitable to such rediscovery. . . . Thus, the transference phenomenon is used so that the patient will completely re-experience the original frames of reference, and himself within those frames, in a truly different relationship with the analyst, to the end that he can discover the invalidity of his conclusions about himself and others (p. 151).

According to this viewpoint, the therapist is *more* than a sympathetic listener who interprets the patient's transference distortions, and his interpretations are not regarded as the only or the most effective factor in therapeutic success. Rather he must strive to create an emotional atmosphere in which the patient can re-experience significant aspects of his early life in which something went awry. By the same token, "countertransference" reactions are interferences with the therapist's positive emotional contribution—that is, instances in which the therapist's own personality through unresolved emotional problems impedes the full realization of the therapeutic goal.

When Freud (1910) introduced the term "countertransference," he revised his earlier view of the analyst as an impersonal mirror by recognizing that "blind spots" in the analyst's personality structure might interfere with his usefulness as a therapist. The emphasis of Freud's original formulation and that of subsequent elaborations has been on *interferences* with the analytic process occasioned by deficiencies, shortcomings, and characterological distortions within the analyst. This led to recommendations about dangers to be avoided, attitudes to be discouraged, and so on. The objective was to keep the analytic field clean and uncontaminated by minimizing unwarranted intrusions and involvements of the analyst in the patient's transference maneuvers. There is no doubt that this did much to augment the objectivity of observations in the analytic situation and to decrease the possibility of influencing the phenomena under scrutiny. Furthermore, it approximated a definition of the analytic situation as a laboratory situation for studying and modifying interpersonal processes (see, in this connection, Janis, 1958). The research potentialities of this method, it seems to me, have remained largely unexplored.

It is instructive to note that in the earlier formulations, countertransference was defined in relation to transferences of the patient, with little regard for the healthy or realistic aspects of the therapist's personality and attitudes. Even today, as Orr (1954) points out, there is widespread disagreement about the meaning of the term. For example, distinctions have been made between "positive" and "negative" countertransference; some writers insist that all feelings of the therapist should be included; others differentiate between whole and partial responses to the patient; still others restrict the term to the therapist's unconscious reactions. Berman (1949) suggests a distinction between countertransference in the classic sense and the therapist's reasonable and appropriate emotional responses, which he calls "attitudes." He also addressed himself to certain contradictions in Freud's writings, and reasons that "The answer could simply be that the analyst is always both the cool detached surgeon-like operator on the patient's psychic tissues, and the warm, human, friendly, helpful physician" (p. 160).

According to orthodox analytic principles, the therapist must not influence the transference situation by any means other than interpretations, which thus become the primary therapeutic agent. Furthermore, Freud and Fenichel imply that differences in the analytic atmosphere created by the analyst's personality do not exert an influence upon the transference situation and the therapeutic results. According to this view, *the* transference neurosis evolves more or less automatically, provided the therapist does nothing to interfere with its development.

In his last formulation Freud (1938) viewed the analyst as a new superego, who corrects errors in the patient's early upbringing. Strachey (1934), writing in the same vein, observes that

The principal effective alteration consists in a profound qualitative modification of the patient's superego, from which the other alterations follow in the main automatically. . . . This modification of the patient's superego is brought about in a series of innumerable small steps by the agency of mutative interpretations, which are effected by the analyst in virtue of his position as object of the patient's id impulses and as auxiliary superego (p. 159).

The dosed introjection of good objects is regarded as one of the most important factors in the therapeutic process.

Bibring (1937) recognizes that the therapist makes a positive contribution through his own personality, but considers this to be essentially nonanalytical:

[T]he therapeutic changes which take place in the super-ego are effected by purely analytical means, i.e., by demonstrating contradictions in structure and development and by making an elucidation of them possible. . . . In my opinion the analyst's attitude, and the analytical atmosphere which he creates, are fundamentally a reality-correction which adjusts the patient's anxieties about loss of love and punishment, the origin of which lies in childhood. Even if these anxieties later undergo analytical resolution, I still believe that the patient's relationship to the analyst from which a sense of security emanates is not only a precondition of the procedure but also effects an immediate (apart from an analytical) consolidation of his sense of security which he has not successfully acquired or consolidated in childhood. Such an immediate consolidation—which, in itself, lies outside the field of analytic therapy—is, of course, only of permanent value if it goes along with the coordinated operation of analytic treatment (pp. 182–183).

Why is the atmosphere created by the therapist in which a "reality-correction" takes place to be divorced from the interpretive essence of analytic treatment? It may be that both are integral parts of analytic psychotherapy and that they operate conjointly as therapeutic factors. To tease out their relative contributions is a research task of the first magnitude, the solution of which may approach an answer to the question of what is effective in psychotherapy.

A major factor in the revival of interest in the therapist's personality was Alexander's conceptualization of the "corrective emotional experience," and it is fair to say that during the past decade this renewed interest in the person of the therapist has gained momentum. (See Strupp, 1962, for a review of typical research studies.) In his attempt to isolate the therapeutic factors in psychoanalysis, Alexander (1950) stated:

No doubt, the most important therapeutic factor in psychoanalysis is the objective and yet helpful attitude of the therapist, something which does not exist in any other relationship. . . . To experience such a novel human relationship in itself has a tremendous therapeutic significance which cannot be overrated. . . . This attitude, combined with correct interpretation of material which is about to emerge from repression, together with the analysis of the ego's defenses, is primarily responsible for the therapeutic effectiveness of psychoanalysis (p. 487).

The essence of the "corrective emotional experience" involves an experential contrast between the therapist's attitude and the original parental attitude, which were presumably pathogenic. In a more recent essay, Alexander (1958) forcefully restated this emphasis:

The theory of corrective emotional experience leads to still another technical conclusion. This concerns the most opaque (in my opinion) area of psychoanalysis, the question of the therapist's influence on the treatment process by the virtue of being what he is: an individual personality, distinct from all other therapists. The evaluation of this most elusive element in the therapeutic equation is at present quite beyond our ken. We know only that the blank screen model is an abstraction, which is too far removed from the actual events during treatment (p. 311).

Frank (1959a) explored the hypothesis that the patient's attitude of trust or faith may play a significant part in his response to all forms of psychotherapy. He hypothesizes that this favorable expectation is fostered by the therapist's own confidence in his ability to help, his ability to inspire confidence in the patient, to care deeply about him, to communicate the message that help will be forthcoming; and furthermore, that "the patient's favorable expectation, which is a major determinant of the therapist's influence over him, may have direct therapeutic effects which are not necessarily transient or superficial" (p. 37). Frank views these ingredients as a common factor in the effectiveness of all forms of psychotherapy. It is my impression that despite his cautions and disclaimers he is inclined to regard this common factor as the *major* factor.

The foregoing hypothesis, if substantiated, would be particularly damaging to the orthodox Freudian position which draws a sharp line between the therapeutic objectives of psychoanalysis and those of other methods, including those of hypnosis, faith healing, brainwashing, etc., which Frank draws upon as analogues.

MacAlpine (1950) postulates the following distinction between the nature of psychological influence in psychoanalysis and suggestion in hypnosis or similar situations:

Both hypnosis and psychoanalysis exploit infantile situations which they both create. But in hypnosis the transference is really and truly a mutual relationship existing between the hypnotist and the hypnotized. . . . One is tempted to say that countertransference is obligatory in and an essential part of hypnosis (and for that matter of all psychotherapies in which the patient is helped, encouraged, advised or criticized). . . . In psychoanalytic therapy alone the analysand is not transferred to. . . . The analyst . . . is never a co-actor. . . . The analytic transference relationship ought, strictly speaking, not to be referred to as a relationship between analysand and analyst, but more precisely as the analysand's relation to his analyst. . . . It is thereby not denied that analysis is a "team work"; in so far as it is, an "objective" relation exists between the analyst and the analysand. Because the analyst remains outside the regressive movement . . . suggestion can inherently play no part in the classical procedure of psychoanalytic technique.

To make transference and its development the essential difference between psychoanalysis and all other psychotherapies, psychoanalytic technique may be defined as the only psychotherapeutic method in which a one-sided, infantile regression—analytic transference—is induced in a patient (analysand), analyzed, worked through, and finally resolved (pp. 535–536).

Frank concedes that his position and the analytic viewpoint need not be mutually exclusive, although I believe that psychoanalytic therapy encompasses considerably more than the "favorable expectancy" envisioned by Frank. For one thing, it requires hard work from the patient and makes similar demands on the therapist. On the other hand, I hypothesize that significant therapeutic progress cannot be made unless the patient is convinced that the therapist is a reliable partner in the enterprise, and that his attitude reflects personal integrity, dedication, honesty, and faith in the fruitfulness of the task. I consider these elements central to psychoanalytic therapy, but they have not yet been adequately conceptualized (Strupp, 1959, 1960b). In this sense, there *is* an "objective relationship" between patient and therapist. I fail to see how its hypothesized existence defiles the "purity" of analytic therapy. Yet analysts have strained to postulate the absence of an interpersonal relationship as a defining characteristic of psychoanalysis in the "orthodox" sense. That interpretations also play an important, though probably secondary, part is not denied, but their curative effect has perhaps been overestimated. At any rate, we have only clinical experience to go on. In saying this, I do not wish to denigrate its value, but neither can it command blind adherence in the absence of hard-core evidence.

Quest for Increased Efficiency of Therapy

The search for ways and means to make analytic therapy more efficient and shorter took its start with the work of Ferenczi and Rank (1925), of which the subsequent efforts by Alexander and French (1946), Alexander (1956), and Rado (1956, 1962) are logical successors. Ferenczi and Rank maintained that the revival of childhood memories in the transference situation was secondary to the re-experiencing of childhood patterns in relation to the therapist, which they considered sufficient for therapeutic change. It had been observed earlier that the "lifting of the infantile amnesia" in and of itself was no guarantee of therapeutic success; contrariwise, therapists noted that interpretation of the transference phenomena, even without recollection of specific childhood patterns, seemed to be the principal and essential condition for therapeutic change.

Alexander made numerous technical suggestions aimed at intensifying the patient's emotional experience in therapy and achieving more rapid termination of treatment. Changing the frequency of interviews during appropriate phases of treatment was one technical device to make the patient more keenly aware of his dependency needs by frustrating them. Alexander also called attention to the problem inherent in any intensive long-term psychotherapy—the danger of excessive regression and the patient's tendency to use the treatment relationships as a means for obtaining significant gratifications instead of attempting to achieve mastery of his neurotic problems in the real world. He recognized—quite correctly, I think—a widespread tendency toward "overtreatment," which he vigorously proceeded to counteract by the above techniques. Alexander's theory of the "corrective emotional experience," a significant departure from orthodoxy in therapy, has already been discussed in the context of the therapist's personality.

The limitations of "the basic model technique" were already recognized by Strachey (1934), and while he drew attention to the importance of the patient's identification with the therapist as an important therapeutic factor, he did not recommend changes in technique. In contrast, Rado took the next step and addressed himself to the problem of how the patient's emotional insight leads to changes in his behavior. He advocated an active re-educational procedure, by means of which the patient hopefully achieves a better adaptation to his life situation. In all of these approaches there is a sharper recognition that the exploration of the past is not a goal in itself in therapy; rather, it represents only a waystation toward mastery and coping with difficulties in the patient's current life.

Rado, much like Alexander, attempted to counteract at appropriate times the patient's regressive tendencies. Of course, analytic therapy considers regression essential to the resolution of traumatic childhood experiences, but there is the ever-present danger that by encouraging regressive trends in the patient, the therapist may unwittingly infantilize the patient and discourage his undertaking the important adaptational tasks which ultimately are the goals of therapy. Systematic research is needed to determine the exact point in therapy at which regression, instead of being helpful, becomes a noxious interference by reinforcing the patient's dependency wishes. To illustrate the absence of hard-core research on most problems of technique, we even lack as yet data on differences between a patient's associations while facing the therapist or reclining on the couch.

A bond uniting a number of modern approaches to analytic therapy, irrespective of divergences in other respects, is the emphasis on the patient-therapy relationships as an interpersonal system, which contrasts sharply with Freud's conception, restated by MacAlpine (1950), in terms of the patient's relationship *to* the therapist. Rado's and Alexander's conceptions fit the former paradigm, which has been elevated to a central position in the writings of Sullivan and those of his followers. Fromm-Reichmann (1950), for example, defines the task of psychotherapy as "the clarification of the patient's difficulties with his fellow-men through observation and investigation of the vicissitudes of the mutual interrelationship between doctor and patient; the encouragement of recall of forgotten memories; the investigation and scrutiny of the anxiety connected with such recall, including the patient's resistance against this recall and his security operations with the psychiatrist who tries to effect it" (p. ix). The patient, according to this view, is suffering from disturbances in his interpersonal relationships, and the therapeutic factor is conceptualized as "discharge of affect plus insight gained by the patient" (p. x). In such statements it is left vague *how* insight changes the character of the patient's interpersonal relationships and leads to the kind of personality changes which are regarded as the goal of intensive psychotherapy. Nor is it clear how the interpretive process, upon which the neo-Freudians also rely, differs from the therapeutic interventions of a Freudian analyst.

Fromm-Reichmann observes in this connection: "There are great differences of opinion, however, among various schools of psychoanalytic thinking in regard to the genetic frame of reference in which interpretation is done and about the patients' selection of content matter for repression and dissociation" (p. 83). She proceeds to note "an interesting transition" in the work of Fairbairn between Freud's psychosexual concepts versus the interpersonal interpretations of Sullivan. According to her, at the turn of the century, when Freud began his pioneering work, "sexual fantasies and experiences were the main entities and phenomena which had to be barred from awareness and to be resolved by interpretation. At the present time feelings of hostility, antagonism, and malevolence between any two individuals seem to be more subject to disapproval in our Western culture, therefore to more repression, than any other unacceptable brand of human experience and behavior" (p. 3). Examples of other "unacceptable thoughts and feelings" are said to include "the infantile overdependence of adults, interpersonal overpossessiveness or magic thinking, ideas of grandeur, etc." The impression is conveyed that these phenomena are taken at face value, rather than as complex resultants of more primitive processes originating in infancy or childhood.

Fromm-Reichmann exemplifies another major departure from Freud's conception of the transference situation. This deviation is rooted in a revised account of childhood development, which places much less emphasis on the Oedipus constellation or at least questions its universality as a causal factor in neurosis. "In my experience," she states, "the wish for closeness and tenderness with the beloved parent and the envious resentment about the authoritative power of the hated one, both without recognizable sexual roots, constitute a more frequent finding in childhood histories of healthy, neurotic, and psychotic people than do their sexual Oedipal entanglements with the parents of their childhood" (p. 99).

In the foregoing, a few examples have been given of prominent attempts to render analytic therapy more effective. These efforts involve changes in the activities of the therapist, regulation of the transference situation, and certain reformulations of the kinds of pathogenic conflicts to be interpreted.[10] Controversy has surrounded all of these innovations, none of which have as yet been subjected to systematic investigation to assess their respective merits. It will be seen in the following sections that efforts to improve the effectiveness of analytic therapy are implicit in other contributions, although ostensibly they may have been written for other purposes.

"Widening Scope" versus Rigorous Selection of Patients

In a series of papers published under the general heading, "The Widening Scope of Indications for Psychoanalysis," Stone (1954) calls attention to Freud's basic conservatism in wishing to restrict the applicability of psychoanalysis essentially to the so-called transference neuroses, coupled with a persistent emphasis on a "basically reliable ego." Yet, a broadening of applications gradually occurred, encompassing the treatment of psychoses, character disorders, perversions, behavior disorders in childhood and adolescence, borderline states, psychosomatic conditions, and numerous others. Furthermore, with the rise of "the affluent society" in America, there is scarcely a human problem which has not been brought to or treated by psychoanalysis, which thus has become the panacea for all human ills. This lack of discrimination may have been partly a function of the great social pressure for psychotherapeutic services, which has been mounting steadily, but therapists as a group must share some of the blame for undertaking tasks that often lay beyond their technical means. This problem was perhaps more severe some years ago than it is today, but it may account, at

[10] In this connection, Alexander (1954) makes the interesting point: "The time has come when our technique must be adjusted to the therapeutic exigencies of each type of patient" (p. 70). In keeping with this assertion, Alexander questions the validity of the time-honored dictum that in psychoanalysis, therapy and investigation run parallel. The reason for this divergence is seen by Alexander in a potentially antitherapeutic result when the therapist pursues his interests in the genetic roots of the patient's illness at the expense of dealing with his oral dependency wishes, which can often act as a powerful and sometimes insurmountable resistance.

least in part, for the disenchantment with psychoanalytic therapy and its potentialities, which currently seems to afflict the public, practitioners, and foundations supporting research.

In this context we again are brought face to face with the problem of defining more clearly the nature of the therapeutic influence as well as the conditions under which it is effective. Anna Freud (1954) comments: "If all the skill, knowledge and pioneering effort which was spent on widening the scope of application of psychoanalysis had been employed instead on intensifying and improving our technique in the original field (hysteric, phobic, and compulsive disorders), I cannot help but feel that, by now, we would find the treatment of the common neuroses child's play, instead of struggling with their technical problems as we have continued to do" (p. 610).

For example, there are as yet no clear-cut demonstrations that the development and resolution of a transference neurosis is the *only* (or indeed the best) method by which lasting ego modifications are achieved, and that the quality and extent of such changes are highly correlated with the therapeutic method. Gill (1954) attempts to draw a sharp line between "psychoanalysis" and "psychotherapy," reserving for the former (1) the development of a regressive transference neurosis and (2) the resolution of this neurosis by techniques of interpretation *alone*. In this connection, the relatively impersonal attitude of the therapist is seen as an attempt to hold constant an important variable—certainly a laudable objective on scientific grounds, and one whose potentialities still remain to be fully explored. Gill notes that in recent years there has been an increase in what he calls "intermediate techniques" which borrow heavily from the "basic model technique," but include departures dictated by various clinical and practical considerations. Nevertheless, Gill believes that psychoanalysis practiced in the strict sense achieves more lasting personality changes than any other technique. With the advent of many new techniques competing with intensive long-term analytic therapy, conclusive answers to this question would be particularly welcome.

The Criterion Problem

In addition to specifications of the "active ingredients" in the treatment method, future progress appears to depend heavily on improved measures of outcome (Strupp, 1963). Clearly, there is no simple relationship between diagnostic indicators and therapeutic outcomes, yet, while much remains to be learned about the problem, in principle it should be amenable to conceptual analysis and empirical research. Traditionally, the "classical" neurotic conditions, like hysteria, have been regarded as ideally suited for psychotherapy and psychoanalysis, whereas severe character disorders and the psychoses have been considered more or less refractory. Such judgments are partly based upon clinical experience; but they also reflect subtle value judgments about the kinds of persons with whom psychotherapists prefer to work, as well as an appraisal in sociocultural terms of the patient's character structure and symptoms. Consequently, a patient meeting the psychotherapist's explicit as well as implicit criteria of a "good" or "promising" patient not only has a better chance of finding a competent therapist, but he may from the beginning elicit greater interest from the therapist, who in turn may become more willing to make an emotional investment in the treatment program and to devote greater energy to the treatment. It is as yet unknown to which extent the patient may fulfill the therapist's unverbalized prophecy.[11] However, it may turn out that a great deal more can be done for certain patients psychotherapeutically once it is possible to approach them and their difficulties in living more objectively.

Once the pertinent variables have been systematically studied, it may turn out that only a relatively restricted band of the population meets "good patient" criteria. The available evidence points to a convergent trend, which was aptly summarized by Luborsky (1959): "Those who stay in treatment improve; those who improve are better off to begin with than those who do not; and one can predict response to treatment by how well they are to begin with" (p. 324). It may be noted that the criteria of suitability which have been identified by research coincide remarkably well with those outlined earlier by Freud. What about the much larger group of people who by these standards are unsuitable for those forms of psychotherapy which place a premium on the patient's verbal skills and his ability to take some distance from his feeling?

From a practical point of view, the answer seems to lie not in making them more amenable to available methods of psychotherapy—sometimes this can be done, although it is a difficult and time-consuming effort—but in becoming more selective about making the limited facilities and the limited professional manpower available to those who can most readily benefit from them. Rather than being "undemocratic," this appears to be a counsel of reality. Research might make an important contribution by refining the selection of particular patients for particular therapists and for particular therapeutic methods. The challenge for the development of alternative techniques and treatment methods for those who cannot readily benefit from analytically oriented psychotherapy of course continues and is beginning to be met (see the section on behavior therapy). There is a strong possibility that a segment of the failure or near-failure cases can be curtailed through more judicious selection of candidates for therapy.

[11] This problem has been studied by the present writer through experimental investigation designed to explore therapists' emotional reactions to patients presented via sound films and in other settings (see Strupp, 1960a; Strupp and Williams, 1960; Strupp and Wallach, 1965).

Before the advent of the "modern era" in psychotherapy research, that is, before sophisticated methodologists and researchers versed in matters of objective investigation and experimental design concerned themselves with these matters, a group of prominent psychoanalysts, including Glover, Fenichel, Strachey, Bergler, Nunberg, and Bibring (Symposium, 1937), addressed themselves to the issue at the 1936 International Congress of Psychoanalysis at Marienbad. While this group did not make any formal recommendation for judging outcomes, they dealt with the aims of psychoanalytic therapy and its modus operandi. Knight (1941) returned to the problem, listing three major groups of criteria:

1. *Disappearance of presenting symptoms*
2. *Real improvement in mental functioning*
   a. The acquisition of insight, intellectual and emotional, into the childhood sources of conflict, the part played by precipitating and other reality factors, and the methods of defense against anxiety which have produced the type of personality and the specific character of the morbid process;
   b. Development of tolerance, without anxiety, of the instinctual drives;
   c. Development of ability to accept one's self objectively, with a good appraisal of elements of strength and weakness;
   d. Attainment of relative freedom from enervating tensions and talent-crippling inhibitions;
   e. Release of the aggressive energies needed for self-preservation, achievement, competition and protection of one's rights.
3. *Improved reality adjustment*
   a. More consistent and loyal interpersonal relationships with well-chosen objects;
   b. Free functioning of abilities in productive work;
   c. Improved sublimation in recreation and avocations;
   d. Full heterosexual functioning with potency and pleasure.

Knight also called attention to certain limitations which may detract from the full effectiveness of the therapeutic method. These will be recognized as the counterparts of the "good patient" variables previously mentioned. Limitations may be due to: (1) the patient's intelligence; (2) native ability and talents; (3) physical factors, such as muscle development, size, personal attractiveness, physical anomalies, sequelae of previous injury of illness, etc.; (4) permanent crippling of the ego in infancy and childhood; (5) life and reality factors which might impose frustrations, privations, etc., against which the patient must do battle, and which might produce relapses; (6) the patient's economic status, whether there is too little or too much money.

Clearly, Knight's criteria go far beyond a definition of disabling illness and in fact attempt a definition of positive mental health. It is also clear that the objectives of psychoanalytic therapy have always aspired to this ideal, and the outcome statistics reported by the various psychoanalytic treatment centers leave no doubt on this point (Fenichel, 1930).

Knight seems to take it for granted that the evaluations are to be made by the therapist. While the therapist's knowledge of the patient provides a unique vantage point for such appraisals, his objectivity is suspect on several counts, such as personal involvement as well as the segmental view he obtains of the patient's life.

In an effort to meet these criticisms, numerous efforts have been made during the last two decades to develop more reliable and valid measures of therapeutic progress. In one group of studies, various aspects of the patient's behavior—notably his verbalizations—have been quantified (see Auld and Murray, 1955 and Marsden, 1965, for summaries of this literature). Another large group of studies has followed the phenomenological approach, by asking the patient to evaluate his own status (e.g., Strupp, Wallach, and Wogan, 1964). A third approach has dealt with assessments by means of psychological tests. Zax and Klein (1960), following a review of several hundred investigations, conclude that the most serious failing of these approaches is that the criterion measures have not been systematically related to externally observable behavior in the life space of the patients. Their own proposed solution is to develop "criteria of sufficient breadth that they are meaningful and representative of a wide range of functioning and yet, at the same time, circumscribed enough to be measured with reliability" (p. 445). They concede that the development of such criteria is in its infancy, largely because there is no unifying set of principles (a theory of "normal" behavior) to guide observations. Finally, they express the hope that it might be possible to develop "a relatively limited number of norms reflecting basic interpersonal environments which can be useful" (p. 446). The basic problem here seems to be one of bridging the gap between the person's inner psychic experience and his adaptation to an interpersonal environment.

Clearly, there can be no single criterion of mental health or illness. As Jahoda (1958) in her review of current concepts points out, mental health is an individual and personal matter; it varies with the time, place, culture and expectations of the social group; it is one of many human values; and it should differentiate between the person's enduring attributes and particular actions. One prominent value in American culture is that the individual should be able to stand on his own two feet without making undue demands or impositions on others.

From the research point of view, Jahoda discerns six major approaches to the subject: (1) attitudes of the individual toward himself; (2) degree to which a person realizes his potentialities through action (growth, development, self-actualization); (3) unification of function in the individual's personality (integration); (4) individual's degree of independence of social influences (autonomy); (5) how the individual sees the world around him (perception of reality); and (6) ability to take life as it comes and master it (environmental mastery).

In discussing directions for further research Jahoda indicates that we must seek better empirical indicators of positive mental health in all of the above areas; furthermore, it is necessary to specify the conditions under which mental health is acquired and maintained. The need for developing outcome criteria in psychotherapy largely overlaps these requirements and must follow a similar course. While the patient's behavior in therapy will scarcely suffice as an ultimate criterion, it will occupy an important place in the cluster of criteria which will undoubtedly emerge. While the therapy situation is a unique "test situation," intratherapeutic criteria must have a counterpart in the external world, that is, a validity beyond the therapeutic situation. It is noteworthy that in discussing various mental criteria, Jahoda assigns the therapeutic situation an important role for gathering empirical data. I agree that the therapeutic situation could be used to a much greater extent for the purpose of generating criteria of outcome because of the unequaled opportunities it offers for making systematic observations over a prolonged period of time. One of the major working hypotheses of psychoanalysis asserts that the patient's relationship to the therapist (the transference is a faithful replica of the patient's patterns of intimate interpersonal relatedness. As a corollary, it is maintained that the patient's adaptation to his human environment outside the therapeutic situation "improves" (in the sense of becoming less conflictual and more satisfying) to the extent that he is able to relate (less conflictually) to the therapist. The skilled therapist is certainly sensitive to shifts in the patient's patterns of relatedness to the therapist and regards them as valuable indicators of therapeutic change and improvement. Research could do a great deal to systematize and objectify these intratherapy observations (Bellak and Smith, 1956; Strupp, Chassan, and Ewing, 1967) and, wherever possible, relate them to the patient's interpersonal performances outside therapy. In this and other respects, the necessity of "calibrating" the therapist-observer is of prime importance. As long as there is poor agreement on the observations made in the therapy situation, any inferences or predictions are on shaky ground.

An Example of a Competing View: Daseinsanalysis

Psychoanalytic therapy clearly has been influenced by a wide variety of developments in the biological and social sciences, and it would be a major undertaking to trace their effect. The theoretical and technical contributions of the various "schools" of psychotherapy have been described by numerous authors, e.g., Munroe (1955) and Ford and Urban (1963). The new "schools" range from basic acceptance of psychoanalytic teachings with various qualifications (e.g., the Neo-Freudians) to more or less complete rejection of Freudian principles (e.g., operant conditioning, behavior therapy, etc.). Perhaps it may be said that the phenomenologists (exemplified in Europe by the *Daseinsanalysts* and in America by Rogers' client-centered therapy) occupy, broadly speaking, a middle ground. In singling out the *Daseinsanalytic* approach for brief discussion, I do not wish to imply either a personal preference or a judgment about its intrinsic importance for the future development of psychoanalytic therapy. The selection merely reflects a desire to present a view which, while recognizing the significance of Freud's contributions to psychotherapy, advances a sophisticated challenge to the naturalistic foundation of psychoanalytic therapy.

Daseinsanalysis, which has enjoyed a certain popularity in America for some years, is a European import purporting "to combine the assumptions of existential philosophy about the nature of man with the phenomenological method, to achieve a more effective understanding and psychotherapeutic treatment of patients" (Ford and Urban, 1963, p. 445).[12] To some extent, existential analysis represents a reaction to the naturalistic approach to psychotherapy implicit in psychoanalysis, which the proponents of existentialism consider inadequate to deal with the "essential concerns" of man as a mortal and finite being. This view is pitted against a normative (nomothetic) approach, which has been the underlying philosophical assumption of psychoanalysis as well as scientific psychology based on the British empiricist tradition. Essentially, existential analysis is a viewpoint, not a system. Indeed, the very notion of system is anathema to its proponents.

The question of primary importance in the present context relates to the operations of psychotherapy, and the extent to which existential therapy differs from analytic psychotherapy as commonly understood and practiced. In this area one gets little help from the writings of the existentialists although a number of case histories have been published. May (May *et al.*, 1958) has made a serious attempt to explain to American readers what the existentialists mean by "technique." "One might infer," Ford and Urban (1963) observe, "that they [the existentialists] have developed a new way of *thinking about* patients, but it does not lead them to *do anything different* in treatment" (p. 469).

Existential analysis, May (May *et al.*, 1958) explains,

> is a way of understanding human existence, and its representatives believe that one of the chief (if not *the* chief) blocks to the understanding of human beings in Western culture is precisely the overemphasis on technique, an over-

[12] For reviews of the background and objectives of this movement, see May, Angel, and Ellenberger (1958), Ruitenbeek (1962), Ford and Urban (1963), Boss (1963), and Binswanger (1963).

emphasis which goes along with the tendency to see the human being as an object to be calculated, managed, "analyzed." Our Western tendency has been to believe *that understanding follows technique;* if we get the right technique, then we can penetrate the riddle of the patient. . . . The existential approach holds the exact opposite; namely, that *technique follows understanding.* The central task and responsibility of the therapist is to seek to understand the patient as a being and as being-in-his world. All technical problems are subordinate to this understanding (pp. 76–77).

The role and function of the therapist are stated as follows: "The therapist is assumedly an expert; but, if he is not first of all a human being, his expertness will be irrelevant and quite possibly harmful" (p. 82). Without rejecting such concepts as transference, it "gets placed in the new context of *an event occurring in a real relationship between two people*" (p. 83). The term *encounter*, frequently used to describe this "real relationship," has a mystical quality setting it apart from the prosaic concept of the ordinary human relationship. In other respects, too, *Daseinsanalysts* charge psychoanalysis with a variety of flaws, of which the encouragement toward intellectualization and cognitive understanding, as opposed to "true insight," is one. *Daseinsanalysis* stresses the now widely recognized truth that ". . . the human being who is engaged in studying the natural phenomena is in a particular and significant relationship to the objects studied and he must make himself part of his equation. That is to say, the *subject*, man, can never be separated from the *object* which he observes" (p. 26). Existential analysis is intended to "heal" the subject-object split in Western thought.

In a real sense, the difference between existential analysis and psychoanalysis reduces itself to a schism between the European approach to psychology as a *Geisteswissenschaft* and the American approach to psychology as an empirical science. Yet, the existentialists deny a lack of interest in the canons of science. They assert that their approach has its own method of investigation and that the frequently voiced countercharge of scientific inexactitude, mysticism, and a terminology which lacks precise meaning is a result of deficient understanding of the basic tenets of existentialism.

No doubt, the existentialists' emphasis on psychotherapy as a deeply personal and meaningful experience is well taken, and the possibility that a system such as psychoanalysis offers an invitation to substitute impersonal formulations about a patient for a human "encounter" cannot be dismissed lightly. Yet these shortcomings are not necessarily inherent in the system. By the same token, there is no guarantee that an unperceptive practitioner following the existentialist viewpoint can successfully avoid the danger of getting lost in the vagaries of a patient's idiosyncratic experience. Nor is it clear that the advancement of an empirical science is possible without efforts to organize the data of observation in terms of a coherent system.

To the person with aesthetic, artistic, literary, philosophical, and humanistic interests, the existentialist position has a powerful appeal, particularly when viewed in contrast to the "empty organism" approach prevalent in American psychology, which impresses the existentialists as "human engineering" and "manipulation." The tradition of American technology demands that the therapist *do* something, "fix" something, or "set things right." On the other hand, being with another human being, sharing his experience suggests a meditative, passive approach, whose intrinsic therapeutic value has face validity, but whose vaunted superiority is as yet undemonstrated. Psychoanalysis, on the other hand, while having very different philosophical underpinnings from American behaviorism, tends to view man as an "object" governed by psychic forces which can be objectively described and conceptualized. The battle between the competing positions is largely fought on philosophical grounds, and there are insuperable divergences in *Weltanschauungen* which are rooted in the culture and history of Western man. For these reasons it is all the more amazing that existentialist thinking has gained a foothold in American psychotherapy (as well as in other areas of human pursuits).

Still, when all is said and done, psychotherapy is not intended to take the place of a new faith, a philosophy of life, nor is it a solace for the inescapable fact of man's mortality, his limited powers, and his susceptibility to existential suffering, loneliness, and anxiety. While firmly supported by humanistic values, analytic therapy *is* a technique and a technology for helping the patient to deal more effectively and adaptively and less conflictually with himself and others. What sets it apart from religion and philosophy is the attempt to discover and apply psychological principles to problems in human living. In short, it aspires to become a science. A patient, for example, who suffers in his interpersonal relationships because of destructive fantasies, often benefits from interpretation of his emerging fantasies. This requires painstaking work, and the result is an achievement in which both patient and therapist share. Is this an encounter? Is there anything mystical about their relationship? To be sure, the relationship must be simply meaningful in a human sense, but there need be no pathos nor a glorification of the "I-Thou." One may well agree with Sullivan's pragmatic dictum that much of psychotherapy is plain hard work. Encounters there may be as well as occasional "peak experiences," but they appear to be the end result, the culmination of work in which resistances have been cleared away and the patient has become amenable to more direct, less defensive, and less complicated ways of relating to another human being. The therapist must possess empathy, but he also must have technical skill. The seeming paradox that the existential therapists do not do anything "different" in treatment may find its resolution in parsimonious formulations which hew as closely as possible to observable clinical data.

It must also be recognized that in all forms of psychotherapy the patient seems to acquire a conviction, a faith, or a system of beliefs which sustains him in the struggle against his neurotic trends and his relationships with other people and the environment at large. The essence of this faith is difficult to define and may take multiple forms. It may express itself as a sense of trust in the benevolence of a superior being (a personal God); a conviction of the strength of one's own powers, a belief that one can master adversity, cope with the vicissitudes of life and retain a sense of integrity and wholeness, a conviction of the truth of a set of scientific principles—all of which may express that *one is not alone in a hostile world.* The root for this faith may lie in the patient's identification with the therapist, which in turn is based upon the child's trust in his parents (seen by Freud as the prototype of the Judaeo-Christian belief in God as a Good Father). Trust, belief in the essential goodness and protective powers of another person, and love with its counterpart, humility (as opposed to narcissism), appear to be essential components of a person's ego strength. It is difficult to see how any form of psychotherapy can be successful which fails to mediate these qualities through the patient's relationship with the therapist. As noted, we are as yet unclear about *how* this process succeeds in producing therapeutic change—terms like identification and introjection do not really explain it—but observation shows that it happens. The task for research is to spell out the conditions, thus insuring a greater likelihood of their occurrence. This sets psychotherapy apart from religions and other forms of psychological influence. It is apparent, however, that the major world religions have a long priority in their recognition of the overriding importance of what for lack of a better term may be called ***basic trust.***

"Behavior Modification": A Challenge to Psychoanalytic Therapy?

Another challenge to analytic therapy has come from a diametrically opposed quarter, a group of scientists who avow a "hard-nosed" approach to psychotherapy. Their banner, "behavior modification," refers to techniques which are broadly related to the field of learning, "but learning with a particular intent, namely clinical treatment and change" (Watson, 1962, p. 19). Major variants include *operant conditioning* (a term used by B. F. Skinner and his followers), *behavior therapy* (whose most vocal spokesman is H. J. Eysenck), and psychotherapy based on *reciprocal inhibition* (a designation preferred by J. Wolpe). The emphasis of these approaches rests on behavior. To quote Ullmann and Krasner (1965):

The working behavior therapist is likely to ask three questions: (a) what behavior is maladaptive, that is, what subject behaviors should be increased or

> decreased; (b) what environmental contingencies *currently* support the subject's behavior (either to maintain his undesirable behavior or to reduce the likelihood of his performing a more adaptive response); and (c) what environmental changes, usually reinforcing stimuli, may be manipulated to alter the subject's behavior (pp. 1–2).

Historically, behavior modification has its roots in the experimental work of I. Pavlov on the conditioned response, in learning theory as developed within American psychology, and in the behaviorism of John B. Watson. Clinical applications have been spearheaded by Eysenck, Mowrer, Dollard and Miller, Wolpe, and the followers of Skinner. A vast literature attests to the viability and popularity of the approach within American (and to some extent British and South African) psychology. For summaries, see Krasner and Ullmann (1965), and Ullmann and Krasner (1965). The appeal to academic psychologists is supported by the behavior therapists' focus on experiment, empirical proof, and the use of concepts that make a minimum of theoretical assumptions. The proponents believe these tenets are continually ignored by therapists following psychoanalytic teachings, of which behavior therapists as a group are highly critical. The attack on the alleged inutility of intrapsychic variables is epitomized by Eysenck (1959): "Learning theory does not postulate . . . 'unconscious causes,' but regards neurotic symptoms as simple learned habits; there is no neurosis underlying the symptom, but merely the symptom itself. *Get rid of the symptom and you have eliminated neurosis*" (p. 65).

Behavior modification, therefore, is aimed at elimination or modification of the maladaptive response itself, which is considered the problem to which the therapist should address himself. Contrary to psychoanalytic therapy, which views any behavioral act as a complex (overdetermined) resultant of motivational forces, behavior therapy rejects all intrapsychic determinants hypothesized by analytic therapy. Neurotic symptoms thus are seen as analogous to habits which are more or less fortuitously learned without subserving important motivational functions for the individual.

If, as psychoanalytic psychology asserts, a symptom is merely a surface manifestation of an underlying intrapsychic conflict, which fulfills an important albeit abortive function in the individual's adaptation, the suppression or modification of the symptom without change in the underlying psychic structure should lead to the substitution of another neurotic symptom. Citing experimental results, behavior therapists assert that symptom substitution rarely occurs, and they consider it of little consequence. The psychoanalytic model of symptom formation is often regarded by behavior therapists as a "medical model" (supposedly because it postulates underlying causes), whereas the behavior therapy model is extolled as a "psychological" one. Without getting involved in semantics, a rather convincing case can be made that the psychoanalytic theory of neurosis, insofar as it is based on purely psychological concepts, is as much a "psychological" theory as a theory based on conditioning principles.

In any event, behavior therapists have attacked psychoanalytic therapy on account of its inordinate length, expense, its narrow range of applicability, and—above all—its alleged ineffectiveness. Beginning with Eysenck's (1952) article questioning the effectiveness of psychoanalytic therapy, increasingly bolder claims have been advanced (Eysenck, 1961; Wolpe, 1958) for the superiority of behavior therapy, particularly in the treatment of phobias, but more recently also in modifying many other conditions. In view of the difficulty of providing adequate experimental controls, the fluid ity of outcome criteria and their consequent noncomparability, the issue, despite the zeal of the behavior therapists, must be considered unsettled at the present time. The fact that a given technique "works" in particular instances does not necessarily prove the superiority of the underlying theoretical system: all systems of psychotherapy can point to successes (as well as failures), and, as pointed out elsewhere in this chapter, the measurement of psychological change is as yet so tenuous that meaningful comparisons in terms of percentage improvements are untrustworthy and have little more than propagandistic value.

To the credit of the behavior therapists it must be said that their insistence on empirical indicators, their critical scrutiny of concepts that resist validation by scientific methods, and their eagerness to experiment with novel techniques are unmatched by any comparable effort on the side of analytically oriented investigators. The utter simplicity of the approach, too, has an enormous appeal.

Behavior therapists aver that analytically oriented therapists, too, employ reinforcement principles albeit in an unsystematic way and that there are common elements in all forms of psychotherapy. Both of these assertions are probably true. For example, the analytically oriented therapist tends to "reward" patients through more active verbal participation and interpretations when they are working on their problems in nondefensive ways, whereas resistance is "punished" by the therapist's silence. A common element in all approaches is probably the therapist's interest, dedication, and conviction of the "truth" of his theories (Marmor, 1962, calls attention to the self-validating character of all therapeutic theories).

By the same token, analytic therapists use the same ploy ("My opponent does the same thing I do, only less effectively or in an inferior manner") by pointing out that the "indoctrination" of patients in behavior therapy achieves its success largely through a crass exploitation of the transference relationship, and they cite historical evidence to show that, for example, persuading patients to expose themselves to phobically avoided situations is an old technique.

One of the most impressive criticisms of behavior modification is its simplistic view of human behavior and neurosis. It has little to say about such complex problems as neurotic depressions, obsessive-compulsive disorders, character problems, and the wide range of difficulties in living which patients typically present to the therapist, in addition to specific neurotic symptoms (like phobias). The number of patients who complain of isolated neurotic symptoms, as any clinician can testify, is exceedingly small. On the other hand, behavior therapists have pioneered in treating patients whose intellectual and personality resources usually make them unsuitable candidates for analytic therapy, which clearly places a premium on the patient's ability to verbalize, to enter into a collaborative relationship with a therapist, and to immerse himself in the "as if" relationship of the transference.

The argument of objectivity, scientism, and the "proven principles" of learning theory, with which behavior therapists buttress the claims of superiority for their position, has recently been challenged from an unexpected source—by psychologists versed in learning theory (Breger and McGaugh, 1965). Characterizing the behavior therapists' position as "untenable" (p. 340), these authors adduce evidence to show that learning-theory principles are not nearly so well established as is maintained by the behavior therapists. They conclude that "there seems to be enough question about what goes on in verbal conditioning itself to indicate that it cannot be utilized as a more basic explanation for complex phenomena such as psychotherapy" (p. 346). Furthermore, "Wolpe's case histories are classic testaments to the fact that he cannot, and does not, apply the symptom approach when working with actual data" (p. 350). Breger and McGaugh argue that the phenomena of neurosis do not fit a stimulus-response theory and that intrapsychic variables are a more adequate way of conceptualizing neurotic disturbances.

> To sum it up [Breger and McGaugh state], it would seem that the behaviorists have reached a position where an inadequate conceptual framework forces them to adopt an inadequate and superficial view of the very data that they are concerned with. They are then forced to slip many of the key facts in the back door, so to speak, for example, when all sorts of fantasy, imaginary [sic], and thought processes are blithely called responses (p. 350).

The therapeutic effectiveness of a system, even if it could be convincingly demonstrated, which at present seems impossible, remains only one criterion by which to judge its value. Perhaps a more important one is its actual and potential explanatory value to account for the major phenomena within its domain. In this realm, I believe, psychoanalytic theory has no serious contender.

Concluding Comments

In critically assessing the current status of psychoanalytic psychotherapy one cannot fail to record a certain disappointment with the achievements and promise of this method of therapy. While continuing to occupy a position of high prestige in the United States, psychoanalysis has sustained a loss in scientific status. This conclusion emerges despite the fact that the last few decades have witnessed the emergence of research studies dealing with aspects of the *general* theory of psychoanalysis. Furthermore, there has been an unprecedented increase in the number of therapists whose training has been deeply influenced by Freudian principles, which in more or less diluted form make up the core of the "psychodynamic viewpoint." The steady rise in the number of therapists has been a result of the momentous growth of psychiatry, clinical psychology, and psychiatric social work. Graduates of these training programs, under the impact of the enormous social need for their services, have broadened their activities to include brief psychotherapy, group therapy, family therapy, and numerous other variants. In this connection, a fair amount of informal experimentation has occurred. Many therapists who have been trained in "orthodox" psychoanalysis, too, appear to treat sizable numbers of patients by forms of psychotherapy other than strict psychoanalysis. Withal, there has been a growing awareness of the necessity to tailor psychotherapy to the needs of an ever-expanding patient population, many of whose members do not meet the rigorous criteria originally postulated for psychoanalytic treatment.

Contrary to a trend of the 1940's, when psychoanalysis was considered the panacea for virtually all of modern man's ills and the "royal road" to the solution of difficulties in living, there is now a reluctance on the part of both patients and therapists to engage in long-term intensive treatment, which seemingly had a tendency to occupy longer and longer time spans. Analyses lasting six, eight, or even ten years were at one time not at all uncommon but now are becoming rarer. This is not to deny the need for intensive therapy in certain cases, but therapists also realize that psychotherapy eventually reaches a point of diminishing returns, beyond which further therapy becomes inexpedient if not positively harmful. However, in the absence of conclusive research, only broad clinical indicators are available to guide the therapist in determining this juncture.

Although there continue to be heard the strident voices of caustic critics who would dismiss the value of psychoanalytic therapy altogether, there seems little question that patients do improve and that they benefit from psychotherapy carried on over an extended period of time. Clinical experience amply documents the value of psychoanalysis and psychotherapy based on psychoanalytic principles with a good many patients. This assertion seems warranted despite the absence of ironclad criteria by which to measure the effectiveness of therapy. The problem is that other forms of psychotherapy can point to comparable successes, and the superiority of any method of therapy remains a moot question.[13] There are no reliable criteria for differentiating "structural changes in the ego" from "transference cures," nor can we as yet explain, except on a post hoc basis, why the outcomes of therapy are sometimes impressive and at other times disappointing.

Among additional factors accounting for the lessening enthusiasm for psychoanalytic therapy is the absence of incisive advances in the technology of psychotherapy during the last quarter of a century. This lack of progress beyond Freud's discoveries is particularly striking in comparison with rapid developments in such fields as psychopharmacology, genetics, and psychophysiology—to name but a few. It shall be left undecided whether such comparisons are relevant or justified; the fact remains that with the increasing recognition of the mental health problem by governmental bodies and the public at large, the clamor for efficient, inexpensive, and "easy" solutions has received a great impetus. In contrast, it is alleged in various quarters that psychoanalytic psychotherapy has failed to answer the challenge, and—what amounts to a more serious charge—has blithely ignored its existence. The accusation has been made that instead of objectively examining its premises and systematically studying its operations in collaboration with cognate sciences, psychotherapy (and particularly organized psychoanalysis) has withdrawn to an ivory tower, from which it contemplates increasingly esoteric problems without paying attention to the societal problems which urgently demand solution.

These feelings of dissatisfaction are voiced not only by unsympathetic or uninformed critics, but also by prominent therapists and theoreticians whose extensive training and experience command respect. It will not do to call their strictures "unresolved transferences" or worse. Too, it must be recognized that the psychoanalytic *mystique* (Glover's term) has exerted an untoward influence on the free development of the field. The close alliance of organized psychoanalysis with psychiatry and medicine, the likelihood of whose occurrence Freud already viewed with foreboding (see Szasz, 1961; Eissler, 1965) and the guild character of organized psychoanalysis in America have been constricting influences which have impeded research and unfettered inquiry. As Shakow (1965) observed, "A scientific area belongs ultimately to its investigators, not to its practitioners. No field can maintain its vitality, in fact, its viability, without such a group. One of

[13] I cannot take seriously Eysenck's contention that a large proportion of patients with serious neurotic problems in living "spontaneously improve" within one to two years of "onset." Such a statement is simply at variance with clinical observation.

the most cogent criticisms that can be made of psychoanalysis at the present is that it has neglected this indispensable rule for growth" (footnote 1, p. 355). Because of its largely self-imposed isolation, psychoanalysis has deprived itself of the help and collaboration of well-trained investigators (notable exceptions notwithstanding) and engendered negative attitudes in governmental and private organizations which control the purse strings of research support. Some of these deficiencies are gradually being remedied (e.g., a somewhat larger number of candidates are receiving analytic training for research purposes), and to some extent thorough training in psychoanalytic therapy and research is available to persons with background training in a variety of fields, from organizations other than the "official" training institutes.

It is quite possible that astounding advances are not to be expected in a field like psychoanalytic therapy. With respect to the problem of personality change, therapists, beginning with Freud, have been impressed with the generally slow rate, and perhaps it bears underscoring that analytic therapy is not aimed at rapid cures but strives for "gradual, unconscious emotional rearrangements" (Hammett, 1965). Precisely, how such rearrangements come about is a problem about which much remains unclear, but they do occur and may be broadly viewed as a function of an emotional learning process.

However, even in the absence of radically new discoveries, systematic inquiries dealing with the selection of patients, the effect of the therapist's attitude, and emotional commitment, the handling of transference manifestations, the problem of making therapy a maximally meaningful affective experience, and so on, are by no means impossible. Many of these problems, despite great technical and practical difficulties, *are* amenable to research, given the good will, patience, and persistence of investigators working in collaboration with therapists. Advances, too, may come from laboratory investigations and from hitherto unsuspected sources. However, I believe that the predictability of psychotherapeutic outcomes can be significantly enhanced by research conducted *within the framework* of the psychotherapeutic situation. While psychotherapy may be destined to remain a clinical art,[14] it seems reasonable to hope that its technical tools can be sharpened by investigative efforts. So far, it must be admitted, objective research in the area has had few practical applications for clinical practice. But it must also be kept in mind that psychotherapy is still a young science, with a long historical tradition but a short scientific history.

If, in conclusion, I may indulge in some speculation about promising areas of advance, I would say that the basic discoveries of Freud relating to the dynamic unconscious, the emergence of transference phenomena and

[14] The high level of skill achieved by some practitioners is truly impressive, and better ways should be sought to communicate this expertise.

their handling in the unique dyadic relationship of the analytic situation continue to hold our best hope for the future. Among the many unexplored but potentially fruitful approaches I would name: (1) investigations aimed at studying characteristics of patients for whom this form of therapy (or empirically proven variants) is most suitable; (2) intensive study of variables in the personality of the therapist which, in conjunction with his technique, mediate the therapeutic influence.

With respect to (1), systematic study may serve to restrict psychoanalytic therapy to patients for whom it is clearly applicable and who are most likely to profit from it. Furthermore, systematic investigation along these lines may lead to the development of more specific therapeutic techniques for patients with particular personality structures and problems in living. Such specification is an urgent requirement.

With respect to (2), we may succeed in isolating better methods for ascertaining "patient-therapist compatibility," thus heightening the chances for an emotionally meaningful experience and re-education. Experimentation with variations in technique (coupled with a clearer formulation of technical principles) should be undertaken in the context of the personality of the therapist, from which technique is inseparable.

Advances in these areas, of course, are contingent upon the solution of a variety of technical problems, including the measurement of therapeutic change (Luborsky and Schimek, 1964), and specifications of the character of the therapeutic influence.

With honest and sustained effort, psychotherapy may show steady, if not stupendous, progress. Just as any educational process is gradual, so psychotherapeutic changes may remain slow and even tedious. As in the field of education, not all persons are equally educable. There seems little doubt that for a long time to come problems in living, created or aggravated by untoward interpersonal events in a person's emotional development, can be effectively resolved by more favorable human experiences as provided through psychotherapy. This is not to gainsay the possibility that personality changes can *also* be achieved in other ways, including techniques of psychotherapy that are based on divergent theoretical assumptions. But analytic psychotherapy, insofar as it remains rooted in empirical observations, aims at a theory of rational and planful personality change which does full justice to the complexities of the human personality. In this respect, it has a great advantage over the variety of simplistic schemes that are tending to pre-empt the contemporary scene. What the field can ill afford is an attitude of smugness, an air of finality, or unsupported claims of superiority over all contenders. It may turn out that pharmacological agents or other measures may be more "efficient" for certain purposes than psychotherapy. However, by working toward realistic goals, and by abandoning grandiose aspirations, analytic therapy seems to be assured of its value as a potent weapon in man's continued fight against neurotic suffering and misery. We may be sure that the future will not be utopia, but neither need there be cause for despair.

Note: I am indebted to the following friends and colleagues for critical and constructive comments: Drs. Ron Fox, Ken Lessler, Lester Luborsky, and Judd Marmor.

References

Alexander, F. "Analysis of the Therapeutic Factors in Psychoanalytic Treatment." *Psychoanalytic Quarterly*, 19 (1950), 482–500.

Alexander, F. "Some Quantitative Aspects of Psychoanalytic Technique." *Journal of the American Psychoanalytic Association*, 2 (1954), 685–701.

Alexander, F. *Psychoanalysis and Psychotherapy*. New York: Norton, 1956.

Alexander, F. "Unexplored Areas in Psychoanalytic Theory and Treatment." *Behavioral Science*, 3 (1958), 293–316.

Alexander, F., and French, T. M. *Psychoanalytic Therapy: Principles and Applications*. New York: Ronald Press, 1946.

Auld, F., Jr., and Murray, E. J. "Content-Analysis Studies of Psychotherapy." *Psychological Bulletin*, 52 (1955), 377–395.

Bellak, L., and Smith, M. B. "An Experimental Exploration of the Psychoanalytic Process." *Psychoanalytic Quarterly*, 25 (1956), 385–414.

Berman, L. "Countertransferences and Attitudes of the Analyst in the Therapeutic Process." *Psychiatry*, 12 (1949), 159–166.

Bibring, E. "Symposium on the Theory of the Therapeutic Results of Psycho-Analysis." *International Journal of Psycho-Analysis*, 18 (1937), 170–189.

Binswanger, L. *Being-in-the-World: Selected Papers of. . . .* New York: Basic Books, 1963.

Boss, M. *Psychoanalysis and Daseinanalysis*. New York: Basic Books, 1963.

Breger, L., and McGaugh, J. L. "Critique and Reformulation of 'Learning-Theory' Approaches to Psychotherapy and Neurosis." *Psychological Bulletin*, 63 (1965), 338–358.

Breuer, J., and Freud, S. "Studies on Hysteria" (1895). *The Standard Edition of the Complete Psychological Works of. . . .* London: Hogarth Press. Vol. 2, pp. 1–305. (Also published as *Studies on Hysteria*. New York: Basic Books, 1957.)

Eissler, K. R. *Medical Orthodoxy and the Future of Psychoanalysis*. New York: International Universities Press, 1965.

Eysenck, H. J. "The Effects of Psychotherapy: An Evaluation." *Journal of Consulting Psychology*, 16, (1952), 319–324.

Eysenck, H. J. "Learning Theory and Behavior Therapy." *Journal of Mental Science*, 105 (1959), 61–75.

Eysenck, H. J. "The Effects of Psychotherapy." In H. J. Eysenck (ed.), *Handbook of Abnormal Psychology*. New York: Basic Books, 1961. Pp. 697–725.

Fenichel, O. "Statistischer Bericht über die therapeutische Tätigkeit, 1920–1930." In *Zehn Jahre Berliner Psychoanalytisches Institut*. Vienna: Internationale Psychoanalytischer Verlag, 1930. Pp. 13–19.

Ferenczi, S., and Rank, O. "The Development of Psychoanalysis." *Journal of Nervous and Mental Disease* (1925), Monograph No. 40.

Fey, W. F. "Doctrine and Experience: Their Influence upon the Psychotherapist." *Journal of Consulting Psychology*, 22 (1958), 403–409.

Fiedler, F. "The Concept of an Ideal Therapeutic Relationship." *Journal of Consulting Psychology*, 14 (1950), 239–245. (a)

Fiedler, F. "A Comparison of Therapeutic Relationships in Psychoanalytic, Nondirective, and Adlerian Therapy." *Journal of Consulting Psychology*, 14 (1950), 436–445. (b)

Fiedler, F. "Factor Analyses of Psychoanalytic, Nondirective, and Adlerian Therapeutic Relationships." *Journal of Consulting Psychology*, 15 (1951), 32–38.

Ford, D. H., and Urban, H. B. *Systems of Psychotherapy: A Comparative Study*. New York: John Wiley, 1963.

Frank, J. D. "The Dynamics of the Psychotherapeutic Relationship: Determinants and Effects of the Therapist's Influence." *Psychiatry*, 22 (1959), 17–39. (a)

Frank, J. D. "Problems of Control in Psychotherapy as Exemplified by the Psychotherapy Research Project of the Phipps Psychiatric Clinic." In E. A. Rubinstein and M. B. Parloff (eds.), *Research in Psychotherapy*. Washington, D.C.: American Psychological Association, 1959. Pp. 10–26. (b)

Frank, J. D. *Persuasion and Healing: A Comparative Study of Psychotherapy*. Baltimore: Johns Hopkins Press, 1961.

Freud, Anna. "The Ego and the Mechanisms of Defence" (1936). New York: International Universities Press, 1946.

Freud, Anna. "The Widening Scope of Indications for Psychoanalysis: Discussion." *Journal of the American Psychoanalytic Association*, 2 (1954), 607–620.

Freud, S. "The Future Prospects of Psycho-Analytic Therapy" (1910). *The Standard Edition of the Complete Psychological Works of. . . .* London: Hogarth Press. Vol. 11, pp. 141–151. (Also in *Collected Papers of. . . .* New York: Basic Books, 1959. Vol. 2, pp. 285–296.)

Freud, S. "The Handling of Dream-Interpretation in Psycho-Analysis" (1911). *The Standard Edition of the Complete Psychological Works of. . . .* London: Hogarth Press. Vol. 12, pp. 89–96. (Also in *Collected Papers of. . . .* New York: Basic Books, 1959. Vol. 2, pp. 305–311.)

Freud, S. "The Dynamics of Transference" (1912). *The Standard Edition of the Complete Psychological Works of. . . .* London: Hogarth Press. Vol. 12, pp. 97–108. (Also in *Collected Papers of. . . .* New York: Basic Books, 1959. Vol. 2, pp. 312–322.) (a)

Freud, S. "Recommendations to Physicians Practicing Psycho-Analysis" (1912). *The Standard Edition of the Complete Psychological Works of. . . .* London: Hogarth Press. Vol. 12, pp. 109–120. (Also in *Collected Papers of. . . .* New York: Basic Books, 1959. Vol. 2, pp. 323–333.) (b)

Freud, S. "Further Recommendations on the Technique of Psycho-Analysis I. On Beginning a Treatment" (1913). *The Standard Edition of the Complete Psychological Works of. . . .* London: Hogarth Press. Vol. 12, pp. 121–144. (Also in *Collected Papers of. . . .* New York: Basic Books, 1959. Vol. 2, pp. 342–365.)

Freud, S. "On the History of the Psycho-Analytic Movement" (1914). *The Standard Edition of the Complete Psychological Works of. . . .* London: Hogarth Press. Vol. 14, pp. 7–66. (Also in *Collected Papers of. . . .* New York: Basic Books, 1959. Vol. 1, pp. 287–359.) (a)

Freud, S. "Further Recommendations on the Technique of Psycho-Analysis. II. Recollecting, Repeating and Working Through" (1914). *The Standard Edition of the Complete Psychological Works of. . . .* London: Hogarth Press. Vol. 12, pp. 145–156. (Also in *Collected Papers of. . . .* New York: Basic Books, 1959. Vol. 2, pp. 366–376.) (b)

Freud, S. "Observations on Transference Love" (1915). *The Standard Edition of the Complete Psychological Works of. . . .* London: Hogarth Press. Vol. 12, pp. 158–171. (Also in *Collected Papers of. . . .* New York: Basic Books, 1959. Vol. 2, pp. 377–391.)

Freud, S. "The Ego and the Id" (1923). *The Standard Edition of the Complete Psychological Works of. . . .* London: Hogarth Press. Vol. 19, pp. 12–66.

Freud, S. "Inhibitions, Symptoms and Anxiety" (1926). *The Standard Edition of the Complete Psychological Works of. . . .* London: Hogarth Press. Vol. 20, pp. 87–156.

Freud, S. "Analysis Terminable and Interminable" (1937). *The Standard Edition of the Complete Psychological Works of. . . .* London: Hogarth Press, Vol. 23, pp. 216–253. (Also in *Collected Papers of. . . .* New York: Basic Books, 1959. Vol. 5, pp. 316–357.)

Freud, S. "An Outline of Psychoanalysis" (1938). *The Standard Edition of the Complete Psychological Works of. . . .* London: Hogarth Press. Vol. 23, pp. 144–207.

Fromm-Reichmann, Frieda. *Principles of Intensive Psychotherapy.* Chicago: University of Chicago Press, 1950.

Gill, M. M. "Psychoanalysis and Exploratory Psychotherapy." *Journal of the American Psychoanalytic Association,* 2 (1954), 771–797.

Glover, E. "Common Technical Practices: A Questionnaire Research" (1940). In E. Glover, *The Technique of Psycho-Analysis.* New York: International Universities Press, 1955. Pp. 261–350.

Goldstein, A. P. *Therapist-Patient Expectancies in Psychotherapy.* New York: Macmillan, 1962.

Hammett, V. O. "A Consideration of Psychoanalysis in Relation to Psychiatry Generally, circa 1965." *American Journal of Psychiatry,* 122 (1965), 42–54.

Harper, R. A. *Psychoanalysis and Psychotherapy: Thirty-six Systems.* Englewood Cliffs, N.J.: Prentice-Hall, 1959.

Hartmann, H. "Technical Implications of Ego Psychology." *Psychoanalytic Quarterly,* 20 (1951), 31–43.

Hollingshead, A. B., and Redlich, F. *Social Class and Mental Illness.* New York: John Wiley, 1958.

Jahoda, Marie. *Current Concepts of Positive Mental Health.* New York: Basic Books, 1958.

Janis, I. L. "The Psychoanalytic Interview as an Observational Method." In G. Lindzey (ed.), *Assessment of Human Motives.* New York: Rinehart, 1958. Pp. 149–182.

Knight, R. P. "Evaluation of the Results of Psychoanalytic Therapy." *American Journal of Psychiatry,* 98 (1941), 434–446.

Krasner, L., and Ullmann, L. P. (eds.). *Research in Behavior Modification: New Developments and Implications.* New York: Holt, Rinehart, & Winston, 1965.

Levy, N. A. "An Investigation into the Nature of Psychotherapeutic Process: A Preliminary Report." In J. H. Masserman (ed.), *Psychoanalysis and Social Process.* New York: Grune & Stratton, 1961. Pp. 125–140.

Luborsky, L. "Psychotherapy." In P. R. Farnsworth and Q. McNemar (eds.), *Annual Review of Psychology.* Palo Alto, Calif.: California Annual Reviews, 1959. Vol. 10, pp. 317–344.

Luborsky, L., and Schimek, Jean. "Psychoanalytic Theories of Therapeutic and Developmental Change: Implications for Assessment." In P. Worchel and D. Byrne (eds.), *Personality Change.* New York: John Wiley, 1964. Pp. 73–99.

MacAlpine, Ida. "The Development of the Transference." *Psychoanalytic Quarterly,* 19 (1950), 501–539.

Marmor, J. "Psychoanalytic Therapy as an Educational Process." In J. H. Masserman (ed.), *Psychoanalytic Education.* New York: Grune & Stratton, 1962. Pp. 286–299.

Marmor, J. "Psychoanalytic Therapy and Theories of Learning." In J. H. Masserman (ed.), *Science and Psychoanalysis.* New York: Grune & Stratton, 1964. Vol. 8, pp. 265–279.

Marmor, J. Personal communication, 1967.

Marsden, G. "Content-Analysis Studies of Therapeutic Interview: 1954 to 1964." *Psychological Bulletin,* 63 (1965), 298–321.

May, R., Angel, E., and Ellenberger, H. F. (eds.). *Existence: A New Dimension in Psychiatry and Psychology.* New York: Basic Books, 1958. Pp. 37–91.

Menninger, K. *Theory of Psychoanalytic Technique.* New York: Basic Books, 1958.

Munroe, Ruth L. *Schools of Psychoanalytic Thought.* New York: Dryden Press, 1955.

Orr, D. W. "Transference and Countertransference: A Historical Survey." *Journal of the American Psychoanalytic Association,* 2 (1954), 621–670.

Rado, S. *Psychoanalysis of Behavior: Collected Papers of. . . .* Volume I: (1922–1956), Volume II (1956–1961). New York: Grune & Stratton, 1956, 1962.

Rapaport, D. "The Structure of Psychoanalytic Theory: A Systematizing Attempt" (1959). *Psychological Issues,* 2, No. 2 (1960), Monograph No. 6.

Reich, W. *Character-Analysis.* New York: Orgone Institute Press, 1949.

Rioch, Janet MacK. "The Transference Phenomenon in Psychoanalytic Therapy." *Psychiatry*, 6 (1943), 147–156.

Ruitenbeek, H. M. *Psychoanalysis and Existential Philosophy*. New York: Dutton, 1962.

Shakow, D. "Seventeen Years Later: Clinical Psychology in the Light of the 1947 Committee on Training in Clinical Psychology Report." *American Psychologist*, 20 (1965), 353–362.

Stone, L. "The Widening Scope of Indications for Psychoanalysis." *Journal of the American Psychoanalytic Association*, 2 (1954), 567–594.

Stone, L. *The Psychoanalytic Situation: An Examination of Its Development and Essential Nature*. New York: International Universities Press, 1961.

Strachey, J. "The Nature of the Therapeutic Action of Psychoanalysis." *International Journal of Psychoanalysis*, 15 (1934), 127–159.

Strachey, J. "Papers on Technique: Editor's Introduction." *The Standard Edition of the Complete Psychological Works of Sigmund Freud*. London: Hogarth Press. Vol. 12, pp. 85–88.

Strachey, J., Glover, E., Fenichel, O., Bergler, E., Nunberg, H., and Bibring, E. "Symposium on the Theory of the Therapeutic Results of Psychoanalysis." *International Journal of Psycho-Analysis*, 18 (1937), 125–189.

Strupp, H. H. "Psychotherapeutic Technique, Professional Affiliation, and Experience Level." *Journal of Consulting Psychology*, 19 (1955), 97–102.

Strupp, H. H. "Toward an Analysis of the Therapist's Contribution to the Treatment Process." *Psychiatry*, 22 (1959), 349–362.

Strupp, H. H. *Psychotherapists in Action*. New York: Grune & Stratton, 1960. (a)

Strupp, H. H. "The Nature of the Therapist's Contribution to the Treatment Process." *American Medical Association Archives of General Psychiatry*, 3 (1960), 219–231. (b)

Strupp, H. H. "Patient-Doctor Relationships: Psychotherapist in the Therapeutic Process." In A. J. Bachrach (ed.), *Experimental Foundations of Clinical Psychology*. New York: Basic Books, 1962. Pp. 576–615.

Strupp, H. H. "Psychotherapy Revisited: The Problem of Outcome." *Psychotherapy*, 1 (1963), 1–13.

Strupp, H. H., Chassan, J. B., and Ewing, J. A. "Toward the Longitudinal Study of the Psychotherapeutic Process." In L. A. Gottschalk and A. H. Auerbach (eds.), *Methods of Research in Psychotherapy*. New York: Appleton-Century-Crofts, 1967. Pp. 361–400.

Strupp, H. H., and Wallach, M. S. "A Further Study of Psychiatrists' Responses in Quasi-Therapy Situations." *Behavioral Science*, 10 (1965), 113–134.

Strupp, H. H., Wallach, M. S., and Wogan, M. "Psychotherapy Experience in Retrospect: A Questionnaire Survey of Former Patients and Their Therapists." *Psychological Monographs*, 78, No. 11 (1964), Whole No. 588.

Strupp, H. H., and Williams, Joan V. "Some Determinants of Clinical Evaluations of Different Psychiatrists." *American Medical Association Archives of General Psychiatry*, 2 (1960), 434–440.

Szasz, T. S. *The Myth of Mental Illness: Foundations of a Theory of Personal Conduct*. New York: Paul B. Hoeber, 1961.

Thompson, Clara. *Psychoanalysis: Evolution and Development.* New York: Hermitage House, 1950.

Ullmann, L. P., and Krasner, L. (eds.). *Case Studies in Behavior Modification.* New York: Holt, Rinehart, & Winston, 1965.

Watson, R. I. "The Experimental Tradition and Clinical Psychology." In A. J. Bachrach (ed.), *Experimental Foundations of Clinical Psychology.* New York: Basic Books, 1962. Pp. 3–25.

Wolpe, J. *Psychotherapy by Reciprocal Inhibition.* Stanford, Calif.: Stanford University Press, 1958.

Wolstein, B. *Transference: Its Meaning and Function in Psychoanalytic Therapy.* New York: Grune & Stratton, 1954.

Wolstein, B. *Countertransference.* New York: Grune & Stratton, 1959.

Zax, M., and Klein, A. "Measurement of Personality and Behavior Changes Following Psychotherapy." *Psychological Bulletin,* 57 (1960), 435–448.

13

Short-Term Psychotherapy

LEWIS R. WOLBERG

With the growing emphasis on community mental health, the psychoanalyst is increasingly being called on to organize, administer, and participate in community programs. Among these are projects to shorten psychotherapy in order to bring its benefits within the reach of the masses of people who are in need of therapeutic services. The abbreviated goals that this undertaking requires, as well as the deviations from classical technique that short-term treatment necessitates, may run counter to the philosophies and habitual practices of the psychoanalyst. A review of the virtues and limitations of short-term therapy and a delineation of the specific contributions psychoanalysis may make to it are the aims of this chapter.

Perhaps the most complete study of the effectiveness of brief therapy is that of Avnet (1962, 1965), who reported on the pioneer pilot project on short-term psychiatric benefits of Group Health Insurance, Inc. Most of the 1,200 participating psychiatrists were analytically trained and long-term oriented. Although skeptical about the potentialities of short-term approaches, they were interested in the medical insurance aspects. A follow-up study on 801 cases was done, averaging about two and one-half years after the project had terminated. Admitting the crudity of measurements and the lack of an available completely reliable scientific instrument for assessing results, 81 per cent of patients reported recovery or improvement, a figure roughly comparable to the 76 per cent figure of assessments of the psychiatrists. There is little question that a strong feeling existed on the parts of both patients and psychiatrists that some changes for the better occurred as a result of the few sessions made available to the patients. It was difficult to identify the denominators that could select the 20 per cent who had failed to show improvement. Diagnosis was hardly a clue, since an equal rate of improvement was scored among psychotic, neurotic, and personality disorders. Sixty per cent of those classified by the psychiatrists in advance as having a poor prognosis responded with "cure" or "improvement."

When we examine the quality of improvement achieved by short-term therapy, it should occasion no surprise to discover that while symptom relief has occurred, and while there has been a more or less rapid return to adaptive functioning, no extensive change has been registered at termination of therapy in the personality organization itself.

Personality reconstruction is a long and difficult pursuit. Required is a taming of archaic impulses, enhancement of the repertory of adaptive reactions, and a reduction of the severity of the conscience to enable the individual to deal more appropriately with his inner needs and external demands. These exhaustive objectives are too often blocked by impregnable defenses, even with extended therapy.

A cardinal principle in short-term therapy is acceptance of modest and nonperfectionistic goals. Actually control, modification, and removal of symptoms are important and legitimate objectives. From the standpoint of the patient they constitute a primary aim. From the therapist's perspective they are rewards that can help both to sustain the patient in the face of continued stress and to promote greater self-fulfillment. Expediency may make mandatory as rapid as possible a restoration to symptom-free functioning.

A dilemma poses itself here. Symptoms often serve as sources of motivation to induce the patient to explore his conflicts and to work through their effects toward a more constructive adjustment. If symptoms are relieved, the patient is presumed to be happy to return to his previous devices, balancing himself precariously until a new stress source unsettles his equilibrium. However, the relief of symptoms and restoration to productive daily operations can have a constructive impact on self-esteem. This may in turn encourage more mature coping mechanisms. Reduction of tension enables the individual to utilize his assets more proficiently and to minimize his liabilities. Nonetheless, it may not be possible to arrange for the control of one's environment at all times to guarantee homeostasis.

A more extensive goal, even where rapid symptom relief is mandatory, would then seem to be in order, in the form of a heightening of the individual's capacities for adaptation at least one notch. Before considering the techniques for accomplishing this, we may realistically appraise what the possibilities are for reversal of deeply imbedded personality traits.

No matter how ambitiously the therapist may pursue treatment, he is confronted with limitations in all patients in their potentials for growth. Three kinds of patterns may clinically be observed. There are those tendencies so deeply buried in the personality matrix that they seem to pursue an autonomous course operating almost like reflexes. No amount of insight, inducement, or authoritative censure seems capable of modifying their expression or lessening their force. These tendencies are probably rooted in conditionings established during the first months of life, before capacities for conceptualization have occurred. They seem as natural to the person as breathing or moving. For instance, where the individual had been separated from his mother for long periods in infancy, he may never have developed feelings of trust. Apathy, depression, a penchant for oral gratification, a suspicion of people, and a consideration of the world as menacing may survive as traits that contaminate the most bountiful reality situation in his adult life. Disintegrative tendencies may follow upon actual situations of deprivation, the ego being structured on an extremely infirm footing.

A second group of tendencies are patternings developed somewhat later which serve spurious functions, and which in execution promote conflict. This group appears to be susceptible to some control through willful inhibition once the individual appreciates the nature and destructive consequences of his patterns. He may then be able to suppress certain strivings or else to rationalize their existence. While they may continue to press for expression, their mastery becomes for him an important objective. Rooted in needs and drives which promote anxiety, they are sometimes relegated to the unconscious. The recognition of the sources of his promptings may, if the individual is sufficiently motivated, enable him to exercise some command over them, and, rarely, even to eliminate them completely. For example, a child whose assertiveness during the second year of life was inhibited by controlling parents insistent that children be seen and not heard may discover that when he mobilizes sufficient aggression and rage he can get his way. "Hell-raising" then becomes a pattern essential to expression of assertiveness. Recognition that his aggression is resented by those with whom he becomes intimately related, and insight into the sources of affiliation of assertiveness with aggression, may enable him to experiment with modes of assertive display dissociated from hostility and aggression. A child fondled too seductively by a parent may become too stimulated sexually and detach from the parent and/or from sexual feelings. Intimate relationships in adult life may precipitate incestuous associations and inhibit sexual expression. Awareness of how his unfortunate conditionings have crippled him may enable the individual to experiment sexually with the objective of establishing new habit patterns. As Freud pointed out, a host of pathological conditionings may invest the sexual and aggressive drives, and the person, as a consequence, may develop inhibitions of function along with distorted and perverse modes of expression. He may be burdened by essentially childish, undeveloped needs, and he may be fixated in activities that survive as outlets for sex or aggression that gratify these drives, but for which he must pay a toll in insecurity, damaged self-esteem, and vitiated potential. This group of neurotic promptings may, with proper therapy, where the individual is sufficiently motivated, undergo some modification. The person may either learn to live with his handicaps or he may be better able to regulate them. With reconstructive therapy, an individual with adequate incentive and flexible defenses may be able to develop more mature ways of feeling and behaving.

A third group of patterns are more malleable, not being subjected to such severe repression. They are not repetitively and compulsively insistent on pursuit beyond reason. These develop in the periods beyond early childhood. Constituting a bulk of the individual's coping mechanisms, they are the most plastic of tendencies. In therapy they may be influenced substantially; they may even spontaneously resolve in the face of productive life experiences.

Disappointment in psychotherapy is often registered when, after an ambitious, carefully designed, and prolonged program of treatment the patient continues to resist giving up the first group of tendencies, and must exercise his will power in keeping the second group in abeyance. One needs to appreciate that all human beings are so constituted that no amount of therapy, as we practice it today, may be able to alter some personality components, since they have become too firmly a part of the neuronal matrix. Acceptance of a therapeutic objective short of complete personality reconstruction becomes a harsh reality.

Apart from limited potentialities for development, with fragility of coping mechanisms and poverty of organized defenses, goal modification is sponsored by other constituents, such as limited incentives, reduced readiness for change, realistic restrictions of available time and finances, secondary gains that put a premium on neurotic behavior, and society's insistence that the individual abide by neurotic standards. Moreover, there are serious qualifications in all of our existing therapeutic methods apart from strictures in skill and personality of the psychotherapist. A short-term therapeutic interlude which accepts an abbreviated goal as its aim attempts to sidestep the dilemma of the psychotherapist who is so often frustrated in bringing his patients to personality reorganization in depth.

Under the pressure of long waiting lists, short-term therapy is often relegated to psychiatric residents who have had a circumscribed training.

On the whole, the results have been not too unsatisfactory, accepting the bounded goal of symptom relief. There are many nonspecific healing factors that precipitate out of any patient-therapist relationship that may, apart from the specific techniques employed, reduce anxiety and permit spontaneous reparative forces to restore the habitual defenses. Exposure to any kind of an interview situation is of potential help to a patient. The more skilled the interviewer, the greater the benefit. But, irrespective of the sophistication of the interviewer, the effects of interpersonal contact can have important therapeutic values. Among the intercurrent factors that precipitate out of the interaction is the placebo effect, inspired by faith, hope, and trust which in itself may suffice to suppress anxiety. Additionally, the interview situation provides the patient with an opportunity for emotional catharsis, the ability to relieve himself of fearsome emotions and burdensome thoughts in an accepting rather than punitive atmosphere, and thus enables him to revalue the malignancy of his past experiences and present impulses. It presents an opportunity for support from an idealized parental figure, a means of subduing helplessness through dependency, thus to become enveloped in a protective gauze. It gives the patient an opportunity to obtain some guidance and direction as to ways of overcoming stress from a person who is more objective than himself about his chances for a better adjustment. It exposes him to the bounties of suggestion which permit him to pursue actions with a diminished neurotic deterrent. It allows him to experience the impact of dyadic group dynamics with its potential of modifying aberrant values. It fosters some clarification and understanding into what is happening to him, establishing greater mastery over inner conflict, evolving healthier inhibitions, and providing more rational controls. It exposes him, where the therapist is drug-minded, to the adjunctive instrumentalities of tranquilizing and energizing medicaments, or to hypnosis and other devices to lessen his tension. These combined agencies may in themselves serve to release spontaneous reparative forces and to restore the homeostatic equilibrium. In persons with fairly intact ego structures, short interaction with a therapist may restore customary modes of adaptation. Assuming that the initiating external stress situation or existing inner conflict can be tempered, or a new and better adjustment subsidized, no further therapy may be needed.

A word of caution is justified. Where one depends on the bounties of a short-term supportive approach as described above, it is usually expedient to interrupt treatment at the peak of therapeutic gain, particularly where the therapist is not dynamically oriented and does not know how to deal with transference and resistance. However, the temptation is great to continue therapy beyond the short-term time limits, in the hopes of spreading the benefits to deeper strata. Where this is done the placebo element may lose its effect, and the idealized relationship may become displaced by an image of the therapist as a nonmagical figure with human frailties. Disappointment with and resentment toward the therapist substitute for expectant trust. Transferential contaminants will then come into operation, particularly where the therapist utilizes probing techniques. Should defenses be challenged, resistances will rear themselves, stirring up tension and reviving symptoms.

The analytically trained psychiatrist has a great advantage here, for he may advantageously move beyond the supportive phase toward a penetration of the defensive armor, in the hopes that the patient will gain sufficient understanding to alter some underlying value systems. In doing this, the therapist is under no illusion that he can duplicate in the short treatment span the extensive changes possible in motivated patients where oceans of time are available for working-through. Yet, it is essential to remember that time spent formally in therapy is not the only variable involved in therapeutic gain. It is but one, and perhaps not the most important, of the many factors that enter into the ingredients of cure. A proficient therapist can accomplish more in five sessions than a bungling therapist can in five hundred.

Since there is little time available in brief therapy to resolve therapist-patient entanglements and misunderstandings, the therapeutic climate must be as consistently warm as possible. Only then can it survive random outbursts of stormy weather developing when resistances are challenged. The therapist must be so constituted that he can maintain an equitable climate in the face of turbulent winds. Perhaps the most disabling barrier to good short-term psychotherapy are personality promptings in the therapist that interfere with a warm working relationship. These may show up only under unique conditions and with certain kinds of patients, and, when they occur, the therapist may not be aware of their presence.

If we were to attempt to outline personality qualities that sponsor the proper therapeutic climate for short-term therapy, we might categorize them as follows:

1. The therapist must be sufficiently skilled and sensitive to recognize important trends from the patient's productions, verbal and nonverbal, both in relation to the reality situation and to inner feelings and conflicts. He must be able to discern his own anxieties and defensive operations as they are extended toward the patient and toward the material that is being discussed.

2. Essential is a tolerant, nonjudgmental attitude toward the patient's neurotic interpersonal operations. This kind of objectivity encourages the avoidance of emotional involvement with the patient, and permits of the handling of demands for unqualified love, acceptance, support, preference, omniscience, and omnipotence. It allows for constructive management of hostility, antisocial impulses, and unwholesome transference projections, without counterhostility, disgust, ambition, power drives, and perverse sex-

uality. The therapist may without awareness encourage the expression of neurotic drives in the patient, such as a hostile defiance of authority and an inordinate striving for fame, power, and perfectionism. An inability to tolerate the expression in the patient of those impulses that mobilize anxiety in the therapist may cause him to circumvent important areas like sexuality, aggressiveness, and hostility, to divert the patient when he approaches these painful zones, and to obstruct the working-through of his conflicts. Neurotic concerns over his self-esteem may make it difficult for the therapist to accept the patient's acting-out tendencies and resistances. A compulsion to be liked and admired may prevent the therapist from challenging the patient's defenses. Perfectionistic tendencies, unresolved hostilities, inability to take criticism, lack of humor, and failure to acknowledge self-limitations are other destructive traits. Where the therapist possesses traits that make him relate to the patient in ways similar to those of the parent with whom the patient is or has been neurotically involved, a therapeutic impasse may be expected. It is, of course, impossible for any one person not to possess some of the untoward constituents mentioned, but these must be blended with a good measure of constructive characteristics if the therapeutic process is to develop ultimately toward reconstructive objectives.

Of necessity the analytically trained short-term therapist will have to modify his classical technique in order to be effective with his patients. Free association must be abandoned in favor of the focused interview. One may be able to tease out of the content of the patient's verbalizations the precipitating stress factors (Harris, Kalis, and Freeman, 1964) that presumably initiated the present illness, or the current symptoms or problems that plague the patient and cause him distress. Sensitivity to nonverbal communication, to slips of speech, and to the revelations of dreams will quickly affiliate the current complaint factor with the underlying character structure, and then establish the connections with the genetic underpinnings of personality rooted in early experiences with important authorities.

Activity must substitute for the traditional passivity and noninvolvement (Bonime, 1953), in the course of which it will be necessary to deal with emerging transference as well as countertransference reactions to avoid smothering the patient by playing God. Flexibility of approach presupposes the employment of drugs where necessary (Lesse, 1960, 1962; Linn, 1964), hypnosis (Wolberg, 1948), group therapy (Keeler, 1960; Philip and Peixotto, 1959), family therapy (Goolishian, 1962), behavior therapy (Wolpe, 1958), and other procedures.

It will be obvious from this that eclecticism in method is the keynote of short-term therapy, even though the orientation is a dynamic one. A limitation of sessions to once or twice weekly replaces the frequent appointments essential in the orthodox technique. Interviewing is face-to-face, the recumbent position being avoided. Whenever transference begins to crystallize, it is handled as rapidly as possible to prevent the development of a transference neurosis. Therapist interventions are not confined to interpretation and purely informative actions as reality testing; active guidance and advice are given where necessary.

A number of models of short-term therapy are now in operation. For example, Levy (1966) reports a crisis-oriented program of psychotherapy in a mental health clinic, limited to six sessions, geared to the needs of severely disturbed individuals who have lost their ability to function. The results indicate how useful strategically timed short-term therapy can be and accent the importance of utilizing available manpower in such a program. The first session lasts forty-five minutes; the remaining five sessions are only thirty minutes each. Medication, environmental manipulation, active family involvement, and coordination of the services of many involved community agencies are among the techniques employed. Of 500 patients treated in 14 months, only 7 required institutionalization!

A total staff mobilization for short-term therapy in an outpatient clinic to render immediate help for patients rather than to put them on a waiting list has been described by Gelb and Ullman (1966). A prompt identification is made of (1) the patient's mode of neurotic functioning and the elements of reality distortion which are producing stress, (2) alternative modes of interaction available to the patient that can lead him to a more constructive adaptation, and, (3) nascent environmental disturbances that are provocative of the patient's disorganization as distinguished from those he is creating. Flexibility of approach with avoidance of a preconceived and limiting theoretical framework, emphasis on the patient-therapist relationship with activity and spontaneity being encouraged in the therapist, the use of experienced co-therapists temporarily teamed with less experienced team members, and the employment of family therapy, group therapy, as well as other indicated therapeutic modalities has made this approach a most effective one, rapidly eliminating waiting lists. Sixty per cent of treated patients improved and completed their treatment within five visits.

Attempting to differentiate two kinds of psychotherapy of short duration, Sifneos (1966) has described an "anxiety provoking" psychotherapy on a once-a-week basis, utilizing psychoanalytic concepts, geared toward reconstructive goals, which lasts from two months to one year, for patients with circumscribed neurotic symptoms. Employing transference feelings explicitly, it focuses on conflicts underlying the patient's symptoms. Improved self-esteem and acquisition of new adaptive patterns have been observed in follow-up visits. Prior to the organization of a neurosis from a current emotional crisis, "crisis intervention" may be undertaken in sessions that last up to two months, with a preventive impact. "Anxiety suppressing" psychotherapy, using various supportive techniques, is the second kind of short-term therapy described which helps severely disturbed patients achieve marked symptomatic relief without any evidence of dynamic change.

Many other models of short-term therapy exist or are now being experimented with, conditioned by the experience and theoretical orientation of the professionals and the policies of the agencies under whose supervision the work is being done.

The principal goals toward which a short-term treatment effort is directed are these: (1) to modify or remove symptoms and to relieve suffering, (2) to revive that level of adaptive functioning the patient possessed prior to the outbreak of his illness, (3) to promote an understanding of the most obvious problems that sponsor symptoms, sabotage functioning, and interfere with a more complete enjoyment of life, (4) to present ideas of how to recognize these problems at their inception, (5) to provide some way of dealing with such patterns and their effects toward a more productive adjustment.

An examination of effective operative tactics reveals the following:

1. Even at the first session an attempt is made to establish a working relationship while getting as complete information from the patient as possible.

2. At the end of the first session, the patient is given some explanation for his symptoms in language he understands, employing concepts with which he has some familiarity.

3. There is an emphasis that the treatment period will be limited, and that results will depend on how the patient applies himself to the guidance given him. He is told that if he does so there is no reason why he should not experience relief from his symptoms.

4. During the succeeding visits an attempt is made, if possible, to establish patterns that have been operating in the patient's life of which the current stress situation is one immediate manifestation.

5. There is an exploration to see if these patterns have roots in how the patient was reared, particularly in his early childhood and his relationship with his parents and siblings.

6. By pointed questioning the patient is encouraged to put the pieces together for himself, particularly to figure out why he was no longer able to make an adjustment prior to coming to treatment.

7. There is an exploration as to why the patient is now unable to work out his present difficulty, bringing him to an awareness of how and why he is resisting or is unable to resolve his trouble.

8. The patient is encouraged in self-observation and he is taught how to relate his symptoms to precipitating happenings in his present environment as well as to conflicts within himself.

9. In the event tension, anxiety, or depression are too severe, tranquilizing or energizing drugs may temporarily be utilized.

10. Hypnosis may be introduced when adaptational collapse is present or resistance is obdurate.

11. In phobic symptoms that do not resolve with interpretation, behavior therapy may be employed.

12. Dream exploration may be instituted where advantageous.

13. The patient is helped actively to execute insight into action, and to desensitize himself to painful situations.

14. He is encouraged to develop a proper life philosophy.

15. Therapy is terminated with the recognition that the immediate accomplishments may be modest, but that the continued application of self-understanding will help bring about more substantial changes.

It is generally recognized that the sicker patients will need some helping resource, perhaps for the remainder of their lives. This may be in the form of (1) occasional visits to the therapist (brief 15-to-20-minute sessions every two weeks may suffice), (2) group therapy where multiple transferences will help lessen the intensity of the hostile dependency, a consequence of prolonged individual therapy, or, (3) a social group in which relationships are relatively casual, defenses are supported, and energy outlets supplied.

Short-term therapy, even where the methods are supportive or reeducative, is much more effective where it is executed in a psychodynamic framework (Alexander, *et al.*, 1946; Wolberg, 1965). Even a few therapeutic interviews may unbalance the adaptive equation that has ruled the patient's existence, to make possible permutations that register themselves in the intrapsychic structure. Where the individual has been brought to an optimal level of functioning with amelioration or abolition of his symptoms, where he has achieved some understanding of the initiating factors in the difficulties for which he sought help, where he becomes aware of the presence of some pervasive personality problems that sabotage his happiness, where he relates aspects of such problems to his current illness, and where he gains a glimmer of awareness into early sources of difficulty in his relationship with his parents and other significant agencies, he will have the best opportunity to proceed beyond the profits of symptom relief.

At the Tavistock Clinic, an experiment under Michael Balint addressed itself to the reconstructive potentialities of insight-oriented brief psychotherapy (Malan, 1963). Patients were selected on the basis that they seemed able to explore their feelings; the therapists were psychoanalytically oriented. The study concluded that in from ten to forty sessions "it is possible to obtain quite far-reaching improvements not merely in symptoms, but also in neurotic behavior patterns, in patients with relatively extreme and long-standing neurosis." There was strong evidence that early interpretation of transference played an important part toward a favorable outcome, particularly the negative transference and the connection of the current feeling toward the therapist with the attitudes toward both parents. Helpful also was interpretation at termination of grief and anger responses.

A follow-up study of a large group of private patients receiving from one to thirty sessions revealed extensive personality changes in many individuals (Wolberg, 1965). These patients had apparently been able to utilize their brief therapeutic experience as a catalyst for growth.

The fact that the various kinds of short-term psychotherapy in the hands of competent therapists bring about approximately the same proportion of cures persuades one that the techniques and stratagems that are employed are among the least important elements responsible for improvement. The proposition is inviting that therapeutic maneuvers merely act as a means through which the therapist encourages the emergence of positive and the resolution of negative healing elements (Marmor, 1966). Thus if a therapist feels most comfortable with a more active approach than with a less active one, with hypnosis rather than formal interviewing, with behavior therapy rather than analytically oriented therapy, he will probably be able to help more patients than were he to force himself to use a procedure with which he is not at ease. This is not to depreciate the virtues of any of the existing techniques, nor to indicate that supportive tactics have the reconstructive potential of evocative and depth approaches; however, we tend to overemphasize technical virtuosity while minimizing the vital healing processes that emerge in the course of the helping relationship as a human experience. In many cases, insight acts merely as a placebo.

The nonspecific windfalls of insight do not invalidate the specific profits that can derive from a true understanding of the forces that are undermining security, vitiating self-esteem, and provoking actions inimical to the interests of the individual. In opening up areas for exploration, the short-term therapist must confine himself as closely as possible to observable facts, avoiding speculations as to theory so as to reduce the suggestive component. The more experienced the therapist, the more capable he will be of collating rapidly pertinent data from the patient's verbal content and associations, gestures, facial expressions, hesitations, silences, emotional outbursts, dreams, and interpersonal reactions toward assumptions that, interpreted to the patient, enable him to reflect on, accept, deny, or resist them. Dealing with the patient's resistances to the acceptance of interpretation and to the utilization of his expanded awareness toward change, the therapist continues to examine his original assumptions and to revise them in terms of new data that present themselves. A hopeful prospect is that therapeutic change will not cease at termination of the short-term contact, but that it will continue the remainder of the individual's life.

References

Alexander, F. *et al.* *Psychoanalytic Therapy*. New York: Ronald Press, 1946.

Avnet, H. H. *Psychiatric Insurance: Financing Short-Term Ambulatory Treatment*. New York Group Health Insurance Company, 1962.

Avnet, H. H. "How Effective Is Short-Term Therapy? Appraisal of Mental Health after Short-Term Ambulatory Psychiatric Treatment." In L. R. Wolberg (ed.), *Short-Term Psychotherapy*. New York: Grune & Stratton, 1965.

Bonime, W. "Some Principles of Brief Psychotherapy." *Psychiatric Quarterly*, 27, No. 1 (January 1953), 1–18.

Gelb, L. A., and Ullman, M. " 'Instant Psychotherapy' in an Outpatient Psychiatric Clinic—Philosophy and Practice." Paper presented at the 122nd Annual Meeting of the American Psychiatric Association, Atlantic City, New Jersey, May 13, 1966.

Goolishian, H. A. "A Brief Psychotherapy Program for Disturbed Adolescents." *American Journal of Orthopsychiatry*, 32 (1962), 142–148.

Harris, M. R., Kalis, B. L., and Freeman, E. H. "An Approach to Short-Term Psychotherapy." *Mind*, 2 (1964), 198–205.

Keeler, M. H. "Short-Term Group Therapy with Hospitalized Nonpsychotic Patients." *North Carolina Medical Journal*, 21 (1960), 228–231.

Lesse, S. "Psychotherapy in Combination with Ataractic Drugs." *American Journal of Psychotherapy*, 14 (1960), 491–504.

Lesse, S. "Psychotherapy in Combination with Anti-Depressant Drugs." *American Journal of Psychotherapy*, 16 (1962), 407–423.

Levy, R. A. "A Practical Approach to Community Psychiatry in a Remote City—What Is Six Session Psychotherapy?" Paper presented at the 122nd Annual Meeting of the American Psychiatric Association, Atlantic City, New Jersey, May 13, 1966.

Linn, L. "The Use of Drugs in Psychotherapy." *Psychiatric Quarterly*, 38 (1964), 138–148.

Malan, D. H. *A Study of Brief Psychotherapy*. London: Tavistock Publications, 1963.

Marmor, J. "The Nature of the Psychotherapeutic Process." In G. L. Usdin (ed.), *Psychoneurosis and Schizophrenia*. Philadelphia: Lippincott, 1966. Pp. 66–75.

Philip, B. R., and Peixotto, H. E. "An Objective Evaluation of Brief Group Psychotherapy on Delinquent Boys." *Canadian Journal of Psychology*, 13 (1959), 273–280.

Sifneos, P. E. "Crisis Psychotherapy." In J. H. Masserman (ed.), *Current Psychiatric Therapies*. New York: Grune & Stratton, 1966. Pp. 125–127.

Wolberg, L. R. *Medical Hypnosis*. New York: Grune & Stratton, 1948.

Wolberg, L. R. (ed.). *Short-Term Psychotherapy*. New York: Grune & Stratton, 1965.

Wolpe, J. *Psychotherapy by Reciprocal Inhibition*. Stanford, Calif.: Stanford University Press, 1958.

14

Family Development

JOAN J. ZILBACH

It is the customary fate of new truths to begin as heresies and to end as superstitions

—T. H. HUXLEY

It follows from the nature of the facts which form the material of psychoanalysis that we are obliged to pay as much attention in our case histories to the purely human and social circumstances of our patients as to the somatic data and the symptoms of the disorder. Above all, our interests will be directed towards their family circumstances—*and not only, as will be seen later, for the purpose of inquiring into their heredity*

—S. FREUD, 1905a, p. 18

Introduction

Family therapy as a distinct clinical area of interest, therapeutic practice, and research is recent in origin. However, it is neither so new as to be regarded as heresy nor yet so staid or established as to have given rise to many superstitions and traditions. As with all developing fields, disagreement and strife are to be expected, and even encouraged, in the interest of stimulating its growth and clarification. It is sometimes said that psychoanalysis as a field has not been concerned with this new clinical area and that intrapsychic concerns must be left behind if we are to understand and work directly with families. It is the intent of this chapter to indicate that certain aspects of psychoanalysis or a psychoanalytic orientation to family therapy are not only useful, but even essential in facilitating a deeper understanding of family dynamics and therapy.

Freud's interest in family life represented a new trend in psychiatric or psychological thinking during the early part of the twentieth century although his primary interest was in the effects of family patterns on the individual rather than in the family as an interacting and structural social unit. It was not until after several decades of psychoanalysis that he began to focus on some of the system properties of groups in his "Group Psychology and the Analysis of the Ego" (1921) although, somewhat earlier, his interest in this problem had already manifested itself in "Totem and Taboo" (1913b). Nonetheless, it is worth examining the many ways in which the significance of family life and family relations recurred in his work.

In 1905 he stated that "above all, our interests will be directed towards the family circumstances"—of our patients (1905a). In the case of "Little Hans" (Freud 1909b), the actions and statements of both parents were utilized to understand the development of the phobic illness and the actual family circumstances were considered in some detail. In several other early papers (1907, 1908, 1909a) Freud referred to parents in the course of his primary concern with the early development of children. A direct effect on children of parents is indicated briefly (Freud 1913a) when he mentions the easily understood lies told by children who are "imitating the lies told by grown-up people."

In "Totem and Taboo" (1913b) Freud confronts more directly the intense emotional currents among members of the primitive family. Whether or not one accepts the speculative historical explanation of the formation of strains and counterstrains in the family, this primitive level of intrafamilial dynamics involves impulses and affects that must be acknowledged as a substrate if we are to understand more deeply the complexities of family functioning.

Still later, in "Group Psychology and the Analysis of the Ego" (1921), Freud continued his concern with extra-individual matters. The opening paragraph of this essay deserves careful consideration:

> The contrast between individual psychology and social or group psychology, which at first glance may seem to be full of significance, loses a great deal of its sharpness when it is examined more closely. It is true that individual psychology is concerned with the individual man and explores the paths by which he seeks to find satisfaction for his instinctual impulses: *but only rarely and under certain exceptional conditions is individual psychology in a position to disregard the relations of this individual to others* [italics mine—J.J.Z.]. In the individual's mental life someone else is invariably involved, as a model, as an object, as a helper, as an opponent; and so from the very first individual psychology, in this extended but entirely justifiable sense of the word, is at the same time social psychology as well (Freud, 1921, p. 69).

Freud's early awareness of the complexity of family relationships and their bearing on developmental processes was evidenced in the formulation of the Oedipus complex. The Oedipus complex has been recognized as a momentous struggle in the life of the individual, but we must be reminded that it involves family members and has many ramifications in later family patterns. The structure and the development of the superego also brings us directly into contact with family influences, particularly that of the parents (Freud, 1923).

In later work Freud continued his concern with the *primal* family and its origins in his efforts to understand the function of communal relationships. It is worth noting that not only did Freud's concern extend beyond the individual to the impact of family relations, but also that he attached profound significance to extrafamilial systems such as those of the community. This concern and some of his most important thought about the relation between man and society are clearly stated in "Civilization and Its Discontents" (1930), where he introduces the issue of the complex patterns of relations between family and community. These primitive forces in family development and the links both to individual and extrafamilial forces have been largely overlooked in much the same way as sexual development was initially ignored in the understanding of the development of an individual. These forces in the family lead to an inevitable potential for conflict between the family and the larger society (similar to the Oedipus complex between the individual and his parents) which must be resolved. These are largely dealt with not by the individual, but in the family as a group over time (that is, in the course of family development).

Another relevant factor is Freud's important reminder that a child has a different estimate of his parents at different periods of his life (Freud, 1933). Certainly the child presents new issues in family life at different stages of its development, but a consideration that has received less attention and has seemed less self-evident is that changes also occur in the parents over time. Thus, although there is little question that a child's estimates of his parents change as a function of *his* development, some of these altered estimates result from the realistic changes the *parents* undergo as a function of their own development as adults and as a function of changes in the family as a whole. More generally, as we shall elaborate in the next section, the family as a whole undergoes developmental changes over time, many of which are a result of changes in life cycle and the life situation although one should not neglect the effect of intrapsychic and extrafamilial factors.

Building on Freud's fundamental early contributions, the systematic advance of psychoanalytic ego psychology has provided a larger framework for understanding the individual in relation to the external world. In "The Problem of Anxiety" (1926) Freud devoted his attention to the defensive maneuvers of the ego. Following on these suggestions, Anna Freud (1936) carried these considerations further. Although her formulations represent a relatively early statement of the problem, the importance of the "influences of the outside world" on ego formation emerged explicitly and led inevitably to greater attention to direct "extra-analytic" observations of the child as seen in the nursery. This, in turn, led to greater concern for the mother-child relationship. This is still far from the observation of total families, but it signifies a basic shift in orientation to include a wider range of socal units as relevant to the understanding of behavior and functioning.

Subsequent developments in psychoanalysis provide further links to family theory and therapy. Hartmann expanded enormously the range of psychoanalytic ego psychology in understanding many facets of the ego in relation to the social environment (Hartmann, 1939). Erikson's attention to the influence of social and cultural institutions on development and his formulation of a "widening social radius" place the family in a series of interacting social relationships (Erikson, 1959). A number of other studies offer specific contributions for our understanding of family interactions: the importance of unconscious parental wishes on the child's behavior (Bruch and Touraine, 1940; Johnson and Szurek, 1952); the impact of social and family relationships on the reactions to crises (e.g., Lindemann, 1952; G. Bibring, 1959; G. Bibring *et al.*, 1961). The trend seems clear in recent papers that include family issues explicitly in the discussion of psychoanalytic cases (for example, Lomas, 1961; Ellis, 1962). Simultaneously, in recent years a number of analysts have moved more directly into the arena of the family and have dealt directly with families and family relationships (Ackerman, 1958, 1962; Bowen, 1959; Grotjahn, 1959; Jackson, 1957; Lidz, 1958, 1962, 1963; Wynne, Ryckoff, Day, and Hirsch, 1958; Wynne and Singer, 1963). These analytic students of the family have attempted to understand various aspects of families and have largely focused on conceptualizing some particular theme or conflict in family dynamics. Some have given particular attention to communication patterns, others to family structure and substructure, and yet others to patterns of equilibrium and disequilibrium.

Psychoanalysis had its origins in a developmental approach and developmental considerations have remained a major core of psychoanalytic theory and practice (Freud 1905b). The usefulness of the developmental approach in the understanding of human behavior and malfunctioning is by now almost taken for granted, but it is interesting that this approach has so far been confined mostly to the understanding of individuals. *Family developmental* considerations are relatively unfamiliar and warrant our fullest consideration. On the one hand, these have considerable significance in their own right in clarifying family processes, in helping to integrate diverse concepts in family analysis, and in providing an essential consideration in family therapeutic intervention. On the other hand, a clarification of family development has much to contribute to our understanding of, and our specific interventions with, individuals.

Family Development

The term "development" refers to an orderly sequence of changes occurring over time: the progression or unfolding of one expectable stage of organization or function from a previous stage. As psychoanalytic clinicians we usually acknowledge that a patient is in or from a family, but we do not directly concern ourselves with the family as such, except in passing or in a fragmentary way. A question such as "What stage of development has the patient's family achieved?" would strike us as most unfamiliar. Nevertheless, it is possible with families, as with other biological, psychological, or social structures, to speak of development as a process of change over time around expectable life-cycle patterns.

Are there clear-cut patterns that we can describe as stages of family development? If so, what are they? If stages of family development can be specified, are they general or typical either within a given society or cross-culturally? Clearly, family development is a complicated process that involves a number of individuals and many psychological and social forces. The family is a small group, composed of two or more individuals.[1] The development of the family as a unit can be described and understood as a very special type of small group and can be formulated as independent from the development of the individuals within the family.

In a general way families have an early or initial phase (Stage I), subsequent years of growth and development (Stages II–V), later years (Stage VI), and an end. There are certain universal, "normal" characteristics that can be described for each stage of family development.[2] The features of pathological family development may then be seen more clearly. It is important to distinguish pathological from sub-cultural variants around common family themes.

STAGE I

A family starts with the marriage of two individuals (or when two individuals establish a common household).[3] Even at this early stage, the family

[1] The family in this chapter refers to the group living in the household, "under the roof." There are other definitions, particularly in the sociological literature, i.e., family of orientation, family of procreation. For clinical purposes the household definition has empirical advantages as the most general conception of the group in most frequent interaction. This definition is similar to that used in some sociological family research and by the Census Bureau (Christensen, 1964).

[2] By *universal* we mean patterns or themes that apply to many or all societies despite variations in detail. "Normal" or typical characteristics may be universal within our society but may vary cross-culturally. Pathological family development would then have to be related to deviations from the norm of the particular society.

[3] Every family has a prehistory in the form of a courtship, engagement period, etc., which will affect, in many ways, the early days of the family (Rapoport, 1964).

unit may consist of two or more people. A particular family as a household may start with three persons, for example, with the addition from the outset of an in-law, or a child from a previous marriage, or another relative. In many instances the marital couple is incorporated into an already-existing, larger family structure. However, even in an extended kinship pattern the conjugal unit has basic tasks that must be accomplished as a unit partly independent from other household members. The form and timing of task resolution may be modified according to the particular kind of family and household structure.

There are certain *basic family functions* which represent needs or tasks that must be accomplished by any new and distinctive social unit in order to attain a modicum of stability around fundamental social issues (Fried and Fitzgerald, n.d.). These basic family functions continue as a substrate through all stages of family development. Inadequate development, distortion, or omission may occur in any or many of these basic family functions at any stage of family development, but for several of them the earliest phase of family development is most crucial.

Four basic family functions must be established in the first stage of family development: housing-shelter, food, finances-employment, and family health.

1. *Housing-shelter.* There are a variety of arrangements that can adequately establish this basic family function at the outset of a marriage. These arrangements for housing and shelter can vary with personal preferences, with cultural expectations, with economic status, with other social commitments. But the fact that shelter or housing must be established for the family as a common (and distinguishable) unit is quite general. Whatever the arrangement, there are also certain basic qualities that must be fulfilled. Ideally these include (a) adequate size, based on number in the family unit; (b) adequate basic structure so that (c) and (d) are possible; (c) facilities for food preparation; and (d) provisions for other essentials such as heat, light, water, and bathroom facilities. Other qualities such as neighborhood are not so critical but may contain potentials for satisfactory family-community relations or hints for later difficulty.

Although social, cultural, economic, and psychological factors will determine the conception of "adequacy" for each of these housing-shelter requirements, once these are defined and choices made, the actual physical arrangements determine many subsequent features of family behavior and interaction. For example, a lower-class family may accept or tolerate an arrangement with three or four children sleeping in the same room, but this arrangement influences the degree and kind of interaction, the level of conflict, compromise, or consensus that is possible or likely.

An expanded or extended household arrangement can provide adequately for the function of housing, and the two individuals may become a part of a larger household. But the issue of housing must be settled, and the actual and adequate designation of family space for the family unit in the larger household must be made. Such an expanded arrangement is one which seems open to difficulty, but this cannot be assumed without actual evaluation of such arrangements.[4]

2. *Food.* The second family function is that of providing food. Again there are certain minimal standards in terms of (a) adequate consistency of supply, (b) amount consistent with size of family, (c) adequate quality and kind so that minimal nutritional requirements are met, and (d) preparation so that it is edible. Although arrangements for this may vary, this is a universal and continuing need in all starting families. Beyond basic nutritional and preference requirements, it is clear that the significance of food and its association with family and household have many biological and psychological implications. Moreover, the arrangements for purchase, cooking, serving, and cleaning up touch on fundamental psychological issues of reciprocity, of giving and receiving, that are of great general importance in family life.[5]

3. *Finances-employment.* This third basic family function has two subcategories: (a) consistent and adequate supply, from whatever source and (b) adequate distribution, planning, and management of resources (finances). This set of family economic tasks also subserves the first two family functions in providing the source (in a money economy) for the purchase of housing and food.

There are many variations in the way family finances are handled, from a common family fund to separate budgets for different family members (especially husband and wife). A common family fund carries a different affective tone with it into other areas of family functioning than do separate or independent funds. It is also important to note that, since the area of finances-employment is so basic to the family's household functioning, priority in earnings and in rights of distribution carry with it many other influences on family and household arrangement.

Finances may be provided by employment, but there is great variation in how this particular aspect of the larger family function is accomplished. Also, employment should be distinguished from finances in order to see these issues in a more universal way. There are many families for whom finances come from sources other than employment, such as from parents and siblings, from agencies (particularly public ones), or from other sources such as trusts.[6]

[4] This can be seen in certain foreign cultures in which a new room is built onto the existing house for the newlyweds. In many societies in which an expanded household arrangement is frequent (for example, among peasantries, aristocracies), there are fairly rigid social arrangements maintaining boundaries to the relationships between people that might otherwise lead to irresolvable conflict.

[5] The primary needs of an infant bear a striking similarity to those of a family, that is, warmth, shelter, and food.

[6] In this age of early marriages, this can be seen particularly in marriages of young

4. *Family health.* This function is a complex one and should be broadly understood as the family equivalent of public health. This family function can be divided into two subcategories: (a) maintenance of minimal physical and emotional health requirements and (b) recognition of health problems, the special needs of disabled or ill persons, and the utilization of proper facilities. Acute and chronic health needs have different patterns and may require the use of different facilities. This is important in estimating the adequacy of this function in a particular family. In acute conditions the outcome should be the disappearance of the problem and discontinuance of use of facilities. With chronic health needs—the opposite pattern is most effective and adaptive—the recognition of needs should be followed by the continued use of facilities as indicated.

Maintenance of health is an important basic function in a family. In its earliest phase this may be provided primarily on a continuing individual basis as a hold-over from earlier prefamily years, although the pattern may rapidly become a more interlocking and familial one because of the variety of health needs in the family. The recognition and equilibrium within family functioning around both special physical abilities and disabilities is not only a necessary basis for effective performance, but carries with it a host of emotional connotations that are significant in creating a familial sense of reciprocity and appreciation.

5. *Other family functions.* There are many additional family functions, some which are important during this earliest phase of family development and others which emerge as central only at later phases of development. They move in two opposite directions: some potentially create increased closeness and intimacy between family subgroups (for example, husband-wife, or mother-child), and others involve the family in extrafamilial relations as a family unit. In the former category, the establishment of the relationship of the newly formed couple is most critical during the earliest phase of family development. Its fundamental interpersonal features, including the establishment of sexuality in marriage, the development of affectional ties, and the overt and covert authority patterns are of the utmost importance in creating the initial family environment. Moreover, the form and effectiveness of these relationships, although primarily a matter for the marital pair, have considerable significance for the development of the family as a unit. However, it raises highly specialized issues, and the development of the marital unit is itself so large an issue that it goes beyond the confines of this chapter.

---

college students. The arrangement of financial support is a task of the early or initial phase and assumes many forms—total family support of both students (by one or both in-laws), support by a working wife, or various admixtures. The working through of these arrangements must be accomplished, either with or without emotional complications.

In a similar way, it is important to note that the family as a unit develops patterns of relationship with the "outside" world of relatives, friends, and community. Patterns of leisure and recreation are established as a family function in these early years. The actual patterns may, of course, continue to be primarily based on individual rather than on family arrangements since familial patterns of association with other people are not universal. Indeed, this function and the extent to which it is carried out on an individual or on a familial basis vary markedly by social class and cultural pattern. As with interpersonal ties in marriage, however, this is a large and significant topic in its own right, and a full discussion of different patterns during different stages of family development is beyond the scope of this discussion.

The pattern of provision for these basic family functions may manifest flexibility or rigidity, progressive or static characteristics from the very outset, and it may continue progressing and changing or remain relatively unaltered during all stages of family development. But there is no simple relationship between the establishment of effective methods of dealing with these issues at any one stage of development and the adaptability of the approach to new problems and issues posed by changes in the family situation. Thus, the patterns may be established satisfactorily for the earliest period of family organization and then continue to function on that same level, remaining fixed and inflexible. On the other hand, the patterns may appear quite inadequate during the first stage of development, and yet prove adaptable and increasingly (or varyingly) effective during subsequent developmental family phases. Moreover, the patterns of provision for basic family functions may not be uniform; there may be difficulties in only one, or two, or in all of these functions that emerge in the earliest stage of family development. An important area for investigation, however, is the extent to which it is possible to anticipate or predict the potential for adaptation among different families from an examination of the early patterns of marriage and marital organization and of the profile of difficulties and achievements.

The basic family function of provision of family finances is recognized more often than the first two basic family functions of food and housing-shelter as a source of problems in early family development. It is common for families or individuals to recall during a later discussion, "Oh, we've always had trouble with money." However, direct scrutiny of the first two functions will often reveal interesting and significant material. Thus, a middle-class family with two children was worried about their older adolescent daughter, and she was referred for school difficulties. Initially this family indicated that they were otherwise comfortable—financially and socially. Further investigation revealed that the mother had always worked and the father, who contributed "when he could," was in one of his longest and most consistent working periods. When in the course of diagnostic family sessions the girl indicated some feelings of deprivation, the issue of food was specifically pursued. The girl indicated that she never had breakfast. This was not an adolescent whim. *There was often no food in the house.* The mother bought food sporadically, and, since she did not get up in the morning, breakfast food was often omitted. The mother's working arrangement fitted with this pattern, and the father had arranged his life accordingly. Superficially, housing seemed adequate, but further questioning revealed that the apartment, furniture, and so forth had been chosen at the start of marriage and had never been changed. There were still only two chairs at the small kitchen table of this family of four, and the family members were rarely all at home at the same time.

The pursuit of the issue of food revealed a pattern of insufficiency dating back to the early days of this family. The mother never cooked, and the father was free to eat many meals out. Housing became inadequate later in the development of this family, and finances had a long history of difficulty. The school difficulties that resulted in a treatment referral were related to the effects in this family of the emergence of both children into adolescence. Adolescence, with its increased emotional and financial demands, tipped the precarious equilibrium in this family. The early profile of basic family functions was crucial in understanding the current difficulties.

STAGE II

The first junction point or next stage begins with the entrance into the family of the first child. The first child's dependent state as an infant has been the subject of much study. However, little attention has been devoted to its impact on changes in family organization and functioning. During this second family phase, the first three basic family functions of housing-shelter, food, and finance-employment must undergo many changes and reorganization for satisfactory family development.

Housing must undergo many changes to accommodate new needs, such as the rhythm and sleeping patterns of an infant, and the need for physical separation of the infant from adults. Food needs change not only in amount, but also in kind, and the adaptability of the family in handling divergent food needs becomes tested. Financial arrangements may also involve new pressures for changes. Finances may have to undergo a necessary expansion in amount of income or readjustment or redistribution of available financial resources must take place.

A young artist and his wife provide an example of difficulty at family Stage II. An infant was brought for a diagnostic evaluation. Lengthy infections had been treated by a pediatrician with unsatisfactory results, and there was a question of developmental retardation. After marriage this couple had lived in their studio and the wife continued to work. Food, housing, and finances were satisfactory until the birth of the first baby. The wife returned quickly to work as planned since she provided the stable income. No question had arisen for these parents about the provision of food, shelter, or finances since she had made an adequate sum for the two of them. The increased demands due to the baby resulted in pressure on the artist to sell his work, pressures which previously had not existed. He was not willing to do this. Pursuit of questions about provisions of food and housing revealed that the father often lost track of time and heard nothing when involved in his artistic endeavors. When lost in his work, medication, food, and the cries of the baby went neglected. After these patterns were revealed and more adequate arrangements for baby care were made, the infections improved and development proceeded more satisfactorily. Later the father was able to release his works for sale and the mother was able to decrease her out-of-the-home jobs. The inflexibility of the family in meeting this new demand for family development was not an individual psychological matter, nor was it explained by the "symbolic meaning" of the baby in the family. This couple had developed effective basic family functions in Stage I, but not in Stage II. Treatment pursued these issues as family developmental blocks and a positive family outcome ensued.

During this phase the fourth function of maintenance of family health becomes truly a family function. The health characteristics of the parents or of the child no longer are individual matters. They affect other members of the family in a complex and interlocking fashion. The artist's family that has just been described illustrates this point.

A fifth family function, that of leisure-recreation, also changes markedly during this stage. At this phase a new set of functions enters into family patterns: socialization and other family child-rearing needs. Many of the significant developmental experiences of a child can be fully understood only on a family level. Socialization is an interactive process which begins in the home, in family member-to-member interactions, in the daily experience of eating together and being together. With the expansion of the family, siblings begin to take on important socializing functions as models (positive or negative) and as auxiliary teachers. Toilet training, for example, is markedly influenced by the family structure. The proud first child who has "taught" the second child reflects this. Similarly, Oedipal experiences are modified by the number of siblings with whom they may be played out. Siblings also alter relationships to parents in other ways by offering opportunities to express sexual or aggressive feelings with a larger number of objects.

Stage II of family development establishes the marital couple more thoroughly as a family. Indeed, in many societies a husband and wife are hardly viewed as a family unit until they have a child. Even among some subgroups in our society (for example, among the working class), a sharper distinction is made between a couple and a family (that is, one that includes a child) than is typical in the middle class. Not only does this stage involve an additional member and new family functions, such as socialization of the child, but it implies a reorganization of existing functions and of prior interactions and relationships. Additional children introduce further elements of reorganization in family development and a much wider range of interactions and relationships, but do not require the initial and basic transition to a totally new stage of developmental functioning as does the birth of the first child.

STAGE III

The entrance of the first child into the larger community is the next landmark in family development. Here the development of socialization must take a big step to include the provision of education and other forms of transfer of information from one generation to the next. Education, as part of the sixth basic family function, has some distinctive characteristics in modern industrial societies: (1) regular attendance in school is a minimal requirement; (2) steady, consistent, and appropriate grade progression is expected; and (3) special needs, such as retardation, must be provided for by special facilities.

Here, too, complications from the family viewpoint can take place so that steady attendance of the child at school does not occur. If other family functions are operating precariously the additional needs of the school-age child—getting dressed, breakfasted, and transported—may be too great and the child may frequently stay home. Frequent or prolonged absences from school have often been discussed in terms of the individual developmental problem of the separation of child from mother and vice versa, but the influence of family members other than mother also may be important. The attitudes toward schooling of other important members of an extended household—including those of the maid or nurse in upper-class socioeconomic families—may be crucial and are often overlooked.

The entrance of the child into the larger community also takes place in another arena. Peer relations begin to assume greater importance, and there is a social and emotional trend away from the family with the development of independence and social initiative on the part of the child. The patterns of peer relations vary from the street orientation of working-class neighborhoods, to groups of children in and out of many houses as in some suburban communities, to the more structured schedules and activities of other urban neighborhoods.

The movement of the child away from the home, both in the form of finding new authority figures in school and in the form of establishing new social and emotional relationships with other children in school and in the community, has many implications for family development. On the one hand, it adds a new dimension to family patterns, in the sense that the child now also has an "extrafamilial" life and in the sense that it provides a further (and often a first) link of the family to the local residential community. This link frequently involves the parent in a wider range of social relationships. On the other hand, this trend implies a developmental change within the household itself that may include making physical and psychological room for child visitors, accepting the absence of the child during his play with other children, and a different conception of the family's relationship with the wider world. This can become a serious problem for those families that are unable to accept either new authorities in the child's life or new emotional relationships that may lessen the intensity of ties to the parents.

The addition of other children into the family does not affect the fundamental nature of these various family functions, but rather tests their expandability, their flexibility or rigidity, and their basic effectiveness.

The sequences and details of the next phases of family development become quite complex, and instead of elaborating each phase and the changes that they bring about, they will be mentioned only briefly.

STAGE IV

Pursuing the family along a developmental line, the next steps may vary in sequence. The entrance of the last child into the larger community makes a significant difference in the family. As the last child expands the range of his social and emotional ties beyond the family, basic family functions begin to narrow and the parents begin to take on a wholly new position in family organization. But it is not in any sense a return to the early years of marriage since the family remains as critical a base for functioning as ever although it spills beyond the confines of the household more freely.

STAGE V

The exit of the first child from the family by marriage or by other establishment of an independent household is the next milestone. Until recently there was a widespread impression that the family as a functional entity began to terminate with this event in urban, industrial societies, particularly in the United States. It is now clear that this is far from the case, and there is a striking continuity in ties at all social class levels and for many ethnic groups, between the parents and the new nuclear families developed by their married children. However, there is little understanding of this phenomenon as a "stage" of family development or the ways in which earlier family development patterns affect the organization of these relationships.

STAGE VI

This is signaled by the exit of the last child from the nuclear family. The so-called "shrunken" family in later years may bring with it a new set of family functions. The role of grandparents has been discussed as perceived by the grandchild. Ideally, however, the grandparents' function should encompass the entire family with provision for varying needs. Problems are common. There are grandparents who can deal comfortably with babies and who in their own nuclear family dealt adequately with Stages I and II, but who had many difficulties in Stages III through VI, which are recapitulated in their relationships to grandchildren. Conversely there are grandparents who were incapable of dealing effectively with later stages of development in their own nuclear families and whose growing perspective is an asset during these stages in the family development of their married children's families. The relationships, at a familial level, between parent-child and grandparent-grandchild patterns remain a relatively unexplored area of family-development investigation.

We have been pursuing the issues of family development and basic family functions in an intermingled fashion. This has led to some complexity, but it is not possible to discuss these independently or simply. It is obvious that families change, and by now it may also be evident that families go through meaningful developmental sequences. In the next section we will indicate how the field of family therapy has not usually included family development as a basic concept. Similarly, the existence of basic family functions themselves is not new, but their integration in a systematic fashion, organized and developmental, into the understanding of families is a task yet to be accomplished.[7]

Other Aspects of Family Development

MOTOR ACTIVITY

Keeping in mind the entire social unit, a family level of activity can generally be identified. Individual patterns often seem to predominate, but certain situations make the family motoric level observable. For example, sitting on a beach where many family groups can be scanned, the differences in the activity level of each family group can be seen. Every family has a motor activity level. The families at each end of a spectrum, the very active families and the very inactive, will be noticed most easily and prominently. In early stages of family development, particularly during Stages I and II, an inactive motor level may be harmonious with the development of the family. But for the inactive families varying amounts of strain may enter as the middle stages are reached and as increasing numbers of children enter the larger community.

[7] Family development has been an integral part of the conceptual framework for some family investigators (Rapoport, 1964; Rapoport and Rapoport, 1965; Goodrich, 1961; Rausch, Goodrich, and Campbell, 1963). Family development has been more extensively developed in the field of family sociology (Duvall, 1957, and Hill, 1964).

AFFECTIVE TONE

There is a range of affective expression available to a family group. One may note a particularly striking or predominant affective tone in some families. For example, in the waiting room of a clinic, a somewhat anonymous atmosphere, the affective tone of the entire family may be observed more easily than in the therapy room itself. An observation like, "Gee, they're a happy family," reflects the predominant affect expressed by this family and not the inner state of individual family members. A family may be noisy, sad, even occasionally joyous, and may be consistently characterized in this manner. Here, as with the motoric level, the situations in which this can be observed are those in which other characteristics of the family are submerged. In the middle ranges, a wide and changing range of affective expression will be utilized. When there is a predominant affective tone this may indicate a constriction or exaggeration of available affects.

Sad families are rather easy to identify. In these families the positive and happy affects are relatively absent. There are other predominant affective tones such as cranky families, sharp families, bitter families, and others. The stresses of any period of family development may precipitate such a pattern. Certain affective tones may also be more characteristic for one period than for others. An inability to describe or identify any affect other than an extremely limited range has been observed in delinquent families (Minuchin, Auerswald, King, and Rabinowitz, 1964).

COMMUNICATION PATTERNS

Normal communication patterns vary with the stage of family development. Communication in Stages I and II will have certain characteristic patterns of verbal/nonverbal distribution. In Stage II there must be a necessary progression to increase the amount of nonverbal communication. Families that do not establish these simple lines will carry the deficiencies on into the next stages.

Communication gaps, monopolies, or exclusions of individual family members may be carried on throughout all family stages. For example, a mother brought an adolescent boy for a treatment because of "obnoxious behavior." All family members were seen in family diagnostic sessions. It very quickly became apparent that all verbal communications progressed through the mother who openly said, "I speak for everybody." The family pattern in many other areas along with verbal communication was one of "mother-doing." The request for treatment, which could then be understood, was brought about by an adolescent surge against this pattern of "mother-doing" which included a monopoly of verbal communication with the external world by the mother. The boy's "obnoxious behavior" was a primitive and nonverbal expression of revolt against the family pattern.

This boy had been silent in two previous years of individual treatment. This could then be understood not as "resistance," but rather as a part of a family pattern. Out of the mother's range, where she could no longer do the speaking, all members of this family were insecure, incompetent, and inefficient. In family sessions she spoke first, and they then agreed. In Stages I and II this might be tolerable as primitive nurturance and care. But beginning in Stage II there are inevitably increasing difficulties with such a pattern. In adolescence, particularly, as part of individual development there is a necessary movement away from the family and difficulties with the parent-dominated communication pattern will come into their ascendance.

FAMILY COPING DEVICES

There are family coping devices, normal or abnormal, that may be used in some or all stages of family development. "Coping devices" is a term to be used only on a family level. The equivalent in the individual is "adaptive pattern" or "defense." It is very important for conceptual clarification and development in the field to have terms which are different for use on a family level (Ackerman, 1958). "Splitting off" is one such coping device. When this is prominent it will be used in turn by the family as a whole and by all members.[8] These alignments may take place along any axis in the family, and then regroupings will occur providing there are no factors making the alliance too difficult or too dangerous.

The stage of family development is very important in understanding this family mechanism of "splitting off." In the early stages if splitting occurs the alignments should be short-lived and changing. As the middle stages are reached any fixed alignment of a particular child with a parent may be a problem. In normal family development the pattern of various groupings of children against one or the other parent should predominate. As more children reach adolescence, in the middle stages of family development an alignment of children against parents should predominate. For example, in early family sessions with the T. family a split was observed with mother and daughter aligned against son. Son versus daughter was also observed at times with the son allied with the mother. Later, as the family treatment progressed, the pattern became and remained adolescent daughter and son against the mother. This was a change in the pattern of alignments and must still be identified within the family as splitting. Only by looking at each variation as part of a family pattern could the pieces be understood as they progressed and became parts of a normal family coping device.

There are other aspects of family relationship that have not been discussed in any detail, such as the development of the marital relationship as

[8] There are pathological family situations with intensive and extensive "splits." For a particularly vivid description see Minuchin *et al.* (1964).

it changes over the course of family development and sibling interrelationships as they develop through the life cycles of the family. But we must turn now to a consideration of certain principles underlying family treatment.

Family Dynamics

Disease is from the old and nothing about it has changed. It is we who change, as we learn to recognize what was formerly imperceptible.

—CHARCOT

The recent rapid growth of interest and the expansion of therapeutic endeavors in family therapy and family research by large numbers of therapists with varying backgrounds and orientations make our first task clear, that is, to attempt to open pathways of communication among the various ideas and concepts in these fields. This task requires agreed-on definitions. As a start, the following seem to be reasonable distinctions: (1) *Family* has been defined here as those living together "under the roof," the household group of parents and their children. This is a definition which "works" clinically, recognizing the several variations of this basic nuclear family pattern. (2) The broadening therapeutic interest which involves going beyond the individual patient to other members of the family might be called *family-oriented therapy*. There are approaches in which the basic tool of treatment is some kind of individual session, but the therapist moves from time to time and in various ways to include the other members of the family as part of the diagnostic interest or formulation. In this sense, then, family therapy can be more accurately called family-oriented therapy. This would be used when the primary object of treatment is the individual but there are some attempts to understand the family as a whole as well as component parts of the family. (3) The more specific term, *conjoint family therapy*, could then refer to the treatment process in which the predominant form of treatment session is with all members of the family. Partial conjoint family therapy is family treatment in which only some members are included but the predominant therapeutic focus is still with family members. (4) *Concurrent family therapy* could then refer to concurrent treatment of individual family members.

Several recent bibliographies have made the task of surveying the family literature an easier one (Mishler and Waxler, 1965; Haley and Glick, 1965; Gerver, Peterson, and Arrill, 1965; and Bell and Vogel, 1960). It is not the purpose of this chapter to review all of the numerous articles on various aspects of family-oriented therapies. Rather, after briefly discussing a few of the major publications and extracting some of the concepts found in the family therapy literature, these concepts will be reviewed in light of the implications of family development.

Historically, the first case of family-oriented therapy was the case of "Little Hans" (Freud, 1909b). This deserves careful rereading by all family therapists or people interested in understanding families. This case might be termed a variant of family therapy, partial conjoint family treatment, since the father and the boy were involved in all sessions and the entire family of father, boy, and mother in some of them. This case is unique in the father's being both the analyst and parent. This important characteristic is noted by Freud at the beginning of this case when he says,

> No one else, in my opinion, could possibly have prevailed upon the child to make many such avowals; the special knowledge by means of which he was able to interpret the remarks made by his five-year-old son was indispensable, and without it, the technical difficulties in the way of conducting a psychoanalysis upon so young a child would have been insuperable (Freud, 1909b, p. 95).

And then later:

> Surely there must be a possibility of observing in children at first hand in all the freshness of life, the sexual impulses and wishes which we dig out so laboriously in adults from among their own debris. . . . With this end in view, I have for many years been urging my pupils and my friends to collect observations of the sexual life of children—the existence of which, as a rule, has been cleverly overlooked or deliberately denied (Freud, 1909b, p. 96).

Freud indicated a great curiosity about what, more recently, would be termed "extra-analytic observation" and the direct involvement of relatives. If we extend these comments from material on sexuality which was, at that time, new and in the process of being discovered, we find ourselves today in much the same situation regarding work with total families, and we might employ the same encouragements that Freud used. We need the freshness of on-the-spot observations of families in order to get at the richness of these complex materials. This should be done without reluctance or reservation, and we are better equipped, presumably, these days to move forward in this direction by virtue of our extensive understanding of individual psychodynamics and of group processes. The field of family therapy and family research has indeed moved in these directions after overcoming some of the same hesitation and conservatism that Freud at that time encountered in understanding the inner life of individuals.

At a relatively early date, Flugel (1921) wrote what might be termed a family-oriented book in which he attempted to utilize some psychoanalytic concepts in the understanding of families. The pioneering work of Ackerman in the 1930's had a family orientation which involved concurrent family treatment. His recent work has moved steadily in the direction of increasingly using conjoint family therapy, and his contribution to the field is a most important one (Ackerman, 1958, 1962; Ackerman, Beatman, and Sherman, 1962).

There were several groups of family researchers and therapists who started their family endeavors at about the same time, during the 1950's. These were the groups involved primarily in working with the families of schizophrenics in Palo Alto and elsewhere (Bateson, Jackson, Haley, and Weakland, 1956; Wynne *et al.*, 1958; Wynne and Singer, 1963; Bowen, 1959; Brodey, 1959; and Fleck, Lidz, and Cornelison, 1963). As a whole this work progressed steadily from studies of the individual members of the family group toward studies of the family as a unit and has provided us with some of the most extensive data on family processes and problems of family intervention. In 1961 Bell published a monograph entitled *Family Group Therapy* that was a true conjoint family-therapy venture. By 1964 a summary text of conjoint family therapy had appeared (Satir, 1964).

In the work of Jackson and the Palo Alto group there are two concepts that stand out to date. These are: (1) the concept of family homeostasis and (2) "the double bind."

FAMILY HOMEOSTASIS

The term *family homeostasis* was defined by Jackson as follows:

> The term *family homeostasis* is chosen from the concepts of Claude Bernard and Cannon because it implies the relative constancy of the internal environment, a constancy, however, which is maintained by the continuous interplay of dynamic forces. Another way of considering the topic of "family homeostasis" would be in terms of communication theory: that is, depicting the family interaction as closed information system in which variations in input or behavior are fed back in order to correct the system's response (Jackson, 1957, p. 79).

The idea of the family as a homeostatic system has certain limitations. As it has been used so far, even though it is termed dynamic, there is often a static quality in family system analyses. The very concept of homeostasis implies a series of alterations in function, initially set off by a major internal or external change, resulting in a return to a previous form of stability. Indeed, even on the surface, complex patterns such as those of the family are rarely homeostatic in this sense and the underlying dynamic of family relationships is more consistently one of continuing change, of movement to new (functional or dysfunctional) levels of family development. In a similar way, the use of the concept of the system tends to take for analysis of family behavior a particular slice in time. For example, a recent publication from the Palo Alto group states: "We assume that the family is a system and that the behavior of its members is, therefore, patterned. We assume that these patterns are consistent over *time* [italics mine—J.J.Z.] and that a few minutes of a family's overt interaction will contain the family's basic style" (Riskin, 1964, p. 485). This is an excellent example of the stress on consistency and stability and, thus, of the static quality that is often implicit or explicit when the term "system" is used. In any small segment of time the family's actions are undoubtedly patterned, but if developmental concepts are utilized this pattern that appears in a single short period of time may prove to be an integral feature only of a particular period of family development. The concept of family development implies a *changing* system over time, and perhaps some of the disparity and disjunctiveness of some of the family data would begin to diminish if these concepts were utilized in the analysis of data. "Life is not characterized by stasis but by dynamic progression" (Galdston, 1959). This indicates the necessity for greater conceptual complexity. The family "system" itself is not identical over time; it involves different components (members), different interactions between these components (relationships), and different sources of external influences (extrafamilial patterns), as well as different sources of internal influence (intrafamilial patterns). In a very real sense, therefore, a developmental family framework stresses the changes in family systems over a period of time rather than the phenotypical consistencies of pattern.

DOUBLE-BIND

The concept of the "double-bind" is one of many in the family therapy literature concerned with communication patterns. Although the concept of the double-bind has been used primarily as a component of family communications that account for the development of schizophrenia, it is of more general interest both as a mechanism of family interchange and as a focus of family intervention. Indeed, one of the important questions we might pose is the range of occurrence of double-bind communications in families. Are they limited to the families of schizophrenics or of particular kinds of schizophrenics? Or do they occur quite widely? Are there differences in the frequency or consistency with which it occurs or in the familial subgroups among whom it is evident?

In the earlier section on family development there was some discussion of the changing patterns of communication in the course of this development. The "double-bind" pattern or double-bind messages probably can occur in any period of family development. The form of these messages and perhaps their impact will vary depending on the development of the verbal/nonverbal communication patterns within the family. The identification of double-bind messages has been reported in families as expressed primarily verbally and in the middle stages of family development. It would be interesting to trace these double-bind messages in earlier stages of family development. Are there actually earlier forms of these messages in which *nonverbal*, contradictory communications play a major role? And, if so, what does this do to later patterns of development of family communication?

PSEUDO-MUTUALITY

Pseudo-mutuality is another concept that frequently appears in the family therapy literature. It is defined by Wynne and his co-workers as follows: "In describing pseudo-mutuality, we are emphasizing a predominant absorption in fitting together, at the expense of differentiation of the identities of the persons in the relation" (Wynne *et al.*, 1958, p. 207). This development of the identity of the individuals based on the stability of the family is seen as basic in the formulations of Wynne *et al.* Pseudo-mutuality is then a disordered form of family structure. A "predominant absorption in fitting together" can hinder the progress of family development. Another way of stating this issue is that in a society that places a premium on individuality, individual competence, and initiative, the focus on family equilibrium can lead to an inflexibility in family patterns so that there is little accommodation to divergent needs of individuals or, in the developmental framework, little ability to change adaptive patterns in response to changing contexts of family life. It might be extremely useful to analyze the patterns of "fitting together" and their relationship to the family's methods of coping with individual needs and desires as they can be specified for the various basic family functions during different stages of family development. Pseudo-mutuality has been reported in families of schizophrenics that are grossly disturbed. Does it occur in other types of families as well in which there is little apparent gross disturbance? Does it characterize certain developmental stages of family life more often than other stages? Does it affect, quite globally, all the basic family functions? Or is it possible to clarify patterns of deficiency, fixations, or rigidities in a more differentiated way for different family functions and during different developmental phases? To what extent, in particular, does the pattern of pseudo-mutuality emerge quite early in family development or does it result from subsequent efforts to cope with changes in family situation? These are quite critical issues and the utility of the concept hinges, to a considerable extent, on our ability to specify its conditions and consequences in family interrelationships.

Lidz, in *The Family and Human Adaptation* (1963, p. 76), emphasizes the importance of "the continuing influence of the family environment through the years." It is this continuing family influence which is the subject of family development. It is essential to note that, though this influence is not static or constant, the issues around which this influence operates are predictable in a fashion to which we have previously not paid much attention. To emphasize this point, it is possible to consider Lidz's concepts in developmental terms. He discusses three principles involved in understanding families: (1) the parental coalition, (2) the maintenance of generational boundaries, and (3) the maintenance of sex-linked roles.

PARENTAL COALITION

Within a framework of family development the "parental coalition" can be understood in its full dynamic development, beginning in Stage I of family development with precursors in the courtship and engagement phase (Rapoport, 1964). Subtly examined, it contains indications of later developmental problems or potentials for progression. This parental coalition, once established, ordinarily changes as development proceeds to meet new family issues, interactions, and relationships. At each stage of family development the parental coalition will have a specific range of characteristics. In brief, although the parental coalition forms a focus for observation and analysis, it can only be understood in relation to other changes in family patterns and situations over time. A matter of particular importance is the ways in which the parental coalition is maintained in response to new family demands and expectations at different stages and how it is affected by differences in individual parent reaction to these changes. Thus, the birth of a new baby (Stage II) can be experienced quite differently by both parents without fundamentally altering a relatively flexible form of parental coalition, but the same pattern of individual difference in response can make serious incursions on a parental coalition predicated on a rigid conception of husband-wife relationships. In a similar way, the emergence of adolescent children in the family (Stages III–V), representing a new focus of power and demand in the family, can be a basis for expanding the range and conception of a coalition between the parents or conversely it can threaten the entire arrangement by the development of new coalitions between one parent and an adolescent child. Although one can say, in a very general way, that our society places a premium on flexible arrangements even in the form of parental coalition, it is clear that the nature of the challenges and the particular kinds and areas of flexibility will differ both with the basis of coalition formation and with the stage of family development.

MAINTENANCE OF GENERATIONAL BOUNDARIES

The "maintenance of generational boundaries" becomes particularly important in the middle stages of family development. The development of the family function of socialization in this period of family development will be affected by maintenance or blurring of these boundaries. This critical stage during which there are many challenges to generational boundaries occurs during middle to late adolescence and the child's moves toward establishing a life separate from that of his parental family. The extent to which these boundaries are defensively and rigidly maintained can be as much of a problem during this stage as can the lability of boundaries that destroy the meaning of differentiation of parenthood and childhood.

MAINTENANCE OF SEX-LINKED ROLES

The "maintenance of sex-linked roles" will exert its effect also as some of the children reach the age of adolescence and attempt to exit from the family (Stage IV). Stage III, the entrance of the children into the larger world, will also be affected. The resolution of the Oedipus complex is crucial in enabling children to move outward and has been considered primarily as an individual matter. But "maintenance of sex-linked roles" will affect the strength and distribution of all family ties including not only father-mother but mother-other siblings, father-other siblings, and intersibling relationships. However, while it is possible to say, in a general way, that progression, distortion, adaptability, and rigidity are critical for the ways in which these fundamental family issues are carried out during the life cycle, it is also important to begin to document this more precisely. It is quite evident that parental coalitions, generational boundaries, and sex-linked roles have different consequences depending on the stage of family development, and some of these differences have been suggested previously. Yet, it remains relatively unknown how the importance of these various features of family patterns change during different stages. A developmental framework provides a basis for examining these issues and utilizing the number of important family concepts more carefully than we have yet been able to do.

FAMILY IDENTITY AND FAMILY MYTH

Other recurring concepts in the literature on family therapy include those of family identity and family myth (Ryckoff, Day, and Wynne, 1959). There can be no single family identity or family myth. The characteristics of "family identity" change from stage to stage of family development. The family myth likewise may have certain progressive or static qualities. Indeed, even if we could designate a single "family identity" or a single "family myth" that could be said to characterize different families over time, its function and meaning would inevitably vary depending on the stage of family development. The very same identity or myth might at one stage open up an entire new world of potentials and at another close issues off prematurely and retard both individual and family adaptation. Moreover, unless the family identity and the family myth could change over time in response to the alterations in family and individual functioning, it would appear to represent a form of rigidity that could hardly prove effective to the inevitable life-cycle changes that families undergo.

BASIC FAMILY FUNCTIONS

An analysis of basic family functions is particularly useful in understanding the seeming chaos in very disturbed families. In a discussion of treatment of families with multiple acting-out children, Minuchin and his co-workers comment that

> the everyday problems of existence in these families are immense, and such emergencies as paying the rent, acquiring clothes for the children or food for the next week make up a large part of their lives. In order to work with them toward our goal of eventual autonomous family function, it was necessary to take an intense personal interest in these problems in an effort to extricate families from constant emergency operations. The families responded as if this were a new experience, as perhaps it was. We found ourselves paying for baby-sitters, for shoes for a child so he could go to school, and lending money to be paid as security on a new apartment or for a child's coat when he needed one, etc. Although we were aware of the danger of supporting the collective dependency of the families in question, we found that such actions opened many doors and immeasurably enhanced our effort to enter the family system because our commitment was not suspect. We chose consciously to capitalize on this observation, and to worry about the additional difficulty of extricating ourselves later in the phase aimed at development of family autonomy (Minuchin *et al.*, 1964, p. 10).

These emergencies and numerous practical necessities are manifestations of disturbances that often exist from the beginning, in the first stage of family development or, at the very least, occur in the second stage with the birth of a child. These disturbances can be systematically understood in terms of failures in the development of certain basic family functions.

"Paying the rent, acquiring clothes . . . or food for the next week . . ." are indications of difficulties in the first three basic family functions of food, finances, and housing. The family worker is entering on a basic and primitive family level. As historical material is revealed in these chronic problem families, it soon becomes clear that these areas have never been satisfactorily developed in the life of this family. They may have moved beyond Stages I and II of family development, and these difficulties frequently will be carried into the later phases. (And often these will have been present in the grandparent generation.) This consideration emphasizes another point. Despite the fact that adaptation to life-cycle changes is not wholly predictable on the basis of methods of coping with a previous stage, certain levels of ineffectiveness and the response to them tend to prevent major change. To a considerable extent, the failure to resolve some of the very pedestrian features of handling fundamental, bisocial needs retards a family's ability to cope with new problems and new issues. Under these circumstances, the kind of reorganization required by a new stage of development appears to superimpose only a new set of burdens which can only be handled by familiar methods which, more often than not, involve a retreat from active problem-solving. If, in addition to this, the family atmosphere is dominated by a form of tolerance closely akin to pseudo-mutuality, the level of dissatisfaction necessary to motivate change is not present. In turn, this combination leads to a continuing and increasing passivity within the family, and each new stage of development is confronted as a threat, not only to functional effectiveness, but to the very existence of the family itself. Since this degree of failure in carrying out basic family functions during the first two stages of family development implies a very primitive level of deficit, it is not surprising to find, as we often do, that there is a tendency for this pattern to be carried on from one generation to another.

Though all multi-problem families can be described generally as deprived and disturbed, groups of these families will show different patterns of insufficient or distorted development of basic family functions.

In some of these families all areas will contain serious problems: Mrs. J. sat in the midst of a dilapidated, filthy apartment with her feet up on a soiled hassock which was one of her few pieces of furniture, uttering constant commands to her adolescent daughter. Mr. J. sat motionless and quiet. An evaluation revealed that *food* had never been consistently available and often was particularly bad in the winter when teachers reported that the children were very hungry in school. The fire in the stove and the only cooking in the house were done by the adolescent daughter. *Housing-shelter* was grossly inadequate in a small wooden unrepaired private house. In the past the family had been evicted from several housing projects. *Finances* had been a constant problem with very sporadic employment by the father. Even when funds were supplied by public agencies the income was variable since budgets were changed often and the mother's reports to the welfare agency managed to cause funds to be reduced until the needs of the family would produce a periodic crisis and another budget change. As the children grew older there were difficulties with local community agencies, schools, and courts; that is, with the emergence of new basic functions at different stages of the life cycle, there arose new areas of difficulty and new spheres of involvement with social and welfare resources. The early family life of both parents indicated insufficiencies and severe deprivation in many stages.[9]

Extreme examples can easily be found among the poor, but basic family functioning can be impaired in a significant though less severe and more

[9] Further description and analysis of different groups of chronic problem families or multi-problem families can be found in another publication (Stone, Zilbach, and Hurwitz, 1962).

differentiated fashion in other troubled families. In the family who referred their adolescent child for "obnoxious behavior," food was an unreported and unobserved area of difficulty until it was pursued. The father went out for meals while mother worked. The mother, who controlled everything, also bought all the food and oriented her buying toward the father who had stomach trouble. She felt his special needs were very important; for example, there was often a supply of bland cereals, but no dry cereal or eggs for the children. Thus the basic family functions of *food, housing,* and *finances* which had been resolved in Stage I began to alter in Stage II, where food suffered a differentiated but still important deficiency. This inadequacy in regard to the children continued unaltered and unimproved through the next stages of development.

A middle-class, economically comfortable family had indicated no awareness of problems in their basic family functions. A diagnostic home visit done to assess these functions indicated that one adolescent girl's bedroom was dark, small, bare, and in the basement next to the heater. Finances contained a subtle problem. There was a younger daughter in this family with medical problems, and money was channeled in this direction to the detriment of the needs of the older adolescent girl. This was revealed in following the clues provided by the housing arrangement. The room of the younger girl was upstairs, large, overdecorated, and clearly oversupplied with equipment. Mother indicated that the care of the "ill" child left little time for food buying or cooking. While the tended child continued her slow development, the older girl, who had been referred for school problems, desperately described her life as a "dark narrow hall with a television set at the end" and was severely disturbed. Thus, *food* was a markedly impaired family function, *housing-shelter* contained a problem which adolescence brought out more clearly when the older girl attempted separation from her sister, and *finances* also contained a problem not of gross amount, but of distribution. Thus development in earlier stages of family life cycle showed a differentiated pattern of problems and progressions, but the middle years had brought on an accentuation of difficulties. This was clearly seen in the emerging disturbance in the older adolescent girl.

Conclusion

The goal of increasing our understanding of human behavior is difficult to attain. In a certain sense it is an ideal never to be fully realized because every significant answer or increase in knowledge leads to many more questions. Few question the role of psychoanalysis in increasing our understanding of individual inner psychic functioning and in providing a new conception of man and his development. Historically psychoanalysis first concentrated on intrapsychic functioning. The gradual expansion of ego psychology enabled psychoanalysis to broaden its concerns and to begin to deal with the impinging environment. The family is an adjacent and most crucial area of the social environment lying between the individual and the society at large. In a developmental sense, the family as a representative of the social environment and as a socializing force serves to transmit information about and to facilitate the internalization of major social expectations. In the world of the individual it represents a small, relatively private social group in which informal and personal patterns and relationships exist in contrast to the more formal and impersonal patterns and relationships at work or in the community.

Until the last decade or so, much of our psychoanalytic knowledge of families was indirect and largely based on information reconstructed from the psychoanalytic study of individuals. With the more recent development of extensive work in family therapy and research (although its origins go back, in a tentative way, to quite early psychoanalytic considerations as well as those in social work and sociology), a broader background of knowledge and concepts has emerged. These have often occurred either completely outside the framework of psychoanalysis or, in varying degrees, influenced by psychoanalytic ideas. One of the more general contributions of a psychoanalytic vantage point, however, that has received relatively little attention is the integration of dynamic and developmental conceptions. It is to this issue that this chapter has been primarily addressed.

A complete explanation of human behavior requires understanding far more than the family. There are three major areas that require consideration: (1) the intrapsychic or individual area, (2) the extraindividual or family area, and (3) the extrafamilial social interaction including the areas of community, work, and friendship.

From a larger point of view, it has become clear that intervention in any of these areas may produce changes in behavior. Intervention in the form of family therapy concerns itself with the extraindividual area and focuses on the family as a social unit of central importance. The new area of social psychiatry has attempted to deal with and intervene in some extrafamilial or community areas. Only after considerably more knowledge has been amassed can we begin to know which intervention or treatment technique involving which areas is most useful in a particular instance, or, for that matter, which combinations of approach are most effective. This would seem to be a more fruitful approach than the exclusive commitment either to old and familiar or to new and challenging areas of investigation. The fact that any given approach is useful does not really provide an adequate comparison with other approaches and is certainly an inadequate basis for clarifying the conditions that should determine the choice among a host of alternatives.

There has been a tendency among family therapists and in the family-therapy literature, excited about the potentials of family approaches, to dismiss the individual system in an effort to progress in therapeutic work and in understanding the familial system. The conception of the family as a system *necessarily* means that changing one part of the system is bound to bring about changes in other parts. The real question—and one that has yet to be answered—is which point of intervention, for any given unit and under which set of conditions, has the greatest "multiplier" effect. One or the other, the individual or familial system under certain sets of conditions may be more susceptible to change. But, all of these systems are continually in a dynamic state of interaction.

Dynamic changes over time largely responsive to life-cycle changes in families have been defined and described as a sequence of stages in family development. Certain tasks during these stages of family development, the changes in these tasks, and the changing character of the same tasks have been specified as development in basic family functions. It is largely through the analysis of these basic family functions as they expand, contract, and get modified in coping with changing family situations that a developmental family approach can most usefully be applied and serve as a focus for family study and treatment. The normal development of a family requires the satisfactory and effective resolution of these tasks. In the process families undergo progressive changes and alterations or, in pathological instances, reveal an inability to change the patterns of basic family functioning in response to new demands.

Tolstoi once said, "All happy families resemble one another, every unhappy family is unhappy in its own way." The formulations of family development may help us to understand *how* happy families resemble one another as they satisfactorily accomplish the necessary tasks of each phase. Unhappy families can also be better understood as they meet but do not surmount the challenges posed by those new tasks or family functions required for effective functioning during successive stages of family development.

Note: The development of ideas and their expression in this chapter have been aided immeasurably by Dr. Marc Fried, Research Professor, Institute of Human Sciences, Boston College. Continuing stimulation, clinical material, and encouragement have been provided by the members of the family-therapy research unit at the Judge Baker Guidance Center, Dr. E. Bergel and Mrs. C. Gass.

References

Ackerman, N. W. *The Psychodynamics of Family Life: Diagnosis and Treatment*. New York: Basic Books, 1958.

Ackerman, N. W. "Family Psychotherapy and Psychoanalysis: Implications of Difference," *Family Process*, 1 (1962), 30–43.

Ackerman, N. W., Beatman, F., and Sherman, S. (eds.). *Exploring the Base for Family Therapy*. New York: Family Service Association of America, 1962.

Bateson, G., Jackson, D. D., Haley, J., and Weakland, J. "Toward a Theory of Schizophrenia." *Behavioral Science*, 1 (1956), 251–264.

Bell, J. E. *Family Group Therapy*. Public Health Monograph No. 64, Public Health Service Publication No. 826. Washington, D.C.: U. S. Government Printing Office, 1961.

Bell, N., and Vogel, E. (eds.). *A Modern Introduction to the Family*. Glencoe, Ill.: The Free Press, 1960.

Bibring, Grete. "Some Considerations of the Psychological Process in Pregnancy." *The Psychoanalytic Study of the Child*. New York: International Universities Press, 1959. Vol. 14, pp. 113–122.

Bibring, Grete, Dwyer, T. F., Huntington, Dorothy S., and Valenstein, A. F. "A Study of the Psychological Processes in Pregnancy and of the Earliest Mother-Child Relationship," *The Psychoanalytic Study of the Child*. New York: International Universities Press, 1961. Vol. 16, pp. 9–27.

Bowen, M. "Family Relationships in Schizophrenia." In A. Auerback (ed.), *Schizophrenia: An Integrated Approach*. New York: Ronald Press, 1959. Pp. 147–178.

Bruch, Hilde, and Touraine, G. "Obesity in Childhood. V: The Family Frame of Obese Children." *Psychosomatic Medicine*, 2 (1940), 141–206.

Christensen, H. T. *Handbook of Marriage and the Family*. Chicago: Rand McNally, 1964.

Duvall, Evelyn R. *Family Development*. New York: Lippincott, 1957.

Ellis, G. "The Mute Sad-Eyed Child: Collateral Analysis in a Disturbed Family." *International Journal of Psycho-Analysis*, 43 (1962), 40–49.

Erikson, E. H. "Identity and the Life Cycle," *Psychological Issues*, 1, No. 1, (1959), Monograph No. 1.

Fleck, S., Lidz, T., and Cornelison, Alice. "Comparison of Parent-Child Relationships of Male and Female Schizophrenic Patients," *American Medical Association Archives of General Psychiatry*, 8 (1963), 1–7.

Flugel, J. C. *The Psychoanalytic Study of the Family*. London: Hogarth Press, 1921.

Freud, Anna. *The Ego and Mechanisms of Defence* (1936). New York: International Universities Press, 1946.

Freud, S. "Fragment of an Analysis of a Case of Hysteria (1905a)." *The Standard Edition of the Complete Psychological Works of*. . . . London: Hogarth Press. Vol. 7, pp. 7–122. (Also in *Collected Papers of*. . . . New York: Basic Books, 1959. Vol. 3, pp. 13–146.)

Freud, S. "Three Essays on the Theory of Sexuality" (1905b). *The Standard Edition of the Complete Psychological Works of*. . . . London: Hogarth Press. Vol. 7, pp. 125–234. (Also published as *Three Essays on the Theory of Sexuality*. New York: Basic Books, 1963.)

Freud, S. "The Sexual Enlightenment of Children (1907). "An Open Letter to Dr. M. Furst, Editor of *Soziale Medizin und Hygiene. The Standard Edition of the Complete Psychological Works of*. . . . London: Hogarth Press. Vol. 9, pp. 131–139.

Freud, S. "On the Sexual Theories of Children (1908)." *The Standard Edition of the Complete Psychological Works of. . . .* London: Hogarth Press, Vol. 9, pp. 205–226. (Also in *Collected Papers of. . . .* New York: Basic Books, 1959. Vol. 2, pp. 59–75.)

Freud, S. "Family Romances (1909a)." *The Standard Edition of the Complete Psychological Works of. . . .* London: Hogarth Press. Vol. 9, pp. 235–245. (Also in *Collected Papers of. . . .* New York: Basic Books, 1959. Vol. 5, pp. 74–78.)

Freud, S. "Analysis of a Phobia in a Five-Year-Old Boy (1909b)." *The Standard Edition of the Complete Psychological Works of. . . .* London: Hogarth Press. Vol. 10, pp. 3–153. (Also in *Collected Papers of. . . .* New York: Basic Books, 1959. Vol. 3, pp. 149–287.)

Freud, S. "Infantile Mental Life: Two Lies Told by Children (1913a)." *The Standard Edition of the Complete Psychological Works of. . . .* London: Hogarth Press. Vol. 12, pp. 303–311. (Also in *Collected Papers of. . . .* New York: Basic Books, 1959. Vol. 2, pp. 144–149.)

Freud, S. "Totem and Taboo (1913b)." *The Standard Edition of the Complete Psychological Works of. . . .* London: Hogarth Press. Vol. 13, pp. 1–161.

Freud, S. "The Unconscious (1915)." *The Standard Edition of the Complete Psychological Works of. . . .* London: Hogarth Press. Vol. 14, pp. 151–209. (Also in *Collected Papers of. . . .* New York: Basic Books, 1959. Vol. 4, pp. 98–136.)

Freud, S. "Group Psychology and the Analysis of the Ego (1921)." *The Standard Edition of the Complete Psychological Works of. . . .* London: Hogarth Press. Vol. 18, pp. 69–143.

Freud, S. "The Ego and the Id (1923)." *The Standard Edition of the Complete Psychological Works of. . . .* London: Hogarth Press. Vol. 19, pp. 12–69.

Freud, S. "The Problem of Anxiety: Inhibitions, Symptoms, and Anxiety (1926)." *The Standard Edition of the Complete Psychological Works of. . . .* London: Hogarth Press. Vol. 20, pp. 77–175.

Freud, S. "Civilization and Its Discontents (1930)." *The Standard Edition of the Complete Psychological Works of. . . .* London: Hogarth Press. Vol. 21, pp. 64–149.

Freud, S. "New Introductory Lectures (1933)." *The Standard Edition of the Complete Psychological Works of. . . .* London: Hogarth Press. Vol. 22, pp. 5–184.

Fried, M., and Fitzgerald, Ellen. "Role Structure and Interpersonal Interaction in Marriage," unpublished.

Galdston, I. "Panel Discussion of Papers." In J. H. Masserman (ed.), *Science and Psychoanalysis.* Vol. 2, *Individual and Familial Dynamics.* New York: Grune & Stratton, 1959.

Gerver, Joan, Peterson, R., and Arrill, Mildred. *Family Therapy: A Selected Annotated Bibliography.* Maryland: National Clearinghouse for Mental Health Information, U. S. Department of Health, Education, and Welfare, December 1965.

Goodrich, D. W. "Recent Research in Early Family Development and Child

Personality." In Ralph H. Ojemann (ed.), *Recent Research Looking toward Preventive Intervention*. Proceedings of the Third Institute on Preventive Psychiatry. Iowa City: State University of Iowa Press, 1961. Pp. 41–87.

Grotjahn, M. *The Psychoanalytic Treatment of the Family*. New York: Norton, 1959.

Haley, J., and Glick, I. *Psychiatry and the Family: An Annotated Bibliography of Articles Published 1960–1964*. Palo Alto: Family Process, 1965.

Hartmann, H. *Ego Psychology and the Problem of Adaptation* (1939). New York: International Universities Press, 1958.

Hartmann, H. "Psychoanalysis and Developmental Psychology." *Psychoanalytic Study of the Child* 5: 7–17. New York: International Universities Press, 1950. Vol. 5, pp. 7–17.

Hill, R. "Methodological Issues in Family Developmental Research." *Family Process*, 3 (1964), 186–206.

Jackson, D. D. "The Question of Family Homeostasis." *Psychiatric Quarterly*, 31 (1957), Supplement, 79–90.

Johnson, Adelaide M., and Szurek, S. A. "The Genesis of Antisocial Acting Out in Children and Adults," *Psychoanalytic Quarterly*, 21 (1952), 323–343.

Josselyn, Irene M. "The Family as a Psychological Unit." *Social Casework*, 34 (1953), 336–343.

Lidz, T. "Schizophrenia and the Family." *Psychiatry* 21 (1958), 21–27.

Lidz, T. "The Relevance of Family Studies to Psychoanalytic Theory." *Journal of Nervous and Mental Disease*, 135 (1962), 105–112.

Lidz, T. *The Family and Human Adaptation*. New York: International Universities Press, 1963.

Lindemann, E. "The Use of Psychoanalytic Constructs in Preventive Psychiatry, Part I." *Psychoanalytic Study of the Child*. New York: International Universities Press, 1952. Vol. 7, pp. 429–448.

Lomas, P. "Family Role and Identity Formation." *International Journal of Psycho-Analysis*, 42 (1961), 371–380.

Minuchin, S. "Conflict Resolution Family Therapy." *Psychiatry*, 28 (1965), 278–286.

Minuchin, S., Auerswald, E., King, C. H., and Rabinowitz, C. "The Study and Treatment of Families Who Produce Multiple Acting-Out Boys," *American Journal of Orthopsychiatry*, 34 (1964), 125–132.

Mishler, E., and Waxler, Nancy. "Family Interaction Processes and Schizophrenia: A Review of Current Theories." *Merrill-Palmer Quarterly*, 11, No. 4 (1965), 269–315.

Rank, Beata, and Macnaughton, Dorothy. "A Clinical Contribution to Early Ego Development." In Phyllis Greenacre (ed.), *Psychoanalytic Study of the Child*. New York: International Universities Press, 1950. Vol. 5, pp. 53–65.

Rapoport, Rhona. "The Transition from Engagement to Marriage." *Acta Sociologica*, 8 (1964), 36–55.

Rapoport, Robert, and Rapoport, Rhona. "Work and Family in Contemporary

Society." *American Sociological Review*, 30, No. 3 (1965), 381–394.

Rausch, H. L., Goodrich, D. W., and Campbell, J. D. "Adaptation to the First Years of Marriage." *Psychiatry*, 26 (1963), 368–380.

Riskin, J. "Family Interaction Scales." *American Medical Association Archives of General Psychiatry*, 2 (1964), 484–494.

Ryckoff, I., Day, Juliana, and Wynne, L. C. "Maintenance of Stereotyped Roles in the Families of Schizophrenics." *American Medical Association Archives of General Psychiatry*, 1 (1959), 93–98.

Satir, Virginia. *Conjoint Family Therapy: A Guide to Theory and Technique*. Palo Alto: Science and Behavior Books, 1964.

Stone, E., Zilbach, Joan, and Hurwitz, J. *A Place in Darkness*. 3 vols.; Boston, Mass.: United Community Services, 1962. Mimeographed.

Wynne, L. C., Ryckoff, I. M., Day, J., and Hirsch, S. I. "Pseudo-Mutuality in the Family Relations of Schizophrenics." *Psychiatry*, 21 (1958), 205–220.

Wynne, L. C., and Singer, M. T. "Thought Disorder and Family Relations of Schizophrenics. Research Strategy." *American Medical Association Archives of General Psychiatry*, 9 (1963), 191–198.

15

Family Therapy

FRANK S. WILLIAMS

Introduction

During the past fifteen years most of the pioneer work and writings about family interaction and psychological disturbance have stressed the insights afforded by family therapy into interpersonal dynamics, communication disturbance, and the "here and now" problems of affect expression; and there has been a tendency in many family approaches to minimize the exploration of genetic material, intrapsychic life, and the utility of psychoanalytic principles. In our family studies at the Cedars-Sinai Department of Child Psychiatry during the past six years, my colleagues and I have placed emphasis on the need for a continued regard for understanding and dealing with genetic and intrapsychic phenomena and their reciprocal relationship to the dynamic object relationships of interpersonal life. Some family therapists stress the concept that intrapsychic conflicts do not cause disruptive family relationships, but on the contrary are the result of such disruptive family relationships (Bell, 1961). The emphasis thereby has been to utilize family meetings to work primarily with such disruptive family relationships. We prefer to study the interaction between intrapsychic and interpersonal factors—the cycle in which pathogenic family relationships cause intrapsychic conflict and maladaptations; once ingrained, these conflicts and maladaptations generate further disruptive familial relationships. Thus we choose not to limit ourselves to the interpersonal portion of the cycle, but rather to explore the interactions between the individual and his family as a unit, and between the individual's psyche and family role assignments, and the adaptations that evolve in that psyche in exchange for love and security.

In addition to stressing the maintenance of sound psychoanalytic regard for intrapsychic phenomena during family therapy, I suggest that family therapy also can serve as a catalyst in individual psychoanalytic treatment. Family theory and observation can enhance psychoanalytic understanding by enlarging our focus on a patient's mental life to include the many fields of influence impinging on him. Spiegel and Kluckhohn (1954) have outlined five such fields of influence: (1) the family as a collection of individuals; (2) the family as an organized small primary group within itself; (3) the major social system; (4) the system of values for the culture; and (5) the effect of geographical setting.

In family therapy we have a vital diagnostic tool for broadening our understanding of psychopathology in children and adults. At the same time, the family approach is one of the best methods of reversing psychopathology in young children, at a time when the roots of emotional conditioning and character adaptation are still fluid and more readily subject to corrective emotional experiences. Family therapy, moreover, via demonstration and interpretation, can enlist parents as effective full-time providers of such experiences.

Technical Considerations

FLEXIBILITY OF METHOD

Flexibility of approach allows us to use various combinations of individual therapy and family techniques. If during individual treatment a child's resistance should either persist or not be fully understood, the introduction of several family meetings often can be of much value in elucidating the nature of the resistance. Brown (1966) has described how treatment of a child and his parents together offers a modality to view the parents' resistance to change as it appears at each step of the child's therapeutic gain. We have used individual meetings with children or parents, as well as conjoint sessions with parents, during the course of an ongoing family therapy to reinforce certain insights or to work on untoward individual reactions. Especially when a family member seems in need of exploring certain deeply rooted intrapsychic conflicts such as embarrassing sexual problems, we have felt free to introduce individual sessions for that member, rather than to rigidly insist on family interviewing exclusively.

The many theoretical constructs and technical approaches in family therapy by pioneer workers in this field have been of great value when utilized in various combinations. Techniques and models that we have integrated into our family therapeutic armamentarium include the approaches to communication problems by Ruesch and Bateson (1951), Jackson (1957), and Haley (1963); problems with family roles and "pseudomutuality" described by Wynne, Ryckoff, Day, and Hirsch (1958); the concepts of "schism," "skewing," and disturbed "generational boundaries" (Lidz, Cornelison, Fleck, and Terry, 1957); Minuchin's educational "task-oriented" family approaches with socially disadvantaged groups (1966); attention to family disorganizing forces such as "emotional divorce" (Bowen, 1960); Ackerman's unraveling of family secrets supposedly "unknown" to family members, as well as his emphasis on scapegoating mechanisms, reversal of roles, and disturbed alliances (1962); sociocultural forces and problems with affect expression in the interactional sphere (Jackson and Satir, 1961; Haley, 1963); and Bell's treatment of the family as a primary unit capable of a gradual enhanced awareness (1961).

RESISTANCE TO CHANGE

We have paid particular attention to those many factors in the family and sociocultural environment that cause resistance to change and have tried to deal with this resistance by guidance and interpretation. Brown (1966), Boszormenyi-Nagy (1965), and Framo (1965) have elaborated on the power of such resistances to block psychological improvement—resistances such as the rigid homeostasis that Jackson (1957) described in the matrix of schizophrenic families. If this resistance is not recognized and dealt with, the therapist may push patients to express certain affects prematurely and, in so doing, may provoke even more rigid maintenance of the psychopathological homeostasis in both the individual and the family.

GENETIC INTERPRETATIONS

In addition to the flexible utilization of the above types of intervention, we explore and interpret *genetic, psychodynamic* material as it is reflected in the family meetings. Our family approach differs from many others in this pointed attention to intrapsychic factors. At a certain point in a family treatment we may focus on any one member, in the presence of the others, in an attempt to draw out certain affects related to traumatic childhood relationships. Our hope is that the spouse, parent, or child will develop empathy for his fellow family member's conflicts, and thereby better understand the meaning of that individual's annoying or disturbing behavior. Paul and Grosser (1965), in reporting conjoint family therapy, have described the stimulating therapeutic effects of the revival of intense affects related to early trauma from an individual's past.

Rather than insisting on primary maintenance of the family group as patient throughout the treatment, as advocated by some workers in the field (Boszormenyi-Nagy, 1965, and Framo, 1965), we have alternated and combined individual analytic therapy with family therapy in a manner similar to that described by Messer (1966). Although it can be most helpful for the rest of the family to learn about the roots of conflict in other family members, a severe intrapsychic block can sometimes cause a stalemate unless it is handled by separate individual sessions. Haley (1963) has stressed the family approach as one in which psychodynamic exploration is not so important as changes in behavior and communication. In contrast, we have noted in many cases that attempts at corrective experiences, corrective identifications, and interpersonal interpretations alone have not significantly altered the disturbed behavior or communication pattern without some concomitant psychodynamic, genetic exploration. Thus, one can, at times, observe certain pathogenic mother-child communication patterns, interpret them, and offer corrective approaches without resultant change. For example, a mother says to her four-year-old autistic boy, "Good-bye, you can go now, it is time to leave the room," while she holds him tightly, rubbing her nose against his, and making accompanying endearing sounds. Confronting her with this contradictory communication pattern and demonstrating corrective approaches may not be successful unless some uncovering work is also done on this mother's deeply rooted problem of separation anxiety. Similarly, a double-bind communication in which a mother verbally says, "I love you," but physically withdraws from her child, may require a working through of the roots of this ambivalence in addition to merely pointing out the double bind and demonstrating more appropriate communication techniques. Again, in an ongoing family treatment where it has been ascertained that a husband's masochistic character structure prevents him from showing any enthusiasm toward pleasurable experiences with his wife, we may, at first, attempt to demonstrate his self-punishing needs within the family setting. Should this not prove effective, however, we might then offer him analytically oriented individual sessions to help him work through his masochistic needs. In either event, we would not ignore the individual intrapsychic aspects of the problem (Williams, 1967b).

Some workers in family therapy do not concern themselves with the genetic "why" of a patient's rage during a family meeting, but choose to deal solely with those "here and now" factors involving the therapist and family members; they stress the provocative and interactive effects immediately recognizable. In contrast, we would further seek out whether a wife's rage was due only to her husband's or the therapist's provocation during a session or whether, for example, it stemmed from some childhood sibling rivalry with a brother, which left within her a chronic readiness to blow up at all men.

TRANSFERENCE AND COUNTERTRANSFERENCE

Transference and countertransference phenomena exist in family therapy, but are frequently more complicated than those in the psychoanalytic one-to-one relationship. Depending on the intrapsychic needs of the various family members, transference and countertransference phenomena increase or decrease in family meetings. In situations of great "oral" emptiness in several family members, the simultaneous demands of several "hungry," deprived, dependent persons on the therapist-parent-surrogate may evoke within the therapist much anger and a sense of being drained. Such demands, as well as the chaotic impact of a deteriorating leaderless family, may cause the therapist to react unwittingly with counteraggression or detachment. Such situations may influence a therapist to recommend individual therapy with therapists other than himself as the "treatment of choice." In contrast, however, we have noted some severe Oedipal rivalry situations to which the therapist may respond with a *preference* for working with the family as a group. For instance, when, following a divorce, a mother and teenage daughter vie erotically for the therapist's love, the seductive elements of the transference may be neutralized when the two females are together. Less countertransference anxiety may be aroused in the therapist than if he were to see either of the women alone.

ACTING OUT BY THE THERAPIST

The potential for the *therapist's acting out* of unresolved conflicts is great in family treatment techniques. A therapist with a need for omnipotence may, under the guise of guidance, cater to the dependency needs of an entire family to the extent of neglecting the family's own potential for self-strengthening and development. Although it is essential for a family therapist to empathize with various family members, a family may sometimes be used as a vehicle for a sadistic attack on a parent, through an over-identification with a child. This is particularly apt to be so if the therapist has unresolved childhood sadistic conflicts. We have on occasion seen an aggressive provocation by a therapist which, in our estimation, was no more than an expression of sadism, technically rationalized as necessary for the encouragement of family interaction and expression. The danger of acting out by the family therapist of unresolved early Oedipal conflicts is great; it is easier for an Oedipal reaction in the therapist to be stirred up when three of the family triangle are present in the same room than it is when a patient reports or fantasies Oedipal material in analysis. A family therapist is often in the very responsible and delicate position in which he can tilt an off-balance marriage toward either consolidation or divorce. Should he have a severe underlying marital conflict in his own life, he might precipitate the tilt in a nontherapeutic direction. Framo (1965) similarly has stressed the therapist's past and present personal life as important in both transference and countertransference reactions during family therapy.

ACTUAL TECHNIQUES

Since what we do in family therapy combines many approaches and variations, it is difficult, without offering direct demonstration, to answer a frequently posed question: "What do you actually do in your family meetings?" I shall, however, try to offer some descriptive material. In addition to the above-mentioned general considerations, we work toward mutual understanding of interpersonal dynamics and intrapsychic conflicts by interpretation and encouragement of expression of feelings. By clarification of familial obstacles to more wholesome adaptations and demonstration of corrective attitudes, we attempt to establish order and consistency in a family's life. Regard for the individuality of the various family members as well as improved family group interest also are exemplified in the therapist's approach to the family.

We especially encourage the expression of anxiety, hidden angers, and hurt feelings which are not apparent to the family members. We point out nonverbal cues toward certain acting-out behavior and encourage empathy for the other person's problems. We interpret to couples, parents, and children the dovetailing of their neuroses. There is an attempt to make confusing communications between husband and wife explicit. An example of the latter is a situation to which the therapist reacts to a couple by saying, "You, the husband, keep telling her to be a loving, submissive little girl, yet at the same time you want her to be a strong, domineering mother. You, the wife, tell him to be a strong, protective father, but at the same time you give him many cues to be a good little boy who will be taken care of and mothered by you." Hidden envies and competitiveness are brought to the surface. For example, a wife may become extremely anxious in a session about the possible failure of a party she and her husband have been planning for members of his office. When sufficient data are available, the therapist may be able to point to her envy, her competitiveness, her wish for the party to be a failure, and the resultant guilt-laden anxiety.

When there is a destructive *family style*, we try to clarify the underlying basis for it. For example, a borderline sixteen-year-old psychotic boy was unable to separate from his mother, and it soon became apparent that mother, father, and son each had a very deep, exquisite sense of internal weakness. Each tried to gain strength by making another member of the family weak. We labeled this mechanism for them as "the family myth of weakness" and pointed out how each of them blossomed in the others' misery, hoping to gain strength from the others' weakness. This interpretation brought the mother and son to verbalize that each feared the other would die if there was a separation. They were then able to see that the fear was related to the need for each to believe that he was the stronger one whose strength would help keep the other one alive. In keeping with our orientation toward appropriately timed analytically oriented individual psychotherapy, this mother, in a series of separate interviews with her therapist, recalled and experienced with affect many of the genetic influences from her own relationship with a domineering mother. She could soon see a force from her background contributing to the conflict in her present-day family life.

Diagnostic Values of Family Therapy

CLARIFICATION OF ETIOLOGICAL DYNAMICS

Family therapy is of enormous value in the assessment of the etiology of children's emotional disturbances, as well as in the understanding of certain forces within families or marriages which perpetuate adult psychopathology. We have come to the conclusion in recent years that one or two family interviews have an essential place in the total intake evaluation of children and can serve, too, as a pivotal vantage point from which the diagnostician may rapidly assess what next steps need be taken to enhance the total diagnostic process (Williams, 1965).

Thus, an adult has long forgotten, and a child is unable to perceive consciously, those unconscious cues by mothers and fathers which move in the direction of corrupting otherwise strict superego attitudes. In family interviews the therapist can observe these cues. A mother may protest the need for sexual abstinence on the one hand, but in a family session may indicate tremendous curiosity about her child's sexual life and may make light of "evil" sexual activities via laughter, jokes, or other subtle, permissive techniques. A mother who is unable to understand her ten-year-old boy's dishonesty in light of the strict principles concerning truthfulness with which she has raised him is seen in the family interview to be quite corruptible herself when it comes to slightly breaking the rules for convenience' sake. Although some of these parental attitudes might be elicited in separate interviews with each parent, the family interview offers an opportunity to observe the child's reactions to these aforementioned cues, either spontaneously or by direct questioning. The family interview—regardless of the etiology of symptoms in the child—helps the therapist observe in vivo those forces which foster the perpetuation of symptoms and also provides him with clues to potential cooperation that may be available from other family members in helping to overcome the child's symptoms. Family techniques offer rich diagnostic observation of the contrast between unfolding variable object relations in terms of the child and the fixed object relations in terms of how the parents see and use the child.

REDUCTION OF GUILT AND FEAR

Child therapists, when interviewing a child for the first time, usually meet, as major obstacles to ventilation of feelings by the child, strong elements of fear and guilt. No matter how angry a child is with his parents, there is usually great concern about talking behind their backs. The anxiety over guilt for betraying their parents often leads children to underplay their affective feelings toward their parents, to deny these feelings, or to whitewash the family environment. This is not only true in child psychiatry; it is seen quite regularly in the early stages of psychotherapy or analysis with adults.

With a family approach, in many cases we have seen, the elements of guilt and fear are markedly reduced for the child. The fact that the parents are present relieves the tension about discussing them behind their backs. Then, too, we have noted a strikingly frequent attitude on the part of parents in family sessions of encouraging the child to talk about them. The parents will usually say, in direct response to a child's hesitation or reluctance to talk, "Go ahead, it's all right for you to talk about us; you won't be punished; that's what we're here for; we can't understand how you feel unless you tell us." At times the parents are the first to discuss more openly their own feelings toward each other or toward the children. This gives the child an opportunity to see that the air is clear for ventilating feelings of anger and disappointment without having to experience immobilizing guilt. I have been very impressed by a child's smile, mild hesitation, and direction of his gaze toward his parent as he is about to be critical. The child moves slowly, and tests the parents by asking permission via hesitation. The parents, both verbally and nonverbally, encourage the child to go on or cue him to stop. This opportunity to observe the parents' rejective or permissive attitude toward his critical ventilations is not available to the child or to the therapist in an individual diagnostic interview.

PROTECTION OF SELF-ESTEEM

Adults come to the psychiatrist for help. Children are brought. This usually means to them that they are "nuts." A strong resistance against offering any information that might attack their self-esteem is a frequent obstacle to obtaining diagnostic data.

With an initial family interview, the therapist can shift attention from merely understanding the child to understanding the entire family. This helps loosen up a child's defensiveness as he is no longer the singled out, criticized, freakish or defective one. We have noted several instances of children, who were almost completely silent in prior individual diagnostic approaches, opening up quite readily in a family session.

CLARIFICATION OF NONVERBAL ATTITUDES

Many attitudes of the parents which affect the child's emotional make-up are not consciously known to the parents themselves. Seeing a parent individually gives one a completely different picture from that seen in a family meeting, in terms of the parents' expectations, standards, and relationship with the child. In an individual session a mother may tell you, and truly believe, that she does not expect her son to be too grown up, or too intellectual. In a family meeting this same mother may, through many nonverbal attitudes, express scorn toward dependency needs and physical activities and show much approval of intellectual and independent strivings on the child's part. A father may feel that he is not overbearing toward his son when you meet with him in an individual session. In a family meeting, however, one may see the same father giving the child incisive stares when the boy fiddles in his seat, telling the boy, "Don't twiddle your thumbs!" "Sit up straight!" Some of the attitudes present themselves so casually that they would be completely missed if one were to question the child or parent about them in individual meetings.

Ten-year-old Ernest and his parents constitute an excellent case example, where the image of family life that the therapist gained from individual sessions was in marked contrast to the actual dynamic interactions observed in a later family interview. Ernest was initially referred for "psychotic temper tantrums," dishonesty, belligerence toward mother and school authorities, and impulsive behavior. In the initial individual contact with the mother, she convincingly presented herself as a warm, maternal figure, who catered to her child's needs for both dependency and autonomy. She spoke highly of his sensitivity, her love for him, and her feeling that she didn't push him toward independence or adult accomplishments. She spoke of the close "buddy-buddy" relationships between her husband, herself, and Ernest. She, and later the husband, also in an individual session, stated that they felt that Ernest's father definitely wore the pants in the home and implied that he was an excellent model for masculine identification. The marriage was painted as a very happy one, and all problems were seen as relating only to Ernest, the problem child. Father in his individual meeting with the therapist appeared to be an emotionally strong, firm, and kind man. Two clinical interviews with the boy and psychological testing presented great problems in that both the psychologist and therapist felt him to be very friendly, agreeable, generally sensitive, nondemanding, and quite honest. His ego appeared strong, and neither psychotic disorder nor potential could be elicited, in spite of a previous psychiatric diagnosis of psychosis. In individual sessions both parents stressed how much they imbued the boy with honesty training which made it very difficult for them to understand his dishonest acting out.

After the individual meetings and psychological testing failed to demonstrate sufficient cause for the boy's behavioral problem, or any psychotic core, one family interview was held in which mother, father, and Ernest were present. The diagnostic impact of the one family interview was most impressive. The mother, who previously had stated she was noncritical of her son and that she did not have excessively high standards for him, spent the entire hour criticizing him in a sweet-tongued, but nonetheless undermining, fashion. When the boy stated he was jealous of his father and father's responsibilities, his mother accused him of lying, telling him that he did not deserve responsibility because he did not show respect for his parents. Her voice was very sweet but biting in its calmness as she depreciated Ernest. By the end of the hour, after excessive critical bombardment from his mother, the boy withdrew completely and showed much regressive symptomatology, moving closer to mother and engaging in a seductive kissing game with her. Any attempt on Ernest's part to gain support from mother during the session was thwarted by critical demands for him to grow up. It was only with complete regression, to an infantile state, however, in which the boy was as much as saying, "Ga, ga," that mother was able to offer dependency gratification. Father, who had previously appeared strong, assertive, and positive, turned out in the family interview to be a mild, submissive man, who catered to every one of mother's wishes and statements. In relation to the education for honesty that the parents had given Ernest, and their dilemma regarding his dishonesty, there were many hints of subtle, unconscious encouragement toward corruptible superego standards, readily observed in the family meeting. The boy climbed into an area where he should not have gone without the therapist's permission. It turned out that mother had previously said aloud, "I wonder what it is like up there?" After the boy had gone where she had subtly encouraged him to go, she then became very critical of his not having asked direct permission from the therapist. The family interview in this case gave the therapist an excellent opportunity to understand Ernest's difficulty with masculine identification, the reactive causes of his hostility toward mother and other figures of authority, his dishonesty as an attempt to carry out mother's unconscious wishes, and his denial of his dependency needs as an attempt to meet mother's high standards for maturity, intellectuality, and independence. None of the individual sessions brought out this material. It was also noteworthy that both parents, when viewed individually, presented themselves as adequate objects for identification and emotional support; however, within the context of the family interaction, their pathogenic roles became quite evident.

UNCOVERING OF UNDERCURRENT MARITAL CONFLICT

Unconscious conflict between parents who lack affective warmth and communication with each other frequently leads to an acting out of the marital conflict through a scapegoat child. This focus serves to shift attention away from the underlying marital disharmony. When seeing such parents individually, or even conjointly, they may paint an idyllic picture of their marriage in order to deny feelings of mutual resentment and disappointment. As one observes them with their children in a series of family meetings, this picture soon begins to break down, and one sees how the child has served as a scapegoat for the parents' problems. In the case of Ernest, mentioned above, it was of note in the described family interview that his father was quite unaware of his wife's needs for attention and dependency supports. When he did not compliment her on her new hair-do, she looked angry and sad, but then, in response to her husband's quizzical gaze, quickly stated that she really did not care for compliments and that she did not expect her "over-worked husband" to be bothered noticing what she wore or how she did her hair. She then abruptly turned toward Ernest and, seemingly out of context, accused him of not having any feelings for other people's needs. She stated how much she resented that when her husband came home from work he "had to be bothered" with hearing about Ernest's bad behavior, when he really needed to relax after a hard day's work. As father evinced surprise at mother's use of "resentment," she quickly drew back in her seat and then emphasized that she did not resent her husband for his lack of participation, but just resented the fact that he was such a loving and kind husband who had to be faced with the burdens of such a problem child. It was very clear that this woman was unable to face her disappointment and hostility toward her husband. In an effort to preserve the fiction of marital bliss, she turned most of her resentment toward her son. Too, much of the husband's passivity, which she resented, led her to encourage in the boy an acting out of assertive behavior, which she then had to condemn. These and many other nuances of marital tensions which are disguised and filtered off into a child's disturbance can be readily observed in family interviews, whereas they are often successfully concealed in individual diagnostic sessions.

DISCRIMINATION BETWEEN FANTASY AND REALITY

Some analytic thinking maintains that in psychopathology it is not the actual attitudes of the parents that matter, but the patient's fantasies of what his parents are, or were, like. I would take exception to this in terms of proper diagnostic assessment, particularly in relation to children.

When one sees a young teenage boy pushing his mother away, not trusting her, belittling her, and generally distancing himself from her, it is extremely important to know more than the boy's fantasy about what his mother is. If in family interviews mother appears to be a warm, understanding person and there are clues that there is potentially a very close physical relationship between mother and son, one can readily see the Oedipal discomfort behind the boy's distancing behavior. If, on the other hand, she turns out to be truly rejecting, threatening, and nonperceptive of the boy's needs, one can then more readily infer that he is pushing his mother away to achieve self-survival or aggressive retaliation. This is an important diagnostic distinction that must be made in planning proper therapy for this type of situation. What is critical is whether or not a child's fantasy about his parents is truly representative of reality or a distortion of reality in the service of warding off threatening affects and impulses. Family interviews help to elucidate this distinction.

One of the implications of studying family diagnostic techniques can be related to the many types of short-term family therapies that have been undertaken in community child psychiatry programs (Williams, 1967a). Kaffman (1963) has described definitive change occurring via a direct or indirect interference on a stressful and pathogenic parent-child interaction. A one- or two-family interview method, if perfected, could become an economic and effective way of assessing the pathogenic parent-child interaction and thereby quickly underscoring what interventions are needed.

Treatment of Children

Family treatment, as an increasingly important approach to the psychotherapy of disturbed children, should lean heavily on Alexander's concept (1957) of the corrective emotional experience. It was Alexander's belief that, in the gamut of human reactions available to the therapist, the therapist would sort out and manifest those reactions which most corrected the original pathogenic parent-child relationship. Thereby the analyst could emotionally recondition his patient within the setting of a new human involvement, different from the one in which the neurosis had its roots. With children, where the intrapsychic problems are still flexible, we have an excellent opportunity to offer corrective emotional experiences at the most optimal point. In individual therapy with a child, however, such corrective experiences several hours per week may be negated by important family members, during the many other hours of the week. It can be much more effective to encourage the parents themselves to become the agents of the new emotional experiences by helping them to alter their part in the pathogenic interaction. The family therapist can enlist the parents as *allies*, who can learn—via identification with the therapist and working through of neurotic conflict—to relate to the child in a more wholesome way.

Parental sabotaging of therapy when change occurs in child patients is well known. In conjoint sessions with the child and the parents, there is a chance to work through the parents' resistance to change at critical points. Instead of becoming "saboteurs" of the therapy, the parents can eventually ally themselves with the therapist toward a common goal. Thus the therapist no longer remains a substitute parent who proves that the real parents have been failures; he can empathize more directly with the parents and, in turn, the parents can see that he is human and that he, too, is vulnerable to their child's frustrating behavior and provocativeness. There is no doubt in my mind, having worked both with more classical child-therapy techniques and with family therapy, that the family approach encourages a greater alliance between therapist and parents.

A dramatic case in point is that of Donald, a thirteen-year-old schizophrenic boy who was never permitted to leave his home or go outside alone for fear he would run away or be physically harmed. Initially I found myself extremely angry with what appeared to me to be extremely controlling and restrictive parents. However, as family treatment proceeded, I, too, began to have some anxiety about Donald's tendency toward self-carelessness when away from his parents. One day I encouraged him to go for a walk alone. I became prematurely anxious when he did not return within ten minutes from the time of his departure. My anxiety mounted in spite of my having pointedly given him a twenty-minute deadline for his return to the office. I was soon able to understand and meaningfully share with the parents their chronic panic. The parents developed a sense of comradeship with me in terms of our now common experience of not trusting Donald. It was of note in this particular case that Donald actually returned ten minutes later, exactly on schedule. This type of experience which occurs frequently in family therapy affords renewed starting points, at various stages of the process, for reconsidering unnecessary anxieties (Williams, 1967b).

I have been impressed with the capacity of many parents, once given some demonstration and guidance, to provide the very corrective parental attitudes that one might initially have felt could only be provided by a substitute parental surrogate. It has been quite striking to see how some initially cold and rejecting mothers, who never seem to reach out or hold their children, begin to show great warmth and acceptance once encouraged to do so. The positive response evoked in their children seems much greater than that which the therapist might evoke on his own. We have especially noticed this in our work with very young, psychotic children. We are beginning to have evidence of faster and more significant strides by using family techniques with some severely disturbed atypical children, including cases of autistic ego development. The therapist is able to demonstrate to parents of such children certain corrective attitudes with which the parents hopefully can identify. He can relate to the disturbed psychotic child in ways which appropriately frustrate inordinate omnipotent demands; he can insist on word language and eye contact in return for gratification of the child's request. When the observing parents are not able to carry through with similar corrective approaches, the therapist is then in a position to interpret both intrapsychic and interpersonal conflicts which seem to be interfering. In my opinion (Williams, 1964) individual analytic or even anaclitic intensive work with an atypical child does not allow for so much reinforcement from the total field—particularly from the parents—as does family therapy.

An empirical clinical finding we have begun to encounter frequently in our interviews with the families of autistic children is the great difficulty the parents of these disturbed youngsters have in expressing angry affect. As we work through their resistance to such expression, and also help them to learn more about their children's nonverbal communication patterns, these parents often can become of great aid in eliciting more interpersonal human responses from the restricted repertoire of expression in these children. We have had the opportunity, in several cases of autistic children, to observe the part that their fathers play in their over-infantilization, via obedience to the autistic child's mechanical commands. Too, we have been impressed in several situations with the pathogenic input by older siblings. On two separate occasions, as the therapist and parents began to attain a measure of success in evoking some natural responses from the autistic child, an older brother minimized the gain and directly attempted to interrupt or sabotage it. For example, as four-year-old Teddy began to make prolonged eye contact with the therapist and his parents, his eight-year-old brother, Peter, looked at him, and with Svengali-like hand motions proclaimed, "You must remain my robot. Do what I tell you! Do not talk!" The family interview approach affords an optimal setting in which to note such obstacles to development and to enlist the total family's help in overcoming them.

Conjoint Marital Therapy

Conjoint marital therapy affords an opportunity for a couple to work through their reciprocal neurotic needs and to learn how their interactions perpetuate each other's neurotic symptoms as well as the marital discord. Psychoanalysts know too well the common story of a man or woman completing a successful analysis, only to face the resultant consequence of a divorce, in light of the spouse's inability to tolerate the change. Although such consequences can be averted by concomitant psychoanalysis for the spouse, there are many situations in which it may save time and be more effective for a couple to approach their marital disharmony and resistance to each other's psychological progress in a conjoint fashion. The effect of a spouse in symptom perpetuation can be strong even in certain psychotic states. Fenichel (1945), in discussing delusions of persecution, significantly stressed that hatred was never projected at random, but rather had a basis in reality. I recently treated a borderline psychotic woman whose paranoid outbursts were difficult to understand in terms of precipitating factors until I began seeing her with her husband. After a few sessions I was able to predict—in relation to the husband's subtle critical remarks and emotional withdrawals—when her paranoia would flare up. Although individual analytic therapy may be greatly needed by one or both partners in a marriage, a series of conjoint meetings can often help elucidate the range of positive adaptation available between the partners as well as the extent of the irreversible loss of potential for intimacy. A recent clinical example which underscored the value of conjoint marital therapy concerned a woman who for four years had psychoanalytic treatment in which she worked through a basic intrapsychic feeling of "I am loved only when I am weak." Following her analysis—partly by circumstance and partly by conscious choice—she married a man who she felt would love her for her strengths instead of her weaknesses. The man she married did love her for her strengths, but unfortunately he demanded super-Herculean strength from her, rejecting even the appropriate interdependency she sought. A series of conjoint meetings with this couple was undertaken in an effort to help them recognize and alter the elements underlying the growing rift between them.

The literature abounds with material on communication distortion in schizophrenic families. We have been impressed, in our work with neurotics, by the frequent marked lack of communication—the dearth of frankness in relation to emotional, romantic, and dependency needs. Often the mutual frustration of each other's needs evolves from a lack of experience in knowing how to ask for what they expect from each other. Conjoint marital therapy stimulates a beginning freedom of such expression.

Family Therapy with Adults

Other than conjoint marital therapy, I have not been impressed with family therapy as the primary treatment of choice for adults with major neurotic conflicts. However, this matter needs further exploration. Some questions worthy of further consideration are: Should, perhaps, every diagnostic evaluation of an adult, even one seeking psychoanalysis, include at least one family interview as part of the diagnostic work-up? In analytic therapy, do we neglect the impact of the interpersonal reactions between our patients and their family members? Generally, I feel that the more severe the intrapsychic disturbance is in the adult, the greater the need for individual support and working through of conflict in a one-to-one corrective therapeutic relationship, at least as the major first step.

Reintegrating the Family in Crisis

At times of acute crisis, or chronically in certain very disturbed families, there exists extreme chaos and a lack of cohesiveness. This chaos can so outweigh the individual psychopathology in given family members as to render individual work useless and secondary to the need for order and structuring. The family approach, in which the therapist serves as a model for leadership, strives for a sense of organization.

Compared with the rather rigid adherence to fixed roles and rules often seen in schizophrenic families, we have noted that in neurotic families there frequently exists an extreme absence of rules, with much shifting of roles. This can, at times, lead to confusion and loosening of structure. In family meetings, a parent in the midst of such chaos, with its resultant or precipitating lack of leadership, can observe the therapist functioning as a leader and has the opportunity to identify with that leadership. Such demonstration of family leadership is not directly available in the one-to-one individual encounter of psychoanalytic therapy.

Community Psychiatry

With the growing demand for psychiatry to serve larger segments of the population and to offer means of prevention of mental illness at a preschool level, the use of family interviewing can be most economical and helpful. When a family doctor, pediatrician, teacher, or agency worker refers a problem child for evaluation, we have explored the use of family intake interviews which the referring person is invited to observe. Later he shares in the diagnostic discussion (Williams, 1967a). A goal of this approach is to help pediatricians, teachers, and family doctors enlarge their understanding of familial dynamics and potential for change. Hopefully we can promote their understanding of the many socioeconomic, cultural, and psychological forces which affect a family's integration and, in turn, impinge on or alter a child's expanding ego functioning.

We have begun to study the value of family interviewing in certain *crisis* situations. One or two family meetings are offered when family cohesiveness and integration begin to falter, such as with a first nursery school experience, a move to a new school or home, a divorce, death of a family member, or serious illness or trauma in a family member. The temporary loss of familial integration which can occur during such crises can signal the beginning of severe psychopathology or deviant development in a child. If one can move in quickly at such points of tension and shorten the duration of the stress, one should be able to ameliorate or minimize the untoward effects.

Contraindications to Family Therapy

Flexibility of method should also include assessment of contraindications to the family approach, at any given time. Generally speaking, when there are severe intrapsychic disturbances in either one of the parents I feel that individual therapy may more effectively bolster the severely disturbed member's ego. When faced with a psychotic parent, it may become necessary to do everything possible to separate an adolescent from the parent's therapy in order to avoid perpetuating a *folie à deux* situation. Such adolescents need a great deal of support, reality testing, and adaptational guidance as they learn to deal with their ambivalence toward the disturbed parent; a trusting, stable, one-to-one relationship to counterbalance the inconsistent parent-child encounters may be more useful than family meetings. I do feel, however, that in such situations, interspersed family meetings, singly or in series, can reinforce therapeutic gains by helping the patient and therapist evaluate the actual familial field. This clarifies the adolescent's reality testing and distortions as his treatment progresses.

When a member of a family, particularly an adolescent or adult, has a problem with underlying severe sexual conflicts, individual therapy is generally preferable. Family approaches attempting to deal with severe sexual deviations may only serve to depreciate the person concerned and precipitate new conflicts in other family members. I am not opposed to discussion of certain sexual conflicts in family meetings, but I doubt the value of any attempt to explore the genetic and symptomatic details of such problems within the family group setting.

The question is often raised as to whether or not the family approach, by nature of its very structure, promotes certain pathogenic symbioses, particularly in situations where adolescents have not yet separated from a close-knit family tie. Our work and results in this area, thus far, have been varied and need further exploration. There are points in such an adolescent's individual psychotherapy at which a crisis emerges around the imminent separation from the parental symbiosis. Several family meetings at such points can be catalytic in the direction of loosening the pathogenic tie and averting the adolescent's regressive pull. On the other hand, we have had several situations of ongoing family therapy with parent-adolescent symbioses where, after long treatment, we recognized that we may have helped perpetuate the overly close involvement between child and parents. The parents unwittingly used the family mode of treatment as just one more experience in functioning as a unit, without due respect for the uniqueness and individuation of their adolescent son or daughter.

Dangers of Family Therapy

INADEQUATE TRAINING OR SUPERVISION

Family therapy is a difficult undertaking because of the multitude of transference demands on the therapist, as well as the different levels within the family of ego strength and weakness. The possible decompensation of a family member in the face of change in certain rigid homeostatic familial patterns requires competent clinical awareness. Optimally, family therapy should be conducted by, or closely supervised by, therapists or teachers with a strong background in psychodynamic principles and psychopathology. Particularly in view of our orientation toward interchanging modalities of treatment, the family therapist should be able to handle, or at least recognize, the need for individual or conjoint measures. Family therapy is not counseling and should not be conducted by people who have had no intensive training. Too, because of the enhanced potential for acting out by the therapist of unresolved familial and marital problems, family therapists should have thorough insight into their own neurotic conflicts and impulses.

DISCARDING PSYCHOANALYTIC PRINCIPLES

As mentioned earlier, I feel critical of any premature discarding of sound analytic principles in family formulations and approaches. The danger of displacing certain analytic concepts lies in potential shift of focus away from the importance of intrapsychic forces. I certainly recognize the many observable familial phenomena so well described in the literature, such as shifting alliances, role diffusion, pseudo-mutuality, and skewing. I feel it is premature, however, to discard psychoanalytic constructs when they apply. Thus, some workers in family therapy have found the term "Oedipal" to be outdated and not descriptive in terms of a family approach. From my own frame of reference, "Oedipal" is "Oedipal" whether it represents itself in an individual one-to-one relationship or in a family meeting. When, for instance, all kinds of familial maneuvers take place so that an underlying seductive potential between a sixteen-year-old girl and her father should not come to the surface, it is clearly a familial defense system against the overt appearance of the "Oedipal" closeness with all of its implications. When that same sixteen-year-old girl lifts her skirt, pats her thigh, and gets much eye contact and smiling response from her father, following which her mother berates her for lack of loyalty relationship to the neighbors at home, we are again seeing manifestations of the Oedipal situation. I find no need for a new construct to describe it.

Conclusion

In the many fields of reference concerning human behavior, no one approach can be complete unto itself. Most of the forces and fields effecting the total human being cannot be directly observed in children and adults, but rather need to be inferred. A fantastic investment of unavailable time and manpower would be required to properly observe and assess the effects of constitutional factors, school life, friendships, church life, recreational activity, and employment matters. Family therapy offers an excellent opportunity for studying a segment of family life as it is re-created within the psychotherapist's office. Just because we have found such a valuable method of studying this segment of human life, we should not, however, discard a method that has been most helpful in studying another segment —the individual's intrapsychic life, a very potent force in his total adaptation.

A major danger in a premature separation of intrapsychic and interpersonal approaches to studies of human behavior lies, I believe, in the area of training. Psychiatric training programs of the future could become individually or interpersonally one-sided in their teaching of techniques and theoretical models. It would be clinically and scientifically short-sighted, I feel, to leave the psychiatric practitioner of the future at a disadvantage in his work because he could deal only with family group dynamics, or only with individual intrapsychic problems via psychoanalytic techniques.

With family therapy barely inside the door, and community psychiatry now on the doorsteps, we need more than ever to strive for synthesis of the many approaches to our understanding and enhancement of the individual and his functioning in relation to his inner life, to his family, and to the larger group around him.

Note: Appreciation is noted for both the initiation and continued guidance of the family studies by Dr. Saul L. Brown, Chief, Department of Child Psychiatry, Cedars-Sinai Medical Center, Los Angeles.

References

Ackerman, N. W. "Family Psychotherapy and Psychoanalysis: Implications of Difference." *Family Process*, No. 1 (March 1962), 30–43.

Alexander, F. *Psychoanalysis and Psychotherapy*. London: Ruskin House, 1957.

Bell, J. "Family Group Therapy." U. S. Public Health Service Monograph, 1961.

Boszormenyi-Nagy, I. "Intensive Family Therapy as Process." In I. Boszormenyi-Nagy and J. L. Framo (eds.), *Intensive Family Therapy*. New York: Harper & Row, 1965. Pp. 87–142.

Bowen, M. "A Family Concept of Schizophrenia." In D. D. Jackson (ed.), *The Etiology of Schizophrenia*. New York: Basic Books, 1960. Pp. 346–372.

Brown, S. L. "Family Therapy Viewed in Terms of Resistance to Change." American Psychiatric Association, Psychiatric Research Report No. 20, 1966, pp. 132–139.

Fenichel, O. *The Psychoanalytic Theory of Neurosis*. New York: Norton, 1945.

Framo, J. L. "Rationale and Techniques of Intensive Family Therapy." In I. Boszormenyi-Nagy and J. L. Framo (eds.), *Intensive Family Therapy*. New York: Harper & Row, 1965. Pp. 143–211.

Haley, J. *Strategies of Psychotherapy*. New York: Grune & Stratton, 1963.

Jackson, D. D. "The Question of Family Homeostasis." *Psychiatric Quarterly*, Supplement 31, 1957, pp. 79–90.

Jackson, D. D., and Satir, Virginia. "A Review of Psychiatric Development in Family Diagnosis and Therapy." In N. W. Ackerman, Frances L. Beatman, and S. M. Sherman (eds.), *Exploring the Base for Family Therapy*. New York: Family Service Association of America, 1961. Pp. 29–51.

Kaffman, M. "Short Term Family Therapy." *Family Process*, 2, No. 2 (September 1963), 216–234.

Lidz, T., Cornelison, Alice R., Fleck, S., and Terry, Dorothy. "The Intrafamilial Environment of Schizophrenic Patients. II. Marital Schism and Marital Skew." *American Journal of Psychiatry*, 114 (September 1957), 241–248.

Messer, A. A. "Successful Family Treatment of a Patient Who Failed in Psychoanalysis." Paper presented at American Psychiatric Association, Atlantic City, New Jersey, May 1966.

Minuchin, S. "Adapting Therapeutic Styles to the Low Socioeconomic Group." Paper presented at American Orthopsychiatric Association, San Francisco, California, April 1966.

Paul, N. L., and Grosser, G. H. "Operational Mourning and Its Role in Conjoint Family Therapy." *Community Mental Health Journal*, 1, No. 4 (Winter 1965), 339–345.

Ruesch, J., and Bateson, G. *Communication: The Social Matrix of Psychiatry*. New York: Norton, 1951.

Spiegel, J. P., and Kluckhohn, Florence. "Integration and Conflict in Family Behavior." Group for the Advancement of Psychiatry, Report No. 27, August 1954.

Williams, F. S. "Family Therapy with a Severely Atypical Child." Paper presented at Regional American Association of Psychiatric Clinics for Children, Los Angeles, California, April 1964.

Williams, F. S. "Family Interviews for Diagnostic Evaluations in Child Psychiatry." Paper presented at American Orthopsychiatric Association, New York City, March 1965.

Williams, F. S. "Community Treatment Services and Prevention—What Are the Issues?" Paper presented at American Orthopsychiatric Association, Washington, D.C., March 1967. (a)

Williams, F. S. "Family Therapy: A Critical Assessment." *American Journal of Orthopsychiatry*, 37, No. 5 (October 1967). (b)

Wynne, L. C., Ryckoff, I. M., Day, J., and Hirsch, S. I. "Pseudo-Mutuality in the Family Relations of Schizophrenics." *Psychiatry*, 21 (May 1958), 205–220.

16

Toward a Taxonomy of Marriage

WELLS GOODRICH

Recently we have completed a five-year study using a combined social science and clinical approach which defined eight patterns of early marriage. The study is the first[1] on early marriage relationships as they exist among average couples living in the community, based on combined clinical and experimental methods. The sampling procedures meet most of the criteria stated or implied by Hartmann for "average expectable developmental states." Hartmann (1958) postulated that within any relatively homogeneous subculture there would be a limited number of expectable patterns of adaptation at any particular stage in the life cycle. It seems likely that some of the eight marital patterns we[2] have discovered will be demonstrable as being average expectable adaptive patterns in this sense.

[1] Some follow-up data exist on the study of 1,000 couples by Burgess and Wallin (1953); their sample was first studied during engagement and then followed up by 15 to 20 years later; questionnaires only were used. In 1928 E. Lowell Kelly (1955) studied 300 engaged couples for which data on 368 individuals followed up 20 years later have been reported.

[2] This study was carried out under the direction of Harold L. Rausch, Ph.D., and Robert G. Ryder, Ph.D., and the principal investigators, besides the author, were Arden Flint, M.D., Paul Blank, M.S.W., Walter Sceery, M.S.W., and John D. Campbell, Ph.D.

After describing this study, and the eight patterns of marriage, this chapter will discuss some requirements to be met before such patterns can be considered as taxonomic types. Finally, the data from our study will be used as a basis, within the framework of psychoanalytic theory, for raising a number of questions about the longer-term adaptive significance of these newlywed patterns. For example, we will consider whether certain patterns of early marriage indicate the presence of severe *latent adaptive difficulties* which, in the long run, might demand some kind of therapeutic intervention more than those marital patterns which, though presently full of *open conflict,* nevertheless also show strong adaptational resources.

There is a public health need for a psychiatrically oriented taxonomy of marital and family development. Present-day epidemiology in psychiatry, tied as it is to the incidence and prevalence of diagnosable, overt symptom disorders, focuses our attention on disorders far beyond that point in time when the patient's early maladaptive processes have become rigidly structured. Recent studies of the interplay between culture and psychiatric disorder have indicated that there are differential rates of certain illnesses among certain populations. For example, Caudill (1963) has discovered that in the contemporary Japanese culture there is a higher rate of hospitalized schizophrenia among first-born sons than with later-born sons or daughters. Alcoholism is prevalent among the Swedes and rare among the Chinese. Depression is common among the Hutterites (Eaton and Weil, 1955). The Japanese have the highest rate of joint suicide in the world (Ohara, 1963). Antisocial and hyperaggressive behavior disorders among adolescent males are particularly prevalent among those living in the heart of large American cities.

One approach to these disorders is not to treat the symptomatically disturbed patients with expensive clinical methods, but rather to view such patients as a sample subgroup which manifests psychological and social processes prevalent within a significant portion of the total community or culture. The question then becomes how to separate those larger "subclinical" populations within the total community who have a significantly higher risk of developing overt symptomatic disorders. This kind of judgment about susceptibility at this stage of our knowledge is a most speculative undertaking; when applied in the form of further developmental and epidemiological studies, however, such speculations may lead us to more adequate concepts of preventive psychiatry and to better notions of how to identify the subpopulations-at-risk within the community. It should be emphasized also that, in principle at least, it should not be so difficult to make predictions about the susceptibility of *groups* of families as it would be to make predictions about the idiosyncrasies of a single individual or a single family.

The Study[3]

This report concerns the first stage of a longitudinal investigation of fifty middle-class marriages, couples who, after having been married for three months, volunteered to spend four evenings of their time with our procedures. In previous publications (Goodrich, 1961, 1963) I have considered the event of getting married for the first time as a developmental turning point which introduces a new stage of the life cycle. This new stage demands a variety of adaptive changes, some similar for husband and wife and some sex-specific. These stage-specific "developmental presses" toward change lead to a variety of adaptive response patterns; this interplay between stage and persons has been referred to as the *developmental transaction of early marriage*. The patterns to be described are conceived as different forms this developmental transaction may take within this sample.

Couples' names were obtained from local marriage license records. Those who subsequently agreed to participate constituted about 60 to 80 per cent of couples who both were approached and fitted our screening criteria, which were as follows: Couples had to be white, to live within a reasonable drive from us, and to have completed high school; but not to have obtained any postgraduate degree, and not to be presently a full-time student. Husbands had to be between the ages of 20 and 27, and wives between 18 and 25. It was required that wives were not knowingly pregnant as of three months after marriage. The couples were studied during the fourth month after marriage. The general intent of our screening criteria was to reduce the impact on our data of ethnic and socioeconomic differences so that relationships among other variables might be more closely revealed.

During this newlywed period, procedures used included six interviews of one to two hours in length, about three hours worth of questionnaires, Goodrich and Boomer's *Color Matching Test*, and a quasi-role playing procedure called *Improvisations*. Interviews were administered by highly skilled and experienced social workers, and were semi-structured. There was a specific set of questions to be asked, but interviewers followed up answers as much as was necessary to achieve clarity. By means of these interviews and questionnaires, certain situations were investigated in depth: the sequential history of the courtship, current aspects of the marriage providing intense satisfaction or dissatisfaction, the sexual relationship, keeping the home, food purchasing and serving, relationships with friends and relatives, occupation, and planning for parenthood. Other situations were investi-

[3] For more detailed reports of this study, see Goodrich and Boomer, 1963; Goodrich and Ryder, 1966; Rausch, Goodrich, and Campbell, 1963; and Ryder and Goodrich, 1966.

gated more cursorily: early childhood history, history of developmentally disruptive situations or events, adolescent school achievement or failure, sexual development, as well as current educational, recreational or religious activities, budget management and health. After the fourth evening, the interviewer rated each couple on 21 variables encompassing a global evaluation of the marriage and aspects of their communication and relationship: empathy, support, decision-making effectiveness, and degree of mutual satisfaction.

The interviews were tape recorded, and the typed transcripts were then subjected to an intensive content analysis. The questionnaires were scored for amount of participation and decision-making by each spouse in these various life situations; scores were also obtained for reported yielding to the marital partner during disagreements as well as for self-restraint, social conformity, and satisfaction with marriage. There were also scores reflecting economic, occupational, educational, and ethnic variables.

The direct observations of husband-wife interaction generated information about qualities of patience or impatience, accuracy or inaccuracy, humor or hostility, and rational modes of discussion as husbands and wives sought to analyze why they disagreed and tried to find a consensus.

Each technique was analyzed systematically: interviewer ratings, interview content codes, questionnaire scores, and color-matching test scores. Factor analytic techniques were employed to eliminate method factors and to differentiate maximally between scores. In all, Robert G. Ryder, Ph.D., developed 164 stable variables which were found to group themselves within 37 clusters. The final factor matrix was subjected to a profile rotation procedure in such a way as to maximize the tendency for each couple to have an extreme score on one and only one factor and to be middling on all other factors.

These procedures identified eight patterns of marriage, corresponding to the positive and negative ends of the four final factors. In presenting the four factors we will list those 10 or 11 variables with highest loadings, namely those variables which provide most of the information accounting for the differences between couples. It is well to remember, in interpreting these data, that these patterns were found in couples who were only two to three months post-honeymoon, were finding much excitement in the relationship, and were facing an uncertain future, as regards occupation, income, residence, and parenthood.

Here an interesting conjunction of four kinds of variables is seen: the husband's dependency on and involvement with his family, the wife's relatively greater sex interest in her husband, absence of spontaneity in the husband's communications with the interviewer (as well as little husband-wife laughter), and much anticipated activity by the husband with his first child. As in Factor IV (to be described), the data point up a basic contrast between spontaneity in relationships on the one hand, and cross-genera-

Factor I Closeness (vs. Distance) from the Husband's Family

Source	*Loading*	*Variable*
Interview Codes		
	positive	Interactive ties with H.'s family
	positive	H. remained living at home until marriage
	negative	H.'s strong sex interest (relative to W.'s)
Interview Ratings		
	negative	H. liked by interviewer
	negative	H.'s communication with interviewer
	negative	H.'s spontaneity with interviewer
Questionnaires		
	positive	H. report of contacts with H.'s family
	positive	W. report of contacts with H.'s family
	positive	H.'s anticipated activity with baby
Observed Interaction		
	negative	W.'s laughter

tional involvement between the couple and their parents and also with their first child to be on the other. The issue here is similar to that reported in a recent provocative study of 457 marriages by Cuber and Harroff (1965). Couples are characterized by them as "utilitarian" or as "intrinsic." That is to say, the utilitarian marriage places higher value on maintaining wider social and family relationships, whereas the intrinsic marriage places higher value on qualities of emotional exchange within the marriage as well as with a small number of intimate friends.

For those couples, identified by Factors I and IV, who show an unusual degree of participation with their parents during the newlywed phase and who, in addition, lack spontaneity and expressiveness, the concept of delayed identity formation may be useful. A firm sense of one's identity implies a combined awareness of inner and outer direction. There is clarity with oneself about those aspects of old and new roles with which one does and does not identify. With a firm sense of identity there is a tendency to enter into expressive interpersonal engagements, positive or negative, with close associates.

In essence this factor appears to be one of role orientation with, at one end, husband interest in occupation (but not household) matters and low wife interest in occupational matters. At the other, or nontraditional, end husbands claim more involvement with housework and wives claim more involvement with occupational pursuits.

The conjunction here of two other variables with the contrasting role orientations lends special interest to this factor. These are rationality of observed task discussion and the husband's recall of various kinds of difficulties with his family of origin and during his development. As we shall

Factor II Marital Role Orientation

Source	*Loading*	*Variable*
Interview Codes		
	positive	H.'s recall of difficulties with his family
	positive	H. expresses occupational and economic ambition
Questionnaire		
	positive	Couple is Jewish
	negative	H. involved in housework at present
	negative	H. anticipates future involvement in housework
	negative	W. involved in job activity at present
	negative	W. anticipates future involvement in job activities
	negative	W.'s mother is involved in job activities
Observed Interaction		
	negative	H. eliminates disagreement by making an error
	positive	W.'s rational discussion of task

see, Factor III points up the association between the wife's recall of difficulties with her family of origin and the presence of marital difficulties during the newlywed period. Here, in Factor II, there is the association of husband's recall of developmental difficulties, and the adoption of an extreme (relative to the other couples in our study) lack of sharing between the couple, the selection by the husband of a stay-at-home type of wife and mother-in-law, and high investment by the husband in occupational strivings. Ryder and I have hypothesized (Goodrich and Ryder, 1966) that this sex difference reflects a sex-specific developmental press characteristic of the initial stage of marriage. The psychological challenge implicit in the situation of being newly married, particularly for the insecure young husband, appears to be to establish himself as economically secure and not to risk too intense an emotional involvement with his wife. For the insecure wife the challenge appears to be to express and work out her emotional life in a freer and more deeply expressive manner with her husband and to use the marital relationship as a situation within which to enact, and perhaps to resolve, her earlier internalized frustrations.

In the long run, of course, each spouse will tend to express within the marriage conflicts derived from early development. It may be plausible, however, to suppose that during the fourth month of marriage there are greater opportunities and psychological pressures for husbands to erect defenses against the open expression of these difficulties within the marital relationship than there are for wives. Our data are consistent with this hypothesis.

In Factor II we also see that husbands with no complaints about difficulties in their family of origin tend to marry wives who want to work (and whose mothers have worked) and wives with whom there is a great deal of sharing in all sorts of activities.

The tendency for these role-sharing husbands to eliminate disagreements during the Color Matching Test by making perceptual or conceptual errors may be associated with a wish to maintain harmony at any price. There also may be a wish to maintain the romantic illusion of a honeymoon kind of relationship. This impression was suggested by the sentimental attitudes and romantic behavior of a number of couples who made such errors during this test situation.

Factor III *Open Conflict (or Harmony) in Marriage*

Source	*Loading*	*Variable*
Interview Codes		
	positive	W.'s recall of difficulties with family
Interviewer Ratings		
	negative	Easy marital decision process
	negative	Couple (vs. individual) identification
	negative	Overall evaluation of the marriage
	negative	H.'s empathy with wife
	negative	H.'s support for wife
	negative	W.'s support for husband
Questionnaire		
	positive	H.'s report of unhappiness and doubts about marriage
	positive	W.'s report of unhappiness and doubts about marriage
	positive	W.'s report of many disagreements with spouse
	negative	W.'s report of yielding to husband in disagreement

It can be seen that this factor is clearly a dimension of reported and judged evaluation of the marriage, in which there is agreement between the spouses' evaluations and those of the interviewers. Early marriages full of doubts, unhappiness, and disagreement tend to have wives who report difficulties with their families of origin. There probably is some correspondence, although how much is hard to tell, between these openly conflicted marriages identified by the positive end of Factor III and Cuber and Harroff's (1965) conflicted marriage pattern. Cuber and Harroff identified a relatively small group of couples who spend much of their time together quarreling and disagreeing, often violently and dramatically. Many of these couples have satisfactory sexual experiences together and, underneath the overt conflict, actually are quite involved with and fond of each other, although these tender feelings usually are not admitted openly.

The negative end of Factor III presents a couple idyllically mated, with high mutual identification, much mutual support and happiness, no doubts about the marriage, few disagreements, and easy decision process. The interesting thing, as noted above, is the high association with absence of wife's recall of difficulties growing up with her family.

Factor IV Closeness (or Distance) with Wife's Family

Source	*Loading*	*Variable*
Interview Codes		
	positive	Interactive ties with W.'s family
	negative	Current difficulties with W.'s family
	negative	Preference for breast (vs. bottle) feeding
Questionnaire		
	positive	W.'s report of contacts with W.'s family
	positive	W.'s report of anticipated future contact with W.'s family
	positive	W.'s recall of her parents' involvement with their relatives
	positive	W.'s recall of her parents' involvement with their friends
	positive	W.'s recall of self-restraint
Observed Interaction		
	negative	H.'s laughter
	negative	W.'s open disapproval of (or hostility to) H.

As noted in our discussion of Factor I, here also is found evidence of emotionality and spontaneity in the early marital relationship among a group of couples who are *not* closely and harmoniously involved with the previous generation. It may not be amiss to interpret the anticipated preference for breast feeding over bottle feeding with the firstborn infant as evidence of value placed on affective intimacy in relationships. In commenting here about this contrast shown in Factors I and IV, it is important to keep in mind that I am considering only that *initial* period during which the couple is establishing the new marital situation, a period when many new couples feel a particular need to be by themselves and temporarily to place limits on participation with relatives.

To summarize, our study suggests that an eventual psychosocial taxonomy of early marriage may include dimensions of complaints about the husband's or wife's family of origin, marital role orientation, degree of current marital harmony or disharmony, degree of involvement with the husband's or wife's family during the newlywed period, and a rational versus affective style of communication between husband and wife. The study, which requires replication on a larger sample, found that wives who report problems with their families in childhood or adolescence are to be found in those couples who report unhappiness, doubt, and diffuse marital conflict. Husbands who report problems with their families tend to take a less involved position within the marriage and to strive most toward occupational and economic goals. There also seems to be a connection between close family involvement during this early marriage period and low affectivity in the marital relationship.

Toward a Taxonomy of Marriage and Family Patterns

Clinical experience is consistent with the idea that families have systems of defenses which interact within and between individuals in a concordant or complementary fashion. The system of family defenses tends to be reproduced across generations in a very general way. Introjects and identifications with their attendant ego ideals, anxious fantasies, and a limited repertory of defenses seem to be shared or to show considerable similarity between members of the same family. Jan Ehrenwald (1963) has described several different patterns of family defense, notably his description of the "Obscomp Family." [4]

Very little work so far has been done with longitudinal monitoring of family defensive and adaptive patterns across stages of the life cycle. Judging from existing longitudinal research publications from the field of child development, one is justified in anticipating that such continuities may be documented by future family research. Studies of the development of intelligence, assertiveness, dependency, and other individual personality patterns from early childhood to adulthood have shown two types of continuity across developmental stages, namely isomorphic and metamorphic continuity. Bayley and Schaefer (1964) report that when a boy is treated with warmth and granted autonomy by his mother in the first three years of life he is apt to have a low developmental score in infancy but a high I.Q. in the years following age 5. This is an example of metamorphic continuity. Sontag, Baker, and Nelson (1958) report that between the ages of 3 and 10 years, three-fifths of 140 children showed a variation of 15 points or more in I.Q. This is an example of significant isomorphic change.

At this point in our knowledge of family developmental patterns across stages of the life cycle it remains to be seen which functions will show substantial isomorphic continuity and which will tend to show fairly predictable or unpredictable shifts. In order to discover family development

[4] The writings over the past decade of Lyman Wynne, Theodore Lidz, Donald Jackson, Murray Bowen, and others are also consistent with this point of view (see Mishler and Waxler (1965) for an excellent review of this literature).

patterns which will have meaningful continuity through time, certain conceptual orientations and investigative strategies are indicated. The first principle is to look at the family holistically; by this I do not mean attempting to assess everything that conceivably may be relevant on any level from the biochemical to the sociological. Rather I mean being open to investigate *obvious* signs of adaptive adequacy or inadequacy wherever they may be found, intrapsychically within family members, interpersonally within the family or between the family and the wider culture. Handel (1965) has recently surveyed and evaluated psychological studies of families carried out from this point of view. An essential interest here is in making judgments about the functional appropriateness of ongoing psychosocial and psychodynamic processes in a family, even though at the moment neither the family nor the wider community may in any sense define any one in this family as "ill." By doing this we may be able to identify those subgroups of the population in which there is a greater tendency to develop overt symptomatic disorders.

With regard to research strategy aimed at defining marriage and family patterns, it is important to combine a social science approach using brief assessments of large groups of families with a clinical approach which uses intensive assessments of small numbers of families. Without the social science approach, one will not know how significant the patterns are from an epidemiological standpoint; without the clinical approach, one will not really understand what is going on within a family, or group of similar families, which may account for the observed pattern of functioning. By linking the two approaches, by designing studies in which the same families are studied by both approaches, one can compare the data of social science with the clinical evidence. This comparison provides the basis for speculations about the psychodynamic and adaptive significance of relatively inexpensive and brief observations of family functioning on larger groups.

In one such study, Harrower (1956) carried out identical psychological tests on the husband and wife for 40 couples receiving psychotherapy. She used the test data to formulate the interaction of defenses within the marriage. For example, using the five subtests of the Wechsler-Bellevue as a personality profile describing ego functioning and sources of anxiety, she described how psychotic deficit in one partner evoked panic in the other and how this process was reflected in complementary deficits in cognitive functioning. She then made some interesting clinical speculations about the prognosis of each marriage.

A variety of foci for investigation, as well as standard controls, are useful if family research of this kind is to differentiate between immediate situational influences and family defense patterns which have structure and continuity. The assessment of adaptive adequacy in families is concerned with their ability to cope with what is novel or strange in life situations, as well as with other kinds of frustration. This assessment can be approached using experimental and interview methods, the two methods serving as a check on each other. We are also concerned with identifying major satisfactions and major anxieties. Styles of communication and relationship between family members in situations of high satisfaction or of high tension or conflict need investigation. An attempt to identify major defenses, values, and attitudes which come into play in response either to an ambiguous reality or to inner anxiety is important. Then it is important to obtain information on the influence of the developmental stage, as well as of the ethnic, religious, economic, and educational influences. Doing all this, however, and obtaining some consistent patterns of marriage or family adaptation is but the first step. Before such patterns can be dignified by the term "types" within a formal taxonomy, it will be necessary to replicate the patterns and to show the range of occurrence of each pattern under various developmental and environmental conditions. That is to say, until a given pattern has been studied under a wide variety of conditions, one is not justified in saying that one has discovered its "typical" manifestation.

The above considerations about the assessment of adaptational patterns were applied in our study. It appears that the eight patterns of marriage can provide a tentative baseline for longitudinal studies of middle-class marriage and family development followed up at later stages of the life cycle.

Fitting Together and Speculations about Adaptation

We are now ready to approach some speculations about the significance of these early marriage patterns for later family adaptation. These speculations will point to new questions for future research on a taxonomy of family development. To study the wider psychosocial phenomena of adaptation, such as the occupational values of the family, as well as the psychodynamic phenomena of anxiety and defense, is consistent with Hartmann's concept of "fitting together" as described in *The Ego and the Problem of Adaptation* (1958). *Fitting together* is to the totality of forces accounting for adaptation in an individual what the *synthetic function of the ego* (Nunberg, 1961) is to the totality of the individual's intrapsychic functions. That is to say, the concept *fitting together* recognizes that at any given moment the individual's ability to adapt psychologically in his situation depends not only on his own inner resources and conflicts, but also on the interpersonal and cultural and developmental situation within which he finds himself. The concept of fitting together recognizes the possible relevance for adaptation of all sorts of combinations of variables: the equilibrium between inner drives, the balance between drive and defense, between the constitutional and the cultural, the intrapsychic and the interpersonal, and so forth, at various levels of generalization. About fitting together Hartmann (1958, pp. 40–41) states:

> We are justified in saying that *adaptation* and *fitting together* are interdependent; fitting together is usually the prerequisite of an adaptation process and vice versa. This correlation also includes the psychophysical relations, and its psychological expression is the synthetic function (cf. Nunberg, 1930), which is thus a special case of the broader biological concept of fitting together. . . . Thus fitting together (in the psychological realm, the synthetic function) gains in significance in the course of evolution. If we encounter—as we do in man—a function which simultaneously regulates both the environmental relationships and the interrelations of the mental institutions, we will have to place it above adaptation in the biological hierarchy: we will place it above adaptive activity regulated by the external world, that is, above adaptation in the narrower sense, but not above adaptation in the broader sense, because the latter already implies a "survival value" determined both by the environmental relationships and the interrelations of mental institutions.

Applied to the problems of this essay the concept of fitting together challenges us to think in terms described by Erikson (1959) and to try to visualize the sequence of psychosocial and adaptive issues which, expectably for many, will face our eight different types of couples. Differences in adaptive style with regard to spontaneity of close relationships, amount of unhappiness and disagreement, involvement with relatives, degree of marital role-sharing and awareness of difficulties during childhood and adolescence all may have long-term implications. The psychoanalytic task here is different from the usual one of assessing the ebb and flow of defenses in relation to an individual patient's impulses, fantasies, or anxieties. Here we are concerned with groups and with assessing, somewhat abstractly, adaptive patterns as they may be reinforced by family relationships, or be challenged by the demands of parenthood and the events of later maturity.

Surely there is no simple relationship between the amount of inner neurotic conflict in a young adult and his or her ability, during a short sequence of clinical interviews, to report an awareness of emotional stress or difficulties while growing up. Nevertheless it may be that our Factor II and III couples include a majority of those individuals from our sample who have neurotic problems. This is supported by an interesting similarity on the Color Matching Test between wives scoring positively on Factor III and husbands scoring positively on Factor II. These scores indicate prolonged conflict, stubborn adherence to the marital differences provided by the experiment, and resolute avoidance of consensus over a long period of time. The data indicate that the *developmental timing* for the open expression of neurosis in the form of a marital problem is likely to be much earlier in the course of the marriage for women than for men.

It would appear then that until the woman begins to bear children—and nearly all our young wives wanted to get pregnant in the fairly near future—her own needs for intimacy and self-expression within the marriage relationship will tend to be greater than her husband's. The significance of work during the early marriage period is different for each sex. For the middle-class woman it is a temporary function adjunctive to her main identifications. For the middle-class man it is a central identification and offers alternatives to investing himself fully in the marriage and the family. It would seem that there may be three resolutions for the early marriage pattern of diffuse disagreements and unhappiness connected with the wife's developmental difficulties. These are: (1) a chronic, openly-conflicted marriage, as described by Cuber and Harroff (1965), in which the couple develops a high tolerance for this style of interaction; or (2) the wife, like the husband in Factor II, may become sufficiently uninvolved, defensively, in the marriage and sufficiently invested in her own children or in occupational opportunities, so that her neurotic conflicts can be displaced, and thereby she is enabled to protect her marriage; or (3) there will be an early separation, probably during the first year. Monahan's research (1962) indicates that the highest rate of separation and divorce is during the first year. It would be interesting to know if many of these early separations are from marriages in which the wife had been aware of difficulties with her family of origin.

The above discussion has been concerned with alternative ways in which several dimensions of the total adaptive situation might fit together. In the main the concern has been with unresolved neurotic conflict within a marital partner, the question of acting out this conflict within the marriage, and the differential press from this developmental stage for each sex as regards investments in family intimacy versus occupational achievement.

It may be that unresolved neurotic problems for many couples are not presented within the marriage until later years, after the novelty, uncertainty, and interest attached to the husband's occupational struggles and to their joint parental experiences have become less demanding. Our Factor II pattern suggests that this is likely, especially for men who have difficulties growing up, and who maintain less involvement in the marriage from the beginning. Contributing to the developmental timing and the locus for expression of conflict is the value placed on intimacy as a source of life satisfaction in contrast to work achievement or other orientations with a greater emphasis on stability of relationships. The critical nature of the *hierarchy of inner values* for patterns of ego adaptation has been discussed by Hartmann (1958). Cuber and Harroff (1965) also comment on the changes in values about marriage which attend occupational success or altered economic circumstance or exposure to new relationships outside of marriage. Relevant here is E. Lowell Kelly's (1955) observation that, over the first twenty years of maturity, attitudes and values about marriage are one of the most changeable aspects of personality, far more than attitudes toward occupation, politics, religion, or other areas of living. A twenty-year follow-up study of these Factor II males, who have awareness of emotional difficulties during childhood and adolescence, might show a higher prevalence of late marital problems and/or late separation than in other husbands in our sample. In the fit between the defense against the conflict, the conflict itself, and the locus of expression for conflict, the influence of changing ego ideals is obviously but one of many significant kinds of changes in ego function, but it is one which may be sufficiently widespread within a particular population that its influences can readily be identified.

It is interesting that one can distinguish with brief experimental observations (Ryder, 1966; Ryder and Goodrich, 1966) and questionnaires couples who communicate with humor, hostility, and other affective expressions from couples who communicate primarily with logic and reason. That this difference also relates to other easily identified information, such as involvement with relatives, suggests that we may be separating out by means of Factor I and IV two significant family adaptive and defense patterns. Perhaps one is the impulsive-expressive family pattern and the other the rational-controlled pattern. It is tempting to speculate that the one kind of family will have a higher incidence of disorders of a hysterical or impulsive sort while the second will have a higher incidence of obsessional disorders. The probability, however, is that we shall need more specific assessments before this kind of extrapolation will be possible.

It is safe to speculate that, if we are interested in locating Cuber and Harroff's "intrinsic marriages," we will find them at the negative end of all four factors. Perhaps we are particularly apt to find them at the negative end of Factor III. This is the pattern rated by our interviewers as showing the most mutual support, empathy, ease of decision-making, mutual identification, and spontaneity. Cuber and Harroff's study (1965) of marriages after ten years indicates that when a couple have enjoyed the deep satisfaction and excitement of a high degree of intimacy and mutual identification, any disturbance of this situation—disturbances which would be nonthreatening to another couple—tends to be experienced as such a loss that this kind of marriage may be more unstable than less involved marriages. This paradoxical conclusion is consistent with the notion that greater intimacy makes for greater "adaptive work" for the ego, greater challenge to inner potentials for anxiety, and a greater tendency to perceive expectable frustrations as threatening to the marriage. We arrive, then, at the unexpected speculation that both the positive and negative end of Factor III may identify groups of couples with a relatively decreased likelihood of stable marriages.

If marital difficulties do arise in couples who score at the positive end of Factors I and IV, perhaps they will arise because of an identity crisis in which a spouse experiences greater need for autonomy from the family. It is impressive how involved with their parents some of these young people are early in marriage: taking meals at their home, using closet space of the parents, consulting the parents about many ordinary matters. It does not seem farfetched to speculate that sooner or later one spouse may experience this state of affairs, so apparently comfortable at the time of our study, as uncomfortably rivalrous. This is more likely in the nuclear-family based American middle-class culture, which values individual choice and self-direction and which sanctions social and personal change, than it would be, say, in the Italian or Japanese extended-family based cultures. Since a break away from involvement with relatives is apt to be initiated by one spouse rather than by both spouses simultaneously, the conjunction of American culture with this kind of marriage contains the seed of future conflict between husband and wife.

We have speculated that the positive end of all factors and the negative end of Factor III have identified various latent or overt marital conflicts and/or developmental problems. It follows that the negative end of Factors I, II, and IV may have the greatest degree of marital harmony and stability.

Except for this latest speculation, much of what has been considered has included what John Benjamin (see his discussion [1959] in "Prediction and Psychopathological Theory") might have termed positive, long-term, inductive, and deductive predictions. (Perhaps he would consider the last speculation as fortune-telling.) Benjamin emphasized the usefulness of predictive speculations so long as an effort is made to evaluate their nature and the evidence on which they are based. He suggested that the criteria to be used at follow-up be specified in advance.

It is hard to escape the impression that early in adult life—barring death or disaster—a certain life course is set up. This is partly a result of choice of marital partner, partly it is a result of other major life decisions, such as occupational choice, and partly it is a result of unforeseeable events. This is not to say that the adaptive pattern will remain the same; it is simply to say that for sizable groups of psychologically similar families certain problems in adaptation will tend to follow, in a somewhat expectable fashion, as a result of the defensive and adaptive patterns structured in the beginning of the marriage.

This chapter has followed Hartmann in using nonclinical data to consider adaptive patterns as average expectable developmental states. Using the concept of fitting together, a few hypotheses have been formulated about the adequacy of family defense patterns in the light of past or present neurotic problems and of future expectable psychosocial issues.

References

Bayley, Nancy, and Schaefer, E. S. "Correlations of Maternal and Child Behaviors with the Development of Mental Abilities . . ." *Child Development*, 29, No. 6 (1964), Monograph 97.

Benjamin, J. D. "Prediction and Psychopathological Theory." In L. Jessner and E. Pavenstedt (eds.), *Dynamic Psychopathology in Childhood.* New York: Grune & Stratton, 1959.

Burgess, E. W., and Wallin, P. *Engagement and Marriage.* Philadelphia: Lippincott, 1953.

Caudill, W. "Social Background and Sibling Rank among Japanese Psychiatric Patients." *Psychiatria et Neurologia Japonica*, Supplement No. 7, 1963, pp. 35–40.

Cuber, J., and Harroff, P. B. *The Significant Americans.* New York: Appleton-Century, 1965.

Eaton, J. W., and Weil, R. J. *Culture and Mental Disorders.* Glencoe, Ill.: The Free Press, 1955.

Ehrenwald, J. *Neurosis in the Family and Patterns of Psychosocial Defense.* New York: Harper & Row, 1963.

Erikson, E. H. "Identity and the Life Cycle." *Psychological Issues*, 1, No. 1 (1959), Monograph No. 1.

Goodrich, D. W. "Possibilities for Preventive Intervention during Initial Personality Formation." In G. Caplan (ed.), *Prevention of Mental Disorders in Children.* New York: Basic Books, 1961. Pp. 249–264.

Goodrich, D. W. "The Developmental Transaction. A Basic Unit for Research on Child Mental Health." *Proceedings of the Joint Meeting of the Japanese Society of Psychiatry and Neurology and the American Psychiatric Association*, Supplement No. 7, 1963.

Goodrich, D. W., and Boomer, D. "Experimental Assessment of Marital Modes of Conflict Resolution." *Family Process*, 2 (1963), 15–24.

Goodrich, D. W., and Ryder, R. G. "Patterns of Newlywed Marriage." Paper presented at the Annual Meeting of American Psychiatric Association, May 1966.

Handel, G. "Psychological Study of Whole Families." *Psychological Bulletin*, 63 (1965), 19–41.

Harrower, Molly. "The Measurement of Psychological Factors in Marital Maladjustment." In V. Eisenstein (ed.), *Neurotic Interaction in Marriage.* New York: Basic Books, 1956. Pp. 169–191.

Hartmann, H. *The Ego and the Problem of Adaptation.* New York: International Universities Press, 1958.

Kelly, E. L. "Consistency of the Adult Personality." *American Psychologist*, 10 (1955), 659–681.

Mishler, E. G., and Waxler, N. E. "Family Interaction Processes and Schizophrenia: A Review of Current Theories." *Merrill-Palmer Quarterly*, 11 (1965), 269–315.

Monahan, T. P. "When Married Couples Part: Statistical Trends and Relationships in Divorce." *American Sociological Review*, 27 (1962), 625–633.

Nunberg, H. *Practice and Theory of Psychoanalysis.* New York: International Universities Press, 1961. Pp. 120–136.

Ohara, K. "Characteristics of Suicides in Japan, Especially of Parent-Child Double Suicide." *American Journal of Psychiatry*, 120 (1963), 382–385.

Rausch, H. L., Goodrich, W., and Campbell, J. D. "Adaptation to the First Years of Marriage." *Psychiatry*, 26 (1963), 368–380.

Ryder, R. G. "Two Replications of Color Matching Factors." *Family Process*, 5 (1966), 43–48.

Ryder, R. G., and Flint, A. A. "Vicissitudes of Marital Disputes: The Object Matching Test." Paper presented at the American Orthopsychiatric Association Meeting, San Francisco, April 1966.

Ryder, R. G., and Goodrich, W. "Married Couples' Responses to Disagreement." *Family Process*, 5 (1966), 30–42.

Sontag, L., Baker, C. T., and Nelson, V. L. "Mental Growth and Personality. . . ." *Child Development*, 23, No. 2 (1958), Monograph No. 68.

17

Psychoanalysis of Children: Problems of Etiology and Treatment

STUART M. FINCH and ALBERT C. CAIN

Introduction

This chapter will deal with what we consider to be the most advanced aspects of psychoanalytic thinking about etiologic factors in the psychological disturbances of childhood. We must, however, immediately note some major omissions. Substantial restatements of the major theoretical formulations of psychoanalytic developmental psychology, of the theory of mental functioning, and of the principles of symptom formation are excluded. They have been spelled out fully and cogently elsewhere (Arlow, 1963; Rapaport, 1960; Fenichel, 1945). We have also omitted the vicissitudes, normal and aberrant, of individual drives, of ego and superego constituents, and of psychosexual stages. Acquaintance with them is assumed. Little space has been devoted to looking backward, either to revisit old controversies or to acknowledge and detail the historical foreshadowing of the newer formulations presented here. Similarly, space limitations do not permit elaboration of all points or documentation with research findings and case material: but wherever possible we have provided relevant references.[1]

[1] We have also resisted the temptation to overemphasize developmental/etiological

Lastly, we have excluded from consideration childhood disorders based on rather clear-cut organic pathology (cerebral pathology, endocrine disorders, and the like), while including and indeed emphasizing the etiologic contribution of constitutional "givens" that are within the broad boundaries of individual differences.

Etiological Considerations

It is perhaps a matter for historical understanding and interpretation that so little has been added to our general concepts of and approaches to the psychoanalytic etiological point of view by direct child analytic efforts. There have, of course, been excellent psychoanalytic contributions to the understanding of the etiology of a wide variety of syndromes of childhood psychopathology (psychosis, tics, enuresis, delinquency, feeding problems, sleep disturbances, chronic aggressive behavior), but from such studies have come relatively few larger contributions to psychoanalytic etiologic concepts per se. This cannot help but seem strange, given the occurrence of childhood syndromes that are not manifested by adults, the complex, significant interrelationships between infantile neuroses and adult disorders, and the fascinating but virtually totally unexplored theoretical riches to be gleaned from studies in comparative psychopathology (Cain, 1965).

In part this state of affairs is the consequence of too blind a devotion among child analysts to a libido theory at best vaguely diluted with ego psychology. Perhaps more important, however, is the fact that until the late 1950's concepts of personality development, etiology, and psychoanalytic technique derived essentially from adult psychoanalytic work have been the controlling concepts in child psychoanalysis. But however short of its potential contributions child analysis has fallen, we are now in the midst of an outburst of fruitful conceptual and empirical contributions. It is our hope that what follows adequately capsules this major upheaval.

REQUIREMENTS FOR AN ETIOLOGICAL THEORY

Before proceeding into more specific etiological concerns, it seems worthwhile first to set forth the basic requirements for an etiological theory of children's psychological disorders. By basic requirements, we mean the kinds of tasks and data that any comprehensive etiological theory must meet and encompass, and thus the criteria against which any etiological theory may be assessed.[2]

---

concepts which are closest to our hearts—or prejudices (preferred sensory modalities, inherent modes of self-soothing, object loss experiences, critical periods in ego formation as well as in the development of object relations, and the vicissitudes of identifications).

[2] Assumed here, of course, are the general requirements for theories and theory construction well formulated in the philosophy of science.

First, explanatory efforts must embrace the full clinical phenomena of disorders rather than just selected aspects. One major reason that after over 2,000 articles and a number of books on childhood psychosis we remain so pitifully far from an adequate etiological understanding is that many of our theorists have chosen quite circumscribed aspects of the full range of clinical phenomena from which to draw their etiological inferences. Thus, one investigator focuses and builds his total explanation almost exclusively on disorders of object relations, another on perceptual and cognitive processes, and another on equilibrium, homeostasis, and orientation in space and time. Each more or less neglects the spheres of functioning that the other emphasizes, and most ignore still other spheres such as disorders of affect.

Any etiological theorist, before plunging into those selected clinical data most accessible to this theory, needs to recognize the full range and specifics of the disorders of structure and function manifest in the condition: one must match the etiologic explanation against the full clinical data.

Second, an etiological theory must also conceptually encompass the *non*pathological or undisturbed aspects of functioning present in a condition. Even more exacting, what also requires compatible explanation is not only the existence of nondisturbed areas in the personality, but also the coexistence of *advanced*, precocious, or particularly adaptive functioning in some syndromes—for instance, the excellent academic work of many school-phobic children, the special isolated advanced abilities noted in a number of psychotic children, or the advanced functioning in certain academic areas of the group once referred to as "overprotected" children.

Third, basic etiological conceptions must surely comprehend the developmental vicissitudes of a given syndrome. That is, the specific explanatory concepts must deal with the knowns of the "life history" of a syndrome, be they deviant sensory thresholds or aberrant states of consciousness and muscle tone in certain subgroups of child psychotics in early infancy, or the alleged findings of lack of toilet-training difficulties in phobic children, or the significant portion of the delinquent population that leaves the delinquent group in late adolescence and merges into the general not-too-antisocial population. The etiologic formulation must be able to encompass the typical "premorbid" developmental status, as well as typical time of onset, precipitating factors, and occurrence of spontaneous remissions of a disorder. Thus, were it true that obsessive-compulsive neurosis in children truly did not occur until the latency period (Mahler, 1955), or that enuresis disappears on a child's reaching pubescence, or that certain forms of phobia cannot and do not occur prior to specific developmental achievements (Escalona, 1961), crucial etiological considerations obviously would emerge. If this suggests the importance of considering the hard data of a syndrome's developmental vicissitudes, it equally points to the need for more numerous, as well as more refined, longitudinal studies of syndromes.

Fourth, etiological explanations must comprehend a variety of related "actuarial data," too often uncollected or neglected, for example, such factors as differential male/female incidence of a particular syndrome. Similar considerations arise with regard to cross-cultural data, for example, the etiological significance of other literate cultures with minimal evidence of reading disability, or of subcultures with reports of virtually no adolescent delinquency, or of subcultures richly productive of childhood hysteria. Eventually, such consideration will need to be given to demographic data on children's psychological disorders, such as class, ethnic, and rural/urban variables. These data are rarely in the focus of psychoanalytic researchers' consciousness and investigations, but there has been ample opportunity to learn from investigations of adult disorders how far awry research findings and etiological theories may go if such variables remain neglected in data collection and explanatory efforts.

Fifth, etiological constructs must have a basic developmental anchorage; they must have clear, meaningful connection and compatibility with generally accepted developmental concepts and data. In those instances where they diverge, and where clinical data force different conclusions on us, we are faced with the necessary revision of generally accepted developmental norms of concepts. It is hardly convincing to invoke superego-based explanations to explain headbanging in infants, or an eight-month-old's anaclitic depression, or to apply the concept of mourning to infants before object constancy is established. On the other hand, etiological formulations stimulated by clinical data (Bergman and Escalona, 1949) have led to long-overdue revival and refinement of the stimulus-barrier concept and helped trigger awareness of and research into neonatal individual differences in sensory thresholds.

Sixth, etiological constructs should permit an advance in understanding of the murky problem of the differential "choice" of symptoms and neurosis. Again and again our etiological theories fail us at the point of explanation—even retrospectively—of why in a particular case a given disorder occurred rather than a series of other disorders or possible resolutions.

Seventh, and parallel to the previous point, etiological constructs must be able to manage conceptually those many instances wherein the individual's history includes a heavy loading of highly "pathogenic" elements without visible or marked manifestations of psychological disturbance. We have come to recognize the remarkable numbers of children (and adults) who have endured striking individual traumas or extremely stressful environmental circumstances (such as exposure to severe bombing, early childhood bereavement, repeated sexual seduction, severely psychotic or alcoholic parents, and frequent surgical interventions) without significant pathological manifestations. Simultaneously, we have become increasingly aware of the variety of adaptive, coping, integrative mechanisms available to children (Murphy, Heider, Toussiang, and Moriarty, 1960). But we have advanced little in interrelating the two matters and have rarely faced, let alone made inroads on, this crucial etiological problem. While such a challenge further burdens already inadequate etiological constructs, it also represents an exciting path toward the exploration of man's adaptive capacities, and one that promises to yield many lessons for our preventive efforts.

In assessing the current status of much of our child analytic etiological work, we recognize that the above requisites for an etiologic theory are highly demanding. They suggest that our basic perception of psychoanalysis is not just as a psychology of the unconscious, nor as a psychology of the neuroses, nor even as a psychology of conflict alone. Rather, these requisites reflect our commitment to the role and the promise of psychoanalysis as a general theory of behavior. We believe such a conception of the ultimate goals of psychoanalytic theory, although indeed demanding and far from fulfillment, is well within the tradition of psychoanalytic thought; and if the above requirements imply a long journey ahead, hopefully they at least also provide a rough map for the trip.

CONSTITUTIONAL ELEMENTS

During much of the history of psychoanalysis and even today, the concept of constitution or constitutional factors has been badly used. Oddly enough, despite all of its rich contributions to the study of individual differences, psychoanalysis until the 1960's has been relatively cavalier and inattentive toward individual differences in constitutional "givens." [3] Worse yet, the concept of constitution was particularly prone to three major forms of abuse. First, it was often used to "throw a bone" to biology—as a half-hearted recognition of the role of biological factors and, at the same time, as a waiving of psychoanalysis' responsibility for exploration of such factors and their relevance to personality development and psychopathology. Second, constitutional factors were regularly invoked by psychoanalytic writers as a "fudge factor," to use Blum's happy phrase (Blum, 1953). That is, whenever experiential determinants of certain features of personality formation or psychopathology were puzzlingly absent after intensive study, or whenever a particular manifestation (especially in the psychosexual realm) could not be readily explained from fairly substantial information available, there would be brief, dead-end references to the probable import of unspecified constitutional factors. Third, in a few instances, a crude linkage between one limited and poorly specified aspect of constitution was posited to have an absurdly direct, one-to-one etiological relationship to a particular form of psychopathology.

Within the last decade, however, as psychology and biological sciences have been reviving and clarifying their concepts of constitution (Montagu,

[3] This is far less the case when one turns to European psychoanalysis.

1950; Williams, 1956), psychoanalysis also has made rapid strides. Perhaps most of all it was John Benjamin who revived and gave new life to Freud's concept of the "complemental series" (S. Freud, 1905). Benjamin further refined our conception of the role of constitutional factors in psychoanalytic theory, and in his own research studies began brilliantly to elucidate and illustrate the role of specific constitutional factors (Benjamin, 1961a, 1961b, 1965). In addition to the abandonment of previously fruitless uses of the constitutional concept, the theoretical clarifications attained, and the sheer increase in research activity in this realm, several aspects of current constitutional work are particularly salient for etiological considerations.

First, our conception of the developmental, potential etiologic role of constitutional factors has become highly *interactional* in nature. Thus, any constitutional given is not invariably nor magically related to a particular pathological condition or related to a particular personality trait. Rather, it is assumed to be but one element operating in a field of interaction with a host of other intrinsic and environmental variables, with any particular developmental outcome pending the nature, strength, and interaction of other relevant variables. Further, psychoanalytic writings now emphasize the reciprocal roles of constitutional and environmental factors, with strong emphasis on the impact of constitutional variables on parents' attitudes and behavior toward the child which, in turn, may further modify those (or other) constitutional variables. Equally important, by their very nature some constitutional variables themselves determine what is registered or experienced from a wide variety of environmental stimuli and influence. "Not only can innate differences in drive organization, in ego functions, and in maturational rates determine different responses to objectively identical experiences, but they can also help determine what experiences will be experienced and how they will be perceived" (Benjamin, 1961a, p. 34). Thus, the interactionalism or "interpenetration" now conceptualized and investigated between constitutional and environmental factors is both marked and highly differentiated.

Correspondingly, we have moved from previous vague global references to constitutional factors, toward increasing specification of them and toward neonatal research into them. Psychoanalytic investigators remain far from a consensus as to what the most crucial personality-relevant constitutional variables are: indeed, that may prove to be a misleading phrasing of the matter. In fact, we have not yet assessed our own theoretical structure sufficiently to draw implications as to what factors are particularly salient. Glover early presented his list: sensitiveness to stimulation, anxiety readiness, variations in the inheritance of instinctual disposition, variations in the distribution of component and reactive impulses, variations in affective readiness, particularly the threshold for painful and pleasurable experience

(Glover, 1953). Psychoanalytic investigators and their colleagues have begun to study and specify both ego and libidinal givens, ranging widely from variations in drive endowment (Alpert and Neubauer), sensory thresholds and preferred sensory modalities (Escalona), autonomic reactivity (Lipton), mechanisms of working through stimuli (Meili), congenital activity level (Fries), response to novel situations (Thomas), and styles of dealing with internal and external stimuli (Korner).

Neonatal measurement of these variables is not easily accomplished. There is a host of variables with which such constitutional elements are interdigitated, and it will be a huge task theoretically to outline and empirically to construct the bridges between early neonatal and later behaviors. Nevertheless, the concept of constitutional factors as important determining agents in personality development and psychopathology now has been recast in forms more fruitful for psychoanalytic exploration.

EXPERIENTIAL DETERMINANTS: EXPANDED CONCEPTIONS OF THE ENVIRONMENT

Just as our architects and ecologists increasingly recognize the relevance of man's environment to his behavior, and personality theory in psychology increasingly becomes interpersonal theory, so revised and expanded conceptions of the individual's environment increasingly take hold in psychoanalytic etiological thinking. Where once we might have spoken in relatively single-track fashion of personality development in terms of unfolding maturational stages, now we also attend to the developmental implications of man's task of adaptation to his environment. Proposing the adaptive point of view, emphasizing the organism's "coming to terms" with its environment, Hartmann (1958) suggests that one cannot assess the individual's level of adaptation or state of adaptiveness without full consideration of the external environment to which the organism is adapting. The reference to the role of the environment is not simply in the sense of summating the stress agents in the environment, but the comprehensive picture of what stimuli are present in what patterns and with what salience; what human objects and in what relationships; what adaptive tasks are required, avoided, facilitated; what values and ideals are in commanding position; what defense organizations and coping behaviors are acceptable; what inducements toward growth exist; what cognitive patterns are preeminent; and what discharge opportunities and methods are available or blocked. With this more meaningful conception of the environment and its role in the genesis as well as maintenance of adaptation or maladaptation, psychoanalytic theory is better prepared to move toward adding what G. H. Pollock has termed an *ecologic* point of view to supplement our current economic, structural, dynamic, genetic, and adaptive points of view.

Hartmann has employed the concept of the "average expectable environment" with respect to assessments of an organism's current or future functioning, and it is clear that this concept ultimately will be employed genetically. It will be necessary to delineate the average expectable environment *coordinate with* and related to expected sequential phases of development. S. T. Cummings (1963), following Erikson, has furthered this effort with an appraisal of basic parental intrapsychic as well as child-rearing tasks consequent on and necessary to the child's sequence of developmental tasks. In some developmental stages, for instance that of the early nursing mother and infant, there are reasonably well-articulated conceptions of the average expected human environment, but in other spheres and phases this is woefully lacking.

In discussing this expanded conception of the environment, it is to be noted that our appraisal of the role of parents in personality development and psychopathology has begun to change radically. Although psychoanalytic concepts of personality development still leave a huge gap between late adolescence and senility, what psychoanalysts have long known, through their clinical work, about personality development during adulthood has begun to find its way into formal theory (Benedek, 1959; Erikson, 1950). Increasingly we recognize that, generally, a parent is an importantly different "person" with each of his children at different points in their development, due not only to his own ongoing maturation and development and many other internal and external forces, but also to what is differentially evoked within him from his own past as each of his children moves through the accented psychic drives, strains, and conflicts of each phase of development.[4] Phrased in terms of our daily clinical etiological puzzlements and endeavors, the parent of the seven-year-old we are seeing today may have been strikingly different in general and in relation to that child when the child was three; and the fact that other children in the family appear well adapted does not—contrary to some points of view—necessarily suggest that the parent's behavior could not have been a major pathogenic agent with *this* particular child. The relevant variables here are not merely the crude ones of the child's age and sex, but rather the unresolved or easily restimulated conflicts of the parents' serial developmental phases, and the parents' readiness for transference of old imagos onto their children, making use of sometimes substantial, sometimes small, sometimes nonexistent aspects of the child for the projections (much as the child does with his parents). Thus we begin gradually to sketch out the etiologic role of parents in a manner that is both more longitudinal and more differentiated than the stereotyped ones so frequent in our literature and case discussions (seductive mother; weak, passive father; phallic mother). Similarly, we speak less generally of a given mother's method of child rearing, and ask

[4] This has not yet significantly affected our continuing neglect of counter-Oedipal involvements.

more specifically about which aspects of her personality were reflected in what particular behavior toward the child at what phase in his development and in interaction with what elements of the child's own specific predispositions.

So, too, siblings have been retrieved from their neglected peripheral position in psychoanalytic theories of personality development and psychopathology. For long periods the study of the role of siblings was lost to oversimplified speculations and research about ordinal position, derived from Adlerian psychology, or retarded by valid but stereotyped and limited conceptions of siblings as primarily representing rivals and vehicles for Oedipal displacements by children. Siblings are now perceived, to an increasing extent, in their proper roles as potentially crucial agents in a child's development, a role visible in a rich variety of ways: both in *direct* sibling interaction (as models for identification, as parent surrogates, external superegos, seductors, spokesmen, provocateurs, and as objects who present opportunities for learning a wide repertory of patterns of interpersonal relating); and *indirectly*, by their particular set of interlocking roles in complex, and at times tautly balanced, family structures. Regarding the latter, one need only look at families from which one sibling suddenly has been removed to recognize how many determinants of previous and current modes of adaptation were inherent in the particular interrelated roles and functions of each sibling.

For all our typically American inability to focus much beyond the nuclear, nonextended family, as clinicians we have not failed to recognize the frequently crucial etiologic roles played by additional family members or "significant others," whether this be a sadistic, tyrannical grandfather in the home, or a symbiotic, dependency-breeding grandmother to whom the mother has essentially abdicated child-rearing responsibilities, or an aunt who has moved in and lovingly buffered a child from the ravages of a mother's prolonged postpartum depression, or a beloved "gramps" dying quietly in a room upstairs. Increasingly, the question "who else was in the home" appears early in our diagnostic assessments, rather than emerging later in treatment material.

We have also come, perhaps only late and grudgingly (as so many parents do), to recognize the important role of individual peers and the child's larger peer group in his development. We refer here not only to adolescents—the evidence suggests that in most cultures the peer group has an influential role starting well before adolescence—nor to a notion of peers as merely presenting opportunities for the playing out of intrafamilial dynamics or for object attachments defensively chosen to escape from conflict-engendering parents. We recognize, rather, that peer groups are often heavily determinative in molding interests, attitudes, and values, at times actually *defining* adaptation and maladaptation for a child and in presenting models and opportunities for experimenting with different styles of relating, promoting sublimations and shared defenses, making certain types of transient regressions acceptable, presenting new perceptions and expectations about the world and its objects, and variously contributing to the child's definitions of himself. Special note ought be made here of the incompleteness of relatively widespread points of view which consider children as offering one another mainly egocentricity, cruelty, and initiation to pecking orders. Whether one observes normal child development, or carefully assesses his own child analytic data, or turns to the experimental work of the Harlows (1962), or Anna Freud and Sophie Dann's classic paper (1951), one cannot help but recognize more clearly Sullivan's early suggestion in his discussion of the "chum relationship"—namely, that individual peers may offer significant opportunities to master, undo, and redo disturbing, pathogenic elements in the child's life, and may readily represent or facilitate major growth experiences and opportunities above and beyond introducing the child to a new "subculture" with somewhat different norms, perceptions, modes of relationships, and values than his nuclear family.[5]

This section probably ought not be concluded without briefly commenting on what represents to many clinicians one of the more exciting developments in understanding and treating child psychopathology, namely, the "family interaction" approaches (Ackerman, 1958): this topic is fully dealt with elsewhere in this volume, but some cautions seem appropriate. There are now a multiplicity of family interaction approaches, each at a different stage of formalization, each with a distinct, contrasting emphasis. Although such approaches have unfortunately achieved an almost faddish acceptance, and have gathered adherents with near religious zealotry, they represent a move toward a more clearly formulated theoretical stance for developmental-interpersonal approaches within psychoanalysis. They also may simultaneously help us avoid the Scylla of the "unfolding flower" analogy of normal and pathological development, and the Charybdis of the approach to the "child as a passive vessel (even victim) of experience."

The family interaction/family dynamics approach has suffered the disservice of becoming widely associated with its most dramatic case material as etiologic contributions to child psychopathology. We hear and read much clinical case discussion which represents a return in a new context to the older, substantially discredited psychoanalytic "meaning of symptom" approach. Thus, children's symptoms are seen simply as direct transmissions of an unconscious parental demand, or the direct embodiment, repre-

[5] We leave to other chapters of this book an intensive analysis of the relationship between cultural-subcultural variables and psychoanalytic approaches to the individual in his social context.

sentation, or acting out of a parental wish; or the family is seen as wanting, needing, and producing a particular symptom or disturbed mode of behavior; or the family is pictured as ferociously resisting therapeutic efforts to dissolve or "take away" a symptom. Although the relationship between family dynamics and children's symptoms is sometimes almost as clear, simple, and "one-to-one" as the above suggests, for the most part such an approach utterly neglects the question of the relationship between character structure and symptomatology. It loses the distinction between elements contributing to the *formation* of a symptom versus later accretions and contributions to the symptom's *maintenance;* and the developmental distinctions between what a family "needed" at an earlier point in its history and what its much-changed family dynamics "require" at a later point are frequently neglected.

This dramatic symptom orientation overshadows the basic richness of the family interaction approach's unique contribution: the demonstration that each parent and child is reciprocally related to all other members of the family system, that major aspects of the relationships often are in sufficiently delicate balance that changes in the psychic state of one family member or in the relationship of two of them will immediately reverberate through other members of the family and their relationships, that each family member plays for every other a multiplicity of roles and functions, conscious and unconscious, and that these interdependent roles and functions consist of interlocking aims, perceptions, modes of behavior, identities, impulse gratifications, superego counterpoints, and that once these patterns have consolidated, shared defense organizations and homeostatic-like mechanisms are evolved to maintain them unchanged.

We have not as yet clarified at what point, quantitatively or qualitatively, aspects of family interaction become pathological or pathogenic per se or at least strongly tend to disturb a child's development. The answer in part seems to consist in determining when such pressures on a given family member produce unconscious conflict, when they run sharply counter to an individual's constitutions, predisposition, and prior developmental trends, and when they exacerbate the particular vulnerabilities and stresses of a developmental phase. Integration of family interaction approaches with psychosexual theory or Erikson's broader epigenetic theory—much less its integration with developmental ego psychology—deserves extensive investigative efforts, and will require much careful theoretical refinement, but it promises eventually a far more comprehensive psychoanalytic theory of personality development and pathogenesis. It also provides a fertile field for the integration of intrapsychic and interpersonal trends within psychoanalysis.

SOME BASIC DEVELOPMENTAL-ETIOLOGICAL CONCEPTS

1. *Fixation.* Although basic to psychoanalytic considerations of etiology, the concept of fixation until recently has received surprisingly little conceptual attention and revision. For a long time, psychoanalytic writings simply noted and underscored its classical position in our theory of psychopathology, and listed a number of circumstances leading to libidinal fixation (excessive gratification, excessive frustration, traumatic experiences, swift oscillation between gratification and frustration, and so forth); there seemed little more to say. Then the point was emphasized that fixation, rather than occurring only globally in relation to a psychosexual stage, may pertain either to the particular *zone* or to various *modes* within a given psychosexual stage. In a further revision, Khan (1963) pointed out that the term fixation has been variously used with reference to fixation to a component instinct, fixation to a particular type of object choice, fixation to a phase of libidinal and/or aggressive development, fixation to a traumatic experience, and fixation to a type of object relationship. His observation about the term's usage is correct, but Khan is referring perhaps more to loose usage of the term than to actual different types or foci of fixation. Yet if one attempts to extract the essence of the concept of fixation with its emphasis on relative cessation of further development and tying of energies if not specific behaviors to a particular stage in development, then Khan is essentially correct.

Similarly, important differentiations are emerging between more typical fixations and various other kinds of arrests, failures, and curtailments of development. Thus, there is now an awareness that there are a variety of factors or conditions which may halt or retard development in certain spheres, that these developmental arrests may be highly different, and that the differences may encompass crucial etiological as well as therapeutic considerations. Hopefully, the next decades will also witness intensive psychoanalytic study of the normal and abnormal development of a host of individual ego elements such as sensory thresholds, perceptual differentiation, mechanisms of delay, cognitive categorization, memory utilization, affect modulation, symbolization, verbalization, hierarchicalization of functions, and a wide variety of adaptive or coping mechanisms. We are also on the verge of conceptualizing and exploring the potential adaptive strains or warping produced by intrasystemic or intersystemic asynchrony of development and early imbalances of development (A. Freud, 1965; Spitz, 1959, 1965).

Close analysis of clinical material also reveals what can appropriately be labeled fixations in superego development. We refer here not so much to earlier descriptions of an essential "sphincter morality," although such clinical evidence foreshadowed the concept of superego fixation. The *con-*

tent of superego fixation may vary considerably and to some extent independently, or it may be the form of the superego: e.g., its concreteness, or overinclusiveness, or rigidity, from a particular earlier phase of superego development; or the fixation may be less in the realm of the punitive aspects of the superego than in the ego ideal which, for instance, may still have too close a connection with early forms of narcissism and infantile omnipotence.

It should be clear, first, that the above considerations in no way diminish the significance of fixations as etiological factors and, second, that we have urgent need to study the manner in which fixations in these different spheres interact with one another and variously affect—inhibit, facilitate, distort—development across spheres. Efforts in the past have centered mostly on studying the effects of fixations within the sphere of origin, but essential developmental and etiologic knowledge awaits us in forthcoming studies of the impact of fixations (or precocious or advanced developments) in one sphere on structures and functions in related spheres (A. Freud, 1965; Katan, 1961), and studies of the factors determining the selective impact of conflict, deprivation, fixation, or trauma on some spheres but not others.

2. *Regression.* Investigations also confirm the need for revision of the concept of regression in etiological formulations. First, it is clear that regressive movements may take place within any of the three "structures" of the personality and that, as with fixation, ego, and superego, regression may well (as Anna Freud suggests) follow somewhat different principles than libidinal regressions. Child analytic clinical work and normal child development demonstrate even more clearly what has also been recognized in adult psychoanalytic work: that it is not regression per se that is pathologic or even pathogenic in nature, but the type and perhaps most of all the sequelae of regression (Glover, 1939). With children another factor is also prominent, namely, the essential tolerance or intolerance of regression by the child's immediate environment (in addition to the child's internal readiness for shame over regression).

Perhaps three major types of disturbance-breeding parental reactions to a child's regression can be distinguished. One can regularly find parents so generally condemnatory toward regressive slides in their children's behavior that the child gains little opportunity for using, or for learning, the normal, safety-valve *adaptive uses of transient regressions* which serve us all so well early in development and throughout life. These children are typically pressed toward ever more woodenly "good," correct behavior, or even advanced (pseudomature) behavior. They are reminiscent of those adults described as intolerant of anxiety (Zetzel, 1949) who are forced toward rather massive disintegrations when stresses accumulate beyond the limits of their severely constricted defensive and adaptive mechanisms. In a second group, the problem is more that of parents becoming frightened and engaging in various forms of combat and struggle over individual fragments of children's regressive behavior. The outcome, not surprisingly, often is embattled maintenance, heightening, and spreading of what otherwise was destined to be a relatively transient regression. Fritz Redl has put it well in informal discussion: speaking of preadolescents he noted that if parents did not "panic" and overreact to certain preadolescent regressive behaviors a goodly portion of the cases in which parent and early adolescent are locked in prolonged mortal combat would never arise. The last of the three gross types of distorted environmental reactions to children's transient regressions is well known: reinforcement of the regression by parents who obtain vicarious gratifications through its impulsive or expressive features, or through narcissistic identification with their child's reflection of an earlier image of themselves, or through certain highly cathected roles that it permits them to play once again in their child's life.

Following Anna Freud's further differentiation of regression with regard to object, aim, or method of discharge (A. Freud, 1965) we are once again well reminded that all but the most devastating regressions are only partial. As clinical investigations of regression continue, a series of related concepts come to the fore as highly relevant dimensions regarding regression: the question of developmental forces' role in the *differential vulnerability* to regression of various psychic structures or subsystems, different individuals' often strikingly different *rates of* regression, and factors *mobilizing progressive recovery* from regressive moves; those factors which determine at what point a downward regression halts—the nature of the *regression "support level"* that does not permit regression to proceed too far. Similarly, what factors differentiate the triggering of partial versus widespread regressions must be determined.

3. *Trauma.* The concept of trauma as a basic etiologic agent in psychoanalytic theory of development and of psychopathology has had a long, checkered careeer. Early psychoanalytic writers were, and some still are today, highly impressed with the essential etiologic role of even a single, individual trauma, especially when its nature and timing are unfortunately matched to particular stage-specific vulnerabilities or preexisting "flaws" in the individual's personality structure. Yet many writers beat a hasty, perhaps too complete retreat as they either learned that presumed and reported traumata (for instance, sexual seductions) had not in fact occurred but were fantasied by their neurotic patients, *or* found that such traumata had occurred among many individuals who showed no evidence of related neuroses. Moreover, the essential concept of trauma, highlighted in the study of traumatic neuroses and particularly the traumatic war neuroses, was that of the organism's being abruptly overwhelmed by stimulation or excitation, in quantity far in excess of what the psychic apparatus could

adequately bind or discharge, thus "flooding it with excitation." Unfortunately, as time passed (and as psychoanalysis has been increasingly popularized), even within psychoanalytic usage the term has frequently slipped over to the more popular lay usage which is focused *outside* the organism, that is to say, which defines trauma as existing in the magnitude or disruptiveness of an environmental situation or event, rather than on its relationship to the psychic apparatus. Studies such as Bonnard's have demonstrated how striking this distinction may be (Bonnard, 1951). Even the most "stressful" external circumstances in which a child may find himself may *or may not* be traumatic for a child. Cognitive or affective elements of the presumed stressful environmental situation may have little or no threatening meanings for the child; he may selectively experience only aspects unrelated to the actual threat present in the situation, or he may have adequate coping devices and discharge capacities to manage effectively the disturbing stimulation involved. The traumatic quality of an event ultimately can be assessed only by the *internal* state of the organism, not by the "objective" qualities of the environmental event. Further, the precise meanings of the trauma, where trauma occurs, can only be determined (so to speak) through the child's eyes, through what the child selectively experiences, in terms of his particular developmental stage, defensive organization, current object relations, modes of perception and thought. Nowhere has this been more vividly illustrated than in Bergen's well-known case report (Bergen, 1958).

While in no way minimizing the potential pathologic import of a particular traumatic state, brief or prolonged, psychoanalysis increasingly turns from conceptions of single trauma as etiologic agents to a conception of series of traumata, and especially series of interrelated traumata; witness Khan's emphasis on what he terms "cumulative trauma," and his harking back to Kris's distinction between "shock trauma" and "strain trauma" (Khan, 1963; Kris, 1956). Referring to the effects of lesser traumata on development, Khan notes that these traumata cumulate quietly and invisibly, and don't so much halt or distort as they do *bias* development. The concept is one of repeated sequences of minor scale traumata whose effects become manifest only as they gradually establish a pattern and rise across a threshold at which psychologic development is damaged. There is serious question whether *trauma* is even an appropriate phasing of this. To some extent what seems to be meant by Khan and others adopting this point of view is that a series of frustrations, minor or at least not individually gross, by their repetitive occurrence over a period of time have pathogenic effects. Quite aside from our preference for retaining the conceptual purity of the trauma concept, the phenomena which Khan describes seem to be referring to events involving *neither* trauma *nor* significant frustration, but rather to repeated sequences which pattern and mold the shape of the individual's object relations, defensive configurations, and ego functions in maladaptive ways. Clinical evidence confirms that just such patternings are of fairly pervasive etiological significance, and, as Khan indicates, are distinct from but complementary to fixation and regression as etiologic agents.

To conclude this section we shall only raise the theoretically fascinating, etiologically important, and virtually totally unexplored question of what factors differentiate regressive or various distorted reactions from progressive, adaptive reactions to traumatic experiences. As noted elsewhere (Cain, 1964) we have had available for some time such concepts as "traumatic progression" and related developmental phenomena, but have yet to plumb their significance for etiological theories.

By this point it is evident that in assessing children's disorders, even aside from those with major organic involvement, we are dealing with far more categories than psychotoxic disorders versus emotional deficiency diseases, ego weakness versus ego disturbance, infantile neuroses versus character problems, or external versus internalized versus truly internal conflicts. Rather we are addressing ourselves to a broad range of childhood disorders which are by nature quite resistant to classification and classification systems.[6] They include innumerable permutations and combinations, and few clear-cut clinical entities (we are particularly impressed with a number of cases initially appearing to be typical or even classical infantile neuroses which nevertheless contain what have been called "silent ego defects").

Child psychoanalysts have, over the years, come to observe, study, and treat a much broader range of childhood disorders than originally envisioned in child analysis. Similarly, psychoanalysts have turned to systematic observation of normal children and have had increasing opportunity for microscopic analysis of familiar children's disturbances. No surprise, then, that far more types of disorders and, particularly important to our present purposes, additional etiologic roots to childhood psychopathology have come to be discriminated beyond those originally conceived.

Thus, our formulation of etiological factors in children's psychological disorders includes not only the basic concepts of (1) fixation, (2) regression, and (3) trauma, as revised above, but also:

4. Constitutional elements, with special reference to either those aspects of constitution which may inherently *tend* toward maladaptation (e.g., marked hypoactivity, low pain threshold, aberrant drive endowment) or those which are sharply discordant with the needs, interaction patterns, and styles of relating of the primary objects in the child's environment.[7]

5. Lack of necessary "stimulus nutriment" and related experience for

[6] Note Nagera's suggested new classification system including infantile neuroses, neurotic conflicts, developmental conflicts, and developmental disturbances or interferences (A. Freud, 1965, p. 164).

[7] One also might include here the speculative references in our literature to alleged constitutional defects such as inherent deficits in the perceptual apparatus, "lack of sending power," defective capacity to neutralize or distribute psychic energy, and similar concepts.

ego formation and development. Here we include not only understimulation but lack of adequate or appropriate objects for ego identification, absence of necessary input during critical periods, and variously inadequate opportunities for normal learning. Perhaps also here we ought list problems of ego distortion based on asynchrony and imbalance of ego structures.

6. Prolonged repetitive patterning in the organism's interactional experiences involving the progressive, warping accumulation of minor frustration, unbound tension, and maladaptive modes of relating or methods of discharge, as previously elaborated in the discussion of ego-strain and "cumulative trauma."

7. Overloading of the organism with internal and external tasks at a given point in development. If one conceives of the individual proceeding through a series of developmental periods each with its characteristic ("phase-specific") tasks, strains, conflicts, and vulnerabilities, it becomes obvious that where the summation of these tasks is, for whatever reasons, excessively heavy, then disturbance, disruption, and maldevelopment, if not symptoms, will likely follow. It may well be, as some clinicians suggest, that such developmental disturbances will typically disappear as the developmental phase with its intrinsic stresses pass, leaving at most potential vulnerabilities for a later period. But our clinical data suggest that such developmental disturbances sometimes contain the seeds of self-perpetuation and further neurotic elaboration.

8. The stage of development, the qualitative nature, and the "match" with the environment of the child's coping mechanisms (Murphy *et al.*, 1960) will be a further major determinant of his level of adaptation. Psychopathological conditions will more likely result, quite apart from quantitative considerations, when the child's coping mechanisms at any given point (especially a stressful point) in development are: (1) generally inadequate, underdeveloped; (2) more or less structurally adequate, but of a qualitatively inappropriate or ineffective form for the current adaptive task (for instance, stress that requires motoric coping mechanisms, but where the particular style of the individual's coping mechanisms is more reliant on perceptual and cognitive modes); (3) structurally adequate to the stresses involved but where, for whatever reasons, the current environment is unaccepting, condemnatory, or punitive toward their usage.

It is equally important to state the obverse of the above; that is, if the environmental stresses do *not* interlock with specific developmental conflicts and vulnerabilities or if the coping methods are qualitatively quite relevant to the stresses, there is far less likelihood of psychological disturbance. Cognizance of this principle furthers our understanding of instances where even severe environmental conditions do not produce significant intrapsychic disturbance.

9. Often the final determination of whether or not a child's develop-

ment is significantly disturbed or not is accidental, in terms of the sheer timing of such stressful events as the birth of a sibling, parental absence, rapid successive changes of residence, surgical intervention, hospitalization, moving next door to a frightening new neighbor, or a death in the family. Although their timing may be quite fortuitous, nevertheless such events can have fateful consequences developmentally. They may be even more potent as etiological factors when they are damagingly coordinated to particular developmental strains present at that time.[8]

It is obvious from the above that even the concepts of multiple causation and a complemental series do not do full justice to etiological realities. Given this approach to the etiology of children's psychological disorders, it can be predicted that careful, qualitative clinical syndrome investigations or more rigorous objective research will *not* find simple or direct relationships between, say, parent psychopathology and children's level of adaptation; parent personality type and specific children's disorder; particular form or content of parental child-rearing practice and particular children's disorder; specific trauma or severe environmental stress and specific resultant disorder. Rather, what we most typically find, as expected, in most syndromes are a few major subgroups with common basic fixations, developmental elements, or patterns of environmental strains—and a substantial number of children with similar disorders reached by a wide variety of other pathological routes, as previously described. And if one looks beyond the syndrome one also finds large numbers of children with essential characteristics similar to those encountered in the major subgroups who do *not* manifest the syndrome in question, but another syndrome or constellation of difficulties entirely—or perhaps a state of relative adaptation. It attests to the advances in psychoanalytic etiological theory that such empirical data no longer need be denied.

Child Psychoanalytic Technique

Child psychoanalysis, both as a subspecialty within psychoanalysis and as a specific theory of technique, has been and remains grossly underdeveloped. On this there is general agreement, whether it is traced back to warring camps among its early practitioners, or to long-standing difficulties in the organizational structure and training programs for child analysis in the United States, or to the fuzzy boundaries between child psychoanalysis and child psychotherapy, or to the overshadowing development of adult psychoanalysis. A series of surveys have shown (Lewin and Ross, 1960; Hendrick, 1958; Rexford, 1962) that in the United States little child analysis is taught,

[8] Analysis of children's disorders suggests even other routes to psychopathology not readily fitting into these categories, for example, discrepancies between parental superegos, or lack of necessary phase-specific frustrations.

even less child analysis is practiced, and remarkably little is written on child psychoanalytic technique. One small symbol of this is that there has been no significant book or monograph on child psychoanalytic technique since the early classics written by Anna Freud and Melanie Klein in 1928 and 1932, respectively. The unhappy result of this state of affairs will be briefly illustrated rather than painfully catalogued in this section. Our comments will be focused more toward some major issues and hopeful new perspectives for future developments in child analysis.

RELATION OF DIAGNOSIS TO TREATMENT

Anna Freud noted some years ago a series of crucial problems faced in the diagnostic assessment of children's psychological disorders (A. Freud, 1945). Others have supplemented the list of problems inherent in the diagnosis of disturbed children: our limited conception of what psychological normality, adaptation or "health" is in children; a totally inadequate nosological system, essentially borrowed from adult disorders; difficulties in the assessment of an organism still highly fluid and amidst rapid physical and psychological changes; the lack of full, extended cumulative evidence of patterned behavior; the more ambiguous nature and uncertain referents of children's symptoms; the quite incomplete state of our norms for development at various ages; and the greater "openness" of children as a system, immediately responsive to numerous potent influences in their environment. Most of these difficulties continue to plague child analysts (Neubauer, 1963) and nonanalysts alike (Jenkins and Cole, 1964). In a rather sketchy paper on the diagnostic profile, Anna Freud (1962) made a focused effort to meet the problems inherent in the assessment of children's disorders. In her later book (A. Freud, 1965) she recognizes that serious theoretical as well as pragmatic problems in child diagnosis remain, while simultaneously emphasizing that painstaking differential diagnosis is crucial to the choice of appropriate treatment technique.

Inevitably related is the problem of selection of patients for child psychoanalysis. Once the early striking differences in the approach to this problem by the Freud and Klein groups are put aside, there is no question that the childhood disorders most amenable to and appropriate for child psychoanalysis are the classical infantile neuroses based on intrapsychic conflict of primarily Oedipal origin, as described originally by Anna Freud and restated by James Anthony with reference to the more circumscribed infantile neuroses: "Phase specific, predominately intrapsychic, nonconstitutional and set in an affectionate familial environment" (Kaplan, 1962, p. 575). Truly a wide range of disorders has been reported to be treated by child analysis, and of course child analysis once was zealously recommended for all children. As with adult psychoanalysis, there has been a widening of the scope of application of child psychoanalytic technique, but often this is with such gross modifications of technique that in no meaningful sense can the resultant approach be called child analysis.

Fraiberg, however, has demonstrated that on the basis of gains in our understanding of ego structure and defense mechanisms one can successfully apply virtually unmodified child psychoanalytic technique with types of disorders hitherto considered totally unamenable to child analysis (Fraiberg, 1962). Similar exploratory efforts will be necessary to assess empirically those disorders for which child psychoanalysis is the "treatment of choice."

As we have begun to delineate those characteristics of a disturbed child necessitating[9] the employment of child analytic technique, we have also recognized the need to assess with equal care the parents of a prospective child analysand in terms of their capacity for sustaining the child's analysis (Bernstein, 1958). Child analysts are all too well acquainted with the potential and actual sources of parental interference with child analytic treatment. But given the lengthy, psychologically arduous task that child analysis presents to parents, it has been well suggested that we ask not only why parents may interfere with or disrupt a child analysis. Rather, we can equally fruitfully begin to ask the reverse: what psychological characteristics of parents sustain them in supporting or at least tolerating their child's analysis?

COUNTERTRANSFERENCE

The prominence of countertransference phenomena in child analytic work is visible in a multitude of fashions. Child psychoanalysis starts with a unique set of countertransference pressures in the very fact of the child analyst's real or fantasied relationship with the child's parents (not to mention the sporadic pressures on the analyst of pediatricians, school systems, and juvenile courts). Thus the child analyst begins with the need to manage virtually three sets of interrelated potential countertransferences to the child and the child's parents, and in some instances the additional problems involved where a colleague is seeing the parent. Such elements as the reenactment of the analyst's affective relationship to his own parents on the child's parents; guilt and anxiety-shrouded jealous competitive desires to psychologically "steal" the child from his parents; needs to be a better parent to a child patient than the child's own parents; rescue fantasies; needs to be a better parent than one's own parents were: all are well known to child analysts in terms of their choice of profession as well as their day-to-day countertransference awareness.

Other special strains of child analytic work are equally apparent: tendencies to overidentify with the child; children's frequent sexual and aggres-

[9] More than occasionally, in the quest for analyzable child patients, the differentiation is lost between childhood disorders that can be analyzed versus childhood disorders which *require* analysis.

sive acting out within sessions; their open, difficult-to-avoid physical provocations; their less developed observing ego and frequent obliviousness to a "therapeutic contract"; and their more primitive regressive behavior. The child analyst must not only manage the aforementioned and deal with the child's repeated insistence on his participation in the child's play, but must also at the same time keep unhampered both the freely hovering attention and the more active reflection and formulation intrinsic to analytic work. In addition he faces the unpleasant bind of feeling a heightened responsibility for his child patient's welfare while vulnerable to many therapeutic defeats of an essentially extra-analytic nature.

It is little wonder, then, that E. James Anthony (Abbate, 1964) strongly recommends regular, intensive countertransference analysis as an absolutely crucial element for child analytic work and views countertransference problems as a primary obstacle to child analytic treatment. The paucity of child analytic countertransference literature suggests that active countertransference analysis in child analytic work is the exception rather than the rule. This problem is all the more grave in that we have no clear model of child analytic technique in the context of which countertransference-based deviations can be properly assessed.

THE ROLE OF PARENTS

Again and again when questions are raised regarding contact with parents, as one observes the practice of child analysis or reviews its literature, it almost invariably emerges that the reference is not to parents but to one parent, the mother. For all our awareness of fathers' crucial role in children's personality development and psychopathology, and the frequency with which the child's father is a key factor in either sustaining or disrupting (even terminating) child analytic treatment, fathers are regularly and repeatedly disregarded. The relevance of this phenomena to "institutionalized countertransferences" and the obvious matriarchal tone and organization of child analysis need further exploration. Meanwhile it will be of interest to see whether this obviously distorted relationship to the fathers of child analytic patients will change with the increasing presence of male child analysts in the field.

Arguments—indeed rather fierce arguments—continue regarding the role of parents in child analysis. The debate covers *whether* the parents are to be seen and *if* they are to be seen, *by whom,* and with what *frequency,* and with what *focus* to the contact. Points of view on this matter vary widely (Littner, 1964; Anthony, 1963). Thus some child analysts avoid seeing the parents at all during the analysis except for the initial diagnostic sessions or for a brief, although sometimes intensive, preparatory period. Others insist that, given the nature of parents' often continuing distorted pathogenic relationship to the child, and the impact of the changes effected by child analysis, in most cases the only way to prevent parents' interference with treatment is to work with them quite regularly. Some child analysts state that direct contact with the parents is unnecessary; others insist that it is not only unnecessary, but that they are far more likely to be able to analyze successfully a child if they do *not* see the parents.

There is similar broad variation regarding who, if anyone, should see the child's parents. Among the varied recommendations are that the child's analyst see the parents, that another analyst see the parents, or that the parents be seen by a caseworker. Lastly, recommendations sometimes are made in cases with prominent interlocking parent-child psychopathology, for simultaneous analysis of parent and child either by the same analyst or by different analysts.

One source of these disagreements is that "environmental manipulation" has taken on almost malevolent connotations in some psychoanalytic circles. More important, there is too little differentiation of types of activity that the analyst or his colleague may appropriately undertake with the parents. The focus of the interventions with parents can range widely from exclusively obtaining information regarding the child's current behavior and environment to giving specific advice in a quasi-educational role, changing specific parent behaviors toward the child, resolving limited aspects of the parents' own difficulties, or diverting from the child those parental difficulties being destructively worked out on the child, helping the parents not to get entangled in the child's provocations or in his attempts to externalize his inner difficulties and transform them into battles with his parents, aiding the parents to understand and permit the child's inevitable regressive behavior and sporadic "transgressions" during analysis, assisting the parents to recognize the child's need for the privacy of his analytic sessions, and initiating the parents with regard to "every step" of the major phases of child analysis and preparing them for continuing changes in the child's behavior.

The questions that need to be asked regarding the child analyst's relationship to the parents are not where, on the above continuum, each child analyst places himself once and for all. Rather, the relevant questions are:

1. What type of intervention with the parents—if any—does a given case *require* in order to permit or facilitate a particular child's analysis?

2. What effects are such interventions likely to have on the analytic process with a given child; and, as with the introduction of any parameter, how can such effects be minimized, or undone?

The nature of the contact with the parents will depend on crucial variables such as the type of disorder, the degree to which conflicts are internal, the age of the child, the nature of the parents, their relationship to the child's disturbance, situational determinants, and the phase of the treatment (Buxbaum, 1954).

SELECTED PROBLEMS OF TECHNIQUE

Discussion of essential elements in child psychoanalytic technique more than occasionally lapses into dispute over such matters as the role of sweets, gift-giving to child patients, or the analyst's mobility in the office. In the process, a number of significant issues have, for the most part, been delicately avoided: for instance, the varied aspects of the child's regression within the transference; the analyst's stance toward permitting regression; the obviously important but almost verboten subject of the implicit structure of rewards and punishment for the patient in analytic work (Piers and Piers, 1965); and the analyst's role as an object for nondefensive, enduring identification by the child.

Most of the central issues of child analytic technique reveal virtually the same range of positions visible in our previous considerations. We will restrict ourselves here to listing briefly some of these issues,[10] then proceeding to more vital underlying considerations. One such issue is whether child analysis typically requires an initial preparatory period, none at all, or preparation only for the parents. Positions vary, and have shifted substantially over the last thirty years. At one end of the continuum is the view that given the child's symptomatology, his strong tendency to externalize his difficulties, and his being brought rather than coming of his own will for treatment, a preparatory period is necessary, often involving much wooing of the child into recognition of his difficulties, and into something akin to a therapeutic alliance. At the other end of the continuum is the view, now perhaps more widely held, that with the exception of special problems or special age groups, such a preparatory period is not only unnecessary but damaging: that the same effects may be produced by active interpretation and an immediate analytic posture. This approach claims that a preparatory period may heavily distort the remainder of the analysis, make it impossible to achieve a full shifting of gears into an analytic relationship, and abort a full development of the transference.

The basic attitude toward negative and positive transference and their interpretation also varies considerably. From one viewpoint there is emphasis on the necessity immediately to undermine negative transference manifestations, on the grounds that they quickly escalate, permit no analytic work, and may represent a totally insurmountable resistance. Another point of view assumes that negative transference is to be expected and dealt with in no unusual way—which is to say, dealt with by appropriately timed interpretations. Similarly, some child analysts insist that a significant positive transference is an absolute necessity for sustaining prolonged analytic work

[10] Other issues would include the nature and depth of interpretation, therapist activity level, approach to resistances, role of "education," and attitude toward play as communication.

and that major therapeutic work with a child can be accomplished only during periods of reasonably strong positive transference. Others insist that positive transference is to be allowed to develop only in the general movement toward the transference neurosis, that it is to be actively interpreted when it forms a resistance, and that it is highly dangerous to woo, seduce, or gratify the child with the aim of manufacturing or maintaining a strong positive transference.

Perhaps the most studied attention regarding technique has been given to the question of whether children are capable of developing a full transference neurosis, and the related questions of the degree to which the child analyst serves as a new, real object vs. a transference figure for the child, and whether the child's object-related attitudes and images are extended, externalized, or fully transferred to the analyst. The gap is far from closed between the positions taken earlier in the history of child analysis (Freud, 1928; Klein, 1932)—positions which characteristically ranged from statements that children did not develop classical transference neuroses to insistence that the development of a full transference neurosis could be obtained regularly with child analytic patients. But we have increasingly if not unanimously come to realize that the question is not one of either-or, nor one of whether perhaps a transference neurosis might possibly develop if the child is placed in very special situations (Bornstein, 1945; Brody, 1961; Casuso, 1965; Fraiberg, 1951; Kut, 1953; Sandler, 1964).

Rather, we have come to assess whether a transference neurosis is likely to develop or not in a particular case by virtue of the child's age, more crucially his developmental stage, the type of disorder involved, the nature of the child's situation and extra-analytic influences upon both the child and the treatment. Such determinants as the therapist's very expectations of transference neurosis development and the child analytic techniques—and parameters—employed have come to the fore. In corollary fashion, there is growing recognition that certain forms of intervention (ingratiatory preparatory periods, overemphasis on maintenance of positive transference, the analyst's adoption of gratifying or educational roles) may themselves make the development of a transference neurosis impossible.

Rather than further addressing ourselves to these individual issues, we would assess the current status of child analytic literature and practice in the following fashion. To overstate for emphasis, child analysis as currently practiced generally consists of the application of a multiplicity of unanalyzed and unresolved parameters. There is a wide variety of positions and points of view surrounding almost every essential aspect of child analytic technique, and a remarkable range of behavior termed proper analytic technique by child analysts. Progress beyond this state will occur only if we can leave behind residuals of combat over principles of technique based on the personalized, hardened, and institutionalized positions taken by the

Anna Freud and Melanie Klein groups. Similarly we will have to undo the past decades' countertransference-based transformation of child analytic techniques into those more befitting tea parties and "play ladies," with their extremely unfortunate emphasis upon gratifying, wooing, and educating the child, and related unrealistic fears regarding the necessary regressive and negative transference aspects of the child analytic process.

Perhaps even more fundamentally, child analysis has been almost paralyzed by its need to assume that it is psychoanalysis and worthy of respect only to the extent that it is virtually identical with adult analysis. This crippling comparison with adult analysis is visible in the constant absurd strain to demonstrate that a particular aspect of child analytic technique or patient behavior is equivalent to its counterpart in adult psychoanalysis. Once again we are dealing with the stepchild role that child analysis has played in the organizational history of psychoanalysis, and with major problems in the child analyst's own professional identity. No solution to the manifold problems of child analytic technique is to be found in a rote identification with psychoanalytic technique as practiced with adults. Achievement of a theoretically and therapeutically viable position with regard to child analytic technique will require that it be based on: (1) a revised, extended formulation of etiological factors in child psychopathology; (2) differentiation of the crucial aims and essential principles of psychoanalytic technique from secondary or tertiary aspects of its practice; and (3) a conceptually clearer, more empirically based understanding of child development and its direct implications for child psychoanalytic technique.

Although Weiss (1964) still proceeds too heavily from the adult model of psychoanalytic technique, he nevertheless states the problem cogently when he suggests that *parameters* have been transformed into the model of child analytic technique; he also insists that we detail precisely what specific aspects of child development require specific changes in analytic technique (and, we add, what effects those required changes in technique will have on other aspects of the psychoanalytic situation). He asks that a clear, basic model and theory of child analytic technique be established and emphasizes that it is only in the context of such a model that we can with deliberate awareness introduce, and then appraise, required parameters of technique. What shall be the constituents of that basic model?

Surely the basic aims of psychoanalysis as a therapeutic measure, child or adult, include goals of broad change in the patient's character structure with particular emphasis upon extension of the sovereignty of the ego and the ultimate heightening of the individual's psychic integration. Clearly, the basic role of the analyst is that of objectivity and his most important activity that of interpretation, not censoring, gratifying, supporting, or educating. The essential process of the analysis must consist of permitting the patient's limited regression, and the gradual appearance and evolution of various stages of transference, with the systematic analysis of defenses and resistances leading to the expression and working through of all major conflicts within the transference. The process should facilitate and be facilitated by the strengthening of the patient's observing ego, his increasing affective awareness of unconscious forces and fantasies, and linkage of his earlier experience with the present—all accomplished over an extended period of time with the analyst's central focus on intrapsychic conflict, with minimal interference in the patient's external world.

These crucial dimensions of the psychoanalytic process must be set within the context of an accurate conception of the child's developmental state and achievement. Thus, these basic dimensions must be translated into a theory and practice of technique consistent with developmental realities such as the child's relatively undeveloped capacity for self-reflection and self-observation; his still weak ego-synthetic forces, in contrast to his strong tendency toward splitting and externalization; his relatively undeveloped capacity for abstract thought; his greater tendency toward motoric discharge rather than talk; his limited understanding of causality (especially of psychological causality and unconscious forces); his still somewhat shaky distinction between fantasy and reality; his relatively tenuous dominance of ego forces over drive organization; his lack of a firm commitment to the reality principle and indeed his still delicate balance between primary and secondary process mental functioning; his continuing interaction with the objects who have been significantly involved in the development of his psychopathology; his different time perspective; his early stage in the modulation and differentiation of affects; and his basic situation of immaturity and dependency on his parental objects. The list is a long one—much longer than briefly presented here. Depending on the child's developmental stage, many of these elements have an important bearing on the very nature of the transference, on interpretive activity, on working through, and on obtaining verbalized insight.[11]

It is no less a mistake, in the process of "giving the child as much pure analysis as it can tolerate," to ignore his developmental state and impose upon him an ersatz, compliant pseudo-secondary process functioning within the analytic sessions than it is to mistake his many capacities for analytic work and deteriorate into unnecessarily seductive, gratifying, non-interpretive modes of therapeutic work. The above developmental considerations have been recognized in generally accepted sharp modifications of technique with preschoolers, and Fraiberg's recent paper, "A Comparison of the Analytic Method in Two Stages of a Child Analysis" (1965), is a par-

[11] To highlight this, one need only remember that in certain ages or developmental stages the aims of child analysis are significantly opposed to the basic direction of normal developmental processes and that one may appropriately refer in child analysis to "developmental resistances."

ticularly telling illustration of what even relatively small age differences and related developmental shifts imply for psychoanalytic technique with children.

The specific implications of these developmental differences for child analytic technique will only gradually be worked out conceptually and in practice. So too, given the increasing tempo of reconceptualizations of etiological factors in children's psychological disorders, the years ahead will witness the move to adapt child analytic technique to more appropriately deal with significant aspects of children's disorders based on etiologic agents other than trauma, fixation, and regression. Such tasks and opportunities make the next decades in the history of child psychoanalysis potentially exciting ones indeed.

References

Abbate, Grace M. (Reporter.) "Panel Report: Child Analysis at Different Developmental Stages." *Journal of the American Psychoanalytic Association,* 12 (1964), 135–150.

Ackerman, N. W. *The Psychodynamics of Family Life.* New York: Basic Books, 1958.

Anthony, E. J. "The Parent and the Child Analyst." Unpublished review, 1963.

Arlow, J. A. "Conflict, Regression, and Symptom Formation." *International Journal of Psycho-Analysis,* 44 (1963), 12–22.

Benedek, Therese. "Parenthood as a Developmental Phase." *Journal of the American Psychoanalytic Association,* 7 (1959), 389–417.

Benjamin, J. D. "The Innate and the Experiential in Child Development." In H. W. Brosin (ed.), *Lectures on Experimental Psychiatry.* Pittsburgh: University of Pittsburgh Press, 1961. (a)

Benjamin, J. D. "Some Developmental Observations Relating to the Theory of Anxiety." *Journal of the American Psychoanalytic Association,* 9 (1961), 652–668. (b)

Benjamin, J. D. "Developmental Biology and Psychoanalysis." In N. S. Greenfield and W. C. Lewis (eds.), *Psychoanalysis and Current Biological Thought.* Madison: University of Wisconsin Press, 1965.

Bergen, Mary E. "The Effect of Severe Trauma on a Four-Year-Old Child." In *The Psychoanalytic Study of the Child.* Vol. 13. New York: International Universities Press, 1958.

Bergman, P., and Escalona, Sybelle K. "Unusual Sensitivities in Very Young Children." In *The Psychoanalytic Study of the Child.* New York: International Universities Press, 1949, Vols. 3–4.

Bernstein, I. "The Importance of Characteristics of the Parents in Deciding on Child Analysis." *Journal of the American Psychoanalytic Association,* 6 (1958), 71–78.

Blum, G. S. *Psychoanalytic Theories of Personality.* New York: McGraw-Hill, 1953.

Bonnard, Augusta. "Some Examples and Consequences of War Injury, Real and Imaginary, in Children." *Quarterly Journal of Child Behavior,* 3 (1951), 1–14.

Bornstein, Berta. "Clinical Notes on Child Analysis." In *The Psychoanalytic Study of the Child.* Vol. 1. New York: International Universities Press, 1945.

Brody, Sylvia. "Some Aspects of Transference Resistance in Pre-puberty." In *The Psychoanalytic Study of the Child.* Vol. 16. New York: International Universities Press, 1961.

Buxbaum, Edith. "Technique of Child Therapy: A Critical Evaluation." In *The Psychoanalytic Study of the Child.* Vol. 9. New York: International Universities Press, 1954.

Cain, A. C. "Special 'Isolated' Abilities in Severely Psychotic Young Children." Paper presented at the Annual Meeting of the American Orthopsychiatric Association, March 1964.

Cain, A. C. "Generality vs. Specificity of Training: Professional Preparation of Child Clinical Psychologists." In *Pre-conference Materials: Conference on the Professional Preparation of Clinical Psychologists.* Washington, D.C.: American Psychological Association, 1965.

Casuso, G. (Reporter.) "Panel Report: The Relationship between Child Analysis and the Theory and Practice of Adult Psychoanalysis." *Journal of the American Psychoanalytic Association,* 13 (1965), 159–171.

Cummings, S. T. Unpublished presentation, 1963.

Erikson, E. H. *Childhood and Society.* New York: Norton, 1950.

Escalona, Sybelle K. "Problems and Opportunities in the Application of Psychoanalytic Knowledge of Normal Development." Unpublished paper, presented at the Fall 1961 Meeting of the American Psychoanalytic Association.

Fenichel, O. *The Psychoanalytic Theory of Neurosis.* New York: Norton, 1945.

Fraiberg, Selma. "Clinical Notes on the Nature of Transference in Child Analysis." In *The Psychoanalytic Study of the Child.* Vol. 6. New York: International Universities Press, 1951.

Fraiberg, Selma. "Technical Aspects of the Analysis of a Child with a Severe Behavior Disorder." *Journal of the American Psychoanalytic Association,* 10 (1962), 338–367.

Fraiberg, Selma. "A Comparison of the Analytic Method in Two Stages of a Child Analysis." *Journal of the American Academy of Child Psychiatry,* 4 (1965), 387–400.

Freud, Anna. *Introduction to the Technique of Child Analysis.* New York: Nervous and Mental Diseases Publishing Co., 1928.

Freud, Anna. "Indications for Child Analysis." In *The Psychoanalytic Study of the Child.* Vol. 1. New York: International Universities Press, 1945.

Freud, Anna. "Assessment of Childhood Disturbances." In *The Psychoanalytic Study of the Child.* Vol. 17. New York: International Universities Press, 1962.

Freud, Anna. *Normality and Pathology in Childhood: Assessments of Development.* New York: International Universities Press, 1965.

Freud, Anna, and Dann, Sophie. "An Experiment in Group Upbringing." In *The Psychoanalytic Study of the Child.* Vol. 6. New York: International Universities Press, 1951.

Freud, S. "Three Essays on the Theory of Sexuality (1905)." *Standard Edition of the Complete Psychological Works of. . . .* London: Hogarth Press. Vol. 7. (Also published as *Three Essays on the Theory of Sexuality.* New York: Basic Books, 1963.)

Glover, E. *Psychoanalysis.* London: Staples Press, 1939.

Glover, E. *Psychoanalysis and Child Psychiatry.* London: Imago, 1953.

Harlow, H. F., and Harlow, Margaret K. "Social Deprivation in Monkeys." *Scientific American,* November, 1962.

Hartmann, H. *Ego Psychology and the Problem of Adaptation.* New York: International Universities Press, 1958.

Hendrick, I. *Facts and Theories of Psychoanalysis.* 3rd ed.; New York: Knopf, 1958.

Jenkins, R. L., and Cole, J. O. (eds.). "Diagnostic Classification in Child Psychiatry." Psychiatric Research Report No. 18, American Psychiatric Association, 1964.

Kaplan, Elizabeth B. (Reporter.) "Panel Report: Classical Forms of Neurosis in Infancy and Early Childhood." *Journal of the American Psychoanalytic Association,* 10 (1962), 571–578.

Katan, Anny. "Some Thoughts about the Role of Verbalization in Early Childhood." In *The Psychoanalytic Study of the Child.* Vol. 16. New York: International Universities Press, 1961.

Khan, M. M. R. "The Concept of Cumulative Trauma." In *The Psychoanalytic Study of the Child.* Vol. 18. New York: International Universities Press, 1963.

Klein, Melanie. *The Psychoanalysis of Children.* London: Hogarth Press, 1932.

Kris, E. "The Recovery of Childhood Memories in Psychoanalysis." In *The Psychoanalytic Study of the Child.* Vol. 11. New York: International Universities Press, 1956.

Kut, Sara. "The Changing Pattern of Transference in the Analysis of an Eleven Year Old Girl." In *The Psychoanalytic Study of the Child.* Vol. 8. New York: International Universities Press, 1953.

Lewin, B. D., and Ross, Helen. *Psychoanalytic Education in the United States.* New York: Norton, 1960.

Littner, N. "Contact between the Child Analyst and the Parents of His Child Analytic Patient." Unpublished paper, 1964.

Mahler, Margaret S. "Discussion of Papers." In P. H. Hoch and J. Zubin (eds.), *Psychopathology of Childhood.* New York: Grune & Stratton, 1955.

Montagu, M. F. A. "Constitutional and Prenatal Factors in Infant and Child Health." In M. J. E. Senn (ed.), *Symposium on the Healthy Personality.* New York: Josiah Macy, Jr., Foundation, 1950.

Murphy, Lois B., Heider, Grace M., Toussiang, P. V., and Moriarty, Alice. "Methods of Coping with Stress in the Development of Normal Children." *Bulletin of the Menninger Clinic,* 24 (1960), 97–153.

Neubauer, P. B. (Reporter.) "Panel Report: Psychoanalytic Contributions to the Nosology of Childhood Psychic Disorders." *Journal of the American Psychoanalytic Association*, 11 (1963), 595–604.
Piers, G., and Piers, Maria W. "Modes of Learning and the Analytic Process." In *Selected Lectures, Sixth International Congress of Psychotherapy*. New York: Karger, 1965.
Rapaport, D. "Psychoanalysis as a Developmental Psychology" (1960). M. M. Gill (ed.), *Collected Papers of*. . . . New York: Basic Books, 1967. Pp. 820–852.
Rexford, Eveoleen N. "Child Psychiatry and Child Analysis in the United States." *Journal of the American Academy of Child Psychiatry*, 1 (1962), 365–384.
Sandler, J. "Notes on Child Analysis." Unpublished paper, 1964.
Spitz, R. A. *A Genetic Field Theory of Ego Formation*. New York: International Universities Press, 1959.
Spitz, R. A. *The First Year of Life*. New York: International Universities Press, 1965.
Weiss, S. "Parameters in Child Analysis." *Journal of the American Psychoanalytic Association*, 12 (1964), 587–599.
Williams, R. J. *Biochemical Individuality*. New York: John Wiley, 1956.
Zetzel, Elizabeth R. "Anxiety and the Capacity to Bear It." *International Journal of Psychoanalysis*, 30 (1949), 1–12.

18

Action and Family Interaction in Adolescence

ROGER L. SHAPIRO

I

In the summary statements of "Youth: Fidelity and Diversity," Erik H. Erikson (1962a, p. 24) says:

> To enter history, each generation of youth must find an identity consonant with its own childhood and consonant with an ideological promise in the perceptible historical process. But in youth the tables of childhood dependence begin slowly to turn: no longer is it merely for the old to teach the young the meaning of life, whether individual or collective. It is the young who, by their responses and actions, tell the old whether life as represented by the old and as presented to the young has meaning; and it is the young who carry in them the power to confirm those who confirm them and, joining the issues, to renew and regenerate, or to reform and to rebel.

In this chapter I will consider the crucial role of adolescent action and interaction between the generations for identity formation. I will discuss adolescent cognitive development and its consequences for action. I will then re-examine the psychoanalytic theory of action, the place within it of various conceptualizations of acting out, and the importance of a more comprehensive formulation of the meaning of action for personality development. Finally, I will describe a method growing from these considerations for investigating the consequences of the behavior of adults on the actions and personality formation of youth, and of actions of youth on the older generation.

The movement of youth away from a position of childhood dependence requires new behavior and specific actions. These actions are an expression of the emerging identity of youth and to a significant extent determine identity consolidation. These actions become possible through the maturation of psychological capacities in adolescence which have been conceptualized by Anna Freud (1936, 1958), Erikson (1956, 1958), Blos (1962), and others. Adolescence is characterized both by maturation of ego capacities reflected in change in the nature of cognition and by change in the id seen in the manifestations of the drive development of puberty. An altered relationship to reality occurs which is determined by these changes. A consideration of these psychological developments, the manner in which they are integrated, and their manifestations led Erikson (1950, 1956) to the formulation of identity crisis as the psychosocial crisis of adolescence and identity formation as the ascendant task of the adolescent ego.

The basis in ego growth for the establishment of identity can be characterized by defining the new cognitive capacities which develop in adolescence and their relationship to action. Inhelder and Piaget (1958) have described a consistent change in the ability to conceptualize and to generalize between ages eleven to fourteen, with a progression from concrete operations in the thinking of the child to a capacity for abstract thought in the adolescent. A new capacity for hypothesis formation develops, with the utilization of hypothetico-deductive reasoning and experimental proof. I have postulated that the consistency of this finding in early adolescence justifies an extension of Hartmann's (1939) assumptions about autonomous ego development to the period of early adolescence, to account for the maturational events of this phase (Shapiro, 1963). Autonomous ego development can thus be assumed to be one determinant of personality growth in adolescence conceptualized as remodeling of psychic structure and increasing secondary autonomy of the ego by Jacobson (1961), as the establishment of ego identity by Erikson (1956), and as the consolidation of the sense of self by Blos (1962).

The assumption that there is autonomous ego development in early adolescence has important implications for the understanding both of cognition and action. It provides an alternative theoretical basis to the classical psychoanalytic formulation that abstract thought and system building in adolescence grow out of defensive needs deriving from the drive development of puberty (A. Freud, 1936). Intellectualization as an ego mechanism of defense in adolescence can then be accounted for as an example of an autonomous ego capacity being drawn into conflict and utilized as a defense. Furthermore, the capacity for abstract thought and formal reasoning in the adolescent gives rise to a new relation to reality, and consequently to a new basis for action in reality. Thus, the foundation of action may lie, on the one hand, in logical processes which are a consequence of autonomous ego development, or, on the other, in unconscious conflict in which intellectualization is the rationalization for defensive acting out. The hypothesis that there is autonomous ego development in the cognitive sphere makes it possible to differentiate in theory between these possibilities. Action, the determinants of which can be found in the psychological characteristics of the adolescent and his relationship to current reality, can be differentiated in theory from action, which represents the defensive acting out of an unconscious genetic conflict. These are theoretical extremes and the analysis of actual action will generally involve complex combinations of these elements.

In "Reality and Actuality," Erikson (1962b, p. 457) differentiates between what he designates "age-specific action" and the acting out of an unconscious genetic conflict:

> Each stage of development has its own acuteness and actualness, because a stage is a new configuration of past and future, a new combination of drive and defense, a new set of tasks and opportunities, a new and wider radius of significant encounters. Our question, then, concerns the possibility that at each stage, what appears to us as "acting out" may contain an element of action, that is, an adaptive if immature reaching out for the mutual verification by which the ego lives; and that, in *young adulthood*, the pursuit of factual or historical truth may be of acute relevance to the ego's adaptive strength.

Here action is differentiated from acting out on the basis that particular behaviors in reality in a developmental phase may have current and acute relevance to the personality functioning and development of that phase. This phase-specific action utilizing the new drive and ego potentialities of the phase can be defined, and behavior understood in terms of its current meaning and validity in addition to consideration of its genetic roots and those determinants which are a repetition of the past. To formulate such behavior as acting out unduly emphasizes its genetic determinants and ignores the new pattern of verification in reality required by the particular cognitive gains of a developmental phase determining age-specific action.

A recent work by Peter Blos, "The Concept of Acting Out in Relation to the Adolescent Process" (1963), attempts an expanded conceptualization of acting out in an effort to encompass the significance and the determinants of action in this phase. Blos calls acting out a phase-specific mechanism of adolescence and includes in it acting out in the service of the ego, acting out in the service of progressive development, acting out in the service of ego synthesis, and acting out in the service of temporal ego continuity. These conceptualizations serve the valuable purpose of acknowledging the importance of the actions under discussion for adolescent personality development and the psychic restructuring which occurs in the ego at this phase. At the same time, however, the designation "acting out" tends to emphasize the unconscious organization determining the action and its defensive meaning and to imply some disturbance in the adolescent's sense of reality. It tends to obscure the reality importance of these actions for the facilitation of the definitive formation of the self which Blos describes as a major effort of the adolescent ego.

With the advent of ego psychology it has been possible to develop highly useful structural theories of thinking and affect, as well as important bridges between them (Rapaport, 1951a, 1953). By comparison, the theory of action has been meager, and the relationship between the theory of action and the theories of thinking and affect has been less well defined. This may reflect the setting of the observations from which classical psychoanalytic theory has evolved. The psychoanalytic situation is designed in such a way as to make possible more extensive observations of thinking and of affect than of action. Those actions which it is possible to observe directly in the psychoanalytic situation, the interactions between the patient and the therapist, have been formulated in a particular way to which Freud gave the designation "acting out in the transference" (Freud, 1905, 1914). This designation was a formulation of resistance in analysis, specifically a resistance to remembering and a repetition in action of behavior determined by past experience now in repression. Here the emphasis on genetic insight gave an impetus to the theory of thinking but inhibited the growth of a psychoanalytic theory of action. The relation of action to resistance in clinical theory, based on a particular theory of therapy, led to uneasiness in psychoanalysts about action and the psychology of action. Although Freud's formulation of acting out was explicitly the formulation of a particular type of resistance in psychoanalytic treatment and a part of the clinical theory, it is now applied as an explanatory concept to a wide variety of actions outside of the analytic situation. This tends to emphasize particular meanings and determinants of action and to minimize others which may be extremely important from the point of view of personality development and personality theory. This is not a necessary consequence of the designation "acting out," as can be seen by the expanded use Blos makes of the term, but it is a consequence of the implications of the historical definition of the term, which has led to an emphasis on unconscious genetic determinants in psychoanalytic conceptualizations of action. The relation of action to cognitive development specifically and its importance for personality development generally have not received sufficient formal consideration. The reality determinants of action and inhibition of action, and the consequences of these for personality development have not been adequately conceptualized.

In "The Conceptual Model of Psychoanalysis," David Rapaport (1951b) discusses the dynamic, economic, and structural considerations behind the primary and secondary models of action, thinking, and affect he constructs. His models allow one to postulate a hierarchy of actions, from action determined primarily by drive to action determined predominantly by considerations of reality. The determinants of action can be conceptualized on a continuum from a drive organization, to an organization determined by unconscious conflict, to an organization determined by reality. This provides a comprehensive framework within which to analyze action. It allows for complex combinations of drive, unconscious genetic conflict, and reality motivations on this continuum from drive to reality organization. It allows for economic considerations as they pertain to action (Rapaport, 1959), from action which is peremptory and closely related to drive discharge to action which is the product of delay and is oriented to objective reality.

This conceptualization of action provides a framework for the analysis of so-called "acting out." This would refer to action with determinants in unconscious conflict which lead to repetitive, compulsive, and stereotyped behavior which is more influenced by unconscious conflict than by reality considerations. It would also include action which is impulsive and related more closely to peremptory drive discharge than to reality considerations. The term acting out is also used loosely to designate behavior which is considered antisocial; this can be particularly misleading because it implies that action which is antisocial has more compelling unconscious determinants and less important determinants in reality than action which is not. This may or may not be the case. All action has unconscious determinants, and the importance of these cannot be assumed to be invariably greater in action which is antisocial than in socially acceptable action.

The conceptualization of action discussed here derived from Rapaport's comprehensive framework, also provides a theoretical framework for action which is relatively autonomous either from drive or from reality. It permits an analysis of action in the light of age-specific considerations, from the point of view of its reality meaning for personality development as well as its genetic meaning.

An elucidation of the determinants of the adolescent's ability to act in reality is essential to a comprehension of identity formation. One foundation of the consolidation of ego identity in adolescence is change in the capacity to act. Action requires a crystallization of identity sufficient to integrate such action, and confirms the identity both in interaction with others and through others' recognition of the action and their response to it. Since the capacity to act is an aspect of ego identity even as it is a prerequisite to the confirmation of a particular identity, an understanding of action or of inhibition of action in adolescence is a part of the understanding of the determinants of consolidation or diffusion of ego identity.

Erikson's statement that individual identity must be consonant with the experience of childhood and consonant with an ideological promise in the perceptible historical process points to two large areas of action in reality which must be examined to understand identity formation in youth. Experience in childhood and specifically action and interaction within the immediate family are major areas of determination of ego identity. The individual's action in society and exposure to particular social response and social ideologies are others. In a study of personality development in adolescence at the National Institute of Mental Health, we have selected for more detailed observation an aspect of one of these areas, that of current interaction between the adolescent and his parents.

II

Our vantage point for the study of parent-adolescent interaction is a weekly hour-long group session attended by the adolescent, his parents, an adolescent sibling if there is one, plus the psychiatrist who is also the individual therapist of the adolescent, and the psychiatric social worker who is also the therapist of the parents as a marital couple. The adolescents we are studying are hospitalized on an open fourteen-bed psychiatric unit at the National Institutes of Health. They have all had a severe emotional decompensation in the first prolonged separation from their families in the first year of residence at college, which made it impossible for them to continue their academic work. We have hospitalized thirty adolescents selected by these criteria and have seen a wide range of disturbances from psychoses, to borderline states, to severe neuroses and character disorders. We have made extended observations of parent-adolescent interaction in family group sessions, which are a part of our therapeutic program as well as a situation for research observations.

The family group session constitutes a highly relevant reality situation in which action pertinent to adolescent personality development and identity formation can be studied. The study of interaction of parents with adolescent over issues reflecting phase-specific development provides one basis for understanding the crystallization of the sense of ego identity in the adolescent, its integration or diffusion, its content, and its consonance with action or with prominent areas of inhibition. The relationship of the adolescent's self-concept to the concept of him which is implicit in the behavior of significant other persons toward him is the basis from which ego identity grows; in short, the relation of self-definition to social definition is the core of individual identity in every psychosocial phase. The relevance of parent-adolescent interaction to identity consolidation or diffusion, of parental delineation to adolescent self-definition, is a central issue in identity formation. The family group session, therefore, is a psychosocial situation in which events which contribute to identity consolidation or diffusion can be observed.

The capacity for a new order of abstract thinking provides the adolescent with a new potentiality for assessing positions taken by his parents and relating these to the rest of what he sees in reality. It provides him with a new basis for differentiating himself from his parents and aligning himself with new objects, ideologies, and institutions. Parental reaction to this new potentiality in the adolescent has great effect on the nature of the development of autonomy in the adolescent. Parent-adolescent interaction over issues of autonomy then becomes another phase-specific focus for observations relevant to identity formation and the capacity for action in adolescence.

The family group session also lends itself to observations relevant to the drive epigenesis of puberty. The relationship to the parents is in the center of these alterations, with drive development reviving old patterns of Oedipal anxiety and stimulating defenses which have a new characteristic. These are defenses against the existence of the Oedipal objects themselves (A. Freud, 1958) and attempts at solution of this problem by finding new objects. Withdrawal of libidinal investment from parents and reinvestment in new objects is one of the complex tasks of adolescence. The characteristics of parent-adolescent interaction over this issue provide data of great relevance for an understanding of the libidinal meaning of the parents to the adolescent and the structure of the libidinal problem in the adolescent.

These are aspects of personality development in adolescence and associated action which can be studied in the actuality of the family group session. The adolescent's impact on his parents, his confirmation of them or rebellion against them and their response to this can be observed. The family group session is a situation of interaction between the generations, in which action of one member may be viewed in terms of the response and further action of the others.

We have developed the concept of delineation as a basis for organizing our observations of behavior within the family group. A central hypothesis of our study has been that there is a significant relationship between parental delineation of the adolescent and adolescent identity formation. By delineation we mean the view or image one person has of the other person as it is revealed explicitly or implicitly in the behavior of the one person with the other person. This is behavior which expresses how the one person identifies the other person. It includes behavior which expresses attitudes about the actions of the other person, as well as behavior which reveals expectations of the other person. A highly important subgroup of delineations consists of those which we call defensive delineations. When behavior of an individual with an object contains evidence of distortion of the object related to the individual's defensive organization, then defensive delineation exists. It is a response to behavior of the other person which stimulates anxiety in the one person and gives rise to defensive operations which are revealed in the nature and style of their delineation of the other person.

Defensive delineation exists in parental behavior where definition of the adolescent is distorted by the parent's defensive needs. These are superimposed on the adolescent's actual behavior and result in characteristic emphases, biases, idiosyncrasies, and distortions in the parent's definition of the adolescent. If characteristic parental delineation can be demonstrated to satisfy particular psychological needs of the parent, we have a basis for argument that it is of long standing and has a determinant in the parent's psychology independent of actual behavior of the adolescent.

The concept of defensive delineation includes a wide range of parental responses toward anxiety-engendering adolescent behavior. Parental distortion and the inference of defense are most clear when, instead of parental delineation constituting an accurate description of adolescent behavior, it is not congruent with the behavior as described by observers. Defensive delineation can also be inferred when despite correct parental perception of the adolescent there is a consistent selection of adolescent characteristics which are perceived and responded to by the parent, and others which are not attended to. Defensive delineation may be inferred from contradictions in parental definition of the adolescent, or in behavior or attitudes which contradict explicit definition of the adolescent. Defensive delineation is behavior determined by the parent's intrapsychic defensive operations and manifested in an interpersonal field with a potential effect on the adolescent. Examples of denial may be seen in a definition of the adolescent that is directly contradictory to the behavior the adolescent is manifesting. Repression can be inferred from characteristic parental delineation which does not acknowledge prominent areas of adolescent behavior. The grossest distortions of reality are seen in those parents where the defensive delineation is no longer selective, but is an aspect of a more general thought disorder in the parent involving a pervasive autistic interpretation of reality. These are the kinds of parents described by several research groups studying the families of schizophrenics (Wynne and Singer, 1963, 1965; Laing, 1962)—parents with gross misinterpretation of reality and whose delineation of the adolescent is confused, pervasively idiosyncratic, and dictated predominantly by internal needs.

The parent's delineation of the adolescent contains clear expectations about the actions of the adolescent. We study the manner in which this image of the adolescent is communicated to him. We observe his response in action to parental delineation of him in the family session, and consider the relationship of the parental delineation to his capacity for action in a variety of spheres outside of the family session. We formulate the relationship of adolescent action or inhibition of action to his problem in identity formation. Research interviews and psychological testing of the parents provide a more complete psychodynamic understanding of them. We formulate the identity problem of the adolescent from material we obtain in research interviews and psychological testing of the adolescent. We examine characteristic parental delineations of the adolescent in the family group session to see how they relate to the capacity for action and the related identity problem we find in the adolescent.

III

A case example will illustrate the utilization of this method. It will emphasize the relationship of action and inhibition of action in the adolescent to parental delineation of him. The capacity to act has a decisive relationship to other aspects of the ego identity of the adolescent. Until action is possible any partial identity element is only potential. Action confirms it in the eyes of the adolescent. Recognition of this action by significant other persons constitutes complementary action which carries this confirmation one step further. These steps will be exemplified in this discussion of case material.

This is an example of defiant and passive aggressive action against the parents on the part of a young man of nineteen years. The defiant action was consistent with long-standing delineation of the patient by both parents as lazy, stubborn, apathetic, withdrawn, and uncommitted to useful activity. However, it was in contradiction to another less overt and explicit delineation of him, that of an expectation that he would be compliant to their demands. The patient's behavior asserted his right to freedom from the demands of his parents. Although it was in harmony with his picture of himself as passive, withdrawn, and abhorring responsibility, it contradicted another aspect of his feeling about himself, that of being controlled by his parents, afraid to defy them, and unable to assert any feeling of his own in active opposition to the ideas of those on whom he depended. He felt that he was being treated by his father as if he were the latter's property, although he knew he could disappoint his father by failing at something he tried, thus expressing resentment; active opposition was another question. He felt that he had to acquiesce and could not express overt defiance or contrary feelings of his own. He felt even more afraid to contradict the expressed wishes of his mother and felt great anxiety at her expressions of rage.

The issue in question arose after the patient had been in the hospital for eight months. Although he was working twenty hours a week on a job, which is a requirement of our program, his parents were disturbed that he did nothing to contribute to the family when he was at home. They made the demand that he work for eight hours in the house or on the grounds if he were home weekends. They tended to discount the possibility that he was doing anything useful at the hospital, despite their awareness of his job in a biochemical laboratory. The patient did little to counteract this evaluation. During the previous months of his hospitalization the father characteristically delineated him as a time-waster, as lazy, as ineffectual and disorganized, as impractical, as unwilling to fulfill his obligations to himself and to society. His mother was less consistent in her delineations of him. At times she defended the patient in a way which made it clear that she saw him as fragile, that she felt she understood him, and that she sympathized with his feelings. At other times, and particularly when the patient was unresponsive to her, she sided with the father in criticism and condemnation of the patient. She seemed to identify with the patient in her empathic responses to him, but he tended to ignore these in behavior in which he seemed to defend against feelings of identification with her.

Research interviews with both parents provided data about their attitudes toward activity, work, and social obligation which made the issues clearer at the same time that they highlighted their complexity.

The father's highly explicit and developed social ideology, with great emphasis on service, social obligation, and doing socially useful work, had a foundation which was consciously ambivalent. After many years of living on inherited income, with repeated failures to complete his graduate education or to find a career direction, he began to work in a social agency where, through unconventional methods, he achieved a high position. He himself saw the work as a reaction against his inclination to live a life of passivity and pleasure. He also saw it as a situation in which he could effectively compete with men, something that had always been a problem, and something that had been impossible with his own father into whose successful business he had avoided going. In relationship to his son, he described a long-standing inability to work cooperatively with the boy, a tendency to take over and to do everything himself, and a great tendency to be critical. The father provided much data consistent with the formulation of an unusual concern over passivity and a pronounced reaction formation against this. He was sensitive to any threat to his masculinity, and aggressive, competitive behavior was quickly mobilized in relation to other men or challenging women.

In interviews with the mother a picture of chronic depression and low self-esteem emerged. She had a conscious awareness of intense wishes for inactivity, rest, and situations of no demand. These wishes were alarming to her and she characterized them as infantile. When she gave in to her passive inclinations, remained in bed, and did not work, she felt immense gratification. However, this was soon complicated by intense guilt and by feelings of worthlessness. Her pattern was then to plunge into activity from which she temporarily derived an increased self-esteem and feeling of being worthwhile, but this did not compensate for the frustration of her passive wishes. When she worked she felt torn, exhausted, and angry. She made increasing demands on herself, felt less satisfied with what she could accomplish, and had periodic periods of decompensation with extreme agitation and depression. Her work was consistent with her ego ideal of social usefulness and service. She was apprehensive of passive and infantile tendencies in herself and intolerant of them in her children. Her response to her children from infancy had fluctuated between an empathic understanding of their infantile needs and an enraged resentment of their passivity or their childish or irresponsible behavior. She considered herself self-centered and self-preoccupied and felt guilty about her maternal behavior, which she characterized as destructive to her children. She felt that her son was extremely vulnerable to her, and she was troubled by this quality in him at the same time that she was certain she would be violently enraged if he were defiant of her.

Research interviews with the patient made explicit his concept of himself as compliant and as afraid to initiate action in opposition to those he depended upon. He saw himself as fearful, childish, and withdrawn and described feelings of passivity and compliance in relation to his peers as well as to his parents. He described a pervasive inability to feel any activity as his own and a tendency to feel controlled by others. Even when he was initially motivated toward accomplishment, as he had been at the beginning of college, he soon began to feel that too many external demands were being made of him and experienced precipitous loss of interest and initiative, with consequent guilt and depression. Although this resulted in his performance becoming so poor that he was asked to leave school, he did not see his behavior as rebellious and felt that he could not be openly defiant. He felt lonely, vulnerable, and afraid of the overt rejection and anger of those on whom he depended. He felt that there was nothing about him which would interest others or be a reliable basis for relationship with others.

In discussing his actions at college he said:

I guess I was pretty lonely there . . . they really left you quite alone there . . . I guess it was a pretty grown up place . . . not a lot of, not any taking care of you . . . I didn't dislike the people there and I didn't dislike the school. I pretty much liked both, but I didn't do anything about it. I would just sit around in my room and go someplace if I could think up something to do. At the end it was better because I was beginning to get famous for cutting so many classes and so kids would come up to me and say, "You are the guy who cut so many classes," and then you know, there was some sort of start or go-between foundation in which I could—you know, be friendly with. It was still a pretty passive type thing, you know, I didn't do much. . . .

The patient related inhibition of action to two areas of concern. He experienced anxiety over the possibility that action would result in his doing something wrong; he also felt emotionally too much like a child to act in a manner appropriate to his age. Doing something wrong meant doing something which would violate his own aspirations or would anger or disappoint other people. He felt it was better not to act than to act in an ineffectual, clumsy, inept way or to demonstrate incompetence in an important situation. He characterized himself as a "goody-goody boy" when describing his compliance and his concern over others' reactions of anger and contempt. His expectations of himself were perfectionistic, and his dread of the reaction of others reflected his feeling that they too had high expectations of him. These attitudes all contributed to anxiety over his childish feelings, and to concern over their being revealed in his actions.

The patient described some variability in his feelings about himself. Although those just described were the most pervasive and most current, he also described a state of mind in which he felt far freer and more capable of independent action. He described the emergence of new feelings about himself at age fifteen in the context of a two-day seminar he attended sponsored by a youth organization.

It seems to me that I used to think of there being quite a change in myself during the tenth grade . . . I went to this . . . seminar here in Washington for a couple of days, and you know, talked to the kids . . . I don't think of it this way any more but at the time I thought of it as a great awakening. Up until that time I—you know, I had been asleep sort of, a little kid unconscious, and this was when I was waking up and seeing that I am here and that I can take conscious decisions and decide what I want to do and so on . . . It stood out in my mind and I would think, "Gee, it's been a year now since the awakening," or whatever it was, but you know, it gradually wore off. I guess I think of it more now as a little upheaval but not any great change, you know, more that I didn't really get any more conscious or anything. . . . It was an experience, in sort of an intellectual way mostly, having to do with having opened up with some of the kids at the seminar, I guess . . . just first it was a great feeling of well-being, happiness or something, very silly . . . we were in a boardinghouse and it was just completely cut off from my regular world for those two or three days . . . I felt very let down at having to come back to my regular old world. I can remember saying this to one of the kids, saying, "It's all mine to do with what I want, I can go anyplace I want. Even what's strange is no different from what I know and I can plan and do things whatever I want—think about anything." It's just that I was sort of going along up until then, almost always afterwards too, just doing what came along. For a moment I had visions of, you know, not just doing what comes along but doing what you want to do or something like that . . . but by the time I was up at school I started right back in again, not talking to anybody.

In this material reported by the patient, long-standing problems of depression and feelings of inadequacy and apprehension with others were intensified in the situation of separation from his family and attendance at college with its new requirements for greater maturity and adjustment to a new group. He was unable to take initiative in forming new relationships, and only when his withdrawal resulted in the establishment of the negative identity of "the guy who cut so many classes" did he feel that he had a basis for establishing himself in relationship to others. He was unable to find sufficient comfort in the new situation to maintain the initiative required to re-establish the feelings of freedom, of ability to do what he wanted to do, of ability to make conscious decisions which had emerged for a short time earlier in his adolescence. He did not feel that the negative identity he achieved in college was earned by conscious choice. It was rather an example of an identity which developed as a consequence of what he called just going along, unable to take initiative or to implement any decisions. He felt the same way about much of his behavior in the hospital. He saw his working in the biochemical laboratory as acquiescence to the demands of our program. However, when his parents demanded that he also work at home on the weekends he took a different stand. He did not go along with their demand, nor did he go home, and, without explicitly disagreeing with their request, simply fail to carry it out. He instead made it explicit in the family group session that he would not acquiesce to the demands his parents made as they seemed to him unjustly coercive and too gross an attempt to control him. He agreed that he should contribute something to the welfare of the family. He felt, however, that this was not the important issue at this time. The more important issue to him was whether in a disagreement between his parents and himself they had the right to bar him from the house if he did not concede to them. Excerpts from two family group meetings illustrate interaction in the family over this issue.

FATHER:

Are you coming home this weekend?

PATIENT:

I was thinking about that. It seemed to me that, that I should be able to come home regardless of my performance and that you shouldn't go around setting conditions like that.

FATHER:

I am not setting conditions.

PATIENT:

Yes, you are.

FATHER:

I am just saying that the family is a unit in which everybody has to take some responsibility.

PATIENT:

So when one of them doesn't, does that mean they have to get out, or maybe they should be able to stick around anyhow.

BROTHER:

That's what they told me to do. That's why I go over to Carl's for a week or so.

FATHER:

No, I don't see anything that is setting conditions.

PATIENT:

But you are.

FATHER:

Well, all right, do you deny that I have a right to set some?

PATIENT:

No, I was thinking of denying your right to kick me out if I don't fill your conditions. . . . If I was busy doing something else you wouldn't have thought of asking me to. . . .

FATHER:

If you were studying for an exam or something else, or if you were inventing something, or doing some. . . .

PATIENT:

Then I wouldn't have to contribute to the family.

FATHER:

That would be a contribution to the family.

PATIENT:

In what respect?

FATHER:

In the same respect that Mother's working on the school board is a contribution to the family.

PATIENT:

Does it? I thought her contribution was the housework and the meals.

FATHER:

Well, that's her immediate contribution but her contribution to society is working for the school board.

PATIENT:

Society? And the family? Well, there's one ground of contention. It seems to me that you don't, that one isn't always demanded to contribute to the family, so why should I, just because I happen to be doing different things of my own. My second area of contention would be that even if I don't contribute to the family, does that mean I'm supposed to be kicked out?

This interaction contains an implicit delineation of the patient by the father as someone whose behavior the father has the right not only to evaluate, but to control. This is in contradiction to the father's initial explicit statement that he is not trying to set conditions, but is only trying to point out to his son what his responsibilities are. He later acknowledges that he is setting conditions, and he asks whether his son denies his right to do this. His delineation of the son is clear, as someone who loses all right to the home if he doesn't acquiesce to the father's demands, and this is perhaps the central psychological issue under discussion. Further delineation of the son as someone whose activities are of no value either to the family or to society is seen in this excerpt. The patient is arguing effectively with his father over these issues, a form of behavior which has been seen with increasing frequency in recent family group sessions. The father's contentiousness under these circumstances derives from a usual delineation of the patient as acquiescent, with the expectation that he conform to his father's values and judgments. Implicit in the exchange are delineations of the patient which ignore his own ways of looking at things and which imply that he is hurtful to his father and does not love him when taking a stand in opposition to the father.

An excerpt from the family group meeting one week later reveals more of the mother's reaction to this situation. She has sided with the father over the issue of the patient's working at home, and the patient has remained at the hospital for the weekend, but had gone home for further discussion with his father the evening before the family group session.

MOTHER:

I think it is time for him to leave this program. I really don't think that it is helping him any further. . . .

PATIENT:

I can sit around home for a while.

MOTHER:

Well, I don't think it will be quite so easy, dear, for you to sit around home. It will be at least a different kind of problem that you will have to cope with and you will have a little more strain put on your natural facilities and talents . . . in the last few weeks the point has been reached where—what you need in order to move at this point is the experience of doing for yourself.

PATIENT:

The only difference the last few weeks is that I've been letting down my shield a little bit more. . . .

MOTHER:

You think so?

PATIENT:

Yeah.

MOTHER:

I don't think so.

PATIENT:

Showing you more the way I feel inside.

MOTHER:

I think I've felt, I don't have any different feeling about how you felt inside, pretty much all along.

PATIENT:

Well, what made you change now? . . .

MOTHER:

It's just that perhaps I have acquired more confidence in my feeling that things are with you about the way they felt to me before, where I wasn't so sure of it. . . .

PATIENT:

I don't know, I have a feeling that—it may not be related to this but I get the feeling that if I let myself go a little more and show them I am not so goody-goody around the house and show them the way I actually feel, which is not like working and so on, why then what happens, things do start happening in return for this; that I'd better put my shield back up again and be goody-goody and not show them how I really am feeling and so on, everything will be all right.

THERAPIST:

Well, what are the dangers now of letting the shield down?

PATIENT:

They start talking about kicking me out.

THERAPIST:

Kicking you out where?

PATIENT:

Home.

THERAPIST:

And here?

PATIENT:

And here too I guess.

MOTHER:

You think this is the result of your having acted differently at home?

PATIENT:

Well, when we start talking about it, it goes away, conveniently or unconveniently enough.

MOTHER:

Perhaps—perhaps you are right. I mean I try to think would it have been different . . . that may have fortified my feeling that you are all there . . . there is something maturing behind there somewhere.

PATIENT:

I don't see that at all, to tell you the truth. . . .

THERAPIST:

What was it like to let your shield down so low? . . .

PATIENT:

. . . letting myself go more and more, less respectful and not hanging on every word they say quite as much and not worrying as much about doing the thing they like or approve of, doing more what I felt like. . . . It was just a little bit and when I got any reaction I would stop it. Like when you got mad about my complaining about the dessert, or if you actually take the car away, why then I can pull in enough to get the car back or something.

FATHER:

That's a mean kind of bargaining business, that you don't want to do anything, and just do enough to get what you really want very much.

MOTHER:

I don't think that's what he is saying, bargaining; he is saying. . . .

PATIENT:

Bargaining with my life, that's what I am bargaining with . . . the quality I deal with is Me, the person Me. I fix Me up the way you like it so that I can. . . .

MOTHER:

How do you know what we like? I like it better, frankly, if you fight . . . I don't like it better but I . . . I don't like it exactly, but I . . . I suspect that you are going to go on for at least a couple of years trying to push the world back and seeing what it is going to do if you lie down and pretend to be dead. I just want to at this point remove myself from having a part in it. . . .

FATHER:

Well, that's what we got into two weeks ago—wanted him to face up to realities and either make himself useful or stop getting free board.

MOTHER:

Whereupon he responded by saying he guesses he would come home and leave us with the choice of, well—what? Should we lock the door and he stand on the outside and shake the door and we stand on the inside and hold the door? I'm not going to do anything like that. If he wants to come in and out of the house and stay there, I'm not going to get into that kind of trouble with you. Well, it's time to go.

THERAPIST:

The time is up.

BROTHER:

What a session!

FATHER:

Will we see you tomorrow?

PATIENT:
Yeah, I guess so.

Here the delineations by the mother are complex and contradictory. In her initial statements that the patient should leave the hospital there is behavior which points to an implicit delineation of the patient as someone who must either be compliant to her or pay the penalty of drastic action being taken to enforce compliance. He is delineated as someone who is idle, who does not seek out situations which place any demand on his capacities, and whose stay in the hospital is promoting this. The patient argues with this and contends that what is really upsetting his mother is recent behavior on his part where he has revealed more of what he feels about things, even if he knows this will displease her. The mother disagrees with this. The argument then develops, with the patient emphasizing his mother's intolerance of any independent behavior on his part, her insistence that he be goody-goody and not express behavior of which she does not approve. The mother insists that it is only the particular behavior of idleness to which she takes exception. Again the possibility that the patient is doing anything useful in the hospital is ignored. This is partly a consequence of long-standing delineation of the patient as idle, uninvolved, and not utilizing his abilities and partly a response to hostile provocative behavior of the patient who characteristically minimizes the usefulness of any of his activity. When the patient takes exception to her evaluation of the situation the mother exhibits a characteristic uncertainty and her thinking becomes more confused. The therapist supports the patient in the conclusions the patient draws that when he lets his shield down he is in the double danger of being kicked out of the home and kicked out of the hospital. It is the drastic nature of these consequences of noncompliance that gives this interaction its characteristic quality. It is not simply a situation of anger on the part of parents at being unable to mold and control the behavior of a child. It is the rapid emergence of threats and imagery of desertion and withdrawal of emotional support as the consequences of noncompliance which are of great psychological relevance in this family.

The mother now shifts in her delineation of her son, agreeing with his statement that he has changed in his behavior at home and justifying her decision that he should leave the hospital on this evidence of his greater maturity. The patient immediately disagrees with this delineation of him as more mature. He goes on to qualify his change in behavior at home, saying that he continues to gauge how much he can get away with and stops any independent or aggressive action when it is challenged. He states that he is bargaining with his life, "fixing me up" so that he won't be totally rejected by his parents.

A contradictory element in the mother's delineation is now introduced. Her ambivalence about his aggression is seen in the difficulty she has enunciating a delineation of the patient as someone she would like to see fight back. She cannot develop the idea that she would welcome aggression from her son nor can she state it clearly. She finds unacceptable the kind of aggression of which he is capable. This is reflected in the exasperation in her concluding statement about refusing to get into trouble with the patient by trying to keep him out of the house if he refuses to work, and by her initiative in terminating the session. It is clear that she expects her son to choose his weapons and methods and to fight in a way which is compliant to her requirements. This is no longer a real fight. The patient implies this in his statement that he is bargaining with his life. He experiences so much of his behavior as compliant and as meeting the demands of others that action feels like something assertive only in an area which contradicts a parental expectation. But here he feels endangered by the imminence of precipitous loss of emotional support. It is in this area that he tries to arrive at a bargain, at a direction for action which feels self-assertive, but which is not completely alienating and not completely self-destructive.

IV

To return now to the theme of adolescent action and family interaction, I should like to consider the relevance of the kind of observations I have been discussing for an understanding of action in adolescence.

The family group setting brings that aspect of action into focus which has to do with the consequences of the action in the reality of a particular nexus of relationships. These consequences may range from alienation, to condemnation of action without destruction of relationship, to acceptance of action, to positive approval with heightening of relationship. This range of consequences of action, from alienation to confirmation of relationship, is the basis of powerful emotional forces which are reality determinants of action.

The parent-adolescent interaction provides data illuminating the emotional consequences of particular actions of the adolescent in relation to his parents. These data can be taken as representative of a long-standing pattern of relationship between these personalities, providing a basis for inference, from characteristics of parental response, about the origin of particular patterns of action or of inhibition of action in the adolescent. In addition, the parent-adolescent interaction reflects parental receptivity to the manifestations of new age-specific action of the adolescent. In practice these two perspectives must be considered together: the genetic implications of parental response to adolescent action, and the current implications of this response for the adolescent's development in his actuality.

The complexities of this assessment cannot be minimized. If the adolescent has had a lifelong experience with parents whose emotional responses threaten to alienate him from relationship when his actions threaten their defensive structure, pictures of massive inhibition of action in adolescence can be expected. The case example I have presented illustrates this situation. Here current parent-adolescent interaction exemplifies this longstanding pattern. At a time when age-specific action in an adolescent who has for years felt tightly controlled by the parents' attitudes would entail an exploration of patterns of behavior to which the parents may be opposed, the parents' intolerance of such behavior is seen in drastic responses containing the threat of alienation. The age-specific energies and the support of a therapeutic relationship and setting allow some movement into a new and more explicit initiative and aggressivity toward the parents on the part of the adolescent, but the underlying anxiety is great, rooted in years of experience with them as primary objects of relationship. The parents have reacted with intense feeling in response to the patients' action of defiance of parental regulations, and his insistence on his rights to the home without meeting requirements. The father has denied him the right to the home. The mother has attacked his right to the hospital. Both react with great anxiety to the patient's insistence that their concern for him should not exact the price of compliance and contribution. This is an issue with both genetic and phase-specific implications. The genetic interpretation of the patient's behavior would relate it to the acting out of a demand for nurture and care which had been repeatedly frustrated in his childhood, with current repetition of the demand as an effort both to undo a repeated frustration and to achieve a gratification which was frustrated in childhood. The phase-specific interpretation of the action in reality would provide a different emphasis. Here consideration of the patient's new capacity to establish the truth of his relationship with his parents would provide the basis for formulations of action in the service of elucidation of characteristic parental faults in the area of nurture and care, and action to establish autonomy. The action would establish one basis of parental responses of rejection and alienation, in parental anxiety over noncompliant behavior on the part of the patient. It would demonstrate the nature of the repeated pressure for compliance which the patient felt, which went counter to phase-specific action crucial to identity formation: the effort to establish an autonomy from the parents. In the effort to establish his autonomy, the patient was repeatedly pushed, as he was in this episode, into a direction of negative identity. Only in action antagonistic to important explicit parental expectation could the patient be sure his phase-specific action was autonomous and not compliant. Once this was established he could begin to act on more positive elements in his personality, elements related to the feelings about himself which he first had the capacity to formulate at age fifteen in the reported experience of self-awareness and awareness of choice and freedom. Having now demonstrated to himself that autonomous but defiant action was not necessarily catastrophic, that the threat of alienation from his parents did not materialize, he felt a confirmation of an identity that was no longer rooted in the inevitability of compliance. He could begin to act on positive elements in his identification with his parents, without destruction of the feeling necessary to his sense of identity, of differentiation from them.

In adolescents where the longitudinal relationship with the parents does not contain a prominent threat of alienation in response to anxiety-engendering action, such pictures of massive inhibition would not be expected. Here too, analyses of interactions over issues of action reveal complex, but specific and definable, interrelationships between areas of conflict and configuration of defense in the parent, and inhibition or reinforcement of particular patterns of action in the adolescent. An elucidation of all of these variables allows some definition of the experience that is the basis of the ego identity of the adolescent and the capacity for action implicit in this identity.

Erikson points out that it is the young who carry in them the power to confirm those (in the older generation) who confirm them. Observation of parent-adolescent interaction can reveal this mutual confirmation as it can elucidate reactions of alienation. These interactions between the generations of confirmation or alienation are powerful determinants of the capacity for action in the adolescent.

References

Blos, P. *On Adolescence: A Psychoanalytic Interpretation*. New York: The Free Press of Glencoe, 1962.

Blos, P. "The Concept of Acting Out in Relation to the Adolescent Process." *Journal of the American Academy of Child Psychiatry*, 2 (1963), 118–136.

Erikson, E. H. *Childhood and Society*. New York: Norton, 1950.

Erikson, E. H. "The Problem of Ego Identity." New York: *Journal of the American Psychoanalytic Association*, 4 (1956), 56–121.

Erikson, E. H. *Young Man Luther: A Study in Psychoanalysis and History*. New York: Norton, 1958.

Erikson, E. H. "Youth: Fidelity and Diversity." *Daedalus*, 91, No. 1 (Winter 1962), 5–27. (a)

Erikson, E. H. "Reality and Actuality." *Journal of the American Psychoanalytic Association*, 10 (1962), 451–474. (b)

Freud, Anna. *The Ego and the Mechanisms of Defence* (1936). New York: International Universities Press, 1946.

Freud, Anna. "Adolescence." *The Psychoanalytic Study of the Child*. New York: International Universities Press, 1958. Vol. 1, pp. 255–278.

Freud, S. "Fragment of an Analysis of a Case of Hysteria" (1905). *The Standard Edition of the Complete Psychological Works of. . . .* London: Hogarth Press. Vol. 7, pp. 7–122. (Also in *Collected Papers of. . . .* New York: Basic Books, 1959. Vol. 3, pp. 13–146.

Freud, S. "Recollecting, Repeating and Working Through" (1914). *The Standard Edition of the Complete Psychological Works of. . . .* London: Hogarth Press. Vol. 12, pp. 145–156. (Also in *Collected Papers of. . . .* New York: Basic Books, 1959. Vol. 2, pp. 366–376.

Hartmann, H. *Ego Psychology and the Problem of Adaptation* (1939). New York: International Universities Press, 1958.

Inhelder, Bärbel, and Piaget, J. *The Growth of Logical Thinking from Childhood to Adolescence.* New York: Basic Books, 1958.

Jacobson, Edith. "Adolescent Moods and the Remodeling of Psychic Structure in Adolescence." *The Psychoanalytic Study of the Child.* New York: International Universities Press, 1961. Vol. 16, pp. 164–184.

Laing, R. *The Self and Others: Further Studies in Sanity and Madness.* Chicago: Quadrangle Books, 1962.

Rapaport, D. *Organization and Pathology of Thought.* New York: Columbia University Press, 1951. (a)

Rapaport, D. "The Conceptual Model of Psychoanalysis" (1951). In M. M. Gill (ed.), *Collected Papers of David Rapaport.* New York: Basic Books, 1967. Pp. 405–431. (b)

Rapaport, D. "On the Psychoanalytic Theory of Affects" (1953). In M. M. Gill (ed.), *Collected Papers of David Rapaport.* New York: Basic Books, 1967. Pp. 476–512.

Rapaport, D. "The Structure of Psychoanalytic Theory: A Systemizing Attempt" (1959). *Psychological Issues,* 2, No. 2 (1960), Monograph No. 6.

Shapiro, R. "Adolescence and the Psychology of the Ego." *Psychiatry,* 26 (1963), 77–87.

Wynne, L. N., and Singer, Margaret. "Thought Disorder and the Family Relations of Schizophrenics: Parts I, II, III, and IV." *American Medical Association Archives of General Psychiatry,* 9 (1963), 191–206; 12 (1965), 187–212.

19

Special Problems of Late Adolescence and the College Years

RAYMOND SOBEL

The emotional problems of late adolescence and the college years are basically no different from those of younger or older persons, despite the fact that the presenting symptoms are at times difficult to understand. The same unconscious dynamics occur at fifteen or at twenty-five years of age. The depressions of adolescence have essentially similar psychodynamics as depressions in middle age. Both are the result of loss, helpless dependency, and repressed rage. Disturbances of interpersonal relationships, psychic conflict, guilt, anxiety, and attempts to cope through mechanisms of defense are relatively constant in any given culture, despite age, and tend to be more alike than different. If this were not the case, every psychiatrist would have to learn a new psychodynamics and psychopathology for each epoch of personality development, of which young adulthood is but a five- or six-year span.

Relationship to the Social Milieu

However, there *are* special problems of this age group. They are rooted firmly in the social matrix in which the young adult lives, plays, and works. These problems are important because they are not only crucial to the career of the individual involved, but also because they have a vital relationship to his milieu. This origin in the milieu is of considerable significance when therapeutic intervention is contemplated, since far-reaching modifications of both psychotherapeutic and psychoanalytic technique are called for. Although the late adolescent presents no new or different mechanism of coping with anxiety, the social role which he chooses (and which the culture assigns to him) is of a special nature, produces specific and unique stresses upon him, and brings about a different kind of patterning of psychiatric symptomatology. In the case of the college student whose major dedication is the pursuit of learning, emotional disturbance almost invariably interferes with his studies and affects his scholastic performance. A result of this particular effect of anxiety on ego functioning is that difficulties shift from the private to the public sphere, and, even though the student may not be failing his work in college, his symptoms become a matter of concern to his family, his instructors, and the college administration. In times of national emergency, the widening circle of effects may include the likelihood of being drafted for military service through the loss of his student deferment status.

In general, when ego functioning becomes impaired in an area that brings about real sanctions from the society at large and that also has been highly charged emotionally by years of conditioning, one can expect considerable turmoil in interpersonal relationships even though the basic disturbance may be relatively minor. Indeed, the effect of an adolescent's disturbance on the environment may be the critical factor in creating difficulties for him, rather than the depth and severity of his own psychopathology. Thus, an inability to study or, more properly for a vast number of undergraduates, an inability to mount a passable academic performance can eventuate in psychiatric referral, whereas a paranoid psychosis or ritualistic obsessionalism often evokes no such thought of psychiatric intervention from parents or mentors. In such cases as mild depression or writing blocks, the psychiatrist is likely to feel that he is dealing with a tempest in a teapot unless he keeps himself reminded of the seriousness of the symptomatology when considered in its context.

Special Characteristics of the Late Adolescent

Before delineating the major syndromes which the psychiatrist can expect to encounter when called upon as therapist or consultant to this age group, it is necessary to consider the special characteristics of late adolescence and young adulthood and to dwell a little longer on the situation of the college student. During recent years there has been a considerable literature dealing with college students and college life emanating from psychoanalysis, psychiatry, psychology, sociology, and cultural anthropology (Blaine and McArthur, 1961; Farnsworth, 1957; Green, 1966; Sanford, 1962; Smith, Hansell, and English, 1963; Segal, Walsh, and Weiss, 1966; Sobel, 1962; Sommers, 1964; Sprague, 1960; Wedge, 1958). Almost all of the contributors concern themselves with the self-image, social role, or identity formation of the adolescent, and all point to the period of adolescence as the time in which the identifications of childhood are revised in the light of the new social expectations. These include independence of family, personal individuation, peer group loyalties, and, in the case of the vocationally directed youth, the assumption of adult work responsibilities. Erikson (1959, 1963) discusses the moratorium aspects of these years and describes how society grants the adolescent some extra time to postpone final commitment to a social role. The adolescent leaving high school to work as an apprentice carpenter or as a secretary or waitress is granted this moratorium to a lesser extent. For him (or her), passing from adolescence into adulthood is more structured than it is for the counterpart in college since the occupation is clear cut and identifiable. A college freshman stated this problem of ambiguity of identity in a colorful way. "I wish I lived in the Middle Ages," he said with an unhappy expression. "You know, all you had to do then was to slay a couple of dragons and rescue a maiden and you *knew* you were a man." He reached into his pocket and whipped out his wallet. "All I have to show for it is this damn driver's license." The salesgirl or the garage mechanic is better off than this young man for whom work is *summer* work or *vacation* work and who feels more often than not that this work has no relevance to his eventual identity except as it contributes to paying his tuition bill at school. In contrast, the lower-class adolescent who is vocationally occupied rather than educationally oriented, although not totally immune to what Erikson calls "role diffusion," is more likely to avoid suffering such ambiguity since at meaningful work he *knows* who he is and what he is doing and has tangible evidence that it is of significance. With full employment in our society, the adolescent from lower socioeconomic circumstances has considerably diminished susceptibility to this problem, but where economic conditions are such that the young person cannot find useful and, above all, meaningful work, the dangers of identity diffusion are increased. It is in this connection that the psychiatric problems of the underprivileged and the culturally deprived are of special significance.

The effects of poverty and emotional deprivation on the ego are well known and the cognitive defects of the youth reared under these conditions have been documented in detail (Riessman, 1962). Presently available psychotherapeutic measures seem to be of little help in modifying the ego impoverishment, the short-term hedonism, and the impulsive action orientation of culturally deprived adolescents since the ego characteristics seem to be developmental in origin rather than the result of later warping. Approaches which are addressed to the individual alone, and do not take into consideration the modification of the immediate family and social environment in which the young person lives, seem to be relatively ineffectual in producing better self-esteem and a firm sense of identity. Restoring an individual youth's sense of worth and effecting the re-establishment of trust in others cannot be accomplished in an atmosphere of economic depression and chronic unemployment. In the case of the youth from a minority group, the issue is made doubly difficult since the realities of racial discrimination and segregation conspire to undo the ego-building effects of traditional psychotherapy. Thus we come to the first of our conclusions regarding the psychiatric problems of late adolescence and early adulthood: *their content is determined in great part by the social role of the patient, and this in turn determines the therapeutic intervention appropriate for cure.*

There are two major social roles of this age group, determined mainly by economic circumstances and social class: the role of worker and the role of student. But as I have already indicated, the mechanisms by which the basic conflicts concerning identity and self-image are worked out do not differ substantially from other age groups. More specifically, the dynamisms of neurosis and psychosis operate in much the same fashion even though the focal points tend to cluster around the issues of work, study, peer group relationships, and emancipation from the family circle. Depending upon the young person's past history and predilected mode of problem-solving, the conflict may be manifested as primarily intrapsychic, that is, as a private symptom such as a work block, or more clearly interpersonal, such as masochistic behavior in which a student becomes the scapegoat for an entire dormitory.

What are the special areas of difficulty for young persons between the age of seventeen and twenty-two who have left or are about to leave high school and who are either attending college or beginning a vocational career? By far, the major concern of this epoch is the need to establish one's independence from one's family and to renounce or cope with the dependent roles of childhood and early adolescence. Secondary to these problems are a host of other conflicts played out in a variety of ways and in a multitude of social arenas. Due to the limitations of space, I have chosen to illustrate the major issues involved in the diagnosis and treatment of this age group by discussing in some detail the problems of identity formation as seen in work and study, and the crisis problems related to the academic institution.

Problems Related to Work and Study

Productivity is not only a major institutional value in our society, but has become such a categorical imperative that the young adult who "fails to achieve his potential" is immediately subject to sanctions and criticism, particularly from his teachers and mentors whose orientation toward achievement is uniformly that of the middle class. Their attitude is a derivative of the Protestant ethic and emphasizes long-term goals, delayed gratification, and the enjoyment of work for its own sake. The middle-class adolescent has already incorporated this outlook of the world. He has introjected the value system of his parents and, in most cases, wants to be what he should be in order to achieve or maintain middle-class acceptance, social status, and prestige. The prototype of this personality development is the medical student who spends long years of hard work, as well as financial and social deprivation, in the pursuit of a course of study which often bears little relevance to his final vocation. A striking contrast is afforded by the adolescent from a lower-class background who is far less motivated by the distant rewards of academic pursuits and whose concerns tend to be with more immediate gratification and with tangible results. Though middle-class ideologies are being increasingly adopted by lower socioeconomic groups, young adults from disadvantaged and culturally deprived homes usually have as their *meaningful* guidelines a different set of values, standards, or ego ideals. They may pay lip service to the need for more education, for long-term goals, for commitment to a vocational life plan, but in actual practice they usually do not carry out their intentions. They show the "proper" attitude toward the learning process, enroll in higher education, but "underachieve" and "drop out." The commitment to study and to what is essentially a middle-class style of life is ego-alien. More than that, it is a source of anxiety and of a sense of self-betrayal, sometimes experienced as being "hypocritical" or "phony." Due to a different cognitive style, these adolescents are not accustomed to introspection and to verbalization of their feelings and as a result are hard put to understand the feelings of internal dissonance and frustration which plague them during their last years of high school and in college, should they continue that far. They have not been socialized in the same fashion as their middle-class contemporaries and even though their idealized image of themselves includes a college degree, their basic conception of what is worth working for does not include the abstract and long-term goals of the studious life.

What makes these individuals of interest to the psychoanalyst is the conflict between the eventual identity to which college studies lead and the self-image previously established in childhood. The latter identity is derived from the adolescent's childhood experience within the framework of lower socioeconomic status. In many cases, there is an unconscious equation of physical activity with masculinity and of intellectual activity with femininity. The end result of such a conflict in a male is anxiety and withdrawal from the scene, often accompanied by acting out. Nonetheless, his teachers and parents do not understand his dilemma and continue to impress upon him the desirability and necessity of further education. A vicious cycle results and the adolescent who is *not* firmly anchored to his peer group is likely to be shaken by this experience. Goodman has written most eloquently about this in *Growing Up Absurd* (1956). The manner in which this conflict is solved is, of course, a function of the youth's previous methods of coping with anxiety, the degree of identification with his peer group, and the degree to which he feels pressed to move away from the value systems which characterize his origins. When we consider that acting out of impulse tends to be the life style for a large proportion of these adolescents, it is not at all surprising that asocial or antisocial behavior becomes the presenting symptom in the situation just described. Also, since these adolescents may have been the victims of the self-fulfilling destiny so characteristic of the poor, their educational disabilities and poor work habits seriously limit them in the availability of meaningful work. Thus they are forced to take those unskilled jobs which only reinforce their limited aspirations and short-run hedonism. Denial and projection tend to be frequent mechanisms of coping with conflict, but avoidance seems to be the major one. It results in extremely nonfunctional work habits which lead to chronic unemployment. When this avoidance is used in a compulsive or impulsive fashion in the academic area, the symptom of "underachievement" is frequently encountered. However, for reasons which have become obvious, these youths from lower-class socioeconomic backgrounds select themselves out of the academic area long before college; it is only the occasional individual who reaches this level of academic achievement to drop out of college, usually in the first part of his freshman year.

The Problem of Underachievement

Moving on to the problems of the college student himself, one of the major difficulties in living is "underachievement," again role-determined and relating to the adolescent's main life task. This disturbance in functioning may range from mild degrees of "underachievement" to work-blocks which lead to suspension from college because of flagrant neglect of studies. The underlying psychopathology in most instances has a monotonous uniformity and reappears in case after case of scholastic "underachievement." It is characterized by passive dependency as a mode of coping with stressful relationships, particularly with authorities, specifically with parent surrogates. As one might expect, this passive-dependent reaction has its roots in early childhood. It stems most often from confusion of assertiveness with hostility and of activity with destructiveness. For children brought up under such circumstances, the anticipation of normal independence becomes associated with anxiety and results in a pervasive dependency upon authorities, the main purpose of which is the avoidance of anxiety. The original confusion arises from identifications with a parent who has difficulties in coping adequately with his or her own anger and who resorts to neurotic mechanisms. As a result of the identification, the child does not learn to handle anger in appropriate ways, and, since self-assertion and hostility are intimately interrelated if not synonymous for such individuals, severe problems in these areas develop early in life. Typically, they are reinforced by the mother's discouraging attitudes toward independent achievement and by the failure of the father to reassure the child that independent activity and assertion are worthwhile. One might say that their fathers fail to lead them into active manhood and that their mothers pull them back toward childhood dependency. When the same syndrome is seen in girls, the parental roles are reversed. However, this disturbance is confined mainly to males. These young men seem to be much more comfortable when uncurious, uninquiring, and uninformed, since past experience with independent thought has been so unprofitable. Their generalized passivity seems to be a response to the years of constant inhibition of their activity by a controlling parent. In such cases, the "underachievement" can be traced back in an unbroken line to the third grade. As one might expect, an enormous amount of resentment toward the originally inhibiting parents develops over the years and produces a severe conflict between the need for dependency and protection on the one hand, and the need for autonomy on the other. The "underachievement" may be interpreted as the neurotic compromise solution. These mechanisms are unconscious and frequently disguised by reaction formations. As a consequence, direct interpretation of the underlying psychodynamics to the college student in treatment may provoke excessive anxiety with which he cannot cope save by withdrawal from the situation. In these cases, premature termination of therapy may be precipitated since the defenses against anxiety have not been worked through beforehand.

Certain cases of college "underachievement" and "drop out" may be traced to unconscious identification with a parent who has the same psychopathology as the student. It is well known to college deans that there is a high correlation between the parents' failure to complete college degree requirements and similar difficulties in their children. A similar situation in family psychopathology is described by Levenson and Kohn (1965) who found that scholastic "underachievement" was often a response to a disturbed family's "cry for help" and served the purpose of bringing the student back home to resume his old role of maintaining the family's homeostasis.

Another more serious form of the passive-dependent reaction in the college student is seen in the symbiotic adolescent who has never learned to be self-actualizing and who has grown to rely upon the parent or parent substitute for the most minor commitment to action. These individuals prove to have been involved in a symbiotic relationship with one or the other parent for many years. Often it has been negativistic and has given their overt behavior the appearance of independence, but closer analysis of the relationship reveals its true nature. It is actually regressed, dependent, magical, and prelogical. Many of these patients prove to be severely psychopathologic, often schizophrenic, and conceal themselves with a façade of correct social behavior. Detailed history-taking and family-interviewing reveal the long and unbroken symbiosis with the parent and presages considerable reconstructive work. If such a student and his parent as well are able to tolerate the separation from each other, intensive psychotherapy is the treatment of choice.

The more talented of these individuals are able to function well academically because of their tendency to obsessionalism, but their breakdown occurs when they are separated from their symbiotic partner by living away from home in a residential college or, in a more figurative sense, by their assumption of the college student's role. Without the partner to provide a sense of being or, to a lesser degree, to "wind them up," they flounder and seek a substitute. Commonly, they find that the college faculty is unwilling to play such a parental role or to give them inspirational lectures on the need to study. Sometimes a roommate will serve this purpose, but usually the symbiotic personalities are unable to effect the transference necessary for accomplishing their academic work. As a result, they frequently regress to infantile "doing-nothing-at-all" and weeks to months later are forced to leave college. An acute psychotic episode may precede withdrawal, but this is rare. More often there is a kind of "fading out" which literally and symbolically satisfies the regressive infantile trends through relief of responsibility and through return home to the symbiotic mother. In cases of less profound ego disorganization, this outcome represents the acting out of a rescue fantasy: the action of the college administration or the psychiatric services is experienced in the transference as the good parent saving the beleaguered infant.

Unfortunately, the unmasking of such long-standing symbiotic tendencies usually does not occur until the adolescent reaches a social situation in which he is unable to find an adult to play the complementary dominating role to his own helplessness and lack of autonomy. In the past, this was carried out with primary and secondary school teachers who reinforced the symbiotic mode of existence through excessive coaching and taking over of the student's responsibilities. Similar collusion in pathological symbiotic behavior by parents may continue into late adolescence, and it is not at all uncommon for parents to come to residential colleges for weekends in order to help their children with their assignments! This tends to disappear with advanced standing in college. Whether this is due to increased independence or to embarrassment is difficult to assess.

Patterns of Rebelliousness

Closely allied to this form of "underachievement" is that seen in the young adult attending college whose patterns of conflict resolution are characteristically rebellious. Individuals in this group have attracted considerable attention during the past few years. Their difficulties are often related to the problems of alienation and cannot be divorced from the social milieu in which they occur.

The progressive tendency of our society to become more and more impersonal and to produce alienation of the individual from his institutions and fellow men has been discussed by Fromm (1955) and Wheelis (1958), who find alienation to be a source of anxiety and conflict and, one might add, of resentment and hostility as well. On the academic scene, the *group* manifestation of this anger and dissatisfaction appears as the student protest: the content of the protest is determined by idiosyncratic and local considerations. For reasons to be taken up later, the psychiatrist is well advised not to write off these protests as neurotic manifestations of the conflict of generations since they may be appropriate and germane to the student's real life situation. It was not too long ago that academic observers were being critical of what they called the "apathetic college generation." At that time it was felt that the students showed insufficient dissatisfaction with their society and that they were too passively accepting the status quo. However, our concern here is not so much with the group expressions of appropriate disaffection due to alienation, but rather with the pathological disturbances of the individual student. Although rebellious "underachievement" is but one manifestation of the psychopathology of late adolescence, it is of considerable importance from the viewpoint of our topic.

Briefly, rebellious "underachievement" appears as a disturbance of academic functioning ranging from conscious neglect of studies to flamboyant defiance of the college's academic and social requirements. Those students who engage in active and overt mechanisms of this sort are easily identified by other rebellious manifestations as well, and for the most part psychotherapy is useful and uncomplicated if the student wishes to modify his or her behavior. In these cases the therapist should attempt to help the patient free himself of his dependent and spiteful coping mechanisms so that he will be in a position to make a free choice based upon rational insight and awareness. Persuasion to remain in college, or to discontinue education, should be avoided since such efforts only induce intensification of the negativistic transference. As might be expected, the basic unconscious mechanisms are neither new nor different than those uncovered in older adults, and they are worked through either in the transference or in the student's relationship to the faculty and the administration. If the therapist is employed by the college or university, a rebellious transference is likely to be intensified, but this need not be an insuperable obstacle as long as the therapist is aware of this contingency.

Passive-aggressive rebellion, on the other hand, presents a more difficult therapeutic problem. Here the young adult most often arrives with a long history of "underachievement" despite adequate ability and what appears to have been considerable application. Most of these students are male and present what one might call the "slipping clutch syndrome." They manage to spend an enormous amount of time going through the motions of studying and working but never get much done. They are often genuinely despairing and are at a loss to explain their failure and have found introspection to be of no help, since the sources of their difficulties are unconscious. Their problems in this respect are no different from those in the passive-aggressive neurosis of adult life in which hostile passive resistance to the expectations of significant persons becomes a way of life. Likewise, therapeutic work with such students is slow and often unrewarding due to the deeply repressed hostility and the highly organized patterns of defense against its arousal. Long periods of time elapse before the compliantly defiant failure pattern becomes ego-alien in therapy, but by this time the student has usually accomplished his unconscious purpose and has dropped out or been suspended for academic failure. Accordingly, in the more severe cases, the therapist is best advised to recommend a medical leave of absence to allow sufficient time for the patient to undergo reconstructive psychoanalytic therapy, if feasible.

Akin to rebellious "underachievement" is offbeat and deviant behavior, often colorfully manifested in hair styles and dress. Long hair, beards, unusually short or unusually long dresses, inattention to personal hygiene or grooming make up the more socially visible behaviors. Among male students such sartorial and tonsorial extremism has a long and venerable history. In the present, no less than in the past, the concern aroused generally reflects the rigidity of the adult observer more than the psychopathology of the student.[1] To my mind, these extremes mirror the general tenor of this period of development and mark the outer swings of the adolescent's at-

[1] Our youth today . . . have bad manners, contempt for authority, disrespect for older people. Children nowadays are tyrants, they contradict their parents, gobble their food and tyrannize their teachers (Socrates, 5 B.C.).

tempt to equilibrate himself in relation to authority. It has been my experience that in therapy it is best to leave the peculiarities of hair style and dress alone unless the patient spontaneously brings them up for discussion. They are really minor issues in the patient's life as compared to the more important ones of commitment and autonomy. Second, they are so overdetermined that the therapist's intrusion evokes such frank anxiety or such elaborate security operations that the effects of such exploration make the effort unpleasantly nontherapeutic. Lastly, such adolescents have been heckled and lectured to so many times by their parents and other adults about cutting their hair or washing up that they are conditioned to react to any mention of the subject by others as tantamount to an attack. As a result, the therapist is likely to fortify a negative child-parent transference. It is my feeling that the therapist has more effective avenues of exploration open to himself and the patient. However, if the patient himself brings up the issue—for example, the girl who says: "The boys are not dating me; could it be related to my appearance?"—then forthrightness is called for, inasmuch as the patient has given the therapist assurance of her willingness to listen and of her intentions to cope with her security operations.

Akin to the student who espouses this type of deviant behavior is the student activist involved in a variety of protest causes such as civil rights, free speech, and pacifism. At the moment of writing, there are a large number of campus "causes" which may serve as lightning rods for what is actually a displaced *rebellion* against parental authority, rather than an *emancipation* from it. It is not outside the psychoanalyst's *expertise* to judge on the unconscious origins of protests which demand the unlimited use of four-letter words! On other social issues, however, the regressive elements are not so clear, and the psychiatrist is cautioned to analyze the situation most carefully before jumping to the conclusion that a student's involvement in pacifist or civil rights activities is a poorly disguised sublimation of unresolved childhood hostility to the parents. At these points, the determination of what constitutes psychopathology and what constitutes deviant belief may prove to be very difficult. Jacobs and Landau give many clues in their descriptive summary of *The New Radical* (1966). In these instances caution and prudence should be the watchwords of the therapist, for if he is wrong and diagnoses illness where there is reasonable belief or vice versa, his therapeutic usefulness may be at an end. It is the characteristic of this age group to tolerate poorly misunderstanding by older persons, and idealistic young adults become exceptionally concerned and indignant when their altruistic motives are placed in question. As Sullivan (1957) has pointed out, there is nothing so righteous as a maligned obsessional! Thus, if the therapist's interpretation should be incorrect, a situation is created in which the adolescent is given a ready-made and realistically justifiable reason to show how unfair and unsympathetic the authorities are. For this reason, any investigation of the roots of political and social activism in the college student should begin with a firm collaborative contract, should proceed in an exceptionally dispassionate fashion, and should occur within the context of a positive transference. It should also be noted at this point that the world outlook of many of these students is considerably different from that of the therapist and may be the source of considerable misunderstanding. These young adults are already sensitive to the failure of the adult world to understand their view of the world, and it is essential that the therapist give them the assurance of an open mind. For a detailed description of the *non-committed* but rebellious adolescent, the reader is referred to Kenniston (1966).

Crisis Problems Related to the Academic Institution

As mentioned previously, colleges and universities are able to absorb considerable behavioral deviance as long as it does not interfere with their specific functions of teaching and research or as long as their relationships with the community on whom they rely for support are unaffected (Group for Advancement of Psychiatry, 1965). Grossly psychotic individuals have not only attended college and graduate school, but in many instances have distinguished themselves and their alma mater in the process. As indicated previously, the crucial factor bringing them to the psychiatrist is not the degree of emotional disturbance, but rather its effects on the milieu. In many respects the manner in which the emotionally disturbed student is brought to the attention of the university authorities parallels the manner in which a mentally ill family member is hospitalized, i.e., the pathology interferes with the family's homeostasis to such an extent that the behavioral deviance can no longer be tolerated. To state it another way, the pathology no longer is congruent with the family's functioning. As a result, social visibility and interference with academic functions are the major factors in determining whether a psychiatric crisis exists in the college or university. The pathological conditions which are critical in this sense prove to be suicide and suicidal preoccupation, acute psychotic reactions with manifestly abnormal behavior, delinquent behavior, and homosexuality. These are very different syndromes, but they do have in common the disruptive effect on the institution and the arousal of anxiety in the faculty and administration. The psychiatrist involved in the diagnosis and treatment of college students is thus placed in a difficult position if he believes that emotional disturbances and mental illness do not occur *in* a person, but reflect disturbed interpersonal relationships or, in fact, *are* disturbances of the field of interaction between the patient and his environment. For such a therapist the task is doubly difficult since he is called upon to intervene in the disturbance not only by his theoretical orientation, but also by the practical realities of parental and administration concern.

In effect, this means consultation with parents and with the institution as well. Analysts who have never conducted treatment in other than the classical dyadic relationship are critical of this type of intervention for they feel that it destroys the confidentiality of the relationship, muddles up the transference with the therapist's quasi- or actual administrative role, or prevents the assumption of a neutral posture toward the patient. On the other hand, analysts accustomed to working with families in conjoint and other types of family treatment do not find these difficulties to be inevitable and have learned that they are mainly the result of the therapist's own anxiety and countertransference (Boszormenyi-Nagy and Framo, 1965). As a result of my previous experience in child psychiatry and family therapy, I have, for some time, handled critical incidents through the direct confrontation of all concerned. This is done by means of a joint interview in which the presenting problem is discussed in detail, and all parties are given a chance to elaborate their position. Where this is not physically possible, a conference telephone is used. In this fashion the chances of garbled communication are lessened, and there is little or no problem with confidentiality since all those involved are present at the time of the conference.

It has been my experience that exploration of the critical problem by means of this technique provides a maximum of information in a minimum of time and also produces a quicker resolution of the spirally mounting anxiety being generated in all quarters. The relief of anxiety seems to be related to the face-to-face confrontation of the patient with his parents and the institutional authority in a neutral atmosphere. Commonly, the student has concealed his difficulties from his family out of guilt and fear, and, as in the case of disciplinary infractions, he and the dean of students may know about the situation but the parents may never have been informed. Joint confrontation not only restores communication, but prevents the parties involved from maintaining the obscurity so favorable for denial and projection. Discussing the problem in detail under medical auspices lessens the possibility of ambiguity and clarifies the intent of the administration to help the student rather than to punish him. Anxiety is lowered and a new direction of activity becomes possible, namely, problem-solution. In the case of suicidal preoccupation or attempt, the mobilization of the adult world on his behalf answers the student's cry for help even though he may, at first, misinterpret the motives. This alone may be sufficient to tide the patient over until definite therapy of the underlying depression can begin. The same method of confrontation can be used in a crisis where a student has been accused of deviant sexual behavior such as exhibitionism or homosexual seduction. Rather than mobilizing punitive reactions from the parents and administrative faculty, the joint confrontation actually diminishes them and steers the energies of the persons concerned into the more useful channels of finding help. It is not sufficiently appreciated how anxious the faculty and administration become when such a critical incident arises involving normally dissociated and repressed impulses, i.e., homosexuality or the bizarre aggression of an acute psychosis. A major gain achieved by the direct involvement of parents and faculty is the relief of anxiety and the reassurance which immediately follows. Last but not least, the therapist's own anxiety is diminished!

A common concern is that one will be caught in the emotional cross fire between the patient, family, and administration. This is not borne out in fact. The question, "How can you expect to conduct such interviews when the parents live at great distances from the college or university?" is often raised. I have found that parents seldom object or refuse when *asked* and will always come for consultation when the seriousness of the situation is made clear to them on the long-distance telephone. Obviously, one should not call in parents for a minor incident nor should the psychiatrist allow the student's guilt and fear to persuade him that the parents would be disinterested or would so overreact that nothing would be accomplished.

Once the crisis has been identified, if not resolved, the issues of hospitalization and medical leave of absence may arise. The indications for the former are clear: the threat of danger to the patient or to the milieu. Typical examples are suicidal depression or homicidal excitement. Although student health services range enormously in the psychiatric assistance which they offer, none has facilities for long-term psychiatric hospitalization. This is particularly true of residential colleges, of which few provide more than the most rudimentary counseling or diagnostic services. However, arranging hospitalization may prove to be less of a problem to the psychiatrist treating the college student than the decision regarding the student's readiness to return to his studies. It has been the experience of psychiatrists in highly selective colleges and universities that the demands and stresses of the present-day college are more taxing than they appear on the surface and that a high degree of ego functioning is required not only to survive academically, but to make the experience at all worthwhile. The therapist about to send a student back to school after recovery from a psychotic episode or following a medical leave for incapacitating neurosis should keep in mind that there is more to be accomplished than a passing grade in courses. The college years are a period of growth and development and the college experience is likely to be wasted if the student does not have the ability to do more than attend classes and get good grades. If a student has not recovered sufficiently to function socially as well as academically, returning to a residential college and a full schedule of work is ill advised. Should the initial psychopathology relate specifically to interpersonal conflict experienced in college, the therapist and the patient should be reasonably certain that these areas are worked through adequately before considering return. Illustrative of this is "homosexual panic" engendered by the student's first experience in intimate living with a peer group of the same sex. Removal from the necessity to use communal bathing and toilet facilities may relieve the acute episode, but the likelihood is that the anxiety will return on re-exposure to the traumatic situation, unless a personality change has occurred in the meantime. In this connection the college psychiatrist may be of considerable help to the patient and his therapist by carefully delineating in writing the changes in behavior and personality which he feels should be accomplished before readmission is considered. Ordinarily, such changes are not rapidly achieved, and several schools require a minimum of a year's absence before readmission procedures can be instituted. I have found it wiser to insist on behavioral change rather than psychotherapy as a condition for psychiatric "clearance." This places the burden of change on the patient rather than on his therapist and avoids the lip-service-going-through-the-motions of the passive-dependent and passive-aggressive types discussed above.

Conclusion

There is a community of psychoanalytic principles underlying the diagnosis and treatment of emotional disorder in all age groups. The problems of late adolescence and early adult life are not different in this respect, and a thorough grounding in the basic mechanisms relating to anxiety and its defenses and to the vicissitudes of transference and countertransference is essential to the diagnostician and therapist.

The special problems of this epoch in the life cycle are keyed to the issues of identity and social role. Although the major characteristic disturbances of late adolescence and young adult life are not unique, they are concerned with these issues and manifest themselves primarily in symptoms of identity diffusion and maladaptation to work and study. Recent developments in psychoanalytic theory call for a new approach to these problems, quite different from that of classical one-to-one psychoanalysis. This new approach views the student's emotional disturbance as but one of the manifestations of a larger interpersonal disturbance involving the student, his family, and the significant persons in the academic institution. Therapeutic techniques derive naturally from this theoretical base and involve a variety of interventions in all areas of the disturbance. Such multiple contacts place an added burden on the therapist's capacity to recognize and handle the transferences and the countertransferences of the involved persons, including himself. Consultation and treatment of individuals in this age group is often frustrating, always challenging, and never dull!

REFERENCES

Blaine, G. B., Jr., and McArthur, C. *Emotional Problems of the Student*. New York: Appleton-Century-Crofts, 1961.

Boszormenyi-Nagy, I., and Framo, J. L. (eds.). *Intensive Family Therapy*. New York: Harper & Row, 1965.

Erikson, E. H. "Identity and the Life Cycle." *Psychological Issues*, 1, No. 1 (1959).

Erikson, E. H. *Childhood and Society*. New York: Norton, 1963.

Farnsworth, D. *Mental Health in College and University*. Cambridge: Harvard University Press, 1957.

Fromm, E. *The Sane Society*. New York: Rinehart, 1955.

Goodman, P. *Growing Up Absurd*. New York: Random House, 1956.

Green, M. R. "The Problem of Identity Crisis." In J. H. Masserman (ed.), *Science and Psychoanalysis*. Vol. 9. New York: Grune & Stratton, 1966.

Group for the Advancement of Psychiatry. *Sex and the College Student*, 6, No. 60 (1965).

Jacobs, P., and Landau, S. *The New Radicals*. New York: Random House, 1966.

Kenniston, K. *The Uncommitted*. New York: Random House, 1966.

Levenson, E. A., and Kohn, M. "Some Characteristics of a Group of Bright, Emotionally Disturbed College Dropouts." *Journal of the American College Health Association*, 14, No. 2 (December 1965), 78–85.

Riessman, F. *The Culturally Deprived Child*. New York: Harper & Row, 1962.

Sanford, N. (ed.). *The American College*. New York: Wiley, 1962.

Segal, B. E., Walsh, M. T., and Weiss, R. J. "Emotional Maladjustment in an Undergraduate Population." *Journal of the American College Health Association*, 14 (1966), 3.

Smith, W. G., Hansell, N., and English, J. T. "Psychiatric Disorder in a College Population." *American Medical Association Archives of General Psychiatry*, 9, No. 4 (1963), 351–361.

Sobel, R. "Conflicting Values and the Psychopathology of Adolescence." *Mental Hygiene*, 46, No. 4 (1962), 618–625.

Sommers, Vita S. "The Impact of Dual-Cultural Membership on Identity." *Psychiatry*, 27, No. 4 (1964), 332–344.

Sprague, H. G. (ed.). *Research on College Students*. Berkeley: University of California Press, 1960.

Sullivan, H. S. *Clinical Studies in Psychiatry*. New York: Norton, 1957.

Wedge, M. (ed.). *Psychosocial Problems of College Men*. New Haven: Yale University Press, 1958.

Weiss, R. J., Segal, B. E., and Sokol, R. "Epidemiology of Emotional Disturbance in a Men's College." *Journal of Nervous and Mental Diseases*, 141, No. 2 (1965), 240–250.

Wheelis, A. *The Quest for Identity*. New York: Norton, 1958.

20

Analytic Group Psychotherapy

MORRIS B. PARLOFF

That groups appear to have powerful emotional effects on their members, effects which may be utilized in the furtherance of the psychotherapeutic process, is now widely accepted. Group psychotherapy has moved out of its earlier defensive position and no longer appears to be preoccupied with establishing its effectiveness as a treatment modality. It has been accepted as one of the appropriate and respectable forms of psychotherapy and the prospects for its even wider adoption as a treatment form are excellent.

A review of the broad field of group therapy today reveals considerable diversity in practice and technique; however, such variations rarely represent either "change" or "originality." The diversity and the reaction to it are perhaps best summed up in Slavson's statement, "Group psychotherapy is plagued, more than any other endeavor in the field of mental treatment, with . . . a 'psychotic need to appear original' " (Slavson, 1962, p. 64).

Our purpose here is not to catalogue all positions or all changes, but instead to highlight those movements which may reasonably be classed as important to the field of "analytic" group psychotherapy. The differentiation of an "advance" from a change or modification should ideally be based on a criterion more substantial than the biases or arrogance of the reviewer. Unfortunately, this is not an ideal world. Ideally, the criterion for assessing change in psychotherapy would be directly relevant to the principal responsibility of the psychotherapist, namely, to be more effective and more efficient in his treatment efforts. Unfortunately, objective standards and techniques for assessing the outcome of any form of therapy—group or individual—are not yet available. Like beauty, therapeutic effectiveness is in the eye of the beholder. No form of psychotherapy has ever been initiated without a claim that it has unique therapeutic advantages, and no form of psychotherapy has ever been abandoned because of its failure to live up to these claims. Although the earlier self-consciousness of the group therapists has subsided, the quiescence may be attributed more to the power of positive thinking and boredom with the issue of outcome than with the fact that compelling evidence has finally resolved the issue.

In the absence of adequate guidelines based on criteria of outcome it is not possible to evaluate movement in the field as forward, backward, or merely windward. We must therefore search for other bases to assess the significance of developments in analytic group psychotherapy. Do the proliferation of techniques and the broadened application of group psychotherapy qualify as evidence of meaningful change?

The widening range and acknowledged ingenuity of group therapy techniques may seem to offer an attractive area for review. However, the broad range of techniques appears to derive, in large part, from the fact that clinicians who enter the field of group psychotherapy are identified with a variety of schools of psychotherapy, each of which includes a repertoire of favorite techniques. The group therapist, naturally enough, attempts to employ these techniques in group psychotherapy. Thus, the range of Freudian, neo-Freudian, and Existentialist forms of therapy is fully represented in the field.

Another basis for the seeming plethora of techniques is the fact that the group setting confronts the therapist with a variety of dimensions and parameters that are novel to him. This novelty invites invention, fantasy, and the modification of old techniques. Although the consideration of the variety of techniques currently employed is of intrinsic interest, it is secondary to our major concern. Any technique is an epiphenomenon of the therapist's conception of the "pathology" that is to be treated and his theory concerning the processes by which the desired changes may be best achieved.

To most patients and many therapists, it may appear to be an important advance that forms of group psychotherapy are increasingly being made available to almost all patients. Practitioners now report success with patients, independent of age, mental, social or physical status, and disability

(Berger, 1962). It is similarly impressive that views regarding the acceptability of group constellations appropriate for treatment now range from the indiscriminate selection of all who present themselves, as suggested by Berne (1966, p. 379), to the patient and his real family.

Increasingly, group therapy is viewed as the treatment of choice with some patients and no less effective than most other treatment forms with other patients. Therapists such as Ziferstein and Grotjahn (1956) are so convinced of the efficacy of group analytic treatment that they predict that it will become the primary therapeutic tool and that individual analysis will be used primarily as a research tool and a training device. We are not prepared, at this point, to assign to this view the status of a "significant trend," but forces other than clinical experience support the prediction that the number of group psychotherapists may soon exceed the number of individual therapists. The normal increase in the demand for psychiatric service will soon be augmented, for psychiatric treatment will be available to a broad segment of the population through the expanding, federally supported, community mental health programs. If serious effort is to be made to provide psychiatric services to those in need of such treatment, the current method of dealing with psychiatric cases will be inadequate and group psychotherapy will be called on even more.

In the absence of any generally accepted criteria by which to assess the field's progress we must adopt our own. This chapter will deal with those theorists who have attempted to integrate group processes into analytic group psychotherapy. We deal then with "directions" rather than clearly evident therapeutic advances. In adopting the posture of the trend-seeker and the historian it is difficult to be certain that one's conclusions are an accurate reflection of how things are rather than merely a representation of one's beliefs about how things ought to be. In looking at the same data this writer and Locke have arrived at different views regarding the trends in the field of analytic group psychotherapy. Locke finds that the field is gradually becoming more psychoanalytic. He states that group therapy has moved through the phases of "group psychotherapy, to psychoanalytically oriented psychotherapy . . . and now the first steps are being taken toward group psychoanalysis" (Locke, 1961).

In my view, the field is moving toward the treatment of groups as entities; rather than tending in the direction of psychoanalytic orthodoxy, it seems to be heading toward the broader reaches of general psychology and group psychology. Regardless of which of these positions more closely approximates the truth, neither commits the offense that Moreno decries, namely, that of implying that group therapy is merely an elaboration of psychoanalysis (Moreno, 1962). That the group has gained widespread acceptance among analytically trained therapists is not disputed, but whether this indicates a trend toward the adaptation of psychoanalytic practice to group psychotherapy is very doubtful. I believe that one can make at least as good a case for a position that group therapy as practiced by analytically trained therapists represents a progressive dilution of psychoanalytic concepts of practice.

For those who by training and affiliation have earned the designation of psychoanalysts, and to those who aspire to such identification, it is important that treatment practices be viewed as conforming with psychoanalytic principles and techniques. Since the practice of group psychotherapy does not permit rigorous adherence to all aspects of psychoanalytic practice, a rather free translation, if not distortion, of theory and techniques to fit the psychoanalytic model has resulted. Although the tensile strength of psychoanalytic concepts is admittedly great, the strain is beginning to tell. Only the credulity of journal editors appears to have survived intact. It is appropriate, therefore, to indicate how the term "analytic" is used here.

The boundaries which separate analytic from nonanalytic psychotherapies are far from clear, and we do not propose to alter this unhappy state. There are today no agreed-on definitions which readily differentiate psychoanalysis from analytically oriented therapies, or analytically oriented treatment from other forms of psychotherapy. A committee of the American Psychoanalytic Association, after a concerted and prolonged effort, concluded that it was "impossible to find any definition of psychoanalysis that was acceptable to even a large group of members of the American Psychoanalytic Association." Moreover, the Committee was unable to draw any firm distinction between psychoanalysis and psychoanalytic therapy (Cushing, 1950). It may be assumed that the committee was cognizant of Freud's liberal definition of what he would accept as analytic, i.e., treatment that deals with transference and resistance (1914) and includes an investigation of the genesis of the neurosis (1938). Yet this knowledge did not aid them.

The intervening years since the APA report have done little to develop consensus. In fact, the problem has been further compounded by the growth of ego psychology and the spread of the neo-Freudian and Existentialist viewpoints. If we turn from authority to practice in searching for a basis for definition, we still find little to guide us.

One finds that a therapist may continue to be viewed by colleagues as a psychoanalyst despite the fact that he rejects the classical libido theory, substitutes social psychological development for the biological bases of psychosexual growth, rejects the role of sexual and aggressive instincts, questions the existence of the primary innate unconscious, etc. (Fromm-Reichmann, 1950).

In our view one of the best and most useful attempts to differentiate psychoanalytic, analytic, and nonanalytic psychotherapies is offered by Gill. He recognizes three major forms of treatment: (1) psychoanalysis, which he describes as concerned with the analysis of transference and resistance back to their genetic dynamic source; (2) analytically oriented psychotherapy, which recognizes transference and resistance but utilizes goals which are intermediate between rapid symptom resolution and character change. The techniques are intermediate in that there is not a full development nor a full analysis of transference neurosis; moreover, interpretation is not the principal vehicle of the therapist's interventions; and (3) supportive, non-analytic psychotherapy which is aimed primarily at strengthening defenses (Gill, 1951, 1954).

With this definition of "analytic" in mind, we will accept here only those acknowledged theorists in the field who have made explicit efforts to effect change in their patients by interpreting unconscious elements of the patient's group participation. This will include theorists who are variously classified as adherents of analytical group psychotherapy, group analysis, and psychoanalytic group analysis.

We propose to view as possible advances in group psychotherapy the efforts of those theorists and practitioners who have attempted to integrate knowledge of group phenomena into analytic group treatment. More precisely, we will focus on theorists who have attempted to go beyond the application of individual psychotherapy to the group setting. We shall review contributions which purport to describe and to specify the dynamic structure of psychotherapy groups and the role of such structure and processes in the conduct of analytic group therapy. This decision is based on the plausible expectation that further advances in the field of analytic group psychotherapy may depend on our ability to integrate individual psychodynamics with a fuller appreciation of the as yet ill-defined dynamics of groups. This is a conviction which has motivated the work of such students of analytic group psychotherapy as Scheidlinger (1952), Ackerman (1961), Bion (1959), Ezriel (1950), Foulkes (1964), and Whitaker and Lieberman (1964).

The present state of the field of analytic group psychotherapy reflects the dynamic interaction between two contrasting beliefs concerning the role of the group in the treatment of the individual: (1) adaptation of the principles and techniques of individual analytic treatment to the group; and (2) the identification, development, and utilization of forces and processes indigenous to groups to facilitate treatment. The resolution which is sought by many is the development of a genuinely distinct form of psychotherapy which utilizes group phenomena as an integral part of the treatment, yet retains the insights and powers of analytic theory and practice.

Although the basic elements believed to be prerequisite for effecting therapeutic change may be independent of the treatment setting, the manner in which these elements are interrelated is different for individual and group treatment. It is appropriate for the group therapist, therefore, to investigate the interrelationships between group process and the individual.

The group therapist is obligated to understand the group as well as the individual in order to maximize the therapeutic potential of group psychotherapy.

In recent years serious efforts have been made to bridge the gap between the research findings provided by the students of small groups and by their application by group psychotherapists (Parloff, 1963). To be candid, the liaison and rapprochement achieved has been casual, desultory, and unimpressive; nor does this situation give promise of changing soon.

It is not our purpose here to review the potential for group therapists of the widely known works of such social scientists as Lewin, Lippitt, Argyris, Mills, Bennis, and Schutz, to name but a few, but rather to report the current utilization of group dynamics by practitioners of analytic group psychotherapy. The clearest integration of group phenomena and group therapy is represented in the work of those who have extended their treatment focus to include the group as an entity.

Despite the fact that we have many reservations concerning this trend, for reasons that will be elaborated later, we have no reservations in saying that a viable trend has been established which must be recognized by the group therapy community. With few exceptions, American group psychotherapists, in contrast to the British, have adopted a skeptical attitude toward "group dynamics." This attitude may be represented in a paraphrase of Judah Halevi's warning against the acceptance of the Hellenistic philosophy, "Let not the wisdom of the group dynamicist beguile thee. It hath not fruit, but only flowers."

Three major approaches to group psychotherapy will be described here, as illustrative of the major positions and directions of the field of analytic group psychotherapy.

1. *Intrapersonalist.* This designation is applied to those therapists who appear to have transposed their views regarding individual treatment processes to the group setting. They maintain their focus on the individual and seek to effect changes in intrapsychic structures and in their internal balance. Proponents of this approach to treatment insist that since intrapsychic change may best be affected by analytic methods, then analytic theory and practice should be adopted insofar as possible in the group treatment setting. Such theorists appear to acknowledge that the group setting represents a challenge to the application of such formal techniques of the analytic method as free association, genetic review, dream interpretation, and the establishment of a transference neurosis. They respond to this challenge in two contrasting ways: by conceding that the aims and patients appropriate for analytic group therapy are restricted (Slavson, 1952); or by admitting no important differences yet reinterpreting the meaning of various psychoanalytic concepts to fit group treatment practices (Wolf and Schwartz, 1962; and Locke, 1961).

2. *Transactionalist (Interpersonalist).* This category encompasses those who attempt to focus on the dyad or subgroup. They deal primarily with interpersonal relationships and "transactional" units.

It is difficult to designate the theorists who best represent the Transactional position since there is no single individual or group that is acknowledged as a spokesman for this wide-ranging "school." The Transactionalists include such divergent views as those held by Frank (1957a), Bach (1954), Berne (1966), and Mullan and Rosenbaum (1962). All these perceive the group as providing stimuli which permit the individual member to demonstrate his idiosyncratic modes of relating and responding to a broad range of individuals. Psychotherapy depends in part on the therapeutic potential of the interrelationships among patients and between therapist and patients. Therapists of this persuasion recognize to a far greater degree than Intrapersonalists that there are properties of groups which facilitate a productive therapeutic experience.

Although the Transactionalists believe that patients' behavior in groups may be understood in part as a manifestation of properties of the group, they are much more concerned with the personality characteristics of the patients than with the dynamics of the total group. Intrapersonalists and Interpersonalists both appear to assume that the major advantage of the group is that it permits the study of the individual as he responds to a number of other individuals and provides the opportunity for therapeutic change by means of the relationships effected.

3. *Integralist.* This term is applied to those who place major emphasis on group processes. They believe that study of the group as an entity reveals the functioning of the individual member in his full complexity, since all group activity reflects overt or covert aspects of the behavior of the individuals composing it. The group as a unit engages in activities which provide the individual with experiences and responses which are different in degree and perhaps in kind from those found in the dyad. The Integralist believes that a major aspect of the patient's problem is his inability to be an effective member of a task-oriented group.

These three classifications do not represent equally popular approaches. On the basis of publications and an informal evaluation of the views expressed at professional meetings, we believe that the Transactionalists have the largest number of adherents and the Integralists the smallest number. Since we are concerned here with trends and directions, the criterion of popularity need not be invoked. As in all fields, relatively few therapists possess the necessary fortitude and acrobatic skill to assume and maintain extreme positions. Yet, by attention to the extremes represented by these few, we can more clearly discern direction. For purposes of this review, which concerns theory of group psychotherapy rather than technique, we will limit ourselves to an examination of some acknowledged leaders in this area.

Consistent with the purpose of this chapter, we intend to place major emphasis on the Integralist's position since it represents a relatively new direction in analytic group psychotherapy. This emphasis stems from the view, which we share with many, that advances in the field require self-conscious efforts to incorporate elements of group process in analytic group psychotherapy. The Integralists have made such efforts, and these we believe are finding growing interest and acceptance. Our emphasis represents neither a conviction that important therapeutic advances have been demonstrated by the Integralists nor that the theoretical positions advanced are compelling. They deserve detailed study, however, because they represent directions which are necessary ones for group psychotherapy to explore. The changes which are represented by the Integralists may best be highlighted by first reviewing briefly the major tenets of the Intrapersonal and Interpersonal positions. The latter two will be presented here as a single unit.

The Positions of the Intrapersonalist and Transactionalist

The analytic group therapist who seeks to base his treatment on the authoritative statements of Freud finds surprisingly little that is supporting. He may be encouraged by the fact that Freud believed that individual psychology was a derivative of the more fundamental group psychology: "We must conclude that the psychology of groups is the oldest human psychology; what we have isolated as individual psychology, by neglecting all traces of the group, has only since come into prominence out of the old group psychology, by a gradual process which may still, perhaps, be described as incomplete" (Freud, 1921). However, Freud's further observation that members of groups appear to show heightened suggestibility, mutual identification, and repression of aggression is far less encouraging to the analytic group therapist. Such effects might indeed be interpreted as evidence of inherent limitations of the group as a setting for analytic treatment, since analytic therapy abjures conformity and repression and seeks to promote insight, freedom, and conscious choice. Freud may also be interpreted as implying that the patient's wish to be accepted by members of his group and to be in harmony with them may produce an antitherapeutic pressure, for he stated, ". . . experience has shown that in cases of collaboration, libidinal ties are regularly formed between the fellow workers which prolong and solidify the relation between them to a point beyond what is merely profitable" (Freud, 1921).

For many analysts, group psychotherapy has seemed sufficiently attractive to warrant making the broadest interpretation of Freud's comments on groups in an attempt to justify analytic group therapy. So great is the concern of some with establishing a Freudian precedent for group practice that the import of Freud's statements regarding groups has on occasion been modified to make them appear more palatable. For example, Freud's statement that group formation is antagonistic to psychoneurotic symptoms and therefore appears to induce a temporary remission of such symptoms has been offered as evidence of the inherent therapeutic value of groups (Anthony, 1966).

The explication of a Freudian framework which justifies the application of analytic principles to group psychotherapy is well presented by Scheidlinger (1952, 1960a, 1960b) and need not be repeated here.

The ingenuity of an analyst determined to demonstrate the applicability of psychoanalytic method to the group is most impressive. However, despite the effort to maintain the psychoanalytic orientation, such spokesmen as Locke grant that psychoanalytic theory cannot be lifted *in toto* and applied to the group, since the group represents a significant change from the individual therapy situation. "We moved into another universe when we moved from the individual to the group, and we must reorganize our thinking to the requirements of our new integration" (Locke, 1966, p. 297).

The "new integration" for the Intrapersonalists appears to refer mainly to adaptation of psychoanalytic principles to the group rather than the integration of "group dynamic" principles to group psychotherapy. The reports based on investigations of small group dynamics have received a very cool reception from the Intrapersonalists, but have achieved more acceptance from Transactionalists. The usual objection is that the group phenomena described by the students of small groups are, at best, irrelevant for the therapy group and, at worst, antitherapeutic. Moreover, the dimensions which have been studied by the social scientists have been deemed to be superficial, for they have not dealt with the unconscious.

The nagging question of whether the treatment of patients in a group requires an awareness and utilization of group processes has most frequently been interpreted by American practitioners as an invitation to extend to the group the theoretical concepts and techniques derived from individual psychotherapy. With the notable exception of Whitaker and Lieberman (1964), American group psychotherapists have done remarkably little in the area of applying group process or group dynamics theory to the practice of group psychotherapy.

It appears that the more Intrapersonal the group therapist the more skeptical he is concerning the relevance of group dynamics to group psychotherapy. Writers such as Wolf and Schwartz (1960) and Slavson (1962) are scornful of any deviation from psychoanalytic procedures for the purpose of attending to group processes or of individual response to group problems. Such interests are, they believe, diversionary or of secondary importance at best.

Wolf and Schwartz assert unequivocally that the "use of group dynamics in psychoanalytic therapy is based upon an illusion, a distortion as to what is appropriate to select in psychotherapy" (1962, p. 209). Although Slavson, too, has protested that group dynamics are psychonoxious and must be "nipped in the bud" lest they interfere with therapeutic process, in practice he is somewhat less intolerant of the possibility that under specified conditions group phenomena may have a therapeutic value. Other Intrapersonalists remain adamant. Granting that so-called group dynamics may be present in the psychoanalytic groups, as in any group, Locke asserts that they play no conscious or directed part in group therapy. Further, it is the individual who is being treated, not the group (Locke, 1961).

Helen Durkin has adopted a tolerant view regarding group dynamics consistent with the belief that they are natural phenomena, inherent in all groups, and will occur whether the therapist attends to them or not. Hers is a benign view of group dynamics based on the observation that since group therapy was effective even before the group therapist was called on to acknowledge the work of group dynamicists, a knowledge of group dynamics is of secondary importance to the achievement of the aims of psychotherapy. She reassures those concerned with the possibility that group dynamics may have psychonoxious effects by stating that "in those instances when they [group dynamics] work in an opposite direction, the therapeutic process will effectively counteract them" (Durkin, 1957, p. 127).

To facilitate presentation and comparison of the major positions taken by analytic group therapists, we shall pay particular attention to each school's conception of the role of the group in three phases of the therapeutic process: (1) stimulation of the patient's typical "pathology" and defenses; (2) enhancement of the patient's accessibility to new experience; and (3) introduction of specific procedures believed by the therapist to have the potential of effecting desired change.

It is generally recognized that in order for attitudes and behaviors to be changed in psychotherapy they must first be given expression in the treatment setting. The effectiveness of the patient's characteristic defenses must be thwarted. It is necessary, however, that therapy provide conditions under which the patient can tolerate the anxiety consequent to the frustration of his usual behaviors and defenses, without resorting to even stronger defensive behavior and without experiencing a disruptive dissolution of his defenses. The patient's accessibility to new experience in therapy requires a commitment to treatment which may be assisted initially by the patient's identification with the therapist. The patient must also have some confidence in the power of the therapeutic agent. Depending on the particular theoretical orientation of the therapist a variety of procedures, techniques, and aims will be introduced as the prerequisite procedures and norms of the group.

STIMULATION

Intrapersonalists agree on the importance of approximating psychoanalytic procedures in the group, yet there is considerable discrepancy between the hopefulness of Wolf and Schwartz and the skepticism of Slavson concerning the degree to which analytic procedural goals can actually be achieved in the group. This leads to marked differences in their approaches.

Wolf and Schwartz (1962) insist that they engage in formal psychoanalysis in the group setting and that the stimuli provided by the group facilitate the accomplishment of psychoanalytic aims. They believe that the usual analytic procedures are fully available in the group.

That the concepts underlying the procedures must undergo considerable revision does not dismay these writers. The distinction between transference and transference neurosis is lost. Free association is redefined so that it no longer refers to the uninterrupted free flow of associations of a single individual, but includes all content and interventions of members of the group during a specified time sequence. Similarly, association to dreams is not restricted to the dreamer, but may include the fantasies and thoughts of fellow group members who free associate to one another's dreams. Such free associations to another's dream are believed to provide additional material which may bear on the latent meaning of the dream. The associations of others are viewed as an extension of the associations of the dreamer, and in this sense the associative process is not interrupted.

Slavson, considerably less sanguine about the effectiveness of these modifications, concludes that patients suffering from massive psychoneuroses, requiring the establishment of a transference neurosis as part of treatment, are poor candidates for analytic group psychotherapy (Slavson, 1964). Slavson reasons that the presence of individuals other than the therapist may diminish the intensity of the transference which can be established with any one person, even though the total "quantum" of affect may be multiplied many times, and that therefore the intensity of the therapy is reduced. As a consequence the group may not be conducive to deep regression and may hamper the emergence of fantasies.

The fact that the group may be viewed as evoking "family transference," and thereby permitting analysis of relevant family relationships, is not accepted by the Intrapersonalists as an endorsement of the recently developed family therapy, since the presence of the actual members of the family is believed by these theorists to limit the expression of fantasy, which is vital for psychotherapy. The group is already too reality-focused for Slavson's tastes. He complains that not only are distortions and fantasies less available for analysis, but also that the reality factor may become so intense that interactions produce "real" conflicts rather than the desired attenuated representations of earlier conflicts with others (Slavson, 1964).

In brief, Slavson is quite adamant in his view that the group presents very serious obstacles to the establishment of the basic prerequisites of analytic psychotherapy: "The single most important condition for successful therapy is the development of positive-negative transference attitudes towards the therapist which are worked through in the course of treatment. . . . Any setting, process, or set of reactions that blocks or dilutes the fantasy-laden, distorted and ambivalent feelings of love and hate, dependence and rejection, dilutes the intensity of the transference and hence also that of the therapy. This situation is unavoidable in groups" (1964, p. 154). As if to dispel any lingering hopes in the minds of his readers that these serious limitations may yet be overcome by the effective use of interpretation, he adds that the effectiveness of the group therapists' efforts to deal with such phenomena as displaced transference feelings is seriously impaired (1964, p. 155).

The Transactional therapists are less concerned with establishing the pristine orthodoxy of analytic procedures, but utilize the group setting to further the analysis of observable interpersonal relationships and transactions. They share with the Intrapersonalists the view that the group offers a unique opportunity for stimulating relevant affects, thoughts, resistances, and defenses. This category of therapist includes the full range of neo-Freudian theorists and encompasses the vast majority of all analytically oriented group therapists.

Within the limits of such variables as composition, orientation, leadership, and the like, the group is viewed as providing a setting in which individuals are confronted with: (1) conflicting values of other members; (2) a wide range of life experiences; and (3) an intensified rivalry for the doctor's attention. All three factors stimulate the individuals to respond verbally and nonverbally with typical sensitivities, anxieties, defenses, and resistances. Members of the group may be provoked into expressing their agreement or disagreement with the ideas of others. The group provides an opportunity for the patient to become aware not only of his own reactions to others, but also of the reactions of others to him. In addition to recognizing such stimulating effects of groups, the Transactional theorists point out that all individuals by virtue of membership in the group must cope with the problems of (1) inclusion, (2) control, and (3) intimacy. Inclusion involves the patient's fear of being left out or not being accepted, but can also refer to his fear of becoming overly involved with the group. The patient must deal with the attractive and repellent features of the opportunity to control others and of the possibility of being controlled. He must also cope with the threat and the potential satisfactions of experiencing his own and others' personal emotional feelings, such as resentment, hostility, warmth, and sympathy (Schutz, 1958; Bennis and Shepard, 1956). These three concepts appear to be extensions of the group phenomena described by Bion as the Basic Assumptions of Dependency, Fight-Flight and Pairing (see page 514).

The Transactional therapists may or may not speak directly in terms of transference, free association, regression, and projection, but the transition from the extreme psychoanalytic position to their own has been made much easier by virtue of the modifications of analytic theory accepted by even the most orthodox group therapist.

ACCESSIBILITY

Stimulation of characteristic patterns of ego functioning and defenses would be of little value if the therapy setting did not provide conditions which permit the patient to utilize the new experiences. The patient's accessibility to therapeutic influence is initially attributed by all Intrapersonalists to his identification with the therapist. This is consistent with Freud's belief that the essence of group formation consists of the libidinal tie which the group member experiences with the leader. With the development of the group, fellow patients as well as the therapist provide multiple models and objects of identification. The behavior attitudes and values of others who are cathected may be imitated and ultimately internalized.

Among other therapeutic assets of the group cited by both categories of therapists is the fact that the self-esteem of members may be increased by the experience of mutual acceptance. The group also helps to reduce the patient's self-alienation, self-criticism, and self-depreciation by revealing that others have the same or similar problems and are victims of similar impulses and feelings (Frank, 1957b; Durkin, 1964).

When the appropriate group mores have been established, the patient may realistically recognize that the risks involved in revealing one's conflicts, fears, and doubts are reduced, for the likelihood of damaging rejection or retaliation has been lessened. As a further consequence, defensiveness and fear of self-revelation are reduced, which makes the repressed and suppressed more accessible to investigation.

Despite the objections of Intrapersonalists to such concepts as cohesiveness, they recognize that a patient's satisfaction with his group membership may facilitate treatment. The satisfaction and support that accrue from membership in a group are dependent on the patient's perception and evaluation of the group. As the patient feels increasingly secure and as his self-esteem rises—partly because of the others' acceptance of him and partly because of his own satisfaction with his performance—he becomes more willing to learn about himself and to investigate the bases of his anxiety.

Although the group provides more opportunity than individual treatment does for experiencing wholesome, loving feelings, sympathy and positive relatedness, patients in groups occasionally treat one another with harshness and cruelty. It is necessary, therefore, that the therapist assume responsibility for supervising the kinds and degrees of interactions.

If the therapist believes that unsupervised patient relationships may be potentially dangerous or antitherapeutic, then he would view with considerable skepticism the wisdom of "alternate" sessions at which the therapist is not present. Wolf and Schwartz (1962) and Mullan and Rosenbaum (1962), however, believe that alternate sessions may permit the expression of direct and effective group support. Because patients' comments in such sessions are spontaneous, and even impulsive, they may carry far more weight than do the more circumspect and discriminating interventions of the therapist. The experience of shared pain as well as pleasure may integrate the group into a generally accepting, permissive, and supportive unit. Again, it must be emphasized that Intrapersonal therapists do not view this kind of experience as therapeutic in itself, but rather as facilitating potentially valuable analytic explorations.

While acknowledging the fact that positive transference to the therapist increases the patient's amenability to the treatment process, Intrapersonal therapists believe that the therapist's enhanced power for influencing the patient is not to be utilized to persuade or directly to influence the patient to conform to or adopt certain standards or modes of conduct. Intrapersonal therapists place great emphasis on the principle that patient change should not be effected as a consequence of conformity either to the therapist or to fellow patients, but should be the result of the patient's increased freedom to exercise conscious control over those behaviors and feelings which had previously been out of his awareness.

One of the areas of disagreement between the Intrapersonalists and Interpersonalists is the role each assigns to the group phenomenon of cohesiveness for aiding the patient to become more accessible to therapeutic influence. The Intrapersonalists believe that cohesiveness implies both an antitherapeutic collusion of mutual good fellowship and a pressure to accept group norms which may be antagonistic to analytic psychotherapy. Although such theorists may admire the elegance of the research performed by social scientists in the area of cohesiveness, they question its relevance. The Transactionalists tend to interpret the term cohesiveness in a manner consistent with its usage by social scientists to refer to the degree of attractiveness which membership in a particular group has for its members (Cartwright and Zander, 1960; Borgatta, Bales, and Hare, 1955). Such attractiveness not only may be based on mutual liking, but also may evolve from the experience of considerable conflict and antagonism in the group (Frank, 1957a).

Transactionalists believe that the attractiveness of the group may be enhanced not simply by the establishment of warm personal relationships among group members, but also by the following: (1) patient's assumption that the therapist is competent; (2) evidence that other group members are deriving "some benefit"; (3) indications that the standards of equality and justice will be maintained by the leader; (4) evidence that the patient's own participation in the group is recognized and valued; (5) derivation of some help with the patient's own problems; (6) respect for members of the group; (7) feelings understood by the group; (8) discovery that others in the group share similar conflicts and fears; and (9) recognition that the group imposes a reduced penalty for inappropriate behavior.

The Transactionalists recognize that the more attractive membership in the therapy group becomes to the patients, the greater will be their concern with maintaining their membership and their roles in the group. This fact implies that the cohesive group has the power to exercise some control or influence on the behavior of each member. Unlike the Intrapersonalists, the Transactionalists do not view such potential pressure as necessarily evil (Durkin, 1964). Granted that cohesiveness may exert pressure on the members to conform to the group standards, norms, and goals, they hold that the value of such compliance depends on the nature of the standards rather than on the pressure.

All forms of psychotherapy are based on the assumption that the patient will make an effort to conform to the requirements of the particular therapeutic procedures employed. The patient may be required, for example, to report dreams, to express his associations as freely as he can, to express his reactions to others, etc. In addition, he must present himself for the group sessions at a specified time and place and at a frequency set by the therapist; he must, of course, pay the fee set by the therapist. The therapist sees no grave issues of conformity involved in his requiring patients to accept his treatment standards. He attempts to facilitate the establishment of those norms and practices which he believes are conducive to effective psychotherapy. If such standards are adopted by the group as part of its norms, there can be no objection that the cohesive group exerts influence on its members to conform to the group norms. The danger lies rather in the possibility that cohesiveness will operate to thwart conformity to such standards. Therapists such as Wolf and Schwartz oppose the development of group cohesiveness on the assumption that since emotionally ill persons tend to cling to their symptoms and disturbed perceptions of self and others, all such groups may reasonably be expected to develop antitherapeutic norms. They are not reassured by Foulkes, who optimistically believes that this will not occur since collectively patients constitute the norms from which they individually deviate (Foulkes, 1948).

Transactional therapists tend not to assign any such universal characteristics to groups, but are interested instead in the conditions that affect the establishment of the appropriate norms. Cohesiveness, like other group phenomena, is not assigned the label of "therapeutic" or "antitherapeutic" independent of the particular matrix of circumstances. It is part of the leader's task to provide conditions that will assist the group to utilize its opportunity for achieving the aims of therapy.

The Intrapersonalists' concern that a group, unless carefully checked, will exert strong pressure toward conformity among its members can be attributed to the multiplicity of research reports which appear to support such a fear. Among the most frequently cited works are those of Lewin and his students, who report that it is usually easier to change the opinions of a group than to change the opinions of individual members separately; moreover, opinions formed by groups are more resistant to change than those formed by individuals independently (Lewin, 1947, 1951).

Researchers such as Sherif (1935), Asch (1952), and Crutchfield (1959) have all produced impressive studies indicating that powerful influences are exerted on the individual group member by internalized reference groups as well as by an apparent group consensus. All researchers stress the fact that such findings are the consequence of complex interrelationships among variables which affect conformity. Particularly noteworthy are studies which specify the differential influence of a member's relative status in the group (Harvey and Consalvi, 1960) and members' perceptions of the influence agents (Kelman, 1963). The Intrapersonalists appear to be more impressed with the general conclusions about groups than with the forces that produce the group phenomena.

A further danger to the individual's autonomy, according to Intrapersonalists, is implicit in what Redl (1942) has called "group emotional contagion." This refers to the communication of emotional feelings from one individual to another even when the content or the cause of the group feeling is contrary to the individual's apparent intellectual convictions and standards. In effect, the group, by common consent or approval, reduces the ego and superego restraints of its members and therefore may make the patient more accessible to experiencing and expressing hostility and aggression. The motivation for such loss of self is further enhanced by the desire for social acceptance. From this point of view, the more an individual becomes a part of the group, the less he can retain his autonomy, his individuality, and his responsibility for self-determination. This view is not shared by Existentialists and Transactionalists such as Mullan and Rosenbaum (1962), who believe that the group represents a lifelike setting in which the patient can aim at becoming more and more "human" without concern as to whether he becomes more and more individualistic. They state further that they have not found the group process to be a conforming force, but rather an "impelling" force that exposes the person to his responsibility as a member of the human society. The definition and role of group dynamics in analytic group therapy, as performed by Intrapersonalists and Transactionalists, remain ambiguous and confused.

MECHANISMS OF THERAPEUTIC CHANGE

Intrapersonalists place great emphasis on the analysis of resistance and defenses by means of interpretation. While therapists of this school recognize the value of catharsis as "a way of purging one's self of noxious states of the psyche" (Slavson, 1964, p. 142), the experience is not valued if it is unaccompanied by insight. This is in sharp contrast to the recent well-publicized formulations of Mowrer (1964), a nonanalytically oriented therapist, who believes that one of the principal values of the group is that it provides an opportunity for "confession" and atonement.

Intrapersonal therapists all acknowledge the utility of the recall of repressed or suppressed material, in that it may be effective for the patient and may also benefit other members of the group. Other patients may be assisted to recall some of their own experiences and to bring them into awareness.

These therapists also believe that the group is particularly effective in analyzing resistances. Group members frequently make frontal assaults on other patients' resistances, and challenge such behaviors as silence, withdrawal, lateness, absence, monopoly, autism, or pseudo-relating. Some therapists believe that this role of the group in treatment derives from the fact that members are particularly sensitive to behavior in others which they tend to reject in themselves. In addition, it is acknowledged that group analysis of resistances represents the acceptance and implementation of therapeutic models and mores introduced by the therapist.

Both Intrapersonalists and Interpersonalists recognize that the group may at times appear to share resistances and may attempt to subvert the therapeutic forms of self-revelation and examination by maintaining interactions at a nonanxiety-provoking level. Such techniques may include changing the subject, interrupting, offering premature support, diffusing anxiety by humor, etc. Although the Intrapersonalists are quite aware of this phenomenon they do not view the analysis of group-shared resistances as a central mechanism of analytic group psychotherapy.

Intrapersonal theorists acknowledge the value of the group for testing reality, yet decry exclusive emphasis on this aspect. They do not believe that any technique which addresses itself predominantly to reality or the analysis of group tensions, or limits itself to the immediate here-and-now situation, can be viewed as effective analytic group psychotherapy. This belief is based on the assumption that neuroses are essentially autonomous and that effective therapy requires that the basic sources of neuroses be worked through by dealing with memories, early relationships, anxieties, and guilt. Intrapersonal therapists believe that efforts to effect changes in interpersonal relationships by means of interpersonal techniques alone can be successful only with those patients whose disturbances are of a surface nature. Since the intrapsychic conflict underlies the manifest interpersonal problem, it must be resolved. Treatment of the interpersonal or transactional relationships is secondary to this aim. Only after the expression and clarification of the dynamics underlying pathology can the patient benefit from confrontation with realistic alternatives in behavior. Following insight into conflicts the process of working through may be effected.

Although therapists such as Slavson believe that the efficacy of treatment depends on the achievement of "affective" insight, they express grave reservations regarding the level of insight which can be achieved in groups. They believe that, because of the limitations on the development of transference and the restrictions on the variety and degrees of cathartic processes in groups, the level of insight that a patient can attain is generally less deep than in individual therapy.

Another frequently cited limitation on the effectiveness of group therapy is the fact that interpretations supplied by fellow members are often not appropriate to a patient's current ego state and psychological readiness (Wassell, 1959). Wolf and Schwartz minimize this objection by asserting that in their experience patients appear to be able to cope with insights offered by their peers, either "by resisting or integrating them in non-toxic doses" (1962, p. 291).

Although both types of therapists assume that psychotherapy takes place primarily through the activity of the psychotherapist, some acknowledge that even untutored patients may make insightful comments and observations. The group plays a particularly important role in the interpretation of transference and distortions by virtue of the impact of group consensus. The group may agree about the nature and appropriateness of recurring behavior patterns which are manifest as patients relate to one another and to the therapist. Frequently, the unreality of a transference reaction may become apparent when several patients have contrasting transference reactions to the same person (Ziferstein and Grotjahn, 1956).

Intrapersonal therapists acknowledge that patients can perform a valuable function as therapeutic adjuncts, but they stress that patients who represent "transference-objects" may not respond in a neutral, objective manner. In such cases, the essential dynamic of transference analysis may become fragmented and diluted.

Intrapersonalists are acutely sensitive to the modification that psychoanalytic concepts must undergo when applied in the group setting; nevertheless, their insistent efforts to apply the techniques and theories of individual psychoanalytic therapy to the group seem to other group therapists to result in a failure to make the best use of the specific advantages provided by features indigenous to the group.

In contrast, the Transactional therapist concentrates on the immediate observable interaction of group members. Eliciting personal history material is neither consistently encouraged nor discouraged, but such material is sometimes effectively used to document and underscore a behavior pattern which has been highlighted in the immediate group situation. The reality-testing aspect of the group is emphasized. The group, in effect, provides a laboratory in which each member has an opportunity to learn how he affects others and how they stimulate him. Depending on the therapist's orientation, the treatment may stress conscious awareness of one's behavior and feelings or emphasize the understanding of the motivation behind the behavior. The level of interpretation frequently aims at uncovering the immediate gains served by the patient's behavior in the group, rather than at attempting to identify his underlying conflicts or "basic motivations" (Berne, 1961).

Another approach to Transactionalist therapy is represented by Frank. He states that as the patient experiences successes due to his more effective way of handling his interpersonal and internal conflicts, his new ways of behaving are reinforced. As a consequence of such repeated experiences, the maladaptive patterns are extinguished and the successful interactions are strengthened. This theory of psychotherapy suggests that the dynamic of treatment is the self-reinforcement value of new behavior which more adequately deals with conflicts. He does not assume that such specific behavioral change is the end point of therapy, but hypothesizes that these changes will enable the patient to experience further emotional growth (Frank, 1961).

For most of the Transactional therapists psychotherapy does not consist of the teaching of more efficient social roles, but instead is aimed at improving social skills through a corrective emotional experience in the context of an interpersonal situation (Bach, 1954). Such change is aimed at modifying neurotic needs. Transactional therapists believe that the patient's motivation for modifying his current behaviors may be stimulated by the forceful recognition of their essential ineffectiveness. Interpretations are concerned with aiding the individual to recognize his role in maintaining ineffective behavior patterns in the present situation. The concept of "working through" is here not concerned exclusively with the patient's eventual acceptance of the reality of his own instinctual conflicts, but instead refers to the period during which the patient tests the therapist, practices skills in more clearly differentiating present situations from past, and utilizes and applies his new understanding of self and others.

In brief, the Transactionalist attempts to provide a treatment situation in which new interpersonal relationships may be developed which are more effective and more satisfying. For some, interpersonal change is believed to be sufficient to represent durable progress (Mullan and Rosenbaum, 1962). For others the emphasis on the interpersonal is based on the assumption that such changes will ultimately effect appropriate intrapsychic changes (Bach, 1954).

One of the most provocative recent theoretical developments among Transactional therapists is that described by Berne. "Transactional analysis," according to Berne, includes four phases: structural analysis, transactional analysis proper, game analysis, and script analysis. Structural analysis concerns the identification and labeling of the moment-to-moment ego state which characterizes the individual patient's functioning (Parental,

Child, Adult). Transactional analysis proper consists of determining which ego state is active in the agent and in the respondent. The ego states of the protagonists may be complementary, crossed, or ulterior. Game analysis refers to the identification of the "game" which the individual is playing, i.e., "a series of ulterior transactions with a gimmick, leading to a usually well-concealed but well-defined pay-off" (Berne, 1966, p. 227). Script analysis concerns the unconscious life plan of the individual, which is based on decisions made in early childhood.

In Berne's approach, the major focus is not on uncovering the etiological bases of current problems, but on identifying the gratifications, the pay-off, which the behavior provides the individual. The uncovering of unconscious material is not dismissed but is not emphasized. The dynamics which effect change are hypothesized to include the patient's learning to control his free energy to a degree that enables him to "shift his 'real self' from one ego state to another by an *act of will* [italics added]. . . . At first he relies heavily on external stimuli to bolster such shifts, but he learns more and more to effect them through autonomous acts of volition" (Berne, 1966, p. 307).

Berne is perhaps the most outspoken advocate of the principle that an intimate knowledge of group dynamics is an important prerequisite for the effective functioning of the group psychotherapist. "A sound knowledge of group dynamics is as important to a group therapist as a knowledge of physiology is to a physician" (Berne, 1966, p. 138).

His view of group dynamics does not propose any listing of specific forces. Nor does it propose any phenomena uniquely characteristic of therapy groups. It offers instead a general checklist of areas which are commended to the therapist's attention and interest. It does not suggest what the therapist will find when he looks there. No forces are assumed to be inherent in the group, save perhaps the dynamic struggle that occurs in all groups between cohesive and disruptive forces.

Berne's approach has the assets of simplicity and directness. These are very appealing to both therapist and patient. It also has the handicap of its own cleverness. It offers the patient a pocketful of wry characterizations which are to be applied to each group member's behavior. The task of therapist and patient is to name the ego states and identify the covert games with these labels. The risk, of course, is that "transactional analysis" may be dismissed as the fastest slogan-therapy in the West.

The Positions of the Integralists

This section reviews the current thinking of leading group psychotherapists whose view of the process of analytic group psychotherapy gives primary emphasis to dealing with the group as an entity. As in the previous section, after a general overview, the presentation will follow three major rubrics concerning the process of psychotherapy: Stimulation, Accessibility, and Mechanisms of Change. The positions of such Integralists as Bion, Ezriel, Whitaker and Lieberman, and Foulkes and Anthony will be described and compared. Since Bion's theory regarding group processes has stimulated many therapists and researchers, his thinking will be reported in some detail.

Integralists hold the view that membership in a therapy group evokes shared unconscious or preconscious conflicts and motivations. The therapist, by attending to such shared group concerns, may effectively treat each patient in his group. This conception of the group as guided by common unconscious forces is consistent with Freud's observation that to the degree that a group lacks formal organization, its members are stimulated to display basic similarities in their unconscious drives. Such groups encourage members to throw off, albeit temporarily, the repressions which constrain the expression of their instinctual impulses (Freud, 1921).

In attempting to treat the group as a unit, the Integralists tend to ascribe to it characteristics of an individual. As a consequence, psychotherapy of the group concerns the analysis of interaction and transactions between the group as an entity and the therapist, or between the group and one of its members. Since the group is treated as if it were an individual, the familiar conflict and tension-reduction models of individual psychotherapy are applied to the group as a whole. Among the clinicians and theorists who attempt to treat the group as a unit, Bion is preeminent.

Bion's formulations are concerned primarily with the description and specification of the common motivational elements of all groups. In his efforts to develop a framework for describing and conceptualizing dimensions which organize the seemingly discrete behaviors of each of the patients, he has carefully avoided the imposition of psychoanalytic concepts. As a consequence, unlike such students of group psychotherapy as Mann (1955) and Semrad and Arsenian (1951), Bion does not utilize concepts like "group ego" or "group superego." Although Bion has applied his theories to the treatment of patients, the major focus of his interest and his writings is in the identification and description of group phenomena relevant to all groups. Bion is far more concerned with explicating group phenomena than with presenting any compelling evidence concerning the therapeutic consequences which follow the application of his theory or techniques of analytic group psychotherapy.

The implementation of Bion's views by clinicians was facilitated greatly by the work of Ezriel and of Sutherland, who in effect bridged the gap between Bion's group dynamics and the group therapist's views of the analytic group psychotherapy treatment process. Perhaps the fullest theoretical statement concerning the role of the group in the treatment process is that presented by Whitaker and Lieberman (1964). Although they were initially greatly influenced by the thinking of both Bion and Ezriel, Whitaker and Lieberman have developed an original and effective theoretical position which integrates their own clinical and research experience with groups.

Foulkes and Anthony (1957) occupy the rather anomalous position of maintaining an orthodox Freudian point of view comparable to that found in the Intrapersonalist, while earning a position among the Integralists by their insistence on treating the group as a unit. Their group focus, however, is neither so narrow as that represented by Bion nor so broad as that of Whitaker and Lieberman.

An important test of the value of any theory is the amount of empirical research which it generates. Although the over-all field of group psychotherapy is notoriously lacking in systematic research on treatment or related areas, the criterion of research stimulation is nonetheless supportive of the emphasis which we place on Bion's contributions. His theoretical conceptions have been seminal for students of small groups, such as Stock and Thelen (1958), Bennis and Shepard (1956), Schutz (1958), Trist and Sofer (1959), Stock and Lieberman (1962), and Whitman and Stock (1958).

Bion's work answers the serious objection which group therapists have long expressed regarding the work of "group dynamicists"—namely, their failure to deal with psychotherapy groups or to represent group phenomena in terms of unconscious motivational states. Despite this, Bion's work has not been widely accepted by clinicians in the United States. Perhaps one of the factors which has acted to dampen the enthusiasm in this country is Bion's use of Kleinian rather than Freudian concepts to expound his theory. In addition, the sociological notion that groups are organized around a shared task—rather than by libidinal ties to a central person as postulated by Freud and amplified by Redl (1942)—is not accepted as tolerantly in the United States as it is in England.

The popular belief that group psychotherapy requires an integration of group processes with individual psychodynamics in their genetic complexity is not shared by Bion or his closest followers. They believe instead that group psychotherapy is best focused on the group processes per se, since these will more effectively reveal the pertinent aspects of the individual. Bion does not accept the distinction between individual and group dynamics and rejects the position that "group psychology" comes into being only when a number of people are collected together in one place at one time. He believes that group phenomena exist in individuals, since no individual, however isolated in time and space, can be regarded as outside of a group or lacking in active manifestations of group psychology. "The apparent difference between group psychology and individual psychology is an illusion produced by the fact that the group brings into prominence phenomena that appear alien to the observer unaccustomed to using the group" (Bion, 1959, p. 169).

STIMULATION

The Integralists who have been influenced by Bion assume that a primary source of stimulation inheres in the fact that therapy groups, like individuals, are motivated not only by manifest overt aims, but also by latent covert purposes which may conflict with the accomplishment of the overt purposes. Such covert motivations appear to be shared unwittingly by the group membership. Bion, in contrast to other Integralists, postulates but does not emphasize or utilize in his theory individual predispositions to behave in idiosyncratic fashion; instead Bion attempts only to describe characteristic group phenomena. On the basis of his observations, Bion concluded that each group appears to behave as if it were in fact two groups—or, more precisely, as if it had developed two quite different cultures. The aims of the covert culture, although apparently inconsistent with the stated purposes of the group, might coincide, on occasion, with the primary task. The two cultures are identified as the work group and the basic assumption (Ba) group. The term "work group" is used to describe the facet of a group's functioning that seems to be purposeful and effective in achieving the primary task. Members cooperate with one another in formulating and implementing a program for realistically achieving the group's aims. Participation in such a group requires effort and utilization of relevant experiences and learned skills.

The Ba group appears to be less reality-oriented, seeks instantaneous satisfaction, and is characterized by the impulsive expression of uncritical fantasy. Participation in such a group requires no special training, skills, or self-conscious effort. Such group behavior may be understood as a reflection of a shared, unverbalized, yet tacitly accepted assumption which motivates the group. Bion has identified three such assumptions or emotional states, all three of which are oriented around the issue of leadership. Leadership is a salient issue in Bion's groups and in all other Integralist groups since the therapist usually appears to the patients to have abdicated his leadership role. This leaves the group members to deal with an apparent leadership vacuum.

Bion's three basic assumptions are dependency, fight-flight, and pairing. Bion insists that his descriptions of the motivations underlying each Ba group are to be taken quite literally rather than metaphorically. The dependency group behaves as if the group's purpose is to obtain protection, comfort, and nurturance from a leader whom it has endowed with godlike qualities of wisdom, knowledge and power. The group members act stupidly and helplessly, as if to underscore their desperate need for an omniscient and omnipotent leader. In the group treatment setting the group turns first to the therapist for such assistance. The leader cannot fulfill this assignment, and, in the view of Bion, should not attempt to undertake it. As a consequence the group's wish for a dependency leader will be frustrated. When the group has exhausted its repertoire of techniques for inducing the leader to fill its dependency needs, it will attempt to seek out an alternate leader from among the membership. He, too, will inevitably fail to live up to the group's expectations. When the emotional state of dependency prevails, the group experiences a sense of closeness and "groupiness" which it attempts to maintain.

With regard to the second basic assumption, fight-flight, the group acts as if its aim is to preserve itself. It seems to see its alternatives as either attack or flight from someone or something. Unlike the Ba dependency group, the fight-flight group appears relatively unconcerned with the welfare of the individual and shows little if any tolerance for "sickness." Such groups appear to be pointedly unconcerned with self-study or rational thought. They are preoccupied with action. The group seeks out a leader who can mobilize it for attack or for flight. Candidates for leadership who do not lead in these directions are disavowed or ignored.

The third Ba group, which uses the assumption of pairing, behaves as if its purpose is to produce a new leader and savior. The relationship between members, regardless of sex, is treated with an air of hopeful expectation that this "sexual" union will produce a new leader or a new concept which will bring about the desired ideal state. When this Ba is operative, the group does not actively seek a leader but appears to wait for one to emerge. The group is characterized by optimism, but Bion emphasizes that the state of hopeful anticipation can be sustained only as long as the group does not in fact produce either a leader or an idea. Reality, apparently, cannot sustain imagination's promises.

Although the differentiation between the affective and cognitive states may appear to be too sharply drawn, it has a certain heuristic value. It avoids the usual problem which confronts theorists who attempt to characterize groups and founder on descriptions which deal with only one aspect of the group's functioning: They see the group as either manifesting a high level of cognitive functioning or else as offering gross interference with man's creative nature. According to proponents of "brainstorming," such as Osborn and Parnes, groups are believed to increase the creative performance of their members (Osborn, 1953; Parnes and Meadows, 1959). Jung, on the other hand, states, "When a hundred clever heads join in a group, one big nincompoop is the result, because every individual is trammeled by the otherness of the others" (Illing, 1957, p. 80). Bion's descriptions do permit a more differentiated view of the group, and therefore encourage more sophisticated generalizations.

To deal with the problem of how the group comes to accept a particular basic assumption, Bion postulates the existence of a universal innate capacity to enter into one or another of the basic assumptions. This capacity he terms "valency." It may vary in the degree to which it is represented in individuals, but it is never absent. The term valency is also used by Bion to indicate a force which irresistibly draws group members into participation in any of the basic assumptions once they have been manifested in members of the group. Valency is seen as analogous to tropism in plants.

Bion's concept of valency suggests that the very fact that some members move into a basic assumption attitude might be sufficient to induce other members to follow. However, Bion is also careful to note, as are his followers, that although the individual may experience a strong inclination to merge with the group, he sharply confronts his counterwish to maintain his own individuality. Part of the anxiety which group members experience in a relatively unstructured group is attributable to their conflict regarding being drawn into a Ba culture. The patient experiences an intensification of emotions, which are associated with his unconscious anxiety that the basic assumptions will become dominant and his intellectual capacity will be reduced. The individual is impelled to seek satisfaction of his needs in the group "by total submergence in the group," yet is simultaneously inhibited by the fears that such activity will sacrifice his sense of "individual independence."

A second source of conflict inheres in the clash between the individual's need to maintain his view of the group as a source of security and his recognition that the group also produces anxiety and frustrations within him. To reconcile the apparent discrepancy between the "good" and the "bad" groups, the group member may, according to Bion, invoke massive denial and projection. The members may split off the negative aspects of the group. The source of frustration may be attributed not to the group but to members, the therapist, subgroups, or events and individuals outside of the group. Projection permits group members to identify rejected aspects of themselves in other individuals. Members may also split off their own competence and invest it in another, such as a leader.

A third source of conflict, which acts to stimulate group members to manifest their predispositions, distortions, and defenses, derives from the hypothesized opposition between the cognitive and affective states represented by the two major group cultures: work and basic assumptions. These two group states appear to be expressions of the conflict represented in an individual patient between his conscious wish to learn about the source of his personal difficulties and to alter his behavior, and his preconscious and unconscious resistances against any such efforts which threaten to heighten anxiety. The work group is concerned with reality, exposing inappropriate ego-functioning and attempting to uncover the source of such disturbances.

The Ba represents an attempt to escape from reality into group-shared assumptions and regressive affective states.

Bion has not undertaken to define the circumstances or the conditions under which the group may move from one affective state to another or from the affective to the cognitive culture. He does indicate that in general the shift from one basic assumption to another is due primarily to the fact that the assumptions are unrealistic and cannot be met satisfactorily. The members of the group are constantly frustrated, and the anxiety aroused is so intense that a new defense must be invoked; the new defense is represented in another basic assumption, but since the new defense is itself inadequate, the inevitable anxiety will force the shift to yet another defense.

Integralists such as Ezriel and Whitaker and Lieberman, while sharing Bion's focus on the group, do not attempt to follow his efforts in treatment to avoid any reference to the individual's psychodynamics and experiences prior to entrance into the group. Although Ezriel shares Bion's Kleinian orientation, he utilizes the concepts of individual psychodynamics to explain the origins of the shared unconscious preoccupations of the members composing a group (1956).

Whitaker and Lieberman, with some modifications, subscribe to Ezriel's view that each patient, on entering the group, projects his own unconscious fantasy-objects onto other group members as he attempts to manipulate the group members into assuming assigned roles. In effect, each member attempts to influence the group in order to make it correspond to his fantasy group. To the degree that the individual's internalized objects do not coincide with reality, or the assigned roles are not accepted by members of the group, the underlying unconscious dynamics of the patient are stimulated and his particular defense mechanisms for coping with such tensions are manifested. Although each individual plays a "private game," the impact of these separate acts on each other provides the basis of common group tensions which reflect the unconscious fantasies of all of the group members. The unconscious group tension produces interactions which are aimed at resolving or diminishing some aspect of the individual's unconscious tension. The group thus stimulates each member to adopt a particular role which corresponds to his own way of defending himself against unconscious fears. The intrapersonal conflicts or relations with internalized objects express themselves in interpersonal relations as the internalized objects are projected onto group members.

Whitaker and Lieberman, in common with Ezriel (1950, 1952, 1956, 1959) and Sutherland (1952), have accepted a conflict resolution model as descriptive of group behavior but do not attempt to identify a finite number of motivations to explain all group phenomena. Movement in groups is not perceived as primarily a consequence of successive frustrations. Instead the group movement consists of more or less effective attempts at conflict resolution. The quality of group movement is a function of the nature of the resolutions which have been achieved. Group behavior is interpreted not simply as evidence of a direct attempt at wish-fulfillment, but also, as pointed out by Ezriel, as a compromise between conflicting motives. The group is a moment-to-moment balance of forces. A change in one aspect of the system will effect changes in the entire equilibrium. Ezriel views the group tension as stimulated by impulses toward unacceptable, threatening relations that are usually avoided. Whitaker similarly postulates that the conflict is between (1) a disturbing motive and (2) a reactive motive. The group's efforts to resolve the conflict are characterized by Whitaker as the "group solution" and by Ezriel as the "required relationship."

Whitaker and Lieberman accept Bion's and Ezriel's view that the wishes and fears of group members evolve into a group-shared unconscious conflict. Increasingly direct analysis of the nature of the impulses and of the defenses against their expression is facilitated by "enabling solutions" achieved by the group. The contrary is true of groups that have a history of accepting defensive or restrictive solutions. An enabling solution is one that is directed at alleviating fears and at the same time allows for some expression of the disturbing motive; a restrictive solution aims primarily at alleviating fears, and does so at the expense of satisfying or expressing the disturbing motive. Whitaker and Lieberman identify group themes as a series of focal conflicts centered around a single disturbing motive. These themes are reminiscent of Bion's basic assumptions in that they are described as dealing with sex, aggression, and dependency. Whitaker and Lieberman also use the term "group culture" in a manner analogous to the way in which Bion uses it, but they refine it. They define culture as the collective effect of group-accepted solutions (whether enabling or restrictive) on group focal conflicts. Group culture concerns the character of the relationship among patients and between patients and therapists, the freedom with which affect is expressed, the acceptability to patients of a wide range of content, and so forth.

Consistent with the British theorists, Whitaker and Lieberman believe that under the conditions of the therapy group, shared group emotions occur immediately on exposure to common stresses among group members. Such reactions need not be viewed as transference phenomena based on experience with previous groups. These theorists do not agree with Freud and Redl that shared group emotions develop through a special relationship with the leader or other members of the group—that is, they do not view the primary functions of the group as the stimulation of family transference or as the provision of an arena in which interpersonal behavior may be observed and interpreted.

Foulkes and Anthony (1957) represent yet another approach to the group as a unit. Although British, they differ from the Tavistock Institute theorists Bion, Ezriel, and Sutherland. Foulkes and Anthony adhere so closely to the Freudian idiom that they may be related to the Intrapersonalists as well as to the Integralists. Despite the fact that they stress the group as the focus of treatment and the main therapeutic agent, they see the individual member as the object of treatment. In practice, Foulkes seems to assume that interpretations addressed to the individual are simultaneously addressed to the group and may therefore be classed as group-oriented interventions.

Although Foulkes and Anthony share the view of the other Integralists that the group responds to the unconscious needs and motivations of the individual members, they believe that this kind of response develops slowly, rather than precipitously and spontaneously. The sharing of unconscious motivations, according to Foulkes, occurs only in the advanced stages of group formation. Anthony does not accept the fact that group members may appear to be dependent on the therapist during the early phases of the group as evidence of shared unconscious group motivation. He believes instead that such leader-centered activity occurs during the phase when the group members are acting more like a collection of individuals than a group. If groups are permitted to remain at this level of development, then, according to Anthony, the relevant group phenomena will not be manifested (1966). It is for this reason, he believes, that many group therapists are unaware of the unique potential of the group therapy setting and persist in dealing with individuals. The evidence accepted by Anthony that the group is guided by the members' sensitivity to or understanding of one another's needs is somewhat different from that proposed by the previously mentioned Integralists. He believes that the shared group unconscious is demonstrated principally in the fact that some patient behavior and needs appear to represent the complement or the supplement of the behavior and needs of other patients. Thus, dominance of one is supported by the submissiveness of the other, activity in some is enhanced by the passivity of others, and so forth (Anthony, 1966).

The development of this alleged unconscious symbiotic relationship is facilitated by confrontation, growing imitation, and identification.

ACCESSIBILITY

The Integralists have added very little to the material presented by the Intrapersonalists and Interpersonalists regarding the conditions which make the individual more accessible to change. The circumstances which enable patients to tolerate their anxieties and permit them to respond with reduced defensiveness are not adequately developed by the Integralists. It may be inferred that membership in the basic assumption groups provides cohesiveness and a sense of belonging which facilitates the patients' accessibility as described previously. However, although these feelings of closeness may provide support for the patients, they may also strengthen resistances. The major therapeutic benefit, according to Bion, lies not in such cohesiveness, but in the conscious experiencing of a high order of work group activity—that is, learning to cooperate in a work group.

MECHANISMS OF CHANGE

The principal technique for effecting change, according to Bion, is the therapist's confrontation of the group with the basic assumption it appears to have accepted. The therapist in effect interprets the group's transference toward him and toward others in the group. Interpretations are made primarily by the therapist. They are used when the therapist is reasonably clear about the group's attitude toward him or toward a patient. Interpretations are also made when a patient acts as if he believed the group had a definite and specific attitude toward him. The focus of interpretations is on the here-and-now, highlighting group-shared behavior concerning the issue of securing leadership that will provide fulfillment of primitive wishes.

Two major approaches to effecting therapeutic changes are implied by Bion: (1) efforts to work through, very thoroughly, the primitive "primal scene" as it is disclosed in the group, and (2) the repeated confrontation of the group with its efforts to manipulate the therapist and group members. The effectiveness of confrontation and interpretation is assumed to result from the fact that when an individual is confronted with reality such contact compels regard for truth, and the work group culture is reinstated.

Bion apparently believes that as the patient becomes increasingly aware that his basic assumptions cannot be met, he is induced to adopt a more realistic and hopefully a more satisfying mode of functioning. The aims of treatment are facilitated to the degree that the individual's appraisal of the group's attitude toward him and expectations of him becomes more realistic. By virtue of repeated and consistent confrontation, the group's basic assumption behaviors are brought under conscious control, gradually lose their threatening nature, and interfere less with the accomplishment of the primary work goals.

By interpreting to the group rather than to the individual, Bion assumes that the effects will be wider and more appropriate, since each individual will find all interpretations relevant to some degree. The aim is not individual treatment in public, but a focus on the actual experiences of the group—that is, the way in which the group and the individuals deal with one another. The ultimate goal of therapy is to aid the patient to become more effective in the groups of which he is a member. This is a relevant goal since all men are impelled to be members of groups and group-functioning is required of all individuals.

A serious limitation of Bion's presentation of his theories, to date, is his incomplete account of therapeutic movement. This aspect of the theory has been dealt with more fully by Ezriel and Whitaker and Lieberman. These writers view the therapist's role as principally that of influencing the processes whereby group solutions may be established, maintained, or modified.

They believe that the occurrence of a given group conflict may permit the achievement of more useful solutions provided that the culture of the group has shifted appropriately. This view of group-functioning represents a considerable deviation from Bion's, since he believes that the same Ba issue, no matter how often repeated, leads to inevitable frustration unless the therapist's interpretations are accepted.

Whitaker and Lieberman assume that groups are capable of dealing with new aspects of old conflicts, feelings, and relationships in the course of time. Conflicts are always associated with anxiety and the solutions to them do not progress in a linear fashion from unsuccessful to successful-restrictive, and finally to successful-enabling. The cultural context which has been established, however, will affect the nature of the solutions which are acceptable to or required by the group.

An assumption underlying their view of the treatment process, based on the thinking of the psychoanalyst French, is that the group focal conflict is a derivative of each individual's nuclear conflict (1952). Although they accept Bion's conviction that attention to the shared group conflicts will usefully influence the individual, they believe it is appropriate to deal also with the individual psychodynamics and with observed interpersonal relationships.

Whitaker and Lieberman seem to represent a transition phase between the extreme Integralist position and an Interpersonalist approach. The essential mechanism of change according to them is learning by reality-testing. As the patient copes with anxiety, he learns that his habitual solutions, which he has heretofore believed necessary for survival, are not required.

This theory of the therapeutic process assumes, of course, that the group provides experiences which objectively demonstrate that the anticipated disasters do not in fact occur. It is the combination of common group tension and a setting which affords the group member a sense of safety that permits him realistically to change his views and expectations. In addition, the patient may benefit by observing the position which others take with regard to the group focal conflict and the consequences of such positions. He can re-examine his own position with or without verbalizing the consequences of such a review.

Ezriel is more similar to Bion than to Whitaker and Lieberman in his insistence that the therapist attend closely to the group's transference to the therapist. Ezriel believes that interpretations of an individual's transference must be deferred in favor of identifying a shared group tension. Having identified the common issue, Ezriel moves away from Bion's insistence that interpretations be limited to the group as a unit, and undertakes to demonstrate to each individual in the group how he has been dealing with the shared tension. In this manner the therapist highlights the individual's contribution to the development, maintenance, and attempted resolution of the tension (Ezriel, 1950).

Among the Integralists we include Foulkes, who represents an approach to groups derived from Freudian theory. The mechanisms of change stressed by Foulkes concern the interpretation of the group's contributions as equivalents of free association. When all conversations in the group are presumed to be equivalent to free associations in their unconscious aspects, interpretations of such group free associations are believed to give access to the repressed unconscious of the members. The interpretations are aimed at enlarging the group's area of awareness by bringing unconscious components into consciousness.

Although Foulkes recognizes that group therapy can be used to communicate insights regarding unconscious problems of each individual, he is diffident about assuming this as the relevant mechanism for analytic group psychotherapy. He insists that interpretations are to be group-oriented and hypothesizes that even interpretations addressed specifically to an individual may be interpreted as directed toward the group, since, like any other communication, interpretations are of a multidimensional and multipersonal consequence. Thus, Foulkes sees interpretations directed to the individual as relating also to the group, while Bion sees interpretations directed to the group as relating to the individual.

Foulkes and Anthony believe that analytic group therapy does not compete with psychoanalysis in the area of analysis of transference neurosis: "It is not that group-analysis does less; it does something different . . ." (Foulkes and Anthony, 1957, p. 22). Foulkes places emphasis on the analysis of transference in the sense of distortions. Like most group therapists he is concerned with the relationship between the therapist and the patient in the present rather than with uncovering the psychogenesis of illness. Anthony appears to have moved toward a model approaching that of "discrimination-learning." He suggests that an essential dynamic of therapeutic value may derive from the fact that the individual in the group is confronted with the discrepancy between his expectations regarding the group behavior or the leader's behavior and his actual experience with the group and the leader. From such a discrepancy the patient may learn that his expectations are inappropriate and that other more relevant attitudes and behaviors can be utilized (Anthony, 1966).

Discussion and Conclusions

Integralists appear to have extended the Intrapersonalists' and Interpersonalists' observation that the verbal and nonverbal participation of group members may be interpreted as free associations around a common theme, conflict and basic motivation. The Integralists believe that the contributions of the group members deal not only with the analysis of the idiosyncratic conflicts of the individual, as believed by the Intrapersonalists and Interpersonalists, but with the shared conflicts. The value of the group is based on the assumption that the group shares the same conflicts and irrational aims and can, therefore, be treated as a unit rather than as a set of individuals. Interpretations and confrontations with reality are believed to be effective for each member to the degree that he participates in the group-stimulated and -shared problem. The Integralist places more emphasis on the immediate conditions which stimulate and maintain the conflicts than on their genetic origins for each individual.

It is clear that the therapist who attempts to deal with the individual patient has no shortage of stimuli to occupy him in his treatment efforts. When the therapist is confronted with a number of patients in a group, the stimuli that are presented to him are multiplied not arithmetically but geometrically by reason of the multiplicity of interactions. As a consequence, the group therapist has a great need to adopt a simplifying principle that will permit him to treat the patients with economy of effort and no loss of effectiveness. That the solution is simply the recognition that a group of diverse individuals represent a composite "single patient" is, at the very least, one of the most fortunate therapeutic coincidences yet discovered. The need for such a solution has been more adequately demonstrated than has the effectiveness of the solution.

Integralists other than Bion do not appear to assume that *all* group behaviors reflect shared conflicts, but believe that it is more useful to deal *only* with those aspects of group behavior which can convincingly be interpreted as shared. A problem which is shared by all group-oriented therapists is that of deciding when they have identified a common unconscious group tension. The process is essentially a deductive one based on the behavior of each individual. There is the "clear and present danger" that the greater the therapist's conviction regarding the nature of the conflicts which may be found in the group, the less evidence he requires for confirmation of his expectations. It is therefore possible that the behavior of an individual may be interpreted as evidence for a group conflict or of a "basic assumption."

One of the more dubious conventions adopted by Bion and other Integralists is that silence and nonparticipation of group members may be interpreted as agreement and consent to the group activity. As a consequence two people who are interacting in an otherwise silent group provide the therapist with the basis for an interpretation of a group-shared conflict. The silent members, by not actively opposing or commenting on the activity, share responsibility for it. The danger of generalizing to the group from the behavior of one or even a few group members is somewhat reduced, however, by the procedure introduced by Ezriel. He requires that group interpretations be documented by explicit reference to the individual ways in which patients respond to the group-shared conflict.

A related problem is that the Integralist, by offering interpretations of presumably unconscious group-shared phenomena, is by definition the only uninvolved member of the group. He is, therefore, the only one capable of making and judging the accuracy of the interpretation. This is a problem which is not unfamiliar to the individual treatment setting. One of the frequently cited advantages of the group therapy treatment form is that the group provides the opportunity for a more objective analysis of transference and countertransference. Among Intrapersonalists and Transactionalists, particularly the latter, it is assumed that patients and therapist all share the opportunity to observe and to evaluate the interpersonal interactions and transactions of others in the group. A consensus thus achieved regarding the behavior and the "meaning" of such behavior carries considerable weight. The likelihood that a therapist's countertransference would go undetected is lessened in Transactional groups.

It must also be recognized that the group-therapy setting provides a uniquely powerful social influence situation. It combines the conditions of ambiguity of treatment process, authority of the therapist, and the suggestibility of patients. The group rarely is able to achieve complete agreement on any issue, even on the rejection of an interpretation offered to the group as an entity. One of the important pressures operating to produce acceptance of a group interpretation is the fact that the group presents a seemingly diffuse set of data and stimulation; the interpretation offers to bring order out of this chaos. This is a very attractive offer. However, when a member seems to offer documentation of an interpretation (post hoc), it must be remembered that this "confirmation" can also be a function of suggestion.

The theoretical advances in analytic group psychotherapy represented by the Integralists appear to be: (1) the formulation by Bion that the seemingly divergent and individualistic concerns of the group members represent a fairly narrow range of shared issues; (2) the modification by Ezriel and Whitaker and Lieberman that behavior of the group (like that of the individual) may be conceptualized as centering around motivational conflicts and their attempted resolutions; and (3) the idea that group-centered interpretations of shared unconscious and preconscious motivations can be made with no loss of power and with considerable gain in efficiency. What now remains is the demonstration that this theoretical "advance" has been accompanied by therapeutic advance.

Although Integralists have relatively little to add to what Intrapersonalists and Interpersonalists have previously stated regarding the utility of the group in facilitating the patient's accessibility to new experience, Bion's descriptions of group phenomena which he regularly encounters raise some serious questions. Most theorists believe that the treatment situation must develop and maintain an optimal level of anxiety in patients. The extremes of panic or apathy are to be avoided as they are not conducive to the development of either curiosity or insight about one's self. The Ba groups are described, however, as evoking a high degree of anxiety, sufficient in some cases to precipitate a psychotic-like regression. It is not clear, therefore, why such states are considered as conducive to analytic work. According to Bion's own descriptions of the Ba groups, the patients in such affective states become less accessible to verbal communications and to rational thought and, indeed, may actively resist any efforts at rational thought.

Bion's unique emphasis on maintaining all therapist interventions at the group level rather than the individual has been tempered by his followers to a point which may be more acceptable to Intrapersonalists and Interpersonalists. The problem remains, however, whether interpretations of generalized motivations and conflicts can be effective in producing individual change independent of explicit efforts to specify their unique relevance to each member of the group. We do not quarrel with the view that the concepts of pairing (sex), fight-flight (aggression), and dependency may adequately classify the motivational states of patients in a group. Psychoanalysts have long contented themselves with only the concepts of sex and aggression, and the addition of dependency may be useful. The problem, however, lies in the implication that these three concepts adequately represent the basic dynamics of groups.

Bion has in effect undertaken to describe characteristic group processes which are independent of group composition, stated goals, size, leadership, etc. This approach to groups appears to be analogous to that of the "trait" theorist and suffers from all the limitations that have been experienced by such personality theorists.

The value of group dynamics for the advancement of the field must lie in the further specification of the variables which influence the development of such group phenomena. One of the least developed aspects of the theory is the description of the conditions which permit the individual and the group to move from one group culture to another or from one basic assumption to another. The concept of valency and the assumption that exposure to reality has a compelling effect have no more explanatory power than coincidence or a *deus ex machina*. What is lacking is a detailed theory regarding therapeutic change.

The three types of therapists appear to encompass two distinct, yet quite familiar, traditional approaches to the conception of mental health and well-being. The Intrapersonalists and Interpersonalists believe that mental health is represented by man's expression of his unique individuality and by his ability to free himself from the constraints of his environment, the group, the culture, and the like. The Integralists take the diametrically opposed position that man's well-being depends on his full participation and integration in the group, the culture, and society. An additional, overlapping view is represented by Existentialists, who are concerned with preserving and enhancing man's ineffable humanness and are less concerned with the aims of individuality or "finding oneself by losing oneself" in the group.

At the present state of the art of psychotherapy, the practitioner's use of what may be therapeutic is based more on the congeniality of the philosophy he adopts than the empirical evidence of its therapeutic consequences. It may be dreary and possibly mischievous to recapitulate the now familiar exhortation that the field cannot resolve its theoretical differences until it undertakes to specify what it will accept as evidence of meaningful outcome. Such a complaint is frequently interpreted as an invitation to specify the aims of therapy, which becomes yet another exercise in rhetoric without referent and grammar without syntax. The fact remains that the therapist cannot defer treatment pending receipt of the ultimate answers from the ultimate researcher.

Group therapy's widespread popularity is further evidence of the therapist's courage, which permits him to "bash on regardless." After some thirty years of claiming success, group therapists find themselves in the rather anomalous position of only now becoming preoccupied with understanding in what ways—if any—the group contributes to the therapeutic process. The need to cope with the multiplicity and complexity of group phenomena requires that the therapist adopt some simplifying principles. Some have found it convenient to maintain their gaze fixedly on the individual; others, on the interaction, the transactional unit, or, more recently, the group as an entity. To treat the group as a unit requires the assumption either that the group members share, albeit unconsciously, the same motivations or that the leader will deal *only* with those issues which can be identified as shared, and will ignore all others. In the face of complexity, the clinician, like the scientist, tends to invoke Occam's razor, but in group therapy, as in any other enterprise, the principle of adopting the most parsimonious explanation may not lead to clarity but only to simplicity.

In our view, the fundamental task for group therapists and individual therapists alike is increased understanding of the treatment process as it relates to the particular patients and particular problems that are to be treated. The premise has direct implications for the therapist's growing interest in group dynamics and group processes, which is based on the seemingly plausible assumption that students of small groups have accumulated information that, if made available to the group therapist, would make treatment in the group setting more effective. The group therapist who immerses himself in the vast literature of group dynamics may be rewarded by recognizing phenomena and principles which can be utilized to facilitate the therapeutic process. The probability of making such discoveries would be significantly enhanced, however, if the therapist's approach to the literature and to his social science colleagues were more focused. The question is not simply what has the researcher learned about groups, but rather what has the researcher learned about groups that would facilitate the achievement of specific events that the therapist believes appropriate and necessary for treatment. The therapist must be quite explicit regarding his hypotheses, not only about the ultimate aims of therapy, but also about the mediating goals—that is, the clinician's assumptions about the steps and stages which must be achieved if treatment is to be effective.

The group therapist, like all therapists, is interested in advances in basic research; however, he cannot expect that the researcher, by sheer serendipity, will stumble on principles which will make the therapist's job easier. The therapist must himself be in a position to recognize and to utilize such basic contributions. Such recognition depends on the "prepared" mind.

The fundamental problem which confronts the group psychotherapist is not the process of group psychotherapy, but the process of any and all psychotherapy. The aim of the psychotherapist, independent of the setting, remains the same—namely, to increase the patient's social effectiveness and personal comfort. When a general theory of change is achieved, it will be necessary only to devise adaptations of the general theory to the group setting. The special conditions to be developed or the unique attributes which inhere in a particular setting could then be identified. This step is contingent on the development of clear criteria of therapeutic change. It is unlikely that we shall recognize answers if we do not recognize the questions.

Note: I am deeply grateful to Mr. Barry Wolfe and to Drs. Merton Gill, David Shakow, Margaret Rioch, and Pierre Turquet for their generous assistance in the preparation of this chapter. They do not, however, assume any responsibility for the accuracy of the reporting, nor may it be assumed that they share the author's formulations and interpretations.

REFERENCES

Ackerman, N. W. "Symptom, Defense and Growth in Group Process." *International Journal of Group Psychotherapy*, 2 (1961), 131–142.

Anthony, E. J. "The Generic Elements in Dyadic and in Group Psychotherapy." Presented at the American Group Psychotherapy Association Meeting, January 28, 1966.

Asch, S. E. *Social Psychology*. New York: Prentice-Hall, 1952.

Bach, G. *Intensive Group Psychotherapy*. New York: Ronald Press, 1954.

Bennis, W. G., and Shepard, H. A. "A Theory of Group Development." *Human Relations*, 9 (1956), 415–437.

Berger, M. "An Overview of Group Psychotherapy: Its Past, Present, and Future Development." *International Journal of Group Psychotherapy*, 12, No. 3 (1962), 287–294.

Berne, E. " 'Psychoanalytic' versus 'Dynamic' Group Therapy." *International Journal of Group Psychotherapy*, 10 (1960), 98–103.

Berne, E. *Transactional Analysis in Psychotherapy*. New York: Grove Press, 1961.

Berne, E. *Principles of Group Treatment*. New York: Oxford University Press, 1966.

Bion, W. R. *Experiences in Groups*. New York: Basic Books, 1959.

Borgatta, E. F., Bales, R. F., and Hare, A. P. *Small Groups*. New York: Knopf, 1955.

Cartwright, D., and Zander, A. (eds.). *Group Dynamics: Research and Theory*. 2nd ed.; Evanston, Ill.: Row, Peterson, 1960.

Crutchfield, R. S. "Personal and Situational Factors in Conformity to Group Pressure." *Acta Psychologica et Pharmacologica Neerlandica* (Amsterdam), 15 (1959), 386–388.

Cushing, J. G. N. "Report of the Committee on the Evaluation of Psychoanalytic Therapy." *Bulletin of the American Psychoanalytic Association*, 8 (1950), 44–50.

Durkin, Helen E. "Toward a Common Basis for Group Dynamics." *International Journal of Group Psychotherapy*, 1 (1957), 115–130.

Durkin, Helen E. *The Group in Depth*. New York: International Universities Press, 1964.

Ezriel, H. "A Psychoanalytic Approach to Group Treatment." *British Journal of Medical Psychology*, 23 (1950), 59–74.

Ezriel, H. "Notes on Psychoanalytic Group Therapy. II. Interpretation and Research." *Psychiatry*, 15 (1952), 119–126.

Ezriel, H. "Experimentation within the Psychoanalytic Session." *British Journal of Philosophical Sciences*, 7 (1956), 29–48.

Ezriel, H. "The Role of Transference in Psychoanalytic and Other Approaches to Group Treatment." *Acta Psychotherapeutica*, 7 (1959), 101–116.

Foulkes, S. H. *Introduction to Group-Analytic Psychotherapy*. London: Heinemann, 1948.

Foulkes, S. H. "Group Analytic Dynamics with Specific Reference to Psychoanalytic Concepts." *International Journal of Group Psychotherapy*, 7 (1957), 40–52.

Foulkes, S. H. "Group Process and the Individual in the Therapeutic Group." *British Journal of Medical Psychology*, 34 (1961), 23–31.

Foulkes, S. H. *Therapeutic Group Analysis*. New York: International Universities Press, 1964.

Foulkes, S. H., and Anthony, E. J. *Group Psychotherapy: The Psychoanalytic Approach*. Baltimore: Penguin, 1957.

Frank, J. D. "Some Aspects of Cohesiveness and Conflict in Psychiatric Outpatient Groups." *Bulletin of the Johns Hopkins Hospital*, 101 (1957), 224–231. (a)

Frank, J. D. "Some Determinents, Manifestations, and Effects of Cohesiveness in Therapy Groups." *International Journal of Group Psychotherapy*, 7 (1957), 53–63. (b)

Frank, J. D. "Therapy in a Group Setting." In M. I. Stein (ed.), *Contemporary Psychotherapies*. New York: The Free Press of Glencoe, 1961. Pp. 42–59.

French, T. M. *The Integration of Behavior*. Chicago: University of Chicago Press, 1952. Vols. I, II.

Freud, S. "On the History of the Psycho-analytic Movement" (1914). *The Standard Edition of the Complete Psychological Works of. . . .* London: Hogarth Press. Vol. 14, pp. 7–66. (Also in *Collected Papers of. . . .* New York: Basic Books, 1959. Vol 1, pp. 287–359.)

Freud, S. "Group Psychology and the Analysis of the Ego" (1921). *The Standard Edition of the Complete Psychological Works of. . . .* London: Hogarth Press. Vol. 18, pp. 69–143.

Freud, S. "An Outline of Psychoanalysis" (1938). *The Standard Edition of the Complete Psychological Works of. . . .* London: Hogarth Press. Vol. 23.

Fromm-Reichmann, Frieda. *Principles of Intensive Psychotherapy*. Chicago: University of Chicago Press, 1950.

Gill, M. M. "Ego Psychology and Psychotherapy." *Psychoanalytic Quarterly*, 20 (1951), 62–71.

Gill, M. M. "Psychoanalysis and Exploratory Psychotherapy." *Journal of the American Psychoanalytic Association*, 2 (1954), 771–797.

Harvey, O. J., and Consalvi, C. "Status and Conformity to Pressures in Informal Groups." *Journal of Abnormal Social Psychology*, 60, No. 2 (1960), 182–187.

Hill, W. F. "Therapeutic Mechanisms." In W. F. Hill (ed.), *Collected Papers on Group Psychotherapy*. Provo: Utah State Hospital, 1961.

Illing, H. A. "On the Present Trends in Group Psychotherapy." *Human Relations*, 10 (1957), 77–84.

Kelman, H. C. "The Role of the Group in the Induction of Therapeutic Change." *International Journal of Group Psychotherapy*, 13, No. 4 (1963), 399–432.

Kubie, L. S. "Some Theoretical Concepts Underlying the Relationship between Individual and Group Therapy." *International Journal of Group Psychotherapy*, 8 (1958), 3–19.

Lewin, K. "Frontiers in Group Dynamics: Concept, Method, and Reality in Social Sciences: Social Equilibria and Social Change." *Human Relations*, 1 (1947), 5–41.

Lewin, K. *Field Theory in Social Science*. New York: Harper, 1951.

Locke, N. *Group Psychoanalysis: Theory and Technique*. New York: New York University Press, 1961.

Locke, N. "Group Psychotherapy, Group Psychoanalysis, and Scientific Method." In J. L. Moreno (ed.), *The International Handbook of Group Psychotherapy*. New York: Philosophical Library, 1966. Pp. 294–298.

Mann, J. "Some Theoretic Concepts of the Group Process." *International Journal of Group Psychotherapy*, 5 (1955), 235–241.

Moreno, J. L. "The Group Psychotherapy Movement, Past, Present and Future." *International Journal of Group Psychotherapy*, Vol. 15, No. 1 (1962), 21–23.

Mowrer, O. H. *The New Group Therapy*. Princeton, N. J.: Van Nostrand, 1964.

Mullan, H., and Rosenbaum, M. *Group Psychotherapy*. New York: The Free Press of Glencoe, 1962.

Osborn, A. F. *Applied Imagination*. New York: Scribner's, 1953.

Parloff, M. B. "Group Dynamics and Group Psychotherapy: The State of the Union." *International Journal of Group Psychotherapy*, 13 (1963), 393–398.

Parnes, S. J., and Meadows, A. "Effects of Brainstorming Instructions on Creative Problem-solving by Trained and Untrained Subjects." *Journal of Educational Psychology*, 50 (1959), 171–176.

Redl, F. "Group Emotion and Leadership." *Psychiatry*, 5 (1942), 573–596.

Scheidlinger, S. *Psychoanalysis and Group Behavior*. New York: Norton, 1952.

Scheidlinger, S. "Group Process in Group Psychotherapy. Part I." *American Journal of Psychotherapy*, 14 (1960), 104–120. (a)

Scheidlinger, S. "Group Process in Group Psychotherapy. Part II." *American Journal of Psychotherapy*, 14 (1960), 346–363. (b)

Schutz, W. C. *FIRO: A Three Dimensional Theory of Interpersonal Behavior*. New York: Rinehart, 1958.

Schwartz, E. K., and Wolf, A. "Psychoanalysis in Groups: The Mystique of Group Dynamics." In *Topical Problems of Psychotherapy*. New York: Karger, 1960. Vol. 2, pp. 119–154.

Semrad, E., and Arsenian, J. "The Use of Group Process Group Dynamics." *American Journal of Psychiatry*, 108 (1951), 358–363.

Sherif, M. "A Study of Some Special Factors in Perception." *Archives of Psychology*, No. 187 (1935).

Slavson, S. R. *Analytic Group Psychotherapy*. New York: Columbia University Press, 1952.

Slavson, S. R. "A Critique of the Group Therapy Literature." *Acta Psychotherapeutica*, 10 (1962), 62–73.

Slavson, S. R. A *Textbook in Analytic Group Psychotherapy*. New York: International Universities Press, 1964.

Stock, Dorothy, and Thelen, H. A. *Emotional Dynamics and Group Culture*. New York: International Universities Press, 1958.

Stock, Dorothy, and Lieberman, M. A. "Methodological Issues in the Assessment of Total Group Phenomena in Group Therapy." *International Journal of Group Psychotherapy*, Vol. 12, No. 3 (1962), 312–325.

Sutherland, J. D. "Notes on Psychoanalytic Group Psychotherapy." *Psychiatry*, 15 (1952), 111–117.

Trist, E. L., and Sofer, C. *Explorations in Group Relations*. Leicester, Eng.: Leicester University Press, 1959.

Wassell, B. B. *Group Psychoanalysis*. New York: Philosophical Library, 1959.
Whitaker, D. S., and Lieberman, M. A. *Psychotherapy Through the Group Process*. New York: Atherton Press, 1964. P. 305.
Whitman, R. M., and Stock, Dorothy "The Group Focal Conflict." *Psychiatry*, Vol. 21, No. 3 (1958), 269–276.
Wolf, A., and Schwartz, E. K. *Psychoanalysis in Groups*. New York: Grune & Stratton, 1962.
Ziferstein, I., and Grotjahn, M. "Psychoanalysis and Group Psychotherapy." In Frieda Fromm-Reichmann and J. L. Moreno (eds.), *Progress in Psychotherapy*. New York: Grune & Stratton, 1956. Vol. 1, pp. 248–255.

21

Psychoanalytic Therapies and the Low Socioeconomic Population

SALVADOR MINUCHIN

Psychoanalytic therapies have evolved slowly from the classical Freudian model for analyst and patient. The theoretical changes introduced by the culturalist school of psychoanalysis and the works of Hartmann, Kris, and Lowenstein, with their emphasis on ego processes, became a point of departure for a new look at therapeutic techniques. The one-to-one therapeutic relationship has expanded to include the therapeutic group, the family group, and groups of families. The couch has been replaced in some instances by the face-to-face transaction, and on occasion the session moves from the analyst's office to the home of the patient. The shared case and stereoscopic therapy have expanded to multiple therapists working with one patient and to multiple impact therapy.

Nonetheless, for all their present variability, psychoanalytic therapies and psychotherapy have consistently failed to reach the low socioeconomic population. Explanations for this failure have generally stressed lack of motivation and an inability to introspect in this population. It is the purpose of this chapter to consider the characteristics of this population in greater detail, to view these characteristics against the implicit requirements of most psychoanalytic therapies, and to consider models and adaptations for therapeutic work.

Implicit Requirements of Psychoanalytic Therapies

It is important to review first the assumptions on which psychoanalytic therapy usually proceeds. These are formal and mainly implicit requirements that the patient must fulfill to be a suitable candidate. These criteria must be openly considered in relation to the low socioeconomic population (Bernstein, 1964; Riessman, 1962).

In general, it is assumed that to use psychoanalysis and psychoanalytic therapy successfully, the patient must have a minimal ability to

(1) observe his participation in events;

(2) observe his affective-cognitive inner reactions and processes;

(3) remember past events;

(4) be able to establish a relationship between past events and present feelings and behavior;

(5) use communication in verbal channels and with the intention to share information; and

(6) agree with the therapist that solutions to his present problems can be found by transactions at the verbal level. Further,

(7) verbal meanings should have a shared significance between patient and therapist; and

(8) patient and therapist should be able to develop a meaningful and effective relationship.

Three basic characteristics emerge from this roster as necessary for the use of psychoanalytic therapy: a capacity for self-observation; an ability to communicate the observed; and a capacity to use another person as a helper.

Can the low socioeconomic population fit into the mold of the psychoanalytic techniques? If this is not easily done, is it possible to develop analytically based therapeutic techniques useful to the very heterogeneous group that comprises the 9.4 million families of the poor in the United States (Bernard, 1965; Gould, 1967)?

Characteristics of the Low Socioeconomic Population

It is obvious that the population we are considering is not monolithic. It has been classified according to religion, ethnic affiliation, geographic subcultures, stable and disorganized qualities, working-class and low socioeconomic groups, level of family organization, and so on. It will be necessary in the near future to clarify its further subgroupings, clinical and dynamic as well as sociological. For the present, our generalizations should be made with some caution and with the acknowledgment that they cannot possibly be applicable to all of the people who fall into this socioeconomic group. From my own work with severely disadvantaged families (Minuchin, Auerswald, King, and Rabinowitz, 1964) and from the work of others who have observed and described segments of the lower-class population, both stable and disorganized (Malone, 1963; Pavenstedt, 1965), it seems clear that some of the characteristics considered necessary for successful therapy are different in this general population. Within the scope of this chapter we shall concentrate particularly on the capacity for self-observation, and the ability to communicate what has been observed—two processes which seem sufficiently different in this population to deserve exploration. To understand these psychological differences we turn to socialization processes in the family, where these capacities are ordinarily learned. Their failure to develop needs to be understood as a basis for therapeutic planning.

The Development of the Capacity for Self-Observation

We posit that the epigenetic development of self-observation in a normal child requires: (1) a grasp of reality as organized along a certain order, and (2) the experience that "I am affecting my environment."

The development in the normal child of object constancy, which is essential for the grasp of reality, requires the experience of repetitive encounters with things and people in similar situations. A child needs to develop trust that the significant objects in his environment continue to exist and retain their basic characteristics even when they cannot be seen or touched. Schachtel (1959) focuses on the progressive interrelation between the following factors:

> a) the discovery of object constancy; b) the power to make an object reappear—be it the mother, by crying, or the spool, by pulling at a thread; c) the capacity to recover an object by going after it and finding it in reality; d) the confidence that an object will continue to exist and eventually will be available again even if, for the time being, one can neither make it reappear nor go and look for it; and e) the capacity to keep hold of an object in *thought*—that is, to develop focal attention to the idea of an object even when the object is not available for present need satisfaction, manipulation, perception, and exploration (p. 264).

In other words, the child's developing sense of reality and of himself in action in this reality depends on the predictability of his environment.

The concept of the discovery of "myself" through "my effect on my environment," which has been explored by so many writers, takes a meaningful new slant in White's (1963) concept of competence and the feeling of efficacy in the child. White points out that the child's sense of self-esteem grows with his competence in mastering and affecting his world of things and people. "Knowledge consists of the several consequences of our several actions. It is a knowledge of action possibilities. Concepts consist of information coded for action . . . efforts produced without focalized attention, intention and directed effort are experienced as *happening to us*; they are not felt as products of ourselves as agents" (White, 1965). It becomes important, therefore, in the development of the observing ego that the child have a focused experience of himself as an agent of change.

In what ways are these processes different in the lower-class population? Various writers have described the immediate environment in which the lower working-class child grows up, pointing up some of the factors that would tend, in our terms, to block the development of a strong sense of self and the capacity for self-observation. Deutsch (1964), for instance, has observed that in the overcrowded living conditions of this population privacy is nonexistent; families are large with little opportunity for individualization. Further, he points out that these children are restricted in the variety of stimulation. In a world in which the child is insufficiently called upon to respond to stimuli, his general level of responsiveness will diminish and he learns inattention. This learned inattention will have an effect on his ability to recall. The relationship among the adults and the children is such that the underlining of shared experience is infrequent and, therefore, the child is unfocused on his experience.

Bernstein (1964) has pointed out that in this population the authority relationship between parents and children supports an externally organized perception of structure and power:

> Where the child is subject to status-oriented appeals which change swiftly to a power relationship then a whole order of relationships is not learned (p. 200).
>
> Further, if it is the case that authority relationships within the family tend to be status and power relations rather than person-oriented relations then the focus of the discipline of relation will be upon the consequences of the act rather than upon the intent of the child (p. 201).
>
> In situations which elicit perceptions of ambiguity or ambivalency the individual may be unable to tolerate the resultant tension involved in loss of structure. He will tend to move towards a well articulated social structure where hierarchy, age, age relations, and sex will provide clear unambiguous prescriptions for appropriate behavior as a means of controlling stress (p. 202).

The child does not develop the sense that he is himself either responsible or effective.

Melvin L. Kohn (1964) has also stressed the external nature of the child's developing standards. In dealing with the value system of working-class parents he has noted that their values in socializing their children are traditional. These parents want their children to be neat and clean, to obey and respect others, and to conform to *externally* imposed standards. He points out that the values involved in parental education come from the lower-class occupations that rely traditionally on obedience, manipulation of things, standardization, and supervision. In socialization for this type of occupation, the important thing for the parents is that the child should not transgress externally imposed rules.

My own experience has been with an even more disorganized and unstable section of the low socioeconomic population, in which these patterns are seen in a more exaggerated and destructive form. In working with disorganized families my colleagues and I have been impressed by certain qualities of the physical and human environment and by the reaction patterns which they seem to foster.

The essential feature of the environment is its impermanence and unpredictability. These characteristics make it difficult for the growing child to define himself in relation to his world. In home visits we encountered a world in which objects are moved around: beds shared by two or more children can be turned over to a different child or to a transient or semipermanent visitor, while the child is crowded into a section of another bed. The geography of the house and its arrangements handicap development of a sense of "I have my place in my world." Meals have no set time, order, or place. The same mother who prepares four individual and different dinners one day, according to the wishes of the children, will prepare nothing on another day, during which the children have to look in the closets for available food, making their meals out of potato chips and soda.

Interpersonal contacts have these same erratic and impermanent qualities. In these large families the care of young children is divided among multiple figures. Mother, aunts, and grandmother, as well as older siblings, care for the young child. Sometimes they shower him with stimulation, and at other times he is left for long periods wandering through the house unattended. There can be elements of security in this multiple care, but danger lurks in those periods when the child is lost between the interstices of responsibility. Multiple erratic nurturant figures can increase the child's sense of an unstable world and hinder his movement from a diffuse to a more focused sense of self.

In socializing the child, these families seem to be characterized by two major features: the parents' responses to children's behavior are relatively random and, therefore, deficient in the qualities that convey rules which can be internalized; and the parental emphasis is on control and inhibition of behavior rather than on guiding responses.

One sees in these families a pattern of parental reactions that operate like traffic signals: they carry the instructions of "don't" at the moment, but they do not carry instructions for behavior in the future (Hess, Shipman, and Jackson, 1965). The unpredictability of parental controlling signals handicaps the child's development of rules. He cannot determine what part of his behavior is inappropriate, and he learns to search out the limits of permissible behavior through inspection of the parents' mood responses. He learns that the "don't's" of behavior are related to the pain or power of mother or other powerful figures. "Don't do this because I say so," or "Don't do this because you make me nervous," or "Don't do this because I'll beat you." Lacking norms to regulate behavior and caught in experiences that hinge on immediate interpersonal control, the child needs continuous parental participation to organize interpersonal transactions. These transactions are inevitably ineffective; they perpetuate a situation in which an overtaxed mother responds erratically to a confused child, who behaves in ways that will assure him of reorganizing controlling contact.

In these families, life experiences are characterized by impermanence, randomness, fast changes in mood, accelerated tempo in interpersonal transactions, control boundaries that shift with parents' moods, lack of guidance and orientation to norms. This kaleidoscope of moving and shifting stimuli hinders the ability of the child to develop the object constancy essential for keeping hold of an object in thought, and it hinders the development of control over impulsivity. Fast, action-oriented impulsive reactions continue to characterize the child who grows in this environment, even at ages where more complex and reflective controls are possible. The kind of reactivity perpetuated in the child represents both an emotional organization and a cognitive style. The child is impulsive and global in his responses, tends to search the immediate reactions of others for clues to the solution of conflict situations, and remains relatively unexercised in the use of focal attention for observing himself or the specific characteristics of a situation.

That these qualities form a coherent syndrome has been suggested by the reports of several investigators working with different populations. Wolff (Wolff, 1965; Wolff and White, 1965), working with infants, has noted a correlation between attention and inhibition of motor discharge. Kagan and Wright (1963), who studied middle-class children of various ages, noted a relation between response time, focal attention, and cognitive style. The ability to inhibit motor discharge and modulate behavior in the face of irrelevant stimulation is correlated in his studies with analytic cognitive style. The tendency toward motoric impulse discharge is associated with poor focal attention and a conceptual style that is global and nonanalytic. It is this latter syndrome that seems more characteristic of the children we have seen. This is an observation corroborated by Bernstein, whose study of time reactivity in speech (Bernstein, 1962) related the fast tempo and "lack of hesitation" of the deprived, working-class child to a restricted type of language that encourages unfocused, nonanalytic behavior responses.

If we consider the kind of growth experiences that normally foster a capacity for self-observation as described earlier, it is clear that a sizable proportion of the low socioeconomic population does not have these experiences and cannot develop this capacity. Circumstances do not allow members of this group to develop either an increasingly objective grasp of reality or a sense of efficacy in interaction with their environment. The inconstancy of the environment, the features that make it difficult to internalize a sense of power and identity, the fast and externally geared resolution of cognitive-affective stress that becomes the dominant coping style—all make for multiple difficulties, including a poor capacity to focus attention and to observe the self, with an attendant inability to make use of most therapeutic efforts.

Ability to Communicate the Observed

A child growing into an increasingly complex and confusing world needs for his development significant adults to process necessary information in ways that will help him in the ordering of his universe. Though for the young child learning of basic emotions and of simple realities can occur in nonverbal modalities, transmission of complex information to the child will require the use of language and the development of dialogues. Parents, in communicating to the child, orient their attention toward certain prevalent segments of the surrounding world that therefore achieve a special affective tinge. The clarity, order, and degree of differentiation in parental communication will affect the child's ability to grasp the nuances of his inanimate and interpersonal surroundings. The model presented to the child will affect his evolving style of interpersonal communication and, more significantly, his inner dialogues and the quality of his self-observation.

When the child exchanges information with his parents, his concern for his relationship with them sometimes outweighs the informational content of his message. To communicate his observations, thoughts, and feelings, the child will need to learn to express himself in ways in which the relationship messages and the content messages do not obscure each other. We will later contend that the child growing up in a disorganized low socioeconomic family is frequently handicapped in the development of this communication skill.

In the process of communication between parents and children, where exchange of information and reciprocal learning occur, there is normally a development of a body of implicit shared rules among them regulating their communication. These rules deal with formal aspects of the "how" of communications. These formal processes eventually develop to the point where they occur on "automatic pilot," allowing for such economy of interaction that parents and children can take for granted the rules of communication and move their attention to content without having to negotiate again *how* content is going to be transacted.

In general, the formal rules that participants share in a dialogue have to do with how to signal that one has heard, understood, agreed, or disagreed. Then the possibility of carrying themes to conclusions becomes realizable. The signaling of closure is shared by others, and there are possibilities for reviewing and recovering information and for signaling shifts in content matter. Important in this process is the capacity to differentiate relevant information from accompanying static which may blur clarity of information. Communication of content is by then autonomous and useful for those problem-solving functions which sustain and express self-corrective processes. A lack of differentiated development in these implicit rules leaves any communicational system handicapped in its self-corrective processes.

Most middle-class people coming for therapy have developed to a viable point a system of rules in communication that are similar to the therapist's. This allows them to exchange information with minimal regard for the implicit formal rules that regulate their communicational flow. The situation with the low socioeconomic patient is quite different. Many treatment attempts, abandoned after the first session, have left therapist and patient frustrated and wondering about the intent of their "opponent."

Bernstein (1963) has explained the difficulty of communication transaction between a middle-class therapist and a low socioeconomic patient in terms of the structural differences in their language. He states that the restricted language code used by low socioeconomic English adolescents is not appropriate for use in the psychotherapeutic relationship because it does not facilitate a verbal elaboration of meaning, and the people who use this code do not verbalize their intent, belief, or motivation. The restricted code is used as a vehicle for expressing and receiving global descriptive relationship messages organized within a relatively low level of conceptualization. Language is not a means to verbalized experience of separation and difference, and affect conditioned by the concreteness of the language is available to be triggered off in a diffused manner. Deutsch (1964, p. 177), with similar emphasis, points out that the low socioeconomic child is reared "restricted to a segment of the spectrum of stimulation potentially available; he is handicapped by a verbal training that doesn't encourage the development of a differentiated language."

Both authors have been concerned with deficits of the structural organization of language and its influence on cognitive organization and learning. Our work with multiproblem low socioeconomic families has given us an additional perspective. We have increasingly highlighted the entire process by which people relate to one another and are affected in their interpersonal transactions by the characteristics of their communication.

The low socioeconomic disorganized family shows deficits in the articulation of implicit rules that regulate the communicational flow. In the overcrowded conditions of these large families, parents pay less attention to the request of the individual children and the children in turn accept the fact that they will not be heard. In the development of necessary techniques for attracting attention to themselves, the children find that intensity of sound is more effective than the power of the themes; assertion by power is more important than knowledge.

Ways of transacting power operations occupy a large part of the siblings' interaction, and "ranking" [1] of one another can occur around an infinite variety of subjects. They attempt to resolve conflict by a series of escalated threats and counterthreats. This process frequently maintains the conflict, unresolved, as an issue that will reappear in another context. Diffuse affect is communicated through kinetic modifiers, through the pitch and intensity of the tone of voice, and the like. Indeed, sometimes it seems that in the resolution of conflict it is unnecessary to hear the content of what is being transacted.

The variety of words, the vocabulary, available in the family is usually scarce. The parents are not only limited by maldevelopment in their verbal education, but tend to employ the best of their verbal equipment in situations outside the family. In the one-parent family, this trend has even more deprivational significance. The model of adults communicating among themselves is unavailable to the child. The role of verbal negotiation in solving interpersonal situations remains undeveloped and the opportunity to sharpen capacities for relationship thinking is largely unexercised (Smilansky, 1965).[2] The child is also trained to be unable to attend to the continuity and development of themes. Specific subject matter will rarely be carried to conclusion. A small number of interactions around a topic is usually interrupted by a disconnected intervention of another family member. It is rare for more than two family members to participate in an interaction around a specific point. When another member intervenes, the subject usually changes. The family threshold for accepting shifts in content matter is much higher than that of most middle-class therapists.

The result is a style of communication in which people do not expect to be heard, in which they assert themselves by yelling, in which conflicts do not have closure, and in which there is faulty development of themes, a

[1] Ranking: a process by which children assign one another to positions in the hierarchical order according to criteria of power.

[2] Smilansky's work is pertinent to our observations. She points out (1964) that among primitive Israeli children whom she served what seemed significantly lacking was not quantity of labels, but an inability to establish relationships between labels. She implied that any teaching aimed at increasing the number of labels really acted as added confusion in a warehouse full of single, unrelated objects. She recommended training in fundamental ways of relating subjects.

restricted affective range, and a lack of training in the elaboration of information-gathering questions. This style, that can be adequate for the transaction of gross nurturing and power relationships, is insufficient to deal with chronic and more subtle conflicts requiring the search for, ordering of, and sharing of different or new information.

There is a strong interaction between characteristics of communicational exchange in the family and the style of control exercised by parents through immediate erratic reactions. The child is trained to pay attention to the person with whom he is dealing, rather than to the content of the message received. This focus on the hierarchical organization of the social relationship in the family handicaps the child's freedom to address himself to the more autonomous aspect of the transaction, namely, the content of what is being transacted at the moment. What seems prevalent in our population is that the constant defining of interrelatedness between people outweighs the meaning of the content of messages. This type of communicational exchange (developmentally correct in interactions between young children and parents) seems to achieve dominance in the low socioeconomic population. It remains an important part of the communication process among such adults. People uncertain of their boundaries, unclear about their effectiveness and their impingement on other people, need continuous use of other people for definition of themselves and of their social situation.

In summary, our observations of the disorganized low socioeconomic population emphasize a communication style characterized by poor development of the formal rules facilitating the flow of exchange of information, and an overfocus on the relationship messages that determine status orientation at the expense of the content of the messages. This style of communication frequently does not have shared meaning with the therapist, trained in a different way of communicating. Thus it often happens that the therapist, who is concerned with understanding symbolic conceptualization, and the low socioeconomic patient, who is involved in structuring an unambiguous interaction with the therapist, engage in pseudodialogues that have a different meaning for each of them and that frustrate therapeutic effort.

Models for Therapeutic Work

Can we adapt our therapeutic techniques in ways syntonic to the perceptual, cognitive, and communicational styles of the low socioeconomic population? The experiences of a number of sociologists, social workers, and psychiatrists point to the probability that the low socioeconomic population can respond to therapy organized along different lines. It seems to us that the effectiveness of these new therapeutic techniques is related to their degrec of success in: (1) narrowing the transactional field around concrete tasks, increasing focused attention; (2) training people in the process of self-observation; and (3) increasing shared communication.

Riessman (1964), for instance, has employed *role playing* as a therapeutic maneuver and also as a way of training people to face areas of difficulty with some knowledge of the future event. He says that if a client "fears an approaching job interview, role playing the part of the employer makes the latter a less threatening person" (p. 41). He points out that in role therapy the roles of the patient and therapist are clearly defined and a setting is provided where the style is concrete, the problem directed and therefore syntonic with the low socioeconomic style of communication.

In an interaction with another person the ability to determine the way in which "you see me" will influence my responses in ways that will attempt to influence "your perception of me." Playing the role of the other person is a way of identifying the nature of his messages, the quality of his affect, the way in which "he sees me." This process fundamentally trains the ego of the patient in the process of self-observation and observation of others. "Me" is externalized and then "I" see myself played by "you."

Levine (1964) describes her work with low socioeconomic families through home visits in which games were used as a medium through which conflict between members was revealed. The therapist acts as "catalyst to dramatize the particular conflict or intervenes to break into the destructive pattern of interaction, and proceeds to demonstrate on the spot ways and means of settling the dispute" (p. 330). In this technique the narrowing of the transaction to the rules of the game allows for an increased differentiation in the areas of interpersonal conflict by presenting the conflict around a specific task (Minuchin and Montalvo, 1966).

The work of my colleagues and myself has been along similar lines. We have developed special therapeutic techniques in *group therapy, remedial learning therapy* and *family therapy*. These techniques are designed to "meet" the low socioeconomic patient where he is, but, more important, to create the conditions that will allow the therapist and patient a "shared therapeutic journey."

LIVING GROUP THERAPY [3]

We have, for instance, been using a technique of "living group therapy" in work with delinquent boys resident at a halfway house.[4] In this technique the therapist and the group counselor meet with a group of eight adolescent children 12 to 14 years of age. The counselor's function is clearly delineated. He acts in group therapy as he does in daily life with the children, fulfilling parental functions and controlling their behavior. He also pays

[3] This technique was developed by S. Fochios, S. Minuchin, and S. Pavlin.

[4] Floyd Patterson House of the Wiltwyck School for Boys, New York City.

special attention, however, to the formal characteristics of their verbal communication: loudness of speech, adherence to the theme, ability to listen and to question, intrusiveness, and so forth. The therapist and counselor decide previously on the theme of the session, which the counselor introduces at the beginning of each session. The theme is usually related to some immediate experience of the group: for instance, scapegoating of a boy, homosexual experiences, or other such problems. The counselor participates, framing the behavior of the children. He focuses the discussion on a subject that is significant in the present, narrows the area of intervention to this particular field, and, by focusing on formal aspects of the communication in the group, increases the ability of the children to continue with the exploration of a theme. The therapist, however, has freedom to operate along more interpretive lines, exploring "why's" and helping the participating children into increased self-awareness and differentiated awareness of others.

Other features are sometimes introduced into these sessions; all serve the function of increasing the sharpness with which behavior and feeling are observed. For instance, a mother of one of the children sometimes participates in the sessions with functions similar to the counselor, while other mothers of the participating children observe the functioning of this mother through a one-way mirror. A therapist observes with them, guiding them into the process of observing their children's participation among "siblings" with a "substitute mother" and with other adults. At times, children from the group join the group of mothers or the group of observers in the process of observing the other children. A session with the mothers follows the session with the children and concentrates on discussion of the mothers' observations as well as the feelings elicited by what may have been seen and experienced. The introduction of the mother into the group and the encouragement given to her to talk about her own family origin lift the taboo on discussion of family matter among the children and bring the "idealized" or shameful family into scrutiny.

REMEDIAL LEARNING THERAPY [5]

A pilot study of children with learning difficulties illustrates some possibilities of our line of inquiry. Six disturbed children 12 to 14 years of age met with a teacher for a series of ten sessions. The curriculum of these ten sessions was the teaching of formal elements in communication. The children were told that it was essential for learning in school that they should master some of the necessary formal characteristics of dialogue. These included differentiation of noise level, how to ask a question, how to follow a theme, pathways in communication, ways of describing a thing, how to select questions in the search for particular answers, and so forth. The chil-

[5] See Minuchin, Chamberlain, and Graubard, 1966.

dren and teacher met in a room with a one-way mirror for one hour bi-weekly meetings. Each meeting centered around one theme, such as noise or listening, and the teacher engaged the children in a series of games designed to give them a clear experience of the significance of this particular concept in efficient communication.

Of special interest were the apparent effects of a procedure in which the children assumed alternate roles as participants and observers. Two children of the group rotated weekly in the roles of observers beyond the one-way mirror. The two observers were trained in the process of rating and judging the other children's ability to respond to the teaching by staff members who joined them in the observation room. The emphasis in judging was put on performance in relation to the learning rather than on conforming or being "well behaved," which was these children's blanket view of almost any adult expectation. At the end of the session, the "judges" would tell the other children their rating and the reason for each one, and a small monetary reward was given for each point by the educational director. In the next lesson the "observer's" role apparently continued to operate in the children who now were the "participants" in the classroom; it became an intermediary to higher processes of self-observation. The children would talk among themselves in terms of the need to organize their behavior along the rules of the classroom. They were conscious of being observed and by *focusing on the particulars of their "observed" behavior* were learning to internalize an attitude of awareness toward their thinking processes and behavior. The level of disruptive noise in this group diminished sharply around the sixth lesson. The subculture of the group changed toward one of concern for achievement about the same time, and the appearance of a much more differentiated language was manifested.

FAMILY THERAPY

Our most sustained explorations of technique have been within the modality of family therapy. This has seemed to us a particularly suitable modality for treatment of the low socioeconomic population. Participation of the total family brings familiar groups into the session, the therapist being the only stranger to the subculture. The patient's familiarity with the interpersonal transactions that characterize his family partly allay his fears of the therapist's interventions. Furthermore, interactions remain in the "here and now." Problems are seen in context similar to the everyday occurrences among family members, and the nature of the situation is such that the therapist more naturally intervenes along lines of communication usual to the family. The prevailing style of interpersonal contact in these families has determined our strategy of therapeutic tasks. These families shift from situations of disengagement in which one member talks while listless parents or siblings are engaged in a variety of isolated and isolating activities—

to situations of engagement, in which everybody talks and shouts at the same time, diffuse affect bouncing from person to person and theme to theme and obscuring the nature of the issue at hand.

These families focus on the end product of behavior rather than content. They are oriented toward externalization and projection, are unskilled in the difficult readings of interpersonal causality, and are untrained in self-observation. They are unable to delineate interpersonal tasks and problems clearly. Their conflict is expressed in a global and pervasive way that renders them inaccessible for problem-solving. It therefore becomes the first therapeutic goal to frame clear-cut interpersonal situations in which family members experience in a differentiated fashion the effect that they have on one another.

We have developed a procedure of focusing part of the session on specific problems or "tasks." The use of tasks narrows the transactional field and forces a family member to address himself to a problem in a very delineated framework. The ways in which family members adapt and respond to the task allow a precise identification of the problem, at the same time that the focused conditions for the interaction facilitate the repair of amorphous family communication.

The tasks are presented within the spontaneous flow of therapy and are around salient and recurrent interchanges which underline family problems. They can be simple and aimed at generic, shared problems. For example, a family comprised of members who never listen to content is asked to pay attention to what is said, not to how it is said. Tasks can remain close to problems on family structure. For example, several members who actively reject and isolate a scapegoated member are stimulated to engage him. A more difficult task is presented when the isolated member is stimulated to reach actively out to the group of rejecting members. The task can also become quite complex and more two-dimensional. A father who continuously derogates his son is asked to find positives when talking to his son, while the wife's assignment is to avoid a customary attack upon the husband.

Devising the strategies of task assignment requires a clear understanding of individual dynamics and how these are manifested in family transactions, as well as in the family's patterns of communication. These strategies must be flexible, continuously responding to the changes the family is undergoing. At this point it should be emphasized that when an interaction in an unfamiliar modality is sought, the attempt is not to break a habit by the simple formula of creating another. The vivid awareness of hidden patterns and underlying motivations is being increased at the same time that experience is offered in alternative ways of attacking a problem.

While some members of the family are engaged in the resolution of interpersonal tasks, the therapist engages other members into the process of observation beyond the one-way mirror, or asks them to move their chairs to a farther part of the room, signifying the change in their roles from participants to observers. The observing members could be asked by the therapist at different times to join the participant members in the resolution of interpersonal conflict.[6] Let me caution the reader that in our description of the use of tasks we are calling attention only to certain general characteristics of technique that we consider necessary in the therapy of the low socioeconomic population. The only road for the development of meaningful tasks is deep understanding of the dynamics of these families: of the meaning, for example, of the mother's investment in the mother's role while keeping an undifferentiated relation to her children or the role of the grandmother and aunts in the evolution of the mothering functions; of the significance of the sibling subgroup as socializers; or of the effect of the transient adult male in children's sexual identification.

In our work,[7] we have paid special attention to the training of therapists in the use of a language and communication style (along concrete, enactive[8] lines) familiar to family members. The therapist diminishes his probing and his ambiguous "umhums," and develops a direct style conducive to actualizing problems around the task situation. Therapists' styles of cognition and communication tend to be abstract, symbolic, oriented toward highly differentiated nuances of verbal transaction. Unless specifically focused, gaps develop between their cognitive communicational styles and those of the families. Manifestations of this gap occur in clinical examples of "pseudodialogue," when therapists and family members "talk" in parallel monologues, while assuming that they are relating and communicating with each other. At other times, family members strain to decipher therapist communications and escape through disruptive actions, mutism, or statements of "I don't understand you" or "I don't know." Therapists tend to interpret such verbalizations as "resistance." We find, in the same vein, family members labeling the therapist communication styles as "social worker talk," and the therapist labeling in equally derogatory terms the family communication as "noise."

Therapists require awareness of this communication gap as well as skill in transforming their messages into a communicational modality which is similar to that of the patient family. To properly understand what we mean by "communicational modality" it must be remembered that a message can be coded in a highly symbolic, verbal manner or in action. The therapist

[6] For more details on these techniques, see Minuchin (1965) and Minuchin and Montalvo (1966).

[7] I wish to thank Mr. Braulio Montalvo, M.A., for allowing me to quote from work he and I are doing collaboratively.

[8] Bruner's classification of the cognitive developmental ladder (enactive, ikonic, and symbolic) is useful for describing the communication styles of family members (Bruner, 1964).

can express a meaning by saying something or by doing something, or preferably by both. For instance, in one family session a therapist found himself heavily attacked. He then changed his seat and sat among the family members. Pointing to the empty chair, he said, "It was very difficult to be there being attacked by you. It makes me feel left out." The therapist might have described in words alone that he felt left out of the family, rather than changing his seat to one between family members and then commenting on his feeling. He sensed that his verbal statement would pass unnoticed by all but the most verbal member of the family and that the "movement language" would be attended to by everyone. The immediate result of this modality of "speech" lies in that it opens the possibilities for further therapeutic interventions.

Communications to our families which "tune in" the enactive modality seem to make accessible avenues of direct communication previously unavailable. Instead of asking a family member, "How come your mother doesn't talk with you?" the therapist challenges by saying, "Could you make your mother talk to you?" Stimulation toward the actual "enactment" of problems, let us note, does not imply that the therapist precludes the task of assisting family members to avoid their tendency to constant action. It simply implies that the participants are moved gradually, rather than abruptly, toward more representational and symbolic levels.

Focused formulations on the part of the therapist are especially relevant during the initial periods of therapy; they actualize the working grounds around which to intervene usefully. Let us illustrate by means of an example from the Wilson family. In this family, composed of the mother, grandmother, and three children, the therapist's interpretations were directed toward pointing out the grandmother's domination of the mother. Interpretations to the grandmother in terms of her "domination" and to the mother in terms of her "passivity" and acceptance of the grandmother's control were felt by them as criticism of their way of being and both responded with resistance. Another interpretation was successfully tried later on, one which remained closer to the operationally observed phenomena.

Grandmother was asked behind the one-way mirror to observe interaction between her daughter and her grandson. She reacted to the daughter's passivity toward her grandson's disruptive behavior (loud banging on chairs) with, "I would have stopped him right there." Two minutes later her daughter did stop the boy in a calm, nonaggressive fashion by questioning him about his day at school. The therapist stated descriptively to the grandmother, "You are always two minutes ahead of your daughter."

This temporal emphasis captured the specific way in which mother was dominating daughter. "Domination," as an interpretation, required unaccustomed inference and more introspection from family members than "two minutes ahead," which retained manifestations of the problem almost as it was visually presented. The latter interpretation remained closer to the actual occurrence, requiring mostly an "ikonic" [9] exertion, a remembering of what was seen.

In general, then, interpretations which employ an almost physical or territorial language, which are grounded on more primitive, cognitive, and communicational systems, seem to be more syntonic with the way in which our families communicate among themselves and are more likely to be effective.

It is, therefore, the therapist's communicative flexibility that is essential for therapeutic effectiveness. The blending of communication, both syntonic and dystonic, to the style of the low socioeconomic family creates both the conditions for patient and therapist "meeting" in the family's "home ground" and moving along in therapeutic exploration. The therapist times his shifts from concreteness to abstraction, from proximity to distance, from others to self. He leaps from focal observation and description of behavior to analysis and evaluation. The appropriate therapeutic tension seems to follow a zigzagging line between attunement to a style of concreteness and directness, and a style of analytic evaluation. The therapist has learned to create situations of dramatic intensity sometimes as a way of calling the attention of the participant members to what he wants to say. This need for projecting the therapeutic message above the threshold of inattention of the participant member will take a variety of forms that will depend on the therapist's artistry in working with this population.[10]

Summary

This chapter has been concerned with the applicability of the psychoanalytic therapies to the low socioeconomic population, an area of therapeutic endeavor generally considered unfruitful and unrewarding. I have examined some criteria considered essential for successful therapeutic work along the analytic model and the characteristics of the population under discussion in terms of their success or failure in fulfilling these criteria. In particular I have focused on the development of the capacity for self-observation; the ability to communicate the observed; and the verbal and behavioral methods of communication. The typical communication styles of (middle-class) therapists have been compared and contrasted with those of the population who "cannot use treatment appropriately." Specific types of "communication gaps" have been described and illustrated.

[9] Bruner's term for perceptive processes.

[10] The use of this modified approach of family therapy has resulted in a sharp diminishing of broken appointments, an increase in family participation and engagement, and clinical improvement of a number of families that were previously considered unreachable.

The need for developing new therapeutic techniques specifically tailored for this population is imperative, as traditional techniques rely on the use of verbal and cognitive skills which remain undeveloped within the families of the poor. Equally important are methods of assessing and evaluating results obtained. Some new models for therapeutic work have been presented, including studies and treatment conducted by my colleagues and myself. We have centered our efforts on developing techniques within family therapy, "living group therapy," and remedial education which train family members or peers in self-observation and in communication. We have focused attention on helping therapist and patient to understand the other's communicational styles and to increase their shared communication. It is our belief that beyond analytically oriented theoretical understanding of individual or family dynamics these aspects of therapeutic intervention need to be understood and emphasized in the process of treatment in order to increase the chances for successful outcome with the low socioeconomic population.

Note: A major portion of this chapter appears in *Families of the Slum: An Exploration of Their Structure and Treatment* by Salvador Minuchin, Braulio Montalvo, Bernard Guerney, Bernice Rosman, and Florence Schumer (New York: Basic Books, 1967).

References

Bernard, Viola. "Some Principles of Dynamic Psychiatry in Relation to Poverty." *American Journal of Psychiatry,* 122 (1965), 254–266.

Bernstein, B. "Linguistic Codes, Hesitation Phenomena, and Intelligence." *Language and Speech,* 5 (1962), 31–46.

Bernstein, B. "Social Class and Linguistic Development: A Theory of Social Learning." In A. H. Halsey, Jean Floud, and C. A. Anderson (eds.), *Education, Economy, and Society.* Glencoe, Ill.: The Free Press, 1963. Pp. 288–314.

Bernstein, B. "Social Class, Speech Systems, and Psychotherapy." In F. Riessman, J. Cohen, and A. Pearl (eds.), *Mental Health of the Poor.* Glencoe, Ill.: The Free Press, 1964. Pp. 194–204.

Bruner, J. S. "The Course of Cognitive Growth." *American Psychologist,* 19, No. 1 (1964), 1–15.

Deutsch, M. P. "The Disadvantaged Child and the Learning Process." In F. Riessman, J. Cohen, and A. Pearl (eds.), *Mental Health of the Poor.* Glencoe, Ill.: The Free Press, 1964. Pp. 172–187.

Fochios, S. "The Use of Families as Therapeutic Levers with Delinquent Disturbed Children from the Lower Class." Paper read at meeting of the American Psychiatric Association, Honolulu, Hawaii, 1965.

Gould, R. E. "Dr. Strangeclass or: How I Stopped Worrying about the Theory and Began Treating the Blue Collar Worker." *American Journal of Orthopsychiatry,* 37 (January 1967), 78–86.

Hess, R., Shipman, V., and Jackson, D. D. "Experience of the Socialization of Cognitive Modes in Children." *Child Development*, 36 (1965), 869–886.

Kagan, J., and Wright, J. C. "Psychological Significance of Styles of Conceptualization." *Basic Cognitive Processes in Children*, 28, No. 2 (1963).

Kohn, M. L. "Social Class and Parent-Child Relationships: An Interpretation." In F. Riessman, J. Cohen, and A. Pearl (eds.), *Mental Health of the Poor*. Glencoe, Ill.: The Free Press, 1964. Pp. 159–171.

Levine, Rachel A. "Treatment in the Home: An Experiment with Low Income, Multi-Problem Families." In F. Riessman, J. Cohen, and A. Pearl (eds.), *Mental Health of the Poor*. Glencoe, Ill.: The Free Press, 1964. Pp. 329–335.

Malone, C. A. "Some Observations on Children of Disorganized Families and Problems of Acting Out." *Journal of Child Psychiatry*, 2 (1963), 1–175.

Minuchin, S. "Conflict Resolution Family Therapy." *Psychiatry*, 28 (August 1965), 278–286.

Minuchin, S., Auerswald, E., King, C., and Rabinowitz, Clara. "The Study and Treatment of Families Who Produce Multiple Acting-out Boys." *American Journal of Orthopsychiatry*, Vol. 34, No. 1 (1964), pp. 125–133.

Minuchin, S., Chamberlain, Pamela and Graubard, P. "A Project to Teach Learning Skills to Disturbed, Delinquent Children." *American Journal of Orthopsychiatry*, 37 (April 1967), 558–567.

Minuchin, S., and Montalvo, B. "An Approach for Diagnosis of the Low Socioeconomic Family." Psychiatric Research Report No. 20, American Psychiatric Association, February 1966, pp. 163–174.

Pavenstedt, Eleanor. "A Comparison of the Child Rearing Environment of Upper-lower and Very Low-lower Class Families." *American Journal of Orthopsychiatry*, 35, No. 1 (1965). 89–98.

Riessman, F. "Some Suggestions Concerning Psychotherapy with Blue-Collar Patients." New York: Mobilization for Youth (mimeographed), 1962.

Riessman, F. "Role Playing and the Lower Socio-economic Group." *Group Psychotherapy*, 17, No. 1 (1964), 36–48.

Schachtel, E. G. *Metamorphosis: On the Development of Affect, Perception, Attention, and Memory*. New York: Basic Books, 1959.

Smilansky, Sarah. "Promotion of Preschool, 'Culturally Deprived' Children through 'Dramatic Play.'" *American Journal of Orthopsychiatry*, Vol. 35, No. 2 (1965), 201–202.

White, R. W. "Ego and Reality in Psychoanalytic Theory: A Proposal Regarding Independent Ego Energies." *Psychological Issues*, 3, No. 3 (1963), Monograph No. 11.

White, R. W. "The Experience of Efficacy in Schizophrenia." *Psychiatry*, 28, No. 3 (1965), 199–211.

Wolff, P. "The Development of Attention in Young Infants." *Annals of the New York Academy of Sciences*, 118 (1965), 815–830.

Wolff, P., and White, B. L. "Visual Pursuit and Attention in Young Infants." *Journal of the American Academy of Child Psychiatry*, 4, No. 3 (1965), 473–484.

22

Schizophrenia and Psychotherapy

OTTO A. WILL, JR.

Introduction

All human existence is, in a sense, solitary. At conception each of us is genetically unique. Though others are present and assist at our birth, we draw our first agonizing breath in the solitude of an alien world. At the moment of death we depart in the same fashion. . . . There is no greater loneliness in the universe than that of being confronted by knowledge: knowledge of one's past in a lizard skull, in the sunlit emptiness of a meadow, or the waiting menace of the forest. . . . On the world island we are all castaways (Eiseley, 1966, p. 1).

Each of us, from birth onward, is bound to his fellows in many ways, with ties marked as much by anxiety and fear as by security, and offering little promise beyond their own quality of transience. To fail in becoming related is to die at the beginning of life or to endure as a dreadful caricature of what one might have been, but to dare involvement in the love of others is to give hostages to fate, as the inevitable accompaniment of love is loss and separation. Although one man is like another to the extent that certain of his behaviors can be predicted, influenced, and controlled, no man in his entirety can be known to others—or to himself; he must live largely unknown, accepting loneliness as an essential aspect of his existence.

Loneliness goes by many names, often passing unrecognized, in which case its quality of hopelessness is most marked; in some instances it may be called conformity or rebellion, and again it may be known as normality or psychosis. The mentally ill and the mentally well—designations yet difficult to define and separate—share this aloneness. The psychiatrist, concerned as he is with the attempt to better understand and modify human behavior, can in no useful way separate himself from his patient in their common concern with the nature of human being.

In assuming the task of attempting to change the ways of another's living we accept responsibility for decision regarding what is good and evil; nothing that we do is neutral; all our acts have consequences. We do not exert influence without having a goal in mind. Among many goals we must select at least one, thus arrogating to ourselves power and a presumption of knowledge that could well be tempered with humility, a recognition of life's uncertainties, and an acceptance of the madness to be found in all men—our patients and ourselves as well.

Relevant to this concern is the comment from *The Plague*, by Albert Camus (1937, pp. 229–230):

> [e]ach of us has the plague within him; no one, no one on earth is free from it. . . . All I maintain is that on this earth there are pestilences and there are victims, and it's up to us, so far as possible, not to join forces with the pestilences. . . . I grant we should add a third category: that of the true healers. But it's a fact one doesn't come across many of them, and anyhow it must be a hard vocation.

Our interest now is to consider some aspects of that complexity of behavioral patterns labeled schizophrenia, noting various approaches made during the past thirty or more years for its understanding and amelioration and discussing the possible significance of the psychotherapeutic intervention.[1] In evaluating the present we can learn from the past, the history of

[1] This presentation is concerned with a general discussion of the development of therapeutic approaches to schizophrenic behavior, other patterns of psychotic disorder not being dealt with. However, it is suggested that all forms of human activity are to a large extent learned and that they reflect previous experience, current involvement in a social field and anticipation of a future. From this point of view psychosis may be looked on as an expression of interpersonal phenomena, in part created and perpetuated by such, and to some extent subject to modification (favorable or unfavorable) by interpersonal contact. The psychotherapeutic task is to explore and delineate the nature of the contact that will promote further desirable growth and learning.

It should be noted that no clear distinction is made here between neurosis and psychosis, the varying behavioral patterns being thought of as differing more in degree than in kind. Of interest in this context are the statements by Arlow and Brenner (1964) that "it follows [from their discussion of psychoanalytic structural theory] that there is

psychiatry being found in the events of today as well as those of yesterday. To a great extent what has been is, and will continue to be, into times ahead. In our work we seek both knowledge and change; we want to know more about our patients and we strive for them to get "better"—and to do so as the result of the use of techniques derived from our theories. Knowing that change in itself is not necessarily good, we must determine the direction which we shall, at least for the moment, follow, realizing that through observation and the accumulation of data both theory and technique will require modification. In choosing a direction, and in subscribing to a theory and technique, we commit ourselves—that is, our personalities become involved (often without our recognizing the fact) in the observations that we attempt to make. With such involvement we may come to behave toward our ideas as if they were vital parts of ourselves, not symbolic representations of events that could, perhaps, be symbolized in other and more meaningful ways.

On this subject I quote Sullivan (1927, p. 148):

> The personality of the observer must either be exterior to the scientific observations which he secures or be represented explicitly in their context when it enters into them. . . . How curiously opaque we are to our own observational scotomata. How easy it is to overlook things which do not fit into our tentative explanation. How more than difficult it is to see evidence of an unpleasant theory. It is sad indeed that medical men are so human as to find theories pleasant and unpleasant. There is no scientist but should blush at an accusation that he liked or disliked an hypothesis, on the basis of ethics or aesthetics, or—and this is the important ground—on the basis of his early training. Convicted of such an accusation, he is adjudged no scientist; he is but a bigoted layman thrusting his likes and dislikes into the serious business of observation, the method of knowledge.

(Although I subscribe to this thesis, I cannot claim to put it into practice. At best, I can only keep it in mind as a warning, recognizing that in my work I need to believe, but recurrently reminding myself that strong belief requires as its companion stronger doubt.)

Throughout the past century there have been numerous theories concerning the nature of schizophrenia (or disorders akin to it), and more or less closely associated with these have been a variety of suggestions as to

---

no more a sharp line of division between what is to be called psychotic and what we call neurotic than there is between the neurotic and the normal. Each shades off into the other just as do the colors of a continuous spectrum (p. 147).

"[T]he great majority of the alterations in the ego and superego functions which characterize the psychoses are part of the individual defensive efforts in situations of inner conflict and are motivated by a need to avoid the emergence of anxiety. . . . In the psychoses the defensive alterations in ego functions are often so extensive as to disrupt the patient's relationship with the world about him to a serious degree" (p. 178).

treatment; the relevancy of the latter to the former is often obscure. Basic to all effort has been the idea that the disorder is undesirable and that treatment is to bring about change in it. The goals of therapy are variously defined—to produce good mental health, to bring about a return to normalcy, to deplete the populations of psychiatric hospitals, to remold the personality, to replace destructive with productive behavior, and so on. It is well worth our noting that in the current state of the world there is no general agreement regarding the desirability, usefulness, or attainability of any of the above or many other goals of psychiatric endeavor. In selecting goals we also select and work in accordance with systems of value learned in our respective cultures, marked by irrational qualities to be found in any human organization, and having no verifiable universal (if even transcultural) finality. In the choice of therapeutic goals knowledge may usefully be tempered by wisdom—that blend of experience, learning, and understanding in practical affairs, and philosophical speculation which includes, and is beyond, mere information.

As a clinician I am concerned with the significance of a disorder—its origins, modes of expression, dynamics, accompanying pathological defects, and outcome. I am interested in factors favorably or unfavorably influencing its course, and in the development of a rational treatment procedure. In the field of psychiatry these tasks are difficult to accomplish with any degree of precision, but of each something is to be said, if only in the service of pointing out deficiencies in knowledge.

At this juncture let us turn to a brief consideration of accounts of the early stages of the schizophrenic transaction, the last term referring to behavior which evokes response from its surroundings and in turn restructures itself in terms of anticipated and actual responses—a feedback system. These are old stories, but perhaps worth the retelling.

Miss A.—"Patient"

Some years ago a young woman, known in her family as dependable, good, and lovable, underwent what seemed to be a change in her personality; that is, she began to exhibit behavior inconsistent with her previous public image. Whereas she had been cheerful, companionable, an able student and participant in social activities, she lost interest in her studies during her first college years, looked depressed, withdrew from friends, and complained of fatigue. Solicitous relatives thought at first that she was showing the effects of an unhappy experience in love, and it was recommended that she "get away from things" and rest at a vacation resort. This she did without benefit, and soon returned home to spend much time alone in her room, complaining of malaise and varied bodily pains. In time she was diagnosed as suffering from a neurological disorder, for which the prognosis was bad and treatment inadequate. However, the evidences of neurological disease did not increase, but a state of depression did, and she attempted to kill herself after failing in an effort to resume her studies at college. Miss A. was then hospitalized and diagnosed as being neurotic and depressed. In the hospital she acted frightened and suspicious, and soon became assaultive and hallucinated, at which juncture she was considered as suffering from dementia praecox or schizophrenia. During the following year she remained in the hospital, being treated with insulin coma, electroshock, a variety of ataractic drugs, prolonged drug-induced sleep, special nursing care, and the services of six psychiatrists, each of whom met with her for a period of one or two months. When she did not improve, a prefrontal lobotomy was recommended but not carried out, and not long thereafter I became her therapist in another hospital.

There follows an excerpt from her speech shortly after she had been visited by her mother and an older sister. During this meeting I sat on the floor in the corner of Miss A.'s room. I remember her well—tall, slender, with a long black head of hair, eyes swollen with weeping, cheeks bloodied from self-inflicted scratches, feet bare, dressing gown dirty and torn, pacing the room, speaking hoarsely and acting as if I were only intermittently and partially present.

> I see my grandmother. She's not dead. Why did they say she was gone? (She sits on the floor and looks at the ceiling.) What strange designs—all circles and colored figures with cobwebs hanging down. (She suddenly looks directly at me—or through me.) Don't go away—the room is so large—I am lost. Nothing is stable anymore—it all changes. Peoples' faces change—so horrible—no friendliness at all. (She goes to the window and murmurs.) Mother, you have come back to me. Let me touch your face. (She holds out her hand and touches the window with her finger—then withdraws the hand with a scream.) Mother! Your face is rotting—you are so cruel. Why have you left me? (She kneels on the floor and makes sweeping movements with her hands.) I must sweep up all the pieces. They are gone forever. (Now she comes over to me, crawling on her knees, grasps my hand and holds it against the floor.) Feel the blood. Someone has been killed. You have come to kill me. No one will get out of here alive.

Accounts from Literature

Miss A. was schizophrenic; she was also lonely, frightened, suspicious, and despairing, with a confused and confusing view of her world. There follow other accounts of disturbances, as reminders of how we came to think of certain human activities as representative of a "disease"—as schizophrenia. Some of the reports are by physicians, others by patients, there being a noticeable difference in the experience of the observer and the observed.

There is, of course, no way of knowing that the reporters are talking about the same things.

John Conolly, an English physician, in 1849, said:

> Young persons not infrequently fall into a state somewhat resembling melancholia, without any discoverable cause of sorrow, and certainly without any specific grief; they become indolent or pursue their usual occupations or recreations mechanically and without interest; the intellect, the affections, the passions, all seem inactive or deadened and the patients become utterly apathetic (Noyes, 1954, p. 359).

Next, the Belgian physician Benedict Morel in 1860 wrote: A bright boy of fourteen years

> lost his cheerfulness and became sober, taciturn, and showed a tendency to solitude. . . . [There was] a melancholy depression and a hatred of his father even with the idea of killing him. . . . A kind of inactivity bordering on stupidity replaced his former activity . . . and it looked as if a transition into an irrecoverable state of dementia praecox was taking place (Noyes, 1954, p. 359).

In 1871 Hecker wrote of a disorder of puberty, marked by melancholia, mania, and confusion, and "a characteristic form of final deterioration the evidences of which can be seen in the first stages of the disease" (Noyes, 1954, p. 359).

There follows a report from an autobiography published in 1714, the speaker being a young man of comfortable circumstances:

> I then waking . . . fancy'd I heard some *rushing kind of noise* and descern'd something at the *Bed's-Foot* like a *Shadow;* which I apprehended to have been a *Spirit.* Hereupon, I was seiz'd with *great Fear* and *Trembling* [and] rose in Haste. . . . While I was thus walking up and down . . . I perceiv'd a *Voice* (*I heard it plainly*) saying unto me, *Who art thou?* . . . I verily believe, this *Voice* would have . . . commanded me to cut it [throat]: For I have all Reason to conclude, that the Voice was the Voice of Satan, and that his Design was, to *humble* me as lowest *HELL* (Landis, 1964, pp. 26–27).

Another patient (in the late nineteenth century) speaks of his experience of the onset of disorder:

> . . . the thought came to me how frightfully large and powerful are the questions which disquiet man. . . . I wanted to ask passing people for a way in which I could meet my new misfortune. . . . The facial expressions of the people involved took on a horrible form . . . it appeared to me that I was surrounded by persons who have arisen from the grave. . . . Since I was in-

clined to believe in the actuality of these hallucinations, I assumed then that I did not live any longer, and that I had found myself in the other world (Landis, 1964, p. 28).

The last of these quotations is from the account of a patient in 1860, a man hospitalized in Scotland:

[E]very thought became agony, and I went mad . . . hope fled, and in her place reigned that sleep-hating demon despair. . . . One night . . . a most horrible impulse seized upon me, an impulse impelling me to destroy one who of all living beings most deserved my love. . . . It was uncontrollable. . . . Barefooted . . . I ran through the streets to the Police Office and implored them to lock me up. . . . Then comes a blank in memory's book . . . the first thing I remember was awakening as out of a horrible dream. . . . I thought to myself . . . how long have I been here, when instantly a voice within me replied "a thousand years." Impossible, I could not live so long, I thought, when the voice again replied, "Thou shalt never die." . . . There is a fearful page in the book of human nature, unread by him who judges an insane man by his actions. . . . [A]pparently unnatural conduct does in some cases arise from motives which, could we trace them, would command pity, veneration, and love (Anonymous, 1947, pp. 17–19).

From the accounts of patients, physicians, and others there developed the concept of dementia praecox, a term suggesting a psychosis with apparent onset in adolescence, ending in organic deterioration (not demonstrated), and arising from "degenerative" processes reflecting hereditary "weakness," "primary" brain disease, toxic influence, and "idiopathic" causes.

Emil Kraepelin (1855–1926) grouped together previously described catatonic, hebephrenic, and paranoid states under the rubric dementia praecox, supposedly a disease of the central nervous system, progressive in course, unresponsive to any known therapy, and destined to end in a state of organic deterioration.

In 1911 Eugen Bleuler

described the schizophrenias as a slowly progressive deterioration of the entire personality. . . . [T]hey showed a tendency toward deterioration and, having once appeared, did not permit of a full *restitutis ad integrum*. . . . [He] believes them to be organic; but at the same time, he stressed the interaction of psychogenic features in their psychopathology and development (Hinsie and Campbell, 1960, p. 659).

Adolf Meyer (1866–1950) suggested that schizophrenia might not be a disease entity in the classical medical sense, but might reflect the organism's difficulties in adapting to its environment, with a resultant resort to fantasy in lieu of more simply goal-directed behavior, and with the accumulation of ineffective "habit patterns."

Sigmund Freud (1856–1939) spoke of schizophrenia as a regression to an earlier narcissistic state, a turning away from "reality" and object relationships to a condition in which the ego is poorly differentiated. Although standard psychoanalytic procedures were not considered to be suitable to the treatment of the schizophrenic person because of the difficulty in relating to him, the way had been opened for the psychological study of this disorder.

What had come to be called dementia praedox (schizophrenia) had been moved from the mythology of devil possession to a conceptualization of vaguely defined and unrelated entities in the field of medicine. Through an act of clinical observation and classification these entities had been drawn together into a concept of disease supposedly reflecting biological weakness and doomed to a state of deterioration. Later came the idea that weak though the flesh might be, and hopeless the outcome, the influence of the environment could not be denied. The possibility of a "therapeutic" environment leading to significant alterations in behavior and personality, however, was not widely entertained. Schizophrenia had gained the status of a medical disease, and those who suffered from it were entitled to the care of hospitals, nurses, and physicians, when these were available, and to the protection of laws designed for the disabilities of the sick. In all of this, however, there was little hope.

Early Personal Experience

My first official contact with psychiatry was in a large state mental hospital. I was embarrassed by some of the proceedings there and did not think that I was usefully informed by exhibitions of "waxy flexibility" and other marvels of hospitalism and chronicity. Later I became directly acquainted with management problems in such institutions, learning that major psychiatric concerns can be those of obtaining the rudiments of decent shelter, clothing, food, and humane treatment. The provision of those necessities continues to be a primary task of the hospital physician, and, for that matter, for a goodly part of the world's population.

In the University Hospital the psychiatric staff members were generally uncomfortable in their roles, apologetic for lack of therapeutic "successes," and eager to demonstrate their qualifications as "real" physicians by a preoccupation with neurology. Once the diagnosis of schizophrenia was made interest in the patient declined, and he was shortly sent to another hospital, an unfavorable outcome being assumed. After securing a long history, there seemed little to do, prolonged contact of patient and physician being discomforting for many of us. We saw patients who had been treated with intrathecal horse serum for the production of a meningeal reaction; there were those who had undergone purging as well as the surgical removal of possible foci of infection; and there were some who "recovered spontaneously," as well as others who disappeared into hospitals, their final outcome unknown to us.

In the later 1930's insulin coma therapy roused much enthusiasm. This procedure seemed to be in the medical tradition: one felt "like a physician," there was more contact with the patient, who remained longer in the University Hospital, and some patients came out of their withdrawn states. But there were complications: a few patients died with the procedure, some suffered brain damage, some did not improve, and others relapsed. Then came the use of metrazol, of nitrogen, of electroconvulsive treatment, and prefrontal lobotomy with its various modifications. I had experience, in one way or another, with all of these, and what enthusiasm I had for the logic and value of much therapy declined.

In contrast to the emphasis on organic defect in schizophrenia was the work of Meyer, White, Sullivan, Fromm-Reichmann, and others. There follow some quotations from a study of "parergasia" published by Gladys Terry and Thomas Rennie (1938):

> Beneath the most garbled utterance or bizarre gesture, lies, for those who can understand, a system of meanings, however overindulged or personalized, unsocialized, distorted, crude, fragmentary. No rigid classification is to be expected without doing violence in a material so heterogeneous (p. 156).
>
> Statistical studies can offer only a very limited understanding of such reaction types. Careful analysis of individual cases or family constellations will bring us closer. . . . The childhood of these patients shows early evidence of unusual, unstable, or inadequate behavior, and these same traits conspicuously color later developments (p. 159).
>
> We see in these patients, as they approach the years of synthesis, one avenue of satisfaction after another closed by virtue of personal sensitiveness, timidities, submissiveness, crippling experiences and memories (p. 161).
>
> We do well to forget the terms and to get immediately to the task of understanding the reaction in terms of the person who is reacting . . . (p. 163).
>
> We are studying living men, not yet dead; and man is an experience-conditioned, life-record determined creature (p. 164).

In the introduction to this same volume Adolf Meyer wrote:

> The present movement in the direction of clearness and mastery over what can be done about the hazard not exactly of living death, but of loss of mental health and recoverability, this is what constitutes the study of dementia praecox. It is the study and prevention of individual personal bankruptcy, prompted by the well-founded faith that dementia is not like death; where there is life, there is hope, i.e. there is something to be done (Terry and Rennie, 1938, p. 15).

Since that writing there have continued certain major trends in the study of schizophrenia. As the work of the psychotherapist must be considered in light of each of these, they are briefly reviewed in what follows.

Studies in Biochemistry, Physiology, and Genetics

Studies in biochemistry, physiology, and genetics have continued in the medical tradition with increasing refinement of techniques. I am not qualified to speak on these matters and shall not attempt to do so. I listen to those who carry on this work, and I expect to be informed by them. At the same time I do as best I can that which I can do, recurrently haunted, of course, by the recognition that some of what I do may seem to be not only irrational and unscientific, but may later be revealed by hard research to be inadequate and replaceable. However, one works with confidence in the human relationship as a necessary condition in human development and as a powerful factor in the molding and modification of human behavior.

Kety (1959) published a critical review of the biochemical theories of schizophrenia, in which he pointed out the difficulties in research and the current lack of a definitive biochemical "explanation" for schizophrenic behavior. A year later he wrote:

> I find the evidence for a significant genetic factor in many or all schizophrenias to be compelling. Arguments which indicate that genetic factors do not operate alone but only in association with socioenvironmental ones do not counter the evidence for a genetic susceptibility in many forms of schizophrenia. . . . Even if the biochemical lesion in schizophrenia does not exist or may not be discovered for many generations, present and future research in that area, if it is critical as well as imaginative, cannot help but lead to a better understanding of the nervous system and behavior (Kety, 1960, p. 137).

Gottlieb, Frohman, and Beckett (1966, p. 241) suggest that

> there is a biologic mechanism in certain patients with schizophrenia that is not functioning properly . . . that a protein or a normal substance of small molecular size carried by the protein is not inactivated properly. . . . The metabolic disarrangements so produced are then responsible through ways poorly understood for the manifestations of the illness.

Hoch (1966) states:

> We consider schizophrenia basically to be an organic disorder. Much of the clinical and experimental evidence indicates that what we today call schizophrenia is a special form of integrative disorganization. This disorganization pattern is widespread and as characteristic as the so-called organic reaction types. . . . This predisposition is inherited . . . a preeminently subcortical

impairment occurs in schizophrenia or a disruption of a normal relationship between cortex and subcortex.

Studies of the Family

As has been noted there was an early, almost exclusive, emphasis on schizophrenia as a disease in the traditional medical sense. There was a lack of formal studies of the social and cultural environments in which the disorder arose and had its being, and in which it played a functional part, influencing and being influenced by its surroundings. A brief review of selected studies of the families of schizophrenic patients will illustrate the rise of developing ways for observing a social system.

The following quotations from Ferenczi (1929) are not a bad beginning for this topic:

> I only wish to point to the probability that all children who are received in a harsh and disagreeable way die easily and willingly (p. 127).
>
> The child has to be induced by means of an immense expenditure of love, tenderness, and care to forgive his parents for having brought him into the world without any intention on his part. . . . The "life" force which rears itself against the difficulties of life has therefore not really any great innate strength, and becomes established only when tactful treatment and upbringing gradually give rise to progressive immunization against physical and psychical injuries (p. 128).

David Levy (1931) described what he called "maternal overprotection," in which the mother, through a lack or excess of control, prevented the development of independent behavior in her child. Kasinin, Knight, and Sage (1934) suggested that a biological inferiority of the child was the stimulus for maternal overprotection in the child who was to become schizophrenic. Hajdu-Gimes (1940) described families in which the mother was cold and sadistically aggressive and the father indifferent and passive. In such an environment the child learned to perceive the world as an object of distrust and suspicion, and seemed likely to develop schizophrenic behavior. Fromm-Reichmann (1948) used the term "schizophrenogenic mother," and Tietze (1949) described the mothers of schizophrenic patients as anxious, obsessive, rigid, and nonempathic, whereas the fathers played a passive role in the home. Ellison and Hamilton (1949) described a combination of rejecting fathers and oversolicitous mothers in the families of schizophrenic patients. Gerard and Siegel (1950) stated that schizophrenic behavior was derived from patterns of family relationships and attitudes. Reichard and Tillman (1950) spoke of the mother's inability to meet the needs of her child and to give to him "genuine love"; Wahl (1954) emphasized parental rejection, overprotection, and loss in the homes of pre-schizophrenic children; and Limentoni (1956) described a symbiotic identification of child and mother as a background factor in schizophrenia.

It is well to note that Oltman (Oltman, McGarry, and Friedman, 1952), in contrast to the developing trend, concluded that schizophrenia is a "biological deficiency disease based on heredo-constitutional factors" and unrelated to known external stresses or deprivations.

Within the last decade research in family study has been greatly influenced by groups associated with Bateson, Lidz, and Wynne. (As this is not a review of the field, much significant work of others has been omitted.) Common to each of these groups is the emphasis placed on the social transactions occurring within the family and their influence in developing personality—in terms of anxiety, social role, communicative defects, and behavioral deviations.

Bateson, focusing on schizophrenic communication as derived from patterns of communication in the family, proposes that

> the symptoms of schizophrenia are adaptive responses of an individual to an underlying illness; . . . it appears as if the "pathology" to which the psychosis is a response refers to the distorted pattern of family relationships (Meshler and Waxler, 1965, p. 289).

Haley, associated with Bateson and Don Jackson, describes schizophrenic behavior as purposeful and learned. The patient, faced in the family by incongruent messages that he cannot avoid, deny, or reconcile without losing a needed relationship, refuses to define important human relationships, resorting to speech in which meaning is kept obscure (Meshler and Waxler, 1965).

Wynne describes the desirable family situation as one in which roles are clearly defined, messages unambiguous, and self-identification and reality-testing made possible. The schizophrenic person learns a role suitable to the family, but not to the demands of the larger culture; in adolescence, unable to separate from the family and reconcile his accustomed role with that expected of him by the culture, he exhibits schizophrenic behavior (Meshler and Waxler, 1965).

Lidz and his associates (1956) focused more intensely on the role of the father in the family, the mother hitherto having borne the brunt of investigation, acrimony, and guilt. Lidz pictures the family of the schizophrenic person as having a culture grossly at variance with the society at large; in the family, identity models are poor and irrational behavior is taught. Psychosis develops when the individual feels unable to deal with his own hostile, incestuous impulses and the demands of society for adolescent adjustment (Meshler and Waxler, 1965).

In outlining the above studies I wish to emphasize a shift in the focus of attention. We have observed that schizophrenia has been looked on as a disease within a person, unrelated to the environment save in terms of the hereditary-congenital defect or imposed organic injury. The trend has been from a concern with the relationship of the child (later to become schizophrenic) with his mother, to a recognition of the role of father and siblings, and more recently to a formal consideration of the family relationships as operative in a social field. Here I refer to Gardner Murphy's definition of field as

the psychological approach which regards the barrier between individual and environment as indefinite and unstable, and requires the consideration of an organism-environment field whose properties are studied as field properties. . . . [The] world and self flow into one another. The boundary is often vague or non-existent, but the flow is always *directed* to some extent by the relations between the outer and inner structures" (1947, p. 15).

In simplest terms, the family is looked on as a social organization which has structure, tradition, purpose, and covert and overt ways of behavior, some of which are at least minimally in keeping with cultural requirements and others of which are private, may not be clearly recognized or admitted as existing even by family members, and are not socially acceptable. In this group each person has a role, determined in part by the greater society and in part by the particular family's background and current needs. As the family molds the behavior of the child, so does the child play a part in molding and controlling the behavior of his family group. Within some families—for reasons suggested in the studies reviewed—one or more members develop a type of estrangement, eventually described as schizophrenia.

The family field tends to maintain a dynamic equilibrium, being resistant to major alteration, and shifting in accommodation to behavioral changes in its constituent members. Thus alterations in the beliefs, values, and roles of family members are likely to be more or less overtly opposed, as threatening to the family mythology and its need for stability. In brief, growth and change in a patient may be resisted by parents and siblings unable to make those changes in themselves required to bring about a reorganization and new stability of the social field of the family.

The "Milieu"

The concept of the social field, developed in detail by Kurt Lewin (1951), is relevant to the study of groups living in a psychiatric hospital and has been variously used in studies of social environment, or "milieu," and in the forming of what is often called "milieu therapy."

There follow two quotations from Stanton and Schwartz (1954):

The systematic study of *personality functioning as a part of institutional functioning* in the mental hospital began perhaps with the work of Harry Stack Sullivan at Sheppard and Enoch Pratt Hospital, in Towson, Maryland, 1929–1931. . . . The results were not obtained by special tricks, but rather by the functional organization as a whole (p. 13).

We have assumed . . . that all human beings are continually engaged in social activity, that every recognized "mental phenomenon" is, in fact, treatable as a part of this continuous interaction with other people. . . . Impulses do not function without relation to the current social situation but can be aroused, satisfied, or altered by one's perception and interpretation of it. All aspects of personality are a part of current interpersonal relations but in ways which are by no means clear (p. 27).

The psychiatric hospital ward has been studied as an example of a social field in which the patient plays an active role in structuring his environment and determining his own fate. From this point of view the following can be said about the hospital:

1. It does not exist simply as a shelter, assumed to be benign, designed to protect the public and the patients from each other.

2. Having more than a custodial function, the hospital environment may be destructive to the patient's welfare, despite its constructive purpose.

3. The hospital has its public and private aspects—the "worlds" of the physician, the patient, the nurse, and so on—each influencing the other, frequently in the absence of any open communication between the parts.

4. Formal and informal—often competing—communication systems, power structures, and concepts of value may exist side by side in a social equilibrium marked by a spurious appearance of harmony.

5. The organization tends to perpetuate itself, resisting change threatening to the continuation of its homeostasis.

As the social structure of the hospital was conceived of as possibly therapeutic in itself, it became essential to define a "good" milieu in terms of the goals being set—improved functioning within the institution, discharge to the community, "personality change," and the like.

John and Elaine Cumming (1962) suggested that in order to bring about the restitution of the patient's ego the hospital milieu should provide the following:

1. "[a] clear, organized, and unambiguous social structure, problems to solve in protected situations, and a variety of settings in which to solve these problems";

2. "[a] peer group and a helpful staff to encourage and assist him to live more effectively"; and

3. The aim of "equipping the patient to act in clearly defined roles powered by a variety of motivating forces and governed by different cultural values" (p. 71). "Because the milieu is more lifelike than the controlled

two-person relationship and because it is assumed that synthetic function can be improved through executive function channels, we would argue that milieu therapy is as effective as dyadic therapy and more easily generalized to the total life situation" (p. 61).

The effect of the various approaches outlined above is to invite attention to the interrelationships of the environment-organism complex. Caudill (1958) makes this point in speaking of open systems[2]:

> [S]tress can manifest itself in one or more of a number of linked open systems . . . the strain on one system can be transmitted to others so that several become involved in the process of adaptation and defense. These linked open systems may be thought of as: physiology; personality; relatively permanent meaningful small groups, e.g., the family; and wider social structures, e.g., community and nation or, variously, economic and political structures. The particular characteristics of any of these systems are influenced in differing degrees by, and form a part of, the culture of the society in which they occur (pp. 1–2).

"Social" Psychiatry and the Group

At the present time there is great interest in the application of psychiatric theory and technique to the needs of society outside of the hospital and the private consulting room. It is recognized that no form of therapy has "emptied the mental hospitals" as some had hoped might happen, and that for most people consultation with an individual practitioner is impractical in terms of time, money, and service availability, even if such attention were demonstrably useful. There are not enough practitioners—medical and other—being trained to meet the needs of the current population, to say nothing of population increases. Group therapy in itself, now with its own body of theory and practice, furthers an understanding of social processes but cannot in itself meet current needs.

There is developing a field of community psychiatry, techniques used in a study of the two-group, the small group, the family, and the institution being brought to bear on the disorders of larger segments of society. Whereas "mental disorder" was once private—the tragedy and the isolated concern of individuals and families—it is now becoming a problem of "public health." In years past gods and devils were blamed for mental disorder; then the accusation shifted to constitutional and hereditary defects, to infections and degenerative processes, to chemical and other malfunctions; slowly the family organization was drawn into the field of study—first with attention focused on the mother, later on the father and siblings, and currently on the group; in time the institution was looked on and found wanting; and now the larger community. And through it all there moves

[2] Biological and cultural systems are "open" in the sense that their continuance depends on reciprocal exchanges with other systems.

that relative unknown—"the nature of man." The "blame" for illness has been passed from one possible causative agent to another. Possibly the burden must be carried not by one, but by a number of agents.

The following statement by Sullivan is applicable at this juncture:

This synthesis is not yet complete. The next, I trust, great steps in its emergency [will come] with the realization that the field of psychiatry is neither the mentally sick individual, nor the successful and unsuccessful processes that may be observed in groups and that can be studied in detached objectivity. The field of psychiatry is the field of interpersonal relations, under any and all circumstances in which those relations exist (1953, p. 10).

Behavioral Therapy

Recently there have developed much interest and considerable literature on behavior modification—or therapy—based on learning theory in contrast to the medical model. The focus is on those "activities of an organism that can be observed by another organism or by an experimenter's instruments" (Hilgard, 1962, p. 614).

This focus on behavior has been succinctly stated by Eysenck: "Learning theory does not postulate any . . . 'unconscious causes,' but regards neurotic symptoms as simple learned habits; there is no neurosis underlying the symptom, but merely the symptom itself. *Get rid of the symptom and you have eliminated the neurosis.*" . . . [There is implied] a formulation of what is meant by maladjustive behavior or symptomatic behavior that differs markedly from the conceptualizations that have been popular for the last seventy-five years. . . . [Therapy is] focused on overt subject responses and the stimuli that control these responses. . . . [Foregone are] intrapsychic conflicts, repressions, and other dynamic explanations (Ullman and Krasner, 1965, p. 2).

There are a number of reports of behavior therapy with chronically disordered schizophrenic patients, but I am unable to evaluate the results currently. It should be noted that this approach differs in theory and technique from both the medical and the psychoanalytic models.

Other Dimensions

The study of man is being extended, as he is seen to be a functional component of his environment. And although there is a holistic quality to this development, the whole is, in a sense, fragmented, each segment developing its own experts who may find it difficult to sympathize or communicate with one another.

The psychiatrist concerns himself largely with the forms and vicissitudes of verbal communication. He pays attention to content, noting also phonemal spacing, tone, and the vocal and other gestural accompaniments of speech, but much of what he knows has not been formally taught to him and is used without recognition of the subtleties of his behavior. We are learning about the communicative aspects of odor, sound, taste, touch, time, and space—factors that play important roles in early life but later are often pushed aside and "forgotten." Our attitudes toward these communicative modes, acquired early in life without formal teaching, often seem "natural and God-given," their cultural and biological significances going unrecognized.

The anthropologist Edward Hall (1966) reminds us of the varied aspects of man:

> As an anthropologist I have become accustomed to going back to the beginning and searching out the biological substructures from which a given aspect of human behavior springs. This approach underscores the fact that man is first, last, and always, like other members of the animal kingdom, a prisoner of his biological organism. The gulf that separates him from the rest of the animal kingdom is not nearly so great as most people think (p. ix).
>
> [At the same time] no matter how hard man tries it is impossible for him to divest himself of his own culture, for it has penetrated to the roots of his nervous system and determines how he perceives the world. Most of his culture lies hidden and is outside voluntary control, making up the warp and weft of human existence. Even when small fragments of culture are elevated to awareness, they are difficult to change, not only because they are so personally experienced but *because people cannot act or interact at all in any meaningful way except through the medium of culture* (p. 177).

The traditional psychoanalytic approach has emphasized the intrapsychic aspects of man's living—the interplay of psychic structures evolved through contact of the biological-instinctual given with interpersonal, social, and cultural requirements. In the development of "ego psychology" an effort is made to move beyond explanations of human behavior as simply expressions of the vicissitudes of instinctual drives, greater emphasis being placed on the learned development of behavior. This move requires a concern with such phenomena as physical motility, sensory and perceptual responses, thought, and language, with an increased recognition of the impact of environmental events in eliciting and modifying behavior.

It is evident that in this survey attention has not been given to the remarkable expansion of the use of drugs in the treatment of psychiatric disorders. One reason for this neglect is not only my own ignorance, but the lack of a theory derived from drug usage and generally applicable to the concept of schizophrenia. That many drugs have been helpful to disturbed people at times of stress there is no doubt, but their use—as with other of our procedures—is not curative of the disorders in which they are given. Their use as an adjunct to intensive psychotherapy is currently being determined.

Psychotherapy

Through the years in which I have had any formal contact with schizophrenic behavior there has extended one unifying thread: the patient and the therapist, together, often unhappily and with distrust, two people in a difficult situation, each curious, fearful, and driven to discover something of himself and the other. I know that there are a number of ways in which human behavior can be changed, but at present I see change not only in terms of growth and learning, but as being accompanied by trepidation, uncertainty, pain, and the lingering apprehension that the way one has chosen to go is the wrong way, and permits no return or any alternative. Reasonably, I cannot insist that man is more than what he might seem to be, a conglomeration of attributes traceable to a past and subject to reduction to some form of understanding. Illogically, however, I choose to be unreasonable, seeing man as "more" than what I could rightly expect him to be. For such an act of self-assertion I feel no contrition, for I do as I do with a certain sense of humor. For me—a man—to aspire to conclusive knowledge of what I am is to usurp the role of an almighty power, or to reduce my own living to an absurdity.

Nonetheless, there are a few statements that I can make about schizophrenia and the psychotherapeutic encounter.

I am currently of the opinion that schizophrenic behavior has its social origins in infancy—that is, in the period prior to the acquisition of speech skills and well-defined object identity. At that time in such a person's experience human relatedness is marked by anxiety and excessive ambiguity, there is doubt and uncertainty regarding self-identity and object relations, and there begins the dissociation of systems of sentiments reflecting painful, inadequately perceived and differentiated, poorly formulated experience; such systems must be available to awareness in later life (as in early adolescence) for the integration of complex, intimate attachments to other people. The difficulties originating in early years have interfered with the learning of skills in succeeding development eras and have not been adequately corrected by later experience. The appearance of gross behavioral distortions in the adolescence of some people who have previously made outwardly "good adjustments" may reflect social pressures to find suitable expression of the needs for intimacy and sexuality and to meet cultural demands for a public demonstration of and a personal acceptance of self-identity and of independence from earlier family ties. From this point of view emphasis is placed on the interplay between the sequential unfolding of biologic potential and living experience, without attempting at this stage of our knowledge to define possible inadequacies in terms of a chemical-neurological-structural background. In brief, the person who manifests psychotic behavior has not developed a clear-cut, satisfying, dependable concept of himself or of the motivations and expected behavior of others. He is made anxious by the human relationship that he requires. In dealing with another person his judgment, perception, and foresight are seriously impaired by learning defects, by the dissociation of important motivational systems, and by the recurrent, uncontrollable intrusion into awareness of poorly comprehended and frightening fragments of these latter, adding to familiar and seemingly "normal" processes of thought a quality of the strange, the uncanny, and the mad.

It should be noted that I refer here to people who have managed to pass through the puberty change without evidence of a major psychological disaster. I am not speaking of childhood autism and schizophrenia, which I expect reflect grave disturbance of the social scene in the early months of life, but am referring to an adolescent crisis (in the developmental rather than the strictly chronological sense). As I noted previously I do not clearly distinguish neurosis from psychosis, thinking these groupings to be more different in degree than in kind.

Both schizophrenia and the psychotherapeutic processes are here considered to be manifestations of interpersonal experience and thus, in a sense, suited to each other. However, there is a need to be more specific. I look on the hebephrenic and paranoid modes as behavioral "solutions" of the more acute, confusional schizophrenic episode. Although hebephrenic and paranoid behaviors serve to reduce anxiety, they constitute grave oversimplifications of experience and do not readily yield to a psychotherapeutic intervention which requires further interpersonal involvement, but are not to be labeled as "hopeless."

Patients who have been hospitalized for years may elaborate patterns of behavior that seem to reflect discouragement, low morale, and apathy, accentuated by the realistic loss of opportunity with the passing of time and a dread of returning to a society in which their role for long has been that of the sick and insane. Such people are not simply schizophrenic as I have used the term here, and the therapeutic task in part is one of retraining and rehabilitation.

Much has been written about the technique of psychotherapy with the schizophrenic patient and I have nothing strikingly new to add. For the moment let us recall Miss A., frightened and alone in the room with me, the therapist she never sought and from whom she has little reason to expect help. What can be done? Nothing very complex. I expect to make myself available, to be present as much as possible when needed, to set limits to destructive behavior, and to learn what I can of how Miss A.

experiences her life. I do not see her as "diseased," but as struggling with problems that are hers, but cannot be entirely foreign to me as another human being; and I have confidence in our making sense together. I expect to be angry, discouraged, rebuffed, and troubled by doubts, as well as to become attached to the patient by ties of affection that are likely to endure. And I do not intend to abandon the task.

The above, of course, is very little to say, but we cannot at this stage of our learning tell others—or even be certain ourselves—just "how to do" psychotherapy. However, basic to the content, form, and technique of a therapeutic relationship are the following matters, which must be considered—accepted, modified, or rejected.

1. Human relationships are looked on as important factors in molding human growth and development, be the outcome "normal" or "pathological."

2. The therapeutic relationship is a special form of human relationship, and its establishment is both possible and desirable.

3. Having determined to enter on such a relationship with a patient, the therapist recognizes that the results may be beneficial or otherwise, and therefore must set up clearly defined goals and make decisions regarding courses of action open to him. He cannot be "neutral" and devoid of "values."

4. To develop a relationship there must be meetings between the participants. It is then necessary to decide upon the frequency of the meetings, the length of each session, the places in which they are to be held, and their duration over an extent of time (days, weeks, months, years).

5. The form of contact in the meetings should be recognized and defined, attention being paid to communication through the media of words, sound, sight, touch, smell, taste, and space.

6. As the participants meet over a period of time there will occur varieties of emotional arousal and inevitably, more or less obscurely and for better or worse, relational bonds will form between the two. Much of the therapeutic task lies in the nurturing, defining, and comprehending of these ties.

7. The relationship will have a reciprocal quality in that to some extent the needs and responses of one will be geared to those of the other. Over an extended period of time, marked by recrudescences of intense anxiety and psychotic behavior, both participants will experience discomfort, uncertainty, doubt as to the value of the procedure, and a desire to abandon it. Both are engaged, each in his own way, in an exploration of personality—his own and the other's.

8. As dependency is developed, recognized, and accepted, the desire for, and the strength to accept independence and separation will develop. That is, unless there is a pathological need for a therapist and patient to

cling to each other, aversive behavior will develop that will lead each to seek greater opportunity for his own development away from the other.

The preceding outline is perhaps too general to be of value. It is with such matters as the foregoing, however, that much of our discussion regarding the techniques of psychotherapy is concerned.

In a study of the psychotherapeutic experiences of a number of patients and therapists, Strupp, Wallach, and Wogan (1964) have this to say:

A solid working relationship in which the participants develop a sense of mutual trust is unquestionably a *sine qua non* for all forms of psychotherapy. In its absence there can be no successful psychotherapy. . . . [O]vershadowing this attitudinal-emotional factor is the patient's conviction that he has the therapist's respect. This faith in the integrity of the therapist as a person may be called the capstone of a successful therapeutic relationship subsuming all other characteristics (pp. 82–83).

So for the time being, Miss A. and I must do what we can together. As more knowledge comes we shall try to put it to good use, but the task is present and cannot wait. It is true that few are helped by this procedure in terms of those who need help, but that need not deter one. Perhaps the knowledge gained in these endeavors can be put to good use in helping us understand how we can so easily and destructively become imprisoned in a universe of our self-created symbols.

In conclusion I refer to the numerous concepts and their supporters, seemingly competing to save the schizophrenic person from his variant of the human condition. We often appear to be bitter contestants, set upon the advancement or salvation of personal ambition and prestige. But there is more in all of this than the welfare of any one of us, and despite our differences our enterprise is, in a sense, cooperative.

Again I quote from Camus's book *The Plague*, in which a priest and a physician hold different views of life while they work, each in his own way, in the midst of a dreadful epidemic of the pest.

Says the priest, regretfully: "And yet—I haven't convinced you!"

Replies the physician: "What does it matter? What I hate is death and disease, as you well know. And whether you wish it or not, we're allies, facing them and fighting them together."

References

Anonymous. *The Philosophy of Insanity: By a Late Inmate of the Glasgow Royal Asylum for Lunatics at Gartnavel.* New York: Greenberg, 1947.

Arlow, J. A., and Brenner, C. *Psychoanalytic Concepts and the Structural Theory.* New York: International Universities Press, 1964.

Camus, A. *The Plague*. New York: Knopf, 1937.

Caudill, W. "Effects of Social and Cultural Systems in Reactions to Stress." *Social Science Research Council Items*, 1958, 1–2.

Cumming, J., and Cumming, Elaine. *Ego and Milieu: Theory and Practice of Environmental Therapy*. New York: Atherton Press, 1962.

Eiseley, L. "Call Us Ishmael." Review of E. D. H. Johnson, ed., *The Poetry of Earth: A Collection of English Nature Writings. The Washington Post Book Week*, April 16, 1966, 1–8.

Ellison, E. A., and Hamilton, D. M. "The Hospital Treatment of Dementia Praecox: Part I." *American Journal of Psychiatry*, 106, No. 12 (1949), 454–461.

Ferenczi, S. "The Unwelcome Child and His Death Instinct." *International Journal of Psychiatry*, 10 (1929), 125–129.

Fromm-Reichmann, Frieda. "Notes on the Development of Treatment of Schizophrenics by Psychoanalytical Psychotherapy." *Psychiatry*, 11 (1948), 263–273.

Gerard, D. L., and Siegel, I. "The Family Background of Schizophrenia." *Psychoanalytic Quarterly*, 24 (1950), 47–73.

Gottlieb, J. S., Frohman, C. E., and Beckett, P. G. S. "Biologic Maladaptation in Schizophrenia." In P. H. Hoch and J. Zubin (eds.), *Psychopathology of Schizophrenia*. New York: Grune & Stratton, 1966. Pp. 233–243.

Hajdu-Gimes, Lilly. "Contributions to the Etiology of Schizophrenia." *Psychoanalytic Review*, 27 (1940), 421–438.

Hall, E. T. *The Hidden Dimension*. Garden City, N.Y.: Doubleday, 1966.

Hilgard, E. *Introduction to Psychology*. 3rd ed.; New York: Harcourt, 1962.

Hinsie, L. E., and Campbell, R. J. *Psychiatric Dictionary*. 3rd ed.; New York: Oxford University Press, 1960.

Hoch, P. H. "Schizophrenia." In P. H. Hoch and J. Zubin (eds.), *Psychopathology of Schizophrenia*. New York: Grune & Stratton, 1966. Pp. 283–301.

Kasinin, J., Knight, E., and Sage, P. "The Parent-Child Relationship in Schizophrenia." *Journal of Nervous and Mental Diseases*, 79 (1934), 249–263.

Kety, S. S. "Biochemical Theories of Schizophrenia." A two-part critical review of current theories and the evidence used to support them. *Science*, 129 (1959), 1528–1532, 1590–1596.

Kety, S. S. "Recent Biochemical Theories of Schizophrenia." In D. D. Jackson (ed.), *The Etiology of Schizophrenia*. New York: Basic Books, 1960. Pp. 120–145.

Landis, C. L. *Varieties of Psychopathological Experience*. New York: Holt, Rinehart & Winston, 1964.

Levy, D. "Maternal Over-protection and Rejection." *Archives of Neurology and Psychiatry*, 25, No. 4 (1931), 886–889.

Lewin, K. *Field Theory in Social Science: Selected Theoretical Papers*. New York: Harper, 1951.

Lidz, T., Parker, B., and Cornelison, Alice. "The Role of the Father in the Family Environment of the Schizophrenic Patient." *American Journal of Psychiatry*, 113 (1956), 126–132.

Limentoni, D. "Symbiotic Identification in Schizophrenia." *Psychiatry*, 19 (August 1956), 231–236.

Meshler, E. G., and Waxler, Nancy E. "Family Interaction Processes and Schizophrenia: A Review of Current Theories." *The Merrill-Palmer Quarterly*, 11 (1965), 269–315.

Murphy, G. *Personality: A Biosocial Approach to Origins and Structure* (1947). 2nd ed.; New York: Basic Books, 1966.

Noyes, A. P. *Modern Clinical Psychiatry*. Philadelphia: Saunders, 1954.

Oltman, J. E., McGarry, J. J., and Friedman, S. "Parental Deprivation and Broken Home in Dementia Praecox and Other Mental Disorders." *American Journal of Psychiatry*, 108 (1952), 685–694.

Reichard, Suzanne, and Tillman, C. "Patterns of Parent-Child Relationships in Schizophrenia." *Psychiatry*, 13 (1950), 247–257.

Stanton, A. H., and Schwartz, M. S. *The Mental Hospital*. New York: Basic Books, 1954.

Strupp, H. H., Wallach, M. C., and Wogan, M. *Psychological Monographs*, 1967.

Sullivan, H. S. "The Common Field of Research and Clinical Psychiatry." *Psychiatric Quarterly*, 1 (1927), 276–291.

Sullivan, H. S. *Conceptions of Modern Psychiatry*. New York: Norton, 1953.

Terry, Gladys C., and Rennie, T. A. C. "Analysis of Parergasia." *Nervous and Mental Disease Monographs*, 64 (1938).

Tietze, Trude. "Study of Mothers of Schizophrenic Patients." *Psychiatry*, 12 (February 1949), 55–65.

Ullman, L. P., and Krasner, L. (eds.). *Case Studies in Behavior Modification*. New York: Holt, Rinehart & Winston, 1965.

Wahl, C. W. "Some Antecedent Factors in the Family Histories of 392 Schizophrenics." *American Journal of Psychiatry*, 110 (1954), 668–676.

IV
CULTURE AND SOCIETY

23

Relationship of Psychoanalysis with Social Agencies: Community Implications

LEONARD J. DUHL and ROBERT L. LEOPOLD

Introduction

In recent decades there has been a substantial and growing increase in psychiatric interventions with people who have critical effects on community agencies, institutions, and organizations. These interventions are based on gradually evolving psychiatric concepts that derive from the concern of the modern psychotherapist with the social context of the patient and with the entire social matrix of the community in which patients and nonpatients exist.

Many of the psychiatrists engaged in such interventions are psychoanalytically trained and experienced. Through their work psychoanalysis has come to have a certain set of implications for community mental health activities. Because they are relatively new and unfamiliar, these implications are pertinent to discussions concerning the current frontiers of psychoanalysis.

This movement away from the dyadic limitations of traditional analytic practice has produced a number of substantial problems. The most pressing of these has to do with the changing identity of the analyst, a matter causing considerable anxiety among psychoanalysts. Zinberg (1965), in a well-reasoned and sensitive review of the relationships between psychoanalysis and various aspects of American life, evaluates the danger to psychoanalysis that lies in a dissemination of its theoretical and therapeutic concepts into the community, that is, the danger of its dilution as a professional discipline. It is clear that a potential danger exists and that this danger is increased if one attempts a point-by-point translation of psychoanalytic concepts valid for individual treatment relationships to community interventions. This is particularly true because interventions in the community must, by their very nature, occur outside the traditional psychiatric milieu. The concepts of social psychiatry make it apparent that one must deal not merely with "cases"; that is, with patients whom one sees outside the office. To do so would constitute only a transfer to another geographic setting of patient-focused psychotherapy. Rather, the newer thinking in social and community psychiatry sees the individual patient and his problems as a "flag" signaling something amiss in the patient's social system. For example, Stanton and Schwartz (1954) view any unusual disturbance of the individual patient on a psychiatric ward as signaling a breakdown in the physician-nurse care-giving function in relation to the entire ward. Thus "case" treatment, applied alone, violates such thinking. On the other hand, an attempt to apply psychoanalytic thinking to a total situation, without some adaptation, violates the essential spirit of psychoanalytic therapy in the sense that its very base is an extremely personal relationship between therapist and patient.

This chapter presents no such point-by-point translation. Rather, it attempts a more flexible translation whereby psychoanalytic theory in general and certain psychoanalytic concepts in particular are *adapted* to the uses of social psychiatry. Here psychoanalysis is seen as enlarging and enriching the conceptual framework of social psychiatry, as well as providing additional operational approaches for the social psychiatrist engaged in community mental health activities.

The primary focus of this chapter is not on the ethereal question of whether psychoanalysis has a place in community work. It is a fact that psychoanalytic psychiatrists have been playing, and no doubt will continue to play, critical roles in community work. We believe that the psychoanalytic training and experience of these psychiatrists have been significant factors promoting their effective functioning in these roles. Our purposes here are to examine these factors; to discuss some of the problems connected with the new roles; and to suggest to other psychoanalytic psychiatrists that they may have special values to contribute to community mental health activities, and that participation in these activities may bring them personal and professional enrichment.

Historical Perspective

It is relevant to give some brief initial consideration to the emergence of social psychiatric understanding and attitudes within the discipline of clinical psychiatry itself. At the outset, one must de-emphasize the apparent dichotomy between traditional psychotherapeutic practice and intervention at community levels in the interest of mental health. Everything a patient does and says, including what he does and says as a participant in a social system, falls within the therapist's purview. Thus every psychiatrist and every psychoanalyst who maintains the fundamental one-to-one relationship of individual treatment must also maintain an indirect relationship to the patient's social system. Indeed, following the work of Nathan Ackerman in dealing with the family, direct contact with the patient's total family and other significant figures in his environment has become more common. A modern psychotherapist, then, although he may not practice social psychiatry in the full sense implied here, does, in fact, engage in some aspects of it.

In the twentieth century, new confrontations with social systems have involved psychiatrists in new kinds of relationships with individuals and groups. The experiences of three wars in this century erected the signposts of a new way of working. During these wars, the psychiatrist was asked to lend his special knowledge, insight, and skills in the development of military programs of selection, training, support in the field, and rehabilitation. He soon found that to meet the mental health needs of the military services he could not depend exclusively or largely on classic one-to-one relationships with individuals. He had to become increasingly involved in more complex interactions with many kinds of military and nonmilitary personnel, that is, with the entire social system serving the war effort. Just as he had sought traditionally to intervene in the individual's functioning in the interest of mental health, so he now sought to intervene, in the same interest, in the functioning of a social system.

The psychiatrist's experiences in these new situations, which were created by emergencies and met by improvisation, gave him a foretaste of what it would mean to take care of the psychological needs of total populations, when, again, traditional practice would have to be modified in order to meet vast demand with inadequate manpower. At the same time, social scientists were beginning to see how psychiatry might help them search for an answer to a question brought into sharp focus by the war: "What is wrong with a society that produces so many 'misfits'?" Since the control of certain environmental factors affected the rate of incapacitating mental illness in military situations, it was inevitable that the possibility should be seen for intervention, with the same objective, in nonmilitary situations.

The concept spread to other social institutions, for example, industrial organizations, schools and colleges, philanthropic overseas agencies, and more recently, the Peace Corps (Duhl, Leopold, and English, 1964).

Today, psychiatric participation in such societal interventions is more or less taken for granted. For example, a university psychiatrist may practice not only individual psychotherapy, but may also be deeply involved in the university's social system, where he tries to develop a sound mental health climate. His presence at administrative meetings, and even classes, may seem an unorthodox form of psychiatric intervention, but its roots in traditional psychiatry and its relevance can be demonstrated.

Thus social psychiatry begins to show concerns in common with those of the public health services: in addition to interest in care, treatment, and rehabilitation there is interest in all the environmental factors relevant to the promotion of health. Social psychiatric emphasis is seen as shifting from traditional psychiatric preoccupation with "curing" the sick to improving mental health in the whole community.

Social psychiatrists, like public health physicians, now find themselves working in state and local health departments; in educational systems; in welfare bureaus; and in many other governmental, quasi-governmental, and private agencies that in one way or another bear on the mental health of significant numbers of people. The psychiatrist's role is predominantly that of consultant to those who directly affect the functioning of individuals within a specific part of a social system. But he will also intervene indirectly in the functioning of the whole system in order to promote the mental health of the total population for which the agency is "responsible." For example, a psychiatrist may serve as consultant to the principal and teachers of a public school; in this role, he will help to work out some of the problems of individual pupils without ever seeing them as patients. He may find that many individual difficulties seem to be focused on a particular administrative procedure, and suggest that this be modified throughout the school, and perhaps throughout the local school system. An increase in the number of patient referrals from one part of a system often signals some serious malfunctioning in the over-all system. When the psychiatric consultant's identification of a problem leads to a more careful study of administrative procedure and policy by responsible officials, he can often play an important part in both the prevention of breakdown and the improvement of general conditions of work and the promotion of productivity.

Although psychiatric concern with the social system began, in general, with improvised responses to emergency needs, continued involvement has demonstrated the need for thinking ahead and planning for environments conducive to mental health. Inevitably, such planning requires psychiatric participation in the processes of over-all policy formulation and program development. The psychiatrist's contributions at this level may be primarily theoretical, particularly in relation to new and unprecedented programs, or the total reorganization of old ones, where long-term issues must be decided. But even so, he may be asked to make responses to immediate and pressing needs, and these can still have a significant effect on future developments. In established social systems, his participation on a theoretical basis is more likely to follow intervention in connection with a short-term issue. But it must be stressed here that regardless of how he arrives at the level of policy formulation and program development, the social psychiatrist is not personally responsible for the outcome of decisions made at this level. Such decisions are the responsibility of administration and management, not of medicine. The social psychiatrist participates in decision only to the extent of providing a specialist's professional insight, knowledge, and skills, which, when combined with those of other appropriate disciplines, can be used to facilitate the decision-making process.

Values Derived from Psychoanalysis

What then are the special values that a psychoanalytic background brings to these contributions the psychiatrist makes in community mental health work?

From the broad perspective of *general adaptation*, psychoanalytic psychiatry at present remains the only body of theoretical knowledge held in common by medicine, psychology, social work, and the behavioral sciences in general. Thus psychoanalysis, although it arises from the exploration in depth of individual psychological functioning, has become a cement that holds together, in rather crude form, a disparate group of disciplines many of which focus not on the individual, but on larger units of society. Although often inadequate, the cement serves until a better one is developed to unite on broadly theoretical grounds, at least, the concerns of those who view the individual and his well-being in terms of his relationship to the total social environment. Obviously, groups of individuals and institutions do not "behave" in the same manner as a single human being. However, psychoanalytic theory provides many important insights respecting individual behavior needed for the development of their own understanding and theories by those disciplines whose major concern is group behavior.

Psychoanalytic theory has played a part in the formulation of some important elements of what is called a *general systems model* of society. Psychoanalysis in itself provides, in fact, a general systems model. Such a model places the individual in a vast and interacting network of systems. He himself is a system; all of his sub-systems (vascular, respiratory, muscular, digestive, etc.) are involved in constant and reciprocal interchanges of matter and energy. The individual as a system is in a similar process of interchange with a series of impinging systems. Starting with his immediate family, the network branches out to include systems represented by all the "communities" in which he lives: educational, occupational, religious, political, recreational, geographic, etc. These systems interact with each other both directly and indirectly. To intervene in one part of this complex network is to set in motion a series of reactions in others. Psychoanalysis as a therapeutic technique deals with the individual, but it sets in motion many reactions in other parts of the individual's various social systems. Likewise, changes in other parts of the network (e.g., those in the work situation or in the educational setting) can set in motion reactions that in some cases may be as significant to the individual as the psychoanalytic process itself.

Thus the psychoanalyst, even though he focuses on the individual, has a sense of process with respect to the interactions within the individual and between the individual and the ever-widening social systems of which he is a part. Psychoanalysis was, in fact, one of the first branches of modern medicine to develop a multi-causal theory of disease. It recognizes no single cause for mental disorder either in the individual or in the environment. Rather, illness is seen as the product of complex combinations of, and interactions among, disturbances occurring within the individual and in the environment. A community attack on the problems of mental health is an infinitely complicated task. To approach it realistically, the social psychiatrist must develop such a sense of process. It is likely to be "ready-made" in the psychoanalytic psychiatrist because he has long been oriented to the idea of a general systems model of society and feels quite comfortable with it.

In speaking of *more specific adaptations*, it is useful to think of the conceptual framework of individual psychoanalytic psychotherapy as providing some significant *bridges* to the practice of social psychiatry.

We may first consider social psychiatry's concern, in its community-based preventive efforts, with sociocultural supports required for individual psychological health, especially at critical stages of personality development. A particularly urgent example refers to the weakening or disappearance of social institutions that formerly helped the adolescent find his ego identity. Involved here are the dissolution of the strong family unit; the ever-growing multiplicity of functional "communities" of which the individual is a part; the political and other jurisdictional complexities that blur group identities; the increasing difficulties involved in making a career choice; the gaps between the education generally available and the skills needed to survive; and other problems depressingly familiar to most students of human affairs. The social psychiatrist is called on frequently to assist in planning sociocultural supports that will compensate, it is to be hoped, for these deficiencies in our social environment. The bridge from traditional practice that can be expected to help the psychoanalyst plan particularly effectively is his special orientation to the concepts centering around *levels of ego growth and of socialization.*

Another bridge is the psychoanalyst's sensitivity to the *timing of interventions.* In community mental health work inestimable importance is attached to the community resources that support the individual when his internal resources are inadequate for coping with stress, i.e., when he is in crisis. The social psychiatrist must have a thorough understanding of *crisis theory.* He must be acutely aware that crises occur in social systems as they do in individuals, and appreciate the significant differences.

Certainly an institutional crisis involves people; yet frequently it relates to problems involving administrative structure, legal arrangements, financing, and capitalization. Crises such as these are not the prime concern of the social psychiatrist, but he should be cognizant of them in the process of consultation with key individuals. Conversely, he must be aware that personal crises in the lives of individuals who most affect the functioning of the institution may reverberate throughout the whole social system of the institution.

For the social system, as well as for the individual, a crisis may present an opportunity for growth and maturation as well as a risk of stagnation. The social system in crisis, like the individual in crisis, is more susceptible to influence than at other times of life. Thus the social psychiatrist makes the most of crises, using them to intervene in the social system in the interest of bettering its resources for supporting and promoting mental health.

It is apparent that the concepts of crisis developed by Lindemann, Caplan, and others derived in large measure from classical psychoanalytic theory and from an understanding of the dynamic balances developed in the last three decades by those interested in ego psychology. The concepts of individual psychodynamics were not carried in toto into the understanding of institutional crises, but rather formed a basis for the further observation of institutions during critical times. Similarly, the techniques of intervention, although they are based on the classical psychoanalytic patterns of interpretation, have undergone modification because of the differences between the behavioral processes of individuals and of institutions.

A psychiatrist may know the dynamic structure of a patient's problems many months in advance of his interpretation to the patient. But he must learn how *not* to intervene too quickly in order to avoid a direct attack on the patient's defenses. Teaching this abstention is a conspicuous difficulty in training young psychiatrists. In social psychiatry, it is equally important that the consultant withhold intervention, even though he is sure that he understands a problem and can help find an answer to it, until the social system in question is ready to loosen the defenses it has built up against seeking a solution.

Some psychiatric experience in the Peace Corps is pertinent here. The psychiatrists who were first asked to come to Washington to help with the new agency's planning and early organization—primarily in setting up psychiatric criteria for selection and procedures for screening applicants psychiatrically—were specifically consultants to the Selection Division. However, their activities were sanctioned by the Medical Division, and they were in constant close contact with its staff because psychiatric clearance is administratively a part of general medical clearance, and hence a part of the total responsibility of the Medical Division.

This responsibility, of course, included maintenance of certain aspects of the Peace Corps training program and of a program of overseas health support. Both these concerns were at that time seen by the Medical Division largely, but not entirely, in physical terms. In psychological terms, the Division focused its thinking primarily on the possibility of psychosis occurring during training or in service overseas.

In contrast, the psychiatrists believed, on the basis of previous experience in related fields, that psychological problems would outweigh physical problems and that few psychotic or pre-psychotic persons would apply for the kind of service offered by the Peace Corps. The latter belief was in fact supported by early developments in Peace Corps recruitment history; moreover, the rigors of the initial screening procedures tended to eliminate such applicants rather quickly. The psychiatrists, then, focused their attention less on potential psychoses than on the difficulties they expected even "normal" persons to encounter in adjusting to new and demanding circumstances. Thus, from the beginning, these consultants felt that training should include psychological as well as physical conditioning, and that overseas health support should include provision for on-the-spot assistance to Volunteers who find themselves in emotional difficulties.

No attempt was made, nevertheless, to press this thinking on the Medical Division all at once, for the psychiatrists realized that resistance was inevitable. The role of the psychiatrist in organizational work—so far removed from the role as a psychotherapist in which he is conventionally perceived—was still so unfamiliar that the sheer weight of novelty alone would militate against immediate receptivity to this intervention. Moreover, it was quite natural that the Division should concentrate its attention on psychosis, for public opinion was expressing grave concern that the Peace Corps might attract seriously disturbed persons; thus, psychiatric experience notwithstanding, considerable actual Peace Corps experience was needed to convince both the public and the Peace Corps administration that this concern was exaggerated. As for the adjustment problems forecast by the psychiatrists, the Medical Division personnel had had little experience in this connection; like most people, they could understand problems they had seen in operation more readily than those reported from the experience of other people. Finally, and perhaps most important, it must be remembered that the psychiatrists were primarily consultants in the process of *selection.* If they attempted to operate outside that process without first obtaining full sanction (from both the Medical Division and other appropriate sources), they would lend credence to the negative stereotype of the psychiatrist as a seeker of omnipotence, and thus tend to reinforce resistance to psychiatric intervention.

The psychiatrists, then, despite convictions and enthusiasm, had to bide their time. In developing relationships within the Division, they tried to make clear to key persons that their interest was not to control, but simply to help wherever possible. Meanwhile, their contributions to the selection process were sufficiently effective to demonstrate that psychiatric consultation has its uses—a demonstration supported by some other contributions they made, on request, at certain nonmedical levels of Peace Corps administration. The facts of actual recruitment gradually assuaged the general concern about possible psychosis, so that the Medical Division became more receptive to the idea of focusing its attention on the problems of adjustment. In the course of time, many such problems, as foreseen by the psychiatrists, did indeed materialize, thus bringing into sharp reality certain issues that had been considered only hypothetical by the Medical Division. Motivation to seek psychiatric intervention then followed quite naturally.

One aspect of this intervention deserves special emphasis here. Frequently these problems precipitated organizational (as well as personal) crises, which gave the psychiatrists opportunities to intervene at times when lasting effects, in terms of developing an overall mental health program for the organization, were most probable.

As events proved to the Medical Division that it could safely and usefully extend its sanction to the psychiatrists to function in areas beyond the mere responsibility for selection, the latter were able, little by little, to offer suggestions and plans that eventually enabled well-defined psychological elements to become integrated into both the training and the overseas support programs.

These developments, reported elsewhere (Duhl, Leopold, and English, 1964), need not be recounted here. However, one incident may be cited as an especially striking example of legitimatization, through clinical evidence, of the psychiatrist's role in organizational work. During the Peace Corps' second year of work overseas, one of these early psychiatrists was asked to attend a regional conference of overseas Peace Corps physicians, planned for discussion of their mutual problems in connection with Volunteer health in the field. He was told to expect that physical problems would take up two-thirds of the discussion and psychological problems about one-third. The ratio proved to be the reverse! With this clear preponderance of psychological over physical problems, there could be little further doubt in the Medical Division about the usefulness of psychiatric participation in programs concerned with Volunteer health.

Understanding the timing of intervention is particularly difficult in social psychiatry because there is so little well-defined experience to guide the practitioner. His experience in clinical practice offers some help, but to avoid too early intervention he must familiarize himself with the workings of the social system. But he must also understand *himself* if he is to avoid an intervention timed in the interest of his own needs. The psychoanalytic psychiatrist's personal analysis should equip him to recognize and deal with his own needs.

Still another bridge is the psychoanalyst's concern with *problems of transference and resistance.* These phenomena are as certain to appear in social practice as they are in clinical practice. However, because of the greater complexities of dealing with the social system, they are not always so readily identifiable. The social psychiatrist brings to his relationship with an agency a ready-made series of transference and countertransference problems. He may be seen as a magician or witch doctor with a capacity for working evil; he may be seen as a physician with a symbolic quality of healing. Most often, he is seen as the ambivalently regarded father. Thus, early in his interactions, he is either cursed or overloved. The group he deals with may turn to him with unrealistic expectations and, at the same time, secretly wish that he fail to meet them. When he does fail, he may be castigated, and even excluded from further group transactions. This aspect of the transference relationship in the social interaction develops faster and is much less explicit than it is in the individual therapeutic relationship. It is less dependent for its resolution on analysis of the transference fantasy than on the social psychiatrist's effectiveness in developing a perception of himself as a purposefully functioning and "human" consultant. The development of rapport, to permit interventions to take place, is as necessary with the group in social practice as it is with patients in traditional practice. Without rapport, no matter how knowledgeable the psychiatrist may be, his knowledge cannot be conveyed to the group in such a way as to contribute genuinely to achievement of its goals.

Certain aspects of the countertransference problem must also be stressed. The psychiatrist working in a social setting is even more likely to be involved in negative countertransference feelings than he is when dealing with individual patients. It is more difficult for him to be realistic about his position in the agency or the community than about his relationship to the patient. A distorted perception of his relationship in the social setting can alter the dimensions of the contribution he has to make, alienate his colleagues, and vitiate his usefulness as a consultant. The psychoanalyst, because of his knowledge of the symbolic nature of the transference and countertransference reactions, with particular respect to his personal analysis, should be better prepared to guard himself against these pitfalls than the non-analyst.

Resistance to the psychiatrist in the role of consultant to the social system is probable. This is not the clinical role that the public, despite many misconceptions, has come to expect and accept. In the consultant role, the psychiatrist finds himself in muddier waters. He is expected to contribute his professional skill and also to behave as if he were an active part of the organization, with all the implications of involvement. As in clinical practice, there will be repeated attempts to force him into symbolic roles. The psychoanalyst, because he has dealt in depth with these attempts in individual therapy, is likely to have developed the patience and constraint with which they must be met in social practice.

Perhaps the most significant of these bridges is the psychoanalyst's understanding of the *dynamic transactional process itself*. Psychiatrists who lack understanding of what is happening between them and the significant persons in an organization frequently become overwhelmed with anxiety and have to withdraw from the situation. There is a great similarity between the process of "working through of unconscious material" in the interaction between the psychoanalyst and the individual patient, and the process by which a group works through some of the unconscious resistance to the psychiatrist in the social setting. The latter requires the same careful understanding as the former. The cues that come from the group as to the unconscious process differ from those that come from the individual, but the fact remains that there are such signals. Psychoanalytic techniques offer guides for dealing with them.

Here again some Peace Corps psychiatric experience is pertinent. One of the early psychiatric consultants in Washington visited a training site (one of the first to be established), and found the Trainees were having a rather unsatisfactory experience. An opportunity to seek out the sources of their hostility and disgruntlement soon presented itself. With an old friend who was attached to the training staff—not a psychiatrist, but a sensitive community organization specialist—he attended a meeting of Trainees called for discussion of various projects and plans.

They found little being accomplished at the meeting. Although an attitude of sullen resentment was quite apparent, there was no frank expression of the real reasons for dissatisfaction. Rather, there was an aimless tossing about of small issues and petty irritations. But there were cues as to an unconscious process going on in the group, for those who were trained to pick them up. Occasionally, there would be a remark such as "There's no use talking—we can't change anything," or "Why bother discussing this? Who cares what we think?" Frequently, even when the discussion involved problems that the Trainees easily could have settled among themselves, they avoided arriving at a solution; and they seemed to aim their remarks obliquely toward the psychiatrist and his friend, to the accompaniment of baleful looks or uneasy laughter.

Obviously, the Trainees' resentment had less to do with the subjects under discussion than with a lack of suitable opportunities to express their dissatisfaction to those in authority. (It should be noted, however, that this failure stemmed from the fact that the training staff were as new at their jobs as the Trainees.) To the Trainees, the psychiatrist and his friend represented "The Organization" and its authority; they were trying to convey their anger at the organization through these two men, but at the same time, fearful of evoking retaliatory anger from the organization, they were avoiding an open expression of their feelings.

The community organization specialist, aware that the meeting would be a total failure unless some psychological insight were injected into it, interrupted the proceedings to ask the psychiatrist what he thought was going on, psychologically speaking, in the discussion. The psychiatrist presented an interpretation corresponding to that set forth here, and the two men discussed the subject freely before the Trainees. This precipitated a venting of all their bottled-up hostility, which they now directed openly at the psychiatrist and the community organization specialist. Subsequently, these two men made it clear, both to the Trainees and to the training staff, that the training situation is not unlike a community organization situation: in both, feelings have to be allowed appropriate expression, and then utilized as the basis for frank exploration of the pertinent problems. The incident seemed to turn the tide of feeling at the site. The Trainees continued to have complaints, but they began to express them at suitable opportunities provided for the purpose. They learned how to handle their feelings usefully, and both staff and Trainees learned how to use what the Trainees talked about as a basis for a valuable community organization experience and for developing relevant improvements in the training program.

In working with healthy people, one encounters a considerable amount of ego strength with which the psychiatrist can ally himself in order to expedite the working-through process. Awareness of, and competence with, techniques of modifying ego-adaptive capacity permits the psychoanalyst to alter defense mechanisms and turn them to constructive advantage, with groups as well as with individuals.

The seduction of the therapist by part of the patient's personality, so familiar to the psychoanalyst, has its counterpart in social psychiatry. Individuals or groups representing one part of a social system will seek to seduce the psychiatrist in order to use him for their own ends, and to exclude him from working toward the over-all ends of the total system. Accordingly, the social psychiatrist must be clear about his role as a consultant for the entire agency, rather than for a discrete part of it. He must remain a friendly, but non-aligned, consultant so that he can intervene as necessary in any part of the system. In other words, the social psychiatrist needs the same kind of professional neutrality in dealing with a group or agency in the social setting as he maintains in dealing with an individual in therapy. The psychoanalyst is helped here because he so readily recognizes seduction and, thanks to his personal analysis, understands the part of himself that is most vulnerable to seduction.

The Change in Role Identity

Throughout the foregoing section various problems have been implied that are associated with the change in role identity that takes place when the clinical psychiatrist moves into social practice. These must be given separate and more specific consideration. Here the relevance of psychoanalytic training has negative as well as positive aspects. Both must be taken into account.

Like other psychiatrists, the psychoanalytic psychiatrist working in a traditional clinical milieu has no particular problems in connection with *role definition*. His patients' expectations of him may be distorted by misconception, but they are based at least in part on their perception of him as a physician. This eases his task when he attempts to clarify his roles and functions for them. Thanks to long tradition, his students and medical colleague require little or no definition of his role. But in social practice there is no long-standing tradition to offer role delineation and supports parallel to those of older milieus. The social field, moreover, does not present him with patients in the traditional sense. Hence, although his title does permit some of the physician's aura to follow him into the field, it is difficult to perceive him there as a healing physician. The social psychiatrist, then, in the absence of supportive tradition, must be prepared to deal with skepticism or hostility (or both) concerning his role more often than deference, from his own and related professions and from the general public. He must be prepared to give full attention to the fantasies he creates when he moves into a public arena.

These fantasies may often be revealed in quite blunt messages; for example, in crude jokes about "headshrinkers." But they may be far more subtle, as in transference phenomena that serve in effect as attempts to exclude him from group participation. His psychoanalytic training and experience should enable him to receive and to interpret the less obvious messages with reasonable accuracy. But the process by which he attempts to dispel these fantasies differs markedly from the calm and patient waiting of clinical practice. He must take positive steps to contradict the negative stereotypes and false expectations of his role that the fantasies represent. He must set about immediately building mutually trusting and respecting relationships with individuals within his working group. Only through these relationships, in time and with patience, can he achieve a satisfactory working definition of his new role. Until he does, he may feel as uncomfortable as does anyone else, psychoanalytically trained or otherwise, who is suddenly shorn of a long-established role identity.

As pressure mounts on the social psychiatrist to find an adequate role identity, and as he finds himself feeling uncomfortable in the new and less privileged status as a consultant rather than a therapist, he may be unconsciously motivated to make patients out of consultees. If he is successful in this, he regains his identity as a therapist and becomes more comfortable. At the same time, he vitiates his usefulness to his agency because he is now focusing on the individual problems of people who may not be clinically ill. This danger is not a major one for experienced psychoanalysts. A more subtle and more significant danger is the temptation, when consulting with agencies, to focus on case material and "patientize" this. By so doing, the psychiatrist apparently remains a consultant, but shifts the focus to an individual rather than to the social system. Thus he maintains at least part of his previous identity and likewise feels more comfortable. Nevertheless, he fails in his obligation to focus his attention primarily on the agency and its work, no matter how needy any individual may be. The continuing self-evaluation to which the psychoanalyst is professionally committed should enable him to guard himself against both these dangers to some extent. Supervision, so far not developed for this field, may be expected to help him become more acutely aware of his own motivation and to deal with it realistically.

It is not only in dispelling fantasies that the psychoanalyst must abandon the attitude of calm and patient waiting to which he has become accustomed in clinical practice. Other aspects of social practice also call for more direct action. Activity in social practice means more than verbal interpretations; moreover, it may be interspersed quite frequently with inactivity, so that the psychiatrist may have to shift continuously back and forth between the two. For example, in addition to recommending appropriate therapy, direct action may mean that the psychiatrist must intervene to have a disturbed child removed from the classroom. Likewise, the university psychiatrist, rather than rely on therapy alone, may have to act directly to help alter a student's course of study, to change his particular area of concentration, or to time a certain course differently.

Again, activity may refer to the kind of situation in which the psychiatrist, sensing a group's unrest, may act directly to help uncover its hostility in order to advance the group process. But then he must shift back to an inactive sideline role as an observer and evaluator, to a position of nonjudgmental and receptive waiting, where he is able to maintain distance and impartiality. Unless he can make this shift, he may find himself becoming another administrator instead of a psychiatric consultant.

All this shifting about may cause the psychiatrist some discomfort; the analyst, particularly, may wonder if it is valid for him to intervene actively or to change his posture so frequently. He should remind himself that the psychoanalyst shifts roles in everyday life, although not necessarily within his *immediate* professional context. He shifts from his role with patients to a more active role with students and with various groups of professional colleagues. He learns early in professional life that he had better not play "the psychoanalyst" with his wife and children, with his professional colleagues, or with anybody other than patients in treatment. These everyday life experiences may help ease the shifts required in social psychiatry until he has gained more actual experience in the field, and until supervision further supports his efforts to adjust to his new role.

When he intervenes in social systems, the psychiatrist must retrain himself to deal primarily with conscious data. Analysts in particular, perhaps, commonly look for unconscious meaning; certainly this is a necessity if one is to understand the dynamic transactional process. But in social practice, successful interventions utilize conscious mechanisms *as well as* unconscious conflicts. The social psychiatrist must recognize that these mechanisms are at least partially conditioned by complex processes within the power structures that exist in every organization. He must understand power structures, and power struggles as well, and the part they play in bringing about and in resolving the situations where his consultation and advice are sought.

He must be aware also that he has less control over the eruption of crises and the timing of interpretations than he has in clinical practice. He must be mindful always that he occupies a less than central place in the functioning of the agency he serves; that as a consultant to an agency, he can carry far less influence with individuals and with groups of individuals than he is accustomed to in clinical practice, and particularly in psychoanalytic practice.

To accept these limitations may prove particularly difficult because the social psychiatrist is likely to be personally involved to a very considerable extent with the agency he serves. Indeed, he could scarcely be useful to it without some significant degree of dedication and commitment to its goals, and a personal stake in its effective functioning. When the psychoanalyst deals with an individual patient, he must be aware of his own character structure and defenses in order to achieve the objectivity so necessary to a successful therapeutic transaction. When he deals with a social agency, he must be constantly on guard lest, in his absorption with the cause he serves, he forget the intense and continuing self-evaluation that will permit him to maintain the objectivity and neutrality needed as much in work with agencies as with individuals. To maintain personal commitment and professional neutrality simultaneously may seem virtually impossible, yet experience has shown that it can be done. Supervision, once more, should ease the task.

All the problems and pitfalls discussed in this section are underlined by the fact that the social psychiatrist is more exposed than the private therapist. His personal vulnerability is greater because mistakes are evident to a wider audience. Moreover, errors in judgment may have far-reaching social consequences. The psychoanalytic psychiatrist, although he is as vulnerable as any other psychiatrist, may be enabled by his personal analysis to accept his vulnerability with somewhat more equanimity.

A case illustration may be useful in drawing together some of these rather broad theoretical considerations. One of the authors (RLL) has recently been involved in the establishment of a rather complex Community Mental Health Center. The history of its establishment has been presented in detail elsewhere (Leopold, 1967). In essence, this history records a joint planning effort to form a Community Mental Health Center involving six hospitals, the Department of Psychiatry of the University of Pennsylvania, the School of Social Work of that University, and various other community agencies. Before joint planning was instituted, several of these units, all of which are located in West Philadelphia, had decided independently that they had a vested interest in being designated as the sole Community Mental Health Center for the relevant area, and there was consequently much working at cross purposes among the interested agencies. The people in the West Philadelphia Community clearly wished to have a Community Mental Health Center established, but they had been quite puzzled and somewhat distressed by the fragmented approach displayed in efforts to serve their area.

In some ways, the community could be likened to a patient with a psychoneurosis: it had a clear reality goal, but it had been subjected to what amounted to warring intrapsychic processes. When the author was assigned a leadership role in a group that was trying to develop cooperation instead of competition among the interested units, he found himself in a position similar to that of the psychoanalyst dealing with various intrapsychic neurotic forces. Intervention to promote cooperation had to be timed, just as in the case of therapeutic interventions, in a way that would make possible successive stages in conflict resolution. Yet, at the same time, had the author taken sides with one or another of the individual agencies, or had he been seduced by them, the entire planning effort would have collapsed. The parallel between the conflicts in the community and in an individual patient was striking, as were the intense efforts on the part of the separate elements to enlist the author's (that is, the analyst's) support. Just as the patient's total mental health must be the primary focus in psychoanalysis, so it was essential here to focus on the long-term goal of creating a healthy over-all organization rather than to make any significant sacrifices for short-term gains.

This was particularly true when one of the major institutions temporarily withdrew from the common planning group in order to attempt (somewhat like a rebellious adolescent) to establish a center of its own. If the planning group had allowed this institution to go its own way, the whole planning process might have been speeded up and a large amount of abrasion and frustration might have been avoided. But the net effect would have been a chaotic duplication of effort and waste of resources, with damage to the long-term goal of serving the *total* area as comprehensively and as economically as possible. Obviously, the price of the immediate gain was too high; thus it was necessary to make compromises that persuaded the dissident member to remain affiliated with the planning group.

The term "negotiation" is used more commonly than the term "interpretation" in community organization. This became especially apparent to the author as he helped to develop the West Philadelphia Community Mental Health Center. But despite the difference in nomenclature, the processes by which compromises are reached and integrated into a body politic are similar to the processes by which the analyst deals with the expanding ego of an analysand. The same restrictions that the analyst applies to himself as the patient matures had to be used by the author as the political process developed.

As planning for the Center proceeded, he became increasingly aware that understanding of the dynamic processes at work in community organization is all-important; indeed, such understanding is probably the most critical single factor in the effective development of any complex program. Certainly many people, both professional and nonprofessional, have an acute sense of process, sometimes intuitive, but more often developed through training and experience of various kinds. Nonetheless, we feel that the sense of process acquired in psychoanalytic training and experience is an immeasurable asset.

The knowledgeable use of self is closely allied to this all-important sense of process. The psychoanalyst, uniquely qualified to understand the problem arising from the stimulation of his own unconscious needs and fantasies, is better able to deal with these problems than are most professionally trained people. For example, the author (RLL), during the negotiations for establishing the above-mentioned Community Mental Health Center, had occasion to meet with a community settlement-house leader, and received from him a quiet, but clearly hostile, lecture on the inadequacies of psychiatric and psychoanalytic knowledge in community work. At the same time, the leader extolled his own virtues and his own exclusive right to work in community efforts. During this monologue, the author recognized within himself all the signs of anger that he had become accustomed to recognizing in clinical situations. After some time, he decided to deal directly with the situation: he expressed calmly, but with determination, his anger at what was going on, and confronted the small group surrounding himself and the settlement-house worker with the emotional issues involved. Within a few minutes, the relevant feelings were expressed openly by the group, and a useful dialogue replaced the monologue. Undoubtedly many professional workers in psychiatric, psychological, and social work fields are able to utilize their own feelings satisfactorily in group work. Nevertheless, the author felt that his special psychoanalytic experiences enabled him, in this and similar situations, to utilize his feelings more consistently and benignly to further the process of achieving joint action.

This case illustration is admittedly incomplete, but it is intended at least to suggest, through a brief account of personal experience, the inestimable value to work in community psychiatry that lies in learning, as a psychoanalyst, to watch and wait patiently as a process unfolds. The illustration also suggests that understanding of social and political processes can be learned, just as an understanding of clinical processes can be learned. Supervision can facilitate this learning process.

Supervision in Social Practice

Because the social psychiatry field is so new and possibly because its activities are so diversified, no body of supervisors and no formal procedures for supervision have developed. Yet the need for supervision is as critical here as it is in clinical work, and its lack impedes progress in the field, affecting psychoanalysts as it does other social psychiatrists. Without formal supervision, one is forced to rely on analogies, intuition, and informal consultation with other social psychiatrists.

The classical *approach* to supervision, that is, the detailed presentation of observed and felt clinical phenomena for evaluation and comment by one's seniors in training and experience, needs no radical change for its application to social psychiatry. But the *content* must be vastly different because psychiatric training and experience, whether psychoanalytic or otherwise, do not of themselves prepare the psychiatrist for social psychiatry. He must add to his clinical background various different kinds of skills, knowledge, and approaches, some of them drawn from disciplines that may have little relevance to his primary tasks as a therapist. Supervision must concern itself, then, with content that includes traditional clinical material, but also a large body of material quite outside this context.

At several points in the preceding section, the need for supervision was cited in connection with problems centering around the social psychiatrist's change in role identity. These points, however, represent only one of many critical areas. For example, the social psychiatrist must be helped to distinguish between individual crises and crises occurring in social systems; moreover, he needs help with the specific problems involved in entry into a system and termination of contact with it. These problems are quite different from those of intervention in individual therapy. In the latter, the patient comes to the therapist with an implicit doctor-patient contract. In social practice, no such contract exists to provide the intervener with sanction and support for his choice and timing of intervention. Termination of individual therapy occurs when an individual has grown in ability to cope alone with his problems. The goals of social practice may not necessarily be personal insight, but rather the initiation of a social process that will result in positive action. With an agency or community, termination of a single intervention may, of course, occur when the organization is capable of dealing with the problem at hand without the presence of the psychiatrist; but consultation may well be an ongoing process, in which the psychiatrist is "on call" or "on retainer," and it may, in fact, never terminate.

The intricacies implied here suggest that supervision must deal not only with understanding of social systems and power structures in general, but also, more specifically, with understanding of communication networks and of modes and alternate modes of entry into, and intervention in, social systems.

Again, social psychiatry requires greatly extended understanding of the lives and problems of many and varied social and economic groups. For example, the psychoanalyst in traditional practice rarely has the motivation or the opportunity to acquaint himself with the social and physical settings of socioeconomic groups lower than the middle classes, and of underprivileged minorities in particular, or to observe and study their problems. But if he is to interact with *total* social systems, his effectiveness will be severely restricted by lack of this knowledge. Supervision must concern itself with seeing that he acquires it.

Thus, it is apparent that in social practice, the psychiatrist needs further training and supervision from many people in addition to psychiatrists. Supervision may have to be a task shared by experienced social psychiatrists with sociologists, community organization workers, political scientists, economists, lawyers, and many others. Training programs are being developed throughout the country to take up the slack between training for clinical psychiatry and that for social psychiatry, but until there is far more certainty in the social field, supervision may have to be ongoing, rather than simply a part of the training process. Continuing evaluation of problems and sharing of experience will be necessary to create the solid body of accumulated knowledge on which growth in any field depends.

Summary and Comment

New implications for the community have been brought to psychoanalysis by the work of psychoanalytically trained and experienced psychiatrists currently engaged in community mental health activities. Since we believe that the effective functioning of these psychiatrists has been partly determined by their psychoanalytic background, these implications have been examined here. They have been viewed in terms of an adaptation to social psychiatric practice of psychoanalytic theory in general and certain psychoanalytic concepts in particular, such that the conceptual framework of social psychiatry is enlarged and enriched, and additional operational approaches are provided for the social psychiatrist engaged in community mental health activities.

Special attention has been devoted to certain problems of social psychiatry deriving essentially from the change in role identity that takes place when the psychiatrist moves from clinical to social practice. The negative as well as the positive aspects of the relevance of a psychoanalytic background to these problems have been considered. Supervision, currently lacking in social practice, has been discussed as a major need of the field. It has been suggested that supervision may well involve many disciplines other than psychiatry and that it may have to continue well past the training phase if the field is to build up the accumulated knowledge on which its progress must depend.

We have attempted to demonstrate that the social psychiatrist can use his psychoanalytic training and experience as important, but not primary, elements in the total armamentarium of knowledge, insight, and skills with which he enters into community mental health. This is quite different from treating every problem he encounters as if it were a problem in individual psychoanalytic therapy. Indeed, we have pointed out that the psychoanalyst, like any other social psychiatrist, must specifically avoid treating the persons he deals with in nonclinical relationships as if they were patients, and "patientizing" case material. Although psychoanalytic thinking can be applied to work in the community in the ways outlined here, we do not believe that its independence as a separate professional discipline is thereby threatened. The various branches of physical medicine that have lent their own specialized knowledge and skills to public health work have not thereby been destroyed as professional disciplines. Similarly, there will always be a place for individual psychoanalytic therapy, and for the discrete training and research thus implied—despite the special values the psychoanalyst can bring to community mental health work.

We have attempted to describe these values, but we are aware that some psychoanalysts have no particular interest in the various activities social psychiatry entails and are not cut out for its roles and functions and for the special demands it imposes. For a variety of reasons, they will prefer to remain in more traditional therapeutic fields.

We feel, however, that although among the social psychiatrists now practicing a significant number are psychoanalytically trained and experienced, many more could be added to that number. As a professional discipline, psychoanalysis has not yet assumed its full responsibility to deal with the problems of the social environment in their relation to individual mental health. To explore the reasons for this is not within our province here. We do, however, express hope that the situation will change as evidence mounts that the mental health issue must be attacked on a community-wide basis as well as at the level of individual treatment. Instead of laboring the matter of responsibility, we should like to suggest that beyond the gratification of meeting a social responsibility, there are other rewards for the psychoanalyst who goes into community work. He will add important new dimensions to his understanding of human behavior because he can observe and study it at close range in groups and in nonclinical settings and because he can draw from the accumulated knowledge of other disciplines. He will learn new techniques, find new ways to communicate his thinking, establish new kinds of relationships. These professionally enriching experiences, far from destroying his identity as a therapist, will help to reinforce it because they will be valuable in developing his therapeutic competence.

Note: This chapter is an adaptation of the authors' "Contributions of Psychoanalysis to Social Psychiatry," presented at the 1964 meeting of the Academy of Psychoanalysis and published in J. H. Masserman (ed.), *Science and Psychoanalysis* (New York: Grune & Stratton, 1965), Vol. 8. The assistance of Dorothy S. Kuhn is gratefully acknowledged.

REFERENCES

Duhl, L. J., Leopold, R. L., and English, J. T. "A Mental Health Program for the Peace Corps." *Human Organization*, 23 (1964), 131–136.

Leopold, R. L. "The West Philadelphia Mental Health Consortium: Administrative Planning in a Multi-Hospital Catchment Area." *American Journal of Psychiatry*, 124, No. 4 (1967), Community Psychiatry Supplement, pp. 69–76.

Stanton, A. H., and Schwartz, M. S. *The Mental Hospital: A Study of Institutional Participation in Psychiatric Illness and Treatment*. New York: Basic Books, 1954.

Zinberg, N. E. "Psychoanalysis and the American Scene: A Reappraisal." *Diogenes*, 50 (Summer 1965), 73–111.

24

The Impact of Psychoanalysis on Sociology and Anthropology

SOL LEVINE and NORMAN A. SCOTCH

It is no easy task to find the right yardstick to assess the nature and magnitude of the impact psychoanalysis has had on sociology and anthropology. At first glance, psychoanalysis has far from fulfilled its once auspicious promise to become an integral part of the social sciences and to make a profound contribution to the scientific study and understanding of society and its institutions. From the vantage point of its ardent proponents, the failure of psychoanalytic theory to become a cornerstone of sociological and anthropological analysis must appear disappointing indeed. And yet, on further examination, one can summon abundant evidence to testify for its success. Surely, no other intellectual discipline or body of thought which has emerged outside of the social science tradition (with the possible exception of mathematics) has entered the daily parlance and consciousness of social scientists or has so visibly pervaded their work. It is the intent of this chapter to consider some of the reasons for this paradox—the success and failure of so remarkable an intellectual achievement as psychoanalysis in its dialogue with the social scientists.

In these few pages our scope is necessarily restrictive and selective, illuminating some of the dominant factors affecting the differential reception of psychoanalysis by sociology and anthropology. No attempt will be made to review the many writers in each of the disciplines, but instead we will try to point up issues and junctures which are more typical and representative in the dynamic interaction between psychoanalysis and the two social sciences. We will omit from our analysis consideration of the impact of psychoanalysis on psychology, though we will touch on the field of social psychology, which is the bridge between psychology and sociology and, in fact, is the domain of each discipline. Our coverage of the literature will be confined to that of the United States where, except for the writings of Sigmund Freud, each discipline has attained its highest fruition. As John Seeley (1962a) had written so eloquently, only in America has psychoanalysis flourished so abundantly.

The relationship between psychoanalysis and the social sciences has been dynamic and pulsating. Reactions by social scientists have ranged from enthusiastic acceptance to cool skepticism to outright rejection, and these reactions have varied with time. To Pitirim Sorokin, writing in 1928, psychoanalysis held little interest for sociologists. He stated: ". . . the theory is utterly inadequate and unsatisfactory. It is hard to admit that it has contributed anything to our understanding of social phenomena, or the relationship between the sex factor and other categories of social facts. So much for this group" (Sorokin, 1928, pp. 607–608). To the leading theorist of contemporary sociology, Talcott Parsons, writing some twenty-five years later, the picture looked quite different: ". . . the contribution of psychoanalysis to the social sciences has consisted of an enormous deepening and enrichment of our understanding of human motivation. This enrichment has been a pervasive influence that it would almost be impossible to trace its many ramifications" (Parsons, 1965e, p. 18). It must be remembered too that neither psychoanalysis, sociology, nor anthropology has remained static, but that each has been subject to its own independent flux and development, which, in turn, affected its stance and relationship to the other disciplines. Sociology, for example, in recent years has witnessed a qualitative change in the power of its data collection methods and its degree of sophistication in data analysis. As its own needs and interests have changed and it has developed greater interest and competency in research technology, its posture toward psychoanalysis has been modified. Psychoanalysis, too, has undergone dramatic developments within its own ranks with the emergence of the neo-Freudian school and its emphasis on social and cultural factors and its lesser emphasis on biological and historical forces. This development has altered the image social scientists have of psychoanalysts.

We must differentiate first, then, between what is loosely and perhaps sometimes unjustifiably referred to as orthodox psychoanalysis, on the one hand, and neo-Freudianism, or revisionism, on the other. In many respects, the latter has been influenced by sociological, anthropological, and other social science theory and empirical data. The writings of the neo-Freudians contain many allusions to fundamental social conditions which mold family structure and familial patterns and, in turn, forge individual personality. The neo-Freudians were the ones who drew attention to society, its conflicts and inconsistencies, as the source of individual pathology. In this respect, the major thrust of the neo-Freudians is to be contrasted with that of the orthodox Freudians who were more biological and instinctual in outlook. It is understandable that a number of social scientists who were alienated by the extreme Freudian position were more favorably disposed to such neo-Freudians as Horney, Fromm, and Sullivan.

Second, it is necessary to distinguish between the contribution of the discipline, psychoanalysis, and the impact which individual psychoanalysts and psychiatrists have had whose thinking may or may not have sprung from the main stream of psychoanalytic theory. Harry Stack Sullivan, for example, whose work has been of interest to sociologists and social psychologists, did not derive his major tenets from the body of established psychoanalytic thinking. J. L. Moreno is a more extreme case in point of a psychiatrist whose fundamental contributions to the behavioral sciences cannot be attributed to his grounding in psychoanalytic theory.

Finally, there is need to discriminate between psychoanalysis as a body of thought seeking to explain normal and abnormal behavior and psychoanalysis as a technology, as a repertoire of skills and prescriptions for handling the problems of the mentally ill. It is not our task here to consider the relationship between these two levels. We are mainly concerned with the influences on sociology and anthropology which stem from the psychoanalytic theory of human behavior.

As we turn to sociology and anthropology we must qualify our analysis, for we cannot treat either as a singular, unified field of endeavor. Quite the contrary. Each is cut by a number of dimensions and pervaded by a variety of styles: pure and applied, theory and research, participant observation and statistical analysis. To be sure, they are not hostile to each other, but do reflect different thrusts and emphases and, in turn, varying proclivities toward psychoanalysis. Then, too, there are the different substantive areas, running the range in sociology from demography to social psychology, from industrial sociology to the small group, from theories of the social system to criminal behavior. Similarly, in anthropology we encounter such disparate subject areas as kinship systems, political systems, and linguistics. Here, too, there are different bases for accepting and utilizing psychoanalysis.

At one extreme end of sociological inquiry is the field of social psychology which is in itself broad and diverse, embracing a wide range of substantive interests, theories, and research endeavors. It is difficult to specify clearly the distinctive domain of social psychology, and it is often impossible to differentiate the work of social psychologists from those of sociologists and psychologists (Brown, 1965, p. xx; Inkeles, 1959a, pp. 273–274). In fact, social psychology is often claimed by the two disciplines of sociology and psychology. Nevertheless, it would be fair to say that much of social psychology is concerned with the effects of group membership and social situations on the individual. In this sense, social psychology may be distinguished from much of sociology for which the group or the aggregate is often the object or focus. To the extent that the individual is the subject of attention—his personality, his perceptions, his attitudes, and his mental world—it would seem that social psychology or the social psychological side of sociology would be more receptive to the contributions of psychoanalysis. While any discussion of sociology cannot exclude some specific writers who traverse social psychology, as well, our discussion will focus on the former discipline.

Reactions by Sociology and Anthropology

Although there is much in common in the reaction to psychoanalysis by sociologists and anthropologists, it is the latter which has been more hospitable. Why, then, has sociology been less receptive than its sister discipline, anthropology? One major reason is that sociology has been more committed to a rigorous empirical and quantitative methodology. Accordingly, the relatively qualitative and unrigorous feature of psychoanalysis was less inimical to anthropology than it was to sociology.

In an excellent article which reviews the applications of psychoanalysis to social science, Hall and Lindzey (1954) present a number of additional reasons for the relatively less enthusiastic acceptance of psychoanalysis within sociology as compared with anthropology. They call attention to the fact that Sapir, Malinowski, and Mead, to name a few anthropologists influenced by psychoanalysis, may have been affected not only because they were anthropologists, but also because of

> . . . some accidental factors linked to the particular experience they were exposed to and the kinds of people they were. More important, the anthropologist, by virtue of his fieldwork experience, was in much more intimate contact with the details of human existence than the sociologist. This means that he was exposed to data relevant to psychoanalytic formulation and also that he was more inclined toward acceptance of the methods of the psychoanalyst, as they resembled their own (Hall and Lindzey, 1954, p. 172).

Moreover, sociology was strongly influenced by such theoretical giants as Marx, Weber, and Durkheim whose emphases were at variance with those of Freud. As Hall and Lindzey state (1954, p. 172), "American anthropology under the influence of Franz Boas was much more theory-less than American sociology and there was consequently less likelihood that psychoanalysis would be rejected because of conflicting or competing theoretical convictions." This is not to deny the *potential* enrichment psychoanalysis could bring to the various sociological theories. However, as we will see, theoretical integration is not easily achieved, and, with one or two notable exceptions, the orientation and substance of the major sociological theorists have remained largely unaffected by psychoanalytic theory.

Furthermore, Hall and Lindzey remind us that in its early inception, and to an appreciable extent today as well, American sociology has been "tinged with the goals and values of the Protestant ministry. From such a vantage point Freud's pessimistic and sensate conception of man was certain to be greeted with hostility" (1954, p. 172). To pursue this theme further, there is also a strong social reform tradition among American sociologists who look to factors in the social setting or the individual's present life circumstances which must be modified in order to produce desired outcomes. They are less receptive to the instinctivistic theme pervading Freudian theory, to the overriding priority and importance assigned to infantile sexuality and early life's experiences, and to the belief that the individual's personality is relatively fixed and established as a result of these experiences.

Finally, Hall and Lindzey properly point out that psychoanalytic writers and Freud himself were interested in some of the specific problems of considerable concern to anthropologists, such as incest taboo, ritual, marriage practices, and kinship patterns—topics which were not of primary interest to sociologists. ". . . it is evident that Freud's early excursions into areas specifically labeled anthropological, and subsequent applications by Jones . . . and Reik . . . made it more difficult for the anthropologist to ignore psychoanalysis than the sociologist" (1954, p. 172).

In discussing these various forms and sources of resistance to psychoanalysis by sociologists and anthropologists, we must bear in mind that the relevance of psychoanalysis to its own subject matter of intrapsychic experience is not at issue (though some may even question this). What is definitely questioned is the pertinence of psychoanalysis for understanding the subject matter of sociology and anthropology—the social behavior of people and the social systems into which they are organized. As Inkeles states so clearly:

> Most sociologists probably accept Freud's as the foremost general theory of the human personality of our time, but the acceptance is limited to its application to the individual's psychic development and adjustment, that is, to his inner life. They do not accept it as the prime explanation of the social behavior of the individual—which they attribute more to his culture, his class, his historical time, or his immediate situation, including the network of interpersonal relations in which he is enmeshed (Inkeles, 1959b, p. 334).

Whereas the concept of unconscious motivation would find general acceptance among sociologists and anthropologists as well, a good many of them would take issue with Freud for having assigned undue importance to unconscious factors in explaining a social human behavior. For one thing, sociologists are less concerned with explaining the more distant underlying or ultimate causes, but, as Inkeles indicates (1959b, p. 334), are more concerned with "the proximate causes of behavior." "Indeed, sociologists often feel that Freud dealt less with the causes than with the underlying preconditions of social behavior. The unconscious and irrational in behavior have seemed to them of less compelling interest than the more conscious, purposeful, and rationally goal-directed behavior."

Nevertheless, as we shall see, whatever the contribution of psychoanalysis to sociology and anthropology may be, it is most apparent and most relevant when the unit of inquiry is the individual, not the group, the organization, the systems of authority, or the patterns of relationship. In discussing which people steal and which do not, or which persons are prejudiced and which are not, it is easy to turn to psychoanalytic theory for suggestive hypotheses. While not by any means without relevance, psychoanalytic theory is less readily consulted as a basis for explaining such relationships as different group structures and task performance; organizational structure and kinds and frequency of commuication patterns; modifications of the organizational "blueprint" by informal groups; ecology and community sentiments; and level of parental education and social mobility. In large part, social scientists often focus on levels of data which exclude or make it unnecessary to consider individual psychic phenomena. A great number of sociological and anthropological questions can be answered in group, structural, or normative terms without resorting to psychological explanations.

To pursue this further, sociologists often focus on a different part of the human spectrum or continuum than do psychoanalysts and, for that matter, students of individual psychology as well. Consider, for example, the question of criminal behavior. The psychologist may be concerned with the relationship between superego development or early patterns of child discipline and subsequent criminal behavior. The sociologist, while not oblivious to these variables, may be more interested in varying social and cultural definitions of criminality, factors associated with commission of crimes and who is adjudicated as a criminal, patterned forms of social deviance and criminality, and the relationship between specific social conditions and criminal behavior. Certainly the two foci of concern can be reconciled and integrated. Even more, it is likely that a more comprehensive and satisfactory theory will develop if the two levels of focus are integrated. While there would appear to be real potential in this mutual development, as yet, with some glaring exceptions, very little has taken place.

In the following pages we will consider briefly some of the main currents of psychoanalytic influence on sociology and anthropology. Although the two social science disciplines have much in common with regard to their subject matter and the points at which they have incorporated psychoanalytic thinking, for purposes of clarity we will treat sociology and anthropology separately in this section. In the concluding section of the chapter we will again treat the two social science disciplines jointly and consider their common relationship with psychoanalysis.

Psychoanalysis and Sociology

In view of what has been said, it is not surprising that the impact of psychoanalysis on sociology is not immediately and glaringly apparent. An examination of a number of textbooks in sociology as well as two recent major reviews or symposia on sociology indicate relatively few references to Freud or psychoanalysis (Merton, Broom, and Cottrell, 1959; Gross, 1959). In many cases only a few bibliographical or historical allusions appear and no analytic use is made of psychoanalytic theory. One of the best texts in the field, *Human Society* by Kingsley Davis (1949), makes no mention at all of Freud or psychoanalysis, though there are references to Piaget and the revisionists, Horney and Fromm. In the recent comprehensive *Handbook of Modern Sociology* edited by Faris (1964), Freud's work is referred to only in two of twenty-seven chapters. One outstanding exception in the textbook field is an excellent and very lucid text by Ralph Ross and Ernest Van Den Haag (1957) in which there is considerable coverage and reliance on psychoanalytic theory, particularly with regard to the sections on personality and socialization. Psychoanalytic theory is described at considerable length, and, while the authors are sympathetic to its significance, their account is quite judicial and balanced. Psychoanalytic tenets, which are often viewed with reservation, receive sympathetic hearing with regard to a number of substantive areas including socialization, deviance, suicide, and art and civilization. It is to be pointed out, however, that neither author is from the main stream of professional sociology and that Dr. Van Den Haag is a practicing lay analyst.

Having indicated that, at the present stage of their development at least, the character and orientation of sociology does not easily invite the incorporation of psychoanalytic theory, and having specified the reasons for resistance, it is necessary for us to pause and reverse our field somewhat if we are to present a balanced and circumspect picture. It may be mechanical and atomistic to measure the psychoanalytic impact purely in terms of the frequency with which psychoanalytic theorists are cited in reviews and handbooks or to count the number of times Freud's name or those of his followers appear in the indexes of the most popular textbooks. The influence of a school of thought may take more devious and subtle paths which, while difficult and sometimes impossible to trace, may still be very considerable indeed. For one thing, psychoanalysis has certainly affected the world of art, literature, and philosophy, as well as the popular media, and thereby has transformed the larger social environment as well as the intellectual milieu in which social scientists live and derive stimulation and nourishment. Even more, the psychoanalytic influence on sociology, and on anthropology as well, in large part may have come in through the back door via academic psychology, particularly clinical psychology and social psychology. Then, too, social science has been affected by the mere fact that social scientists have had to deal with psychoanalysis and to come to terms with it, even while rejecting or attempting to demolish it. It may even be fruitful to consider whether a number of sociologists who acknowledge no debt to psychoanalytic thought could have done the work they did without the influence of Freud and his followers.

There are less global and more immediate criteria to assess the impact of psychoanalysis on social science. Has psychoanalysis deepened and enriched interpretations of social phenomena? Has psychoanalytic theory presented new hypotheses, concepts, and insights which have been employed by social scientists? Have additional research questions been formulated and specific substantive areas identified as a result of exposure to psychoanalytic theory? Has psychoanalytic theory stimulated the use of new research methods and techniques?

What is conspicuous at close examination is that despite the relatively narrow inroads of psychoanalysis in sociology, its impact has been strategic and has commanded the attention of some of the most notable and influential names in sociology. We will mention only a few. Talcott Parsons, the dean of sociological theorists, has devoted a major part of his recent professional effort to trying to integrate psychoanalytic and sociological theory. Parsons' reliance on some basic elements of psychoanalytic theory is evident in his consideration of such sociological questions as the relationship between social structure and personality, the socialization process in the family, the role of the patient, the nature of illness, and the structure of the doctor-patient relationship. David Riesman, author of the famed *The Lonely Crowd* (1955), *Individualism Reconsidered* (1954), and other well-known works, clearly shows the influence of Sigmund Freud and Erich Fromm, especially in regard to his concern with the relationship between character and society. Robert F. Bales, a pioneer in the empirical study of the interaction process in the small group, is another sociologist whose work, in collaboration with Parsons and his associates, shows the influence of psychoanalytic theory (Parsons, Bales, Olds, Zelditch, and Slater, 1955). In recent years, Bales and his colleagues have attempted to integrate psychoanalytic concepts with the findings and formulations of small group research. Finally, Alex Inkeles, a sociologist with a major interest in the field of social structure and personality, gives attention to the relevance of psychoanalytic theory for the broadening and enrichment of sociological analysis (Inkeles, 1959a and 1959b; Inkeles and Levinson, 1954).

An examination of the works of these and other writers on socialization and the general area of social structure and personality reveals extensive recourse to basic psychoanalytic Freudian tenets including the role of the unconscious, the operation of defense mechanisms, the structure of personality, the influence of parental figures and early childhood disciplines, and the internalization of social norms and prescriptions. In fact, the greatest impact of psychoanalytic theory on sociology is probably manifest in this general area of socialization and social structure and personality, a field of interest paralleling the anthropological interest in culture and personality, which will be discussed in detail later in this chapter. Socialization may be defined as the process by which the individual becomes an adult member of his society and the groups to which he belongs. Sociologists are concerned with how social systems manage to survive and maintain continuity, particularly through the socialization or the development of conformity among its members. While no individual ever learns all about his entire society and culture, and no one is exactly like another, each "normal" person acquires a number of minimal values, attitudes, motives, and behavior patterns which he shares in common with other members of his society and which allow him to function congruously, or in phase, with his society. The individual's response repertoire appropriate for functioning in a given society is acquired through complex learning processes in which various agencies, such as the school, the church, the peer group, and particularly the family, the main agency of socialization, play an active role.

Sociologists are also concerned with how basic social conditions determine specific socialization mechanisms and practices and, in turn, how such mechanisms and practices affect the personality and behavior of the growing child. It is particularly with regard to the study of the socialization process within the family, and, to a lesser extent, within other primary groups, and how these processes affect personality formation that sociologists have leaned heavily on the concepts and insights of Freud and his followers. Although, as Pitts reminds us, Erikson and Sullivan are among the very few psychoanalysts who have paid attention to socialization beyond puberty, psychoanalysis is still "the most comprehensive theory of human learning that we now possess" (Pitts, 1961, p. 699). It is to be observed, however, that in two excellent discussions of socialization after childbirth by sociologists Brim and Wheeler there is no reliance upon the psychoanalytic literature (Brim and Wheeler, 1966; also see Dager, 1964).

It should be emphasized strongly that such sociological writers as Parsons, Bales, Riesman, and Inkeles have not engaged in mechanical or uncritical application of Freudian tenets to the subject matter of sociology, nor have they attempted to reduce sociological analysis to the allegedly more basic level of psychoanalytic analysis (Inkeles, 1959a, p. 272). What they have set for themselves is the difficult task of integrating at specific points psychoanalytic and sociological theory into a more explanatory conceptual scheme. Parsons states the problem clearly:

On the one hand, Freud and his followers, by concentrating on the single personality, have failed to consider adequately the implications of the individual's interaction with other personalities *to form a system.* On the one hand, Durkheim and the other sociologists have failed, in their concentration on the social system as a system to consider systematically the implications of the fact that it is the *interaction of personalities* which constitutes the social system with which they have been dealing and that, therefore, adequate analysis of motivational process in such a system must reckon with the problems of personality (Parsons, 1965e, p. 20).

No one has devoted more sustained attention to the points of articulation between the two disciplines and has worked more for their integration than Talcott Parsons. In a classic article, "Social Structure and the Development of Personality," Parsons attempts to clarify and sharpen Freudian theory in terms of its own subject matter, the structure and development of personality, and with regard to the understanding of the "relation between the individual and to his social milieu, especially in the process of personality development" (Parsons, 1965c, p. 79). Parsons attempts to demonstrate that a proper reading of the literature reveals that Freud himself made an important contribution to the integration of psychoanalysis and the subject matter of sociology (pp. 80–81). In fact, in focusing on the internalization of cultural norms by the growing individual, Parsons is struck by the "remarkable convergence between Freud's views on internalization and those developed independently and at nearly the same time by Emile Durkheim in France and by Charles H. Cooley and George Herbert Mead in the United States" (p. 80).

Parsons' thesis, in essence, is that the role of social and cultural factors in the development of personality is not confined to the development of the superego, as a number of writers have assumed, but pervades the entire personality system described by Freud. Leaning heavily on the psychoanalytic concept of "object relations" and related Freudian concepts of identification, object-cathexis, internalization and the superego, as well as his own "theory of action," Parsons argues that not only is the ego "socially structured," but that the id itself in Freud's own thinking cannot be viewed as a "manifestation of 'pure instinct,'" but is derived, in good part, from the early socialization experience of the individual. Parsons' view can be summarized in the following quotation:

The distinction between the instinctual and learned components of the motivational system cannot legitimately be identified with that between the id, on the one hand, and the ego and superego on the other. Rather, the categories of instinctual and learned components, cut across the id, the ego and the superego (1965e, p. 20).

As we have already indicated, the family is one field of sociological inquiry in which the influence of psychoanalytic thinking is clearly evident, particularly with regard to socialization. This is manifest in an examination of a number of textbooks on the family which have appeared over the years. What is more, psychoanalytic theorists, in their emphasis on the importance of parental behavior and early childhood training, have undoubtedly provided stimulation for a number of studies in this area. More explicitly, psychoanalytic thinking influenced the choice of variables used by sociologists in their study of socialization. One major research question is the degree to which parents of different social class backgrounds vary with regard to such aspects of childhood training as cleanliness, toilet training, breast feeding, and expression of aggression (Sears, Maccoby, and Levin, 1957; Miller and Swanson, 1958). Another research concern is the degree to which various forms of parental training or discipline are related to subsequent personality development. One of the few serious empirical efforts in sociology to test the relationship between specific early training experiences and later personality development (as suggested by Freudian theory) yielded negative results (Sewell, 1952). In reviewing studies in sociology and psychology, Brim sums up the situation succinctly. He states (Brim, 1959, p. 44) that studies in the United States "find no relation between such parent behavior as early and strict toilet training and subsequent personality, whether personality is measured by paper and pencil tests or by projective tests as the Rorschach and the Thematic Appreciation Test . . ."

The influence of psychodynamic thinking is also evident in a number of studies on social deviance, including delinquency, suicide and homicide, and mental illness. We will cite three illustrative studies. The first, the classic study by the Gluecks on the development of delinquency, leans heavily on psychoanalytic conceptions of superego development (Glueck and Glueck, 1950).

The Gluecks believe that delinquents live in very different home environments from nondelinquents, particularly with regard to the nature of parental discipline and consistency and the definition of ideals and standards of conduct which the growing child can internalize. In addition, the findings of the Gluecks strongly suggest personality differences in delinquents and nondelinquents, with the former being less submissive to societal authority and possessing a less developed superego (see brief discussion of the work of the Gluecks in Inkeles, 1959b, pp. 341–343).

One of the best studies of juvenile delinquency, which also shows the influence of psychoanalytic thinking, is Cohen's work on delinquent boys

(1955). Cohen regards delinquency as one major mode of response which lower-class boys make to their inability to achieve success in the middle-class world which surrounds them. In order to overcome their ambivalence toward middle-class standards, they join with other lower-class boys in rejecting middle-class values and vigorously adopt the standards and behavior of the gang. Cohen thus views lower-class delinquency as a reaction formation against middle-class values.

The third study of interest, the work by Henry and Short on suicide and homicide, was guided by an explicit psychodynamic view of personality. Observing that suicide and homicide vary inversely, Henry and Short agreed that suicide could be viewed as aggression turned inward and homicide as aggression turned outward, and that the characteristic mode of expressing aggression reflected the degree of superego development (Henry and Short, 1954). As Inkeles indicates (1959b, pp. 331–332), by adding their psychodynamic view of personality, Henry and Short were able to enrich and to add a significant intervening dimension to the classic study of suicide undertaken by the famous French sociologist, Émile Durkheim, several decades before.

It is necessary to add a qualifying note to the foregoing discussion. Despite the significant influence of psychoanalysis on study of the family and deviant behavior, to which we have alluded, it must be appreciated that a major part of sociological endeavor in each of these fields is still relatively free of such influence. Most of the review chapters in the extensive volume *Handbook of Marriage and the Family* (Christensen, 1964), except for those in which personality and socialization are relevant factors, show little influence of Freudian thinking. Similarly, the field of deviant behavior at present is not dominated by psychoanalytic thinking.

The field of prejudice or intergroup relations shows the clear stamp of psychoanalytic influence, particularly that of Erich Fromm and the authors of *The Authoritarian Personality.* (Adorno, Frenkel-Brunswik, Levinson, and Sanford, 1950). *The Authoritarian Personality* was a monumental study which was guided by the theoretical view that anti-Semitism was part of a more general prejudice orientation and that this, in turn, was related to a broader social and political outlook. This broader outlook was believed to stem from deep-felt personality needs of the individual which had their roots in early childhood training and experience. *The Authoritarian Personality* of Adorno and his colleagues resembled the sadomasochistic personality described by Erich Fromm in his classic work, *Escape from Freedom* (1941).

Although *The Authoritarian Personality* was greeted by serious methodological criticisms, including the "contamination" of research procedures, questions of sampling and the failure to control for educational differences (Hyman and Sheatsley, 1954), it gave impetus to work in their general research area and led to a number of additional studies which aimed at replication or refinement of the findings (Srole, 1956; Roberts and Rokeach, 1956; Himmelhoch, 1950; MacKinnon and Centers, 1956).

The notion of a rigid, hostile, repressed, morally indignant—authoritarian—personality which projects its needs and hostility to other social objects persists in the sociological literature. A number of scales and test items borrowed from or suggested by the original study (including the well-known "F" scale) have been used widely in studies outside the field of intergroup relations as well. While sociologists have serious theoretical and methodological reservations about the approach embodied in *The Authoritarian Personality,* it has had definite impact on the thinking and research in the field (Simpson and Yinger, 1959).

The contribution to the research technology of sociology understandably has not been psychoanalysis' greatest contribution, largely because sociology has a much more impressive methodology of its own and because sociologists, in their concern with reliability, have a skeptical stance toward the less rigorous psychoanalytic methods. Yet, there has been some impact in the research field. We have already cited one of the contributions of psychoanalysis to the methodology of sociology in the form of questionnaire items or scales which were used or suggested in *The Authoritarian Personality.* The interview as a sociological research tool has also borrowed from or been affected by the general experience gained in the use of the clinical interview. Researchers have incorporated a number of clinical prescriptions or practices, such as the need to establish rapport, the use of unstructured or "depth" interviewing, the importance of the interviewer's role, the need to detect anxiety, and the utility of indirect probes and questions. In our subsequent discussion of psychoanalysis and anthropology, the uses and limitations of projective methods in social research will be considered.

Psychoanalysis and Anthropology

The mutual relationship between anthropology and psychoanalysis seems to have intrigued numerous anthropologists over many generations. Every five years or so, during the last thirty-five, articles have appeared assessing, evaluating, and predicting the potential of the influence of psychoanalytic thinking on anthropology. Landmark papers of this genre include the early articles of Edward Sapir in 1932, M. K. Opler in 1935, Cora DuBois in 1937, and Clyde Kluckhohn in 1944. During the last fifteen years several new papers have been published, with the best of these the recent work by Singer (1961).

There is little need to repeat the early issues which arose in response to attempts by each field to work more closely with the other. Nor need we dwell again on the by now legendary controversies (e.g., the Oedipus complex and Malinowski) which many scholars delight in returning to again and again (Roheim, 1962). Nor is it possible in this brief chapter to provide a detailed history of great turning points in the developing relationship (the Kardiner seminar, DuBois among the Alorese, etc.). These historical events are more than amply described in numerous previous publications and the interested reader's attention is directed in particular to the papers by Kluckhohn (1944) and Singer (1961) for highly objective and lucid presentations of historical materials. In addition, F. L. K. Hsu has provided a useful bibliography, entitled "A Selected Bibliography Bearing on the Mutual Relationship between Anthropology, Psychiatry, and Psychoanalysis" (1961), which should serve the interested scholar well. The present discussion, therefore, will be limited to some brief remarks concerning psychoanalytic influences on the development of the field of culture and personality and on the general methodology of anthropology.

Undoubtedly, the major impact of psychoanalysis has been on the development, particularly in the earlier stages, of the whole field of culture and personality. Though the viability of this field within the general discipline has waxed and waned over the last four decades, there is no question that this area of research has achieved a secure status as a valid and meaningful area of inquiry within anthropology. The field of culture and personality has consolidated its gains, overcome many of its methodological weaknesses, and has already made numerous substantive contributions, not only to its parent discipline—anthropology—but to other disciplines as well, such as psychiatry and sociology.

There are still, of course, many anthropologists who remain skeptical or indifferent. It is of interest that some writers trace their skepticism to the influence of psychoanalysis on this field, as illustrated in these remarks by Wallace:

> But while the strategic importance of culture-and-personality is great, it has not inspired universal confidence among anthropologists. It has to many (including the writer) often seemed to be "soft" in logical structure and in research method. This partial failure to gain acceptance commensurate with its pretensions has been owing to several circumstances. *One circumstance has been the insularity of the brand of psychology which it has chiefly utilized, namely psychoanalytic theory.* Despite the claim of Freud, its creator, that psychoanalysis is based on biological knowledge, his disciples have so heavily emphasized the autonomy of psychological process that two-way bridges between dynamic psychology and physiology have been few. This has tended to reduce the natural affinity between culture-and-personality and the relatively "hard" sciences of neurology, general physiology, biochemistry, and experimental psychology. Personality theory, which emphasizes the affects, has also been somewhat insulated from the academic psychological core-tradition and its concern with perceptual, cognitive, and learning processes (Wallace, 1964, p. 3).

However, our task in this chapter is not to provide a detailed and complete review of the subdiscipline of culture-personality, but to examine some of the major issues in the field, especially those in which psychoanalysis has played an important role. Much of the discussion that follows relies on the splendid review of the growth and development of the field of culture and personality in anthropology by Singer (1961). In his essay Dr. Singer points out that the field of culture and personality is a relatively recent phenomenon which owes its early emergence within anthropology to the influence of psychiatry, particularly Freudian psychoanalysis.

According to Singer there have been several dominant themes in the development of culture and personality to which psychoanalysis has contributed, among them: (1) the relation of culture to *human nature;* (2) the relation of culture to *typical personality;* and (3) the relation of culture to *abnormal personality.*

Regarding the first theme, the relation of culture to human nature, Singer points out that there was a basic difference in the stances taken by psychiatry and anthropology in the 1920's and early 1930's, with the psychiatrists more or less espousing the position of psychic unity, of personality manifesting underlying basic physiological drives which are the same throughout the world. The anthropologists reacted powerfully to this theme with overwhelming evidence of "human nature's plasticity." In this connection Singer offers this apt quote from Margaret Mead:

> It was a simple—a very simple point to which our materials were organized in the 1920's, merely the documentation over and over of the fact that human nature is not rigid and unyielding, not an unadaptable plant which insists on flowering or become stunted after its own fashion, responding only quantitatively to the social environment, but that it is extraordinarily adaptable, that cultural rhythms which they overlay and distort, that the failure to satisfy an artificial, culturally stimulated need—for outdistancing one's neighbours in our society, for instance, or for our wearing the requisite number of dog's teeth among the Manus—may produce more unhappiness and frustration in the human breast than the most rigorous cultural curtailment of the physiological demands of sex or hunger. We had to present evidence that human character is built upon a biological base which is capable of enormous diversification in terms of social standards (Mead, 1938, p. x).

Mead's position on this issue represented the reactions of numerous anthropologists to the early phases of the argument (Mead, Benedict, Malinowski). And it is interesting that the earliest influence of psychiatry on anthropology should be a negative influence which activated many anthropologists, at that time, to prove the psychiatrists wrong. And the anthropologists saw it as a battle:

The battle which we once had to fight with the whole battery at our command, with the most fantastic and now startling examples that we could muster, is now won. As the devout in the Middle Ages would murmur a precautionary "God willing" before stating a plan or a wish, those who write about the problems of man and society have learned to insert a precautionary "in our culture" into statements which would have read, fifteen years ago, merely as "Adolescence is always a time of stress and strain," "Children are more imaginative than adults," "All artists are neurotic," "Women are more passive than men," etc., with no such precautionary phrase (Mead, 1938, pp. x–xi).

However, Singer very correctly declares that "from our vantage point, the issues appear more complex, the victory less decisive." For one thing, he points out, "a good deal of psychoanalytic theory . . . was incorporated in the very process of resistance to it . . . ." And for another thing, the issue was not to be resolved simply by piling up data on the endless varieties of human behavior. Moreover, with the passage of time "the anthropologist's position . . . has been moving closer to the universalism of psychoanalytic theory and away from an exclusive preoccupation with differences (Singer, 1961, p. 19).

It is probably safe to say that contemporary anthropologists no longer regard the question of "human nature" as important. They consider man to be influenced by a number of universal features associated with his being human, but that the influence of culture on human behavior is more important. But the question no longer is put as to which of these factors influences behavior more. Both contribute, and the question now revolves more around the content and nature of the contribution, rather than the amount.

A second major theme of the culture and personality approach involves the relation of culture to *typical personality.* Considerable research has been conducted in this area which has led to a great deal of both interest and controversy. Again the interested reader is referred to Singer's paper for an excellent discussion of the development of the various subareas of this field, including detailed attention to the following schools or approaches: configural personality, basic personality, modal personality, and national character. In discussing the various approaches to the question of typical personality, Singer (1961, p. 22) states:

From about 1935 to 1950 . . . personality and culture theory and research concentrated heavily on the problem of the relation of culture to typical personality. The theories of configurational personality, of basic personality structure, of national and cultural character, and of modal personality were all developed and served as guides to field research during this period. It has become usual to consider these theories as more or less equivalent, and the differences among them as primarily semantic. This is a mistake. Such a view overlooks significant differences in concepts, methods, data, and fields of application. These theories have obviously influenced one another and have some features in common, but there is more to be said about them.

They all agree that every culture has a typical personality which is produced or conditioned by some aspect of culture.

Very briefly the different approaches have concentrated their attentions as follows:

1. The configurational approach generally consists of attempts to apply psychological typologies descriptively to the major values of total societies. The best known exponent of this approach is, of course, Ruth Benedict, who, in *Patterns of Culture* (1934), applied the typology "megalomaniac paranoid" to the Kwakiutl, paranoid to the Dobuans, Apollonian to the Zuñi, and Dionysian to the Plains Indians. Benedict's account has been severely criticized on several grounds, with the most severe criticism directed at her use of secondary data and improper attribution of these typologies, and at her lack of psychological and personality data.

2. The study of basic personality, of all the areas in culture and personality, shows the impact of psychoanalytic influence the most. Important psychoanalysts made a great impact on some of the foremost of American anthropologists. Singer writes, for example (1961, p. 29):

> The theory of basic personality structure marks an important milestone because it was one of the first systematic and explicit attempts to apply a modified psychoanalytic approach to different cultures. It consolidated the previous criticisms and research both of anthropologists (e.g., Kroeber, Malinowski, Mead, Benedict, Linton) and of psychoanalysts (e.g., Fromm, Horney, Rado, Ferenczi, W. Reich, Roheim) into a new synthesis which has been very influential on subsequent personality and culture theory and research.

Essentially, the major concern in basic personality studies has been to assess the impact of primary institutions (e.g., child rearing) on "unconscious constellations," which in turn influence the development of secondary institutions such as art and religion. "The psychoanalyst Abram Kardiner is chiefly responsible for the formulation of the theory of basic personality structure. Several anthropologists participated in Kardiner's seminars, and made important contributions to the theory, but the general formulation is Kardiner's" (Singer, 1961, p. 29). Kardiner's theory was explanatory in nature, attempting as it did to relate and integrate personality types with primary and secondary social institutions. Several anthropologists, such as Linton, DuBois, and West, collected data to test Kardiner's hypotheses, and numerous important publications resulted. There has been some criticism of the Kardiner approach, in terms of unsupported assumptions and data limitations (e.g., Singer, 1961, p. 33): "It is especially difficult to maintain that individual reactions to the same external frustrations are not uniform, and yet to reason from individualized reactions to common institutional causes." Yet we think it is fair to say that Kardiner's influence has, on balance, been extremely useful and stimulating for culture and personality studies specifically, and for anthropology in general. Indeed, the freshness of his conceptual approach has transcended the boundaries of the school of his own anthropological colleagues and collaborators and has been adopted many times by many social scientists. A number of his hypotheses are currently used in field investigations.

3. The study of modal personality is based on the reasonable premise that certain personality types will be found more frequently than others in particular societies, as a result of unique influences of a combined biological, social, cultural, and physical environmental milieu. This concept is essentially statistical and tends to be descriptive rather than analytic, and most frequently is used in conjunction with projective tests. Work in this area began with DuBois's famous study of the Alorese, stimulated by the Kardiner seminar. Other work has been done by Clyde Kluckhohn and Dorothea Leighton (1947), Anthony Wallace (1952), and Bert Kaplan (1961). Problems have arisen as to whether or not projective test protocols should be analyzed blind or in conjunction with minimal understanding of the culture from which they are drawn. In evaluating this approach, Singer writes (1961, p. 40):

> Generally speaking, the program for validating basic personality structure, configurational personality, and other derivations of typical personality from cultural data and social institutions has disappointed early expectations. The introduction of psychological data about individual personalities has not led to demonstrations that the "vast majority" or "the bulk" of individuals in a culture conform to a dominant personality type.

4. The study of national character was stimulated by the desire to understand our "enemies" better during World War II (Benedict, 1946) and led to attempts to understand personality development and characteristics within the complex modern national states. Within this field studies have been conducted by numerous disciplines in addition to anthropology, such as sociology, history, political science, and economics. The major psychiatric influence in this area came, of course, from Erikson and Fromm. The study of national character or social character is a tremendously broad and complex field which, unlike the previous fields discussed, is more viable today in terms of interest, research and conceptual development. Major investigators, such as Inkeles, Levinson, Leites, Fromm, Erikson, Riesman, Mandlebaum, and Mead, from many diverse disciplines continue to conduct important studies. This is a lively and exciting field today, and it certainly

deserves greater discussion than it receives here. Although psychiatrists have contributed and continue to contribute to research in this area, it is probably safe to say that psychoanalysis today derives more from the study of social character in modern countries than it has put in.

Of all the areas of possible collaboration between psychoanalysis and social science one would have expected that cross-cultural aspects of mental disorder would occupy the center of the stage. Strangely, however, relatively little collaboration has occurred in this domain. To be sure, there have been copious words spent on the role of culture in both inducing and in inhibiting mental illness, and there have also been some studies carried out on cultural variations in the symptomatic content of mental disorder. The role of the native healer as a "primitive psychotherapist" has also been studied (Kiev, 1964).

In general, however, tests of etiological hypotheses based on dynamic psychoanalysis in diverse cross-cultural settings have been rare (Mishler and Scotch, 1963). It is true that there have been a significant number of recent studies of psychiatric disorder such as the study of *Psychiatric Disorder among the Yoruba* by Leighton and his group (A. Leighton, Murphy, Macklin, Lambo, Hughes, and D. Leighton, 1963), but such studies are much more heavily oriented toward descriptive and epidemiologic models than they are toward dynamic psychiatry.

In point of fact, the emergence of the whole field of social psychiatry (A. Leighton and Murphy, 1965) probably owes a great deal more to epidemiology, sociology, and anthropology than it does to psychoanalysis. There is some irony in the fact that at a time at which culture and personality studies are more respectable and acceptable than ever before that the once seminal influence of psychoanalysis now plays a minor role. Academic psychology which did not provide any stimulus for the development of the field is today highly influential through the work of such men as Lindzey, McClelland, and Child; and social psychiatry, which did not exist when the field of culture and personality was developing, also plays an important role today.

In the area of research techniques, anthropologists have borrowed freely from both therapeutic and research techniques of psychoanalysis. As a result, interviewing techniques have been vastly refined, especially in the recognition of the role of the interviewer's own needs in such situations, as well as in the techniques of passive interviewing (Carstairs, 1961). The use of personal documents such as life histories is partially traceable to psychoanalytic influence. Edward Sapir, for example, was a great proponent of life histories and in this respect was influenced by his relationship with Harry Stack Sullivan (Langness, 1965). The deep interest in dreams, fantasies, and many aspects of folklore arises partly from the extensive use of such cross-cultural materials made by psychoanalysts, not the least of these being Freud himself (Eggan, 1961; Honigmann, 1961; D'Andrade, 1961).

Of all the methodological techniques borrowed from psychiatry by anthropologists probably the use of projective tests has occupied most attention. DuBois's famous study of Alor (DuBois, 1944) and the subsequent analysis of her Rorschachs by Ernest Oberhalzer and its use by the Kardiner seminar are correctly regarded as a high point in the early development of the culture and personality field (Kardiner, 1944).

The best critical survey of the use of projective techniques in anthropology was published by Gardner Lindzey (1961). Lindzey points out the potential value of such methods—they are relatively culture-free, permit a holistic approach, and fit well with naturalistic observations. Yet in examining in great detail a large number of important studies, Lindzey finds numerous methodological weaknesses, many of which were quite avoidable. Moreover, up to the time of his survey at any rate, he notes little increase in sophistication over the years. He concludes that, in view of the huge number of man-hours spent in collecting, scoring, and interpreting thousands of test protocols, the handful of generalizations that has emerged appears quite puny. Kaplan, in a similar review, concludes:

> My judgments about the cross-cultural use of projective tests have been very harsh. I have looked for the positive values in these tests and have found them very scant. I have looked at the difficulties in their use and found them to be enormous, and have concluded that as these tests are being used and interpreted at present, only a modicum of validity and value can be obtained from them (Kaplan, 1961, p. 252).

It should be emphasized that though the early use of projective tests was stimulated by contact with psychoanalysis, the misuse of these methods can for the most part be attributed to anthropologists themselves, many of whom used them cavalierly to "pick up extra data," and few of whom used them with any sort of thorough grounding in their proper use.

To be sure, many of the techniques taken from psychoanalysis have not been used without attendant difficulties, such as those alluded to by Kaplan in the quotation above, and such as those raised earlier in connection with sociology. On balance, however, the psychiatric influence on the collection of data has been beneficial. When, however, we move from the level of technique to the level of over-all strategy, the meeting of psychoanalysis and anthropology has been a meeting of two disciplines notorious for their lack of scientific rigor, and for their dependence on intuition and insight, description and anecdote. This humanistic reliance on the "art" of data collection rather than the science has been responsible for many accounts rich in depth and insight, but more often has led to explanations of behavior unsupported by solid, replicable data. This resulted in the development of great resistance on the part of many "traditional" anthropologists both to engage in such research and to accept *any* of the findings of workers in this area. There is reason to believe, particularly in the last five or ten years, that concern with this situation has led, and is leading, to significantly greater attention to methodological questions and to many improvements in this sector. In this connection, the important work of the Whitings and their colleagues (B. Whiting, 1963; J. Whiting, 1961; J. Whiting and Child, 1953; J. Whiting, Kluckholn, and Anthony, 1960; Whiting and Whiting, 1960) may be cited in the area of child development. Also cross-cultural studies, such as those by Stephens (1962) on the Oedipus complex, and the critical work of Frank Young (1965) on initiation ceremonies, show vast conceptual and methodological improvement.

Evaluation and Conclusion

Although psychoanalysis has been a definite source of stimulation to sociology and anthropology, it appears that it has far from fulfilled its potential contribution to the two disciplines. The full contribution, if it eventually comes, we believe, will not be in the "reduction" of social science to psychoanalytic formulations nor in the "psychologizing" of social science, but in the mutual growth and refinement of the two disciplines as they are brought to bear on specific problems of analysis—in short, a real integration. This, of course, does not imply that psychoanalytic theory will be pertinent to the entire subject matter of sociology and anthropology, but, as Inkeles has argued so convincingly, effective sociological analysis of social systems will frequently depend on a general theory of personality and will need information on the personality characteristics of the people composing the social systems (Inkeles, 1959a, p. 272).

What are the prospects for integration? After sensitively describing some of the processes which would be involved in the integration between the two disciplines, Van Den Haag concludes: "We are very far from this ideal, in part because neither psychoanalysis nor the social sciences is sufficiently developed to make close integration fruitful. And, as is to be expected of adolescent sciences, boundaries and ambitions are hazily defined, claims are ambitious, and mutual misunderstandings frequent" (Van Den Haag, 1962, p. 168). While we only partly share Van Den Haag's view, there is little doubt that serious impediments exist to the integration and even to the effective cooperation between the two disciplines.

Certainly, there are a number of social scientists unfavorably disposed to psychoanalysis. The strong emphasis on exact and rigorous measurement, the tradition of operationalism, and the concern that propositions be stated which are amenable to testing and replication are some of the reasons the empirically oriented sociologist and anthropologist view the more facile psychoanalytic explanations with suspicion and, at times, even ridicule. This is not to imply that psychoanalysts are the only ones to incur criticism from the social science empiricists. Considerable criticism is leveled against the more facile formulations of their own colleagues. What has been especially vexing to a number of social scientists is that psychoanalysts presumably do not view the rich Freudian formulations as tentative, but as clear and established propositions for all to accept. Indeed, it is on the matter of what constitutes evidence that many rigorous social scientists have thrown up their hands in the belief that it is hopeless to negotiate with the Freudians. Many of them will not deny the richness of Freudian principles, but they view these as insightful and possibly fruitful hypotheses for testing—as a beginning, not as a definite body of knowledge. In discussions with psychoanalysts, the social scientist empiricist will challenge them to set up whatever criteria they wish, but to abide by them; to use independent measures and to avoid circular reasoning; to abandon the posture of possessing a proven body of theory; and to accept the canons and conditions of the scientific community.

Psychoanalysts, for their part, are often disdainful of social scientists whom they view as being naïve and ignorant of basic psychoanalytic theory. Some even say that it is impossible for social scientists who have not undergone psychoanalysis to understand psychoanalytic theory or to test psychoanalytic formulations. Many psychoanalysts contend that the methodology of social science is too narrow and limited to do justice to the depth and richness of Freudian theory. These psychoanalysts are often contemptuous of the puny and irrelevant indicators which they believe sociologists and anthropologists use in testing psychoanalytic formulations.

The psychoanalytic indictment is even shared by a small number of social scientists who are impatient with the social sciences' "detailed knowledge of the trivial or esoteric, together with a curious blindness to vital fact, obvious and near at hand . . ." (Seeley, 1962b, p. 110). The sociologist Seeley poses two challenging questions:

(1) Is psychoanalysis not perhaps pursuing strange and futile gods in its constant attempts to make itself scientifically respectable on the model of the nonhuman science? (2) Would it not be well for the social sciences to ask themselves whether or not they have in psychoanalysis a more apt model for the getting of what they want to get than they have in the dominantly dilute physical science models they now so largely ape? (p. 110).

The problem of developing integration between the two disciplines is further complicated by the actual difficulty of empirically testing Freudian theory. A good case in point is the previously cited work by Sewell on infant training and adult personality. In order to test the general theory, Sewell "computed the relationship between each of seven specific infant training practices and each of the forty-six personality indicators. In other words a total of 322 specific empirical tests was regarded as necessary by Sewell to evaluate the general theory" (Hyman, 1955, p. 359). The point to be made here is that what at first glance might appear to be a simple research procedure becomes a much more complex and difficult process. In analyzing this study, Hyman points up the difficulty of testing Freudian theory because of its generality and ambiguity.

> Sewell's study . . . demonstrates . . . the complexity of testing a theory that is *general*, but *discursive*, and one in which the *component hypotheses* are not explicitly articulated and the initial *concepts vague or non-unitary* in character. We see that a large number of specific tests are needed to comprehend the theory, but that the analyst is faced in turn with the dilemma of how to combine the evidence from the many specific tests, in the absence of a clear directive from the theory (p. 360).

It is ironic in view of all the admirable effort to which Sewell went that LaBarre took issue with Sewell's findings and contended that Sewell was ignorant of the real position assumed by Freudians regarding the effects of training (Hyman, 1955, pp. 361–362). This is just one illustration of how a methodologically rigorous study can still fail to obtain acceptance because of the very ambiguity of psychoanalytic theory and the difficulty of obtaining agreement as to what the theory explicitly states. The same ambiguity and lack of agreement is evidenced in an article by Orlansky which reviewed studies on infant care and personality and in a rejoinder to Orlansky by the psychoanalytically oriented social scientist, Sydney Axelrad (Orlansky, 1949; Axelrad, 1962). It is clear that the two authors disagree as to what are some of the fundamental tenets of psychoanalytic theory.

Despite the obvious problems in developing integration between the two disciplines, problems which are further complicated by different styles, postures, and even faiths of workers in the respective fields, there seems to be little alternative to continue to do some of the familiar right things, perhaps with a little more effort. Although, as some have stated, science and research are not always or necessarily synonymous with knowledge, the general scientific method is still our main tool in building cumulative and systematic knowledge. As long as psychoanalytic theorists argue that their discipline is a science, they must submit to the canons and prescriptions of the scientific method. Even more, they must assert the conditions under which they will accept or reject their own propositions. Indeed, they must be prepared to accept that some of their most treasured beliefs are in need of change or refinement and, in fact, may even have to be discarded.

This does not free sociologists and anthropologists from the important responsibility of knowing psychoanalytic theory intimately and of employing the most sensitive and appropriate methods to tap the full depth and wisdom of psychoanalytic theory. In this respect, sustained joint research efforts by psychoanalysts and social scientists, whatever the difficulties which may be entailed, may help considerably in explicating psychoanalytic hypotheses and in establishing appropriate criteria and methods for the testing of those hypotheses.

Note: We are indebted for comments and criticisms of an earlier draft of this chapter to Lenin Baler, David Lavin, Robert LeVine, Elliot Mishler, Carol Pearson Ryser, and Alvin Zalinger. These colleagues offered so many fruitful suggestions that we were almost sorry we sought their advice in the first place since the required scope and brevity of the chapter prevented us from incorporating many useful suggestions.

References

Adorno, T. W., Frenkel-Brunswik, Else, Levinson, D. J., and Sanford, R. N. *The Authoritarian Personality*. New York: Harper, 1950.

Axelrad, S. "Infant Care and Personality Reconsidered: A Rejoinder to Orlansky." In W. Muensterberger and S. Axelrad (eds.), *The Psychoanalytic Study of Society*. New York: International Universities Press, 1962.

Bales, R. F. "Small Group Theory and Research." In R. K. Merton, L. Broom, and L. S. Cottrell, Jr. (eds.), *Sociology Today*. New York: Basic Books, 1959. Pp. 293–305.

Benedict, Ruth F. *Patterns of Culture*. Boston: Houghton Mifflin, 1934.

Benedict, Ruth F. *The Chrysanthemum and the Sword*. Boston: Houghton Mifflin, 1946.

Bossard, J. H. *The Sociology of Child Development*. New York: Harper, 1954.

Brim, O. *Education for Child Rearing*. New York: Russell Sage Foundation, 1959.

Brim, O., and Wheeler, S. *Socialization after Childhood: Two Essays*. New York: Wiley, 1966.

Brown, R. *Social Psychology*. New York: The Free Press of Glencoe, 1965.

Carstairs, G. M. "Cross-Cultural Psychiatric Interviewing." In B. Kaplan (ed.), *Studying Personality Cross-Culturally*. New York: Row, Peterson, 1961.

Christensen, H. T. (ed.). *Handbook of Marriage and the Family*. Chicago: Rand McNally, 1964.

Clausen, J. A. "The Sociology of Mental Illness." In R. K. Merton, L. Broom, and L. S. Cottrell, Jr. (eds.), *Sociology Today*. New York: Basic Books, 1959. Pp. 485–508.

Clinard, M. B. "Criminological Research." In R. K. Merton, L. Broom, and L. S. Cottrell, Jr. (eds.), *Sociology Today*. New York: Basic Books, 1959. Pp. 509–536.

Cohen, A. K. *Delinquent Boys: The Culture of the Gang*. Glencoe, Ill.: The Free Press, 1955.

Dager, E. Z. "Socialization and Personality Development in the Child." In H. T. Christensen (ed.), *Handbook of Marriage and the Family*. Chicago: Rand McNally, 1964.

D'Andrade, R. G. "Anthropological Studies of Dreams." In F. L. K. Hsu (ed.), *Psychological Anthropology*. Homewood, Ill.: Dorsey Press, 1961.

Davis, K. *Human Society*. New York: Macmillan, 1949.

DuBois, Cora. "Some Anthropological Perspectives on Psychoanalysis." *Psychoanalytic Review*, 24 (1937), 246–263.

DuBois, Cora. *The People of Alor*. Minneapolis: University of Minneapolis Press, 1944.

Eggan, Dorothy. "Dream Analysis." In B. Kaplan (ed.), *Studying Personality Cross-Culturally*. New York: Row, Peterson, 1961. Pp. 551–578.

Faris, R. E. L. (ed.). *Handbook of Modern Sociology*. New York: Rand McNally, 1964.

Fromm, E. *Escape from Freedom*. New York: Farrar & Rinehart, 1941.

Glueck, S., and Glueck, Eleanor T. *Unravelling Juvenile Delinquency*. Cambridge, Mass.: Harvard University Press, 1950.

Gross, L. (ed.). *Symposium on Sociological Theory*. Evanston, Ill.: Row, Peterson, 1959.

Hall, C. S., and Lindzey, G. "Psychoanalytic Theory and Its Applications in the Social Sciences." In G. Lindzey (ed.), *Handbook of Social Psychology*. Cambridge, Mass.: Addison-Wesley, 1954. Vol. 1, pp. 143–175.

Henry, A. F., and Short, J. F. *Suicide and Homicide*. New York: The Free Press of Glencoe, 1954.

Himmelhoch, J. "Tolerance and Personality Needs: A Study of the Liberalization of Ethnic Attitudes among Minority Group College Students." *American Sociological Review*, 15 (1950), 79–88.

Honigmann, J. J. "The Interpretation of Dreams in Anthropological Field Work: A Case Study." In B. Kaplan (ed.), *Studying Personality Cross-Culturally*. New York: Row, Peterson, 1961. Pp. 579–586.

Hsu, F. L. K. "A Selected Bibliography Bearing on the Mutual Relationship between Anthropology, Psychiatry, and Psychoanalysis." In F. L. K. Hsu (ed.), *Psychological Anthropology: Approaches to Culture and Personality*. Homewood, Ill.: Dorsey Press, 1961. Pp. 439–498.

Hyman, H. *Survey Design and Analysis*. Glencoe, Ill.: The Free Press, 1955.

Hyman, H., and P. B. Sheatsley. "The Authoritarian Personality: A Methodological Critique." In Marie Johoda and R. Christie (eds.), *Continuities in Social Research: Studies in the Scope and Method of the Authoritarian Personality*. Glencoe, Ill.: The Free Press, 1954. Pp. 50–122.

Inkeles, A. "Personality and Social Structure." In R. K. Merton, L. Broom, and L. S. Cottrell, Jr. (eds.), *Sociology Today*. New York: Basic Books, 1959. Pp. 249–276. (a)

Inkeles, A. "Sociology and Psychology." In S. Koch (ed.), *Psychology: A Study of Science*. New York: McGraw-Hill, 1959. Pp. 317–387. (b)

Inkeles, A., and Levinson, D. J. "National Character: The Study of Model Personality and Sociocultural Systems." In G. Lindzey (ed.), *Handbook of Social Psychology*. Cambridge, Mass.: Addison-Wesley, 1954. Vol. 2, pp. 977–1020.

Kaplan, B. "Cross-Cultural Use of Projective Techniques." In F. L. K. Hsu (ed.), *Psychological Anthropology: Approaches to Culture and Personality*. Homewood, Ill.: Dorsey Press, 1961. Pp. 235–254.

Kardiner, A. "Introduction" to Cora DuBois, *The People of Alor*. Minneapolis: University of Minneapolis Press, 1944. Pp. 1–13.

Kiev, A. (ed.). *Magic, Faith, and Healing.* Glencoe, Ill.: The Free Press, 1964.

Kluckhohn, C. "The Influence of Psychiatry on Anthropology in America during the Past One Hundred Years." In *One Hundred Years of American Psychiatry.* New York: Columbia University Press, 1944. Pp. 569–617.

Kluckhohn, C., and Morgan, W. "Some Notes on Navaho Dreams." In G. B. Wilbur and W. Muensterberger (eds.), *Psychoanalysis and Culture: Essays in Honor of Géza Roheim.* New York: International Universities Press, 1951. Pp. 120–131.

Langness, L. L. *The Life History in Anthropological Science.* New York: Holt, Rinehart & Winston, 1965.

Leighton, A., and Murphy, Jane M. (eds.). *Approaches to Cross-Cultural Psychiatry.* Ithaca, N. Y.: Cornell University Press, 1965.

Leighton, A., Murphy, Jane M., Macklin, D. B., Lambo, T. A., Hughes, C. C., Leighton, Dorothea C. *Psychiatric Disorder among the Yoruba.* Ithaca: Cornell University Press, 1963.

Leighton, Dorothea C., and Kluckhohn, C. *Children of the People: The Navaho Individual and His Development.* Cambridge, Mass.: Harvard University Press, 1947.

Lindzey, G. *Projective Techniques and Cross-Cultural Research.* New York: Appleton, 1961.

MacKinnon, W., and Centers, R. "Authoritarianism and Urban Stratification." *American Journal of Sociology,* 61 (1956), 610–620.

Mead, Margaret. *From the South Seas.* New York: Morrow, 1938.

Merton, R. K., Broom, L., and Cottrell, L. S., Jr. (eds.), *Sociology Today.* New York: Basic Books, 1959.

Miller, D. R., and Swanson, G. E. *The Changing American Parent.* New York: Wiley, 1958.

Mishler, E. G., and Scotch, N. A. "Sociocultural Factors in the Epidemiology of Schizophrenia." *Psychiatry,* 6, No. 4 (November 1963), 315–351.

Opler, M. E. "The Psychoanalytic Treatment of Culture." *Psychoanalytic Review,* 22 (1935), 138–155.

Orlansky, H. "Parent Care and Personality." *Psychological Bulletin,* 46 (1949), 1–48.

Parsons, T. "Social Structure and the Development of Personality: Freud's Contribution to the Integration of Psychology and Sociology." In T. Parsons, *Social Structure and Personality.* Glencoe, Ill.: The Free Press, 1965. Pp. 78–111. (c)

Parsons, T. "The Superego and the Theory of Social Systems." In T. Parsons, *Social Structure and Personality.* Glencoe, Ill.: The Free Press, 1965. Pp. 18–33. (e)

Parsons, T., Bales, R. F., Olds, Jr., Zelditch, M., Jr., and Slater, P. *Family Socialization and Interaction Process.* Glencoe, Ill.: The Free Press, 1955.

Parsons, T., Shills, E., Naegele, K. D., Pitts, J. R. (eds.). *Theories of Society.* Glencoe, Ill.: The Free Press, 1961. Vol. 1.

Pitts, J. R. "Introduction" to T. Parsons, E. Shils, K. D. Naegele, and J. Pitts (eds.), *Theories of Society.* Glencoe, Ill.: The Free Press, 1961. Vol. 1, pp. 685–716.

Riesman, D. *Individualism Reconsidered.* Glencoe, Ill.: The Free Press, 1954.

Riesman, D. *The Lonely Crowd*. New Haven, Conn.: Yale University Press, 1955.

Roberts, A. H., and Rokeach, M. "Anomie, Authoritarianism, and Prejudice: A Replication." *American Journal of Sociology*, 61 (1956), 63–67.

Roheim, G. "Psychoanalysis and Anthropology." In H. M. Ruitenbeek (ed.), *Psychoanalysis and Social Science*. New York: Dutton, 1962. Pp. 73–101.

Ross, R., and Van Den Haag, E. *The Fabric of Society*. New York: Harcourt, Brace & World, 1957.

Ruitenbeek, H. M. "Psychoanalysis: A Challenge to the Social Sciences." In H. M. Ruitenbeek (ed.), *Psychoanalysis and Social Science*. New York: Dutton, 1962. Pp. 12–27. (a)

Ruitenbeek, H. M. (ed.). *Psychoanalysis and Social Science*. New York: Dutton, 1962. (b)

Sapir, E. "Cultural Anthropology and Psychiatry." *Journal of Abnormal and Social Psychology*, 27 (1932), 234–235.

Sapir, E. *Culture, Language and Personality*. Berkeley: University of California Press, 1956.

Sears, R. R., Maccoby, Eleanor E., and Levin, H. *Patterns of Child Rearing*. Evanston, Ill.: Row, Peterson, 1957.

Seeley, J. R. "The Americanization of the Unconscious." In H. M. Ruitenbeek (ed.), *Psychoanalysis and Social Science*. New York: Dutton, 1962. Pp. 186–199. (a)

Seeley, J. R. "Psychoanalysis: A Model for Social Science." In H. M. Ruitenbeek (ed.), *Psychoanalysis and Social Science*. New York: Dutton, 1962. Pp. 102–111. (b)

Sewell, W. H. "Infant Training and the Personality of the Child." *American Journal of Sociology*, 58 (1952), 150–159.

Simpson, G. E., and Yinger, J. M. "The Sociology of Race and Ethnic Relations." In R. K. Merton, L. Brown, L. S. Cottrell, Jr. (eds.), *Sociology Today*. New York: Basic Books, 1959. Pp. 376–399.

Singer, M. "A Survey of Culture and Personality Theory and Research." In B. Kaplan (ed.), *Studying Personality Cross-Culturally*. New York: Row, Peterson, 1961. Pp. 9–90.

Sorokin, P. *Contemporary Sociological Theories*. New York: Harper & Row, 1928. Pp. 607–608.

Srole, L. "Social Integration and Certain Corollaries: An Exploratory Study." *American Sociological Review*, 21 (1956), 709–716.

Stephens, W. N. *The Oedipus Complex*. Glencoe, Ill.: The Free Press, 1962.

Van Den Haag, E. "Psychoanalysis and the Social Sciences: Genuine and Spurious Integration." In H. M. Ruitenbeek (ed.), *Psychoanalysis and Social Science*. New York: Dutton, 1962. Pp. 167–185.

Wallace, A. F. C. "The Modal Personality Structure of the Tuscarora Indians as Revealed by the Rorschach Test." *Bureau of American Ethnology*, Bulletin No. 150 (1952).

Wallace, A. F. C. *Culture and Personality*. New York: Random House, 1964.

Whiting, B. B. (ed.). *Six Cultures: Studies of Child Rearing*. New York: John Wiley, 1963.

Whiting, J. W. M. "Socialization Process and Personality." In F. L. K. Hsu (ed.), *Psychological Anthropology: Approaches to Culture and Personality.* Homewood, Ill.: Dorsey Press, 1961.

Whiting, J. W. M., and Child, I. *Child Training and Personality.* New Haven, Conn.: Yale University Press, 1953.

Whiting, J. W. M., Kluckhohn, R., and Anthony, A. A. "The Function of Male Initiation Ceremonies at Puberty." In E. E. Maccoby, T. M. Newcomb, and E. L. Hartley (eds.), *Readings in Social Psychology.* 3rd ed.; New York: John Wiley, 1960.

Whiting, J. W. M., and Whiting, B. B. "Contributions of Anthropology to the Methods of Studying Child Rearing." In P. H. Mussen (ed.), *Handbook of Research Methods in Child Development.* New York: John Wiley, 1960.

Young, F. *Initiation Ceremonies.* New York: Bobbs-Merrill, 1965.

25

Psychoanalysis and the "Creative" Arts

LEON EDEL

This chapter is concerned with the relationship between psychoanalysis and those arts we usually designate as "creative"—music, painting, sculpture, and imaginative literature (poetry, drama, and the novel). That such a relationship exists is generally recognized. Its nature, however, has not been sufficiently examined or understood. There is frequent confusion between these arts and their sister arts of criticism, cultural history, and biography—in a word, the analytical arts—where the influence of psychoanalysis is profound and palpable. Confusion has further been created by the use of superficial psychoanalytical formulations on the stage, or in such novels as the once-sensational *Snake Pit* or in so airy a trifle as *Lady in the Dark,* the popular musical about dreams of a quarter of a century ago. This kind of "influence," however, does not suggest for a moment the fundamental relationship between the original Freudian search for the meaning of our subterranean dream life and the effects of Freud's discoveries on the dominating arts—those arts which must exist before criticism and cultural history are even possible.

I would like to suggest that we can best approach our subject by recognizing that we stand on uncharted and even slippery ground. The analysis of the human psyche or "soul," however scientific, continues to be a mixture of physical fact in confrontation with the impalpable imagination. We see all around us creations of this imagination, yet the imaginative processes themselves are as elusive as trying to pin down the flow of our thoughts—a little like trying, as William James long ago remarked, to discover what darkness looks like by turning on a light. We still have only the crudest theories about the genesis of imaginative work, and artists themselves can give only sketchy and skeletonized accounts of it.

The truth of this does not need to be argued, and we know that the link between psychoanalysis and the creative imagination existed from the first in the character and personality of Sigmund Freud himself. He founded psychoanalysis not only out of his knowledge of scientific method, or out of what he had learned in medicine, but also out of the profound humanism of his being; it is doubtful whether a dividing line could ever be drawn between his medical knowledge and his humanistic imagination. The two were inseparable. Freud discovered very early that he was concerned not only with specific medical problems, but, in Shakespeare's words, with "the dark backward and abysm" where man's imaginative existence is rooted. He was concerned, in a word, with man's ability to create and use symbols. This suggests that the practice of psychoanalysis is itself irradiated by certain qualities of the imagination.

I

From the moment psychoanalysis began to explore man's use of symbols, it was exploring man's creative capacities, sometimes in their crudest forms. The equation is simple: as human behavior is related to the unconscious and is influenced by the feelings and memories of our earliest years, so the arts materialize and acquire form and beauty out of such buried states in the artist's past; these give rise to his fancies and dreams. Until recently, the plastic, verbal, or aural powers, the gifts and disciplines of the artist, determined the quality of his creations. In modern times, however, we have been subjected to much of the raw stuff of the unconscious, a great deal of it pathological, and in some misguided way this has been judged to be a form of finished art. It sometimes happens to be sufficiently fanciful to be "documentary" and illuminating, and it sometimes possesses adventitious form and shape. But it must be recognized that such form and shape are as accidental as the shapes assumed by crystals of frost on a windowpane and that which we call art today is in reality inchoate material to which no "process" or discipline has been applied. "Stuff of sleep and dreams," said Coleridge long ago, adding significantly, however, "and yet my Reason at the Rudder." Charles Lamb made a similar observation when he spoke of poets dreaming as other men—but dreaming "being awake." The poet is not possessed by his subject, he said, "but has dominion over it." I think today we would say that he *is* possessed by it, but he can control this possession.

Coleridge was one of the great empiricists of man's "inward turning," which began at the dawn of romanticism, when writers recognized that behind reason there exist many states of sentience. Literature, which verbalized these insights, is fertile in illustrations. We know that the symbolist movement had come into being before Freud attended Charcot's clinics at Salpetrière, that poets, dramatists, and a new school of novelists were beginning to understand the limitations of "realism," and that literary expression had found greater freedom in using language as evocatively as the impressionist painters were using their plastic materials on canvas. Music too —as in the work of Debussy—was finding new clusters of sound and new tonal harmonies that superseded mere "tune" and the art of the fugue. William James wrote his chapter on "the stream of consciousness" in the late 1880's. One could list many such early pre-Freudian insights and explorations. There has never been, so far as I know, a study of the "climate" in which Freud's book on dreams appeared. It was published at a moment when all the arts in Europe were receptive to some rational explanation of the increasingly perceived but as yet misunderstood "unconscious." I find it curious to come upon the following in the letter of a minor American novelist (Constance Fenimore Woolson) written before 1894: "There is a new theory, 'working hypothesis' they call it, which seems to explain many mysteries. It is that we have two minds, one which we feel, another which makes itself known only at moments. . . . I think we are on the eve of great discoveries (Benedict, 1929–30, p. 53)." This novelist may have been reading William James's paper on "The Hidden Self" which he published in 1890; it was William's brother, Henry, the novelist, who a decade later was to use the phrase, much quoted since: "the deep well of unconscious cerebration."

II

The creative arts then might be said, in a certain sense, to have been ready for *The Interpretation of Dreams*, and indeed awaiting it; yet in another sense they had anticipated it. In painting, "futurism" and "cubism" had already sought to capture on canvas distortions akin to dream experience, and not long after, during the years of World War I, the *dada* movement was founded, a nihilist movement in the arts which contained within it the germs of the later surrealism and the even more recent existentialism and some of the neo-modern movements. Was *dada* a product of the early impact of Freud on European thought? Who can say. From the moment *The Interpretation of Dreams* was launched its ideas were in the air, and the artistic imagination, as we know, reaches constantly for hints and suggestions, almost as naturally as plants absorb moisture. It is sufficient to note that the dadaists invoked the unconscious and explored autistic writing and that their assault upon language itself was outmoded, since it expressed man's rationalizations and carried a large hint of early Freud. But if *dada* plucked things out of the air, there is no doubt about the origins of surrealism. André Breton, its founder, was a medical student in Paris when World War I broke out. During the war he served in psychiatric wards, treating the wounded. He had read Freud with care and with respect, and not long afterward he journeyed to Vienna and was received by the eminent doctor. Freud was much moved by this attention from a young Frenchman, since rational and Descartian France had been the one country in Europe that was coldest to his explorations. Returning to Paris, Breton wrote an account of his interview, and in further articles he showed how profoundly *The Interpretation of Dreams* had affected him. He had always been interested in literature and was a gifted writer. He now gave up his studies of medicine to devote himself to the arts. His dream-symbolic *Les Vases Communicants* was dedicated to Freud, and Freud can be said to have directly fertilized the surrealist movement which Breton founded.

Surrealism at first was concerned with dreaming and automatic writing—that is, with attempting the almost impossible setting down of messages directly from the unconscious. Indeed, Breton arrived at his personal discovery of his inner world during his own hypnagogic states and his attempt to record the half-formed words and images that arose at the moment of falling asleep. One of the surrealists who later attracted great attention was Robert Desnos, who could effortlessly fall asleep and utter words and phrases that seemed to come directly from the hidden depths of himself. Louis Aragon has described this:

> At the café, amid the sound of voices, in the full glare, amid the elbowings of the people, Robert Desnos had only to close his eyes, and he spoke—amid the beer-glasses and saucers—and the whole ocean flooded in with its prophetic clatter and its mists decorated with long colorful banners. Those who questioned this formidable sleeper had but to needle him and promptly prophecy and revelation, the tone of magic, of revolution, the tone of the fanatic and of the apostle, emerged. Under other circumstances, if Desnos had used this kind of delirium, he could have become a new religious leader, the founder of a city, the tribune of a people in revolt (Nadeau, 1945, p. 77).

In summing up, Nadeau, the historian of surrealism, points out that what began as an inquiry by the surrealists into the uses of language for poetic ends became a study of "total subjectivity," with language regarded as personal property, which each could use as he wished. This might be said of abstract painting as well, in which the artist gives us a wholly personal symbolism. "The external world," says Nadeau, "was denied at the expense of the world the individual found within himself and which he wished to explore systematically. Hence the significance given to the unconscious and its manifestations, as translated into a new, liberated language" (p. 258).

Anna Balakian, in her illuminating study of surrealism (1959), has described for us the ways in which Freudian ideas were incorporated by Breton into the various manifestoes of the movement. The name itself was derived from Breton's concept of a marriage between the dream states of the unconscious with reality, into "one sort of absolute reality." This he called "surreality." The surrealists had dream sessions, recorded their dreams in their various publications and, in a kind of epidemic of self-analysis, also sought to interpret them. Many forms of these dreams may be seen embodied in the work of Salvador Dali, the painter who embraced surrealism, as well as in surrealist poems, novels, and plays. Miss Balakian summarizes:

> These exercises in uninhibited, and sometimes erotic, writing and exploration of sensations beyond the control of reason were to sharpen, to renovate poetic imagery, and to incorporate into the poet's technique Freud's observations on the role of language in dreams and dream interpretation; the condensation that results in a density of imagery; displacement of the senses of time and space in the vision; the importance of figurative language (Balakian, 1959, p. 99).

One important difference remains which Freud himself voiced after he had a talk with Dali. Freud considered these condensations and distortions as forms by which man concealed from himself the unpalatable truths of his instincts; the surrealists regarded them as a liberation from the conventional and from the clichés of art, and as providing new ways of looking at reality. His most important statement on the subject I deem to be his discussion of the artist's motivations. Embodied within this debated declaration is a significant passage which has been insufficiently noted because it seems to be beyond controversy. The difference between everyone's day-dreams and those of the artist, Freud explained, resides in the fact that the "true artist"

> understands how to work over his day-dreams in such a way as to make them lose what is too personal about them and repels strangers, and to make it possible for others to share in the enjoyment of them. He understands, too, how to tone them down so that they do not easily betray their origin from proscribed sources. Furthermore, he possesses the mysterious power of shaping some particular material until it has become a faithful image of his phantasy . . . If he is able to accomplish all this, he makes it possible for other people once more to

derive consolation and alleviation from their own sources of pleasure in their unconscious which have become inaccessible to them (Freud, 1916–1917, p. 376).

This in effect provides an answer to artists so fascinated by the id-stuff within themselves that they forego all thought of process and discipline. The surrealists who inscribed themselves under Freud's banner did not listen to him. A Pandora's box of mixed blessings had been opened, and the artists found the glimpses of the unconscious enormously seductive. It was capable of wit and humor, of integrations of which the individual artist was not consciously aware; it could offer sudden "inspirations" that emerged out of unknown depths; it had a kind of wild freedom that belonged to the flights of dream; and it could conjure up moments of haunting beauty and of terror. On the one hand, there came greater and more awareness of the hidden powers residing within art, and, on the other, there emerged insane flights and primitivisms, and often the "raw" symbols of pathology. Henry James in alluding to the artistic process remarked that "in the great glazed tank of art, strange silent subjects float." The dredging up of the silent subjects, and other specimens of this submarine life, marked a great stage—a "breakthrough"—into the "modern"; its benefits and extremes are still with us today. At one extreme Freudian analysis was to indulge in a rampage of id-psychology that was to continue in various ways for years, in spite of criticisms and observations by later practitioners, and it was not until Hartmann and others supplied the correctives of ego psychology during World War II that a greater depth of insight was achieved. The automatism, the ink-splattering "chance" effects—plastically, verbally, tonally—of modern art derive in some measure from the "uncorking"—on various levels of the unconscious and the explanation of its role in the imagination, which the art world had known—and experienced—for so long but had not fully understood. The Freudian movement gave a kind of implicit sanction to modern art and also to the successive movements, from later forms of futurism through expressionism and surrealism to existentialism. The effects are to be seen to this day: indeed, the school of the "absurd" is a late re-flowering of *dada*-cum-Freud. This kind of "creativity," as I have observed, is based on a significant misconception: the belief that the direct recording of symbols emerging from the unconscious on canvas, or in poetry and prose, without "process" constitute forms of "creativity," and reveal the buried artistic drives in man, or testify to the depth of his inner vision. There are those who have argued that art as we have known it is false or that id-art is the true art. But as we reassert the role of the ego and the self, we must recognize that cruder emanations of the unconscious have value only as forms of experiment; they represent a kind of impulse-art and a failure to adapt the modalities, techniques, and disciplines which man has learned in so painstaking and difficult a fashion during the centuries. We can perceive that the most successful art of our time has indeed been that which has used the unconscious to constructive ends, tapped it to a greater degree than before, but also united it, as Breton seemed at first to envisage, with disciplines long-learned and cherished. Sometimes new disciplines are achieved in this process.

The entire modern movement, if we examine it retrospectively in the old age of our century, seems to have conformed to the historical forces traced by Bernard Berenson in his studies of Italian art. In primitive or archaic forms of art, no artist strays very far from his goal, Berenson observed. He is in quest of form and movement, and art has not yet learned how to depict it. So he fails. But his quest, from the first, as Berenson liked to say, is "life-enhancing." At a later stage, after many centuries, art achieves classic form; the artists have discovered how to create and use formal beauty; they have solved difficult questions of discipline and technique. And Berenson brilliantly describes the regressive process which at some stage sets in:

> classic art, producing these things adventitiously and never aiming for them, speaks too softly to the emotions, is too reticent in expression and too severe in beauty to satisfy the masses. They therefore greet with applause every attempt which self-assertiveness and the mere instinct for change will inspire the younger artists to make. And this because every variation upon classic art leads necessarily through schematization and attenuation to the obvious. Once the end is mistaken for the means, it will occur to the first clever youth that, by emancipating the oval of the face from the modelling which originally produced it, he would be skimming off all that made it attractive, and would present its attractiveness unalloyed. He thus gets prettiness of oval, and to make it more interesting, the artist of the new school will not long hesitate to emphasize and force the expression. Nor will he stop here, but will proceed in like fashion with the action, and continue with the simple process of neglecting the source of its value, Movement, and accentuating the resulting silhouettes, till they too become accurate, fully representative pictographs. Having got so far, he will then be borne one stage farther along the rolling platform of art-reaction, and will attempt to combine these pictographs, not of course in designs based on the requirements of form and movement, but in arrangements that will be most obviously pretty and eloquent. But that time, without realizing whither his applauded progress—which is really no more than blind energy—was taking him, he will have got rid of form and movement; he will have thrown art out of the door, and, unlike nature, art will not come back through the window (Berenson, 1952, pp. 202–203).

Franz Alexander, in his essay on psychoanalysis and painting (1953), offered us further insights. In discussing the way in which old-time realism yielded to an absence of real objects or to their distortion in painting, he suggests that in some cases this might be a token of withdrawal from the world "as perceived through the sense organs, and substituting for it a newly created different kind of world," which at the extreme allows free play to the id. He suggests further that we might seek possible hostile components in such paintings, that is, denial by the artist of the world as it is commonly perceived. This would particularly be true in any emphasis on the grotesque. Yet he shows also how distortion is often reconciled with earlier forms: "It is like transposing a melody from one key to another." Modigliani illustrates this, Alexander points out, in his "consistent longitudinal distortion of proportion and symmetry" even while adhering to techniques of earlier masters and preserving a flavor of the renaissance in his works. We might make an analogous observation about Stravinsky's use of old materials (as in the *Pulcinella* suite) which he rewrites into his personal musical idiom, and his alternations of rhythm, or his bringing together the classical and the modern in works such as *Apollon Musagète, Orféo,* or his *Psalm* symphony.

III

In our glimpse into some of the mysteries of the unconscious, we find the deepest and most significant relation between psychoanalysis and the creative arts. We are at our greatest ease, however, when we observe the role of the unconscious in the visual and verbal arts, and we encounter difficulties with music and the dance not only because these cannot be translated into language, but also because they are available to us in a time dimension and not in space. Freud could contemplate Michelangelo's Moses at his leisure; it was present constantly before his eyes. But the music of his favorite composers was, in the words of the poet, "momentary in the mind." One recalls how Loïe Fuller, dancing at the Folies in whirling, shining draperies, caught the imagination of painters and poets in the late nineteenth century. Her creations were almost pure symbol—and as evanescent as images thrown on a screen. Perhaps clinical pyschology, with its use of non-verbal and plastic materials in its study of the dynamics of personality, may offer us a valuable approach in the future to the non-verbal arts through thematic apperception, figure drawing, and above all the inkblots of Rorschach.

When we turn to the verbal and visual arts, those which are spatial in form, we are enabled with greater sureness to see the influences of psychoanalysis. The overt influences need not concern us; they have involved the mere copying of the clichés and superficialities of psychoanalytic popularizing. Philip Weissman, in his perceptive study of psychoanalysis in the theater (1965), has described this kind of influence as "documented case history with accompanying therapy on the stage" (p. 233) and has properly asked whether this can be called art. Psychoanalysis has influenced the creative arts in a much more fundamental way than through these often irresponsible borrowings of surface materials.

The relation between the creative arts and psychoanalysis can be sought in a much more rewarding fashion in the areas I have suggested and in the works of the great innovators of our century; what we find there we can apply to the host of lesser talents who have also been enriched by Freudian and Jungian explorations. From the mid-century perspective, I suppose, critics would generally agree that the most fertile and inventive creators in the arts of our time have been—in the Western world—Stravinsky in music, Picasso in art, and Joyce, Mann, and Eliot in literature. (I exclude Proust, who explored memory and association by himself under the apparent influence of Bergson and perhaps some of the Sorbonne psychologists, but outside the influence of the psychoanalytic movement.) We might add the name of one other writer, wholly individual and bizarre, Franz Kafka. Of Stravinsky we can say little, for, as we have seen, music is a subjective language, and words can discuss sounds only in the most limited way. We know that this composer's music contains within it some distinct primitivisms and folk music, a search for variant rhythms and subtle and sometimes violent sound effects and a breaking away from old musical forms which seem to parallel the discoveries of id-art. But it can equally be said that Stravinsky is the most "tuneful" of the moderns and is formidably disciplined. One is as aware of "structure" in him as in Bach. There is no evidence, however, that the Russian composer was particularly exposed to psychoanalysis. His work evolved from nineteenth-century Russian music and folk tunes and contributed to the Freudian *Zeitgeist*. *Sacre du Printemps* is, after all, of 1912—before the influence of Freud had reached the arts.

One might be less hard put to unravel the psychoanalytic sources of Picasso's inspiration, and even less were we discussing Paul Klee, who spoke of "that secret place where primeval power nurtures all evolution." If we find dream distortions in Picasso's work, deformations of figure and faces, we know that these could stem from his enormous grasp of the art movements of our time and that he possessed a strong personality, a discipline and tradition before he shattered his forms. His cubism antedated his "Freudianism." Franz Alexander has remarked that Picasso always finds a consistent formula to transform the world we live in into a world of his own—and we might add that some of his canvases show a kind of dismembered rage-world. But this has many affinities with man's rages and the rages of our century; it has also, in its later and possibly more "Freudian" phases, the harsh light of reality—the same faces incorporating front and profile, the condensations of visage and body, the translation of the human figure into objects and in many instances that of women into misogynic symbols. Picasso has lived most of his creative years in France. He knew the surrealists, who regarded his innovations as in the direct line of their own theories, and psychoanalysis may have reached him through them. It seems to be present in brilliant and often diagrammatic and cruel form in his later phases.

We are as always on the least difficult ground with writers, and James Joyce's work illustrates a profitable absorption of some of the basic ideas of psychology and psychoanalysis in our time. Indeed, it is surprising that "applied psychology" has not found him out: he offers an infinity of "games" for those psychoanalysts who find a constant intellectual pleasure in the exercises of the wit and humor of the unconscious. In his great dream book, *Finnegans Wake*, we find Joyce puns on the "intrepidation of dreams." As early as 1916 Joyce was noting his own dreams, and attempting to interpret them; he often asked his friends for theirs, and cross-examined them minutely on their ways of dreaming. Freud, Jung, the French psychologist Levy-Bruhl, and Krafft-Ebing might be judged his principal sources. A consistently scatological writer, Joyce has in him, we might say, all the "madness of art"; he possessed so great a verbal power that he appears, in a tremendous will to sanity, to have had the fragmentations of schizophrenia and yet created conscious word-salads out of the eighteen languages with which he had some acquaintance. His verbal condensations, his mutilation of language, his incessant puns, his attempts to render the "stream of consciousness," his large grasp of symbol and the nature of phantasmagoria (as in the "nighttown" scenes in *Ulysses*) all speak for familiarity with psychoanalytic literature as well as independent discoveries of his own. His friends used to tell him that the name Joyce in Irish means what the name Freud means in German, and we know that the superstitious ritual-seeking Joyce attached importance to such coincidences. "We grisly old Sykos," the analyst in *Finnegans Wake* joyfully—and joycefully—puns, "have done our unsmiling bit on 'alices, when they were young and easily freudened." Sykos-on-'alices is Joyce's fanciful manner of writing the word *psychoanalysis*, and introducing into it also a reference to *Alice in Wonderland*, a book filled with psychological insights and word-condensations. As for *young* and *freudened*, Joyce delighted in punning on the best-known names in the movement. He might talk in his letters of "Doctor Jung the Swiss Tweedledum who is not to be confused with the Viennese Tweedledee Dr. Freud" (again here associating *Alice in Wonderland*), and he might proclaim psychoanalysis to be "blackmail," but Joyce's casuistic intellect and his word-imagination were endlessly teased by the night world of the unconscious and the myths embodied in hidden memory. He remarked that his imagination grew when he read Vico "as it doesn't when I read Freud or Jung," but he read them all, and he mingled Freud and Jung with Vico, whose *La scienza nuova* (1725) was a seminal book for Joyce in *Ulysses* and *Finnegans Wake*. Vico developed a theory of history based on language and a belief in cycles of development, constantly repeated.

No one has rendered "free association" better in the literature of our time than Joyce, unless it be Proust whose approach to experience was, however, analytical, where Joyce was simply "representational." Freud's dream work thus gave unexpected birth to a fascinating literary dream book, and Jung's "archetypes" fertilized Joyce's awareness of myth and his interest in the "collective unconscious." That Joyce's books are those of a misdirected genius, a colossal illustration of the working of obsession and compulsion in art, does not alter the fundamental fact for us that they are major experiments, and they had as a consequence an extraordinary influence on other writers. In this way Joyce became the funnel for certain psychoanalytic concepts which were spread to a whole generation of writers which never read Freud or Jung, but used Joyce's discoveries.

With T. S. Eliot the use of psychoanalytic knowledge is more subtle. Much of Eliot's poetry, and particularly his *Quartets,* is informed by the insights of psychology. His inquiry into the "dissociation of sensibility"—which profoundly affected his many disciples in criticism—is of 1921. Eliot constantly, and in a truly psychological way, reminded critics of the relation of thought to feeling, and his formulation of the "objective correlative"—the poem as concretion in word and form of the unverbalized and unformed feelings that arise from the unconscious—was one of the most valuable critical formulations of our time. Eliot had read deeply and searchingly in French criticism and was in touch with the new writers and new movements of the postwar period in the 1920's; he was deeply interested, for example, in Jacques Rivière, who had recognized from the first the importance of Proust, and had lectured and written on Proust and Freud. These "connections" suggest that Eliot, for all his formidable intellectuality, was aware of Freud's inquiries into the instinctual side of man and the emotional basis of poetic endeavor. His readings in Dostoevski and Conrad, in the background of his long period of personal despair which gave rise to *The Waste Land* and *The Hollow Men,* suggest his psychological orientation; for he turned to the psychological writers who yielded the greatest insights. The interpersonal strategy used by the psychoanalyst in *The Cocktail Party* springs also out of a familiarity with modern psychoanalytic theory: "I learn a great deal by merely observing you," says the analyst. "And letting you talk as long as you please, and taking note of what you do *not* [my italic] say." Again and again we come upon lines in the poems—and stances in the criticism—which are informed by the century's inquiries into the psyche.

Freud speaks to us most directly through Thomas Mann and Franz Kafka, understandably because his works were immediately available to these writers. They did not have to rely on translations. One critic (Brennan, 1962) has observed that Mann worked out his Freudianism without direct help from Vienna and only after he had written *The Magic Mountain,* but he decidedly grasped what was in the air, for we remember the dream sequence which is the climax of Hans Castorp's education and interest in the new theories of the psychoanalytically oriented medical man at the sanatorium. By the time of the writing of his "Joseph" novels, Mann was familiar not only with Freud, but also with Jung. Certainly Mann's two essays on Freud find him pointing directly to the unconscious as the source of art and to the ego as a transfiguring agent. The first of Mann's essays dealt with Freud's position in the history of modern thought, and the second was titled "Freud and the Future." It expressed Mann's debt to Freud for ideas and themes he had used in his work, particularly in the "Joseph" series. In his first essay he welcomed Freud for emphasizing "the night side of nature and the soul as the actually life-conditioning and life-giving element." This he said represented "in the most revolutionary sense the divinity of earth, the primacy of the unconscious." But he too warned against id-art, against the danger that "these dark precincts do not allure it [art] for their own sake." And he used the word *oubliettes* to characterize the deepest recesses—they were the dungeons in which the artist could lose himself, indeed, imprison himself.

Franz Kafka looms as a lesser talent than those I have mentioned, but he has been a potent influence, and this because unlike most of the modern novelists and poets he understood the nature of dreams profoundly and studied his own nightmares. He had read Freud, as we know from his notebooks; he may indeed have been exposed to some psychoanalysis. The key to his works—which have bewildered so many readers—is to be found in Kafka's method of relating distorted dream material, or material analogous to dream, as if these inner creations of the unconscious were occurring in a matter-of-fact outer world. His stories are thus the equivalent of some of the best canvases of the abstract movement, with the important difference that the absurdities he sets down carry a sense of continuous reality, in the midst of the imagination's extravagances, and touch the wellsprings of our own irrationalities and the bizarre of our own fantasies. Moreover, they are written in a tight and vivid prose; it is hard and "functional." The experimentation is in the content. He restored to the art of fiction the magical and the mysterious. We feel as if a nightmare is taking place in broad daylight, in the streets of town or city, visible to all. Various components of his hero's id, ego, and superego become persons in Kafka and are treated as separate characters as sometimes occurs in dreams. We have only to remind ourselves that the "assistants" in *The Castle* who cling always to the surveyor, and from whom he cannot separate himself, are parts of his inner self cast in individual human forms.

But Kafka's work was incomplete. His novels seem but part of one continuous novel, fragmentary and without end, since he could not achieve an end to his dreamings and redreamings. He will be written down as the prose fiction writer of our time who truly integrated the new knowledge of the psyche with his particular art. His "objectification" of the inner world was done not by uniting literature to psychoanalysis (as if a forced marriage were being performed), but by allowing the buried world Freud uncovered to work through and permeate his art.

IV

I observed earlier that the analytic arts have most naturally derived instruction from the analysis of the psyche. Without attempting to define the exact art category in which we place biography, its relation to psychoanalysis will be at once clear. Psychoanalysis deals with the life of a patient; it attempts to induce the patient to speak, as it were, his own autobiography, and then, by continuous acts of evaluation and interpretation—which is really what the higher criticism is—it enables the patient to bring some of his hidden motivations into the open, revise his life, and find some release. The goals of biography and of criticism obviously are not therapeutic; they deal with texts, paintings, sculptures, music—the "output" of the artist—and there is no confrontation of the creators. Biography and criticism are impersonal, or should be; yet in dealing with the products of the imagination, and of the creative energy of individuals, they can use some part of psychoanalytic knowledge. I have developed these ideas in two earlier papers and need only summarize them here (Edel, 1961, 1965).

The psychoanalytically informed biographer can look today more critically at a slip of the pen in a manuscript; he can study certain verbalizations and seek to determine whether they express truth or rationalization of experiences; he is more aware of family dynamics in the life of his subject; he can see more clearly the nature of ironic statement. As Berenson studied paintings and established their authenticity by noting those fine details which were most characteristic in them, so literary texts may be read in a similar way. In other words, the old argument that a writer's work may not be used by the biographer for biographical purposes is no longer true. The story a novelist makes up may not have happened to that novelist, but the *kind* of stories he makes up and the *kind* of poems a poet writes tell us a great deal about the fantasy and word-world in which these stories had origin. Above all, modern biographers are no longer concerned with making their subjects seem logical, rational, and without contradiction. They know much more about ambivalence in the human being.

In criticism the critic today using the tools of psychoanalysis can more vividly see symbolic meaning and the operation of myth in the given work; he can study motivation and behavior—as Ernest Jones studied the "madness" of Hamlet—and he can also analyze a poem or novel with a firmer grasp of the meaning of style as expression of the personality. By the same token he can be more aware of subjective attitudes within himself which may blur or distort his perception of the literary work; he can tug more systematically at the roots of "creative process."

It seems to me that these will continue to be the areas of greatest influence and most intimate relation between the disciplines and that the relation of psychoanalysis to the creative arts will continue to be more subterranean and difficult of access. We come back to the fundamental fact that in the imaginative arts the artist has access to some of the secrets of his own imagination without the help of analysis, and it remains a moot question whether the psychoanalyzing of an artist by helping to heal his "wound" will help his art. We are led here, if we follow this speculative avenue to the whole vexed question of art and neurosis, to the disequilibrium in an artist's being from which his art is derived and whose art is often a sign not of sickness but of a will and a drive to health and to the enhancement of existence. It is a commonplace to hear psychoanalysts express the belief that their skills can help a writer to improve his work, since they may remove some of his inhibitions and his anxieties. This may be true of certain kinds of writers; it may not be true for others. We remember with what horror James Joyce recoiled when Jung volunteered to analyze him. Jung, having read *Ulysses*, was fascinated by Joyce and felt he had a subject of the greatest interest to the art of psychoanalysis. But Joyce's instincts were probably sound; he wanted to be neither a "subject" nor a patient. We know a great deal about Joyce's life and we can discern in it a series of defenses mobilized passionately against an overpowering sense of guilt and employed with the highest imaginative skill to keep Joyce from plunging into those distortions of madness to which his daughter fell victim. In Joyce we have, as I have suggested, a supreme case of the "madness of art," and the artful word-salads of *Finnegans Wake* may well have kept him from lasping into the unstructured word-salads of the mental wards. No one can guess what break might have occurred if his life's rituals and magical formulas had been disturbed. Joyce had developed an elaborate series of superstitions: he believed in signs and portents; he made extraordinary efforts to have his books published on his birthdays; and if he did not consult the stars, he consulted a highly personal kind of astrological calendar. He had renounced Catholicism, but in his deepest self he believed in the works of the devil, for he was always searching for spells to ward off danger—the nightmare of his inner world.

It is not surprising that many artists intuitively fear psychoanalysis. And while many minor artists and amateurs have been helped by undergoing analysis, we have no evidence at the present time, nor any records, of what it can do or has done for the transcendant genius.

V

In the foregoing I have attempted to sketch very broadly some of the elements involved in the relation between psychoanalysis and creation. The dialogue between the two has been very much at cross-purposes. In criticism and biography psychoanalysts have written papers on the arts which have been diagnostic and therapeutically directed but which have shown great ignorance of artistic discipline and of certain fundamental aesthetic ideas, so that their contributions have been undermined by their ignorance. The same faults have existed in the creative arts where gross errors have often been perpetrated, based on popularizations of psychoanalysis; many critical studies have been rendered meaningless at their inception and in spite of their guise of interdisciplinary wisdom. The only answer to this is a greater exchange between the two disciplines, and a larger attempt at understanding. Certain training institutes have created seminars to provide psychoanalytical orientation for individuals in the critical fields. But what is needed are seminars and colloquiums in which many fundamental ideas can be discussed on both sides and attempts made to clarify the interdisciplinary relationship. It seems to me that the arts have suffered and are suffering from profound misunderstandings by psychoanalysis of the creative process and that psychoanalysis, on its side, suffers from a gross mishandling of its ideas and subtleties by artists and critics. Meaningless and sterile formulations are the result.

I know of few disciplines which have more to give to one another. The best psychoanalysts have been those most deeply grounded in the humanities, as well as in their proper science, and the best creators have been those who have seen most deeply into the wellsprings of their own imagination. Of all the disciplines man has created, these are the two which can claim to be the most humane; they touch most deeply the creative well-being and the imaginative health of the world. We cannot do enough to lessen ignorance on both sides.

References

Alexander, F. "The Psychoanalyst Looks at Contemporary Art." In W. Phillips (ed.), *Art and Psychoanalysis*. New York: Criterion Books, 1957.

Balakian, Anna. *Surrealism: The Road to the Absolute*. New York: Noonday Press, 1959.

Benedict, Clare (ed.). *Constance Fenimore Woolson*. London: Ellis, 1929–1930.

Berenson, B. *Italian Painters of the Renaissance*. London: Phaidon Press, 1952.
Brennan, J. *Thomas Mann's World*. New York: Russell & Russell, 1962.
Coleridge, S. T. *The Notebooks of Samuel Taylor Coleridge* (1718–1719). Kathleen Coburn (ed.). New York: Pantheon, 1957. Vol. 1.
Edel, L. "The Biographer and Psychoanalysis," *International Journal of Psycho-Analysis*, 13 (1961), Nos. 4–5, 458–466; "Literary Criticism and Psychoanalysis," *Contemporary Psychology*, 1, No. 2 (Spring 1965), 51–63.
Eiseley, L. "Theory of Unconscious Creation," *Daedalus*, Vol. 94, No. 3 (Summer 1965).
Eissler, K. R. *Medical Orthodoxy and the Future of Psychoanalysis*. New York: International Universities Press, 1965.
Freud, S. "Introductory Lectures in Psycho-Analysis. Part III" (1916–1917). *The Standard Edition of the Complete Psychological Works of . . .* London: Hogarth Press. Vol. 16.
Nadeau, M. *Histoire du surrealisme*. Paris: Editions de Seuil, 1945.
Trilling, L. *The Liberal Imagination*. New York: Viking Press, 1950.
Weissman, P. *Creativity in the Theater*. New York: Basic Books, 1965.

26

Psychoanalysis, Delinquency, and the Law

LAWRENCE ZELIC FREEDMAN

Twentieth-century culture has fed avariciously on the constructs, models, language, and clinical observations of psychoanalysis. But the corpus, civilization, and its skeleton, the law, have not grown noticeably robust on it. This difference, though paradoxical, is inevitable. Culture is the sum, at any point in time, of the emergent creative values, the fluctuant aesthetic tone, the amorphous manner, the nuances of living style. One man may write a poem, a play, a book, compose music, paint a picture, survive a personal sequence of struggle, live a private life. Any man, through his work, whether physical, intellectual, political, or artistic, may seek solutions to his immediate, idiosyncratic dilemma. When he is creative, his solution is novel. Those who spontaneously associate themselves with him because his emergent solution seems to resolve their own predicaments may absorb a powerful cultural change relatively quickly.

Civilization is the totality of laws, rules, institutions, rituals, mores, and traditions which order the lives of the cives, city-state nations, of communities of organized conglomerates of persons. The formal structure of government, the controlling precedents of a society, maintain continuity and stability. Their primary function is to forestall the chaos of anarchy, whether by social control or by social example. Civilization, so defined, yields slowly to novelty.

One cannot argue seriously against those who hold that the official rituals of a society and the complex, variegated cultural values of its individual participants and aggregate groups are so interdependent as to make any effort to distinguish between them hopeless. Similar ambiguity afflicts the words delinquency, law, and psychoanalysis. We must depend, however, not on a specious and therefore dangerous illusion of semantic precision where none exists, but must acknowledge that we communicate through shared understanding, through apperceptive and empathic communality. However vague and inherently antithetic this may be, a clear awareness of the inherent ambience and limiting finiteness of verbal symbols, whether spoken or written, is preferable to the illusion of exactness where it does not exist. This degree of insightful lucidity is especially important when we attempt to collate the relationship between law, which is essentially a system of social prescriptions semantically defined, and psychoanalysis, which attempts to treat the ineffable, the verbally inexpressible.

In mid-twentieth-century United States, civilization exists within a diversity and heterogeneity of cultures, of ethnic and national origins and recency of arrival, ranging from the indigenous Indians, really Mongolian immigrants from eons past, to Puerto Ricans, still flowing into our urban centers. Both, like the Negroes, are culturally depleted, economically deprived, and politically victimized. There are, in this country, a few men whose riches are unparalleled in world history, and there are whole communities which are chronically impoverished. Our citizens range from aggressive atheists to articulate agnostics, to those who noncommittally withdraw. There are also powerful organizations of ancient religions and a bewildering kaleidoscope of made-in-America variants of religious ritual and churches. A wide spectrum exists, as well, in education, skills, and aesthetic sensibility.

The American civilization whose principles are set out in the Declaration of Independence and the Constitution of the United States and, modified, in our courts, legislature, and referenda during the two centuries since, encompasses all these cultures. It is identical with none. Within this civilization and under this Constitution with its puissant thrust of states' autonomy and separation of powers, how do we educate those whose heritage is discrimination, whose ancestors have been enslaved, and whose skin is pigmented? How do we respond effectively and decently to lawbreakers who, as a consequence of their lifelong estrangement, have become identified with different cultural values than those who apply the sanctions? How do we achieve an equilibrium between equality before the law for the putative offender and protection for victims of harmful persons? What just balance can we achieve between freedom for impulsive expression and legally reinforced inhibitions?

A judge of the Federal Appellate Court asked the Attorney General of the United States to help adapt procedures of arraignment for the poverty-enslaved Negro so he might achieve actual, substantive equality before the law. This request was rejected by the Attorney General on the grounds that the law seeks not equality but justice. The procedural protections of the accused exist, said the Attorney General, not for the defendants' sake but for ours, that is, for our civilization. The law-compliers and the law-enforcers are encased in a sense that justice will be done. The Attorney General did not say so, but he was certainly aware that most men accused of crime who have suffered through their life from social injustice do not expect to get legal justice. The judge was sensitive to the significance of the operations of the law to the men from deprived subcultures. He had expressed a parallel awareness of the wide-ranging distortion of the perspective of the mentally ill toward lawful behavior, when he and his judicial brothers had earlier freed, from century-old legal practice, the narrow cognitive criteria for the determination of responsibility (*Durham* v. *U.S.*, 1954). He had articulated, for the first time in American courts, considerations concerning the relationship between the unconscious motives, described by psychoanalysis, and the legal intent, inferred by prescription of legal codes (*Miller* v. *U.S.*, 1963). Thus, the same judge who had introduced concepts of the unconscious into courts had also widened the arena of relevant psychiatric testimony in criminal cases beyond the unrealistic constrictions of "knowledge of right and wrong." He had indicated as well his awareness that the social context of early development and adult role affects a man's sense of equality, of law, and of justice.

But the law has been concerned with the unconscious determinants of socially harmful behavior for centuries (Freedman, 1965). Acts contrary to the common welfare, to the rights of other individuals or to the prerogatives of the state, have not been judged criminal, however destructive they might have been, unless they reflected evil intent. The Law of Moses provided, as did criminal codes before and since, sanctuary for antisocial acts which were unlooked-for, unintended, or adventitious, as it did for all acts of the unequivocally mad. As civilizations have developed, they have expanded the perimeters of this area of immunity from legal punishment.

The essential, hopeless, and honored task of the law has been to discover how to quantify accident, how to calibrate the degree of madness which exculpates. The limits of accident impinge on the borders of negligence. The frontiers of the democratic freedom to be different merge into the boundaries of psychotic syndromes. In recent decades the increasing diagnostic and therapeutic precision of psychoanalysis has helped to extend the legitimate area of concern of psychiatry from the institutionalized psychotic to the irrational personality, not readily recognized by lawyers as "insane" or by the laity as "mad." Personality deviance, whether subjectively felt or behaviorally expressed, has come within the widening ambit of psychoanalytic concern. In most jurisdictions, however, the law of responsibility remains fixed at a level of psychological understanding which reflects a period in history when the preoccupation of alienists was with the insane in institutions mislabeled asylums, as prisons were mislabeled penitentiaries.

One of the many ironies which make life stingingly unbearable and wryly tolerable is that while impulsivity has, like accident and madness, become legally mitigating, the law's delays have themselves increased. Three centuries ago, Hamlet's suicidal soliloquy keened over the law's delays. And his audience of bumpkins, bourgeois, and orange girls recognized this as a real, legitimate, if insufficient vector toward self-immolation by suicide.

Perhaps the law's delays and the law's tolerance of impulsivity are reciprocally related. Lengthening time lags between the act, the accusation, and the legal judgment in twentieth-century America, while still perhaps inviting but rarely precipitating suicide, any more than it did in the ambivalent prince, is a basic feature of its process and function if not of its structure and intent. We might regard the common bind of compulsivity and impulsivity, inhibition and spontaneity as reaction formations to each other, reflections of the nexus of a human dilemma. This is the crossroad where the essential social stabilizing role of law through compulsion and inhibition meet, sort out, and in some yet unknown and still confused way discover a set of workable balances. If these speculations are justified, then this mix of private impulsivity and public inhibition reflects a sort of essential social symbiosis, which is antipathetic but crudely workable. It is an amalgam of private wishes, initiative, and intents, and public precedent, restriction, and ideology.

Spontaneity, impulsivity, and creativity are always a potential source of danger to the state. But they are also necessary ingredients if the body politic is to escape stagnation and collapse. To legal organizations, the creative person is like the lover or spouse whose fickle partner bedevils and enrages but without whom life has no savor. Through its government, society enforces concordance and imposes order in the service of coherence and continued coexistence of its members. But some individuals require a sense of personal adventure, of emergent boldness, of private novelty if they are to wish for continued existence. Society needs them if it is to make cultural experiments and adaptations in the evolution of its civilizations. If either through its laws or tyranny it stifles them, it risks atrophy and fossilization. But uncontrolled spontaneity and the impulsive power of the mob also threaten orderly government with extinction. The delicate titration of impulsivity is, then, part of the shared chemistry of culture and civilization and law. Somewhere between the fossil and the dodo, viable laws must play their meaningful role.

This imperative need to achieve optimum balance between impulsivity and inhibition is shared as well by mid-twentieth-century psychoanalysis. Once, in a state of bemused if scientific inspiration, Clarence Day (1920) speculated that due to our evolutionary origins as the descendants of monkeys, impulsive, erratic, squealing, simian activity is labeled with some understanding and affection as "human." Even when such behavior is socially harmful, we may excuse it, we often envy it, and we might glorify it through our mass-communications media. Spontaneity carries a positive valence for us in our culture. Similar acts carried out deliberately with what the law calls "malice aforethought" provoke community anxiety and may elicit its vengeance. If, Day fantasied, we had been happily descended from elephants, thoughtful and planned behavior even when socially harmful would be considered elephantinely deliberate. It would, therefore, be humanly understandable, lovable, and forgivable. Simian impulsivity would evoke social fear and legal punishment. The thoughtful, deliberate, and reflective pachydermal criminal would be, at least, predictable, and hence held to be a better social risk than the unpredictable anthropoid delinquent.

Impulsive behavior is contrasted with thoughtful and rational conduct by the conventions of common sense as well as the precedents of the law. When spontaneity gets one into serious trouble with the criminal law, the differential ingredient deciding one's fate is often time. States' and defense attorneys, judges, and juries attempt to ascertain, with exquisite precision, the interlude of time which separated the onset of the conscious idea and intent of harmful behavior and the carrying out of the illegal act. If the interlude is very short, the behavior may be tagged impulsive. The punitive sanctions against such impulsive behavior are far milder than when intent and planning can be proven. Rarely, a legal defense of "irresistible impulse" provides complete protection from punishment. Delay leads to the presumption that conscious cognitive processes have intervened. Harmful acts after deliberation are prima facie evidence of evil intent, of a cold heart and an evil mind. If too long a time has elapsed between the thought and the act, severe punishment may be inflicted.

Impulsive behavior gratifies the immediate wish. It is characterized by minimal lapse of time between self-awareness of the action tendency and its realization. Frequently there appears to be a simultaneity of impulse and idea, kinesic tension and act. Psychoanalysis, like law, does not yet provide a better operational calibrating instrument to distinguish impulsive from other forms of behavior than this measurement of time. For the law, however, the duration of this crucial variable extends from the conscious recognition of the intent to the beginning of the act. Psychoanalysis has demonstrated that an unconsciously or preconsciously impelling motive may anticipate by days, months, or years any conscious self-awareness of its existence. The impulse is an inference retrospectively derived from the act.

A number of states, here and in Canada, have added "irresistible impulse" to the McNaughten "knowledge of right and wrong" and awareness of "the nature and quality of the act," as mitigating and exculpating for an otherwise criminal act. But judges and juries have rarely invoked the irresistible impulse clause because they have been unconvinced by it. The concept comes close to evoking a direct confrontation between Western man's paradoxical insistence on his own free will and his eager acceptance of the benefits of science's working hypothesis of determinism. In practice, the legal decision-makers have found it virtually impossible to distinguish between the irresistible impulse and the unresisted impulse. The anxious cynicism which is engendered by this ambiguity is typified in the comment of Judge Lidell in Ontario to a defendant: "If you cannot resist an impulse any other way, we will dangle a rope in front of your eyes and perhaps that will help." In this country, Judge Darling succinctly summarized the judicial if unjudicious view of this defense: "Impulsive insanity [sic] is the last refuge of a hopeless defense."

From psychoanalytic treatment and from neonatal observation has come persuasive evidence that the milieu of the newborn and his later development are significantly associated with the likelihood of impulsive behavior, and with the probability of social conflict resulting from it. These factors are, however, differently experienced by those with different constitutional endowments. But biologists, the evolutionary theorists, the ethologists, and the physiologists have yet contributed little that is legally relevant to the solution of this problem (Freedman and Roe, 1958). Community-wide studies have, so far, made some preliminary but helpful observations. For example, we have found that among neurotics bodily malfunction and impulsive acting out are much more frequently diagnosed among lower-class patients (Freedman and Hollingshead, 1957). Subjective psychic states such as depressive reactions, indicating the greater potency of restrictive and self-punitive defense maneuvers against them, are more common in the middle and upper-middle socioeconomic levels (Leavy and Freedman, 1956, 1961). By combining scales of classification within society with classification of symptoms, we were able to detect a configuration which stretched along a continuum from impulsive behavioral difficulties and somatic complaints in the lower-class psychiatric patients to inhibited, subjective, introverted symptoms in the mentally ill of middle and upper middle socioeconomic levels. A Social Interaction Index (Freedman, 1957), tracing this spectrum with greater precision, revealed that the focus of conflict progressed also through increasingly wider arcs of social dislocation, ranging from intrapersonal symptoms in Classes I and II, the upper and upper-middle socioeconomic levels, to severe social and legal collisions in the lowest Classes, IV and V. We overgeneralized (Freedman and Hollingshead, 1957; Hollingshead and Redlich, 1958), aphoristically, that the psychopathology of neurotics in the most economically endowed and socially privileged Classes I and II expressed dissatisfaction with themselves. The lower middle-Class III patients defended, anxiously. The Class IV neurotics ached physically. But disturbed persons in Class V behaved impulsively. These latter, disadvantaged by and disenchanted with our society, express their irreconcilable personal conflicts through an impulsive motor pattern of symptoms which often leads them into social conflict. There is a difference in concept of self as patient, in the different social classes, if he is uncomfortable or unhappy, if his body hurts or functions poorly, if he is unable to be effective in his work, if he is in trouble with his social community, or if he is in difficulty with the law. Alternative to or coexistent with impulsive behavior tendencies is the psychosomatic expression of conflict through pain or malfunction, including venereal disease (Freedman, 1948).

Viewed from this perspective, impulsive behavior which provokes legal reaction of men is the concern of psychoanalysts as well as makers of social policy. The successful merchant, bureaucrat, or professional has fulfilled an essential prerequisite for attaining his stake by yielding up or postponing the immediate gratification of numberless wishes. He has set the limits of his expression of spontaneity to the lowest possible tolerance. His conscious desires are vigorously attenuated, his impulses are deflected or submerged. Like the terms of his credit buying, the satisfactions of his biological needs are paid out regularly but fractionally until the postponements within his life merge with eternity at the end of life, still unpaid and unfulfilled. Thus the middle-class patient avoids social conflicts and social diseases, but is afflicted by private anxiety, neurotic syndromes, and semiotic dislocation.

Impulsive behavior, as a life style, is mainly the prerogative of the very rich and powerful, of the very poor, and of a few others, creative and rebellious, who have opted out of, or have been ejected from, the class system. With its immediate satisfactions, impulsive behavior assaults the middle-class model, the law's model, and the psychoanalyst's model of what is permissible. Of those who can and do act impulsively, those who are both threateningly rebellious and very poor are punished. The law invokes punitive sanctions against the most irritating and the most vulnerable.

Any act, verbal or motor, is set in a matrix of confluent and divergent affects, ideas, and motives, at every level of consciousness. The impulsive act which in the neonate is the immediate response of the individual's biological potential to its stimulating environment becomes in the adult the eruptive expression of affects, motives, object relationships, and matrix of defenses which is called personality, and which he has accumulated over his span of maturation. For psychoanalysts it is a truism that human behavior involves unconscious and preconcious as well as conscious ideas, emotions, and motives, and that it employs indirect and symbolic as well as direct techniques of expression. This confluence of endogenous, developmental, and exogenous psychic forces makes accurate conceptualization and precise investigation of socially delinquent personalities almost paralyzingly complex. However, the overt act may be taken as the initial unit of observation. From this base, levels of response may then be delineated accurately, scrutinized closely, and studied meaningfully.

A comparative study of social offenders, grouped according to categories of acts rather than legal statutes, offered some answers concerning the behavioral forms of personally adaptive defenses which result in legal discordance (Freedman, 1961). The men had been convicted of offending against the criminal code of the community. The legal ritual which found them guilty resulted as well in publicly stigmatizing them, and had penalized them further by confinement in prison. We used the phrases Acquisitive Offender, Sexually Deviant Offender, and Violent Offender to delineate the three major groups of behavior which had evoked the punitive action of law enforcers.

These men had behaved illegally as well as impulsively. In the first group were the common chronic thieves, men who had been intemperate and uncontrolled as well as illegal in their acquisitiveness. In the second group were men who had been indiscreet and uninhibited in their sexual deviation, and those in the third group had been excessive and unchecked in their violence. All had been unhindered by characterological or legal checks from the original expression of their various impulses. All had, after the act, been reacted to with criminal sanctions.

Since any personality, be it stalwartly conformist or outrageously criminal, reflects a persistent life style of characteristic defenses, we treated the form which the delinquency took with the same respect that psychoanalysts accord the symptomatic pattern which different neuroses assume. We predicted that the conformation of legally discordant behavior would be reflected in their infantile and childhood development, in the differential qualities of their adult personalities, as well as in the style of their lives, and that the tiny fraction of their acts which was criminal would be consistent with the predominance of their characteristics which conformed to legal precept. We therefore tested an interlocking set of hypotheses, that repeated behavior of a sexually deviant, violently harmful, or acquisitively illegal nature would be symptomatic of associated dimensions of motivation, of affect, and of personality. As the acts were unmistakably different, so too would be their other traits.[1]

[1] The men studied lived in the northeastern part of the United States. Their socioeconomic level was predominantly Class IV, the next to the lowest on the five-level socioeconomic continuum. Obviously, application of observations drawn from any single

We found that the special characteristics of particular offenses were not random. They were fixed and repetitious. Most criminals are homotropically and monogamously wedded to one form of illegal activity. Men whose illegality took a wide variety of forms we called polytropic or polyphasic. They were a very small minority, made up mainly of psychotic offenders. The overwhelming majority were not only faithful to one of the three categories, Acquisitive, Sexual, or Violent offenses, but each was repetitiously bound to a subgroup of his own offense category. Moreover, his judgment of criminals in offense categories other than his own was extremely condemning and morally critical. Not surprisingly, the specific type of each man's delinquent behavior was a symptomatic syndrome. The internal consistency of his traits and defense systems was as predictable as were the obvious and persistent differences between the categories of his illegal aberrances. Any major category of personality characteristics might be used to examine the validity of these hypotheses as well as the observations which flow from putting them to the test. Psychosexual experience in early childhood and level of sexual integration achieved as an adult are considered by many psychoanalysts to be at the core of any man's personality. Let us therefore use psychosexual factors as one paradigm of the more inclusive propositions.

The acquisitive offender exceeded by far the other groups in libidinal precosity and promiscuity. The range of his partners, the frequency, and the apparent spontaneity of his sexual expression from his childhood to middle years, his available sexual energy and his polymorphous propensities, were also higher than those of the other groups. He was younger at the time of his first ejaculation. He had initiated masturbation by puberty. He had participated in coital behavior by early adolescence. The thief, in contrast to the sexual deviant, made the transition from masturbation to interpersonal eroticism before his mid-teens. By sixteen, his predominant libidinal activity was heterosexual intercourse. If married, he initiated coitus with his wife, just as he did with his numerous extramarital casual pickups and prostitutes. The prevalence, but not the frequency, of his homosexual experiences equaled that of the sexual deviants. He did not tolerate sexual fantasy, however; he rejected and denied erotic daydreams as unpleasant.

---

group can be generalized to other strata, periods, and locales only with great caution. To widen the justifiable applicability of knowledge derived from this special group, we developed a set of equipotential hypotheses. Using them, a roughly measurable quanta or intensity of stress within a defined social and familial environment might be demonstrably equipotential with an equivalent quanta or intensity of stress in another similarly defined social and familial milieu. Thus, though two factors might appear to be separated by geography or social or legal context, they might be psychically equivalent. To cite a simple example; growing up as a member of one minority group prevalent in one section of the country might have effects similar to or identical with growing up as a member of quite a different minority group which had settled in another part of the country.

The most obvious psychosexual characteristic of the sexual deviant was the damped-down, truncated, abortive, tardy, and joyless quality of his libidinal life. He began masturbation late and continued persistently but infrequently. Inhibited during childhood in initiating autoeroticism, he perseverated through puberty, adolescence, and adult years in this form of self-stimulation. He rarely yielded it entirely for other forms of sexual activity, either conventional or unconventional. His childhood homosexuality had been lower than those who later became thieves. At the onset of puberty, the quickening of sexual interest and activity noted among thieves and violent offenders and common to most boys of their age did not occur amongst the sexual pre-deviants. Both heterosexual foreplay and intercourse began late and continued, but with comparatively long intervals between episodes.

The violent offender reflected in his sexual life the greatest intensity of ambivalent flux between libidinal impulse and anxious inhibition. He began masturbation earlier than the sexual deviant, but later than the thief. He was least likely to find his autoerotic stimulation either gratifying or satisfying. He rarely experienced or recalled sexual fantasies. For him erotic daydreams were not accompanied by a mood of pleasure; they were disagreeable. The violent offender, then, was as inhibited in his psychic erotic experience as the sexual deviant. His heterosexual behavior reflected equally well his ambivalence of anger and affection, love and hate.

Thus, the sexual impulsive behavior of each of the three major categories of men who are in serious legal trouble with society was found to have particular and persistent patterns from their early life onward.

All these men had been defeated, had tried to cope, but unsuccessfully. Publicly stigmatized, castigated, isolated, and restricted, their difference lay not primarily in psychopathology in its traditional sense but in syndromes of socially inappropriate and legally punishable acts. What crucial variables distinguish them from the socially adapted? Repression, as a defense mechanism, is conveniently, conceptually juxtaposed to expression of an affect, idea, motive, or action tendency. I have, thus far, avoided tackling the tangled skein of the relationship between the concept of impulse and the related constructs of emotions, motives, drives, and cognitive processes. Yet obviously the areas of congruence, difference, and reinforcement between these psychic constructs need to be articulated. The expression or discharge of a compelling cognition, feeling tone, or action tendency is presumably, under "normal circumstances," followed by its disappearance as a dynamic factor in the psychic economy, or its successful incorporation within the consciousness of the person. Its repression, on the other hand, assures its disappearance from consciousness but guarantees it a continuing role in the psychic topography of the person, leading sometimes to its fragmented emergence as mental illness. The particular facet of the personalities of the men whom we are considering reflected disarticulated and differentiated repression of action tendencies. Within the model of adaptation, they suffered from a disequilibrium of motility propensities. If they are considered pathological, their pathology is primarily kinesic. Their deviation from homeostatic balance consisted both of semiotic hypertrophy which is obvious and of its atrophy which is less self-evident.

Any re-direction of behavioral tendencies, whether fantasy, hallucination, or any kind of wish-fulfilling inaction which could avoid social conflict while providing adequate, even if partial, gratification of the impulsive action-tendency, seemed to be unavailable to them. While the deflection to alternative objects or victims of compelling action-tendencies was common enough, sublimation appeared not to be within their psychic capacity. The early familial and later community experiences of these men provided some information which helps to explain how and why each selected and persisted in his particular category of illegal response.

The common chronic thief was often, within this population, a transitional person lost between old-world parental values and unconcerned, because unidentified, with new-world property and personal values. He had never developed a personality capable of forming significant, empathic, personal relationships. With no ego ideal of formidable virtue to measure himself against, and lacking a superego capable of castigating himself to the point of restraint, he was marvelously, but in fact superficially and only apparently, ego-syntonic in his illegal behavior.

The sexual deviant whose familial attachments were stronger and who, in this geographic area, tended to spring from the white indigenous, rural sections of the countryside, in whose cities he later settled, was sexually aberrant for reasons which reflected inner dynamics of his family structure. He was profoundly identified with the dominant values of the community. This identification was reflected partly in the powerful conflictful ego-dystonicity of his impulses.

The violent offender, in contrast to both groups, was likely to be both psychologically and often literally a transient, frequently Negro, raised within a family constellation which was itself fragmented, fatherless, provocative of wide swings of affect with inadequate identifying figures either in the home or in the larger, threatening and threatened community. Both fearful and feared, he exploded intermittently into action, propelled into violence by anxiety which his poorly structured and inadequate ego was incapable of containing.

Psychosexually and characterologically, the life style of the common chronic thief was the most *impulsive*. He was encumbered least by empathic human object relationships. Correspondingly his impulsivity seemed most ego syntonic. From his childhood, the common chronic thief appeared to be sexually an impulsive, free-acting, polyfocal man. He was most active, diverse, most transient, and least concerned about his partners. By overt criteria he was the most immediately responsive to endogenous shifts in his physiological and psychological balance, as in puberty. He adjusted readily as well to exogenous, externally imposed variability of available objects, as in prison. He was the most impulsive activist, the least rigid in his forms of sexual expression, and least likely to admit to any feeling of guilt or shame concerning his sexual mode, style, or nature of partner. Neither his heterosexual nor his homosexual prostitution evoked any expression of concern or anxiety. These psychosexual characteristics of the thief bore striking homology to his pattern of objectless, repetitive, illegal acquisition of money and objects. His thefts too were repetitive and guilt free. The interchangeability, the emphatic insignificance of his sexual objects combined with the persistence of his sexual aims, was matched by the human objectlessness of his obstinate acquisitive aims. His guiltless sexual promiscuity was matched by a life style characterized by explosive, episodic, angry assault which exceeded in frequency but not in harmfulness those of the violent offender.

The sexual deviant, with his low level of sexual activity and general resistance to impulsive behavior during formative years, had nevertheless greater capacity for emphatic human relations than the thief. The sex offender as an adult was the least impulsive and therefore most socially compliant in spheres of activity other than sexuality. He might therefore be appropriately described as *compulsive.* This term, with its connotation of tension, reflects acts carried out in spite of conscious reluctance, or conflict, and of ego-dystonicity. More likely to identify with sexual conventions of the larger community, he experienced shame and guilt as he compulsively violated them.

The violent offender was frustrated and goal inhibited rather than unambivalently heterosexual or even overwhelmingly assaultive. He was least likely ever to be sexually deviant. If through drunkenness or seduction or excitement he behaved deviantly, he reacted with guilt, shame, and denial. In sex as in aggression, he lived a life of ambivalent frustration, intermittently erupting into blindly fierce assault, most often directed against an intimate, a woman. More rarely his victim was a man within his circle of family or friends. In either case his victim had, inadvertently or deliberately, challenged and threatened his tenuous hold on heterosexual balance and masculine identity. Poised precariously between love and hate, lust and destruction emerged sometimes simultaneously, sometimes directed at the same feared and desired partner. This ambivalent dilemma seemed to characterize his sexual as well as his violent acts, which were a reflection and, rarely, a resolution of it. For the violent offender, ambivalence, the fruit of frustration of a life lived on the seesaw of love and hate, of passivity and aggressivity, the assaultive and sometimes murderous act might most accurately be described as *propulsive,* to connote the ego-engulfing nature of its violent resolution.

There are crimes of difference and crimes of dangerousness. Violent offenses are crimes of dangerousness. The sexual deviants commit crimes of difference, with a subcategory of those who combine dangerousness by assault with their unsettling difference. The common chronic thief commits crimes which are nominally different, but his punishment through the lawful apparatus reflects a neutral bureaucratic maneuver designed to maintain social efficiency. Society, through its legal representatives, seems neither appalled by the thief's difference nor frightened by him. His forms of acquisition are simply inconsistent with the tenets of efficient social organization. It is ironic, therefore, that it is the thief who over his life span is penalized most severely, if most routinely.

Conflict between these forms of impulsive, compulsive, and propulsive behavior and socially incorporated inhibition against carrying them out may not be inevitable, but it is ubiquitous. An enormous resonance exists in the general population for impulsive sexual, compulsive acquisitive, and propulsive violent offenses. The criminal and social offender is by no means an isolated phenomenon in our culture. He is a crystallized expression of the omnipresent conflict between private impulse and social structure which is the general concern of psychoanalysis.

Psychoanalysis is based on law. Freud (1895) first attempted to write a value-free theory of human behavior, to create a neuropsychological science. Discouraged, he tried to disentangle functional from organic syndromes of human psychopathology. But it was his discovery of the unconscious, of the bipolar conflict of the pleasure/unpleasure spectrum of hedonism, of the emergence of personality through introjection, imitation, identification, desire, punishment, threat, and reward, which were the beginnings of psychoanalysis. All these are intimately related to law. He treats the play of Oedipus, the myth of Moses, the novelistic characters of Alyosha, Dmitri, and Ivan, the atavistic reconstruction of *Totem and Taboo,* as dramas of man's social evolution toward a rule of law and of his inner reactions to his own emergent civilization (Freud, 1899, 1937–1939, 1928, 1912–1913). A now classic exposition of psychoanalysis was written in the form of an imaginary dialogue, a sort of dialectic, between Freud and a government official who was bent on prosecuting one of his brilliant law protégés on the grounds of violation of Vienna's laws prohibiting quackery (Freud, 1926).

The contributions of psychoanalysis to understanding, prediction of delinquency, and the determinants of the law are still primitive, groping, and insufficiently enlightening when we consider that psychoanalysis in its origins and in its models is steeped in law. For psychoanalysts it may be said that in the beginning was the crime, the parricide of the primitive horde, the parricide and incest of Oedipus. No figure haunted the writings of Freud, not even Oedipus, more than Moses. And Moses was pre-eminently the Giver of the Law. Freud considered that the Jews' selection of abstract monotheism over concrete polytheism was an achievement of profound significance. It predisposed to abstract thinking in areas other than religion, and to the establishment of law based on ethical as well as utilitarian principles. This was a contribution of Freud's hero, Moses.

Freud's literary style of analysis, while graceful and elegant, is also legalistic and talmudic. Concepts are disentangled and clarified from an intuitive and empirical core through progressive analogous, homologous, syllogistic progression to universal laws. Each of them, like the law itself, is contingent on an interlocking meshwork of impinging correlates of laws, mores, and social predispositions. His psychoanalytic detection, based on a virtuoso elucidation of micro-detail as reflected, for example, in his "Interpretation of Dreams" (1899), is reminiscent of a similar concern with seemingly minor clues in criminal detection of the great German criminologist, Hans Gross. His emphasis on words as the overly determined, heavily loaded carriers as well as vectors of human desire and guilt is analogous to legal science, which is essentially a system of semantic definitions. Psychoanalysis' concern with motive and need reflects the criminal laws' preoccupation with intent. Its Hobbesian assumption of inherent human aggressivity and perversity is not unlike that of most lawmakers through time. Indeed if one echoes Freud in saying that religion is an obsessive-compulsive ritual writ large, one must state the reciprocal, that his psychoanalytic theory is the social and legal flux of desire, greed, lust, violence, harm, and punishment writ small in his paradigm of individual human development.

Just as Freud disdained to distinguish between civilization and culture (1930), so he minimized the differences between guilt arising from violations of social mores and guilt aroused by breaking community laws. In his early writings he scarcely distinguished between private and public sources of punishment. Fear of punishment was equally potent as a dynamic element, whether the punishing agent was imposed by parental withholding of love and approval, by condemnation, by alienation from the social group, or by formal sanctions applied by the law.

Yet one of Freud's major scientific as well as personal crises hinged on precisely such distinctions. His early theory of the development of hysteria and obsession was based on his acceptance of his patients' descriptions of their infantile sexual seduction by older members of their own family or other adult intimates of their families. When he realized that these precocious stimulations had in most cases never occurred, that his patients had not been the victims of such premature sexual onslaughts, he was in despair. He believed for a time that this vitiated his empirical method and his theory alike. Out of his despair came his great creative leap. As he had appropriated the language of his earlier efforts to create an anatomical model of psychology, and applied the terms to a mentalistic model, so now he enlarged his complex of hypotheses to include the memory of such early seductions not as recalled fact, but as projected fantasies, as wish fulfillments. This shift from fact to fantasy had profound implications for the development of psychoanalytic theory and method of observation. It represented also a shift from actual overt experience as the preponderant source of a sense of guilt to covert wishes which were incompatible with external reality, or with competing inner drives or defenses. When viewed as fact, the sin, the immoral or illegal act was external, the crime was that of the parent or adult rather than the erstwhile child-become-patient. In the second instance, the "crime," the psychological sin, is the patient's, a retrograde seduction by the adult patient of his parent.

Thus Freud in middle age swallowed his dismay, saved himself from melancholia by shifting the burden of legal guilt from his patient's childhood family environment to the intrapsychic derivatives of the biological, instinctual imperatives of the patient. This crucial blurring of the actors, of blaming the self rather than others, this psychic burdening of the wish rather than the deed, has had significant if possibly unintended effects on the relationship between psychoanalysis and the law.

For although Freud was a wry, acerbic, perceptive, and deadly critic of the mores, institutions, and laws of his time, he was no social reformer. He pointed to the soft and often salacious underbelly of the law. He adumbrated the source and the cost of sexual asceticism; he was aware of the corruption of capitalism; he resented the arrogance of power. He traced unerringly the courses of legal self-righteousness and its suppression of crime and civil disobedience through ritual violence to its anlage in social aggression.

Yet Freud never campaigned for change in the economic, sexual, or governmental, political, and power structure in which he lived. His own life was scrupulously moral, lawful. Courageous in adumbrating the dangers of sexual asceticism, he was himself rigidly monogamous. He never seriously challenged the sexual laws of his community, for example, as did Bloch or as did Hirschfeld in his Institute of Sexology. He considered money an ignoble motive, but he valued it as preferable to a naked struggle for power (1930). He abhorred violence between men, yet he was skeptical of outlawing war (1933).

I think it not excessive to assume that for Freud, codified law and social mores were psychological realities, as inviolable as privately biologically derived impulses and reaction to them. It seemed hardly to have occurred to him that there were ethical, rational, or psychological reasons for psychoanalysis to serve as anything other than an auxiliary to the law. In his only published paper which related to the uses of psychoanalysis in the courts of law, he discussed experimental techniques of eliciting confessions, or methods of eliciting guilt by word-associative techniques and reaction time of Jung, without regard to the nature of the crime or of the law which would thus be served.

The superego is a remarkably faithful reproduction of the body of laws of the legal interdictions of the Western culture of the twentieth century. It is as though psychoanalysis had collapsed the cultural legal incubus of all of the Western Judaeo-Christian tradition. This presumes that the evolutionary phylogenetics of an entire species was incorporated into the law and through introjection of a child's ontogeny, into the psychic homunculus of the human infant (Freedman and Roe, 1958).

The major difficulty of psychoanalysis' present contribution is that while the law is concerned with the act, and with intent as a necessary psychological concomitant, psychoanalysis has become preoccupied with the conflict of motives, and the act has assumed a secondary, corollary significance. Since the unconscious has through the method of free association been shown to harbor all manner of illegal wishes, the distinction between the law evader, the law breaker, and the law abider is, within psychoanalysis, less sharp than in the common-sense judgment of the laity or in the decisions of those officially and legally empowered. It is as though the act is not a potent psychological fact at least as significant as the overdetermined psychic vectors which have predisposed to it. So we have arrived at the paradox that the law with its behavioral and existential sense of the significance of the act is a more sound and sophisticated psychological sounding board than is the most advanced theory of psychology in the mid-twentieth century.

It is within this ironic framework that the radical right of psychoanalysis is able to receive a hearing by denying any legitimate role whatsoever to psychoanalysis within the legal ritual, or indeed, to psychological motivation in the definition of crime, which is a reversal of civilized progress as threatening in its own way as the fascist reversal to feudal structure.[2]

The theoretical implications for the law of psychoanalytic hypotheses and empirical observations must be distinguished from their practical impact. The former are potential, the latter are minimal. It must be fairly said that the impact of psychoanalysis, as a body of clinical observation and as a theory of personality, on procedures, attitudes, and the substance of the law is still a rather pale reflection of the diffuse dispersion of psychoanalytic ambience over the surface of American life.

True, the climate of legal response to sexual crimes has changed, in the United States, in the half century since psychoanalysis was introduced here. But it is not likely that psychoanalysis was the sole or even the most signifi-

[2] For example Szasz, having previously denied the reality of mental illness, has advocated that the mentally ill offenders be sent to prison (Szasz, 1963). He considered mental illness to be a myth, and declared it nonexistent. For him the conflict of values always implicit in a pluralistic democratic society was easily resolved. In an encounter between law in which he believes and psychopathology in which he disbelieves, prison is the only appropriate solution—an extraordinary detour to a primitive ethic (Szasz, 1965; Freedman, 1964).

cant factor in the progressive mitigation of legal attitudes toward sexual activities which are inconsistent with the Judaeo-Christian model of monogamous heterosexual genital pairing within marriage. Freud has stated that the two great crimes in all social communities in all recorded eras of time and, he speculated, in prehistory as well, have been incest and parricide. But these two primal and universal offenses, slaying the father and copulating with the mother, are quantitatively and qualitatively insignificant in the courtrooms of advanced countries of the world. Such incest cases as reach our courts are almost invariably father-daughter relationships which are legally but not biologically incestuous. The man in these cases is most often not the biological parent of the girl but a husband of an older woman who had remarried after the death, divorce, or desertion of the girl's father. It is not unusual for such cases to represent a triangular sexual anaclisis. The mother is at least a tacit participant, tolerating or even approving the sexual relationship between her husband and her daughter, either consciously as a maneuver to maintain the company and affection of a man who she fears might otherwise leave her, or possibly unconsciously as a technique for sharing, by narcissistic projection, the sexual gratifications of her child through a counteridentification and counterintrojection, and occasionally as an intrafamilial mother-daughter example of intense homosexual attraction which can be expressed only by sharing the penis of the same male. Not infrequently, yielding sexual access to her daughter is part of an implicit contract which permits the wife and mother extramarital sexual freedom. The classical Oedipal fantasy and literary theme of son-mother incest is virtually never brought to court, nor frequently seen by analysts. In these few cases, one or both of the participants are likely to be psychotic. Incest, which is a linchpin of psychoanalytic theory, has provided few cases that have been studied in depth.

In most legal codes in the United States, sexual crime is virtually any sexual act outside of genital marital monogamous heterosexual intercourse. Functionally, the law intervenes more discriminatingly. Criminal sanctions are involved when there is a marked age discrepancy between the participants or when sexuality is fused with aggressivity, as when sexual access is gained by violence or its threat. Already the prestigious Model Penal Code of the American Law Institute (1962) has omitted adultery (delightfully labelled criminal correspondence) and homosexuality between consenting adults from its penal sanctions. It is reasonable to assume, although risky to prophesy, that in the next generation the legal codes will more closely approximate the actual practices of the courts. Even the taboo against marked age discrepancy and possibly that against the fusion of aggressivity and sexuality may be discarded. A few years ago the novel *Lolita,* describing the sexual preoccupation of an adult man with a preadolescent girl, became a best-seller. One of America's outstanding literary critics described it as one of the few love stories of our time. Nymphet became a word of affirmative currency. Sadistic sexuality, formerly a term of anathema, has achieved the cachet of approval by leading European intellectuals, particularly existentialists such as Sartre and de Beauvoir. Their exegeses along with the literary works of de Sade himself are now in vogue, and widely circulated in this country.

It can be argued with considerable thrust that the invariant in the patterns of sexual object and aims is not the primacy of genital sexuality nor the goal of maturity. Incest in highly developed cultures such as, for example, the Egypt of the Ptolemies, has been not only socially approved, but the envied prerogative of the elite. The Greeks and other high cultures held homosexuality to be an approved form of relationship, and had built into their myths innumerable examples of incestuous loves among their gods, who were far more manlike creatures than our gods. The congruence of aggression and sexuality has been so widespread that no examples need be given.

The one invariant of sexual practices, however, over time and in the most widely disparate cultures, is the existence of some accompanying taboo. The nature of the taboo has varied enormously and indeed may, at the same time but in different geographical or culture centers, be quite opposite. In any one locale the form of the taboo may change, over time, as to the nature of the forbidden person or type of anathemized act. What persists is the potent prohibition. In our time, in our culture, in our civilization, there persists, to be sure, a codified and a functioning system of legally defined interdictions concerning deviations from acceptable sexual practices. However, even a cursory perusal of the hundreds of sexual and marital manuals being sold in our bookstores and magazine racks reveals that they advise any and all forms of physical interaction leading to erotic gratification, except those which might seriously injure, or interfere with the sexual gratification of, the sexual partner. Most of these suggestions are illegal, but those who follow them are unpunished.

A taboo nonetheless does attach itself to sexual behavior in our culture. In those communities or subcultures or circles in which religious structuring and legal interdiction and conventional ethical considerations apparently play a feeble role, their place has been taken by what I have called a psychological morality. In a study of "normal sexuality" (Freedman, 1966) we found that men and women who were for the most part highly intelectually endowed individuals from middle-class backgrounds had little reluctance to describe their every form of sexual relatedness, other than those which inflicted physical or psychic harm on their partner. Indeed the taboo was a reciprocal, a mirror image of the articulate taboo of our popular culture of just a generation ago. These subjects, be it noted, were not psychiatric patients, but were selected for their "normality." These persons were concerned that they had violated not the law, but the canons of the psychological morality of sexuality. Women who could recall no masturbation apologized, and those who had no sexual affairs to report offered excuses. Women who had not been "fulfilled," who had not experienced a full orgasm, were defensive. Men whose extramarital sexual behavior had been quantitatively deficient explained away this "fault." Most men and women were anxious to know whether they achieved psychological criteria of sexual adequacy as measured by a number of sexual outlets per week. In this country, late marriage also is suspect to the point of a virtual taboo. For both male and female now it subjects most unmarried persons over thirty to the suspicion of at least latent homesexuality, asexuality, or sexual frigidity. Our sexual mores seem to be evolving toward a pan-hedonism which is at least as unrealistic as was the constricted limits of approved sexuality of recent generations.

Indeed, a numerically small but culturally significant minority of our society, in late adolescence and early adult age, has gone beyond the sexual pleasure principle to the principle of sexual apathy. One of the striking features of what, for a short period, was referred to as the "Beat Movement," was that while subdued sexual aims persisted, the ideal in sex, as in many other aspects in life, was to play it cool, to avoid sweaty passion. This seeming apathy may be ascribed to many causal factors. Possibly it is an expression within this "emancipated" group of the entropic energy loss accompanying the freedom to express impulses without external hindrance.

Be this as it may, the apathy, anhedonism, and unpleasurable quality of sexuality following a generation of desperate experimentation in pansexuality involving all sexes and all anatomical possibilities, hints at the adaptive function of the ubiquitous taboo. Apparently, where sexual taboos are minimized, repressed, or denied, sexual expression neither expands the opportunities for pleasure nor leads reactively to pain or unpleasure. Not pleasure but intensity is lost. Sexual gratification apparently requires constraints, not to keep it within limits, but to make it worthwhile. The psychological danger of the fulfillment of the extramarital fantasies of the bourgeoisie is not that the family and society will be unable to survive in the competition for sexual access without restriction or introduction, but that sexuality as a meaningful human expression as well as a sensual gratification cannot survive the loss of taboo.

The twin dangers to the life of man are derivatives of the core drives of sex and violence. With some exceptions, psychoanalysts describe aggressivity as a multidetermined phenomenon usually evoked by frustrations, generally related to affectional or sexual deprivations. Since the model of psychoanalysis is dynamic, that is, based on conflict, it is assumed that aggression and its derivatives, the affect of hatred, the trait of cruelty and the act of violence, achieve symptomatic expression only when they are components of powerful and unresolved conflicts within the personality.

Unchecked sexuality may yet destroy the species of man on this planet or alter its character in some way now unpredictable. Through overbreeding and overpopulation it may bring into play those competitive, adaptive, evolutionary mechanisms which have in the past eliminated species of animals. Unchecked aggression, not, as in the case of sexuality, by billions of copulating couples, but by a few persons in control of hydrogen and atomic bombs, could end the evolutionary experiment called man. In the mid-twentieth century, psychoanalysts are aware of the technical possibility of species-wide human self-immolation. They have faced parricide without flinching. They have embraced incest. But most have looked at death and denied it. Perhaps they had better look again. The delinquency of sexual dalliance and the sociopathy of seizure of property are important and still unresolved puzzles. But if a man can kill a man, then men can murder all men.

And there ought to be a law against that.

References

Day, C. *This Simian World*. New York: Knopf, 1920.

Durham v. *United States*, 214 F. 2d 862 (Washington, D.C. Cir. 1954).

Freedman, L. Z. "Venereal Disease among Naval Prisoners." *United States Naval Medical Bulletin*, 48, No. 5 (September–October 1948), 722–728.

Freedman, L. Z. "Sexual, Aggressive, and Acquisitive Deviates: A Preliminary Note." *Journal of Nervous and Mental Disease*, 132, No. 1 (January 1961), 44–49.

Freedman, L. Z. "Psychiatry and Law." In E. A. Spiegel (ed.), *Progress in Neurology and Psychiatry*. New York: Grune & Stratton, 1964.

Freedman, L. Z. "Social and Legal Considerations of Psychiatric Treatment in a General Hospital." In M. R. Kaufman (ed.), *The Psychiatric Unit in a General Hospital*. New York: International Universities Press, 1965. Pp. 269–280.

Freedman, L. Z. "Sexual, Aggressive, and Anxious Behavior in the 'Normal' Person" (unpublished). Read at Yale Research Seminar, 1958.

Freedman, L. Z., and Hollingshead, A. B. "Neurosis and Social Class. I Social Interaction." *The American Journal of Psychiatry*, 113, No. 9 (March 1957), 769–775.

Freedman, L. Z., and Roe, Anne. "Evolution and Human Behavior." A. Roe and G. G. Simpson (eds.). In *Behavior and Evolution*. New Haven, Conn.: Yale University Press, 1958.

Freud, S. "Project for a Scientific Psychology, Part I" (1895). Marie Bonaparte, Anna Freud, and E. Kris (eds.). In *The Origins of Psychoanalysis: Letters to Wilhelm Fliess, Drafts and Notes: 1887–1902*. 2nd ed.; New York: Basic Books, 1954. Pp. 355–404.

Freud, S. "The Interpretation of Dreams" (1899). *The Standard Edition of the Complete Psychological Works of. . . .* London: Hogarth Press. Vols. 4–5, pp. 1–621, 687–751. (Also published as *The Interpretation of Dreams*. New York: Basic Books, 1955.)

Freud, S. "Totem and Taboo" (1912–1913). *The Standard Edition of the Complete Psychological Works of. . . .* London: Hogarth Press. Vol. 13, pp. 1–161.

Freud, S. "The Question of Lay Analysis" (1926). *The Standard Edition of the Complete Psychological Works of. . . .* London: Hogarth Press. Vol. 20.

Freud, S. "Dostoevsky and Parricide" (1928). *The Standard Edition of the Complete Psychological Works of. . . .* London: Hogarth Press. Vol. 21. (Also in *Collected Papers of. . . .* New York: Basic Books, 1959. Vol. 5, pp. 222–242.)

Freud, S. "Civilization and Its Discontents" (1930). *The Standard Edition of the Complete Psychological Works of. . . .* London: Hogarth Press. Vol. 21.

Freud, S. "Moses and Monotheism" (1937–1939). *The Standard Edition of the Complete Psychological Works of. . . .* London: Hogarth Press. Vol. 23.

Freud, S. "Why War?" (1933). *The Standard Edition of the Complete Psychological Works of. . . .* London: Hogarth Press. Vol. 22. (Also in *Collected Papers of. . . .* New York: Basic Books, 1959. Vol. 5, pp. 273–287.)

Hollingshead, A. B., and Redlich, F. C. *Social Class and Mental Illness*. New York: John Wiley, 1958.

Leavy, S. A., and Freedman, L. Z. "Psychoneurosis and Economic Life." *Social Problems*, 4, No. 1 (July 1956), 55–66.

Leavy, S., and Freedman, L. Z. "Psychopathology and Occupation. Part I: Economic Insecurity." *Occupational Psychology*, 35 (January and April 1961), 1–13.

Miller v. *United States*, No. 17061, United States Court of Appeals (Washington, D.C., June 15, 1963), p. 9.

Model Penal Code. The American Law Institute. Philadelphia, 1962.

Szasz, T. S. *Law, Liberty, and Psychiatry*. New York: Macmillan, 1963.

Szasz, T. S. *Psychiatric Justice*. New York: Macmillan, 1965.

27

Psychiatry, History, and Political Science: Notes on an Emergent Synthesis

ARNOLD A. ROGOW

The relationship between psychiatry and political science, like that between psychiatry and history, reminds us of those long engagements that somehow never eventuate in marriage. The two have known each other for a considerable period of time, and like all tentative lovers they share an uneasy rapport compounded of affection, dislike, dependence, and suspicion. Cohabiting when mutually inclined, they occasionally produce offspring who are feeble and short-lived; if one of these products of timorous coupling survives into adolescence, it is then cast off by one or both parents and dies. Despite, or perhaps because of, such vicissitudes, the engagement continues, with neither party able either to break off the relationship or to set a firm date for the wedding.

But the future is full of promise, since all the evidence suggests that our timid lovers are drawing closer together, indeed, are moving rapidly toward fruitful collaboration. In psychiatry, the increasing concern with social psychiatry and community mental health programs indicates that the broader sociological context of disturbed behavior is becoming a major field of interest in the discipline. A small but growing number of political scientists have revived an inquiry, going back to Plato, into the psychological foundations of political stability. Historians are more aware than formerly of personality variables and motivations as clues to the behavior of figures long since dead. Practitioners in all three disciplines articulate a dissatisfaction with traditional research methodologies and canons of evidence and insist on the need for a more scientific approach. Such trends, and others to be explored in due course, underline the possibilities for productive research within and between the disciplines that constitute the behavioral and humanistic sciences.[1]

The engagement, nevertheless, has been a long one, and its fructification, assuming that optimism on this score is not unwarranted, owes something to more than two thousand years of speculation about the nature of man and the political institutions he could and should establish. Plato showed perhaps the first awareness of the debilitating effect on the individual of passions at war with each other, and he certainly was the first to posit a psychology of social classes when he developed his famous characterological distinctions between the rulers, warriors, and workers in the ideal city-state.[2]

Aristotle, who probably would have accorded psychoanalysis a welcome far warmer than that of many of Freud's medical colleagues, dealt with problems that psychiatrists of all persuasions continue to find challenging: the variety and meaning of dreams, the extent to which instincts (the id) can be integrated with other personality components, and the question of whether frustrations of one sort or another can be sublimated.[3] It was also Aristotle who thought of happiness as a harmonious and focused "energy of the soul," and he saw clearly that the health and stability of the polity depended on friendliness and affection among the citizenry.

Long before Machiavelli, but most explicitly beginning with *The Prince* (1535), political theories have been justified or put forward in terms of a conception of human nature upon which the theory is supposed to rest. Just as psychiatrists differ among themselves as to the proper weighting of biological as opposed to social factors in the etiology of neurosis, so political

[1] This is not to slight a number of past efforts by psychiatrists and psychoanalysts designed to bring psychiatry, history, and the social sciences into closer proximity to each other. The best known examples include Géza Roheim (1947, 1950a, 1950b, 1951), Warner Muensterberger and Sidney Axelrad (1955), Hendrik M. Ruitenbeck (1962), and Bruce Mazlish (1963). See also Carl Binger (1948), J. F. Brown (1941), H. W. Dunham (1948), Lawrence K. Frank (1941), and W. A. White (1942).

[2] *The Republic*, passim. It is of interest to compare Freud's view in "Civilization and Its Discontents" (1930) that culture required some renunciation of instinctual gratification with Plato's insistence that the guardians, or rulers, renounce material rewards, affluent living standards, sexual choice, travel, and other gratifications of ordinary citizens.

[3] In his *Poetics*, Book VI, Aristotle anticipated the psychodramatists in stating that tragedy "achieves through pity and fear a catharsis of these emotions."

theorists have quarreled for centuries about the true nature of man and the degree to which he is shaped by instinctual drives as contrasted with environmental conditioning. One school has always assumed that man is inherently wise and virtuous, or can become so, given a suitable social climate. Its public policy recommendations have sought to maximize freedom and opportunity to acquire the spiritual and material necessities of life. Liberty and equality, its members believe, are part of the human birthright, and therefore they constitute the natural condition of society. This school of thought concerning human nature includes such political philosophers as Locke, Rousseau, and Marx and such American thinkers as Jefferson and Paine. Twentieth-century advocates of an expanded welfare state base themselves on identical or similar assumptions regarding man's behavior, as do psychiatrists who have been influenced by, among others, Fromm and Horney.

The other school of thought concerning human nature broadly assumes that man is a weak and selfish creature whose life without government would be, in Hobbes's phrase, "solitary, poor, nasty, brutish, and short" (Hobbes, 1651). Emphasizing authority and stability rather than liberty, the Hobbesian school believes that inequality is the natural condition of man and society and anarchy the end result unless the political system is strong enough to keep order. These and related assumptions have been shared in the past by such thinkers as Hume, Burke, Hegel, and Spencer and, on the American side, Hamilton, John Adams, and William Graham Sumner. Modern conservatives substantially identify themselves with this tradition of thought, and it is a tradition that is in large part compatible with Freud's own reflections and perhaps the main thrust of psychoanalytic thinking (Freud, 1915, 1930, 1933).

While both liberal and conservative theorists thought of themselves as scientists who had taken the entire world for their laboratory, they in fact derived their conceptions of human nature from observations severely limited in both time and space. They wrote a good deal about "natural man," or man in a "state of nature," but, as Rousseau noted, "primitive man is on their lips, but the portrait they paint is of civil man." Thus Hobbes, observing behavior in an age of wars and revolutions, believed that man was prone to act in an aggressive manner. Locke, writing in support of a new constitutional order, thought that human nature was essentially peace-loving, orderly, and reasonable. Rousseau, who lived during a period of corruption and debasement, maintained that man was basically good, but that he became corrupted by society.

It is easy to treat these observations as gross and naïve simplifications, until we remember how much of current political argument begins: "It is, after all, only human nature to . . ." In effect, Hobbes is no further away than the local Republican party headquarters, and Rousseau no further than the campus rally being held by Students for a Democratic Society. Moreover, while we pride ourselves on the more advanced techniques of research available for the study of human behavior, to what extent are these techniques and the conclusions we derive affected by limited observation and experience? In political science, how many respondents constitute an adequate population sample for purposes of testing hypotheses about behavior? In anthropology, how many cultures? In sociology, how many small and large groups? In psychology, how many controlled experiments and simulations? And finally, in psychiatry, how many patients, of what class and condition, seen how often, treated how, by whom, where? Is it possible that had Freud not had personal experience of wars and revolutions, anti-Semitism and Nazism, he would have been much less pessimistic about the possibilities for peace and progress?

The question of methodology, to which we shall return later, must be squarely faced if collaboration among psychiatry, political science, and history is to be as richly productive as its sponsors would wish. The intention, however, is not to substitute scientific method for insight and intuition, but to merge them; "hard" and "soft" approaches, despite the zeal of some partisans for one or the other, are supplementary to each other and not mutually contradictory. Nor would it be wise to dismiss the earlier theorizing about human behavior, in political science and psychiatry, as mere speculation. Hobbes and Locke, Freud and Adler, seem relevant not because they were closet dreamers and "couch" philosophers, but because they have something profound to tell us about the nature of man and society.

Indeed, what is striking about much of the pioneering work in political psychiatry is its modernity. As early as 1758, for example, J. G. Zimmerman sought to identify the sources of patriotism and to specify the means by which excesses of national pride could be controlled. National pride, he argued, was a universal phenomenon that derived from such attributes as the "great antiquity" of certain peoples, or their putative descent from the gods, or alleged possession of the only true religion, or their supposed liberty, power, valor, or reputation. Although Zimmerman did not propose the total elimination of national conceit, he did favor certain measures that would make pride subservient to "good" purposes. Within a given nation pride could be constrained by diffusing knowledge about other peoples, principally by translating their literature and through the cultivation of self-critical attitudes. One can easily call to mind contemporary treatments of nationalism in which Zimmerman's strictures would not be out of place.

In 1822 another overlooked treatise dealt with political power as a complex of psychological elements. Gottfried Duden, endeavoring to break new ground in his discussion of sovereignty, dispensed with the usual metaphysical abstractions and theological dogmas and bypassed the fiction of contract and unitary theory of force. Sovereignty, he argued, could be understood only as a relationship between the desire to rule, on the one side, and the need to obey, on the other. To the extent the ruler alienated any motive of obedience, he narrowed the base of his power, and, if he acted counter to all motives of obedience, he risked the total loss of his power. In Duden's view, the evaluation of motives, whether of dominance or submission, required consideration of such variables as direction, strength, persistence, and modifiability of the impulse and obstacles to its gratification. It was only a century later that Duden's research perspective, which aroused no interest in his day, became an articulate concern in political science.[4]

Thirteen years after Duden, Tocqueville struck a chord that was not to be fully tuned until Freud began his own research toward the end of the nineteenth century. In 1835, with his customary perspicacity, the great French commentator on America noted:

> A man has come into the world; his early years are spent without notice in the pleasures and activities of childhood. As he grows up, the world receives him when his manhood begins, and he enters into contact with his fellows. He is then studied for the first time, and it is imagined that the germ of the vices and the virtues of his maturer years is then formed.
>
> This, if I am not mistaken, is a great error. We must begin higher up; we must watch the infant in his mother's arms; we must see the first images which the external world casts upon the dark mirror of his mind, the first occurrences that he witnesses; we must hear the first words which awaken the sleeping power of thought, and stand by his efforts if we would understand earliest the prejudices, the habits, and the passions which will rule his life. The entire man is, so to speak, to be seen in the cradle of the child (Tocqueville, 1835).

It is no accident that Zimmerman's and Duden's "forgotten studies" were "discovered" by Harold D. Lasswell, the foremost psychoanalytically inclined graduate of the Chicago school of political behaviorists, led for many years by Charles E. Merriam.[5] During the two decades between the world wars almost the entire effort within political science to relate it to psychiatry emanated from Merriam's former graduate students, several of whom underwent psychoanalysis and received some analytical training. The fortunate result was a number of books and articles making use, for the first time, of the prolonged insight interview as a method of studying the behavior of politicians, judges, and administrators; other writings focused on the implications for politics, especially for mass movements and ideological parties, of guilt, repression, frustration, insecurity, and other personality variables.[6]

[4] This summary of Zimmerman's and Duden's books is based on Harold D. Lasswell, "Two Forgotten Studies in Political Psychology" (1925).
[5] See Lasswell (1930, 1932, 1933, 1935, 1938, 1939, 1948).
[6] Lasswell received his Ph.D. in 1926 and taught at Chicago from 1922 to 1938. Some other Chicago "products" of the Merriam era were Gabriel A. Almond (Ph.D., 1938),

Despite such enterprise, it remains true that political science is the last of the social sciences even tentatively to embrace psychiatry and psychoanalysis and that history has lagged behind some of the other humanistic disciplines in utilizing psychiatric insights. Psychology, anthropology, and sociology were the first behavioral fields to be affected by Freud (the latter two merit and receive a separate chapter elsewhere in this volume), whereas the relations between law and psychiatry, relations always difficult and frequently acrimonious, go back almost to the beginnings of psychiatry (and are also dealt with in a separate chapter). While no economic theory has been significantly modified by Freudian formulations,[7] such formulations have been important in the work of industrial organization theorists,[8] welfare economists (Durbin, 1940; Durbin and Bowlby, 1939), and those concerned with managerial problems and performance, including problems of executive health.

The impact of psychoanalysis on the writing and interpretation of fiction, on painting and sculpture, and on art history and criticism has been enormous,[9] so much so that it suffices to say that Freud's own interest in Balzac, Heine, da Vinci, and Michaelangelo has been more than repaid by Lionel Trilling (1955), Edmund Wilson (1941), Leslie Fiedler (1955), Alfred Kazin (1958), Meyer Schapiro (1956), and other humanists. The American theater, in particular, is permeated by Freudian concepts, and, although the British have been less influenced, the plays of Harold Pinter and John Osborne are hardly free of such influence. In France and Italy, Freud is very much a *metteur en scène* in the work of the "new wave" playwrights, novelists, poets, and cinema directors, as he is also a force in the film creations of Sweden's Bergman and Italy's Fellini.

No analogous claims can be made for history despite repeated appeals by and to historians reminding them that psychoanalysis and history have much to offer each other and, to some extent, use the same approach to human events (Hughes, 1960; Schmidl, 1962). In a frequently cited presidential address to the American Historical Association in 1957, Wil-

---

and Frederick L. Schuman (Ph.D., 1927). See Almond (1954) and Schuman (1939) for their respective psychoanalytic orientations.

7 The relatively few efforts to deal with the implications for economics of psychiatry and psychoanalysis include Louis Schneider (1948) and A. Lauterbach (1950).

8 The so-called Hawthorne studies of Elton Mayo and his associates have had far-reaching effects on industrial organization theory. The studies were based on production experiments carried out at the Western Electric Company's Hawthorne Works in Chicago from 1927 to 1932. See also C. Argyris (1952).

9 See, for example, Irving Malin (1965), Sir Kenneth Clark (1939), and Hendrik M. Ruitenbeck (1964). Psychoanalysts and psychiatrists who have written about literature and art, or about novelists, playwrights, poets, and artists, are too numerous to be listed here. Judging by articles in the professional journals, the perennial favorites among writers for psychoanalytic examination include Poe, Dostoevski, Conrad, Shakespeare (especially such characters as Hamlet, Lear, and Macbeth), Proust, and Melville.

liam L. Langer lamented the fact that "historians have for the most part approved of the iron curtain between their own profession and that of the dynamic psychologists." Recalling that in 1913 a distinguished American historian, Preserved Smith, had published an article on the psychoanalytic interpretation of Martin Luther's early years, Langer suggested that historians cannot afford to overlook "the psychic content" of religion, plagues and epidemics such as the "Black Death," wars, and other social upheavals. He urged younger historians, in particular, to acquire training in the methods and techniques of psychoanalytic inquiry (Langer, 1958).

Perhaps some of them did so, but the following year, when Erik H. Erikson's book on Luther appeared, it was not reviewed in either the *American Historical Review*, the official publication of the American Historical Association, or the *Journal of Modern History*—or, for that matter, the *American Political Science Review*, published by the American Political Science Association.[10] In 1963 it was still possible to say that there were "only a few hardy pioneers in psychoanalytic history" (Mazlish, 1963), and, at the 80th Annual Meeting of the American Historical Association in December 1965, the point was once again made that very few historians have "ventured into the wild continent that Langer opened up to them." Arguing that we "know little or nothing about the history of child-rearing, of the changing attitudes of society toward different stages of the epigenetic cycle —how the various societies have valued childhood, adolescence, old age, for example," Frank Manuel noted that the "psychologist asks these questions of his contemporary world. Why should they not be addressed to the past as well?" (Manuel, 1965).

Of the reasons that may be advanced for the failure of political scientists to respond to Freud, three in particular stand out. The first is the long and tenacious tradition within political science of conceiving of the discipline as consanguinely related to law, history, and philosophy rather than to behavioral science. Emphasizing the study of constitutions and enactments, approaching the state and other political entities descriptively rather than analytically, treating the history of normative political ideas as the sum and essence of political theory, political science for a very long period eschewed a dynamic interpretation of political life. The founding fathers of American political science, many of whom did graduate work in German and British universities, could not conceive of the personality dimension as relevant to political science; most of them, at the beginning of the twentieth century, were unhappy with efforts to view the political process as a function of groups competing and bargaining for power, much less the outcome of individual and group interrelations influenced in part by unconscious motivations. Even today, it is worth noting, political science in Europe and

[10] It should be mentioned, however, that one of the most perceptive treatments of *Young Man Luther* was written by a political scientist (Pye, 1961).

elsewhere remains steeped in legalistic, historical, and philosophical exegesis, although there are exceptions and, indubitably, modernizing trends are underway.[11]

A second cause of resistance to psychoanalysis is the challenge posed by Freudian principles to the heuristic rational and superstructural models which, for a very long time, constituted nuclear political science. Freud's belief that mental processes are essentially unconscious appeared to undermine the Enlightenment view, incorporated into political science, that man was a reasoning calculator of his own self-interest whose judgment of what would benefit himself and society would improve with increasing education and diffusion of knowledge. The conviction of Freud that culture itself was the result of a fragile tension between constructive and destructive tendencies in man, with the latter frequently in ascendancy, threatened the very root structure of the belief in progress and its corollary liberal doctrine of change and perfectibility in human nature. Psychoanalysis, insofar as it was understood by political scientists, seemed to be saying, finally, that the entire political superstructure—conservative and radical parties, ideologies, voting, the state itself—could be "explained" in terms of childhood traumas, Oedipus complexes, father figures, castration fears, libido diversion, and the like. Freud, it appeared, like Marx before him, was suggesting that political institutions were essentially a façade, a veneer, a gloss to mask the real interests and motivations of man, and much of the treatment accorded Freud was similar to that accorded Marx and other demolishers of the superstructure: disbelief, disdain, disinterest. There were also those in the political science profession, the moral views of which have always been closer to Calvin than to Casanova, who shared and still share the opinion expressed in 1910 by the Dean of the University of Toronto that Freud was an advocate "of free love, removal of all restraints, and a relapse into savagery" (Jones, 1955), in short, a dirty old man.[12] After Freud, as, from another perspective, after Hitler and the national insanity of Nazism, it could no longer be maintained that man was cast in the image of God, or, if not God, at least Thomas Jefferson or John Stuart Mill.

The third source of estrangement between psychiatry and political science, and one that constitutes a major threat to continuing possibilities for collaboration, has to do with methodological developments in both disci-

[11] It remains true that such British pioneers as Ranyard West and Roger Money-Kyrle have fared no better than their American counterparts. Most British political scientists and historians are unfamiliar with West's *Conscience and Society* (1942), and Money-Kyrle's *Psychoanalysis and Politics* (1951). A more recent if less successful effort to psychoanalyze certain aspects of politics is R. V. Sampson's, *The Psychology of Power* (1966).

[12] The writer can clearly recall an occasion when he was a graduate student at Princeton in 1948 or 1949, being advised by a distinguished professor of political science that Freud was not worth reading "because he justified every sin you can think of, and some that you don't even know about."

plines. Since World War II political scientists have been increasingly concerned with the discipline's methodological lag behind the other social and behavioral sciences. Doctoral candidates in political science, unlike those in economics and sociology, knew no mathematics or statistics; hence their models and paradigms were verbal constructs, and there was little agreement even within the profession about the words used, especially such words as power, influence, consent, coalition, authority. Few political scientists were skilled in techniques of quantitative and qualitative measurement; therefore they were unable to process aggregate data, such as that produced in sample surveys, or to undertake multivariate analysis. One major consequence of this technological lag was that certain research areas, notably research in public opinion formation and voting behavior, were transferred, as it were, from political science to sociology and psychology. Another result was that studies undertaken by political scientists—for example, studies of interest groups, or local governments, or decision-making processes—tended to be, however illuminating, subjective and frequently idiosyncratic. They were difficult, often impossible to replicate, were not susceptible to proof or disproof, and hence were of little utility in that slow and painful construction process by which a discipline transforms itself into a science.

While this is not the occasion to discuss all the motivations for change, it may be noted in passing that a professional inferiority complex, especially among younger practitioners, has played an important role, as have a number of foundations whose funds are seemingly available without limit for "hard" research. The impact of the Center for Advanced Study in the Behavioral Sciences, where political scientists and historians have been welcomed since operations began in 1954, should not be overlooked; shifts of emphasis within the Social Science Research Council and National Science Foundation have also been important.

Similar currents of thought and development have affected history in recent years, but the continuing reluctance of historians to probe the "wild continent" of psychoanalysis and psychiatry requires a somewhat different explanation than the one advanced for political science. While historians, like psychoanalysts and psychiatrists, argue interminably among themselves as to whether their fields of endeavor constitute art, or science (or philosophy, ethics, or even simply literature), while historians are also familiar with the intuitive, introspective approach and make extensive use of the case method, they are less inclined than analysts to regard inferences as evidence with respect to either individual lives or historical events that lack extensive documentation. In the case of biography, the historian, unlike the analyst, is wary of an interpretation that rests on inadequate and random information about the formative years of an important figure long since dead; his inclination, therefore, is to report what is known rather than to interpret it, much less to "explain" an entire life in terms of one or several isolated childhood incidents. The psychoanalyst-biographer, on the other hand, *if* he feels that the childhood incidents are of great significance—*if*, that is to say, psychoanalytic theory treats such incidents as of decisive importance in any life, great or ordinary—may be satisfied that, although little is known about the formative period, what is known is sufficient. While it is an overstatement to say that "the tendency of psychoanalytic criticism [is] to reduce literature to its lowest common factor, which usually turns out to be the oedipus complex" (Rowley, 1958), there is a tendency in much psychoanalytic interpretation to avoid multiple causation and to substitute for the socioeconomic context of events the phobias, fantasies, and complexes of leading figures. Most historians would accept the thesis that much history is made by great men, but they rightly reject the proposition that history is formed by them.

Moreover, the historian, like the political scientist, who steps foot on the "wild continent" is regarded with suspicion not only by his colleagues, but by psychoanalysts and psychiatrists as well. He may be willing to risk the disbelief, even hostility, of other historians—and the promotion and tenure problems that accompany such disbelief—but he is a bold historian indeed if he dares commit what Erikson has called the "diagnostic fallacy," that is, the attribution to nations and their leaders of "psychiatric conditions" (Erikson, 1962). And if he is less venturesome, he must still disregard to some extent Franz Alexander's warning against the application of psychoanalytic insights to "the fate of nations as they evolve in the wide perspective of history" (Alexander, 1940). Such eminent advice, addressed to a profession that is by force of habit, if not also by force of intellect, cautious, and certainly one not known to plunge boldly even into well-charted seas, is usually sufficient to deter all but the very brave—one is tempted to say all but the foolhardy. Nor is the effect overcome when it is noticed that Alexander did not always follow his own advice, as when he wrote in 1952 that "the concurrent fascist and communist developments in Eastern and Central Europe are the manifestations of unbridled instincts in politics. They also have a regressive character and are basically irrational . . ." (Alexander, 1952).

Finally, it must also seem to the historian, as it does to the political scientist, that the contributions of psychoanalysis and psychiatry to our understanding of history and politics are limited by the inordinate "softness" of much psychiatric research. While in psychiatry, too, there is growing dissatisfaction with traditional methods, what has been said about methodological lag in political science applies with even greater force to psychiatry. Whether or not it is an overstatement to suggest that "psychology can be of use to the social sciences *only* if its use can be reduced to a technique which is verifiable, teachable, and can be corrected or changed in the face of new evidence" (italics added) (Kardiner, 1945), it is plausible to suggest that the limitations of much psychiatric research—for example, the lack of standardization in the concepts and measures employed by psychiatrists, the proneness to generalize findings that are based on a highly selective, nonrepresentative, middle-class population sample, the tendency to minimize the importance of variables found to be significant by political scientists, such as social class, income, education, and religious affiliation—constitute a severe restriction of its utility.[13]

While it is evident that many psychiatrists are more interested than ever before in interdisciplinary methodologies and research efforts, it is far from clear, at least to an outsider, what the effects will be, on the one hand, of the increasing separation between clinicians and researchers, and, on the other hand, of the growing interest in biochemical and engineering approaches to mental illness. No doubt it is too early—it may be totally in error—to say that the most imaginative and competent psychiatrists are gradually abandoning clinical practice for research, instead of engaging in both, but the implications of such a development, especially implications for interdisciplinary training programs that include political scientists and historians, are not all happy ones. Similarly, it may be wrong, or at least premature, to conclude that the interest in biochemistry and psychophysiological research will draw psychiatry back toward medicine and the natural sciences, which is where Kenneth M. Colby and others feel it belongs (Colby, 1960), and farther away from the social sciences. In psychiatry, as in all other branches of knowledge at the present time, there are conflicting trends; the only certain thing is the necessity of continuing discussion and analyzing trends.

But assuming, once again, that psychiatry and political science are drawing closer together rather than farther apart, and psychiatry and history as well, what does psychiatry have most to contribute to political science and history? What can political science and history offer psychiatry? Where are the interdisciplinary frontiers and "cutting-edge" areas, and the richest possibilities for innovative developments?

The contributions of psychiatry to political science and history can be

[13] Thus the social science profession, especially in its current "hard" mood, is not likely to regard as an endorsement of psychiatry the fact that its screening processes are notoriously nonpredictive of behavior. In 1945, for example, in a study of over 100,000 men constituting the entire population at all induction stations in the United States, the proportions rejected on psychiatric grounds varied from 0.5 per cent at one induction station to 50.6 per cent at another, although the test scores had much the same frequency distribution (Stouffer, 1950). On October 21, 1965, *The New York Times* reported that the performances of forty-four Peace Corps volunteers "bore no relation to the predictions of a team of psychiatrists who had rated them before they left [for Ghana]." According to M. Brewster Smith, as quoted by *The Times*, a partial explanation for the lack of correlation was the "over-concern" of psychiatrists for "adjustment and mental health."

roughly classified under the headings of method, emphasis, and insight. In terms of methodology, Freud's most significant achievement was undoubtedly the unstructured, free-association interview. Depending as it does on observational techniques that require special interpretational skills on the part of the investigator, the free-association interview has not been fully exploited by political scientists and historians interested in contemporary affairs and the recent past. Yet it would appear that the psychoanalytic-type interview is an indispensable tool for intensively exploring and theoretically charting areas of political behavior that are not amenable to other methods of inquiry (Brewster *et al.*, 1965; Lane, 1962).[14]

For example, much research by political scientists into the etiology of right-wing extremism suggests that members of such organizations as the John Birch Society are plagued by high levels of anxiety, low self-esteem, strong needs for inviolacy, and hostile and misanthropic orientations toward the social order. Many of them belong to the discontinued classes of society—that is, they are the older residents of burgeoning towns and cities, the proprietors of neighborhood stores and small businesses threatened by the huge chains and shopping centers, the elderly retired who are made apprehensive by small children, non-whites, noise, traffic, and tax increases—and these drop-out citizens are attracted to such subcultures of despair as the John Birch Society. Unfortunately, they are less likely to cooperate with social investigators using survey research and other "hard" instruments of research than individuals who are more sanguine in both personality and outlook. Hence, studies positing a relationship between, say, alienation and extremism are characterized by a high refusal rate for requested interviews and questionnaire returns and consequent failure to demonstrate that the relationship holds at levels of statistical significance. In fact, we know very little altogether about those who consistently refuse to participate in survey studies, whatever their nature. Surely, here is a collaborative area that would benefit from a merger of the "soft" technique of the clinician with the "hard" techniques currently used in political science.

Even less developed than the free-association interview is the application of free association to the analysis of documents, letters, diaries, and written records of all sorts. Although the historian frequently deals with handwritten accounts, almost no effort has been made to analyze changes of handwriting, including sudden changes in the way one signs letters, that are known to occur under conditions of great internal as well as external stress. Hence we are uninformed about the relationship of such changes to life and career experiences. While handwriting, to a great and growing extent, has been replaced by the telephone, typewriter, and tape recorder, it is by no means impossible to search typewritten and spoken messages for

[14] Explorations of nonpolitical behavior based on psychoanalytic interviews are reported by Herbert Hendin *et al.* (1965).

clues to traumatic events. Much could be learned, for example, by approaching taped political interviews, speeches, press conferences, and so forth in a fashion similar to that employed in the analysis of taped psychiatric interviews and group-therapy sessions.

Related to the free-association interview is Freud's emphasis on the "latent, unconscious, irrational, and archaic aspect" of behavior, and the stress he placed "on the formative influence of early childhood, of dreams and of phantasies" (Frenkel-Brunswik, 1952). Little of this emphasis has penetrated research in either political science or history, although efforts are now under way in political science to study the processes by which children become interested, involved, and partisan in politics (Greenstein, 1960, 1965; Easton and Hess, 1960, 1962). So far as is known, no attempt has been made to collect and interpret the dreams and fantasies of political figures. No doubt this is due in part to the fact that what we know of living individuals is by and large what they want us to know and what we know of the dead is by and large what their families and posterity permit us to discover. But it is also true that special skills are required for the analysis of inferred motivations as opposed to those that are manifest; lacking such skills, political scientists and historians tend to confine themselves to that which is conscious, declared, and easily observable. Thus the latent, underlying motivations of both individuals and institutions, in the concealment or disguise of which all advanced societies excel, may be totally overlooked by the political behaviorist and social historian.

If this were not the case, we would know much more about the origins of deviant political and social behavior and the role of such behavior in history. Most political scientists see the universe as conveniently dichotomized into political and apolitical strata. Focusing upon the extended middle range of attitudes and behavior, they find that about 10 per cent of the citizenry are activists, that is, people who vote regularly, join political organizations, contribute money, communicate their opinions to public officials, and even run for office. The activists are usually well informed about public affairs and firmly committed to democratic rules of the game, for example, the protection of civil liberties (Stouffer, 1955).

The great mass of citizens, however, are found to be apathetic and indifferent to politics, and their commitment to democratic rules and procedures may be viewed as tenuous. The prevailing interpretation of such behavior is that these persons remain outside the political arena because they attach a low priority to political affairs relative to other forms of gratification, or because they believe that values allocated by the public sector will come to them even if they do not participate, or because they have a strong sense of political inefficacy or impotence. It is rarely observed that from time to time some of these apathetics venture into the political arena and convert their anger and frustrations into punitive acts directed at political actors and objects—hence the disaffected, lower-class Negroes who convert the community into a phobic sector through street riots and other forms of anomic behavior; the alienated, Caucasian lumpen proletariat who form "patriotic" and paramilitary societies, such as the Minutemen, the American Nazi party, and the Hell's Angels motorcycle clubs, dedicated to overthrowing the democratic rules of the game; and the Lee Harvey Oswalds who endeavor to punish the powers-that-be by assassinating the President. The conditions under which these deviant types of behavior develop can hardly be specified if the political world is seen and studied as a crucible of moderate activism, the characteristic style of which is pragmatic, consensual, brokerage involvement. Because it is this world, not the deviant one, that elects presidents, the deviant zones of society are generally ignored, although they are often decision-making zones at local levels (school boards, for instance) and generate much of the rhetoric that flows through the political main stream. In effect, the truncated and culture-bound vision that dominates American political science is here joined by a "hard" approach that rejects Freud's emphasis as well as his method. As a consequence, it is rare to encounter in the discipline, even in investigations of deviance, that "deep and penetrating study of individuals [that] may often tell us more about the themes of a contemporary society than will a surface description of the existing institutions" (Frenkel-Brunswik, 1952).

The third, or insight, component of Freud's contribution to political science and history is that large body of psychoanalytic and psychiatric literature which deals with politics and history. The term insight is used because such literature is designed to provide an analysis in depth, based on psychoanalytic and psychiatric theory, of phenomena that are only partly explored or understood by political scientists and historians. Most of this literature, for reasons already discussed, has originated with psychiatrists themselves, but an increasing amount is being published by psychoanalytically inclined social scientists, not all of whom have cared to acknowledge their indebtedness to Freud and his progeny. Indeed, in certain areas, notably biography, it is customary *not* to acknowledge a debt to psychoanalysis, however large and conspicuous it may be.

Broadly speaking, the history of insight literature is, like other histories, one of changing times, interests, and intellectual styles. Someone once remarked, in an effort to explain a Supreme Court decision, that the "Supreme Court reads the headlines." In a similar vein it may be observed that psychiatrists read the headlines and are affected by them, at least insofar as their insight writings are concerned. Thus, during the "long twilight" that glowed over Europe between the Franco-Prussian War and 1914, Freud and his colleagues wrote very little outside the area of primary concern, that is, the origins, symptoms, and treatment of neuroses and psychoses. While Freud early demonstrated an interest in literary and artistic themes—his essays "The Theme of the Three Caskets" and "The Moses of Michaelangelo" appeared in 1913 and 1914 respectively—he did not turn his attention to problems of war and peace until 1915, when he published "Thoughts for the Times on War and Death." His preface "Psycho-analysis and War Neuroses" appeared in 1919. During the relatively peaceful 1920's he wrote little on the subject, but in 1930 his *Civilization and Its Discontents* was perhaps more prophetic than anything else that year of the approaching end of tranquility or, in Harding's coined phrase, "normalcy." The Freud-Einstein exchange of letters, "Why War?" was published in 1933 (although the letters were written late in 1932), on the eve of the Nazi long march.

The psychiatric interest in the conditions of war and peace, it need hardly be said, has had no cause to diminish since Freud observed in his letter to Einstein "that owing to the perfection of instruments of destruction a future war might involve the extermination of one or perhaps both of the antagonists All this is true, and so incontestably true that one can only feel astonished that the waging of war has not yet been unanimously repudiated" (Freud, 1933).

During and immediately after World War II the writings of Alexander (1941, 1942, 1943), G. Brock Chisholm (1946), Trigant Burrow (1941), and others argued that war is not inevitable from a psychiatric point of view, although it does serve as a release for frustrations and conflicts of all sorts. Much of the literature of this period built less on Freud's conception of the place of Thanatos in human affairs than on the sequential "frustrations and aggression" theme developed by John Dollard and his associates in 1939 (Dollard *et al.*, 1939).

With the founding of the Group for the Advancement of Psychiatry in 1946, usually referred to as GAP, the attention of psychiatrists was specifically drawn to the problem of war and related problems that beset the national and world communities. Since 1960 the writings of Jerome D. Frank (1960) and Judd Marmor (1964), some of which are addressed to lay audiences, have been influential, and in 1964 GAP itself published a widely read report titled *Psychiatric Aspects of the Prevention of Nuclear War*. Citing as difficulties in the way of nonviolent solutions such factors as psychological defense mechanisms, "primitivising effects of extreme fear or panic," increasing dehumanization, ethnocentric perceptual distortion, and other factors that contribute to the psychological escalation of aggression, the GAP study nevertheless insisted that other ways could be found "of conducting conflict between groups of people, or between nations, that can serve these psychological needs more adaptively in our modern world." War, concluded the report, "is a social institution; it is not inevitably rooted in the nature of man."

A second area of interest between the two world wars and for some years after 1945, although perhaps an area rather more developed by psychoanalysts than psychiatrists, was the concept and dimensions of national character, especially the character of Germany. That Germany received focal attention is understandable in view of the fact that the disruptions attributable to German-provoked wars and, above all, to National Socialism, included the persecution and forced migration of a large number of psychoanalysts including, in addition to Freud himself, Rank, Adler, Stekel, Fromm, Fromm-Reichman, Alexander, Horney, Reich, Erikson, and Reik. Almost all of these prominent exiles from Nazi-occupied territory were of Jewish extraction, and paralleling the interest in the psychopathology of German national character was a deep concern, personal as well as professional, about the possible spread of virulent anti-Semitism. To be sure, the Germans were not the only ones to receive attention. A survey of the relevant literature reveals numerous articles and a few books dealing with the American, British, Russian, Chinese, Japanese, and even Norwegian so-called national characters. But in such books as Richard M. Brickner's *Is Germany Incurable?* (1943) and Wilhelm Reich's *The Mass Psychology of Fascism* (1946), in articles such as Erik H. Erikson's "Hitler's Imagery and German Youth" (1942), and Fritz Moellenhoff's "The Price of Individuality: Speculations about German National Characteristics" (1947), German national character and Nazism, its most virulent expression, were subjected to a psychoanalysis more searching than that accorded any topic or theme in the social sciences. Much of this analysis was devoted to an explication of paranoid tendencies in German history and thought and the means by which these tendencies could be abolished or at least reduced after the war, but there were also efforts, as in the writings of Erich Fromm (1941), to gaze at Germany and the general problem of authoritarianism through spectacles, the right lens of which had been contributed by Freud and the left donated by Marx. Since 1950 interest in Nazi Germany has very largely been confined to historians, some of whom have attempted to apply psychoanalytic categories, while the study of national character as such is now only a marginal interest in both psychiatry and the social sciences.

Ethnic group prejudice, on the other hand, is a continuing concern. There have been shifts of emphasis, however, reflecting changing problems and research needs. A vast literature dealing with anti-Semitism, to which psychoanalysts and psychiatrists have made influential contributions, has succeeded in exposing the roots of anti-Semitism, although precise boundaries are not fixed, for example, between religious, historical, social, economic, and psychopathological causal explanations. Since publication of *The Authoritarian Personality* in 1950, the most significant effort made to link anti-Semitism to a variety of individual and social disorders, most work on anti-Semitism has been in the form of surveys that attempt to measure the distribution of opinions in a given population.

After 1954, the year of the momentous school desegregation decision of the Supreme Court, interest conspicuously shifted to problems in Negro-white relations and related civil rights activities. Prior to the Brown v. Board of Education decision of a unanimous court in 1954, American psychiatry, like American society itself, did not demonstrate much concern for Negroes apart from an occasional article dealing with race riots or with the high incidence of mental illness in predominantly Negro communities. Perhaps this neglect owed something to the relatively small position that Negroes occupy in psychiatry either as doctors or as private patients. Whatever the explanation, not much was known about the psychiatric aspects of either segregation or desegregation prior to a 1956 round table on the subject sponsored by the American Orthopsychiatric Society. In 1957 a GAP publication, *Psychiatric Aspects of School Desegregation*, was an important contribution to the small body of literature on the subject, and since then race relations themes have been dealt with in a number of articles published by psychiatrists. It remains broadly true, however, that psychiatry, much less psychoanalysis, has not given to the civil rights area the attention that it has given to other problems in the social psychiatry field, or the attention that civil rights problems deserve. Partly for this reason, there is as yet no published work as substantial as *The Authoritarian Personality*; indeed, the most significant book on race relations is still Gunnar Myrdal's *An American Dilemma* (1944), and Myrdal was neither an American nor a psychiatrist, nor yet a political scientist or historian, but an economist-sociologist of Swedish nationality.

A fourth dimension of psychiatric insight literature, and one closely related to research on ethnic group relations, has been concerned with democratic and nondemocratic personality types. (Fromm, 1941; Erikeon, 1954; Rokeach, 1960; Alexander, 1942; Lasswell, 1948, 1951).[15] Most psychiatrists who have written on social issues have had something to say about contrasting authoritarian and nonauthoritarian character structures, although it is fair to comment that their work, like that of political scientists with similar interests, is given more to implication than explication, especially with regard to nonauthoritarian character structure. Much of what has been published is also vulnerable to a criticism similar to that leveled at *The Authoritarian Personality*, namely, that the nuclear concept excludes left-wing behavior. While efforts have been made to study individual communists, the personality type occasionally referred to as the authoritarian liberal remains elusive, at least in research terms. Here, too, there may be a reflection of the personal as well as professional environment. The psychiatrist, like the political scientist and historian, is a member of the liberal political community,[16] and he is apt to assume, rather

[15] Aspects of democratic and authoritarian behavior are treated in the writings of G. W. Allport, G. Murphy, H. Cantril, A. L. Edwards, O. Klineberg, R. N. Sanford, T. M. Newcomb, and others.

[16] It is estimated that between 80 and 90 per cent of political scientists and historians vote Democratic or left-of-Democratic, and in the 1964 Presidential election it is en-

than inquire into, his own normalcy and that of his colleagues and friends relative to those "on the other side." He may also believe, having been brainwashed to some extent by his social science brethren, that authoritarian types are those who *very strongly agree* or *very strongly disagree* with it-doesn't-matter-what, whereas nonauthoritarians *agree* or *disagree* or are *uncertain* or *don't know*. The man in the middle of the scale, however, is not always a democrat, as when he is asked, for example, whether he approves or disapproves of genocide, castration of homosexuals, compulsory sterilization of women on relief, imprisonment of war profiteers without trial, and other inhumane measures.

Insofar as authoritarian and nonauthoritarian types can be extrapolated from the diverse body of literature specifying certain essentials of democracy and dictatorship, it would appear that the authoritarian type, from a psychiatric point of view, is a coercive, anxious, and suspicious individual who is oriented toward power and extremely limited in his capacity to give and receive affection. Demanding from others either dominance or submission, the authoritarian type tends to be the total leader in one kind of situation, and the total rebel in another. "Intolerant of ambiguity," in Frenkel-Brunswik's phrase, his problem-solving methods are rigid, quick, and direct, and his preferred solution is always simplistic. He prefers his wife passive, his children submissive, his home life undemanding, his friends deferential, and his employees docile. He is frequently skilled in masking his basic hostility behind a façade of spurious warmth and friendliness, and he is often a master in the art of dissimulation. Enjoying the delusion of rectitudinous grandeur, he may see himself as an honest man who has not been discovered by Diogenes. If he is conservative as well as authoritarian, such phrases and words as communist, socialist, Stevenson, one world, medicare, and beatnik may engender spontaneous combustion. If he is liberal as well as authoritarian, the inflammable terms are capitalism, Wall Street, Hoover (both Herbert and J. Edgar), CIA, military-industrial complex, and Catholic hierarchy.

The democratic type, by contrast, is a persuasive, secure, and trustful individual for whom power is only one of a number of values. Able to give and receive affection, his relations with others are characterized, in Erikson's wording, by "mutuality." Lacking the desire to be either the absolute leader or absolute follower, the democrat as husband, father, and employer does not demand that others strip their own egos in order to clothe his own; his role may require that he be *primus inter pares* in decision-making

---

tirely possible that the Johnson-Humphrey vote approximated 95 per cent. In other words, the overwhelming number of political scientists and historians (and perhaps the majority of all social scientists and humanists) are liberals, as that term is commonly understood, or, at any rate, as understood by the irate Republican parents of undergraduates. In the medical field, so far as is known, only psychiatrists consistently cast a majority Democratic vote.

situations, but he is supportive in such a role, and he takes others into account. He can accept criticism, understand frailty in others as well as himself, and limit his hostile and aggressive impulses or discharge them harmlessly. Politically he may lean to either side, but whether a conservative or liberal he rejects devil theories of politics and controls his emotional reaction to manipulations of symbols irrespective of their plus or minus value in his belief system.

Clearly these characterological types should be of immense importance in the study of political behavior, and yet very little use has been made of them by political scientists and historians.[17] Some reasons for this have already been noted—the "hard" approach infatuation of many political scientists, the reluctance of historians to utilize either the method or the insights of psychoanalysis, and so forth—and, in addition, many students of political behavior feel that the authoritarian and democratic personality models are too vague and imprecise to be of research utility. Some critics go so far as to suggest that such models are more imaginative than descriptive, arguing that the key concepts are not dichotomized terminals between which a given population distributes itself, but points on a personality continuum within individuals. The same person, they maintain, will be authoritarian in one situation and democratic in another. They also express doubts that the authoritarian subculture, assuming one exists, plays a significant role in American life or that it is increasing in size and importance.

These reservations and criticisms may or may not be legitimate; what is certain is that they will not be resolved unless "hard" and "soft" methods are joined in a collaboration between psychiatrists, political scientists, and historians. From psychiatry, for example, we need much more specificity with regard to the interpersonal (family, school, workplace) environments that nourish democratic and authoritarian personalities and recommended measures for strengthening democratic as opposed to authoritarian tendencies. From history we need more information about the economic, social, and political conditions which have given rise to authoritarian subcultures and paranoid pseudo-communities in democratic societies. From political science we need to know more about the extent to which authoritarian tendencies in political life can be modified by role settings and expectations, by interaction between authoritarians and democrats, by enlightenment, and, finally, by restriction and confinement in the larger social environment. These demands made upon the several disciplines hardly exhaust the research needs and opportunities with reference to possible linkages between personality types and political behavior.

Indeed, it is difficult to think of any insight area in social psychiatry, or

[17] Neither political scientists nor historians were involved in *The Authoritarian Personality* study, and few political scientists have made any effort to relate personality variables to opinion and ideological orientation. With one or two exceptions, the most significant contributions have come from social psychology and sociology.

any research in political and historical behavior, that would not benefit from collaboration among the three disciplines. The study of voting behavior, for example, a "hard" research field in social science if ever there was one, would become more exciting and significant if voting motivation and intention underwent psychological scrutiny in depth; adaptations of the psychiatric interview would add an important dimension to research into the behavior of bureaucrats, congressmen, state legislators, city councilmen, and the like. While psychiatrists have gradually become aware of correlations between socioeconomic variables and mental illness (and the treatment thereof), more research is needed on the national cultural aspects of mental health and illness. If biographies are to serve as the rich tapestries of entire lives and not merely as pale sketches of names, dates, and places, historians and others will have to acquire some skills from psychoanalysis in making inferences, reconstructions, and interpretations.

The frontier areas of these disciplines, however, require less an exchange of methods and insights than a merger into a comprehensive science of social behavior. In this development the psychiatrist is likely to find himself working in tandem, not with medical specialists, but with social scientists and historians who share with him a common interest in man's fate. The merger of methods and insights in the future may even extend to practices, treatments, and therapies. It requires little imagination to foresee the time when there are psychiatry members of political science and history departments and when political scientists and historians are attached to hospital and clinic staffs.

The emergent science of social behavior will not lack for challenging research areas; indeed the problem will be to assess priorities among problems that demand attention. But by any test, one urgent problem is bound to be the problem of defining democracy in terms that are meaningful in a twentieth-century world of nuclear weapons, superpowers, gross inequalities of wealth, racial tensions, and, in the so-called advanced portions, of giant organizations that transform men into pigmy automatons and antlike robots. Put another way, the problem is how to make the world safe for democratic character development and unsafe for those authoritarian and destructive tendencies that threaten an end of the human experience. In short, the most urgent question facing the emergent science is the question of man's survival itself.

A collaborative approach to the question of survival might initially focus on those institutions and behavioral patterns, national and international, that create or contribute to neurosis and psychosis. Reference here is not to the concept of "society as the patient," as useful in certain circumstances as that concept may be, but to the belief that a good deal of disturbed behavior, both social and individual, is rooted in societal conditions. While efforts have been made to identify these conditions and relate them to deviant behaviors, much remains to be known about the nature and treatment of such relationships.

It is fairly well established, for example, that the distribution of mental illnesses is inversely related to class and income, that, to take one case, proportionately more of the poor than the rich suffer from schizophrenia and other illnesses. There is also evidence that Americans in general worry more about financial insecurity than about any other problem in their lives. Clearly, the unhappiness of a great many, and the psychoses of some, Americans is to some extent a reflection of the economic and social environment in which they find themselves. It follows that the environment needs changing, and gradually—all too gradually—it is being changed, in some respects. But for the short run, at least, much could be accomplished if we could account for the fact that not everyone in a poverty culture becomes schizophrenic or otherwise mentally ill, and not all Americans are equally worried about financial insecurity. What factors, then, *in addition to environment*, determine whether one does or does not become ill or markedly insecure? Here, surely, is a collaborative area, the exploration of which would save many more from crippling illnesses than are now saved by conventional treatment methods.

Another neglected area of research, and one of equal challenge, is the relationship between sexual and social behavior. While it is a truism, since Freud, to declare that psychosexual disturbances in the individual are a prime cause of neurosis, very little research has been done on the extent to which the sexual aspects of culture promote as well as reflect disturbed behavior in political and social arenas as well as individual lives. Many of those who work with young people are persuaded that they especially suffer from the strains and tensions that are built-in features of American sexual culture—although, again, we cannot discriminate with any precision among the factors that predispose some to suffer more than others. But not only the young people; there is evidence that adults also suffer from what Sullivan called the "lurid twilight" of sexuality in America, a "twilight" made up of unrestricted stimulation, on the one hand, and restricted response, on the other. No doubt Sullivan had in mind some sections of the mass media which, quite apart from their catering to voyeuristic tastes, parade before us a thousand inviting male and female images, although the mores make us do with one husband or wife at a time, inviting or otherwise. Despite sporadic protests, New York is now publishing books banned in almost all other Western countries, and Hollywood is making movies for popular consumption that were formerly reserved for stag evenings at American Legion halls. The unprecedented rise of *Playboy*, the only magazine in its price class ever to reach a three million per month circulation, is a related phenomenon, as is the appearance of the bare-bosomed waitress.

If our sexual mores had changed *as much* as the books and magazines, there would be fewer problems arising from the supercharged erotic atmosphere. The mores, however, while they have undoubtedly changed, still do not endorse premarital or extramarital sexual intercourse, nor are they tolerant of deviant sexual practices. The frequent result of the visual do's and verbal don't's is a psychic state inimical to either physical or mental health. Yet there have been few efforts to study the "lurid twilight" in terms of its relationship to political extremism, delinquency, violence, ethnic group tension, and other problems.[18]

A third important, and somewhat neglected, research area is the relationship between personality and political leadership. The psychodynamics of political leadership is largely unexplored territory despite the efforts of some political scientists and historians to make limited and not always successful use of psychiatric insights in particular cases (George and George, 1956; Gottfried, 1962; Rogow and Lasswell, 1963; Robertson, 1964; Edinger, 1965; Wolfenstein, 1967). For reasons not entirely clear, psychiatrists and psychoanalysts have written relatively little about political leaders; apparently they have preferred to deal with cultural and religious figures. As a consequence, we know relatively little about the role of personality factors in opinion formation and in the shaping of political career patterns. We are even less informed about the influence of physical and mental illness on decision-making processes, although the list of sick statesmen is a long one. It is also thoroughly international, and it may be significant for an understanding of certain key decisions that have had a decisive effect on world history (L'Etang, 1958, 1961; Rogow, 1963, 1966).

It is fascinating to think what might be accomplished by systematic research and discussion of the role of personality variables in the decisions to drop the bomb on Hiroshima, or to intervene in Korea and Vietnam. Much could be accomplished if most of the 266 psychiatrists in the District of Columbia were willing to collaborate with political scientists in studying the consequences of stress, tension, and illness on decision-making. As it is, neither psychiatrists nor political scientists can say much about the factors that predispose particular individuals to successfully tolerate stress in decision-making situations. We simply do not know who breaks down, and why, and what the effect has been in policy terms. Practically nothing is known about the influence of tranquilizers and related drugs; for that matter, nothing reliable is known about the role of psychiatry itself in the nation's capital apart from the fact that Washington, D.C., is a leader in the ratio of psychiatrists to population. Here, again, collaboration between the disciplines could have only the most beneficial results in terms of both public welfare values and research frontiersmanship.

The stability of the democratic community may also be threatened by

[18] The role of psychosexuality in prejudice has been noticed in studies of anti-Negro and anti-Semitic attitudes, especially the tendency of those prejudiced to attribute hypersexuality to Negroes and/or Jews (Myrdal, 1949; Bullock, 1962).

the impact of automation in areas that have always been characterized by warm, face-to-face interpersonal relations. In medicine the day is not far off when diagnosis and treatment will be carried out by computers, and in psychiatry there are those who believe that in the future many varieties of mental illness will be diagnosed and prescribed for by tape-fed machines rather sophisticated in processing somatic data. Within ten years or less the average patient, without leaving his hospital bed, much less his room, will be able to feed and bathe himself, administer certain medications, take his temperature and have it recorded, and even undergo surgery. Clearly the need for confrontations with doctors, nurses, technicians, orderlies, nurses' aides, and other hospital personnel will be sharply reduced.

The automated university is hardly farther away than the hospital. Much of the teaching now done by professors will be done by teaching machines, closed-circuit television, tape recorders, and other devices. Perhaps the day will come when the student, like the patient, need never leave his room to obtain the benefits he has paid for. Students already complain that they rarely see their professors; in the future, at a great many universities, they will *never* see their professors.

All this signifies that in medicine and education, not to mention the factory and office, there will be marked decrease in interpersonal contacts and face-to-face relationships, in short, a decrease in opportunities for rewarding human relationships. What will be the consequences for mental health? Family life? Our economic and political institutions?

If these questions are to be answered in a positive and hopeful fashion, and, before the full consequences of technology are upon us, collaboration between the social and humanistic sciences may have to go beyond research into the practice areas themselves. If it be assumed, for example, that the technological revolution will be accompanied by a rising incidence of psychiatric disorders, notwithstanding the material benefits conferred by technological development, then it is clear that something more is needed than a collaborative research orientation and the conventional treatment methods now in effect in psychiatry. Perhaps what is required is collaboration in broadening and deepening the concept of the therapeutic community to make it apply, not to the mental hospital and psychiatric clinic (M. Jones, 1953), but to any subculture of society that directly or indirectly promotes mental health and democratic citizenship. In this sense, a therapeutic community is one that not only treats those who are ill; it seeks to prevent illness by establishing an environment that is supportive of health, rationality, and creativity. Oriented toward the whole man and not merely one of his roles or functions, a therapeutic community helps develop in everyone the potential for neurosis-free behavior in both the personal and social setting.

One such therapeutic community, in this sense, is the university, although it is rarely thought of that way. For four years or more in the lives of millions of persons, the university constitutes a distinct subculture of society providing not only education, but moral instruction, social life and companionship, physical activity, and aesthetic uplift. Education in terms of formal classroom instruction is perhaps the least important aspect of university life, at least as regards time. Each week the average student will spend between twelve and fifteen hours in class, and the average professor will devote between six and twelve hours to teaching. The remainder of the student's time is spent in the library, dorm or fraternity house, dining room, union, dating, and attending sports events. Professors devote much of their time to reading and writing, department meetings, committee work, advising students, answering mail, and so forth. Evenings and weekends are generally given over to the family, but on many campuses even family life is campus-related: the dinner party guests will be drawn mainly from the faculty, and the children's friends are likely to be the children of colleagues.

Clearly the structure and function of this subculture, the extent to which it satisfies basic needs, are important in considering such campus problems as suicides (the second-ranking cause of death among college students), nervous breakdowns, drugs and alcoholism, theft, sexual promiscuity, failures, and drop-outs; needless to remark, the faculty, too, has its share of these problems, and it is a share that is increasing. Yet within the university these problems are rarely discussed as societal problems, that is, as problems generated by stresses, strains, and tensions in the academic community as such. And when they are discussed, it is comparatively rare for administrators to draw on the specialized knowledge of either behavioral or humanistic scientists. Psychiatrists, political scientists, and historians are usually consulted less often than such other behavioral experts as electrical engi-
sity these problems are rarely discussed as societal problems, that is, as prob-
lems mentioned are invariably approached as administrative problems which, by definition, are problems that can be solved by a new rule or disciplinary action.

But the university is only one type of organization rarely thought of as a therapeutic community. While universities lag far behind corporations and law firms in developing the equivalent of executive health programs, the latter do not yet see themselves as therapeutic communities in which there is a central concern for mental as well as physical health. Existing health programs too often focus on the maximization of productivity, commonly defined in terms of output, job-performance, or some other crude measure of efficiency. It therefore is no surprise that many of these programs function at the expense of health, rationality, and creativity rather than in support of these values.

If the concept of the therapeutic community is to be successfully redefined, there will have to be significant changes in the training of behavioral and humanistic scientists and in the role played by them in society. Since the supply of clinicians is extremely limited, clinical training must be provided for all those whose occupational positions require them to serve as teachers, counselors, advisors, and social planners—in short, for all those who occupy important posts in the therapeutic community. In the university, for example, the larger part of the guidance function is performed by the professors with whom students are in frequent contact; in effect, the professors are called upon by students to act as clinicians, irrespective of whether they have any clinical training or vocation for clinical practice. Moreover, if the university is to be successfully transformed from a learning factory into a therapeutic community, those who plan and direct the transformation must be familiar with psychiatric methods and insights. Decisions about the curricula and degree requirements, the design of buildings and physical settings so as to provide the necessary amounts of privacy and collegiality, rules and regulations, student and faculty housing arrangements, and much else—these decisions require more than the part-time consultative services of a social psychiatrist or clinical psychologist. Ideally those who make these decisions will be generalists, not specialists, and as generalists they will be participant-observers in therapeutic processes that draw on the whole range of the behavioral and humanistic sciences.

The challenge presented by and to the therapeutic community is a formidable one, to be sure. But if the challenge is very great, so, too, is the opportunity presented to increase the potential—individual and social, national and international—for health, rationality, and creativity. Insofar as these values of the therapeutic community are realizable only in a world that has abolished war, peace itself would not be least among the outcomes of a fruitful collaboration among psychiatrists, historians, and political scientists.

But it would be naïve to imagine that collaboration will be either easy or immediately productive, considering that innovative "breakthrough" thinking is not the foremost characteristic of either the clinic or the academy. At least twice in his life Freud observed that there were three "impossible" professions: educating, healing, and governing. He has not yet been proven wrong.

Note: I wish to acknowledge the research assistance of I. S. Ziony. I have benefited greatly from the critical comments of Richard W. Lyman.

References

Adorno, T. W., Frenkel-Brunswik, Else, Levinson, D. J., and Sanford, R. N. *The Authoritarian Personality*. New York: Harper, 1950.

Alexander, F. "Psychology and the Interpretation of Historical Events." In

C. F. Ware (ed.), *The Cultural Approach to History*. New York: Columbia University Press, 1940.

Alexander, F. "The Psychiatric Aspects of War and Peace." *American Journal of Sociology*, 46 (1941), 504–520.

Alexander, F. *Our Age of Unreason*. Philadelphia: Lippincott, 1942.

Alexander, F. "Aggressiveness—Individual and Collective." In *The March of Medicine*. New York: Columbia University Press, 1943.

Alexander, F. "The Psychoanalyst Looks at Contemporary Art," an address delivered to the Society for Contemporary American Art, Chicago Art Institute, Fullerton Hall, March 4, 1952.

Almond, G. A. *The Appeals of Communism*. Princeton: Princeton University Press, 1954.

Argyris, C. *Interpersonal Competence and Organizational Effectiveness*. Homewood, Ill.: Dorsey Press, 1962.

Binger, C. "New Partnerships for Psychiatry." *American Journal of Orthopsychiatry*, 18 (1948), 543–547.

Brickner, R. M. *Is Germany Incurable?* Philadelphia: Lippincott, 1943.

Brown, J. F. "Social Science and Psychiatry." *American Journal of Orthopsychiatry*, 11 (1941), 628–634.

Bullock, A. *Hitler: A Study in Tyranny*. New York: Harper, 1962.

Burrow, T. "Neurosis and War: A Problem of Human Behavior." *Journal of Psychology*, 12 (1941), 235–249.

Chisholm, G. "The Psychiatry of Enduring Peace and Social Progress." *Psychiatry*, 9 (1946), 1–35.

Clark, K. *Leonardo da Vinci*. Cambridge, Eng.: Cambridge University Press, 1939.

Colby, K. M. *An Introduction to Psychoanalytic Research*. New York: Basic Books, 1960.

Dollard, J., Doob, L., Miller, N., Mowrer, O., and Sears, R. *Frustration and Aggression*. New Haven: Yale University Press, 1939.

Duden, G. *Concerning the Essential Differences of States and the Motives of Human Nature*. Cologne: 1822.

Dunham, H. W. "Social Psychiatry." *American Sociological Review*, 13 (1948), 183–197.

Durbin, E. F. M. *The Politics of Democratic Socialism*. London: Routledge & Kegan Paul, 1940.

Durbin, E. F. M., and Bowlby, E. J. M. *Personal Aggressiveness and War*. London: Routledge & Kegan Paul, 1939.

Easton, D., and Hess, R. D. "The Child's Changing Image of the President." *Public Opinion Quarterly*, 24 (1960), 632–644.

Easton, D., and Hess, R. D. "The Child's Political World." *Midwest Journal of Political Science*, 6 (1962), 236–247.

Edinger, L. J. *Kurt Schumacher: A Study in Personality and Political Behavior*. Stanford: Stanford University Press, 1965.

Erikson, E. H. "Hitler's Imagery and German Youth." *Psychiatry*, 5 (1942), 475–493.

Erikson, E. H. "Wholeness and Totality." In C. J. Friedrich (ed.), *Totalitarianism*. Cambridge: Harvard University Press, 1954.

Erikson, E. H. *Young Man Luther*. New York: Norton, 1958.
Erikson, E. H. Unpublished paper, 1962.
Fiedler, L. "Come Back to the Raft Ag'in, Huck Honey." In *An End to Innocence*. Boston: Beacon, 1955.
Frank, J. D. "Breaking the Thought Barrier: Psychological Challenges of the Nuclear Age." *Psychiatry*, 23 (1960), 245–266.
Frank, L. K. "Social Order and Psychiatry." *American Journal of Orthopsychiatry*, 11 (1941), 620–628.
Frenkel-Brunswik, Else. "Interaction of Psychological and Sociological Factors in Political Behavior." *American Political Science Review*, 46 (1952), 44–65.
Freud, S. "Thoughts for the Times on War and Death" (1915). *The Standard Edition of the Complete Psychological Works of*. . . . London: Hogarth Press. Vol. 14. (Also in *Collected Papers of*. . . . New York: Basic Books, 1959. Vol. 4, pp. 288–317.)
Freud, S. "Civilization and Its Discontents" (1930). *The Standard Edition of the Complete Psychological Works of*. . . . London: Hogarth Press. Vol. 21.
Freud, S. "Why War?" (1933). *The Standard Edition of the Complete Psychological Works of*. . . . London: Hogarth Press. Vol. 22. (Also in *Collected Papers of*. . . . New York: Basic Books, 1959. Vol. 5, pp. 272–287.)
Fromm, E. *Escape from Freedom*. New York: Rinehart, 1941.
George, A. L., and George, Juliette, L. *Woodrow Wilson and Colonel House*. New York: John Day, 1956.
Gottfreid, A. *Boss Cermak of Chicago: A Study of Political Leadership*. Seattle: University of Washington Press, 1962.
Greenstein, F. "The Benevolent Leader: Children's Images of Political Authority." *American Political Science Review*, 54 (1960), 934–943.
Greenstein, F. *Children and Politics*. New Haven: Yale University Press, 1965.
Group for the Advancement of Psychiatry. *Psychiatric Aspects of the Prevention of Nuclear War*, Report No. 57, September, 1964.
Group for the Advancement of Psychiatry. *Psychiatric Aspects of School Desegregation*, Report No. 37, May, 1957.
Group for the Advancement of Psychiatry. *Sex and the College Student*, Report No. 60, November, 1965.
Hendin, H., Gaylin, W., and Carr, A. *Psychoanalysis and Social Research: The Psychoanalytic Study of the Non-Patient*. Garden City: Doubleday, 1965.
Hobbes, T. *Leviathan*. 1651.
Hughes, H. S. "The Historian and the Social Scientist," *American Historical Review*, LXVI, 1960.
Jones, E. *The Life and Work of Sigmund Freud*, Vol. 2. New York: Basic Books, 1955, p. 57.
Jones, M. *The Therapeutic Community*. New York: Basic Books, 1953.
Kardiner, A. *The Psychological Frontiers of Society*. New York: Columbia University Press, 1945, p. 23.
Kazin, A. "Psychoanalysis and Literary Culture Today." In Ruitenbeek, *op. cit.*, 1964.

Lane, R. *Political Ideology: Why the American Common Man Believes What He Does.* New York: The Free Press of Glencoe, 1962.
Langer, W. "The Next Assignment." *American Historical Review,* 63 (1958), 283–304.
Lasswell, H. D. "Two Forgotten Studies in Political Psychology." *American Political Science Review,* 19 (1925), 707–717.
Lasswell, H. D. *Psychopathology and Politics.* Chicago: University of Chicago Press, 1930.
Lasswell, H. D. "The Triple-Appeal Principle: A Contribution of Psychoanalysis to Political and Social Science." *American Journal of Sociology,* 37 (1932), 523–538.
Lasswell, H. D. "Psychoanalyse und Sozioanalyse." *Imago,* 19 (1933), 377–383.
Lasswell, H. D. *World Politics and Personal Insecurity.* New York: McGraw-Hill, 1935.
Lasswell, H. D. "What Psychiatrists and Political Scientists Can Learn from One Another." *Psychiatry,* I (1938), 33–39.
Lasswell, H. D. "The Contribution of Freud's Insight Interview to the Social Sciences." *American Journal of Sociology,* 45 (1939), 373–390.
Lasswell, H. D. *Power and Personality.* New York: Norton, 1948.
Lasswell, H. D. "Democratic Character." In *Political Writings of Harold D. Lasswell.* New York: The Free Press of Glencoe, 1951.
Lauterbach, A. "Psychological Assumptions of Economic Theory." *American Journal of Economics and Sociology,* 9 (1950), 27–38.
L'Etang, H. "The Health of Statesmen." *The Practitioner,* January, 1958.
L'Etang, H. "Ill Health in Senior Officers." *The Practitioner,* April, 1961.
Machiavelli, N. *The Prince.* 1535.
Malin, I. (ed.). *Psychoanalysis and American Fiction.* New York: Dutton, 1965.
Manuel, F. Quoted in *San Francisco Chronicle,* December 30, 1965.
Marmor, J. "War, Violence, and Human Nature." *Bulletin of Atomic Scientists,* March 1964, 19–22.
Mazlish, B. (ed.). *Psychoanalysis and History.* Englewood Cliffs, N. J.: Prentice-Hall, 1963.
Moellenhoff, F. "The Price of Individuality: Speculations about German National Characteristics." *American Imago,* 4 (1947), 33–60.
Money-Kyrle, R. *Psychoanalycis and Politics.* London: Duckworth, 1951.
Muensterberger, W., and Axelrad, S. (eds.). *Psychoanalysis and the Social Sciences,* Vol. 4. New York: International Universities Press, 1955.
Myrdal, G. *An American Dilemma.* New York: Harper, 1944.
Plato. *The Republic.*
Pye, L. "Personal Identity and Political Ideology." In Dwaine Marvick (ed.), *Political Decision-makers.* New York: The Free Press of Glencoe, 1961. Pp. 290–314.
Reich, W. *The Mass Psychology of Fascism.* New York: Orgone Institute Press, 1946.
Robertson, P. L. "Cleveland's Personality as a Political Leader." *Psychoanalytic Review,* 51 (1964), 130–154.

Rogow, A. *James Forrestal: A Study of Personality, Politics, and Policy*. New York: Macmillan, 1963.
Rogow, A. "Disability in High Office." *Medical Opinion and Review*, 1 (April 1966), 16–19.
Rogow, A., and Lasswell, H. D. *Power, Corruption and Rectitude*. Englewood Cliffs, N.J.: Prentice-Hall, 1963.
Roheim, G. *Psychoanalysis and Anthropology*. New York: International Universities Press, 1950. (a)
Roheim, G. *Psychoanalysis and the Social Sciences*. Vol. 1. New York: International Universities Press, 1947.
Roheim, G. *Psychoanalysis and the Social Sciences*. Vol. 2. New York International Universities Press, 1950. (b)
Roheim, G. *Psychoanalysis and the Social Sciences*. Vol. 3. New York: International Universities Press, 1951.
Rokeach, M. *The Open and Closed Mind*. New York: Basic Books, 1960.
Rowley, B. A. "Psychology and Literary Criticism." In Warner Muensterberger and Sidney Axelrad (eds.), *Psychoanalysis and the Social Sciences*, 5. New York: International Universities Press, 1958.
Ruitenbeek, H. (ed.). *Psychoanalysis and Social Science*. New York: Dutton, 1962.
Ruitenbeek, H. (ed.). *Psychoanalysis and Literature*. New York: Dutton, 1964.
Sampson, R. V. *The Psychology of Power*. New York: Random House, 1966.
Schapiro, M. "Leonardo and Freud: An Art-Historical Study." *Journal of the History of Ideas*, 17 (1956), 147–178.
Schmidl, F. "Psychoanalysis and History," *Psychoanalytic Quarterly*, 31, 1962.
Schneider, L. *The Freudian Psychology and Veblen's Social Theory*. New York: King's Crown Press, 1948.
Schuman, F. L. *The Nazi Dictatorship*. New York: Knopf, 1939.
Schuman, F. L. *International Politics*. 6th ed.; New York: McGraw-Hill, 1958.
Smith, M. B., Bruner, J. S., and White, R. W. *Opinions and Personality*. New York: John Wiley, 1956.
Stouffer, S. A. "Indices of Psychological Illness." In Paul F. Lazarsfeld and Morris Rosenberg (eds.), *The Language of Social Research*. New York: The Free Press of Glencoe, 1955.
Tocqueville, A. de. *Democracy in America* (1835). New York: Knopf, 1945, Vol. 1.
Trilling, L. *Freud and the Crisis of Our Culture*. Boston: Beacon Press, 1955.
West, R. *Conscience and Society*. London: Methuen, 1942.
White, W. A. "Thoughts of a Psychiatrist on the War and After." *Psychiatry*, 5 (1942), 403–434.
Wilson, E. *The Wound and the Bow*. Boston: Beacon Press, 1955.
Wolfenstein, E. V. *The Revolutionary Personality: Lenin, Trotsky, Gandhi*. Princeton: Princeton University Press, 1967.
Zimmerman, J. G. *Essay on National Pride*. Zurich: 1758.

28

Psychiatry: Revolution, Reform, and "Reaction"

JOHN R. SEELEY

Just as in the "natural" course of events every person knows least about himself, his "real nature," his effect on others, his "function" in the world in which he lives (indeed, what world it is that he lives in) so too, and for analogous reasons, for all social groups, and not least for professions. The view a profession has of itself—or, to be more exact, the shared views the professionals hold, in virtue of which they recognize each other as colleagues—has the same relation to reality, and a similar set of functions, as has a person's unreconstructed self-image. It is to function as a guide to salability, or at least negotiability, internal and external, which is to say that it is to be primarily a polite, politic, and political version of and front for the underlying realities. It is a presentation—a guise in which—a disguise for what is to be presented, partly by selection out of what is present, partly out of what can be made to appear so.

There is the same problem for the profession as for the person of being, in a dual sense, hoist by one's own petard. In the first place, in both cases, the representation taken (for mixed motives) at its face value by others comes to function as a radically coercive set of expectations, so that what it is to be a doctor, a teacher, a John Smith is no longer largely a matter of choice for the doctor, the teacher, or John Smith, respectively. In the second place, and in both cases, the representations "take in" (though they do not include) the representers, so that they come to mistake their masks for their persons. Bankers may really come to believe that bankers are acquisitive, while the most cursory survey may indicate that after a lifetime of dealing in debits and credits (referring even then to very abstract titles) they have acquired little (besides ulcers) and have been able to accept, and thus genuinely acquire, less than an "exploited" blue-collar worker.

The pains and gains of probing any further are also, in the case of person and profession, somewhat alike. There can hardly be a question that in most cases the going pretenses allow the person, social group, or profession to "function well enough." To function well enough means essentially that day-by-day routines can be carried out; some considerable smoothness, coordination, and articulation can be preserved; costs can be overlooked or neglected; forgone possibilities kept at least invivid; and the whole chain of tragedy, destruction, other-crippling and self-truncation that is the attendant upshot can be ascribed and written off to such "other causes" as fate, miscalculation, or the malign propensities of alien or enemy others. But it is in most cases most of the time "a stable system" of a sort; and we do have sufficient reason to value stability that we ought not lightly to disrupt it unless we can show credible cause. Unless things are going very badly—as in psychosis, or family disintegration, or a powerful attack on the medical profession—it is difficult to show such credible cause. We are left with mere faith—which is necessary, but, like love, "not enough"—that things would be plausibly better under or after examination, peculiarly and painfully, self-examination. I believe, however, that things *are* going sufficiently badly—as attested by wars, pervasive fears, chronic and acute, clamorous competing claims by all parties and professions to have a line, if not the line, to salvation, and the like—to justify some self-examination on the first count alone.

Not that we should take it that under social examination, any more than psychological, what is to be discovered need be (except in a very special sense) self-damaging. Just as patients may conceal their tenderness as well as their aggressiveness and turn out to be both better than they feared and worse than they believed, so may professions turn out to serve purposes or perform functions both more and less worthy or needed or self-pleasing than they supposed.

I take it that what is true for other professions, including my own, is true also for psychiatry. And I take it that—even where psychiatric sensitivity is so exquisite that virtually nothing significant in the doctor-patient relation escapes the doctor—I take it, even then, that it does not follow that the relation of the profession to society is necessarily at all clear. It is on this supposition that I make bold, as a would-be friend to and student of both society and the psychiatric profession, to speculate about the two and their relations in the following way.

I beg you to take note at the outset of the magnitude, rate of growth, pervasiveness, reach, and novelty of psychiatry, whether viewed as profession, doctrine, or practice.

I know that, as far as size is concerned, you are sometimes seized with visions in which it becomes clear that even to do the most narrowly defined of your jobs—to care, say, for the frankly mentally ill—you would have to double, treble or *n*-tuple the present size of the certified profession; visions in which you sometimes see yourselves as a beleaguered little sect, lost till recently in general medicine, itself lost in a barbarian, pagan, and superstitious world. You are quite right in these visions. It is so. There are not enough good men to go around. And there never will be, because there never can be, because in this way of figuring, as soon as we came close we would redefine what it means to be a good man.

But what a peculiar way to count—unless you intend it as a professional strategy such as self-deprecation in a patient who knows no other way to ask for praise. It is as though the Church at the height of its power had counted over its saints, seen their insufficiency to the needs of the day for sanctification, and concluded to its own weakness or the world's irredeemability. The saints are not the Church, by definition, and neither are the certified psychiatrists psychiatry. The Church is not even properly bounded by its membership, for that requires commonly a formal act of adherence, and informal acts are functionally no less efficacious. The boundary of the Church is where its sway or influence runs out, where conduct, including belief and the mordant pangs of conscience, is no longer substantially ordered by and conformed to what it stands for and believes in. (It may even be, thus, that in evil times the true church is altogether or substantially outside the Church; and for all I know it may be so even now.)

And this has little to do with whom you will recognize or admit to colleagueship or license to practice. Those are your prerogatives, and the degree of finickyness that is appropriate to a given profession at a given moment is a matter of strategy that I do not wish to enter on here. You may bound your formal or nominal membership as you will, but you cannot easily limit the number of these who judge their attitudes by yours, who seek to pose in your posture, who adhere to and base their conduct on what they take to be your (most recent) doctrine, let alone the growing number of those who do so without self-conscious awareness of the source of their modeling or the capital or Vatican of their "profession." The profession, thus properly numbered by the number of those who profess its professions, perhaps not in all pristine purity, runs into millions, or more likely, hundreds of millions.

Note that this is not an idle distinction, something true for every profession. The mathematician, despite the spread of much low arithmetic and poor algebra, is not followed and attended by a mass following of more or less mathematically thinking and mathematically self-guiding people. Hardly anyone has a clue to what the mathematical orientation is or what it can do, or what it is for, or the beauty and delight of it. Nor is everyone in some notable degree a classic historian, a cytologist, or an expert in Sanskrit. Even a learned psychiatrist might know next to nothing of Sanskrit and be little affected by what little he knew; but our Sanskritologist would have to be ivory-tower to the point of illiteracy to know but little of psychiatry, and uncomprehending to the point of idiocy to be little affected by whatever he did know.

So you have a peculiar profession which has a cloud of witnesses quite uncommon, and, whether you so will or not, a numberless host of co-believers, sharers in the mystery, and, licensed or not, co-practitioners. The ultimate test—that some vast majority of those who oppose you orient themselves not so much on a competitive doctrine but on their opposition to you ("Down with Mental Health!")—indicates the particular place of prominence that, sought or unsought, is yours.

Nor is this a matter of mere externalities—like the Church adopting the habits and manners of the Roman rulers to whose powers it succeeded—though it is that also. These outward signals are indeed signs of inward and invisible graces, even if not so inward nor so graceful as we might wish. People widely, now almost by first nature, do regard themselves, conceive themselves, on the lines of a "psychodynamical psychology," directed in a "therapeutic" direction, and taking for granted as presupposition what is in psychiatric theory given as conclusion. And, as toward themselves, so in degree toward each other. And not necessarily from above downward only, but also and frequently from below upward. So that one may observe adolescent children, for instance, not only making valid and insightful diagnoses—if I may use the term—of their parents' condition, and their own, and the interplay, but additionally taking serious and sometimes weighty, therapeutic responsibility and acting thereupon with quite consummate skill. Or so I judge.

So you have a profession of magnitude and pervasion. As for novelty, I perhaps do not need to press the point. But as someone recently pointed out in reference to King Henry VIII, who left a trail of blood, misery, disease, schism, and divided nation behind him, the very question as to what was wrong with him in the modern, postpsychiatric sense could simply not have occurred to anyone—because the world to which it refers, while it existed, existed in everybody but existed *for* no one. And that is less than fifteen generations back. Grandeur can now in principle be distinguished from grandiosity, and while men do not yet govern themselves accordingly, now that they know that answers are available they will not long content themselves with mere questions.

I have only made these general points in case you are generally insufficiently impressed with the size, reach, depth, and first-order consequence of psychiatry as a movement in the world. Moreover, I wanted these generals as background to and foreplay for some particulars. The particulars have to do with the social consequences, intended or unintended, of your practices.

At this point, I fear, I have to distinguish among your practices, the things you do, in a variety of combinations and mixes. Among them I find prominent the following. Some of you refine and elaborate or extend theory, either directly or as incident to other activities. Some illustrate and enrich theory by the provision of ever fresh or ever more dramatically detailed, and hence in one sense more comprehensible, case material. Some of you educate in these or other ways, by your writing or speaking—or example, even—either in pair-relationships, or in larger groups or aggregations or publics. Some of you practice psychotherapy which, in many cases, is a microscopic but all the more important, for that—mix of all these things. Some of you draw the seeming implications as they appear for public policy of what you observe in your consulting rooms and in the Republic—what Scott Buchanan calls "the public thing." Some of you go beyond drawing implications and publishing them, to other and closer arts of suasion, a more direct intervention in the shared life of institutions. Others of you become administrators. Still others become sorters of men, or assistants or accomplices in their sorting. And some of you, I am sad to say, become keepers of men—in the same sense as zoo-keepers are keepers of animals, and jailers and wardens are of boys and girls, men and women.

I am sure I have slighted you by the omission of vital functions, but, even so, I am forced by the needs of brevity to do further violence by lumping all this vast variety of different activity into three gross categories: your function as theorists and case-reporters; your function as policy-makers and policy-changers; your function as sorters-and-jailers.

Broadly speaking, let me say that in these three roles respectively you appear vis-à-vis the world as revolutionaries, reformers, and reactionaries. By a revolutionary, I mean someone who oversets the fundamental criteria by which men habitually govern themselves. By a reformer, I mean someone who makes or procures changes in the operation of important institutions, in important ways, without however directly challenging the going order at its base. By a reactionary I mean someone who comes along to restore *a tergo* what a society has actually or latently already progressed beyond, someone who not merely stops up the womb of human and humane development, but attempts to cram back into it the already delivered fruit thereof.

Let me deal with the last first, since—quite evidently—I like it least. And briefly.

The presenting problem is the following. In a given society those who have the power to do so exact from those who have not the power to refuse a patterning of conduct (sometimes extending even to speech and the showing of feeling) which bars some lines of behavior and requires others. Some yield to the exaction and some do not. In a sufficiently advanced stage of civilization an attempt is made to distinguish those who cannot yield from those who will not. The distinction is pragmatic: those who *cannot* yield are those who do not do so after every sanction the society is willing to use has been applied, plus those who are somehow judged to be like them. Those who *will* not yield are the residue. In general: those who will not yield, so distinguished, are the criminal and delinquent; those who cannot are the ill and defective. (The difference between the last two is also pragmatic: a defect is a disability—a state of *can*not—that there are no means available and allowable to change.)

Both ways, men are classified and restricted. Both of these are police operations. Police operations, etymologically and otherwise, mean policy operations, politic operations, operations of power, operations directed to discipline, order and control *for* some community, operations then in behalf of some men on and against one man. There are, of course, important differences. But the identities are even more significant. The psychiatrist becomes gentle jailer, polite policeman. His patient is no longer, except marginally, his client. He serves the public order—with such kindness, at best, as that constraint permits. He is open to the corruptions of power, peculiarly so, more so than the more worldly warden. For his ward is—by definition—weaker, and, to escape, must yield not only outerly but innerly. The wildest tyrants in their wildest fantasies have not required more. Indeed, their fantasy is for the first time somewhat filled out: conduct that might be sufficiently convincing of the inner conformity required to pass muster for a Grand Vizier may well not get by the oblique eye of a Rorschach. In preserving and promoting such an institution in the world, in serving or assisting it or what is like it, the role of the psychiatrist is, in the deepest sense, in the service of reaction.

And by "what is like it" I mean all those organizations that "employ" —that is, use—men, conceiving of them as "employees" (useds) or "potential employees" (usables) or personnel (man-*matériel*). Try to hear it, what is being said, with an unspoiled ear: Men have uses! (How would you respond if someone asked: How can I use this baby? Or this little girl? Or boy? Why do you respond if the object is "these men," "these women"?) All the various assistances you give to the sorting, selecting, transfer, and other associated categorizing and locating processes are in principle no different from the labeling and relocation by ward (as reward or penalty) that is provided as a pattern in the mental hospital.

Let me turn with relief from these enterprises to those that constitute your principal effect, what I have spoken of as willingly or unwillingly "revolutionary": your direct effect in psychotherapy (when properly practiced), your indirect effects as you publish in whatever degree the general results or dramatic details that flow therefrom.

The most far reaching effect is, of course, the redefinition of what man is. To be a man, following the vision from Vienna, is to be something else again from what it was before, incredibly more credible, released by several degrees of magnitude from the principal imprisoning pretenses of the past, and, moreover, furnished forever in principle with a key to that prison, though by no means all doors have yet been opened, or even noted. I will not labor the point, for a great deal has been said and written about the Freudian revolution, though, even so, not enough. For in a very real sense not one stone is left upon another in the ancient walls and temples, and such as remain are destined, one may see, for a different use. Let me turn to less obvious but perhaps nearly equipotent effects.

For men do not live by the bread of abstraction alone, but by every word that comes out of the mouth of the concrete actors who constitute history as they speak and act the vast drama of their little lives. So that what it is to be man is defined and enriched no less by those truer autobiographies that come out of the consulting room as case material than by what is inferential in it or explanatory of it, by way of heuristic concepts or metapsychological entities. It is not just the theory of "the vicissitudes of the instincts," nor merely the fascinating forms of the compromises and "resolutions" *in abstracto*, but it is rather all the complex, concrete, unique outworkings as dramatically presented in the ongoing drama that restructure and re-form and redefine our life and our lives. Not the theology only, but the rich and encrusted hagiography of everyman, is and enters into the reconstitution and illumination of the life, lone and shared, of every person-participant.

But beyond—or below—theory and concrete embodiment lies the propaganda of the act, the force of your example. The existence in the world—the same world where men have uses!—of the therapeutic alliance serves to raise an uncomfortable question about every alternative relation. For the core of it is an interpenetration and interplay between the actual best in one person and the latent best in another, with no other aim in view than the release in the one who—momentarily—has the less to give of that latent best crying for its own liberation into reality. And that operation, underwritten not by a judgment of relative worth, but a presumption of absolute value! And the reward not in money (which merely makes it possible), nor affection, which sometimes hampers it, or honor, which is at best a by-product, but in pure joy in pure liberation. For the patient: "And my growth have no guerdon but only to grow . . ." For the true psychocurator: "And the lives of my children made perfect with freedom of soul were my fruits."

I say that that relation, established and re-established, enacted and re-enacted every day challenges and calls into question every other relation and joint enterprise. For, first, it is infinitely generalizable and extensible wherever, as is always the case, there is a difference in degree and kind of need between persons, from moment to moment. And second, it becomes increasingly clear that most of the things we say we value can be had under the sign of that relation and no other, so that we are driven either to abandon age-old hypocrisies or to run the risks of authentic, unarmed, and beneficent encounters in the authentic. And as we do the latter, the domain of the genuine is extended, and the realm of the false and the tawdry manipulative is shown in sharper shadow for what it is. So that the very underpinnings of what most men do most that is most harmful simultaneously to themselves and others are undercut, and the structures erected on them rendered untenable and untenantable. And as the country of the soul is mapped, the country for the soul, the meaning of the long-sought civilization, comes into sight and may be occupied.

Lastly, from this peculiar and most unlikely perspective, the couch, actual and virtual, comes, curiously enough, the crucial information as to how things are going in the ordinary affairs of men. For institutions and customs and social practices are not, or not only, what they patently (and, particularly, rationally) seem to be. A family is not (or is not simply or only) a social "arrangement" for getting sex regulated, children bred, born, and raised, companionship established and cared for, love in its multiple meanings deepened and channeled—or any such list of "functions." For the family—and any other institution—is in one sense consumed by each of its members, and in another sense is the stage for and context of them, and in yet another is an interpenetration with, as well as a mode of expression of, their lives. And the meaning in each of these meanings of what it is, is neither what appears at the face, nor what is to be "more carefully observed"—nor even what can with skill be introspected—but more than these and less, and certainly quite other. The family is most crucially—but so is the state, the school, the colleagueship, the group of friends—a conversation, unconscious to unconscious, direct and indirect, a provision for heredity (continuity and variation) at an ulterior and quite decisive level. And knowledge of what that conversation is—and hence of what the institution *is*—can come or does come to us only by the processes by which we explore the unconscious or its manifestations, prototypically the psychoanalytic methods. And the relation between what men say there—and, indeed, in both senses of the word dis-cover—and what they say in everyday and ostensible conversation is so oblique and multiplex, that we can hardly even regard the two as complementary revelations, and can hardly help but regard the first as giving the "true" or "real"—or certainly, crucial—meaning of the second. However that may be, let us say, conservatively, that the ostensible meanings, serving motives, functions, and effects of institutions from war to monogamy, from courtship to combat—are so little and misleadingly given, both in general and in particular, by their evident and everyday appearance, that social policy founded on such shallowness and distortion is quite inevitably disaster-bound, failing the corrective—let us call it that—that comes to us from that other world.

And that other world is the domain of the psychiatrist as such (and not, let us say of the psychologist, no matter how skilled and "psychodynamic") because knowledge of it is to be had when and only when life is faced as a problem and not as a question. (A beautiful elaboration of the distinction occurs in Abraham J. Heschel, *Who Is Man?*) And where there is a problem—or more specially, *the* problem: Who am I? What must I do?—there is an agony. And where there is an agonist, there is a problem of soul healing in the problem's resolution—a psychiatric contest and opportunity in the widest sense of those words.

So I see you, I am sure, through my own distorting lenses. There must be in my picture omissions and misbalances. But in its large lines I think, after long and tender study of the object, the picture I present is valid—at least in the sense that a vision of the flower's possibilities is possible on the basis of what is only promise in the bud.

Reference

Heschel, A. J. *Who Is Man?* Stanford, Calif.: Stanford University Press, 1965.

Subject Index

Name Index